Crane

(62-15732)

COINS
OF THE WORLD

COINS
OF THE WORLD

R. A. G. CARSON

*Assistant Keeper in the Department of
Coins and Medals at the British Museum*

HARPER & ROW, PUBLISHERS
NEW YORK and EVANSTON

HARPER & ROW, PUBLISHERS
49 East 33rd Street, New York 16, N.Y., U.S.A.

Second Impression 1963

Printed in Great Britain for
Harper & Row, Publishers, Incorporated

To

Meta Fransisca
in gratitude for her help

CONTENTS

Introduction

★

This book sets out to deal with the coins used in the different civilizations and countries of the world but not with the whole field of money. Money is a generic term covering the wide variety of objects which furnish the medium of exchange for goods and services, and coinage is only one of such media, though it has sustained the largest and longest rôle in the history of civilization. Coins, by definition, are objects of metal of a standard consistency and given weight, stamped with a representation guaranteeing this weight and value and consequent exchangeability. Excluded, therefore, from this work is the money of primitive civilizations whether it be the brass armlets of West Africa or the large, flat and circular stone money of the Caroline Islands in Oceania. Equally, paper money, in the shape of bank-notes or cheques of the credit commerce of the modern world, lies outside the scope of this book. Coinage is an index not of a developed civilization but of a stage in its economic growth where specialized production, even if only in its most elementary forms, provides surpluses which form the basis of commerce and create the demand for a convenient medium for their exchange.

As in so many fields, China is credited with the invention and earliest use of coinage; for the earliest Chinese coins, tradition says, date from the second millennium B.C. Early types of coinage were simply small-scale reproductions in bronze of everyday objects such as knives and spades, previously exchanged in barter. These pieces began to be inscribed from about the middle of the first millennium B.C., and, though this form of coinage probably lasted down towards the beginning of the Christian era, coins of conventional round shape, with a square hole in the centre, and inscribed with characters, began to come into circulation some centuries before this.

In the Western world coinage does not make its appearance until the early seventh century B.C. The great civilizations of Assyria and Egypt had, indeed, a rudimentary form of exchange in the shape of bullion in bars or rings. These, though they may have been of a rough standard weight, carried no mark of guarantee and had to be weighed on each occasion of exchange and it is to this class that the shekels and talents, familiar from the Old Testament, most likely belong. The credit of inventing coinage is attributed by Herodotus to the Lydians in Asia Minor, who began to stamp ingots of their native 'gold' with an official mark which rendered repeated recourse to weighing unnecessary. The earliest coins are, in fact, of electrum, originally the local natural mixture of gold and silver. Herodotus believed that the earliest coins of the Lydians were in gold and silver, a form of coinage now associated with Croesus in the sixth century, an erroneous but understandable identification of the beginnings of coinage with this king whose name has become proverbial for wealth. The early form of coinage was quickly taken up by the Greek mercantile cities on the coast and islands of Asia Minor and improved upon with the use of recognizable badges and names as marks of guarantee.

The use of coinage quickly spread across the Aegean to Greece and was carried thence to the colonies established in Italy and Sicily and trading settlements such as Massilia (Marseilles) until the practice was universal round the Mediterranean basin and the Black Sea. This coinage was largely in silver, but the introduction of a rich series of gold issues by Philip II of Macedon in the fourth century started off waves of imitations which brought coinage to Gaul and even to Britain by the late second century B.C., and the empire of Alexander the Great and the kingdoms into which it broke up carried coinage eastwards as far as north-west India. Later the absorption by Rome of the great Hellenistic monarchies and the extension of empire over most of the civilized Western world carried the use of coinage even further.

After the collapse of the Roman empire in the West in the fifth century A.D., the survival of the Eastern Byzantine empire maintained the tradition of coinage, and even western Europe in the Dark Ages preserved some imitation of the Roman gold coinage. Early mediaeval Europe, with its reduced level of civilization, reverted to a silver coinage of a single denomination, the denier or penny of the various emerging states. Increasing prosperity led to the introduction of larger silver pieces in the thirteenth century and to the re-emergence of a gold coinage, initially by the rich mercantile city states of Italy. The discovery of the New World in the late fifteenth century not only extended the use of coinage to the Western hemisphere but uncovered rich supplies of precious metals for the coinage of the old world. Another new source was the development of the silver mines of south Germany and Austria such as that in Joachimsthal in Bavaria in 1518, a place which gave a name to one of the best-known denominations, the thaler. The colonizing activities of the great mercantile nations of western Europe from the sixteenth century onwards introduced coinage to the newly discovered lands of Australasia and the new settlements in Africa and Asia.

Asia itself was not unfamiliar with coinage. The Near East had known the coinage of Greece and Rome and from the seventh century onwards had used the successive forms of Muhammadan coinage. In the sub-continent of India, as well as the coins of the Greek kingdom of Bactria in the north-west and the later Scythic and Kushan kings, native coinages had proliferated and been influenced by the innumerable invasions, such as those of the Moguls in the sixteenth century. Further east, the conservative coinage of China had preserved its outward form and had influenced the development of coinage in Korea and Japan.

The whole of the coinage of the ancient and the mediaeval world and much of the coinage of the East until the last century was 'hammer-struck'. The coins were produced by placing the metal blank on a die, fixed in a form of anvil; a second die held in position on top of the blank was then struck with a hammer. It was not until the sixteenth century in western Europe that machine methods for producing coins were introduced. In England, for instance, experimental issues were made under Elizabeth I and Charles I, but it was not until after the Restoration of Charles II that the practice was permanently adopted. Until the introduction of mechanical striking, the shape of coins, though in general circular, had been somewhat eccentric and with an irregular edge. The features of machine-struck coins are that they are regular in shape, be it circular, square or many-sided, and the edges finished off with a graining or milling.

Coins in one form or another have accompanied the history of the last two and a half thousand years of civilization and have been collected for a good many centuries. As collected pieces coins have a dual character. Quite apart from their obvious attraction as objects of interest or beauty, coins provide an almost unparalleled series of historical documents. Their most immediate contribution is as illustration of history, for in Western civilization from the end of the fourth century B.C. onwards, with the exception of a large portion of the Middle Ages, they supply contemporary portraits of many of history's leading characters. Many famous sculptures and buildings of the ancient world which have since vanished have found their only pictorial record on coins. The contribution of coins to the history of art is too obvious to require more than mention, but from the study of coins much less obvious evidence can be deduced bearing on the political, economic and social history of the world.

Coins have, however, been collected—and still are collected—more often for their own sake than for their contribution to knowledge. Suetonius tells us that the Emperor Augustus, at the beginning of the Christian era, was, in a way, a collector of coins and that he was in the habit of presenting to his friends fine Greek coins which he had acquired. The princes of the Renaissance, with their revived interest in the learning and art of the ancient world, were the first of the modern coin-collectors and by the later sixteenth century the collections of some of the noble houses provided the material for the earlier catalogues of coin-collections. In the eighteenth century a cabinet of coins was as essential a part of the background of the cultured gentleman as his library, and the fashion of coin-collecting was pursued by many royal houses, whose natural national pride added coins relevant to the nation's history and provided the nucleus of most of the great national collections of today.

Changed economic conditions put an end to collections which covered the whole range of coinage and the even more straitened circumstances of the post-war world have brought about the dispersal of the last great private collections devoted to one whole field of coinage. But if the size and range of individual collections have become smaller, the number of such collections has grown apace. The growing curiosity about the past and its monuments is seen in the widespread public interest in archaeology, and a realization of the relative ease with which coins of all places and periods can be collected, both as antiquities in themselves and as a source of illustration and knowledge of the past, has made the collecting of coins no longer the hobby of the few but the pursuit of a large and ever-increasing number of enthusiasts.

The actual collecting of coins is comparatively easy and inexpensive, for coins have been produced with considerable regularity for roughly the last two and a half thousand years and, since they are objects of metal, have survived in some quantity. The modern coin-collector, however, is concerned not with the mere assembly of coins; his interests lie in the correct identification and attribution of the pieces which come his way, in the interpretation of the information which the coins can impart and in the relation of the coins to the particular country and period of history in which his interests lie. To the vast material which is the heritage of well over two thousand years of coinage a literature of corresponding immensity has been devoted, much of it highly specialized. The vastness of the material and the complexity of its literature, these are the two great initial difficulties for the ordinary collector and student; and it is with these difficulties in mind that this book has been written.

The aim of this book is to present an outline of coinage as it has developed in various parts of the world throughout the ages, to present a general picture in which any chosen field of coinage can be related to its historical background. The considerable amount of detailed description incorporated in the account of the several coinages together with the illustration of about a thousand coins, should enable most coins to be attributed to their correct series. The bibliography, divided into sections corresponding to the divisions of the book itself, lists the more specialist works for those who wish to make a more detailed study of any particular field of coinage. The bibliography is itself select and has been restricted to the standard works in each field; these books themselves provide, in turn, even fuller lists of yet more specialist works.

This book is, I believe, the first attempt to deal with the whole sweep of coinage in one volume, and it is only the wealth of research both of contemporaries and of earlier generations that has made it possible to attempt the task. The select bibliography with which the book is furnished is only a very partial measure of my indebtedness to the many scholars whose works I have consulted. I am particularly grateful to my own colleagues for reading various portions of the book and for their helpful suggestions while it was being written.

My final and warmest thanks are to my wife, not for conventional wifely forbearance but for her real encouragement and, even more, for her active assistance in checking details of fact, in typing the whole of the manuscript and in helping to prepare the index.

R. A. G. CARSON

GREECE

★

Greece

THE material to which the term 'Greek coinage' is usually applied defies brief definition. In general terms it is applied to the whole body of coinage which in any way derives its inspiration from Greek culture, and consequently includes the coinage of all the lands of the Mediterranean basin, together with those of the north-west of Europe such as Gaul and Britain to which something of Greek culture was spread by trade and migration. Greek settlements and colonies brought their social and economic culture to the lands round the Black Sea and in the late fourth century B.C. the conquests of Alexander the Great spread Greek ideas across Mesopotamia and Persia as far as the north-west of India. The period of time covered by the general concept of Greek coinage is equally immense. From the invention of coinage about the middle of the seventh century B.C. the pattern of Greek coinage, ever changing but always preserving a continuity of development, stretches through the history of the city states of the classical period, the rise and decline of the great Hellenistic monarchies, to the establishment of the Roman empire covering almost the whole of the civilized Western world at the beginning of the Christian era. Even under the Roman emperors the flow of Greek coinage continued, only restricted now to more local issues, and it is not until towards the end of the third century A.D. that Greek coinage finally disappeared.

The diversity of a coinage covering close on a thousand years of history and a vast expanse of territory lends itself to a variety of arrangements. The most scientific is the chronological classification of coins by style, grouping together the coins of all issuing states in the various regions of the Greek world. Satisfactory though this method is for gaining an overall picture of the development of Greek coinage, it raises at least two major practical difficulties. In the first place, it involves returning to a consideration of the coinage of any particular place, possibly seven times, the number of chronological periods into which Greek coinage is usually divided; secondly, where the object, though only secondary as here, is the facilitating of the identification of coins, it is more practical to have a single treatment of the whole of the coinage of one place.

For such reasons the present treatment of the coinage of the Greeks has been

3

based on the traditional geographical arrangement. Whereas, however, the traditional arrangement has been to trace the various coinages from west to east it is proposed here to begin with the coinages of Asia Minor which saw the invention of coinage in Western civilization, to work counter-clockwise round the Mediterranean in its widest sense and conclude with the coinages in the Middle East and India which derive from Greek influences. In two respects, the strict geographic treatment has been abandoned. Coinages, as for example the Macedonian coinage of Alexander the Great, which were current over a wide area are discussed as an entity though this involves cutting across the geographical barriers. The issues made from local Greek mints which continued to function under the Roman empire have been grouped together in a separate section, for though they continued much of the tradition of Greek coinage, they also contain much of the spirit of Roman imperial issues.

Since the coinages of the different places in the Greek world will each be described as a chronological sequence and since not all coinages began with the very invention of coinage in the West nor continued throughout the whole expanse of ten centuries, it is essential to outline the successive periods into which Greek coinage is commonly divided by reference to changing and developing trends in artistic and technical treatment.

I *c.* 650–480 B.C. *Archaic.* The general characteristic of this period is the development from a certain crudity, both in artistic representation and in workmanship, to a surer and stronger touch and a more finished technical execution. The initial coin types have a stiff angularity and are limited largely to animal forms or inanimate objects. Only occasionally is the human head featured, and though usually seen in profile, the eye is drawn as if seen from the front. The earliest coins are rough bean-shaped lumps but gradually they become more regular and circular in outline. In this period, coins generally have a type on the obverse only, the reverse having only a rough indentation from the punch used to drive the metal blank into the die which produced the obverse type.

II 480–415 B.C. *Transitional.* Both technique and design show a considerable advance. The rough indentation on the reverse is succeeded by a more regular incuse square which often contains a type in relief, an elementary heraldic badge or a name. The incuse reverse continued longer in Asia Minor than in Greece and the West where reverses also with a type in relief were more readily adopted. The designs themselves are more varied and are executed with greater competence, particularly in the drawing of the human figure.

III 415–336 B.C. *Finest art.* The technical process of striking had now been mastered and could do justice to the work of the die engravers. The resultant coin types are the supreme achievement of Greek coin artists. They are compositions of elegant proportion, rich in detail and where the subject is the human or animal form they vividly transmit a feeling of movement and action. To this period belong the coins whose obverses succeed in presenting the head turned almost full-face to the spectator. Contemporary regard for the medallic artists shows itself in the appearance of their signatures on certain coins, particularly those of Euainetus and Kimon on the splendid silver decadrachms at Syracuse.

IV   336–280 B.C. *Later fine art.* The earliest contemporary portraiture makes its appearance on the obverse, gradually ousting the traditional representations of divinities. On the reverse the tendency is to impart a certain slimness to the human form and to emphasize the muscles caught in action. Variety of reverse type there still is, but the seated figure becomes the predominant type.

V   280–146 B.C. *Decline.* The rise of the great Hellenistic monarchies in Macedonia, Syria and Egypt and of Rome in the West put an end to the coinage in silver of many cities and smaller states. The great regal coinages produce a series of magnificent if idealized portraits but less attention is devoted to reverse design which tends to become stereotyped.

VI   146–27 B.C. *Continuing decline.* The continuing expansion of Rome gradually eliminated coinage in silver with the exception of the silver cistophori in Asia Minor. Local bronze issues which continued show a degradation of style and execution.

VII   27 B.C.–A.D. 268. *Imperial.* With some exceptions, coinage in the precious metals was produced at Rome or at branches of the Roman mint in the provinces. Many cities in the East and a few in the West secured the right to produce local coinage in bronze. The obverses show the head of the personification of the local municipality or more usually of the emperor, while the reverses commonly depict local temples, cult-images or legends.

ASIA MINOR AND THE ISLANDS

LYDIA

Coinage in electrum. The credit for the invention of coinage was a matter of controversy in the ancient world, some sources attributing it to the Athenians,

some to Pheidon of Argos and others to the Lydians. Modern scholarship, while
agreeing to dismiss the Athenian claim, continues to argue the merits of the case
for Pheidon and that for the Lydians but for some time consensus of opinion has
favoured the latter. The coinage accepted as the earliest is neither gold nor silver,
the usual precious metals, but electrum, a mixture of gold and silver, found
originally in a natural state in the river beds running down from the Tmolus
range in Lydia. The exact date is not determined at which rough blobs of this
metal of standard weight began to be used as a quasi-coinage but recent research
has ascribed the issue of the first electrum coinage proper to the Lydian kings.
This first series of coins proper qualify for the title for they are not only of a
standard weight but bear on one side as a guarantee the fore-part of a lion, the
device of the Lydian kings, though the other side showed only a rough incuse
punch.

The invention of coinage is now placed no earlier than 640–630 B.C., that is in
the reign of King Ardys (652–625). The mint which produced these coins is not
certainly established but the capital of the Lydian kingdom, Sardes, is the likely
place. The major unit was the stater (Pl. 1) but the most common surviving
denomination is the third of the stater and subdivisions ranging as low as a ninety-
sixth are also found. The distribution of this coinage between Ardys, his son
Sadyattes (625–615) and his successor Alyattes (615–560) is conjectural though
the inscription on some staters is said to read the name of Alyattes.

Croesus (560–546). The amount of gold contained in the electrum staters varied
and the discredit into which the electrum currency fell is made evident by the
numerous private counter-marks placed on coins to denote their acceptance.
Croesus, the son of Alyattes, replaced the electrum currency by a coinage of gold
and silver staters. The device on these was the fore-parts of a bull and a lion facing
each other with, on the reverse, two incuse squares of different size (Pl. 2). The
mint of this coinage was probably also Sardis but, unlike the electrum coinage, this
series had only one sub-denomination, the half-stater. This coinage ended with the
defeat of Croesus by the Persian king Cyrus and the incorporation of Lydia into
the Persian empire.

Coinage struck in Lydia as successively part of the Persian empire, of the empire
of Alexander the Great and of the Seleucid kingdom appears under these headings.
Otherwise, down to the formation of the Roman empire, coinage in Lydia consists of silver cistophori issued at six mints and local bronze issues from these and
an additional eight mints. The cistophori, said to have been originally issued in
connection with Bacchic festivals, were silver tetradrachms of large, spread fabric
showing on obverse a basket, the *cista mystica* with snake emerging from it and on
the reverse two coiled serpents with a bow case between them. The half and

quarter pieces have types of club and lion-skin on one side and grapes and vine-leaf on the other. The cistophori were issued by some Lydian mints after the incorporation of Lydia in the Pergamene kingdom in 189 B.C. and by some after the formation of the Roman province of Asia in 133 B.C.

Cistophori were issued (1) in the time of Eumenes of Pergamum at Apollonis, Thyatira and Stratonicea. The reverse is inscribed with part of the ethnic or place name and the date, e.g. at Thyatira, △, = year 4 of Eumenes = 186 B.C. (Pl. 3); (2) under the Attalid kings of Pergamum before 133 B.C. at Sardes and Tralles with ethnic on reverse; (3) in the Roman province of Asia after 133 B.C. at Nysa, Sardes and Tralles after 58 B.C., with names of Roman proconsuls. Small bronze coins were struck by all these cities and in addition at Blaundus, Caystiani, Clannudda, Hieracome, Magnesia ad Sipylum, Mostene, Philadelphia and Tripolis. These bronzes show the head of one of the gods on the obverse and an associated object on the reverse, together with the ethnic and sometimes, additionally, the name or monogram of a magistrate as on the coin with head of Zeus and eagle reverse at Blaundus (Pl. 4).

IONIA

As the great trade routes from Asia passed through Lydia westwards to the coast, it was natural that the new invention of coinage in Lydia should have been quickly taken up in the coastward cities of Ionia and in the islands. The earlier coins here, too, were of electrum, tariffed at roughly 1 to 10 in terms of silver. In each district the standard coin or stater was adjusted to the particular talent in use in the locality for weighing precious metals. The types appearing on some of the Ionian electrum suggest particular cities as the place of minting, but many electrum coins can be attributed only generally to Ionia where they are found.

Unattributed electrum. The earliest, or at least the most primitive, stater which must be roughly contemporary with the first Lydian staters is a stater on the Babylonic standard with simply a scored or striated surface on the obverse and an oblong sinking between two square sinkings on the reverse (Pl. 5). Staters on the Phoenician standard include types, on obverse, of two lions' heads facing and two lions rampant confronted. On the Phocaic standard are staters with obverse, the fore-part of an ibex (Pl. 6). These are all probably of the later part of the seventh century, but staters, again of the Phocaic standard, with types of a chimaera or a fish decorated with fillets, date from the earlier sixth century before the reform of Croesus in 560. Subdivisions of the Ionian staters are also found, chiefly the half, the third and the sixth or hecte which was in most common use. As in Lydia, other smaller denominations down to the ninety-sixth are also known.

For most of the cities of Ionia coinage begins in the late seventh and early sixth centuries with electrum issues usually uninscribed, which are succeeded by a coinage in silver lasting down towards the end of the fourth century and accompanied in its later stages by series of small bronze coins. The autonomous coinage of some Ionian cities was interrupted for the whole of the third century when it was superseded by the silver issues of the kingdoms of Alexander, Lysimachus and the Seleucids. Following the defeat of Antiochus III of Syria at Magnesia by the Romans, city coinage resumes, though in different form. It is confined mainly to the appearance of the city's device as a symbol on the late gold staters of Philip's types and on the Alexandrine tetradrachms, but bronze coinage reappears using the types familiar from the earlier coinage and bearing the name of the city.

At *Clazomenae* the principal type used first on rare electrum staters and hectae (or sixths) and later, in the fifth century, on silver tetradrachms and lesser denominations is the fore-part of a winged boar. The fourth century brought a brilliant coinage both in gold and silver with a superb three-quarter facing head of Apollo as obverse type and a swan with spread wings on the reverse (Pl. 7). A notable reverse on the second-century bronze shows the seated figure of the philosopher Anaxagoras. At Clarus in the territory of Colophon stood the famous temple of the oracle of Apollo whose head regularly occupies the obverse on the silver coinage of the fifth and fourth centuries. An exceptional type on second-century bronzes is a seated figure of Homer.

A grazing stag, the type of Artemis, the patron goddess of *Ephesus*, is accompanied on an electrum stater by the earliest certain coin inscription reading: 'I am the badge of Phanes', presumably the guarantor of the piece (Pl. 8). The other familiar type, the bee, also appears on electrum coins and is the main type on the silver down to the early fourth century. The alliance which linked Ephesus with Samos, Rhodes, Cnidus and Iasus issued a federal coinage of silver tridrachms. These had a common obverse type, the infant Heracles strangling the serpents, and were inscribed $\Sigma YN(\mu\alpha\chi\iota\alpha)$ = alliance, and on the reverse appeared the badge of the issuing city, in the case of Ephesus, the bee (Pl. 9). Later silver and bronze issues combined the bee and stag types and, in the third century especially, the obverses feature a delicately beautiful head of Artemis herself (Pl. 10). In the last two centuries B.C. Ephesus was the mint for an extensive series of silver cistophoric tetradrachms, the later issues signed with names of Roman proconsuls.

A star-like flower is the badge of the city of *Erythrae* on the early electrum and a naked horseman on the archaic silver. The fine-style coins of the fourth century with both sides in relief combine these two types (Pl. 11). The head of Heracles and the club, bow and other symbols associated with his cult supply the types for the coinage of later centuries. The earliest coins at *Magnesia ad Maeandrum* are connected with Themistocles who, when exiled from Athens in 465, was assigned this city by the Persian king. The name of Themistocles accompanies the obverse type of a naked Apollo on a rare series of silver didrachms. The most impressive coinage from this city is the series of tetradrachms in the second century. These coins of large, spread fabric carry the head of Artemis and, on the reverse, a naked standing Apollo within a Maeander circle (Pl. 12). The electrum coinage of *Miletus* with its type, a lion with head turned back, is probably the next most ancient after the Lydian series struck at Sardes. A lion's head and a star ornament supply the types on the silver down to the fourth century (Pl. 13). Thereafter, on both silver and bronze an Apollo head occupies the obverse and the lion with head looking back is relegated to the reverse.

The device on the rare staters of *Phocaea* is an excellent example of the punning type of coins for the obverse shows a seal (phoca), while below is ⊙ the phocaic equivalent of Φ, the Greek initial of Phocaea (Pl. 14). An extensive series of electrum hectae (sixths) and lower denominations was issued down into the fourth century. There was a great variety of types. The earlier are chiefly animals—seals, lions, bulls and griffins, usually accompanied by a small seal as a symbol; the later types are heads of divinities—Silenus, Hermes, Pan and Athena. Coinage came late to *Priene* though it was one of the ancient cities of Ionia. Not till after Alexander the Great who in 334 dedicated there the famous temple of Athena Polias did a silver coinage appear. The obverse type has a representation of the head of the cult statue of Athena Polias, the obverse usually a trident. Rare electrum coinage with type of lion's head with open jaws is attributed to *Smyrna* before its destruction by Alyattes of Lydia in 585. Spasmodic issues of silver and bronze in the fourth and third centuries attest the restoration of the city but substantive coinage was resumed only in the second century. Alexandrine tetradrachms of spread fabric similar to that used at Magnesia have a fine turreted head of Cybele on the obverse and on the reverse a wreath enclosing the city name, sometimes accompanied by a lion (Pl. 15). Uninscribed silver drachms with type, a seated griffin, were struck before the mass exodus from *Teos* at the time of the Persian conquest in 544. The griffin type continued on the silver coinage with the later addition of the city name.

The three principal islands lying off the coast of Ionia were Chios to the north, Samos further to the south and Icaria lying to the west of Samos. The cities of Chios, Samos and Oenoë, the chief town on Icaria, struck coinage which followed the general pattern of that of the mainland cities of Ionia.

The type, seated sphinx with a peculiarly curled wing, which was to remain the chief device of *Chios* through most of its coinage appeared on its earliest coinage, a rare electrum-stater series, issued about the end of the seventh century. Archaic and still uninscribed silver coins appeared in the sixth century but a second series of electrum staters on the Milesian standard is perhaps connected with the revolt against Persia in the early fifth century. The most striking coinage is the series of silver tetradrachms and subdivisions of the early fourth century (Pl. 16). An unusual revival of coinage in silver and bronze is seen after 84 when Sulla declared Chios a free ally of Rome. The sphinx remains the obverse badge but the amphora which had been a subsidiary type on earlier issues now occupies the reverse.

Unlike Chios and Samos, *Oenoë*, the chief town on the smaller island of Icaria, had only one series of coinage, issued about the beginning of the third century. The types on both silver and bronze are the head of Artemis and a charging bull.

The electrum staters and subdivisions of *Samos* have as type a facing lion's head. The bulk of the coinage probably dates from the decade beginning in 530 when Samos was the chief maritime power in the Aegean. Archaic silver has similar types, but in the fifth century a second type, the head and neck of a bull, appears in the incuse square on the reverse. On the extensive coinage in smaller denominations there is a greater variety of type, a winged boar, a ram's head and a griffin. A similar series, but executed in a more delicate style, belongs to the later fifth century and the presence on the reverse of an olive branch, the symbol of Athens, is a reminder that Samos became completely subject to Athens between 439 and 408 (Pl. 17). The Samian coinage was interrupted between 365, when Athens expelled a large part of the population, and 322, when they were reinstated, but thereafter issues of silver and bronzes with the traditional types continued down into the second century. The prow which was one of the badges of maritime Samos appears as a mint symbol on Alexandrine tetradrachms in the second century.

Although the number of cities in Caria for which coinage is recorded is considerable, there are only a few important series. The cities of the interior did not begin to flourish commercially, and issue autonomous coinage till after the battle of Magnesia in 190. In the earlier period coinage was struck only by coastal cities such as Astyra, the community of Chersonesus, Halicarnassus, Iasus, which is noteworthy for its participation in the federal coinage of silver tridrachms (see p. 8 above), Idyma and Termera.

In the second century autonomous coinage began in the inland cities. Most of these struck a silver series in the second century and, later, usually bronze coinages only. The cities for which coinage is on record are: Alabanda, Alinda, Antiochia ad Maeandrum, Aphrodisias, Apollonia, Attuda, Bargylia, Ceramus, Euromos, Myndus, Orthosia, Stratonicea and Tabae. These city coinages have each their own distinctive types and can be identified from the city name appearing in full or in abbreviated form on the reverse, together usually with a magistrate's name. Most of these cities continued to strike bronze coins into imperial times.

The one Carian series issued consistently and in some quantity was that from the city of *Cnidus* at the western end of the Triopian peninsula. Associated with Cnidus from early times was the cult of Aphrodite and, later, that of Apollo who had a sanctuary there. The chief types on coins of Cnidus, therefore, are the head of Aphrodite and a lion which appears to have been the symbol of the Triopian Apollo. A silver stater with an Aphrodite head in very archaic style may be the remnant of the earliest issues of the late seventh century but it is the forepart of a lion which supplies the obverse type for the earliest substantive silver coinage in the sixth century. The head of Aphrodite appears in the incuse of the reverse. For most of the fifth century Cnidus, under the Athenian hegemony, practically ceased coinage but in the fourth century began the series of tetradrachms and subsidiary silver with a beautiful head of Aphrodite restored to the obverse (Pl. 18). It has been thought that this fine head is a copy from the famous statue of Aphrodite by Praxiteles. The plentiful issues of the next two centuries reflect the prosperity of the city. In the second century the coinage of Cnidus becomes assimilated to that of Rhodes, the three-quarter facing head of Helios on the coinage of the latter replacing the Aphrodite head.

Of the smaller islands scattered off the west coast of Caria there are rare silver issues from Megiste and Nisyrus in the fourth century and earlier silver from Calymna and Carpathus, while only bronze coins of the later centuries are known from Astypalaea. From the larger island of Cos coinage struck by the chief city of the same name extends from the earliest times down to the Roman period. The island of Rhodes has, initially, coinage from the towns of Camirus, Ialysus and Lindus and then a long series of currency of the new capital city, Rhodes, founded in 408.

At *Cos* the oval-shaped archaic silver of the sixth century and perhaps the late seventh has a crab as its emblem. In the fifth century the crab appears on the reverse of tetradrachms, while on the obverse is a discobolus in action, one of the few effective athletic types on Greek coins (Pl. 19). This type probably refers to the games in honour of the Triopian Apollo. Silver, with a wider, spread fabric in the fourth century and later, has a Heracles head. Under the influence of the Rhodian coinage Heracles is shown almost full-face in the early second century. Later in this century the emphasis is on the worship of Asclepius for which the island was later famous. Reverses show either Asclepius or his emblem, the snake-entwined staff.

The fig leaf on the early coins of Camirus, the winged boar of Ialysus and the lion's head of Lindus all vanish with the creation of the new capital of *Rhodes* in 408 and the beginning of the copious issues which lasted down to the Roman period. The types are almost uniform throughout the coinage. The obverse has the head of the sun-god, Helios, to whom the island was sacred and the reverse a rose (rhodon) from which the island took its name. In addition to silver issues there were gold staters in the early fourth century and in the second century. The head of Helios is shown full-face and on some issues from the late fourth century this head is radiate (Pl. 20).

PHRYGIA

Coinage is the expression of a certain degree of prosperity and commerce and in the ancient world such conditions tended to be achieved earlier by cities with access to water transport, the only really efficient means of transport in the ancient world. The history of coinage in the inland districts of Phrygia, therefore, is very similar to that of the inland cities of Caria. There was, in effect, no autonomous coinage by the cities of Phrygia until the development of trade in the second century and, even then, from most of the cities came only local issues of bronze coins. When Phrygia, in common with a great part of western Asia Minor, passed to the kingdom of Pergamum after 190, mints for the production of cistophoric coinage were established at *Apamea* and *Laodicea* and later at *Synnada* after the creation of the Roman province of Asia.

The cistophoric coinage from the first of these two mints has the usual types described above under Ionia but with the addition of the appropriate city name on the reverse. In the Roman period the coinage from these two mints and from Synnada has, in addition to the city name, the names of Roman proconsuls. The only other city with a silver coinage was *Cibyra*. This coinage in the second and first centuries was on the cistophoric standard but had its own particular types, a young male bust in crested helmet and a galloping horseman (Pl. 21). These cities also struck bronze coins from the second century as did a good number of others of which the more important were Acnonea, Ancyra, Appia, Dionysopolis, Eumenea, Hierapolis, Peltae, Philomelium and Prymnessus. These coinages bear appropriate city names and have types of city goddess, the great deities or more local divinities, principally the Phrygian Mên. He is featured on a number of coinages as, for example, at *Philomelium* where he is shown wearing the typical Phrygian cap (Pl. 22).

LYCIA

No coinage was struck in Lycia until after the Persian conquest in 545 when Lycia was formed into a province of the Persian empire and placed under the control of dynasts. A number of series of silver coinage was struck from this time, down towards the middle of the fourth century, when the province fell under the power of the Carian dynasts. After the conquest of Alexander the Great and during the control of the Seleucid kings no local coinage was issued but after 168, when Lycia became a Roman protectorate, a federal coinage of silver and bronze began, as well as some coinage from individual cities.

The early silver coinage of Lycia has been divided into five series: (1) a series of staters and smaller denominations current from *c.* 520 to 480 with the fore-part of a boar on obverse and only a rough incuse square as reverse; (2) a similar series dated to *c.* 500–460 with a like obverse but with an animal - tortoise, crab or bull in the incuse reverse; (3) *c.* 500–460, the same boar obverse but in the reverse a solar symbol, the trisceles, the most common of Lycian reverses; (4) an extensive series running from 480 to 390, again with the trisceles or tetrascles as reverse type but with the heads of deities or dynasts on the obverse. On the reverse and occasionally on the obverse the name of the dynast is given in Lycian characters (Pl. 23);

(5) coinage with a facing lion's head on the obverse and generally the trisceles on the reverse together with the dynast's name.

The number of cities in the Lycian league in the Roman period is given by Strabo as twenty-three and he names as the most important Myra, Olympus, Patara, Pinara, Tlos and Xanthus. The main coinage of the league was, however, issued by the two monetary districts of *Cragus* and *Masicytes*. The principal types on the silver drachms and on bronze are an Apollo head and a lyre (Pl. 24), though types of Artemis and quiver also occur on bronze. The only city to issue autonomous coinage in the early period was the coastal city of *Phaselis* where fifth-century silver staters have the prow and the stern of a galley as obverse and reverse types.

PAMPHYLIA

Like other areas of Asia Minor this district seems not to have been organized politically or economically till after the time of Alexander the Great and, with two exceptions, city coinages in fact date generally from the second century when the area passed first to the kingdom of Pergamum and then to the Romans.

Of the two exceptions, the more important was *Aspendus*. The silver coinage of staters and drachms in the fifth century has a naked but armed hoplite on the obverse and on the reverse a trisceles similar to that on Lycian coins but composed of human legs. The best-known coinage of Aspendus is the fine series issued in the fourth century and later with a pair of wrestlers on the obverse and a slinger on the reverse (Pl. 25). On the reverse, also, is inscribed the native form of the Greek name Aspendus. The coinage ceased sometime in the third century and only some bronze issues appeared from the second century onwards. The second major coinage is that of *Side*. The principal types on fifth-century staters are a pomegranate and a head of Athena in crested helmet. The staters of the fourth century have a more spread fabric providing a larger flan for the finely drawn types of a standing Athena and a naked Apollo (Pl. 26). The Athena head re-appears as the obverse type on the large spread tetradrachms of the second century with their reverse type of Nike or Victory. Bronze coins were issued from the second century by *Attalia*, *Sillyum* and *Perga*. The latter city also struck silver tetradrachms of similar fabric to those of Side but with types, the head of Artemis and a standing figure of Artemis accompanied by her stag.

The only city in this area with a coinage of any continuity and extent was *Selge*. On the silver-stater coinage of the fifth century a facing Gorgon head occupied the obverse and the fore-part of a lion the reverse. Smaller silver had the head of Athena as reverse type (Pl. 27). Selge lay on the Eurymedon, up-river from Aspendus, and appeared to have had a monetary convention with the latter in the fourth century. The silver staters have the same wrestler and slinger types as Aspendus but with the city name in Pisidian letters. Later coins in the third and early second centuries retain these types but give the city name in Greek characters. On bronzes in the last two centuries B.C. the types are a Heracles head and a stag. The coinages of the other Pisidian cities date from the second century and some only from the first, when the district was included in the Roman provincial organisation. The coinage is almost entirely in bronze where the types used are chiefly deities and local divinities and cult statues.

LYCAONIA

Autonomous coinage in this inland area is practically confined to the period of the Roman empire. The cities of *Iconium* and *Parlais* issued their own bronze series but only late in the first century B.C. At the former, the types are heads of Zeus and naked Perseus, at the latter, heads of Zeus, Apollo and Artemis.

CILICIA

There were only six mints of any importance in Cilicia up to the time of Alexander's conquest in the later fourth century. From the mid fifth century these cities had issued silver coinage, partly in their own name and partly in the name of the Persian satraps but this coinage was superseded by the royal coinage of Alexander and then of the Seleucids; and only when the country was organized as a Roman province in the first century did autonomous coinage begin again, and then only in bronze.

The coining cities under the Persians were all ports used as naval bases by the Persian fleet. At *Celenderis* the chief types on the silver-stater coinage are a naked horseman and a kneeling goat, a reverse apt for the surrounding mountainous country rather than for any special cult significance (Pl. 28). The city name is added to the reverse in the issues of the fourth century. A satrapal coinage attributed to Celenderis has a goat as obverse and an owl with spread wings on the reverse. To *Mallus* on the lower course of the river Pyramus has been tentatively attributed a coinage of silver staters of the fifth century with a baetylic stone and bunches of grapes on the reverse and a female figure with wings in a typical kneeling-running attitude. A similar figure, but this time male, occupies the obverse of the staters dated 425 to 385 which have, on the reverse, the city name in its early form, Marlus. The reverse is a swan, more sedate and stately than the lively bird used at Clazomenae (Pl. 29). A satrapal coinage from 385 to 325 has staters with a variety of types, the Persian king with bow, and Heracles strangling the lion, or head of Heracles and the portrait of a Persian satrap (Pl. 30). The staters issued at *Nagidus* from the late fifth century down to Alexander's conquest usually show a seated Aphrodite crowned by Eros and on the reverse Dionysus. The satrapal coinage at *Issus, c.* 385, has unusual types. The god Baal on the obverse is accompanied by the city name in Greek and the name of the Persian satrap Tiribazus in Aramaic. The reverse has the figure of the Persian deity, Ahura-Mazda, cut off by a winged solar disk. Tiribazus issued similar coins at Mallus, Soli and Tarsus. The types peculiar to *Soli* in the fifth century are a kneeling archer and bunch of grapes, though the head of Athena also appears as an obverse type and becomes practically the sole variety later in the fourth century. *Tarsus* as the most important city in Cilicia struck a more prolific series of coins. The first series in the late fifth century, in rather crude style, is in the name of the city only but has Persian types, the king on horseback and a kneeling hoplite. In the fourth century the coinage bears the names of the satraps and presents a rich variety of types, executed in careful detail. The staters of Pharnabazus reproduce on the obverse a facing female head clearly copied from the Arethusa head of Kimon at Syracuse. Later satraps generally place the figure of Baal on the obverse. The vivid reverse of a lion killing a stag used by Mazaeus is copied from coins of Citium (Pl. 31).

CYPRUS

The coinage of this island falls into two separate series. Beginning in the later sixth century is a coinage, inscribed first with Cypriot characters and then in Greek, issued by the kings of Amathus, Idalium, Marium, Paphos, Salamis and Soli. The two Phoenician kingdoms of Citium and Lapethus began striking about the same date a coinage with Phoenician inscriptions. The conquest of the island by Ptolemy Soter of Egypt in 312 ended these local issues and thereafter down to the incorporation of Cyprus into the Roman empire at the end of the first century

Ptolemaic coinage was struck in and for Cyprus. Some of the early issues are unusually primitive in appearance and down to the time of the Persian wars have only a plain reverse. Even in the fifth century, when a reverse type, still in an incuse square, is added, much of the coinage continued to be eccentric in shape. The major denomination was the stater which was divided into thirds, sixths and so on down to a forty-eighth. In the fourth century gold staters and subdivisions were struck with some frequency, particularly at Salamis.

Of the smaller, less frequent coinages that at *Amathus* has as its types a recumbent lion and the fore-part of a lion, at *Marium* an Apollo head and a goddess, identified as Aphrodite, seated on a galloping bull, and at *Soli* a lion's head with open jaws and, as reverse, a bull's head. The more plentiful coinage from *Idalium* has, on the obverse, a seated sphinx, reminiscent of that on coins of Chios, and on the reverse a lotus flower, an allusion to the belief that Cyprus was the lotus land to which Odysseus came on his travels (Pl. 32). At *Paphos* a human-headed bull supplies the obverse type and the reverse usually portrays an eagle, sometimes only its head and fierce beak (Pl. 33), sometimes the bird standing or in flight. The most plentiful issues come from *Salamis*. There the types are a ram lying and, on the reverse, the *ankh*, a ring of pellets round a linear circle (Pl. 34) or a ram's head. In the fourth century appear types of Heracles and goat and busts of Athena and of Aphrodite as on the gold stater of King Prytogaras (351–332).

At Phoenician *Lapethus* the head of Athena appears on both sides of the coins. The earlier more archaic series shows both heads in profile but on the coinage in the name of the king Sidmelk, about 450, the reverse has an arresting full-face head of Athena (Pl. 35). A fighting Heracles is the chief obverse type at *Citium* with, first, a seated lion on the reverse and, in the later fifth century and onwards, a lion killing a stag (Pl. 36). The rendering is more stilted than on the copy used at Tarsus.

GALATIA

There is little coinage of the Greek character from this district and what there is was issued by the local rulers and not by the cities. Only some bronze coinage is known for the earlier tetradrachms following the organization of Galatia by Pompey in 64. Amyntas, who ruled Galatia and a wider area from 36 to 25, struck a series of silver tetradrachms of similar spread fabric and with the same types of Athena head and Nike as at Side in Pamphylia (Pl. 37).

Though the whole of this area cannot be strictly described as in Asia Minor, its proximity and its history make it convenient to consider its coinage at this point. In the Asiatic portion of Bosporus, to the east of the Sea of Azov, there were only small autonomous coinages issued by the cities of *Phanagoria* and *Sinde*. Silver coins of the latter in the fourth century had a horse's head reverse type and either a griffin or a Heracles head on the obverse. At Phanagoria the types on silver in the fourth century were a head in an unusual pointed cap and a butting bull; in the first century a Dionysus head and the city name in an ivy wreath.

The coinage of *Colchis*, the district at the eastern end of the Black Sea, is of base silver issued in the fourth century. The types are a reclining lion and a kneeling human figure with ox's head (Pl. 38).

Of the cities in Pontus, only from *Amisus* and *Trapezus* are there rare silver staters of the fourth century. These cities together with others of which the more important were Amasia, Cabira, Comana and Pharnacea struck a coinage in bronze, particularly during the reign of Mithridates the Great (120–63).

PAPHLAGONIA

Autonomous coinage of the pre-Roman period comes mainly from two cities. There were small coinages in silver in the late fourth century from *Sesamus* with types of Zeus and Demeter and from *Cromna*, also with Zeus head with flowing beard, but, on the reverse, the city goddess with turreted head-dress. These cities were incorporated in the new city of *Amastris*, founded about 300. The silver staters here showed a head in Phrygian cap and a seated female figure.

The only coinage of any extent was issued by *Sinope*, a thriving port on the Black Sea. Staters of the fifth century in primitive style have an obverse type only, the head of an eagle above a dolphin. Later in the century the sea-eagle and dolphin form the reverse and the obverse shows a head of Sinope, an arrangement of types persisting into later centuries (Pl. 39). In the fourth century between 375 and 322 the mint at Sinope struck staters with the same types but the city name was replaced by that of the Persian satrap. In the late third century, though Sinope remains on the obverse but with a turreted head-dress, Apollo and Poseidon appear on the larger tetradrachms. Under the Pontic kings coinage was restricted to bronze.

BITHYNIA

From only some three cities is there an autonomous coinage of note in the fifth
and fourth centuries. From the third century there is a regal coinage issued by the
kings of Bithynia whose rule lasted down to 74 when Bithynia was constituted a
Roman province.

   Calchedon, situated on the Asiatic side of the Bosporus opposite Byzantium
began to coin about the middle of the fifth century. Silver drachms have a bearded
male head on the obverse, while the reverse is a wheel ornament of four spokes
with the first letters of the city name in the intervals. In the fourth century a
stater coinage shows a bull standing on an ear of corn but the reverse is simply
an incuse with a mill-sail pattern (Pl. 40). The coinage of *Cius* began only in the
time of Alexander the Great. Gold staters as well as silver drachms were struck in
the late fourth century, Apollo head and prow being the types on both metals
(Pl. 41). *Heraclea Pontica* was at its most prosperous under a series of tyrants in
the later fourth century but already in the beginning of the century had a coinage
of silver drachms with the head of Heracles as the natural obverse type and a
charging bull on the reverse. The names of the tyrants Timotheus and Dionysius
(345–337) appear on the reverse of their staters, accompanying a design of
Heracles and trophy; the obverse now shows a young Dionysus head. Dionysius
who was sole tyrant down to 305 made use of the same types but signed with his
name only (Pl. 42).

MYSIA

We have now come almost full circle in the tour of Asia Minor, and in Mysia,
lying to the north of Lydia where the earliest coins were issued, it is not sur-
prising to find series of early electrum coins struck by some of the prosperous
cities of this district. The three major coinages in our period were those of Parium,
Lampsacus and Cyzicus, particularly of the latter two. Coinage in electrum from
Cyzicus and in gold from Lampsacus were issued over a long period and provided,
together with the Persian gold darics, the gold currency of most of the ancient
Mediterranean world down to the emergence of the Macedonian empire and its
new gold coinage in the late fourth century.

   The series of electrum staters and hectae at *Cyzicus,* one of the early series of
coins, may have begun towards the end of the seventh century. The most archaic
series of staters is that with a tunny-fish decorated with fillets or ribbons on one
side and on the other, in an incuse oblong, a scorpion. When a tunny is not the

principal type it always appears as a symbol on the Cyzicene coins. Smaller denominations in the sixth century have a variety of marine forms for their types. The electrum series in the fifth and the first half of the fourth century present a whole gallery of types, together forming one of the most varied and attractive series in the Greek coinage. There are three main classes of types; a series of heads—Athena, Heracles, Dionysus; figures such as Heracles with his club and bow, a satyr (Pl. 43), a kneeling Poseidon; and a series of animal forms—lion's head, griffin chimaera or a centaur. All these varieties did not appear continuously but the electrum coinage falls into successive series determined by changing and developing style.

Though some silver was struck at Cyzicus in the archaic period, the principal series is that of the fourth century and the early part of the third. The obverse is usually a charming head of Kore Soteira wearing corn-wreath and veil while a stylized lion's head with bristling mane occupies almost the whole field of the reverse (Pl. 44). Another reverse shows Apollo seated with his lyre beside him. Bronze coins of this period often have heads of either Kore or Apollo. Silver tetradrachms with the spread fabric seen on coinages of other cities in the second century retain the head of Kore, and the reverse is a torch within an oak-wreath.

At *Lampsacus* in the Hellespont, the electrum coinage is probably no earlier than the beginning of the fifth century, the type being the fore-part of a winged horse. Silver drachms of the later fifth century have an unusual double female head in archaic style with a helmeted Athena head in the incuse of the reverse (Pl. 45). The famous series of Lampsacene gold staters is of the first half of the fourth century. The winged horse provides the consistent reverse type but the obverses present a series of heads such as those of Zeus (Pl. 46), Aphrodite and Helios or a variety of figures including Heracles, Helle, Nike and Cabirus (Pl. 47). Silver of the fourth century repeats the peculiar janiform head of the earlier coinage but also shows heads of Athena and Apollo which have the usual reverse of the winged horse. Bronzes of this period use much the same types as the silver coins. In the second century a series of tetradrachms has the head of Priapus on the obverse and on the reverse Apollo playing his lyre.

The coinage at *Parium* is relatively small. Electrum coins of the sixth century, though they bear no city name, are attributed to Parium, for the type, a facing Gorgon head is found with later, signed coins. In the fifth century silver coinage uses the same type as does a coinage of about 400 which has on the reverse a bull with head turned back. In the revival of coinage in the second century at Parium as elsewhere, tetradrachms preserved the Gorgon-head type on the obverse.

Some twenty-three cities in Troas are recorded as having issued autonomous coinages but these vary greatly in extent and importance. The chief coinages in the fifth and fourth centuries before the time of Alexander the Great are those of Abydus, Cebren, Dardanus, Scepsis and the island of Tenedos. From some of these and from Alexandria, Troas and Ilium in addition comes a coinage of tetradrachms in the revival of coinage in the second and first centuries.

Some electrum pieces with the type of an eagle with closed wings have been attributed to *Abydus* about the beginning of the fifth century and in the first half of this century silver coins with the same type carry also the city name; the reverse on the silver is a facing Gorgon head. Between 411 and 387 Abydus revolted from Athens and was a military station of the Spartans on the Hellespont and to this period belong the fine gold staters on which the eagle recurs, but now on the reverse, while the obverse shows a kneeling Nike sacrificing a ram (Pl. 48). On later fourth-century silver, and in bronze also, the almost exclusive types are Apollo head and eagle. The tetradrachms of the second century at Abydus retain the eagle reverse, though it is now portrayed with spread wings; on the obverse, Artemis replaces her brother Apollo.

At *Cebren* the persistent badge is that of a ram's head on the small silver coins of the fifth and fourth centuries which have only an incuse reverse. Bronzes of the fourth century also bear the ram's head on the reverse and usually an Apollo head on obverse.

Electrum staters of sixth- and fifth-century date have been tentatively assigned to *Dardanus* on the Hellespont because of the representation of a cock on the obverse, a type commonly used in later coinages of this city. The cock appears on the reverse of fifth- and fourth-century silver coins which commonly have a naked horseman on the obverse. *Scepsis,* on the river Scamander, has as the types on its silver in the fifth and fourth centuries the fore-part of a winged horse and the stylized representation of a tree, identified as a fir.

Notable amongst the series of tetradrachms of typically wide flan in the second century are those from Ilium,on the site of ancient Troy and from Alexandria, a city founded in the late fourth century by bringing together the inhabitants of a number of cities including Cebren and Dardanus. At *Alexandria* both sides of the coin are devoted to Apollo. The obverse bears his head with long flowing locks; the reverse is a standing figure of Apollo with his lyre. Similarly at *Ilium*, the head and the full length figure of Athena Ilias occupy either side of the tetradrachms (Pl. 49).

21

The island of *Tenedos* off the mainland of Troas minted an extensive coinage from about the mid sixth century down to the early fourth century. The types remain practically uniform throughout the period, a janiform head on the obverse and a double-headed axe on the reverse. The remarkable feature of the obverse type is that of the two heads, the one facing left is a bearded male head, that to the right a female head (Pl. 50). At Tenedos also after about 189 a series of large silver tetradrachms was issued with types similar to those on the earlier coins.

AEOLIS

Of the coinages of this district to the south of Troas the most important is that of the city of *Cyme* which is said by Herodotus to have had a share in founding no less than thirty colonies. Archaic silver without inscription but with the badge of the fore-part of a horse associated with later coins of the city is rare and the most extensive issues date from the time of the Persian wars about 480. These coins and the issues continuing down into the third century continue to have as one of their usual types the fore-part of a horse often combined with the type of an eagle (Pl. 51). On the flat tetradrachms of the second and first centuries the personified head of Cyme supplies the obverse type and on the reverse the horse is shown standing within a wreath.

The other important series in Aeolis are similar tetradrachms from *Myrina* and *Aegae*. At the latter city there is a fine Apollo head on the obverse and a naked Zeus on the reverse; at the former, Apollo holds patera and laurel branch. The Apollo here represented is the Apollo of nearby Grynium where there was a famous temple and oracle of the god.

LESBOS

Of the city coinages of this island the two most important are those of Mytilene and Methymna. These two cities are most probably also the mints of two series of coins without specific mint names. The first of these is a coinage in billon, that is of base silver, in a rather lumpy and eccentrically shaped fabric stamped with the letters Λ E Σ or M. This coinage belongs to the later sixth and earlier fifth centuries and has a design on the obverse only. The more common types are a lion's head and a facing Gorgon head.

The electrum coinage from Lesbos, particularly the long series of hectae or sixths, was the product of the mint of *Mytilene*. The coinage continued from the earlier part of the fifth century down to the middle of the third and falls into three main classes, differentiated by the treatment of the reverse. On the earliest group the reverse type is in *intaglio*, that is sunk into the coin instead of protruding in relief. The other two classes have a more normal relief on reverse, first enclosed in an incuse square then later in a square bounded by lines. The first group of electrum is largely restricted to animal types on both sides (Pl. 52), the second has a number of heads of divinities on the obverse and animal heads (Pl. 53), often in confronted pairs, on the reverse, while the last group in the fourth century tends to have heads of divinities on both sides. This electrum coinage, as well as being one of the most extensive in the Greek series, is one of the most attractive, particularly the later groups which have an appealing freshness and delicacy (Pl. 54).

The silver and bronze of Mytilene of the corresponding period consists of pieces of similar small size and uses a more restricted number of the heads and animal forms from the wider range of the electrum hectae. On the larger silver issued between about 350 and 250 the sole types are an Apollo head and lyre (Pl. 55). Bronze coins of this period present the same types but in the last two centuries B.C. the head of Zeus Ammon with his horn takes over the obverse, accompanied on the reverse by a terminal figure of a bearded Dionysus.

The coinage from Methymna is relatively less abundant. A boar with head lowered to charge is the chief obverse design on silver staters of the earlier fifth century; the incuse reverse has an archaic helmeted head of Athena. This Athena head, but in fine style, becomes the obverse type in the later fifth century and in the fourth, with the lyre of Apollo as the reverse. On bronzes the common reverse is the kantharus or beaker, an allusion to Dionysus of whom there was a cult at Methymna where, also, most of the famed wine of Lesbos was produced.

EUROPEAN GREECE

CRIMEA

The north and west coasts of the Black Sea were dotted with colonies settled by Greek cities chiefly in Asia Minor and these new cities in time issued their own coinages. In the Tauric Chersonese, roughly the modern Crimea, the most important and striking coinage was that of *Panticapaeum* (now Kertch) on the west side of the Cimmerian Bosporus. The earliest coins are silver drachms of the fifth century with a facing lion's head and the first four letters of the city name disposed in the quarters of the reverse, but the most remarkable series is the issue of gold staters in the fourth century. On the obverse the bearded head of a satyr with tousled locks is turned three-quarters facing or in profile, and on the reverse is an unusual winged panther with a horned goats' head (Pl. 56). Fourth-century silver has a similar satyr or Pan's head with a bull or lion's head reverse. The plentiful bronze coins resemble the silver in their types. The only other coinage of any dimensions is that of *Cherronesus* near the modern Sebastopol in the third century. Heracles or Artemis figure on the obverses, with reverse types of a rushing bull (Pl. 57), a stag or a griffin.

NORTH-WEST BLACK SEA

The city of *Olbia* which conducted a prosperous trade with the Scythian tribes of the interior issued silver and bronze coins from the third to the first centuries. The chief types on silver are the head of Demeter and a sea-eagle carrying a dolphin, while on the bronze appears the bearded head of the local river-god, Borysthenes, and a conventional reverse of bow-case and battle-axe. An unusual coinage is a series of cast bronze pieces of various weights showing either Athena or a Gorgon head with a wheel reverse or the sea-eagle as on the silver. Because of their rude fabric these coins were long placed as early as the sixth century but the date now more favoured is the third century. At *Callatis* in what was later the Roman province of Lower Moesia silver coins of the third and second centuries have the not uncommon types of Heracles' head accompanied on the reverse by his bow and club. The silver coins issued by *Istrus* in the fourth century have the sea-eagle and dolphin type which has widespread popularity in this region but the obverse has a most strange representation of two heads; one up, one down (Pl. 58), explained as symbols of the rising and setting sun-god. *Tomi*, famous as the place of exile of the Roman poet Ovid, has a bronze coinage in the first century with the bearded head of an anonymous deity and an eagle in wreath on the reverse. A similar head appears on the silver tetradrachms of about 200 B.C. at Odessus where the reverse shows a full-length, bearded figure identified by the inscription as the 'Great God of Odessus'.

THRACE

Further to the south the coinage of the Thracian cities on the coast of the Black Sea still partake somewhat of the barbaric tinge detectable in the other Euxine coinages. The only city coinage here of any significance was that of *Apollonia* where the persistent type, apt for a seaport, was an anchor. This supplies the type for the obverse of fifth-century silver which has a swastika for reverse. On later coins the anchor is used on the reverse and the head of Apollo, who had a famous temple and a colossal statue in the city, graces the obverse.

The silver coins of the wealthy city of *Byzantium* which was later to achieve greater fame when chosen by Constantine the Great as his new capital under the name of Constantinople are extremely common but begin no earlier than the end of the fifth century. Down to the great siege of the city by Philip of Macedon in 340 when autonomous coinage ceased for a time, the principal type was that of a cow standing on a dolphin (Pl. 59). Byzantium was situated on the shore of the Propontis at the entrance to the Bosporus and had been settled from Argos. The coin type is probably a reference to Io, the daughter of a king of Argos, who was loved by Zeus and who, changed into a heifer and tormented by gad-flies sent by jealous Hera, was driven from land to land and even swam the strait between Asia and Europe which took its name from this event and which is represented on the coin by the dolphin. The connection with the sea is reflected in the types of Poseidon on the silver and bronze coins later in the third century. At *Perinthus* to the west of Byzantium the unusual type, the fore-parts of two horses joined back to back, appears on fourth-century coins with, on the obverse on silver, a Zeus head or a head of Kore in corn-wreath which also was used on bronze.

In the latter part of the sixth century a Miltiades, with a body of Athenian colonists, is said to have established himself as tyrant in the peninsula of the *Thracian Chersonese* and to this period is ascribed a tetradrachm with a facing quadriga, recalling the victory of Miltiades in the four-horse chariot race at the Olympic Games. Tetradrachms issued under a second Miltiades, from about 515, have a lion with head reverted for the obverse, and the Athenian connection is apparent in the helmeted head of Athena in the incuse reverse. The mint of these coins was probably the city of *Cardia* which was originally settled from Miletus, whose badge was the lion used on the obverse here.

With the cities along the Aegean coast of Thrace we come nearer to Greece proper and to coinages which convey the beauty of Greek art, as the matured archaic style blended into the fine classical style. At *Aenus*, on tetradrachms and smaller denominations from 450 to 400, the head of Hermes in his close-fitting *petasus* is seen in profile with, on the reverse, a goat. On the coinage of the first half of the fourth century the same types remain but the Hermes head is shown full face (Pl. 60). At *Maronea* the constant type is a prancing horse. The earliest pieces have only an incuse square on the reverse but fifth- and fourth-century silver coins carry a vine with bunch of grapes within a square inscription giving a magistrate's name (Pl. 61). The city took its name from Maron or Dionysus, and was famous for its wine, recalled by the reverse design of its coins. Dionysus also appears on both obverse and reverse of the large tetradrachms issued in the later second century. Next along the coast was *Dicaea* where the earliest coins have an archaic head of Heracles, joined later by a bull's head as the reverse. About mid fourth century a female head replaced that of Heracles. *Abdera* was settled in 544 by the great exodus of the population of Teos at the time of the Persian conquest of Asia Minor. On the silver octadrachms and tetradrachms of the next century the griffin on the obverse is copied from coins of Teos, and later in the fifth century the city name or the name of a magistrate, arranged in a square, appears on the reverse. A further modification in design added a variety of types in the centre of the reverse (Pl. 62). Silver staters of Abdera after it was subdued by Athens in 408 adopt an Apollo head as reverse type. A very rare tetradrachm of the late fourth century where the magistrate's name is Pythagoras has on the reverse a bearded portrait, thought to be that of the famous philosopher of that name.

Of the islands of Thrace in the Aegean only *Thasos* possessed a coinage of any duration and quantity. Archaic staters show an ithyphallic satyr carrying off a struggling nymph (Pl. 63), a scene repeated in less harsh and brutal style on later fourth-century coins when Thasos came under Athenian domination. Thasos revolted from Athens in 411 and rare gold staters were struck at this time. The types of these and of the silver tetradrachms and subdivisions of the next half-century are a bearded head crowned with ivy and a bearded Heracles kneeling. When autonomous coinage resumed in the second century after the intervention of the Macedonian supremacy, Thasos issued an extensive series of large flat tetradrachms with a Dionysus head and a standing Heracles.

In the troubled times from the Persian wars onwards native tribes under their petty kings extended their influence over most of Thrace. Their names are known almost solely from their rare coinage much of which was struck in imitation of the city coinages of Thrace and the Euxine coast. Coinage of a king called Bergaeus in the early fourth century imitates the type of Thasos, and Amadoccus uses the reverse type of Maronea. Other coinages are original in design, like the silver drachm of a king Seuthes with an armed horseman on the obverse and simply the king's name on the reverse.

MACEDONIA

Lying to the west of Thrace and stretching across the mountainous country from the Aegean to the Adriatic, Macedonia played a critical rôle in the later centuries of our period, for the great Macedonian kings, Philip II and his son Alexander the Great, changed the course of history, not only for Macedon and for Greece, but for the whole of Western civilization, both in Europe and in Asia and Africa. The coinage of Macedonia reflects its development and its place in history. The coinage of the fifth century and of part of the fourth is that of the native tribes together with that of a number of city states. The rise of the Macedonian kings is reflected in the growth of their coinage from the early fifth century onwards and, with the conquests of Philip II in the middle of the fourth century, the autonomous city coinages come to an end. The coinage of the great Macedonian dynasty from Philip II onwards, since it was for a great part of the time not restricted to Macedon but covered a large portion of the Western and Eastern world, is dealt with in a separate section together with the coinage of the other great Hellenistic kingdoms. Finally, with the conquest of Macedon by the Romans in the second century, a semi-autonomous coinage for Macedonia only made its appearance and lasted down to the end of our period and the inception of the Roman empire.

The rough tribes who occupied the mountainous region of Pangaeum along the Aegean coast of Macedon worked the rich gold and silver mines there and, not unnaturally, produced coinage at quite an early date. To the *Onescii* is attributed a rare electrum coinage as early as the sixth century with, as type, a centaur carrying off a woman and early in the fifth century they issued, as well as smaller silver pieces, a series of unusually large silver coins, octadrachms, showing, on obverse, a naked man guiding two oxen; the reverse is still a quartered incuse square. In the district, further to the west, the *Bisaltæ* also struck octadrachms with a naked warrior standing with his horse. The names, presumably, of local kings appear on some series of smaller silver coins with no indication of the people over whom they ruled but one, King Getas, on a series of octadrachms with a naked man guiding two oxen, similar to the type of the Onescii, is clearly stated on the reverse to be the king of the *Edoni*. Yet another tribe, the *Derrones*, struck even larger denominations, decadrachms. The rudely drawn types depict a bearded man driving an ox cart and, on the reverse, a three-legged ornament (Pl. 64).

Of the city states *Neapolis* stood on the Aegean coast opposite the island of Thasos. Its archaic coinage of silver staters has the facing Gorgon head favoured by some other cities in northern Greece. At the end of the fifth century and down to the end of minting in the mid fourth century an Artemis head was used on the reverse on bronze as well as silver. *Amphipolis*, further west on the river Strymon, was founded from Athens in 437 and issued coins from about 424 down to 358. The series of tetradrachms and smaller denominations is one of the great successes of Greek coin design with the sheer beauty of the full-face portrait of

Apollo. The reverse, by comparison, a race-torch enclosed in a square border with the city name is extremely banal (Pl. 65). Amphipolis continued as a mint under the kings of Macedon and under the Romans.

Dotted around the coast of Chalcide, the great promontory with three large tongues of land jutting down into the Aegean, were a number of towns which issued coins from the fifth century down to the conquests of Philip II in the middle of the fourth century. The constant badge on the coinage of *Acanthus* on the west coast is a lion savaging a bull. Herodotus relates that this area abounded with lions and wild bulls and that camels of the Persian expedition under Xerxes were attacked in this district by lions. Archaic tetradrachms (Pl. 66) have the usual quartered incuse but later in the fifth century the city name in a square border appears on the reverse. Almost at the end of the central of the three peninsulas of Chalcide stood *Terone,* famous for its wine and a flourishing port which supplied ships to the Persians in their invasion of Greece. The coinage in the first twenty years of the fifth century included a series of tetradrachms which had on the obverse a wine amphora decorated with a bunch of grapes. During the Athenian supremacy down to 424 the badge was a smaller wine vessel, an oenochoë but the coinage consisted mainly of tetrobols and smaller denominations. A shallow incuse square remained the sole decoration of the reverse till late in the period, when a goat was added as a reverse type. The coinage ceased about 420. At *Olynthus* the coin types seem all to have reference to contests at the games. Archaic tetradrachms of the late sixth century show a quadriga with a bearded charioteer and smaller silver has a remarkable frontal view of a man riding a horse. The same types are repeated after 479 when Olynthus was free from Boeotian occupation but now a flying eagle took its place on the reverse. The confederacy of Chalcidian towns in the first half of the fourth century produced from the mint at Olynthus a coinage of extreme beauty, and, though the city was captured by the Spartans in 379, coinage seems to have continued until the conquest by Philip of Macedon in 358. Gold staters probably issued late in the period may well have been the inspiration of the famous staters issued later by Philip. The types, a beautiful Apollo head and a lyre, are used not only on the gold but on silver tetradrachms and smaller denominations on some of which the name of Olynthus also appears. *Mende* on the westernmost of the peninsulas was, like Terone and Maronea in Thrace, renowned for its wine and hence the choice, as type, of the vine and grapes and representations of the god of wine, Dionysus. On early fifth-century tetradrachms and divisions an ass, the usual mount of Dionysus in legend, stands before a vine with a crow pecking at his tail. Dionysus himself reclines on the ass's back holding a wine cup on coins of the finer period when a reverse type is added showing a vine (Pl. 67). In the later part of the fifth century and down to

Philip's conquest in 358 a young Dionysus head with ivy crown becomes the main type, while the ass is relegated to the reverse. Smaller denominations and bronze carry an amphora on the reverse. An unusual representation of Poseidon, god of the sea, appears on fifth-century coins of *Potidaea*; for the god, holding his trident, is shown mounted on a horse. The famous siege of the city by the Athenians in 432–429 brought an end to the coinage except for some issues in bronze in the fourth century.

At *Lete* the coins, reminiscent of those of Thasos, give a glimpse of the rude and primitive cults of Dionysus in this mountainous area. The types are variations on the theme of a naked satyr seizing a nymph. Staters of the later sixth century are of a lumpy fabric; those in the fifth, prior to the seizure of the area by Alexander of Macedon in 480, are of flatter fabric. The original capital of Macedon was at *Aegae* (later Edessa) and the type of a kneeling goat on its silver staters (Pl. 68) is yet another example of a type punning on the city name and the Greek word for goat. The coinage of Aegae is dated from the accession of Alexander I in 498 to about 480 when he moved his capital to Pydna on the coast.

MACEDON UNDER THE ROMANS

Rome, when she defeated Perseus, the last of the Macedonian kings, at Pydna in 168 divided the kingdom into four districts which, some ten years later, were given the right of issuing coinage. Tetradrachms of the usual wide flat fabric of the second century carry a representation of a Macedonian shield with a head of Artemis in the centre and have, as a reverse, a rather banal design of a club within an oak-wreath and an inscription designating the district issuing the coin. In 148, after the revolt of Andriscus, Macedonia became a Roman province in which only bronze coins were issued with a helmeted head of Roma and the name of the provincial quaestor on the reverse. Between 93 and 88 an unusually plentiful series of silver tetradrachms was issued by the Roman governors. A head of Alexander the Great, with wildly flowing hair, supplied the obverse type and a club between a money-chest and a chair the reverse. The names of the Roman praetor and quaestor appeared one on each side.

THESSALY

To the south of Macedonia lies the great Thessalian plain, almost completely cut off by mountain ranges to the north, west and south. According to legend

Thessaly had once been a great lake until Poseidon, the earth-shaker, opened up the Vale of Tempe through which the waters flowed as the river Peneius. Poseidon accordingly has a place of honour in Thessalian coins for this reason and also as the creator of the horse for which Thessaly was a famous district. Games held in honour of Poseidon took the form of bull fights, which are a favourite representation on coins.

Historically, there appears to have been little archaic coinage struck in Thessaly and the majority of the city coinages date only from the period following the repulse of the Persian invasion in 480. Autonomous city coinages endured down to the invasion of the district by Philip of Macedon in 353 and its final conquest in 344. Some copper coinage is all that probably continued under the Macedonian empire but in 302 Demetrius Poliorcetes of Macedon bestowed liberty on Larissa, Cremaste and Pherae where some coinage was issued for a short time. Coinage lapsed once more and it was not until the liberation of Greece by the Roman general Flamininus in 196 that Thessalian coinage resumed, this time as a coinage of a federation of Thessalian cities. This coinage in turn came to an end in 146 when the district was incorporated into the Roman province of Macedonia.

Larissa, situated on the river Peneius, was the most important city in Thessaly and issued the most extensive and continuous coin series. It is the only city with a rare coinage in the archaic manner, issued before 480. The main coinage, however, begins in 480 with a series of silver drachms and portions using the popular Thessalian types of a youth subduing a bull by grasping his horns, and a free horse in an incuse square (Pl. 69). A number of reverse types in the fifth century feature the nymph Larissa who, according to legend, while playing ball, fell into the river Peneius. The nymph becomes the principal type on the silver coins of the fourth century where she is portrayed full-face in the style of the Arethusa on the coinage of Syracuse. The Thessalian horse still persists as the reverse type. After the subjection of Thessaly in 344 the only coinage of Larissa is in bronze. The next most important town was *Pherae*, not far from Mount Pelion and the famous fountain of Hyperea. The early silver drachms of Pherae have the common bull-fight type and Thessalian horse, accompanied by a lion's-head fountain pouring a jet of water. This same fountain forms the reverse type on fourth-century silver, either alone or accompanied by the figure of the nymph Hypereia with a head of Hecate on the obverse. Alexander, who made himself tyrant of Pherae from 389 to 357, issued a coinage in his own name. Hecate still appears on the obverse of silver didrachms, but now shown full-face, while, on the reverse, is an armed horseman, reminiscent of Macedonian types, and the name of Alexander (Pl. 70).

At *Pharsalus*, famous in later history as the scene of Caesar's defeat of Pompey, there is a departure from the stock Thessalian obverse design in the helmeted head of Athena, though she is accompanied on the reverse, first by a horse's head in the earlier period, and, later, in the period of fine style in the fourth century by a horseman. The *Aenianes* also placed somewhat more original types on their coinage which began only in the fourth century. The obverse shows a head of Zeus and the reverse a javelin thrower. An unusually late resumption of coinage around the mid second century featured an Athena head and a slinger in the act of throwing (Pl. 71).

The coinage of the *Thessalian League* between 196 and 146 presented a series of heads of deities—Zeus, Apollo and Athena as obverse types. The most effective reverse is that of the large silver denomination, tariffed as the equivalent of 1½ Roman denarii, where a helmeted Athena is shown in fighting attitude with spear poised (Pl. 72).

Of the coinage of the islands lying off Thessaly in the Aegean only some bronze pieces survive from *Icus* and *Sciathus*. From *Peparethus* came a larger and more varied coinage. This island was yet another place in Greece famous for its wine and, according to legend, was originally settled by the son of Dionysus and Ariadne. Hence, on some silver tetradrachms of the early fifth century the principal type presents one or more bunches of grapes. The variety of reverse types which recall the badges of other cities, such as the helmet of Corinthian issues, indicates, it has been suggested, close trade relations with such cities. The island was subject to Athens for most of the fifth century and issued no coins of its own, but bronzes of the later fourth century revived Dionysiac types.

ILLYRICUM

Lying on the east of the Adriatic was this mountainous district which was never completely subdued until the Roman period, and the history of coinage here is largely that of the two cities of Apollonia and Epidamnus which were settled as colonies from Corcyra. About 300 an Illyrian kingdom was set up which struck coins at Dyrrhachium but when in 229 Rome interfered in Illyrian affairs and afforded protection to cities such as Apollonia and Epidamnus coinage was resumed and continued down to the reorganization of the area by Augustus.

At *Apollonia* the first period of coinage from 450 to 350 produced a series of silver staters on the Corcyrean standard and with the types of Corcyra's coins, namely a cow suckling a calf and the distinctive double floral pattern on the reverse together with the city name. In the second half of the fourth century the silver staters are of Corinthian weight and types, Pegasus and a head of Athena in Corinthian helmet, distinguished only by the addition of the city name.

Apollonia had no coinage of its own during the ascendancy of the Illyrian kings but after 229 began a new coinage on the standard of the Roman victoriate and with a revival of the cow and calf type of the early coinage. About 100 Apollonia, in conformity with the changed standard of Rome, issued silver on the standard of the Roman denarius, the principal types being an Apollo head and three nymphs with torches dancing round a fire or an Athena head in Corinthian helmet and an obelisk. The coinage issued at *Epidamnus* the capital of the Dyrrhachii follows exactly the pattern of that at Apollonia with the addition of the appropriate name, this time that of the Dyrrhachians. The coinage resumed in 229 had ended before the change in standard and types introduced at Apollonia about 100.

Of the *Kings of Illyricum*, the founder, *Monunius*, occupied the city of Dyrrha-chium and issued a coinage of staters imitating the types of the first coinage of the Illyrian cities but adding his own name and titles on the reverse. Of *Genthius* (197–168) only some bronze coinage has survived but *Ballaeus* (167–135) issued a silver coinage with his portrait and a figure of Artemis on the reverse.

The tribes who occupied the area on the borders of Illyricum and Epirus controlled silver mines and at a mint in the town of *Damastium* produced, in the fourth century, a coinage of silver staters in crude style with types of an Apollo head and a tripod. The names on the reverse are probably those of the local chieftains.

EPIRUS

Lying between Thessaly and the Adriatic, Epirus has a terrain similar to that of Illyricum to the north and its history and coinage follows a similar pattern. The only city coinage of importance here was that of the Corinthian colony of *Ambracia*. The silver staters issued between 480 and 342 were of Corinthian types, differing from the coinage of the mother city in the city name. The Epirote kingdom, however, was a more lasting and more influential institution than the Illyrian.

The Molossi had always been the predominant tribe in Epirus but in 340 *Alexander* extended their dominion over the whole of Epirus. His coinage is, however, largely of non-Epirote origin and stems from his expedition in 332 to help the Greek cities in southern Italy against the Lucanians and Bruttians. The very rare gold staters and the more plentiful silver staters were probably struck at Locri in south Italy. The types are a head of Zeus wearing the oak-wreath peculiar to his worship at Dodona and a thunderbolt. *Pyrrhus* (295–272) also issued coinage in the precious metals during his expedition in Italy and Sicily against Rome. His beautiful gold staters with head of Athena and a graceful

Nike or Victory are, to judge from their fabric, of Syracusan mintage (Pl. 73). From the same mint came also a fine series of tetradrachms and smaller denominations. The tetradrachm has a head of Dodonian Zeus with, on the reverse, his spouse Dione seated on a throne, while the didrachm has a head of Achilles, and Thetis, his mother, riding on a hippocamp. The Sicilian origin of the coinage is reflected in the Persephone head on the drachm which has a fighting Athena on the reverse.

No coins have survived of the successor of Pyrrhus but of the *Epirote Republic* a plentiful coinage appeared from about 238 down to its destruction by the Romans in 168. On didrachms appeared the jugate heads of Dodonean Zeus and Dione with the charging bull of Epirus in an oak-wreath on the reverse. The drachm shows the head of Zeus alone with eagle in oak-wreath as the reverse type.

CORCYRA

On its island of the same name lying in the Adriatic off the west coast of Epirus, Corcyra was one of the few cities together with Athens, Aegina, Euboea and Corinth to issue coinage in the sixth century. It was a wealthy maritime state settled from Corinth and its main series of coins began when it secured independence from that city in 585 on the death of Periander, the tyrant of Corinth. The silver-stater coinage is quite different in fabric from that of other early coinages in Greece and its weight standard is lower than that of the prevalent Aeginetic standard. The obverse type of Corcyra's staters which remains constant for centuries and shows a cow suckling her calf resembles that on coins of Carystus in Euboea; but, though there was a tradition of an early settlement in Corcyra from Euboea, the difference both in fabric and standard of the Corcyrean staters is against this derivation. The reverse design, a double star pattern, is found on early coins of cities in Asia Minor, particularly Miletus and, as the weight standard approaches that in use in Asia Minor, Corcyra's coinage was probably influenced by the city's trade relations with the cities of Asia Minor.

Even earlier than the archaic staters struck from 585 there probably was a small issue of triobols and smaller silver with a cow's head facing as type and a deep incuse reverse. The archaic staters with cow and calf type and double-star reverse (Pl. 74) carried no written indication of their origin down to the middle of the fifth century, when the first syllable of the city name was added to the reverse. Of the smaller denominations most had a single-star design but varying obverses; on the drachm the fore-part of a cow, the half and quarter a head of Hera, an amphora or a kantharos. Between 338 and 300 Corcyra abandoned her centuries-old types and struck staters with Corinthian types but inscribed with her own name or monogram. At the beginning of the fourth century the Corinthian standard of a 40 grain drachm was adopted but the new coinage reverted to older types, forepart of cow and double-star pattern for didrachms and cow and calf or amphora for the drachms.

Bronze coinage in earlier periods had had Dionysiac types, a bunch of grapes, Dionysus and his panther or a satyr with amphora but in the present period lasting down to 229 appeared an additional bronze series showing on the obverse the prow of a galley. These are racing galleys and the names inscribed on them are said to be those of galleys successful in the races. Corcyra became a Roman protectorate in 229 but retained the right to issue autonomous coinage. Didrachms had a young Dionysus head in ivy-wreath for the obverse and Pegasus on the reverse. In conformity with Roman standards a victoriate was also struck with head of Dione and Pegasus. Bronze coins were also struck with similar types.

ACARNANIA

This district on the eastern coast of the Adriatic and south of Epirus had, as its boundary with Aetolia to the east, the river Acheloüs. Like so many other areas on the Adriatic seaboard it derives its coinage standards and to a degree its types from commercial colonies of Corinth established in the territory. An Acarnanian league was in being by the end of the fifth century, the chief town being Stratus on the river Acheloüs.

Of the coast towns of Acarnania which issued a coinage of staters of the Corinthian type one of the most important was *Anactorium* on the Ambracian gulf not far from Actium. The staters here from the fifth century down to 350 were of the conventional Corinthian type but with a digamma F as the distinguishing feature and after 350 the name or monogram of the city was added to the reverse. The city of *Leucas* on the island of the same name separated from the mainland by only a narrow strait began its Corinthian stater series early in the fifth century. After Stratus fell to the Aetolians, Leucas, as the chief city of the Acarnanian League, has a series of staters signed with the monogram ΛK. An extensive bronze series was struck between 350 and 250, one of the most common types being Bellerophon on Pegasus, accompanied on the reverse by a chimaera. Under the Romans, Leucas became separated from Acarnania but continued its autonomous coinage of which the chief piece was the tetradrachm with its statue of Aphrodite and a prow reverse.

The coinage of the inland cities presented their own types on series of small silver. At *Stratus* in the later fifth century the types were the facing head of the local river-god, Acheloüs and on the reverse the head of Callirrhoë his daughter, the mother of the original ancestor of the Acarnanians. From 400 until the city was taken by the Aetolians in the early third century Stratus issued a coinage for the Acarnanian League, retaining its own types but signing them K.

The coinage of the *Acarnanian League* between 250 and 167 was probably struck at Leucas. The most usual types are of local significance for they show the head of the river-god Acheloüs in profile and either a figure of Apollo, who had a famous sanctuary at Actium, or Artemis (Pl. 75). On bronzes in the early second century Acheloüs appears as a reverse type with heads of Zeus, Athena or Heracles on the obverse. *Thyrrheium* which had issued a Corinthian-type stater coinage from about 350 seems to have been the mint of the federal coinage after the separation of Leucas in 167 from Acarnania.

AETOLIA

The reputation of this area in ancient times as the home of a race the least amenable to civilization seems borne out by the absence of coinage until the third century. Against the invasions of Macedon in the late fourth century and of the Gauls in 297 an Aetolian League was created which issued coinage down till 168 and the battle of Pydna, where Rome defeated the last of the Macedonian kings and reorganized the whole region. Unlike other districts which issued a federal coinage no Aetolian cities apparently issued coinage of their own.

The coinage of Aetolia, on the model of that of Macedonia, included a series of gold pieces; the stater had a helmeted head of Athena and the figure of Aetolia seated on shields (Pl. 76), the half the same reverse but a young Heracles head on obverse, and a rare quarter-stater showed head of Aetolus and the Calydonian boar of local legend. In silver the tetradrachms have a similar reverse with either Heracles or Artemis on the obverse. The shields on which Aetolia sits are of two types, Macedonian and Gaulish, a reference to the two invasions, to counter which the League was formed. The figure is a copy of the statue dedicated by the Aetolians at Delphi in honour of their victory over the Gauls. On smaller silver coins one of the most frequent types shows Aetolia weaving the *causia,* a broad-brimmed Macedonian hat, and for the reverse type the Calydonian boar. Bronze coins also reproduce these types, sometimes with a male head, probably Aetolus who appears with additional reverses such as a spear-head, club or trophy.

Locris consisted of two districts; the western, bordering Aetolia and lying along the Gulf of Corinth, was occupied by the Locri Ozolae, while the eastern Euboean was the home of the Opuntii. There was no independent series of coins issued by the cities of the Ozolae, though *Amphissa* and *Oeantheia* struck bronzes in the second century on the pattern of those of the Aetolian League. The coinage of the Opuntii, both quite extensive and of a beauty unexpected in this area, is thought to be not earlier than 387 when, by the treaty with Persia negotiated by Antalcidas, the Spartan, the autonomy of the towns of Greece was guaranteed.

In any event, the upper limit of the coinage is determined by that of the Syracusan issues on which it is modelled. The obverse on the staters, drachms and halves is such a faithful and effective copy of the Arethusa head on the Syracusan tetradrachms by Euainetus (405–367) that it has been thought that the dies for this Locrian coinage were prepared in Syracuse. The reverse also is a copy of the Syracusan type showing the hero Leucaspis. The figure here, however, is, as one variety with his name shows, the hero Ajax, the son of Oïleus king of the Locrians who sailed with the Greeks against Troy (Pl. 77). Silver obols with types of amphora and star may be somewhat earlier than the stater series. After the success of Philip of Macedon at Chaeronea in 338, the Opuntii, who presumably had supported the wrong side, lost their right of coinage, for later fourth-century coinage with similar types bears the name of the Locrians generally and not the Opuntii. Coinage ceased under the Macedonian hegemony from about 300 but when Flamininus restored freedom to the cities of Greece in 197, Opus resumed a coinage in bronze with its old types of Apollo head and bunch of grapes.

PHOCIS

There is practically no autonomous coinage of the cities of Phocis with the exception of Delphi but the twenty-two towns of Phocis were united in a confederacy which issued a coinage from the mid sixth century till late in the fifth century. These small silver coins, triobols, obols and hemiobols had a constant obverse, a bull's head facing, with, as reverse, respectively a female head in profile, a boar's head and a helmet. From 357 to 346 the Phocians seized and held Delphi and used its treasures to strike coin. On the triobols and obols of this period the head of the Delphic Apollo was placed on the reverse. Bronze coins, still with the

36

bull's head obverse, have the names of successive commanders of the Phocians in a wreath on the reverse.

Although the temple of Apollo at *Delphi* enshrined the most famous oracle of the Greek world, the place was only a small town which originally was one of the confederate towns of Phocis, and the claim of Delphi to be regarded as a separate community was resisted by the Phocians. It was, therefore, only from about 520 that coinage for Delphi began and was interrupted from time to time by the stress of political events. The small silver pieces which constituted this coinage were 1½ obol pieces or trihemiobols, obols and three-quarter obol pieces or tritartemoria and even smaller pieces. Of these the most numerous were the trihemiobols with types of ram's head and goat's head facing between two dolphins (Pl. 78) and the tritartemoria with a negroid head with ram's head beneath dolphin (Pl.79). The ram was the symbol of Apollo as god of flocks and herds and the goat refers to the legend that the chasm over which the oracular tripod was later placed was first discovered by the antics of a herd of goats which had sniffed the fumes arising from the chasm. The negroid head probably represents Delphes the legendary founder of Delphi, a son of Poseidon by the nymph Melaine.

A remarkable series of staters and smaller silver was issued when the Amphictyonic Council at the end of the Phocian war was held at Delphi in 346. A fine head of Demeter graces the obverse and Apollo himself is shown on the reverse seated on the Delphian Omphalos (Pl. 80).

BOEOTIA

As in Phocis to the north, the cities in Boeotia early united in an Amphictyonic League and also issued a coinage from about the mid sixth century. In Boeotia, however, the confederate coinage took an unusual form; for, on the staters and smaller denominations, the badge of the confederacy, the Boeotian shield supplied the universal obverse type while the differential of the issuing city in the form first of the initial or part of the city name coupled later with a distinguishing type was placed on the reverse. So at *Coroneia* the site of the great Boeotian festivals a Gorgon head appears on fifth-century coins, at *Orchomenus* in the fourth century a galloping horse and at *Tanagra* a springing horse (Pl. 81).

At *Thebes,* the most important and influential city of Boeotia, coinage probably began earlier in the sixth century. Throughout the coinage the Boeotian buckler remains on the obverse, varying in treatment in the successive periods. On the archaic coinage, the mill-sail pattern incuse is inscribed with part of the city name but in the next period an amphora is added as the reverse type (Pl. 82). On the fine series between 446 and 426, when the Athenians had been expelled and the Boeotian League revived, Heracles and his exploits are the themes of the reverses (Pl. 83). The reverse showing the infant Heracles strangling the serpents, struck now at Thebes, was adopted as a type of the struggle of freedom against tyranny and used in the alliance coinage of Ephesus, Cnidus and other cities in Asia Minor (see p. 8).

Though the ascendancy of Thebes was broken by the peace of Antalcidas in 387, Thebes under Epaminondas in the years from 379 re-established and widened her sphere of influence. To this period belong the finished series of staters with their elegant amphora accompanied by a magistrate's name. The victory of Philip of Macedon at Chaeroneia in 338 over Thebes and her allies ended Theban influence, and coinage, issued at varying times in the next two centuries, was small and mainly in bronze.

EUBOEA

This long island in the western Aegean and lying just off the coast of northern Greece achieved early importance for its commercial activity and the important rôle it played through its two chief cities, Chalcis and Eretria, in establishing colonies and settlements along the coast of Thrace and in Sicily and south Italy. Euboea also gave its name to one of the most widely accepted weight standards for precious metals, and was, accordingly, early in the field in the production of coinage. Since most of the earliest coins are without inscription, there was, in the early stages of coin study, hesitation in ascribing coinage to Euboea but later it was realized that coinage once ascribed to Athens because it was found in Attica has features that distinguish it and indicate its Euboean origin. These features are the existence or a plain linear circle enclosing the obverse type and the division of the incuse of archaic coins by diagonal lines; further the types on such coins appear later accompanied by indications of names of cities in Euboea.

At *Chalcis*, one of two Euboean cities of early importance, there may even have been a small electrum coinage with types of an eagle devouring a hare, but on the archaic silver of the sixth century down to the conquest of the city by Athens in 507 the chief distinguishing badge is a wheel. This wheel forms the obverse type on silver from didrachm down to obol, the reverse consisting of a diagonally divided incuse square. A little later, on tetradrachms and smaller denominations, the wheel, accompanied by letters of the city name, moves to the reverse, the obverse type being an eagle holding a serpent (Pl. 84). During the Theban supremacy from about 370 down to the Macedonian conquest in 336 coinage was resumed with types of female head and eagle with serpent or hare. Similar types were used on the bronze where sometimes the female head is shown full-face. After the restoration of freedom to the Greek cities by Flamininus in 197 Chalcis issued some Attic tetradrachms with a Hera head in a quadriga but the fourth-century types were also used again on other silver.

On tetradrachms of *Eretria* in the fifth century a cow with a swallow perched on her back scratches her nose with her fore-hoof on the obverse and an octopus wreathes its legs on the reverse. The same types but for the absence of the swallow (Pl. 85) were used on the didrachm and drachm and a facing bull's head replaced the cow on smaller silver. While Athens held Euboea between 445 and 411 there was no autonomous coinage but from 411 Eretria struck a coinage in the name of the island as a whole with a nymph's head as obverse and a recumbent or a standing bull on the reverse. Coinage lapsed under the Macedonians from 338 but in the revival after 197 the standing or lying ox appeared again on the reverse and an Artemis bust or head replaced the nymph on the obverse. Bronze coins in both the fourth and second centuries use similar types to the silver in varying combinations. At Chalcis as at other Euboean cities coinage ceased in 146.

Some coinage at *Carystus* probably falls in the later sixth century but the main issues begin after the repulse of the Persians in 480. On didrachms the types are a cow suckling a calf with a cock on the reverse, on drachms and halves a Heracles head and recumbent bull and on smaller silver the fore-part of a bull and palm-tree. The series was interrupted by the Athenian conquest between 445 and 411 and ceased in 336, the earlier series still having the incuse reverse. In the coinage of the second century some gold staters were struck with the Heracles head and bull lying. On silver a beardless head with a diadem and Nike in biga are the types of the didrachm, a Heracles head and butting bull of the drachm. Bronze coins in this period have heads of various deities and reverses of eagle, bull or dolphin.

At *Histiaea* coinage began just before the mid fourth century. A female head in vine-wreath and a bull standing before a vine are the types on the silver, indicating the importance of the local vineyards. In a brief revival of coinage in and after 313 the same obverse was used but on the reverse inscribed with her name the nymph Histiaea was shown seated on the stern of a galley (Pl. 86). In the second century similar types were used. On bronzes of all periods the types were usually a female head and the bull and vine together or separately.

ATTICA

Because of the great and continuing interest of later ages in *Athens* as the greatest single contributor to the development of Greek civilization, the Athenian coinage has naturally been the subject of greater study than any other single series; and the resultant accounts of Athenian coinage have shown great variation both in their view of the content of this coinage and its dating. The proud record of the achievements of Athens in its glory predisposed scholars to attribute to her a pre-eminence in her earlier days also and to single her out in the field of coinage also as one of the earliest to take up and develop the new invention. A similar complex with regard to Rome credited her with a developed coinage at least a century earlier than the date which more recent research has established.

The coinage of Athens, the famous 'owls', the silver tetradrachms with the helmeted head of Athena as obverse and a reverse with a second type, the owl of Athens, and an inscription consisting of the first three letters of the city name was at one time thought to be as early as the early sixth century and associated with the reforms of Solon. A modified view connected this coinage with the time of Pisistratus and the institution of the Panathenaic festival in 566. Other writers, while accepting approximately this latter date as the inception of the 'owls' have attributed to Athens in the earlier part of the sixth century a variety of other coinage. More recent research based on the sober evidence of coin hoards and other art objects has produced a chronology for the Athenian coinage more in keeping with the overall development of Greek coinage.

The earliest coinage at Athens, now placed about 575, is identified as a series of didrachms of what are known as *Wappen-Münzen*, coins bearing on their obverse a variety of devices or family badges and having an incuse reverse, normal in archaic coinage (Pl. 87). This series gave place to a similar series of tetradrachms towards the end of the third quarter of the sixth century and the introduction of the 'owl' tetradrachms described above took place about 525 in the time of Hippias. This coinage, accompanied by smaller denominations with similar types, continued after the restoration of democracy at Athens in 507 with no significant change. The first important alteration in the types was the addition of an olive-wreath to the helmet of Athena and of a small crescent above the owl on the reverse (Pl. 88). The wreath most certainly connotes victory and a recent study has shown that the waning moon in its last phase on the reverse is applicable to the battle of Salamis rather than Marathon. The new variety, then, was introduced about 479, a date in accord with the discovery of new and richer silver deposits in Attica. The series included large decadrachms with similar types, except that the owl faces to front with outstretched wings, and smaller denominations, down to a hemiobol, less than a quarter of an inch in diameter. This silver coinage of Athens, particularly the tetradrachms, became an almost international currency and was widely imitated, particularly in the Near East.

After the disaster of the expedition against Syracuse an emergency gold coinage was struck in 407–406 from metal obtained by melting down the gold statues of Nike in the Parthenon. The types of this coinage, known from the half-stater downwards, remained traditional. This period of stress down to 393 also produced a series of plated bronze tetradrachms. Coinage in good silver, resumed in 393 and extending to about 339, is distinguishable by the replacement of the 'almond' eye of Athena on the archaic coins by a more correct profile eye and by the large heads and more careless drawing of the owls. A second coinage in gold took place probably about 339. The very small silver coins included a denomination as low as the eighth of an obol but these were replaced by bronze coins, largely of similar types, after the mid fourth century. Coinage with an additional symbol on the reverse was issued late in the fourth century.

Athenian coinage practically lapsed during the Macedonian hegemony and it is only in 196 that coinage, mainly of tetradrachms, was resumed. The fabric of these coins is large and flat and the relief considerably lower than on earlier series. The types remain basically the same, though executed in such a different fashion that this coinage is traditionally known as 'New Style'. Athena still holds the obverse and the owl the reverse but the latter is now shown full-face, standing on an amphora. The reverse, carrying two monograms or two or three magistrates' names and a varying symbol, is all enclosed in an olive-wreath (Pl. 89). On the amphora, also, is a numeral and, below it, two additional letters. This coinage together with bronzes in like style and with similar types lasted down to the time of Augustus.

MEGARIS

The capital, *Megara*, though situated advantageously on the trade routes between the Peloponnese and the rest of Greece, produced no inscribed coinage until the first half of the fourth century. A fine head of Apollo in whose honour the lesser Pythian games were held at Megara provides the obverse type for all the silver coinage, with his lyre as the reverse on the larger pieces and crescents, arranged in wheel shape, on the smaller. Megara ceased to coin after the defeat of Athens and her allies by Philip of Macedon at Chaeronea in 339, but after the conferment of freedom by Demetrius Poliorcetes in 307 a second coinage was issued for a short time. Drachms and smaller silver repeat the Apollo and lyre types, which also appear on bronzes, as well as a prow with a tripod and dolphins.

This island with its magnificent harbour situated in the gulf of the same name was ideally situated for trade not only with the states of northern Greece and the Peloponnese but also with the cities of Asia Minor and, from very early times down to its conquest by Athens in 456, was one of the most important commercial states of Greece. In these circumstances the new invention of coinage came early to Aegina. There have indeed been claims that the earliest coinage of the Western world was struck in Aegina, the conception being traditionally ascribed to Pheidon, king of Argos. While the claim of Lydia has been preferred, it remains true that the Aeginetan coinage is the earliest Greek coinage in Europe, its first issues being made in the late seventh century. The uniformity of type on the coinage throughout its history marks it out, in the same way as the Athenian coinage, as not merely a local currency but one intended for international circulation; and down to the Peloponnesian war the coinage of Aegina was the uniformly accepted currency throughout the Peloponnese.

The coinage of silver staters and divisions is of a typically thick, dumpy fabric with a constant obverse type of a sea-turtle, sacred to Aphrodite, whose temple stood above the harbour of Aegina. In the first coinage, the earlier issues show the turtle with a smooth shell, the later with a row of dots down the back and the incuse reverse consists of eight triangular compartments (Pl. 90). In the early part of the sixth century the incuse pattern resembles the sails of a mill, while, on issues down to 456, the incuse is divided up into an irregular pattern by broad bands in relief. Only some of the smaller denominations were struck at Aegina between 456 and 431 when Athens occupied the island and put an end to the coinage.

When in 404, after the ultimate defeat of Athens in the Peloponnesian war, the Aeginetans were restored to their city and coinage was resumed, the obverse type of a sea-turtle was now more shallow and regular with narrower dividing bands. In the divisions of the square appeared the first letters of the city name and a small dolphin. This coinage lasted down to the middle of the fourth century and towards the end of the period bronze coins began to replace the smaller silver denominations. The types were two or three dolphins on obverse and the usual divided incuse, often with abbreviated names. Aegina's coinage in the third and second century was in bronze, the most common types being prow of galley and ram's head.

This city was at least as advantageously situated as a commercial centre as was Aegina. Its isthmus formed the one land connection between the Peloponnese and northern Greece and the city was the meeting point of trade routes from East and West. Through its position on the Gulf of Corinth it monopolized the westward trade, not only with the eastern seaboard of the Adriatic, but with the cities of south Italy. The beginning of coinage at Corinth, accordingly, is only a little later than at Aegina and here too the international nature of the currency is apparent from the constant nature of the coin types.

The obverse type of Pegasus as the sole type on the early issues gave to the Corinthian staters the popular name of 'colts'. Later an Athena head appeared as reverse type, completing the reference to the legend of Bellerophon who was helped by Athena to take and tame Pegasus. The unusually flat fabric of the early Corinthian coinage distinguishes it from most other coinage in European Greece. The earliest staters with the Pegasus type and the archaic letter ? have an incuse reverse divided into eight compartments similar to those on early coins of Aegina. This incuse develops through the sixth century into a swastika pattern (Pl. 91). On the smaller denominations the half-drachm has a half-Pegasus and the half-obol a head of Pegasus as obverse type. By about the beginning of the fifth century the fabric becomes more compact and the coins smaller. A change takes place also in the types, with the addition of a helmeted head of Athena in the incuse reverse on the stater and drachm and of letters on some of the smaller pieces. In the fine-style pieces of the first part of the fourth century, with a relief type on both sides, a changing magistrate's symbol is added behind the head of Athena (Pl. 92). On the full and half-drachm the reverse head is that of Aphrodite, while on coins of the later fourth century and of the third century down to 243 magistrates' letters or monograms are added on the reverse. The issue of Corinthian coinage continued after its occupation by the Macedonians in 338 but came to an end in 223 on its recapture by the Macedonians, after having been freed in 243 by Aratus and the Achaean League. Autonomous coinage was not struck after the freeing of Greece by Flamininus in 196 and in 146 the city was destroyed by the Romans under Mummius. Bronze coinage from mid fourth century to 243 present the traditional types, coupled sometimes with a trident or a head of Poseidon.

A number of cities in the districts on the eastern seaboard of the Adriatic and in south Italy and Sicily modelled their coinage on the Corinthian stater. These copies are distinguished by the omission of the letter ? from the obverse and

43

the substitution of the initial, monogram or fuller form of the city name. The more important of those are as follows:

Acarnania: *Anactorium* (fifth century); *Leucas* (fourth to mid third century); *Stratus* and *Thyrrheium* (*c.* 350–250); *Acarnanian Federation* (*c.* 300–167).
Corcyra: *Corcyra* (later fourth to mid third century).
Epirus: *Ambracia* (*c.* 480 and 432–350).
Illyricum: *Dyrrhachium* (third century).
Sicily: *Syracuse* (late fourth and early third centuries).
Italy: *Locri Epizephyrii* (*c.* 350–268).

THE PELOPONNESE

Up until the Persian wars the currency needs of the Peloponnese were largely supplied either by the Pegasus staters of Corinth, which served the northern area along the gulf of Corinth, or by the staters of Aegina, accepted universally throughout the rest of the area. In the fifth century the magnificent staters of Elis, Sicyon and Argos gained wide currency and there was a considerable increase in the number of Arcadian mints. After the subjection of the Peloponnese by Macedonia in 322, autonomous silver issues largely ceased, though bronze continued to be struck. In the third century as Macedonian hegemony was shaken off the coinage of the Achaean League came to be the chief currency. After the formation of the Roman province in 146 local silver issues finally ceased but bronze continued to be issued by some cities down to the end of the Republic.

ACHAIA

Some archaic staters with a letter Φ between the legs of a trisceles have been tentatively attributed to *Phlius* on the upper waters of the river Asopus, but the main issues from this city run from about 430 to the Macedonian conquest in 322. On the silver drachms the obverse shows a bull, perhaps representing the river-god Asopus, and the reverse a wheel. The name of the city is divided between obverse and reverse. On the smaller silver the letter Φ replaces the wheel. At *Sicyon* the drachms in the fifth century have, as types, a dove with spread wings and a large Σ or a chimaera and a dove, while smaller denominations combine these types. On the handsome staters and drachms of the fourth century down to 322 the types are similar but the dove of the reverse is encircled by a laurel-wreath

(Pl. 93). During the Macedonian period the chief types on bronze are an Apollo head or a dove flying with Σ in wreath as the reverse. Between 251 and 146 a series of triobols continue the dove on the obverse and on reverse Σ surrounded by a magistrate's name.

The series of tribols at *Aegae* begins in the early fifth century but the main series run from 480 to the destruction of the town in 370. The obverse type of a goat is, as at Aegae in Macedonia, a pun on the Greek word for goat and the city name. The principal reverse type is an ivy-crowned head of Dionysus. The first coinage of the *Achaean League* in the decade 370–360 included fine staters with a beautiful head of Artemis and an enthroned Zeus, with sceptre and eagle. The hemidrachms with their laureate head of Zeus and, on the reverse, the monogram of Achaia Χ in a laurel-wreath, were the prototypes of the staple coinage of the reconstituted League from 280 down to 146. As successive towns joined the federation each adapted this coinage, the output of the different mints being differentiated by abbreviated names of the cities, with additional symbols and names of magistrates (Pl. 94). A uniform bronze coinage was also struck with a full-length figure of Zeus and a seated Demeter. On this coinage the name of the participating city appears in full.

ELIS

From the absence of pieces in the archaic style it is apparent that the coinage of *Elis* begins only after the Persian wars about 470. From then until 421 the coinage is of varied and developing style and treatment. Since Elis owed its importance in Greece to the worship of Zeus at Olympia and the celebration of his festival and games there every four years, the coin types naturally refer exclusively to the cult of Zeus. The constant obverse type on staters and smaller silver is the eagle of Zeus. The constant obverse type on staters and smaller silver is the eagle of Zeus, usually shown with a tortoise, a hare or a serpent in its claws; on the reverse Nike or Victory stands or runs, holding the palm branch and the wreath which were the honours awarded to victors in the Olympic Games (Pl. 95). The thunderbolt, the other great symbol of Zeus, is also used as a reverse type. Towards the end of this period only the eagle's head appears on the obverse and the thunderbolt reverse is enclosed in an olive-wreath. In the late fifth century portraits make their way on to the coins with a bearded and laureate head of Zeus with perching eagle reverse or a head of Hera on ornate stephane. Another female head appearing at this time is that of the nymph Olympia. In the fourth century the types of Hera or Zeus and eagle become almost standard and it is the Zeus head of this period which provided the conventional representation, repeated in many subsequent coinages in the Hellenistic period. Elis recovered her freedom from Macedon in 312 and resumed issue of silver coinage with her traditional types down to 191 when she was compelled to join the Achaean League and issue its standard coinage.

Of the islands off the coast of Elis the largest and most important was *Zacynthus* with its city of the same name. On the small silver pieces of the first half of the fifth century the commoner types are either a crescent or an amphora on the obverse and a tripod on reverse. Apollo, to whom there was a temple in the city, is consistently honoured on the coinage for the rest of the activity of the mint down to the middle of the fourth century. On staters and tetrobols early in the period the reverse shows a figure seated on a rock, playing a lyre, identified either as Zacynthus, the eponymous hero of the island or as Apollo himself. On later issues the reverse of most denominations reverts to the tripod of the Apollo cult; bronzes of the later period present similar types.

MESSENIA

The only coinage of importance in this district was that of *Messene* itself. The Messenians, subject to Sparta since the seventh century, were restored after the defeat of Sparta by the Thebans under Epaminondas at Leuctra in 371 and the city refounded. The staters and smaller silver issued between 369 and 330 used, as obverse, a Demeter head crowned with corn, derived from the type designed by Euainetus at Syracuse. The Zeus on the reverse represents the local cult of Zeus whose temple stood on the slope of Mount Ithome where the new city of Messene was established. Similar types, but in weaker style, appear on the large Attic tetradrachms of the next period. With the establishment of the Achaean League in 280 the coinage of Messene adopts a similar style with types of Zeus head and tripod. In 191 Messene began the issue of the conventional coinage of the League.

LACONIA

The traditional Spartan contempt for money is borne out by the absence of any coins struck at *Sparta* until the third century. Rare tetradrachms attributed to King Areus (310–266) show a head with royal diadem and on the reverse the archaic, colossal statue of Apollo at the ancient Laconian town of Amyclae (Pl. 96). Tetradrachms of the later third century have a helmeted Athena head and a seated Heracles. His head and his symbol, a club, provide the types for smaller silver and bronze. King Nabis (207–192) also appears on his own tetradrachms with a seated Heracles. The bronze coinage of Sparta from the third century down to Roman times is more plentiful. The obverse and reverse types are supplied by heads of deities and their symbol such as Athena and owl, Heracles and club.

ARGOLIS

Although one tradition gives the credit for the invention of coinage to Pheidon, king of Argos, it was at Aegina that these early pieces were supposed to be struck. There are in fact no archaic coins of *Argos*, which was heavily defeated by Sparta shortly before the Persian wars, and it was not until about 468 that Argos was sufficiently restored to begin the issue of coinage. This first series, lasting till about 421, consists of silver drachms and fractions, the types being a wolf, the symbol of Apollo Lykios whose worship at Argos was of considerable antiquity. In the following period, extending down to the Macedonian conquest in 322, Argos produced one of the most handsome series in the Greek coinage. The head of Hera on the stater, drachm and some of the smaller silver was probably inspired by the famous statue of the Argive Hera by Polycleitus. The reverse on the stater shows two dolphins swimming in opposite directions with a small symbol between them and, on the drachm, the Argive hero Diomedes grasps a sword and carries the Palladium, the ancient wooden image of Pallas Athena which he had brought back from Troy to Argos (Pl. 97). In the century after 322 the only autonomous silver issues were tetrobols, with the earlier types of wolf and initial letter *A*. Most of the Argive bronze coinage is of this period. The chief types are Apollo head and wolf or tripod and head of Hera with initial letter. On joining the Achaean League in 229 Argos began the issue of this federal coinage.

The coinage of *Epidaurus*, famous for its great sanctuary of Aesculapius, had its own coinage only between about 350 and 323, but Apollo as well as Aesculapius is honoured on the coins. On light-weight drachms the Apollo head on the obverse is accompanied on the reverse by a figure of Aesculapius seated on a throne and holding his hand over a serpent. This reverse is said to be a faithful copy of the statue in gold and ivory of Aesculapius at Epidaurus, the work of Thrasymedes of Paros. Bronze coins of the same period mainly refer to Aesculapius and the objects associated with his cult. Coinage of the Achaean League was struck at Epidaurus from 243.

Although there was no political confederation of the towns of Arcadia with a federal currency such as that of the Achaean League, coinage for Arcadia in general was apparently struck, probably on the occasions of the national festival. Silver triobols dated to the period 490 to 417 were minted at *Heraea* with types of Zeus Lycaeus enthroned and on the reverse a female head with the inscription *Arkadikon*. A later issue was struck at the new capital *Megalopolis* between 370 and 362. The staters show head of Zeus and Pan seated on a rock and the Arcadian monogram. Coinage was struck by these and other Arcadian cities in their own names. One of the most plenteous issues was that of *Pheneus*. On the silver of 421 to 362 Hermes is honoured on the obverse with, on the reverse of the triobols, a bull feeding and, on the obols, a ram. On issues later in the fourth century Demeter, crowned with corn-leaves, occupies the obverse and Hermes is shown on the reverse of staters and drachms running and carrying on his arm the child Arcas, son of Zeus and Callisto and legendary founder of the Arcadians. The famous story of the destruction by Heracles of the Stymphalian birds naturally finds expression on the coins of *Stymphalus*. On triobols and obols of the early fourth century the types are a Heracles head in lion-scalp head-dress and the head of a bird. On staters of about 362 Artemis, who was worshipped at Stymphalus, appears on the obverse while the reverse shows Heracles striking upwards with his club, presumably at the Stymphalian birds (Pl. 98).

CRETE

Although Crete is now recognized as the site of one of the earliest-developed civilizations in the Western world, it had long lapsed from that proud position and the economic circumstances were such that it was not till the fifth century that some Cretan cities began the issue of coinage. The most prolific period of coinage is the fourth century, though a number of city coinages continued in one form or another down to the conquest of Crete by the Romans under Q. Caecilius Metellus in 67. The weight standard generally in use is the Aeginetic and the denominations usually struck were staters (or didrachms), drachms and some smaller portions. In the early second century a number of cities struck imitations of the Athenian new-style tetradrachms, inscribed with the local name, and a number also issued Attic tetradrachms with spread fabric.

The folk memory of the ancient glories of Crete created a store of legends and myths, many of which are the subject of illustration on the coinage. Zeus who was said to have been born and concealed by Rhea in a cave on either Mount Aegaeon or Mount Dicte appears most frequently; and the type of a goat, used on a number of occasions, refers to the goat Amalthea who suckled Zeus in his infancy. The labyrinth built for Minos by Daedalus at Cnossus is the almost constant reverse on the city's coinage. The story of the abduction of Europa by Zeus who, in the form of a bull, brought her to Crete where she gave birth to Minos is featured on the coins of Gortyna and occasionally of other cities.

At *Aptera* on the north coast of the island some of the fourth-century staters are distinguished by the signature of the artist Pythodoros on the obverse. The types of the stater are a head of Artemis and an armed warrior saluting a sacred tree. The hero is called Ptolioikos on the coins, perhaps the *oekist* or founder of the city. On the fourth-century staters of *Chersonesus* the obverse head is that of Britomartis, a Cretan nymph, daughter of Zeus and beloved by Minos who pursued her till she leapt into the sea and was transformed by Artemis into a goddess. The reverse shows Apollo seated with his lyre. At *Cnossus* fifth-century staters illustrate the legend of the Minotaur and the labyrinth. On the obverse the Minotaur runs with a stone in each hand and the labyrinth, in a square maeander pattern, occupies the whole of the reverse. In the early fourth century the labyrinth takes the form of a swastika with a star at centre, while the obverse shows a head of Demeter. On issues between about 350 and 200 the head, on pieces of fine style, is that of Hera and the maze is of the conventional square pattern (Pl. 99). Attic tetradrachms of flat fabric after 200 have either an Apollo head and round labyrinth or Zeus Ammon head and square maze. This latter type was also used on bronzes, as well as an Artemis head with quiver or with caduceus.

The supposed founder of *Cydonia* was Cydon, the son of Apollo and Akakallis, a daughter of Minos. Staters and drachms of the fourth century with a nymph's head for obverse show, on the reverse, a child being suckled by a wolf or hound, suggesting that attached to Cydon was yet another instance of the widespread ancient legend of an unwanted child being exposed to die but being brought up by a wild animal. The nymph's-head staters have another reverse type, an archer stringing his bow. Bronze coins have a young male head and a seated hound reverse. In the period after 200 Cydonia in common with other Cretan cities struck imitation Athenian tetradrachms as well as tetradrachms of similar flat fabric with bust or Artemis with bow and quiver and Artemis in hunting dress accompanied by her hound. Most of the issues in the period down to 67 were in bronze. The most common types were an Apollo head or an owl as obverse and a star within crescent as reverse. Next to Cnossus the most important and wealthy city was *Gortyna*. Here the principal subject of the coinage is the legend of Europa and the bull. Staters of the mid fifth century show her seated on the bull, the reverse being a lion's scalp surrounded by the name of the city in a square inscription. The handsome coins of the period between about 430 and 300 are even more completely devoted to illustrating the legend. A bull forms the reverse while, on the obverse, Europa sits pensive on the branch of a tree (Pl. 100)—a Gortynian facet of the legend of which there is no certain knowledge. On staters later in the series an eagle perches on the branch of the tree or on Europa's knee. On bronzes of the third century also these latter types are used. In the period after 200, as well as imitation Athenian tetradrachms, there are pieces with local types, a Zeus head and standing figure of Athena. Drachms repeat the earlier Europa-on-bull type as well as a naked male figure either seated on a rock or advancing with spear and shield. Bronze coinage down to 67 features Zeus and Europa and bull or Apollo and butting bull.

Another ancient legend is commemorated on the coinage of *Itanus*. The sea-god, half man, half fish, armed with a trident and the two sea-monsters on the two sides of staters and, smaller silver of the late fifth and the fourth centuries is a reference to the story of Glaucus of Anthedon in Boeotia, a fisherman who ate of a divine herb which Cronos had planted and, thus, secured the gift of prophecy. Every year he visited the islands and coasts of Greece accompanied by marine monsters and, as at the seaport town of Itanus, his oracles were much reverenced by fishermen and sailors. The coins at *Lyttus*, staters and subdivisions, in the period 450 to 300 with types of an eagle flying and fore-part of a boar again refer to the legend of the birth of Zeus for Lyttus was close to Mount Aegaeon, one of the claimants to be the birthplace of the god. The same types interchange their positions on the drachms of the third century and bronzes of the period usually also have a Zeus head and standing eagle. At *Phaestus* the early issues in the fifth century illustrate the Europa legend but many of the types, particularly in the fourth century, honour Heracles, the father of the eponymous hero, Phaestus. On one series of staters Heracles stands with his bow, club and lion-skin while on the reverse is a bull—the famous Cretan bull bound by Heracles. On another, the story of the bull is combined with that of the slaying of the Lernaean hydra (Pl. 101). Another of the Cretan legends is shown on yet other staters. The reverse is again the Cretan bull but on the obverse is a naked winged figure, hurling a stone. The inscription identifies him as Talos, the man of brass made by Hephaestos. His task was to traverse the island, warding off strange vessels which approached it.

The artist Pythodorus who worked for Aptera also signs some of the issues in the earlier fourth century at *Polyrhenium*. The reverse is the bull's head, common to many Cretan coinages, and the obverse, the head of Artemis Dictynna whose temple stood in the territory of Polyrhenium. Staters of the period 330–280 show a Zeus head and again a facing bull's head. Coinage of the period down to the Roman conquest include tetradrachms of Athenian type as well as with types a male head with bow and quiver at neck and a seated figure of Dictynna holding Nike. *Praesus* which stood to the east of Mount Dicte, one of the claimants to the scene of the birth of Zeus, naturally honours the god on many of its issues. Staters and drachms show Zeus enthroned, holding sceptre and eagle, and the fore-part of a goat, which, according to legend, suckled Zeus in his infancy. The bull of Cretan legend forms another reverse, linked with heads of Apollo or Demeter. Although *Rhaucus* was an inland town, it had a cult of Poseidon but not in his normal aspect of sea-god but rather as the creator of the horse and the teacher of its management. Staters of the fourth century show Poseidon leading a horse while the reverse is the god's usual symbol, a trident. Silver of the period 300 to 166 has head of Poseidon with dolphins or trident while bronzes combine these two latter types.

AEGEAN ISLANDS

Aegina and not the other great island Crete would seem to have been the model for coinage in the Aegean islands, for the earliest series are of sixth-century date, earlier than the coinage of Crete, and are based on the Aeginetic weight standard. Only the more important and flourishing of the islands have coinage as early as this, the lesser islands not commencing their issues till the third century. Although the Cyclades passed under control of the Ptolemies in 308 they were allowed to continue some autonomous coinage, though in the last two years of our period much of the silver currency was furnished by Athenian and Cretan issues.

The most northerly of the Cyclades was *Andros* and here an archaic coinage of staters and subdivisions in the sixth century has as its sole type an amphora, for Dionysus was the chief deity of the island and a fountain in his sanctuary ran with wine on his festival. Similarly, in the coinage from 308 down to Roman times, Dionysus and his panther appear on silver and, on the bronze, again the head of Dionysus with some form of wine vessel. On the island of *Ceos* three cities issued coins. At *Carthaea* fifth-century staters have an amphora with dolphin or dolphin and grapes, the latter type having the incuse reverse inscribed with the first syllable of the city name. Pieces with the same amphora type, given to Andros above, are possibly also of Carthaea. In the series after 300 the bearded head on the silver may be that of Aristaeus, son of Apollo and regarded as the protector of vine and olive plantations. The reverse is the dog Sirius, encircled by rays. The early issues at *Coressia* illustrate two of the fishermen's catches, either a cuttle-fish or a dolphin. Later issues, in bronze only, have head of Aristaeus with a bee, grapes or a star.

The chief city *Iulis* uses the common type of a bunch of grapes, on both staters and smaller silver, in its sixth-century issues. Its bronze issues after 300 are similar to those at Coressia but have the appropriate city name.

Delos, though the smallest of the Cyclades, had the greatest claim to fame as the place where Leto gave birth to Apollo and Artemis and the site of one of the greatest temples of Apollo. Despite all this, it has no prolific coinage. No coins of the Aeginetic weight standard current in the other islands have been identified for Delos in the archaic period, but didrachms of the Euboic standard with type of lyre and letter Δ may represent the coinage of the island of the sixth and early fifth centuries. Delos was the site of the common treasury of the Greek confederacy for the war against Persia, but during its control by Athens down to about 308 it issued no coinage. In the following centuries down to about 87, using the Rhodian standard, Delos struck silver with types devoted to the cult and legend of Apollo. On drachms and half-pieces the Apollo head on obverse is supplemented by a reverse of a palm-tree in which a swan is seated, a reference to the story that Leto gave birth to Apollo and Artemis in the shade of a palm. Bronze coinage shows Apollo and lyre, and Apollo, or Artemis, and palm-tree.

The early issues at *Melos* are on the Phoenician standard. On sixth-century staters the type is a ewer but in the fifth and subsequent centuries the constant type was a pomegranate (Pl. 102). Melos sided with Sparta in the Peloponnesian war and was taken by Athens in 416. Coinage began again in the restored city about 400 on the Rhodian standard, again with pomegranate obverse, linked with types of wine-cup, trident or ram's head, and, on half-drachms, a naked archer shooting. The latter type also appeared on fourth-century bronze. The coinage from the third to the first century included some Attic tetradrachms showing helmeted head of Athena and Apollo in long robe, playing his lyre and didrachms with the same obverse and pomegranate reverse. Bronzes have the pomegranate obverse and reverses of wine vessels or a lyre. Dionysus was also the chief deity at *Naxos*, the most fertile of the Cyclades, which exercised some measure of hegemony in the sixth century. Its staters and halves of this period have the type of a wine-cup appropriate to Dionysus. After a lapse, while under Athenian control, coinage began again in the fourth century. The types now were head of Dionysus and wine-cup on both silver and bronze. Similar Dionysiac types continued in use down to the Roman period.

The fine marble and its products for which *Paros* was famous find no mention on its coins. On its early coinage a kneeling goat forms the obverse type. After the suppression by Athens of local coinage at Paros, as elsewhere, fourth-century silver and bronze take up the goat type again with an ear of corn as reverse. Didrachms of fine style in the third century have a head of Artemis and standing goat or head of Demeter and ivy-wreath enclosing the island's name. Tetradrachms of the second century gave place of honour to an ivy-crowned head of Dionysos and show Demeter seated with corn and sceptre. On other tetradrachms Archilochus of Paros, one of the earliest lyric poets, is pictured seated playing the cithara.

Siphnos was famous for its mines in the early centuries and was regarded in the time of Herodotus as the wealthiest of the islands. Its permanent coin type was an eagle flying, used on the obverse of its archaic staters and as the reverse on early fifth-century pieces, where an archaic Apollo head supplies the obverse. Similar, types, coupled with an Artemis head, were used on the bronze in the fourth century. The most handsome issues at *Tenos* are the fourth-century tetradrachms with head of Zeus Ammon and, on the reverse, Poseidon enthroned, holding dolphin and trident. Similar coins were issued in the third century and bronzes feature Poseidon and his symbols, for Tenos was famous for its great temple of Poseidon.

ITALY

The coinage of Italy down to the extension of Roman control over the peninsula in the latter half of the third century and the suppression of autonomous coinages falls into two distinct categories. In the south the colonies founded from Greece struck a coinage of silver and small token bronze in the fashion of other Greek cities. In the inland and upland areas to the north in Umbria, Picenum, Latium and Apulia the medium of exchange appears to have been bronze used as a value coinage and issued in large heavy cast pieces, though some of the smaller denominations were struck coins. This type of coinage is similar to the early bronze issues of Rome in the early third century and is discussed together with the Roman issues in the next section. At some cities in intermediate areas parallel coinages in silver with token bronze and in heavy bronze or *aes grave* were issued for a time as at Rome itself.

ETRURIA

Etruscan civilization, influenced by Greek ideas, but yet different and owing little to native Italian culture, reached its greatest heights in the fifth century. Its earliest coinage, a series of gold coins with types of lion's head or young male head with a plain reverse may be of fifth-century date but the main Etruscan series runs from the fourth century down to the mid third century. Gold and silver often bear marks of value ranging from 100 down to 1, indicating on the gold their value in silver litrae and, on silver, the value in bronze. Types on gold coins include a hippocamp with four stars on the reverse or a young male head with, as reverse, a bull crowned by bird with wreath in beak (Pl. 103). On silver the variety of types is considerable, amongst the more common being a Gorgon head with plain reverse, a running Gorgon with a wheel reverse or laureate head of Apollo with plain reverse. In bronze the larger denominations are of cast heavy bronze, the smaller of struck bronze. The most common series are those with wheel both sides or wheel and wine-cup. Some of the issues in all metals bear inscriptions in Etruscan characters of towns such as Populonia, Volaterrae and Volsinii, where the coins were issued, but many issues carry no indication of their origin.

CAMPANIA

This, the most northerly of the Greek silver-coining areas of south Italy, included coin-issuing cities, both those founded originally as colonies from Greece itself and also cities which, as the chief towns of their own areas, issued coinage on the Greek model. *Cales* was a city of this latter type. In the third century it has a series of *aes grave* with the constant reverse, a wine-cup indicative of the two main industries of the city, wine and pottery-making. In the latter half of the same century Cales issued silver didrachms with types an Athena head and Nike in biga. The coinage of *Cumae,* the oldest Greek colony on the west coast of Italy founded from Euboea, begins in the early fifth century. Issues in quantity, however, begin only about 480 with silver staters with the constant badge of Cumae, a mussel-shell, and either a diademed female head, Athena head or lion's scalp facing, between two boars' heads. The series ended in 423 when the Samnites captured Cumae. The fine harbour at *Naples* early attracted a Greek settlement, originally from Rhodes. Initially the site was called Parthenope and later received settlers from a number of cities including Athens. By these settlers in the mid fifth century it was re-named Neapolis and it is about this date that its first coinage of silver didrachms begins, with types, in the period down to about the middle of the fourth century, of a man-headed bull as reverse and an Athena head or head of Parthenope and man-headed bull, crowned by flying Victory (Pl. 104). The next series changes the types to Apollo head and horseman, but the didrachms of the third century revert to the earlier Parthenope and man-headed-bull types. Though Neapolis came under Roman dominion about 290 the silver coinage probably continued down to the end of the first Punic war in 241. The bronze coinage which began in the fourth century may have continued a little later. The usual types are Apollo and Victory crowning man-headed bull.

A number of towns in Campania have a series of silver didrachms issued around the mid third century. At *Nuceria Alfaterna* the types are a young male head with ram's horn and name in Oscan script and Castor standing by his horse; at *Suessa Aurunca* the obverse shows Apollo and the reverse a rider carrying a palm and leading a second horse, while at *Teanum* Heracles in lion-skin occupies the obverse and Nike in three-horse chariot the reverse, again with the city name in Oscan script.

APULIA

The prolific coinage of Tarentum, just to the south in Calabria, served the currency needs of this district until the early third century when coinage by Apulian cities began to be issued. At *Luceria* and *Venusia* only bronze in the form of *aes grave* was issued and at a number of cities the only coinage was apparently small bronze pieces. Of the few cities with coinages of silver didrachms and subdivisions the most important series are those of *Apri* and *Teate*. At the former the types of the didrachm are head of Persephone and prancing horse; at the latter, a diademed female head and a naked horseman crowning his horse.

CALABRIA

The issues of the cities of this area are meagre, with the exception of those of the great and prosperous city of *Tarentum* whose coinage is easily the most prolific of all the Greek cities of south Italy. A colony of Lacedaemonians was settled as early as 708 on the bay on the west coast of Calabria, a site equipped both with an excellent harbour and access to superlative fisheries and also set amidst fertile country famous for its produce and its horses. From the latter half of the fourth century Tarentum called in a succession of adventurer kings from Epirus to aid her, first against the Lucanians and other barbarians and, latterly, against the encroaching power of Rome. The ancient tradition that Taras, the founder of the first settlement, was saved from shipwreck by his father Poseidon who sent a dolphin to carry him to safety provides an almost constant type on Tarentine silver staters.

The earliest staters in the latter part of the sixth century are of an unusual fabric which is employed by a number of cities in Magna Graecia. The type of Taras on the back of the dolphin is in relief on the obverse and the identical is repeated on the reverse in incuse. It is, however, not a question of the obverse relief being punched through from the reverse but of the use of two separate dies, one the normal intaglio die to produce an obverse in relief, the other a relief die producing an incuse reverse. Contemporary with the Taras type is a type of a kneeling Apollo holding lyre and flower. This issue is of like fabric, with the identical type in incuse on the reverse. Later in the century the more usual fabric was adopted with a second type in relief on the reverse, first a wheel of four spokes and then a hippocamp or sea-horse. At the beginning of the fifth century an archaic head, probably that of the founder Taras, appears on the reverse of the staters and smaller silver which have other—but still marine—types of sea-horse or cockle-shell on the obverse. On the establishment of a democracy at Tarentum in 473 a new stater coinage was issued, still with Taras and dolphin on obverse but with a seated figure of the founder holding a wine-cup or other object on the reverse.

About the middle of the fifth century began the great series of Tarentine staters which was to extend, with modifications of style and small changes of type, down to the suppression of local issues by Rome in 228. The basic types are Taras on dolphin on the reverse and, on obverse, a rider on horseback. This long series is divided on grounds of style and change of types into successive periods: (1) 420–380, naked horseman; (2) 380–345, Nike crowning horseman leading a second horse; (3) 344–334, boy crowning horse while another examines its hoof; (4) 334–302, horseman with lance; (5) 302–281, similar but with magistrates' names on obverse; (6) 281–272, boy-rider crowned by naked youth; (7) 272–235, similar types but of smaller module; (8) 235–228, similar types but with complicated monogram in field. The district round Tarentum was famous for its horses and the great variety of horesmen types on the staters, particularly since a Victory crown is associated with many of them, probably illustrate the games in the hippodrome. On the staters of the period 281–272 the symbol of an elephant which appears on the obverse clearly indicates their issue in the period when Pyrrhus of Epirus with his squadron of elephants was campaigning for Tarentum against Rome in south Italy (Pl. 105).

Tarentum also struck a succession of gold staters and subdivisions. From the variety of designs, outstanding is the earliest with head of goddess in stephane and veil, with reverse of Taras as a child, holding out his arms to his father Poseidon. Other issues show head of Heracles and Taras driving a biga or head of Zeus and eagle with extended wings standing on a thunderbolt.

Though Tarentum was finally captured by Rome in 272, the city, as an ally of Rome, was allowed to continue coining till about 228. During Hannibal's invasion of Italy in the second Punic war Tarentum sided with Carthage and issued gold staters and a final series of horsemen staters of low weight in silver between 212 and the recapture of the city by Rome in 207.

The Greek city colonies of this district lying both on the east coast on the Tarentine gulf and on the west coast on the Tyrrhenian sea together produced one of the most interesting and artistically successful coinages in our period. Their early issues are of the unusual fabric noted above at Tarentum, where the obverse type is repeated on the reverse in incuse. Though these cities flourished greatly due to their situation in prosperous terrain and to their commercial activity, the prosperity of many of them was interrupted by destructive strife between themselves and by the attacks of the Lucanian natives, until in the third century the whole district passed under the control of Rome.

On the shores of the Tarentine gulf the most northerly of these cities was *Metapontum*, an ancient settlement destroyed by the Samnites but resettled from Sybaris under the leadership of Leucippus in the early sixth century. The silver coinage here as at other Lucanian cities consists of staters of Achaean weight (8·3 gm.) with subdivisions of a third, a sixth and a twelfth. The earliest series from the latter part of the sixth century down to about 470 is of the typical thin fabric with the distinctive type of a corn-ear in relief on obverse and incuse on reverse (Pl. 106). This type which is the consistant badge of Metapontum may be connected with a cult of Demeter but more probably refers to the wheat crops, one of the sources of prosperity. The staters of the remainder of the fifth century have the more usual type in relief on both sides. The corn-ear, the constant obverse type, is accompanied by a variety of reverses—Apollo standing with laurel branch and bow, or seated playing his lyre, and Heracles with club on shoulder. In the first half of the fourth century, as happens in other coinages in this period of finest art, the city badge is transferred to the reverse, the obverse being given over to heads of divinities inscribed with their epithets, Homonoia, Hygieia, Demeter, etc. The latter half of the fourth century produced first a coinage of staters and di-staters with the helmeted head of the founder Leucippus as the obverse type. Later issues have a head of Demeter with corn-wreath for obverse while the corn-ear reverse is accompanied by a variety of symbols and magistrates' names. Bronzes issued in the late fourth century commonly have a female head and ear-of-barley types. The coinage of Metapontum ended with the capture of the city by the Lucanians just before 300.

Heraclea, further down the coast from Metapontum, was founded only in 432 by Tarentum and Thurium, as another link in the chain of defence against the Lucanians. The first issues in the last years of the fifth century are diobols with a head of Heracles and lion running and only in the early fourth century were larger pieces, didrachms, struck with types of bare-headed Athena and Heracles with wine-cup, reclining on rocks. The best-known series is that of the didrachms between 370 and 281 with the splendid reverse of Heracles strangling the lion, and a helmeted head of Athena on the obverse (Pl. 107). A similar coinage continued to be issued in the third century but on a different weight standard, that of Rome. Bronze coins in the later fourth and the third centuries commonly have types of Athena and Heracles.

On the coast just north of Bruttium stood *Sybaris* which enjoyed such prosperity that it became synonymous with luxury. The sixth-century staters are of the normal archaic fabric for this area with type of bull with head turned back and the name of the city inscribed retrograde. The city, destroyed in the war with Croton in 510, was refounded with help from Poseidonia in 453. In the short period before its second destruction by Croton in 448 Sybaris issued a coinage of sixths of staters which recognized the assistance rendered by Poseidonia, for the coins combine the Poseidon with trident type of Poseidonia but inscribed with the name of Sybaris and the Sybarite bull type inscribed with the name of Poseidonia. After the second destruction of the city the Sybarites, with assistance of colonists from Greece, particularly from Athens, founded a new colony in 443 not far from the old site. It was given the name of *Thurium* from a fountain called Thuria in the vicinity. The new colony had reached a high pitch of prosperity by 425 and the series of staters and portions issued in the remainder of the fifth century reflect the city's prosperity in their artistic excellence. The types are a helmeted head of Athena and a bull charging with lowered head. Though the Thurii were severely defeated by the Lucanians in 390, the city continued to flourish, to judge by the fine series of coins issued in the first half of the fourth century. The types are similar to those of the earlier period and include a number of di-staters on which names engraved on the base below the bull may be those of the die-engravers (Pl. 108). The style of the coinage in the period down to 281 deteriorates and the names of magistrates now appear on them frequently. In common with other south Italian coinages the issues of Thurium in the later third century adopt the Roman six-scruple weight standard. The types on the staters are now either a laureate head of Apollo with the charging bull or an Athena head with owl on branch. On bronze coins of the fourth and third centuries the most common types are those of helmeted Athena and bull.

On the west coast of Lucania the colony of *Poseidonia*, founded from Sybaris in the seventh century, began its coinage about the middle of the sixth with a series of staters of the common south Italian archaic fabric, with types of Poseidon poising his trident (Pl. 109). The weight standard of the issues down to 470 was that of the Campanian stater (7·6 gm.) but the fifth-century issues adopted the

Achaean weight (8·3 gm.) and, at the same time, a fabric with relief types on both sides, the reverse being that of a standing bull. On staters just before the capture of the city by the Lucanians about 390 a facing head of Hera replaced Poseidon on the obverse. The Lucanians changed the name of the city to Paestum. Some rare silver and bronze issues were struck with only semi-literate inscriptions in Greek in the third century before the Roman colonization of the town in 273. From this time onwards bronze only was issued by Paestum which, exceptionally for Italian towns, was allowed to continue her bronze issues even down into the early decades of the empire.

Another colony of Sybaris to the south of Poseidonia was *Laüs*. Its coinage of staters and portions has, as type, the local river-god, represented by a man-headed bull with head turned back, on its issues in the second half of the sixth century. In the fifth century, when a reverse type in relief was adopted, the same bull type was used but with head not turned back. Laüs, too, was taken by the Lucanians about 350 and its coinage thereafter is only in bronze with types, a goddess head and a crow.

Velia owed its foundations to the Phocaeans who had emigrated at the time of the Persian invasion about 540. Early issues in the latter part of the sixth century are uninscribed Phocaean drachms and portions with fore-part of lion devouring prey and an incuse reverse. In the first half of the fifth century Velia produced didrachms of Italic standard with nymph's head and crouching-lion types. The finest coins of Velia are the fourth-century didrachms. On obverse is a head of Athena in a richly worked helmet while the reverse shows a lion in the act of seizing a stag. Smaller silver pieces have as reverse an owl on an olive-branch and bronzes in the later fourth century mainly use the types of the silver issues.

BRUTTIUM

The history of coinage in Bruttium, the district forming the toe of Italy, follows a somewhat similar pattern to that of the areas to the north. There is an archaic coinage for a few of the Greek cities which are joined by others in the fourth century. In the early fourth century these suffered at the hands of the invading Lucanians and of Dionysius of Syracuse. Croton, supplemented by a new mint at Locri, was the principal mint from the mid fourth century onwards but after Rome seized contol of the area about 277 only the Bruttii retained the right to strike gold and silver, the other mints issuing only bronze in the third century.

One of the earliest coinages was that of *Caulonia*. Staters of the normal south Italian fabric have a strange type, a naked male figure holding up a branch or a plant in his right hand, while a small winged figure runs down his extended left arm; at his feet stands a stag. On the staters and portions from 480 to 388 the same figure continues to hold the obverse while the stag is promoted to the principal type, now in relief, on the reverse. The coinage of *Croton* is one of the most plentiful and persistent. In its archaic issues the chief type, in relief and incuse, is a tripod, the city name being spelled with the initial archaic letter ९. In the period 480–420 where both sides of the coins are in relief the tripod continues as the main type, but in the next series down to about 390 an eagle with closed wings perched on the capital of a column or other object forms the obverse with the tripod only as the reverse type. Towards the end of the fifth century some exceptionally elaborate compositions adorn the coins. These include Heracles seated on a rock before an altar with, on reverse, again a tripod, to the left of which Apollo shoots an arrow at the Python. Other staters show the facing head of Hera, and Heracles reclining on rocks, holding a wine-cup. In face of the danger from the Lucanians and from Dionysius of Syracuse the cities of south Italy leagued together and Croton struck an alliance coinage about 390 with types head of Apollo and infant Heracles strangling two serpents, an alliance type used elsewhere both at Thebes and for Ephesus and her allies (see p. 8). Though the success of Dionysius in 388 ended the coinage of most of the cities, Croton, after an interval of about twelve years, began to coin again, at first staters with Apollo head and tripod and, later, eagle with spread wings and the usual tripod. Coinage ended when Croton was taken by Agathocles of Syracuse in 299. Bronze coins, mainly in the fourth century, have as types eagle and thunderbolt or tripod, Heracles and eagle or Persephone and three crescents.

Pandosia, an inland town, was one of the mints which began to strike only in the mid fifth century. The stater types are a nymph's head and a naked figure holding branch and patera. From the inscription this is a personification of the local river-god Krathis. Towards the end of the fifth century staters and thirds of unusual beauty present a facing head of Hera and a scene where a naked Pan sits on a rock with his dog beside him. *Terina*, originally a colony of Croton, began its independent issues about 480. A female head inscribed Terina has a variety of Nike reverses and in subsequent coinages down to the early fourth century these types persist, with heads in finer style and with more elaborate representations of Nike.

Locri Epizephyrii, the ally of Syracuse against the Greek cities, has a double series of coins from the mid fourth century. Corinthian-type staters with Pegasus and head of Athena in Corinthian helmet with the name of the city as a differential on the obverse were used, as finds show, for foreign trade. Coinage for more local circulation used a Zeus head as obverse type with a seated figure, described as Eirene, as reverse in the period down to about 332. Later issues present a new reverse, an eagle devouring a hare. When Locri became an ally of Rome in the third century, she issued staters with a remarkable reverse on which a figure, described as *Pistis*, the good faith of the Locrians, placed a wreath on the head of a seated Roma.

Rhegium, just across the straits from Sicily, has early issues with the same type in relief and incuse on obverse and reverse respectively but the coinage is of drachms not staters, the type being a man-headed bull. About 494 Anaxilas, the tyrant of Rhegium, used a band of Samians and Milesians emigrating to the West to seize the Sicilian town of Zancle and Rhegine drachms of this period make use of Samian types, a facing lion's head and calf's head. Subsequent coins of Rhegium between 480 and 466 show a mule-car with bearded charioteer and a running hare, types said to celebrate Anaxilas' Olympian victory with the mule-car. On the establishment of democracy at Rhegium in 466 issues began of tetradrachms and drachms with, again, the lion's head facing and as reverse a seated male figure. On the striking coinage from about 415 to the destruction of the city by Dionysius of Syracuse in 387 the reverse is a fine laureate head of Apollo (Pl. 110). Bronzes of this period have similar types.

The native people, the *Bruttii*, established their superiority over the area, including most of the Greek cities, by the early third century. Their coinage begins during the Pyrrhic war when they sided against Rome but, even after their submission in 272, coinage continued until the end of the century. Gold drachms have types of Poseidon and Thetis on hippocamp, accompanied by Eros, or Heracles head and Nike in biga. The main coinage is of silver where one of the chief types with busts of the Dioscuri and, on the reverse, the Dioscuri on horseback (Pl. 111) has an affinity with the early Roman denarius. There were plentiful issues of bronze with heads of deities such as Apollo, Heracles and Zeus and reverses of Nike in biga or fighting Athena.

SICILY

The story of coinage in Sicily as in south Italy is largely that of the coinage of the numerous Greek colonies established in the island. The most prosperous and influential city was Syracuse, which at various times practically monopolized the right of coinage for the whole island. A number of events affected the history of the cities and their coinages. In 480, when the Persian threat to Greece was repulsed at Salamis, the Carthaginain invasion of Sicily was thrown back at the battle of Himera by Theron of Agrigentum and Gelon of Syracuse. The fifth century was a period of prosperity for the cities of Sicily and it is reflected in the magnificent coinage of this period. Towards the end of the century came the Athenian invasion, culminating in the disastrous defeat and surrender of the Athenians in 413, an event which was followed by a series of special issues at Syracuse. In 406 the Carthaginians were successful in seizing and holding the western part of the island, bringing to an end a number of city coinages and initiating issues for their own purposes at others. At the request of the Greek cities, Timoleon of Corinth came to Sicily in 344 to oust the Carthaginians whom he defeated at the Crimissus in 388 and who, by the subsequent treaty, were confined to the district west of the Halycus. Under Timoleon most of the tyrants were expelled and democracies established in the cities. The struggle against the Carthaginians was continued mainly under the leadership of Syracuse, until, at the end of the first Punic war, they were compelled to evacuate the western part of the island, which passed to Rome. Syracuse under Hieronymus sided with Carthage in 216 and the city was besieged and taken by the Romans under Marcellus in 212. The whole island from this time was made into a Roman province and city coinages except for some bronze came to an end.

Of the cities along the south coast *Agrigentum*, situated on the heights a few miles from the sea, was easily the most prosperous. Its coinage began in the latter half of the sixth century with a series of didrachms with types of eagle and crab. As a result of the leading part played in the defeat of the Carthaginians in 480 by Theron, who had become tyrant of the city in 482, Agrigentum rose to new heights of importance, and with the death of Theron in 472 began a period of great prosperity which lasted till the Carthaginian invasion in 406. The magnificent and plentiful coinage of this period consists of tetradrachms and smaller silver, still with the eagle and crab types. In the last years of the period between 413 and 406 new splendour was added to the coinage by issues including decadrachms which showed two eagles standing on a hare and on the reverse a quadriga with an eagle flying above (Pl. 112). Smaller silver denominations repeat these types, while bronzes retain the eagle and crab designs. The city was destroyed by the Carthaginians in 406 and it was not till the time of Timoleon that coinage began again but only with small silver pieces and bronze coinage. Under the tyrant Phintias (287–279) bronze coins were struck with his name on the reverse. Agrigentum sided with Carthage in the wars of the third century, her coinage then consisting of small silver with types of Zeus and eagle, and of bronze with types such as Apollo head and two eagles on hare. The city passed under Roman dominion in 241 and for the remainder of the century issued only some bronze coinage.

Eastwards along the coast from Agrigentum lay the city of *Gela* at the mouth of the river of the same name. In earlier times Gela was the most important city after Agrigentum and Syracuse and its tyrant Gelon (491–485) even gained control of Syracuse to which he moved part of the population of Gela. On the coinage of the earlier part of the fifth century the constant type is that of a man-headed bull, representing the local river-god. On tetradrachms the second type is either a quadriga with Nike above (Pl. 113) or a warrior on a prancing horse. This latter type is also used on smaller silver denominations. On the establishment of democracy at Syracuse in 466 and the return of the inhabitants of Gela there ensued a period of prosperity reflected in the fine series of coins which largely continue the earlier types. In the period between the defeat of the Athenians in 413 and the destruction of the city by Carthage in 405 Gela struck some small gold coins; the major piece has the traditional types, another the man-headed bull and head of goddess described as *Sosipolis*, the guardian divinity of the city. On the tetradrachms is the head of the young river-god Gelas with quadriga reverse. On bronzes of this period the most common types are this young river-god and bull with lowered head. The city, recolonized in 338, struck only small silver pieces and bronze coins whose issue extended into the Roman period after 241.

Camarina further along the south coast was destroyed by Syracuse in 552 but rebuilt in 495 by Hippocrates of Gela and, in the decade before its next destruction by Gelon, issued small silver coins with types of Athena standing and flying Nike with swan beneath. Rebuilt in 461 as a colony of Gela, Camarina produced a series of tetradrachms with head of Heracles in lion pelt and quadriga and late in the fifth century outstanding didrachms with a facing head, declared by the inscription to be that of the river-god Hipparis. On the reverse the nymph Camarina rides on a swan (Pl. 114). Camarina did not recover from the Carthaginian depredations until the time of Timoleon when small silver litrae appeared with types of Athena and free horse.

Selinus, furthest to the west, took its name, as did the river near which it stood, from the selinon or wild celery which grew in abundance there and a leaf of which forms the obverse on its early didrachms in the period 480–466. The swampy and malarial land was improved by the draining of the marshes in the second part of the fifth century on the advice of the philosopher Empedocles. This freeing of the city from the pestilence of malaria is commemorated on tetradrachms where in a quadriga stands Apollo as god of healing together with Artemis, while on the reverse the river-god Selinus sacrifices at an altar. Didrachms illustrate the same theme with types of Heracles struggling with a wild bull and the river-god Hypsas sacrificing. The coinage of Selinus ended with the Carthaginian destruction of the city in 409.

In the north-west of the island the town of *Eryx* was famous for its temple of

Aphrodite. Its coinage in the archaic period, with types of eagle and crab, suggest a dependency on Agrigentum. On fifth-century coinage after 480 Aphrodite takes the place of honour. She is usually shown seated, holding a dove and sometimes accompanied, as on a tetradrachm series, by Eros, with the reverse type of a dog and three stalks of corn. The city fell to Carthage and in common with the rest of eastern Sicily remained in Carthaginian hands throughout the fourth century. Silver obols struck in this period still have the head of Aphrodite but, on the reverse, a man-headed bull is accompanied by an inscription in Punic letters. Aphrodite also appears on bronzes of the fourth century with dog reverse and continues on the bronze issues after eastern Sicily passed to Rome in 241.

Though not a Greek city, *Segesta* achieved an equal level of civilization and also began coining in the early fifth century. The chief types on didrachms and smaller silver were the head of the personified city and a dog. Towards the end of the century Segesta produced a brilliant coinage, particularly the beautiful tetradrachms with head of Segesta and a young hunter, accompanied by two dogs. It was a dispute between Segesta and Selinus to the south that led to the Athenian intervention in Sicily and the subsequent Carthaginian invasion in 409 which brought an end to coinage at Segesta.

At *Himera* on the north coast of the island the earliest coinage is just towards the end of the archaic period in the early fifth century. The obverse type is a cock with an incuse square as reverse of didrachms and a hen in the incuse of drachms. Theron of Agrigentum seized control of the city about 482 and it was here, after being blockaded in the town by the Carthaginians, that he gained his great victory over them. The coins of Himera until the death of Theron in 472 still have the cock as obverse type but use the crab of Agrigentum as a reverse. In the prosperous years of the fifth century, tetradrachms have the favourite Sicilian type of a chariot with Victory flying above. Here the coin is inscribed with the name Pelops, the legendary king of Elis where the Olympic games were held. The reverse shows the nymph Himera sacrificing at an altar while a small figure of Silenus stands under the jet from a fountain (Pl. 115). The naked horseman on the obverse of didrachms is probably another type referring to the Olympic games. Bronze coins of the fifth century have a Gorgon type on obverse and a varying number of dots, indicating value, on the reverse. Though Himera was destroyed by the Carthaginians in 408 a new town, built near the thermal springs close by and taking its name *Thermae Himeraeae* from them, coined again in the first half of the fourth century. The head on the obverse of tetradrachms is that of the nymph of the springs, the reverse continuing the well-known quadriga type. Heracles appears on the reverse of smaller silver and bronze for, according to legend, it was for him that the springs first opened. A coinage in bronze began again when Rome took control of eastern Sicily in 241.

Panormus, a Phoenician town on the north coast began to coin after the repulse of the Carthaginians at Himera in 480. The coins are quite in the Greek style with types, as on the tetradrachms, of Apollo and quadriga and even the inscriptions are almost always in Greek. After the successful Carthaginian invasion of the end of the fifth century and the destruction of many Greek cities the importance of Panormus as a mint was enhanced but the coins, now with Punic inscriptions, largely copy the types of Syracuse and other Greek cities. In the fourth and third centuries the coinage is mainly in bronze and after the city was captured by Rome in 254 it continued a steady bronze coinage.

The outstanding quality of the coinages of the cities of Sicily makes this series a contender for the crown of all Greek coinage and particularly is this so in the case of the cities on the eastern side of the island. Just across the narrows from Italy was the city originally called *Zancle* whose early fifth-century coins show a dolphin within a sickle-shaped band, probably representing the harbour. The city, seized about 494 by Anaxilas, the tyrant of Rhegium in Sicily, with a force of Samian and Messenian emigrants, was renamed *Messana*. Tetradrachms of the time of Anaxilas (494–476) use the Samian types of a facing lion's head and a calf's head and the types of mule-car and hare which appear also on the coins of Rhegium. After the expulsion of the tyrants in 461 these latter types were continued, but shortly the driver of the mule-car becomes the city deity, Messana herself (Pl. 116). About the middle of the century the name Zancle reappeared for a short time on tetradrachms with Poseidon and dolphin types. The city was destroyed by the Carthaginians in 396 and later coinage is in bronze only. In 288 the city was seized by a body of Oscan mercenaries called the *Mamertini* who maintained themselves through alliance with Rome and struck a bronze coinage till late in the century. The types are chiefly martial, amongst the most common being a head of Ares, god of war, and eagle on thunderbolt.

Naxus, the oldest of the Greek settlements, has a coinage lasting only from the later sixth century to the destruction of the city by Dionysius of Syracuse in 404 but its issues are amongst the most admired in the Greek coinage. Dionysus is the god most celebrated on this coinage. On the early issues appears his portrait in archaic style with a bunch of grapes as reverse type. The city's inhabitants were transferred to Leontini in 476 but, before the middle of the century, coinage was again being struck at Naxus. On tetradrachms the head of Dionysus is wreathed with ivy and, on the reverse, a bearded Silenus squats on the ground holding a wine-cup (Pl. 117); on later issues a vine grows up beside him. In the last years before the city's destruction, the obverse type is changed on tetradrachms to a Maenad and on didrachms to Apollo.

At the foot of Mount Etna was the town of *Catana*, founded from Naxus. This city issued tetradrachms of an unusually finished style in the period before Hiero of Syracuse removed the inhabitants in 476. The obverse is another example of a local river-god, Amenanus, in the form of a man-headed bull and on the reverse is Nike carrying a wreath. Hiero named the new colony of Syracusans he established here Aetna. With the exception of a unique tetradrachm with a bearded Silenus head and seated Zeus the coinage is of smaller silver with a similar Silenus head and a winged thunderbolt. Catana, restored in 461, struck tetradrachms with a young male head and quadriga. The finest coins of the city are of the period 413 until the destruction of the city in 404 by Dionysius of Syracuse. A magnificent facing head of Apollo graces the obverse of the tetradrachm series, accompanied by a quadriga with horses at full stretch. A number of these pieces carry the signature of the artists who engraved the dies. On smaller silver there is a similar facing head identified by the inscription as the river-god Amenanus. After submitting to Rome in the first Punic war Aetna recovered her prosperity and struck a plentiful bronze coinage down into the second century. At another inland town, *Leontini*, a regular type, a lion's head with open jaws, is another example of a pun on the type and the city name. This type appears on tetradrachms in the first half of the fifth century together with the common Sicilian type of a quadriga with Nike flying above. An alternative to the lion's-head type is an Apollo head which, in the finer style of the later fifth century, is paired with the lion type to form a most handsome tetradrachm (Pl. 118). The city passed into the control of Syracuse about 422 and it was not until that city fell to Rome in 210 that coinage was revived at Catana, though now in bronze on which Apollo and lion continue as frequent types.

The leading rôle in Sicilian affairs played by *Syracuse* is apparent from the above account of the other cities and their coinage. Its own coinage, whether under its tyrants and kings or under a democracy, is both in its quantity and quality an index of the city's status. Coinage imported from Greece must have supplied the earliest needs of Syracuse, for it is only in the latter part of the sixth century that coinage in its own name can be identified. In the archaic period the reverse is an incuse square divided into four parts, usually with the archaic head of a nymph in the centre. The obverse types seem clearly to be related to denominations, for on the tetradrachm appears a four-horse chariot and on the didrachm a horseman leading a second horse. With the seizure of control of Syracuse by Gelon, tyrant of Gela, in 485 there began a new series of coins with a second type in relief, the head of Arethusa, the nymph of the fountain on the island of Ortygia. The dolphins around her head symbolize the sea surrounding the island. The great defeat of the Carthaginians by Gelon at Himera in 480 was followed by an issue of large decadrachms with the now traditional types but executed in exceptional style. These pieces are popularly called Demareteia, for they were said to have been struck from the proceeds of the hundred talents of gold presented to Demarete wife of Gelon by the Carthaginians for her intervention on their behalf in the peace negotiations. Under Hiero who succeeded his father in 478 and under the democracy following Hiero's expulsion in 466 the tetradrachm coinage of Syracuse continued the traditional types in ever-developing style, a number of pieces bearing the signature of the die engraver, a sure sign of contemporary appreciation.

The defeat in 413 of the Athenian expedition to Sicily opened a new period of coinage. The issues included gold pieces, the largest of which with a female head and Heracles strangling a lion were signed by the artists Kimon and Euaenetus. As after Himera, so now, the victory over the Athenians was celebrated by magnificent silver decadrachms with Arethusa head and a quadriga in high action. Below the quadriga are represented the arms taken as booty from the Athenians and given as prizes in the games which celebrated the victory. A number of these decadrachms are signed by the engravers Kimon and Euaenetus (Pl. 119). In addition to tetradrachms reproducing the types of those decadrachms, another series, again by Kimon, presented, as obverse type, a facing head of Arethusa with loose, flowing locks. This coinage gained great acclaim throughout the Greek world and was copied by a variety of cities. Such was the coinage under Dionysius the elder and his son of the same name, until the latter was dethroned by Dion in 357. A novelty in the Syracusan coinage in the brief four years of Dion's reign was a series of electrum coins of 100 litrae and subdivisions. The usual obverse was an Apollo head with head of Artemis, a tripod and a lyre as the reverse type of the various denominations.

With the advent of Timoleon, the liberator from Corinth in 345, the silver stater was established as the standard denomination with a Pegasus reverse and helmeted Athena head, as on the Corinthian staters, but also with other obverse types such as head of Zeus or Arethusa. On bronze coinage of this period the head of Zeus Eleutherios is the most prevalent obverse type with, as reverse, a free horse or a thunderbolt. The coinage of Agathocles who next ruled Syracuse from 317 to 289 in the earlier issues continues to bear only the city name; then the name of Agathocles replaces the city name on gold and silver and finally from 304 the title of king assumed by Agathocles is also recorded on gold and bronze issues. Amongst the finest of the issues are the tetradrachms of the middle period with head of Persephone and Nike erecting a trophy, a reference to Agathocles' victory over the Carthaginians in Africa in 310 (Pl. 120). The name of Hicetas, tyrant from 288 to 279, appears on his gold coins, that of the city only on the silver. In the long reign of Hiero II (274–216) silver coins, still maintaining the traditional quadriga reverse, introduce a series of portraits of Hiero himself, his son Gelon and his queen Philistis. Hiero's grandson and successor Hieronymus also placed his portrait on silver pieces in the single year which he reigned until his assassination brought a final three years of democracy, ended by the capture of the city by Rome. For a considerable period in the second century Syracuse, under the Romans, continued to strike bronze coinage with heads of divinities, mainly Zeus, Athena and Persephone.

CENTRAL AND WESTERN EUROPE

The coinages of the only semi-civilized peoples, including a number of Celtic tribes in the northern hinterland of Mediterranean civilization, are all derived from Greek and, later, from Roman models. Not unnaturally, the earliest series to lend themselves to imitation by such barbaric tribes were the gold staters of Philip of Macedon, with laureate head of Apollo and two-horse chariot and the silver tetradrachms of Philip, with laureate head of Zeus and horseman, for these were amongst the first coinages to gain, as it were, international currency. These coinages and their successive imitations from the later fourth century onwards spread by means of the natural routes of communication up the Danube valley into the valley of the Rhine.

In *Transylvania*, the western part of modern Rumania, in western Hungary and lower Austria finds which are the only means of identifying such coinages with specific areas show that the most commonly imitated coin was the tetradrachm of Philip of Macedon. The horse usually becomes plump and ungainly, far removed from the race-horse of the original, but the obverse, though the indiscriminate mixture of hair and leaves betrays an ignorance of the true original, is still recognizably a Zeus head. Later pieces from some of those areas bear in Roman letters the names of local chieftains. In *Moravia* the coinage imitated was the gold stater of Alexander the Great with types of helmeted head of Athena and figures of Nike with wreath and palm. A most unusual imitative coinage is that of the peoples in the valleys of the upper Danube and Rhine in *Bohemia*, *Bavaria* and parts of *Switzerland*. This coinage of the Boii is of gold and is of an unusual cup-shaped fabric with a peculiar shell-shaped pattern. Because of the fancied resemblance to a rainbow of some of these patterns, these pieces are commonly known by their German name, Regenbogenschüsselchen (Pl. 121). As Roman power expanded and the denarii of the republic gained wide currency, this coinage was also copied in *Pannonia*, an area partly represented by modern Jugoslavia.

GAUL

The only coinage in Gaul in true Greek style is that of *Massalia* (Marseilles), a Phocaean colony founded about 600 B.C. Small silver pieces, divisions of the Phocaean drachm, with an incuse reverse and a variety of obverses such as fore-part of Pegasus, lion's head or boar's head have been suggested as coinage issued by Massalia in the sixth century but the earliest certain series is of fifth-century date. These are silver obols with Artemis head obverse and crab reverse, accompanied by the initial M or Apollo head and wheel reverse. Similar coins with the letters MA dated to the early fourth century confirm the identification. In the later part of the century come the handsome silver drachms with head of Artemis and lion, accompanied by the city name (Pl. 122). The obverse type changes to bust of Artemis with quiver in the second century, while the weight standard becomes that of the Roman victoriate. Plentiful issues of bronze coins in the last two centuries B.C. present types of Apollo head and charging bull, or Athena head and tripod.

The coinage of the Celtic tribes in Gaul is completely imitative, based principally on the model of the Macedonian stater of Philip II and, later, on Roman denarii. Controversy persists as to the means through which the Philip staters which served as models became familiar to the Gallic tribes. The view that these staters found their way up the valleys of the Danube and Rhine into Gaul is militated against by the fact that they are less widely imitated than other series in the areas along the suggested route or become already extremely distorted in these districts, while a number of Gallic imitations are not far removed from the original designs. It is more probable that these gold pieces reached Gaul by trade through Greek settlements such as Massalia.

The imitative coinage of Gaul is of great variety but falls into a number of general geographic categories. The coinage of south Gaul consists principally of imitations of the Massalian drachms of the fourth and third centuries, though in some areas the types of the second-century bronzes provide the models for local coinage. Towards the Pyrenees some coinages such as that of the *Volcae Tectosages* copy the types of the coins of the Greek colony at Rhoda in Spain, a head of Persephone and a rose in full bloom to front. In central and western Gaul the tribal coinages are based on the Philip stater. Obverses range from close copies of the Apollo head to utter caricatures of the human features, while reverses normally show a single horse in place of the two-horse chariot and frequently the single horse is replaced by a boar or other animal as on coins of the *Sequani*. Names, presumably of local chieftains, are inscribed on staters of some of these tribes, for the names of Vercingetorix, the celebrated opponent of Julius Caesar, appears on staters of the Averni. Amongst the peoples on the left bank of the Rhône imitations of Roman republican denarii were widespread. The head of Roma usually remains recognizable on the obverse, but on the reverse the Dioscuri of the Roman original are reduced to a solitary horseman.

A number of general categories are discernible in northern Gaul. Amongst the tribes in the areas eastwards towards the Rhine the staters are slightly cup-shaped and sometimes the obverse carries no type in relief. In the area of the Seine the staters of tribes such as the *Parisii* and *Bellovaci* are thin and extremely flat, and the design of the obverse in many cases is obsessed with an elaboration of the hair and wreath of the Apollo head to the exclusion almost completely of the features (Pl. 123). Amongst tribes in the north-west such as the Aulerci and the Osismi and Curiosolitae in Britanny the Apollo head becomes a nightmarish mask and the horse on the reverse is often represented with a human head. The staters of these tribes, particularly the base billon-staters of the *Curiosolitae* (Pl. 124) also had wide currency in the Channel Islands.

ANCIENT BRITAIN

The earliest coinage which can be attributed to Britain is the so-called tin money, in reality an alloy of copper and tin. The types are degenerate imitations of coins of Massalia (Marseilles). The obverse presents a caricature of an Apollo head and on the reverse a charging bull (Pl. 125). This coinage was current in the south-east, particularly in the Thames valley in the first quarter of the first century B.C. After the first Belgic invasion of Britain about 75 B.C. imitations, at several removes, of the celebrated gold stater of Philip of Macedon became current in the south and south-east. Little more remains of the Apollo head obverse of the original than the laurel wreath and the horse-drawn chariot on the reverse has degenerated into a single disjointed horse (Pl. 126). The second Belgic invasion which followed Julius Caesar's reconnaissance in force in 54 B.C. brought from Gaul the *Atrebates* and *Regni* who installed themselves in Hampshire and Sussex, where they issued imitation staters and a new denomination, the quarter-stater. The descendants of the Atrebatic chief Commius, who is mentioned in Caesar's *Commentaries* and who probably came to Britain a little later, are known from a series of inscribed coins. Staters are inscribed with the names of Commius himself, his sons Tincommius (*c.* 20 B.C.–A.D. 5), Eppillus (*c.* A.D. 5–10) and Verica (*c.* A.D. 10–40).

Of the two latter there are also silver coins which from their fabric and style are clearly copying Roman denarii.

The gold staters of the *Catuvellauni* who lived in the district from London northwards to Oxford present further variants of the imitation Macedonian stater. A number of their chieftains are known from inscribed coins, particularly Tasciovanus (*c.* 20 B.C.–A.D. 10) and his son Cunobelin (A.D. 10–40) whose staters and quarters, inscribed with the name of the town Camulodunum (Colchester) show that his authority extended into Essex (Pl. 127). Bronze coinage of Cunobelin shows a strong Roman influence. Of the other tribes, the *Trinovantes* in Kent and Essex, mentioned in Caesar's despatches, also issued imitation staters. A number of these bear the name of a chieftain Addedomarus (*c.* 15–1 B.C.) and of Dubnovellaunus who was probably his successor.

Further north in the fen country of Norfolk and Cambridgeshire the *Iceni,* renowned for their revolt later, in the time of Nero, struck, at an earlier date, gold staters and silver pieces, some of which are inscribed with the names of chieftains. The *Brigantes* of Yorkshire did not appear in history until the Romans penetrated the north of the country about A.D. 50 but in common with other Ancient British tribes they too issued a coinage of gold staters with almost unrecognizable derivative types and later, in the early first century A.D., silver coins which again record the names of local rulers. To the west in Oxfordshire and Gloucester lived the *Dobuni*, a native not an invading tribe who did not take up coinage until late in the first century B.C. Gold staters as well as silver pieces carry inscriptions and on some pieces the obverse has degenerated into a fern-like design. The *Durotriges* in the south-west in Dorset and Somerset struck extremely crude imitation staters and a series of cast-bronze coins (Pl. 128), whose rough designs are as far removed as it is possible to conceive from those of the Macedonian stater.

SPAIN

The comparatively late political and economic development of the Iberian peninsula is reflected in the history of its coinage. Early coinage needs were presumably served by the plentiful issues from other coining centres in the western Mediterranean and the small divisions of the Phocaic drachm associated with the north-east coast of Spain are, despite their archaic fabric, not earlier than the mid fifth century, if indeed they were in fact struck in Spain. To *Emporiae* (Ampurias), a Phocaean settlement of Massalia of the early fourth century is attributed a series of silver obols with a variety of types, inscribed with the first letter or letters of the city name, struck in the late fourth and early third centuries. The best-known series from Emporiae is that of the silver drachms issued from about the mid third century with head of Persephone and flying Pegasus. These coins and a wider series of imitations, frequently with Iberian inscriptions, continued to be struck down to the early second century. Contemporary with the early drachms of Emporiae were drachms of the adjacent settlement of *Rhoda*, again with a Persephone head but, on the reverse, a rose in full bloom, shown from the front. These drachms also were widely copied both in Gaul and Spain (Pl. 129).

The earliest coinages of southern Spain display their Carthaginian inspiration. Apart from the series struck for the Barcids at Carthago Nova and Gades (see below, p. 76), the latter mint issued, from the later third century, drachms and smaller silver with head of Melkart–Heracles in lion-skin and tunny-fish reverse with Phoenician inscriptions. The island of Ebusus also produced didrachms and subdivisions with types of Cabirus and a walking bull.

Even after the conquest of Spain by the Romans in 206, coinage of these categories continued to be produced in the two main coining areas of Spain. At Rome a new silver denomination, the denarius, introduced about 211 and accompanied by a coinage in bronze of asses and subdivisions on the sextantal standard (see below, p. 101) rapidly established itself as the major coinage of the western Mediterranean and had its effect on the native coinage of Spain. A whole series of hoards of Roman republican denarii found in Spain demonstrate that this coinage formed one of the staples of currency, but alongside the Roman coinage there circulated also series of native coinage during the remainder of the second century, following the introduction of the Roman denarius system and, in the first century, probably down to the Sertorian wars in 80-72.

The native coinage of Spain falls into two general groups, the first coinciding roughly with the eastern part of Hispania Tarraconensis—the coastal area and the valley of the Ebro—the second with Hispania Baetica in the south and south-east. The first group includes issues from something over ninety mints. The full coinage system contained a silver coin of approximately denarius weight standard, a half-piece or quinarius, in bronze an as with its half-piece and occasionally smaller divisions, but few mints appear to have struck the full range. Though the weight system was derived from Rome the usual types in silver are not those of the Roman denarius but have a male head, often bearded, on the obverse and, on the reverse, a horseman with palm-branch or lance, with, in Iberian characters, the name not of the mint city but of the tribal territory in which the coins were struck. The most plentiful issues of silver are from Osca (Pl. 130). The bronze as and its parts, more universally struck than the silver coinage, also ignores the types of the Roman counterparts and normally reproduces types similar to those of the silver. The progressive reduction in weight of the Roman as is reflected in the Iberian issues also, though it is apparent from other criteria that weight is not the overriding factor in determining the sequence of issues. Initially, inscriptions are solely in Iberian script but later at some mints such as Celsa, Saitibi and Osicerda inscriptions are in both Latin and Iberian.

In the southern group the coinage based on the Roman weight standard is principally in bronze. At some mints the types associated with earlier issues under the Carthaginians continued to be used, as at Gades where a Melkart-Hercules head remains on the obverse and two tunny-fish on the reverse, accompanied by a Punic inscription. At other mints such as Obulco the types, again individual designs of a female head on obverse and plough and corn-ear on reverse, have a Latin inscription on one side and a form of Iberian inscription on the other (Pl. 131).

Local coinage which had probably come to an end during the Sertorian wars was resumed at some mints in Hither Spain during the last great civil wars of the Roman republic. The types are either those of the earlier native issues but with the mint name now in Latin only or are adapted from the types of Roman denarii. Under the early Roman empire, particularly in the time of Augustus and Tiberius, a great number of towns struck bronze coinages either as *municipia* or as colonies. These coins normally carry the imperial portrait and titles on the obverse; varied reverse types have the names of local magistrates as well as the mint name. At a few mints coinage continued into the reign of Caligula (A.D. 37–41).

NORTH AFRICA

MAURETANIA

The ancient kingdom of Mauretania coincided roughly in extent with present-day Morocco. The earliest king of whom we have knowledge was Bocchus I who, by espousing the cause of Rome and betraying his son-in-law, Jugurtha of Numidia, further extended his dominion. No coins can be attributed with certainty to Bocchus I or to his immediate successors in the kingdom divided on his death in 81 B.C. into Western and Eastern Mauretania. Silver coins of Bogud, King of Western Mauretania (49–33 B.C.), have as types a head of Africa with elephant-skin head-dress and a griffin or a griffin on either side together with his name and title in Latin. Bocchus II, King of Eastern Mauretania from 49 B.C., united the whole country in 33 B.C. when Bogud, by backing Mark Antony in the civil wars of Rome, chose the losing side. His coinage in bronze carries his portrait and his name in local script with, on the reverse, Bacchus accompanied by a small bull. On the death of Bocchus II in 31 B.C. the country was administered by Rome until 25 B.C. when the Emperor Augustus made Juba II king. In the interregnum a series of bronzes with local types and legends was struck as well as a Roman series with head of Augustus.

The coinage of the long reign of Juba II from 25 B.C. to A.D. 23 is very plentiful. His silver coins, light-weight denarii, have his portrait and name on the obverse and a great variety of reverse types. Many coins bear a regnal date in Roman numerals from year VI onwards (Pl. 132). Bronze coinage is less common and on some of the pieces the king's name is given in Greek. Another series including two unique gold pieces, plentiful denarii and some bronze has on the reverse the name of Juba's queen, Cleopatra, the daughter of Mark Antony and Cleopatra. The king's name and title on the obverse is normally in Latin, that of Cleopatra on the reverse in Greek. Some denarii have portraits of both Juba and Cleopatra. There is also a small issue of coinage in the name of Cleopatra alone and between A.D. 20 and 23 a coinage in the name of Juba and his son Ptolemaeus. The coinage of the latter till his death in 40 follows the pattern of that of his father but becomes steadily more Roman both in types and style.

Late in the history of the Mauretanian kingdom a number of cities issued an autonomous bronze coinage, usually with inscriptions in Punic script. Only rarely, as at Tingis, modern Tangiers, was Latin used for the coin inscriptions.

NUMIDIA

Towards the end of the third century B.C. this country, roughly modern Algeria, consisted of two kingdoms, that of the Massaesylians to the west and that of the Massylians to the east. Of the former the earliest king of whom coinage is known was Syphax (213–202) who, having sided with Carthage against Rome, was defeated by Masinissa, king of the Massylians and an ally of Rome. His bronze coins have a bare-headed and bearded portrait, perhaps of the king himself, and on the reverse a horseman with, on a tablet, a Punic inscription. The greater part of his kingdom was assigned to Masinissa but some portion continued to be ruled by Vermina, son and successor of Syphax, until 192. The latter's very rare silver coins resemble those of Syphax, except that the reverse shows a free horse.

The coinage in bronze of Masinissa, who emerged finally as sole ruler, is reasonably extensive, the usual types being a laureate and bearded head and a galloping horse (Pl. 133). This series carries no royal names and presumably continued in issue under the often-disputed succession to Masinissa. The western portion of the kingdom was assigned to Bocchus I of Mauretania on the defeat of Jugurtha, only a remnant being left to his successors Hiempsal II (105–62) and Juba I (60–46) on whose defeat at Thapsus in 46 Numidia became a Roman province. Of the extremely rare coins of these kings a noteworthy series in silver shows the cuirassed bust of Juba with his name in Latin and a temple façade with the king's name in Punic script.

CARTHAGE

The great commercial empire in the western Mediterranean of which Carthage was the emporium and capital did not begin to issue a coinage in its own name until the end of the fifth century. After the second and successful invasion of Sicily in 410 a number of Greek city mints were utilized to issue a Carthaginian coinage. Issues from Cephaloedium, Eryx, Motya and Panormus continued the types already in use but the mint name now appeared in Punic script. On other series where Punic inscriptions define the place of issue only loosely, as, for instance, *Machanat*—the camp, the types are more definitely Phoenician. The coinage placed in the century between 410 and 310 consisted of both gold and silver pieces. On gold the types are a head of the Phoenician goddess Tanit, assimilated to the Greek Persephone, and a prancing horse (Pl. 134) or a palm-tree or else a palm-tree and a horse's head. The palm-tree is another instance of a punning type, this time on the words for palm and Phoenician. The horse's head is an allusion to the legend recounted later by Virgil in the *Aeneid* that a carving of a horse's head was found by the early settlers digging the foundations of Carthage. Silver tetradrachms of this series have types of a free horse, crowned by Nike and a palm-tree (Pl. 135), a female head in tiara and lion in front of palm or head of Tanit and horse's head with palm. Bronze coins of this series reproduce similar types.

The precious-metal coinage struck at Carthage itself from 340 to the end of the first Punic war in 242 is entirely in gold or electrum, but there were also issues in bronze. The types are the now stock Carthaginian types of Tanit head and horse or horse and palm-tree. Carthage, impoverished by her war with Rome and the consequent loss of Sicily and Sardinia, and further harassed by the revolt of her army of mercenaries, produced for some time only a coinage of shekels of base metal but after Hamilcar Barca's successes in Spain, in the years from 237 onwards, the rich supplies of precious metals from the Spanish mines brought a revival of Carthaginian coinage. An electrum coinage reproduces the stock types. The coinage in silver or in silver alloyed with one of the baser metals has some exceptionally large denominations. The dodecadrachm has, as reverse, a prancing horse, the decadrachm and octadrachm have a Pegasus with a Punic inscription supposed to stand for Byrsa, the citadel of Carthage. The tetradrachms and smaller denominations, all with a Tanit obverse, return to the more usual reverse types of horse, horse's head or horse and palm-tree. Bronze coins, usually with similar types to the silver, include a number of large, heavy denominations. The Carthaginian coinage ended, in effect, with the destruction of the city in the third war with Rome in 146.

In addition to the coinage issued at Carthage itself other series were struck at mints at Gades and Carthago Nova in Spain following the conquests of Hamilcar in 237. The most outstanding of these issues are silver pieces often attributed to Numidian and Mauretanian kings but now identified as coinage of the Barcids in Spain. On triple shekels from Carthago Nova the obverse bust of a bearded Melkart-Heracles with club on shoulder probably represents Hamilcar (Pl. 136), and on a double shekel a similar but unbearded portrait is most likely that of Hannibal himself. This mint continued to strike after its capture by Scipio Africanus in 209 and the Roman-style portraits on some of the shekels may be representations of the Roman general. During Hannibal's campaign in Italy some electrum pieces with the usual Carthaginian types were struck at his base in Capua in 216-215.

CYRENAICA

The coinage of Cyrenaica is largely that of the principal city, *Cyrene* which was settled by Dorian immigrants about 631 under the leadership of Battus I. It was not until a second wave of immigration from Crete, Rhodes and other islands seized more territory from the Libyans in the time of Battus II about 573 that the city reached a sufficient degree of prosperity to require its own coinage. The former attribution of electrum coinage to Cyrene has now been disproved and the earliest issues of tetradrachms and smaller silver belong to the period 560 to 525. This archaic coinage with only an incuse reverse has as its obverse the fruit of the silphium plant which was to remain the standard symbol of Cyrene throughout its coinage. Silphium, a now extinct plant, was the basis of Cyrene's prosperity, for the juice extracted from it and used both as a condiment and a medicine was in great demand in the ancient world.

The successful resistance of Cyrene to Egyptian encroachment in the latter part of the sixth century and the establishment of Persian suzerainty in 525 had no noticeable effect on the coinage. The issues between 525 and 480, in common with the general development of Greek coinage, were struck with two types in relief, the silphium, its fruit or some other portion of the plant continuing as the chief type. In the last period of coinage of the dynasty of the Battiadae until their replacement in 435 by a form of republican government the usual type in addition to the standard silphium was a head of Zeus, identified with the Egyptian deity Amun or Ammon whose celebrated temple was at Ammonium in the Libyan desert (Pl. 137). Down to the end of the first quarter of the fourth century the coinage retained much the same form with the addition of magistrates' names, but gold drachms and hemidrachms with similar types also made their appearance. Gold was more plentifully issued in the later fourth century; staters show a quadriga driven by Nike or Cyrene and a standing or enthroned figure of Zeus Ammon, drachms a horseman and silphium plant and smaller pieces heads of divinities on either side. The main difference in types on the silver coins is the frequent appearance on the obverse of the young beardless head with horn at forehead of Carneus, the god of flocks. Bronze coins of this period, in addition to the stock Cyrenaican types, also have as reverse a wheel design of six spokes.

Cyrene passed into the empire of Alexander the Great in 331 and on his death was claimed by Ptolemy I, but it was not until 308 that the province was finally secured for Ptolemy by his step-son Magas, who governed Cyrene until his death in 258 except for a brief period about 271 when he asserted a temporary independence. The coinage under Magas largely continues the denominations and types of the earlier issues except that magistrates' names are usually replaced by monograms. During his revolt Magas issued coins of the usual Ptolemaic types but with his own monogram on the reverse. Some years of dissension followed the death of Magas, including an attempted federal reorganization about 250 when coinage in silver, still with traditional types, carries the inscription Κοινον. Some time about 247 Ptolemy III reunited Cyrenaica to Egypt and from this time Cyrene issued a coinage with Ptolemaic types. The province passed to Rome in 96 and there after the coinage struck in Cyrene was of bronze with Roman magistrate's names inscribed in Latin.

Barce, a neighbouring Lybian settlement of Cyrene was raised to a position of some importance by a dissident branch of the Battiadae dynasty. Its coinage follows the pattern of that of Cyrene though distinguished from it by the city name inscribed on one or other side of the coin.

The coinage of Egypt before the time of Alexander the Great is represented only by extremely rare pieces. These are principally small silver pieces imitating the types of Athenian coins and, very recently, a fourth-century Egyptian imitation of an Athenian tetradrachm has come to light with an additional inscription in demotic characters on the reverse (Pl. 138). The extremely copious coinage struck in Egypt both under Alexander the Great and the subsequent Ptolemaic kings is described below in the section devoted to regal coinage.

The currency needs of the area from the line of the river Jordan westwards to the Mediterranean and stretching from the Sinai desert in the south to Phoenicia in the north were supplied by the major currencies of surrounding districts; in the fifth and early fourth centuries by the Persian coinage and then by Alexandrine coinage. The ancient seaport of *Ascalon*, first a mint of this latter coinage and then for coinage of the Seleucids, struck a coinage of bronze and tetradrachms with portraits of the later Ptolemies, including the famous Cleopatra (Pl. 139). *Gaza*, as well as minting coinage of similar categories, struck a series of silver drachms in the fifth and fourth centuries with either a janiform head, male and female, or an Athena head on obverse and an owl in incuse square on the reverse. This and similar series, imitative of Greek coinages, principally of Athens, circulated generally in north-west Arabia but were most probably produced by the mint at Gaza. In addition to these two mints in Judaea, *Tiberias* in Galilee issued a bronze coinage for Herod Antipas and Herod Agrippa I in the early decades of the first century A.D. *Caesarea* in Samaria also struck bronze for some of the Idumaean princes, notably Herod Agrippa I whose portrait adorns some of these pieces.

Jewish coinage proper dates from the later second century when Antiochus VII gave permission for the Jews to strike their own coins. The earliest pieces are of the *Hasmonean* kings, John Hyrcanus I (135–104), Judas Aristobulus (104–103) and Alexander Jannaeus (103–76); these are mainly small bronze pieces with a laurel-wreath enclosing a Hebrew inscription on obverse and on reverse double cornucopiae (Pl. 140). Under Alexander began coinage with types, flower and anchor or star and anchor with obverse inscription in Hebrew and the king's name and title in Greek on the reverse. The coinage of the remainder of the Hasmonean princes down to 37 was of similar types. For Herod the Great (37–4), the first of the Idumaean dynasty, large bronzes have as types a tripod surrounded by the king's name in Greek and on reverse a ceremonial head-dress (Pl. 141). Smaller bronzes have a variety of types—caduceus and pomegranate, anchor and two cornuacopiae, or anchor and wreath, types continued by Herod Archelaus until his banishment in A.D. 6.

While Judaea was administered by Roman procurators between A.D. 6 and 66 small bronze of like fabric and similar types to the preceding series continued to be struck, with the name of the emperor and his regnal year in Greek. Some of such pieces are dated to the time of Pontius Pilate, the procurator most familiar to the Christian world (Pl. 142). The Idumaean kings who continued to rule portions of Palestine and, for a time, areas east of the Jordan, issued a bronze coinage mentioning the name of the ruling Roman emperor as well as their own and under Agrippa II (A.D. 48–100) the emperor's portrait and title appears on the obverse.

The final class of coins is that associated with the two revolts of the Jews against Rome between A.D. 66 and 70 and 133 and 135. The coinage of the *First Revolt* consists of silver shekels and halves with types a chalice and a stem with three flowers and inscriptions in Hebrew. The obverse also carries a Hebrew numeral indicating the year of freedom (Pl. 143). Bronze coinage has types of amphora and vine-branch. The suppression of this revolt was commemorated by Rome on bronzes struck in Palestine. The normal types are the portraits of Titus or Domitian, the sons of the Emperor Vespasian on the obverse and a trophy of arms or a palm-tree on the reverse. The coins of the *Second Revolt* in the time of the Emperor Hadrian are of three categories. The first consists of silver shekels showing the screen of the Tabernacle on obverse and a bundle of twigs and citron on reverse (Pl. 144). Other smaller silver pieces, overstruck on Roman denarii, present a variety of types, principally an inscription within a wreath and a one-handled jug or a bunch of grapes and a lyre. On bronze coins of varying size a vine-branch and a palm-tree are the most usual types.

PHOENICIA

The important coinages of this area lying between the Lebanese mountains and the Mediterranean are those of the great commercial cities on the coast. These coinages fall roughly into three groups: independent issues from the later fifth century down to the time of Alexander the Great; coinage of Alexandrine staters and tetradrachms, followed by Ptolemaic and/or Seleucid issues; finally in the early second century a resumed autonomous coinage lasting, in most cases, down to or into the time of the Roman empire.

Tyre, the most southerly of the important Phoenician cities, was originally founded from Sidon which it soon came to rival. Its issues in the second half of the fifth century include tetradrachms and smaller silver with types of dolphin swimming above the waves and, in an incuse square, an owl accompanied by crook and flail. In the fourth century before Alexander's conquest the reverse type remains the same but is no longer contained in an incuse square while the obverse shows the Phoenician god Melkart riding a sea-horse over the waves.

Tyre is an exception amongst the Phoenician cities in that for the remainder of
the century and the first part of the third it continued to strike its own types in
silver and Alexandrine types only in bronze. The mint issued Ptolemaic coinage
from 267 to 200 and Seleucid from then until 125. Autonomous Tyrian tetradrachms and drachms with Melkart head and eagle on beak of ship continued in
issue until A.D. 51 Bronzes of this period have types of Melkart, eagle and galley.
The mint at *Ptolemais-Ace*, the modern Acre opened in 328 and struck successively
Alexandrine coins, Ptolemaic (261–200), and Seleucid down to the first century.

Further northward lay *Sidon*, the most important of the maritime cities of
Phoenicia, with a coinage which matched its status. Its regal coinage in silver
began in the late fifth century with a series of double-shekels and smaller denominations. The obverse, consistent for almost all denominations, is a galley with furled
sail and in the incuse square of the reverse appears the Persian king in his chariot
on the double-shekels, while on the smaller pieces the king shoots with his bow.
In the earlier fourth century the reverse no longer is in an incuse square and on the
major piece the types represent a galley in front of a city wall and the king driving
at speed in his chariot. On the coins of the remainder of the century down to the
Macedonian conquest the 2 shekel pieces show on reverse the Persian king in
chariot followed by the Egyptian king, symbolizing the subjection of Egypt to
Persia (Pl. 145). From 333 Sidon was an important mint for Alexandrine-type
coinage until it was lost by the Ptolemies to the Seleucids in 202. For most of the
second century Seleucid silver was issued by Sidon but about 111 autonomous
coinage again began of tetradrachms with head of the city Tyche and eagle and
didrachms with eagle on prow of galley as reverse. Bronze coinage had similar
types as well as Europa on bull, car containing sacred stone and a temple. This
bronze coinage continued well into the time of the Roman empire.

Byblus on the coast at the foot of Mount Lebanon has a silver coinage of staters
and divisions for its kings Elpaal, Azbaal and Ainel between 400 and about 315.
The obverse shows a galley with horse's head as figure-head, manned by three or
four marines with a sea-horse below; the reverse, a typical oriental motif of a lion
bearing down a bull, with the name of the king in Phoenician letters (Pl. 146).
Byblus did not coin again until the second century when a bronze coinage of the
Seleucids began, continuing into the first century. *Aradus* on an island off the
north coast of Phoenicia began its coinage like the other principal Phoenician
cities in the late fifth century. The types, initially, are a fish-god holding two
dolphins and a galley with sea-horse below, but in the fourth century tetradrachms
and staters show a head of Melkart with galley reverse (Pl. 147). Bronze was also
issued after the middle of the century with similar types. From the Macedonian
conquest coins of Alexandrine types were struck by Aradus and from about 174

coinage in the name of the city was resumed. Tetradrachms have the city Tyche as obverse and figure of Nike within a wreath. Small silver pieces were also struck with a variety of types as well as bronze coinage.

On the coast between Byblus and Aradus a new city, *Tripolis*, was settled from three cities Sidon, Tyre and Aradus in the fourth century. It minted successively for the Ptolemies and Seleucids and from about 112 began an autonomous issue of coins. The principal denomination was the Attic tetradrachm with its broad, spread flan with types of the Dioscuri and a city Tyche, holding rudder and cornucopiae. The most northerly of the coastal towns, *Marathus*, was a mint for Alexandrine-type coinage down to about 229 when its own series proper began. Tetradrachms have the conventional head of the city, turreted on obverse; the reverse shows Marathus seated on shields.

SYRIA AND MESOPOTAMIA

The great number of mints active in these areas largely begin their activity only in Roman times. In our present period the most important coinages are those struck by the Seleucid kings at mints founded by them in Syria at Antiochia on the Orontes, Laodicea ad Mare and Damascus, and in Mesopotamia at Seleucia on the Tigris. These coinages are described below in the section devoted to regal coinage.

ARABIA

Two unusual coinages here require mention. The first is that of the *Nabathaean kings* whose capital was at Petra and who produced a coinage in the first centuries B.C. and A.D. The coinage, at first in bronze then from about 62 B.C. in silver as well as bronze, is basically an imitation of Seleucid types. The most plentiful series is that of Aretas IV (9 B.C.–A.D. 40) with busts of himself and his queen Huldu on obverse and reverse of silver coin and jugate busts of the king and his queen Shaqilath on the obverse of bronze pieces, with crossed cornuacopiae on the reverse (Pl. 148). The second coinage is that of the *Sabaeans* and *Himyarites* in the hinterland of Aden. Their coinage consists of imitations in silver of Athenian tetradrachms. In the third and second centuries B.C. the model for these coins is the 'old-style' Athenian tetradrachm while in the first century the Himyarite coins are clearly imitating the 'new-style' Athenian tetradrachms with their spread flan and owl on amphora reverse type (Pl. 149).

The coinage of Persia provided the staple currency for the greater portion of the Near East from the later sixth century down to the conquest of Persia by Alexander the Great. The Persian kings do not appear to have struck coins until after the conquest of the Lydian empire of Croesus by Cyrus in 546, and the replacement of the gold and silver issues of Croesus probably did not take place until about 515. Both the gold darics and the silver sigloi are bean-shaped pieces with a type on obverse only and an oblong incuse on the reverse. The obverse type always shows the Persian king in a variety of attitudes; either he is shown half length, shooting with his bow, or running with bow and spear. The first two varieties were introduced by Darius not earlier than 515 and the third most probably by his successor Xerxes sometime after 486. All three varieties are found on the sigloi but only the second and third on darics (Pl. 150). A number of rather rare subdivisions of both daric and siglos exist with similar types.

The types of the Persian coinage continued substantially unchanged throughout the centuries but there are some general stylistic differences between the more archaic and the later pieces as well as some differences in the portrayal of the features of the king.

BABYLONIA

After the surrender of Babylon to Alexander the Great by the Persian governor Mazaeus in 328 and his re-instatement by Alexander, a coinage was minted there by Mazaeus and his successors. Babylon is most probably the mint for a series of double gold darics, still with the obverse type of the king running with bow and spear but with the incuse reverse filled with irregular markings. A series of silver tetradrachms with the name of Mazaeus on the reverse in Aramaic script show on the obverse a figure seated in the attitude of the Zeus of the Alexander tetra-drachms but with the name Ba'althars. The reverse is a standing lion with tail curled (Pl. 151). Similar pieces, as well as smaller denominations with like types, were struck by subsequent governors down to Seleucus before his assumption of the royal title in 306. An unusual decadrachm struck by Seleucus shows a horseman charging an elephant on which is seated a mahout as well as a figure with a tall head-dress. On the reverse is the standing figure of Alexander the Great wearing Persian head-dress and cuirass and holding a thunderbolt (Pl. 152). The coin illustrates Alexander's defeat of the Indian king, Porus, at the battle of the river Hydaspes in 327.

REGAL COINAGE

MACEDON

Alexander I (498–454), the founder of the Macedonian dynasty, profited by the conditions arising from the Persian invasions of Greece in the early fifth century to extend his kingdom by conquest and by 480 he controlled the rich mining district of the Bisaltae. Alexander not only adopted their existing coin standards but took over their coin types. He issued a series of silver octadrachms and tetradrachms, retaining the naked horseman standing by a horse as on the coins of the Bisaltae but adding his own name in a square border round the incuse reverse (Pl. 153). Smaller denominations have other equine types—a horse prancing or running free. Of his successor, *Perdiccas II* (454–413), there are only smaller silver pieces similar in type to those of Alexander. Under *Archelaus I* (413–399) the capital was transferred to Pella where were struck his silver staters again with the favourite Macedonian type of a prancing horseman and with the goat badge of the original capital of Aegae on the reverse. Other staters introduce an Apollo head, his hair bound with a fillet, and smaller coins show the young Heracles head which was to become a feature of the coinage of later kings, especially on the prolific coinage of Alexander the Great. *Archelaus II* (396–392) struck mostly with these latter coin types, signed with his real, as opposed to his titular, name, Aëropus. The brief reigns of *Amyntas II* (392–390) and *Pausanias* (390–389) brought only alteration in the regal names on the coins. Under *Amyntas III* (389–369) the Heracles head in its lion-skin head-dress of earlier smaller denominations now appears in the principal piece, the stater, accompanied on the reverse by a standing horse. Similar types but with the horse on the trot were used by *Perdiccas III* (365–359).

Philip II (359–336). The acquisition of the almost untouched reserves of the gold mines of Pangaeum in 356 gave Philip the opportunity of reorganizing the Macedonian coinage. In gold the major piece was a stater of 8·6 gm. with types, a laureate head of Apollo and a two-horse chariot (Pl. 154). Smaller denominations continued the favourite Macedonian type of young Heracles head in lion-skin on the obverse with a variety of reverses. In silver the tetradrachm of 14·5 gm. (a new ratio of gold to silver of 10 : 1) had a laureate and bearded head on obverse and a boy-rider carrying a palm. A Heracles head supplies the obverse on the lower denominations with a youth on horseback as the usual reverse. These types most probably refer to the victories of Philip's chariots in the Olympic games.

Philip's gold coinage rapidly established itself as an international currency and was issued in some areas long after his death. In western Europe the Philip stater supplied the model for innumerable imitative coinages. The tetradrachms were similarly imitated in the Balkans and in the Danube valley (see p. 68 above).

Alexander the Great (336–323). The coinage of Alexander is the first great world coinage of Western civilization, matched, in the ancient world, for its uniform simplicity and extensive distribution only by the issues of the Roman empire. The composition of the coinage followed much the same pattern as that of Philip II. The unit in gold was the stater with, now, some di-staters or double pieces and less frequent smaller denominations. The obverse bore the head of Athena in crested Corinthian helmet, decorated with a griffin, a sphinx or a serpent, while on the reverse was a standing figure of Nike holding a wreath and a naval standard (Pl. 155). In silver the major piece was the tetradrachm; occasional didrachms were struck as well as drachms in some quantity and some smaller pieces. The silver types were the head of young Heracles in lion-skin on obverse, a type used with some frequency in earlier Macedonian issues and, on the reverse, Zeus enthroned holding eagle and sceptre (Pl. 156). The name of Alexander appeared on the reverse of both gold and silver. Token bronze issues also had, usually, the Heracles head and his symbols of club and bow.

As Alexander's conquests swept eastwards and southwards until, with the final defeat of the Persian king and the expedition into India, the Macedonian empire extended from Greece to north-west India and from the Black Sea to Egypt, so a chain of mints was brought into being. These mints had almost all been major coining centres but now they were set to strike the coinage originated in Macedon. The mints have been determined by the evidence of finds in different localities, by differences of style influenced by coinages previously produced and by smaller differentials such as initial letters appearing on some of the coins produced. In the lifetime of Alexander some twenty major mints were in operation striking all or only some of the denominations but principally tetradrachms. In European Greece the two great mints in Macedon itself were at Amphipolis and Pella, while another at Sicyon in the Peloponnese began striking about 330. Across the Hellespont in Asia Minor there were mints at Lampsacus in Mysia, Miletus in Caria, Side in Pamphylia, at the old Lydian capital of Sardes, and one of the greatest, at Tarsus in Cilicia. In Syria the mints were Myriandros, renamed Alexandria-on-the-Issus in honour of the king, and Damascus, while further down the Mediterranean coast the chief mint cities Aradus, Byblus, Ace and Sidon were turned to the production of the new coinage. Only Tyre which had resisted and was destroyed is absent from the list. In Cyprus also Alexandrine coinage was struck at Paphos, Salamis, Citium and Amathus. The new city of

Alexandria in Egypt which Alexander had planned and named after himself was also equipped with a mint active from about 326. Finally at Babylon, the capital of the Persian empire, where the coins are signed with the letter M for the Metropolis the capital of empire which Alexander designed Babylon to become. The title of *Basileus* or king was added to Alexander's coins at Alexandria-on-the-Issus about 329 and subsequently at some other mints.

Even after the death of Alexander in 323 his monolithic coinage system and its types continued to be produced and only towards the end of the century did the kingdoms into which his empire was split begin to produce a coinage, modelled on the Alexandrine, but with individual types. Indeed at some mints tetradrachms of Alexander type continued to be minted down to the time of Mithridates the Great in the second century but these latter are distinguishable by their broad, thin flans in contrast to the more compact module of the true Alexandrine issues.

The two heirs of Alexander, his half-brother Aridaeus and the young Alexander, his posthumous son by Roxana, were taken back to Macedon under the guardianship of the general Cassander. For the first of these, coinage was struck with the traditional types but with the name of Philip, the regnal name assumed by Aridaeus. Following the murder of Philip III in 317 and the imprisonment of the young Alexander IV and his subsequent murder in 311, Cassander assumed rule in Macedon. Coinage in the precious metals continued in the name of Alexander, Cassander's name and title appearing only in bronze. The coinage of the sons of Cassander, Philip IV (298–296) and Alexander V (295), continued the Alexandrine types and titles. In 294 Demetrius Poliorcetes (see below, p. 86) secured the throne of Macedon and issued a coinage of new types in his own name. The gold stater bore the portrait head of Demetrius himself and a horseman with spear. Tetradrachms have head of Demetrius and standing figure of Poseidon.

For some years after the death of Demetrius in 283 the control of Macedon was disputed, but after the defeat of the great invasion of the Gauls in 277 by *Antigonus Gonatas*, son of Demetrius, he was hailed as king by his army. On tetradrachms of Antigonus the obverse consists of a Macedonian shield with head of Pan in the centre and a fighting Athena on reverse (Pl. 157). The Pan head is thought to be a reference to the belief that it was this god who had spread his panic terror amongst the Gaulish invaders. Other tetradrachms with head of Poseidon and Delian Apollo on prow refer to the naval victory of Antigonus over Ptolemy II of Cos in 258, when, before the battle, Antigonus had vowed his flagship to Apollo, if he gained the victory. The reign of *Demetrius II* (239–229) and *Antigonus Doson* (229–220) produced no individual coinage in gold or silver but most probably continued the traditional Alexandrine types which had persisted through the reign of Gonatas also.

The main coinage of *Philip V* (220–179) with individual types is associated with the preparations for war with Rome in which ultimately he was defeated at Cynoscephalae in 197 by the Roman general Flamininus (see below, p. 109). The types on this tetradrachm coinage on broad, spread flans are a magnificent bearded portrait of Philip and the now-familiar fighting Athena (Pl. 158). Another tetradrachm issue about 186 is associated with the second war with Rome. The obverse is a Macedonian shield, similar to that introduced by Antigonus Gonatas but with a Perseus instead of a Pan head in the centre. On the reverse is the club of Heracles in an oak-wreath, together with the king's name. The Perseus head honours the Argive descent of Philip's wife for Perseus was the hero and legendary king of Argos. Philip also gave the name *Perseus* to his son who succeeded him in 179. The types of the tetradrachm coinage of Perseus were his bearded portrait and an eagle on a thunderbolt within an oak-wreath. In the third war with Rome Perseus was defeated and captured at Pydna and Macedon passed into Roman control (see above, p. 29).

ASIA

Another of Alexander's generals, Antigonus, received in the division of the empire the provinces of Phrygia, Lycia and Pamphylia and to these, after his defeat of Eumenes, he added Cappadocia, Paphlagonia and Pontus. In his mints he continued the issue of Alexandrine-type staters and tetradrachms. Following the defeat of the fleet of Ptolemy off Cyprus by Antigonus' son, Demetrius Poliorcetes, in 306 Antigonus took the title *Basileus* though it never appeared on the coins struck in his Asiatic mints but some issues, probably struck at Salamis in Cyprus by Demetrius, accord the royal title to Antigonus. Demetrius also assumed the royal style at this time and struck in his own name gold staters with figure of Nike with trumpet and naval standard standing on a prow and fighting Athena. Silver tetradrachms also used the Nike type as an obverse coupled with a reverse of Poseidon poising a trident (Pl. 159), clear reference to the naval victory of Demetrius. The Nike representation is similar to the famous Victory of Samothrace now in the Louvre. In 301 at the battle of Ipsus the four other kings who had divided Alexander's empire defeated Antigonus, who died in the battle. Demetrius still held Cyprus and later in 294 became king of Macedon.

To *Lysimachus* in the division of Alexander's empire in 323 fell the province of Thrace. While Alexander's nominal heirs, Philip III and the young Alexander IV, still lived, Lysimachus continued the issue of the traditional Alexandrine coinage, but from the death of the latter in 311 the first two letters of Lysimachus' name were generally added to the conventional coins. Following the fashion set by Antigonus in 306 Lysimachus also adopted the title of *Basileus* and initiated a coinage of new types. The types on both gold staters and on silver were a head of the deified Alexander with horn of Ammon and a seated Athena crowning the name of Lysimachus on the reverse (Pl. 160). In the confused years following the expulsion of Demetrius from Macedonia in 287 Lysimachus for a time controlled that country and issued tetradrachms in his own name from its mints. He was killed in 281 in the battle of Corapedium against Seleucus.

Ptolemy I (323–285), who took as his share of empire in 323 the satrapy of Egypt, at first, like the other generals, continued the issue of Alexandrine coins but on the murder of Philip III in 317 Ptolemy produced a new obverse type on his silver tetradrachms, a head of Alexander the Great with horn of Ammon and elephant-skin head-dress. A little later a new reverse, the fighting Athena, was also introduced, the name of Ptolemy being added to that of Alexander on the reverse in some issues. Gold staters struck after Ptolemy adopted the title of *Basileus* in 305 show the diademed head of Ptolemy and Alexander in a quadriga of elephants. On tetradrachms also the royal portrait appeared together with a new reverse, an eagle on thunderbolt, the badge of Ptolemy which was to become the standard type throughout the Ptolemaic coinage (Pl. 161).

Ptolemy II (Philadelphus, 285–246) succeeded on his father's abdication and continued the issue of the established types of a coinage which can scarcely be distinguished from that of his father. By his marriage in 280 to his sister Arsinoe, widow of Lysimachus, parts of Ionia and Phoenicia were added to his domains. Large gold octadrachms carry double portraits on both sides—the deified Ptolemy I and his queen Berenice on one side and Ptolemy II and Arsinoe on the other. In honour of the deification of Arsinoe in 270 prolific issues both of large gold pieces and silver tetradrachms were made with types, veiled head of Arsinoe and double cornucopiae (Pl. 162). *Ptolemy III* (Euergetes, 246–221) by his marriage to Berenice, heiress of Magas in Cyrene (see above, p. 77), secured that province for Egypt once again. In addition to continuing the conventional-type silver tetradrachms and gold pieces of the Arsinoe type, Ptolemy III struck a series in both gold and silver with the portrait of his queen Berenice as well as a similar series with his own portrait with the attributes of the three major gods. He wears the radiate crown of Helios, round his neck is the aegis of Zeus and on his shoulder the trident of Poseidon. Massive issues of bronze in various denominations have a head of Zeus and the traditional eagle on thunderbolt reverse (Pl. 163).

Innovations in the coinage types made by *Ptolemy IV* (Philopater, 221–204) include tetradrachms with jugate busts of the Egyptian gods Serapis and Isis and gold octadrachms with the portrait either of himself or his queen Arsinoe III. Under *Ptolemy V* (Epiphanes, 204–181), who succeeded as a child, the fortunes of Egypt began to wane and most of her provinces except Cyrene and Cyprus were lost to Antiochus the Great of Syria. In this and in most of the subsequent reigns for the next century the coinage continues the types now standard in all three metals and the issues of the various Ptolemies can be distinguished only by minutiae of design, symbols, deteriorating style and fabric. Typical of the changes which had come over the Ptolemaic coinage is the base tetradrachm (Pl. 164) of *Ptolemy XIII* (Neos Dionysos 80–51). Between the death of this king and the conquest of Egypt by Augustus in 30 the Ptolemies XIV and XV were nonenities and effective rule was in the hands of Cleopatra VII, who made that name famous. By her association with Antony control was regained of mints in Phoenicia and Palestine including Ascalon, which struck tetradrachms with her portrait (Pl. 139).

SYRIA

To *Seleucus* (312–281), another of Alexander's principal officers, was allotted the satrapy of Babylon on the division of Alexander's empire. Expelled by Antigonus in 328 he took refuge with Ptolemy but at the battle of Gaza in 312 he regained his dominions and from the autumn of that year is dated the Seleucid era. In common with the other inheritors Seleucus initially continued Alexandrine coinage but after assuming the title of *Basileus* in 305 the name of Seleucus was often substituted for that of Alexander on the coins. By a series of campaigns Seleucus extended his empire until it ranged from the Aegean to the Indus in north-west India. To the mints of his empire Seleucus added Seleucia-on-the-Tigris and Antioch-on-the-Orontes. Amongst new coin types introduced towards the end of the reign were the head of Seleucus in helmet ornamented with bull's horn and Nike crowning a trophy, as on the coins of Agathocles of Syracuse (Pl. 165).

Seleucus associated his son *Antiochus I* as monarch with himself in 293, allotting him the eastern provinces where Antiochus struck silver in his father's name as well as in his own. The main innovation in the coinage of Antiochus as sole king on the death of Seleucus in 281 was the series of tetradrachms with his portrait and a reverse showing Apollo seated on the omphalos, holding bow and arrow (Pl. 166). *Antiochus II* ruled jointly with his father from 266 to 261 and alone until 246. In the joint reign tetradrachms from mints in Asia Minor substituted a seated Heracles for Apollo on the reverse but gold staters as well as silver also continued the Apollo type. In this reign Diodotus in Bactria revolted and set up an independent kingdom.

In the reign of *Seleucus II* (246–226) further portions of the Syrian empire fell away with the establishment of separate kingdoms in Parthia, Armenia and Pergamum. *Antiochus Hierax*, the brother of Seleucus II, also successfully established himself as an independent king in Asia Minor, striking tetradrachms for himself with the traditional Apollo reverse. Seleucus II struck for himself both gold staters, silver and bronze pieces with his portrait and a distinctive standing Apollo. The brief reign of *Seleucus III* (226–223), eldest son of Seleucus II, brought no new types to the coins. His successor and brother, *Antiochus III* (the Great, 223–187), regained some of the territorial losses and conquered Phoenicia from the Ptolemies. He retained the conventional coin types but struck, in addition to the normal denominations, large gold octadrachms. A coinage in gold, silver and bronze with the portrait of Antiochus and an elephant reverse probably commemorates his Eastern campaigns in 206. The traditional Seleucid reverse was carried on under *Seleucus IV* (187–175) and in the earlier issues of his brother *Antiochus IV* (175–164) whose coinage is distinguished by the addition in the inscriptions of his epithet 'Epiphanes'. On later issues in all metals the reverse shows a seated Zeus holding Nike on outstretched hand. Other tetradrachm series have a Zeus head on obverse and seated Zeus reverse or an Apollo head obverse and standing figure of Apollo with lyre on the reverse. Antiochus invaded Egypt and was turned back only by the intervention of Rome; a series of bronzes with the traditional Ptolemaic reverse of an eagle on thunderbolt are connected with his campaign. The infant *Antiochus V* (164–162) was murdered by his cousin *Demetrius I* (162–150) whose early coinage is of the usual types but whose later issues have on the reverse an enthroned Tyche with sceptre and cornucopiae. In 162 Demetrius succeeded in quelling the revolt of *Timarchus*, satrap of Babylon, who revolted and issued coinage in his own name; gold staters with his portrait and Victory in quadriga, tetradrachms with portrait and the Dioscuri charging.

With the death of Demetrius in 150 the history of the Syrian kings and, consequently, of their coinage enters on a period of confusion which extended down to the Roman conquest. In 150 *Alexander I* (150–145), a usurper claiming to be the son of Antiochus IV, seized the throne. His principal coinage in gold and silver preferred the enthroned Zeus reverse of his supposed father, though the earlier Apollo appears on smaller silver denominations. A series in silver, mainly tetradrachms struck in Phoenician mints, has an anonymous portrait head on obverse and the Ptolemaic eagle and royal title on the reverse, types reflecting the influence of Ptolemy VII who aided the usurper and gave him in marriage his daughter Cleopatra. Ptolemy quarrelled with Alexander and replaced him in 146 by *Demetrius II*, the young son of the first Demetrius and his brief coinage reverted to the Apollo reverse type. In 145 the infant son of Alexander was set up as *Antiochus VI* by Tryphon, chief minister of Alexander, and remarkable tetradrachms of the child show his portrait with radiate crown and, on the reverse, the Dioscuri. *Tryphon* killed his ward in 142 and coined in his own name with the additional title of 'autocrator', a series in silver with a reverse type of a helmet with ibex-horn. Tryphon was overthrown in 138 by *Antiochus VII*, brother of Demetrius II, who introduced as a reverse type a standing Athena. He was succeeded in 129 by Demetrius who had been held prisoner by the Parthians. The coins of this second reign of Demetrius II show him with a full-bearded portrait, and usually have the seated Zeus reverse.

Alexander II, set up by Ptolemy VIII as a rival to Demetrius II, reigned only briefly from 125 to 121 but real power rested with Cleopatra, who had been successively the wife of Alexander I, Demetrius II and Antiochus VII. Tetradrachms carry her portrait and the double cornucopiae, typical of Ptolemaic issues. Her son *Antiochus VIII* ruled jointly with her from 125 to 121 and tetradrachms show their jugate busts on the obverse. Antiochus poisoned his mother in 121 and reigned alone, but from 114 shared rule with his brother Antiochus IX. The chief reverse type of the latter is a standing Athena, of the former the seated Zeus. From 96 a swift succession of kings occupied the Syrian throne until in 83 Tigranes, the king of Armenia, was invited to put an end to the perpetual strife. The coinage of Tigranes in Syria lasted until he was compelled by Lucullus to abandon Syria in 69. His tetradrachms show him wearing a tall Armenian headdress and have, as reverse, the Tyche of Antioch with the god of the river Orontes at her feet (Pl. 167). A final Seleucid king, Antiochus XIII, ruled from 69 till Pompey in 64 formed Syria into a Roman province. His poor tetradrachms revert to the conventional portrait obverse and Zeus reverse.

Bronze coinage was issued with some regularity by the Seleucid kings with types of considerable variety. The fashion in types follows roughly that of the precious-metal coinage. Either an Apollo figure or his symbol, the tripod, is common and in the earlier reigns the elephant is a frequent reverse. Somewhat later figures of Zeus enthroned, a standing Athena or Nike are frequent, with occasionally, as under Antiochus IV, the Zeus head and eagle types borrowed from the Ptolemaic coinage. In a number of reigns, of which that of Seleucus IV is the earliest, some bronze issues are of an unusual fabric with a serrate or nicked edge.

PERGAMUM

Philetaerus, who had been appointed in 284 by Lysimachus to be in charge of the treasure he had deposited at Pergamum, used the opportunity and the means thus provided to found a new kingdom of Pergamum. From the time of his successor Eumenes I (263–241) the regal coinage of Pergamum, just as that of the kings of Pontus and of Bithynia, presents on silver tetradrachms a series of impressive portraits which though attributed to successive kings seem rather to be minor variants of one portrait only. The reverse pictures a seated Athena and the royal name (Pl. 168). Attalus III willed his kingdom to the Roman people on his death in 133.

Under the kings of Pergamum the coinage of *cistophori* made their first appearance. These coins were in fact silver tetradrachms and their name means no more than that they bore, as the principal type on the obverse, the sacred chest or *cista* used in the mysteries of the god Bacchus. From the *cista* on the obverse a snake emerges and on the reverse two snakes are coiled around a bow-case. The coinage, begun at Ephesus just before 200, was soon being produced at other mints within the Pergamene kingdom, not least at Pergamum itself (cf. Pl. 3). On the reverse of these coins usually appears the name or monogram of the issuing city. Even after the formation of the Roman province of Asia in 133 the cistophoric coinage continued to be issued, and in the first century the reverse carried also the names of Roman proconsuls.

BITHYNIA

The kingdom of Bithynia was founded by Zipoetes in the first years of the third century, though the earliest coinage on record is of his son and successor Nicomedes I (279–255). As in the case of the Pontic regal coinage, the notable feature is the splendid series of portraits on the silver tetradrachms. The standard reverse throughout most of the series, a standing Zeus crowning the royal name, was introduced by Prusias I at the end of the third century (Pl. 169).

The only coinage of this area of any consequence was struck by the independent kings who ruled Cappadocia from the time of Alexander down to the early first century A.D. when it was incorporated as a Roman province. The coinage of the cities dates almost all from the Roman period.

The first king in Cappadocia established in 330 a dynasty which lasted down to 95. The coinage of this king, Ariarathes I, consisted of silver drachms with types probably derived from some of the satrapal coins of Cilicia. A seated figure of Baal holds the obverse and on the reverse a griffin devouring a stag. The names of Baal and of Ariarathes appear in Aramaic script. All the kings of this dynasty have the same name as the founder and the coinage from Ariarathes III (240–220) is of silver drachms and occasional tetradrachms with a portrait head of the king and a standing figure of Athena holding Nike with the king's name in Greek. One of the most splendid examples was struck by the pretender Orophernes in 158 (Pl. 170). A second dynasty founded in 95 by Ariobarzanes I continued a similar coinage.

PONTUS

The kingdom of Pontus was established by the first Mithridates in 297 but the first coinage of note was the series of silver tetradrachms of Mithridates III (255–185). These coins and, indeed, similar issues by his successors are notable for the realistic and often unflattering portraits of the kings on the obverse. The reverse used by Mithridates III retained the seated Zeus type familiar from the tetradrachms of Alexander the Great but had an additional badge, a star within a crescent, symbolizing the Persian descent claimed by this dynasty. The most extensive coinage was that of Mithridates VI the 'Great' who reigned from 120 to 63 and established suzerainty over much of Asia Minor until his defeat by the Romans and his death in 63. To the period of the first war against the Romans (88–84) are dated a series of gold staters. The types on these and on the silver tetradrachms of the reign are the portrait of Mithridates, with wildly flowing hair, and a stag grazing or Pegasus drinking (Pl. 171).

With the exception of the coinage of Tigranes I as king of Syria, only very rare bronze issues survive of the line of Armenian kings who ruled from the late third century down to the end of the first century. An example is the bronze of Artavasdes I (56–34) which shows the king wearing a spiked Armenian tiara on obverse and riding in a chariot on the reverse (Pl. 172).

PARTHIA

About 250 the peoples in the area to the south-east of the Caspian Sea under their leader Arsaces revolted against their Seleucid overlords. Under successive kings, Tiridates I and Phraates I, the new kingdom was further consolidated but the greatest expansion took place under Mithridates I (171–138) who added portions of the Bactrian kingdom in the East and Babylonia in the West. Since Parthian coins state in their inscription only that they are the coins of the Great King Arsaces with the addition of varying epithets, and only from the time of Volagases I in the first century A.D. have a more explicit regal name in Pehlvi script, the attribution of the series to the successive kings depends on criteria such as the date given in the Seleucid era, a variety of symbols, the epithets applied to particular rulers, portraits and changing styles.

The earliest coins are silver drachms with a bearded head in Scythian cap on the obverse and a figure of the king in Scythian dress, seated on the omphalos and holding a bow. Some of these may be coins of the earlier rulers, but Mithridates I introduced a new obverse type on the drachms where the king wears a diadem in the fashion of the Seleucid kings. The larger denomination, the tetradrachm, was also introduced by Mithridates with, as reverse, a standing figure of Heracles. Coins were also struck in bronze with various reverses but always with the king's portrait as the obverse type. Similar coins were struck by his successors, Phraates II (138–127) and Artabanus I (127–123). The later issues of Mithridates II the Great (123–88) show the king wearing a richly decorated tiara with rounded top (Pl. 173).

Further changes in the otherwise conventional coinage took place in the later first century B.C., notably the arrangement of the king's hair in parallel lines of heavy curls and a reverse type showing the Tyche of the city of Seleucia crowning the seated king. Amongst unusual pieces are the coins of Phraataces (3 B.C.–A.D. 4) with his portrait on obverse and on the reverse that of his mother Musa, the slave girl who had been sent as a present to his father Phraates IV by the emperor Augustus (Pl. 174). Another departure from the conventional is provided by tetradrachms of Artabanus III (A.D. 10–40) where his portrait is shown full-face and on the reverse a Tyche presents a wreath to the king on horseback. In the course of the first two centuries A.D. the Parthian coinage progressively degenerates. The king's portrait loses all realism and the hair and beard are represented by a series of lines while the reverse type is scarcely recognizable and the Greek inscription practically illiterate (Pl. 175). The Arsacid dynasty was finally overthrown by the Sassanian Ardashir in A.D. 224.

CHARACENE

At the head of the Persian gulf and occupying the lower part of the Tigris valley this little kingdom with its capital at Spasinou Charax secured a semi-independence in the second century. The coinage of tetradrachms and drachms is a crude version of Seleucid issues. The obverse has a diademed-and-bearded portrait of the king, the reverse a seated Heracles and name of the king in Aramaic. The coins gradually deteriorate in style and metal but issues seem to have continued until the rise of the Sassanian kingdom in A.D. 224.

ELYMAÏS

This province, also known as Susiana after its capital the great city of Susa, lay to the west of Babylonia and at the head of the Persian gulf. It was at first included in the Seleucid empire but about the middle of the second century it achieved independence under a dynasty whose kings bore the name of Kamnaskires. The coins of the first king of this name are tetradrachms and drachms imitating contemporary Seleucid coins. Kamnaskires II (c. 82 B.C.) also struck tetradrachms and smaller silver with the jugate busts of the king and his queen Anzaze and on the reverse a seated Zeus holding Nike (Pl. 176). Under Kamnaskires IV (c. 72 B.C.) the types became conventional, a bearded bust of the king on obverse, accompanied by the Seleucid anchor symbol and a star or crescent; on the reverse is a smaller diademed head. Under later rulers the coinage is in copper and after the first century A.D. the names which appear on the coins are those of contemporary Parthian kings.

This semi-independent kingdom on the Persian gulf to the east of Elymaïs, though the Parthian king was acknowledged as overlord, struck its own coinage of tetradrachms and drachms in fabric like the Parthian issues but with different types. The coins have inscriptions giving the names of the kings in Aramaic and the earliest coins are attributed to Bagadates I about 222. The types are the head of the king and a figure of the king before a fire-altar (Pl. 177). Later issues become more assimilated to those of the Parthian coins, though other reverses with a trisceles or a star in crescent make their appearance. The Sassanid prince Ardashir of Persis revolted against his Parthian overlord in A.D. 224 and established the new, virile Sassanian kingdom.

BACTRIA

Around 250, about the same time that Parthia was asserting its independence from the Seleucid kings, Diodotus, the satrap of Bactria, the most easterly portion of the Seleucid empire, also revolted against Antiochus II and began an independent coinage. The types on the gold stater, on the silver tetradrachm and smaller pieces are a portrait of Diodotus on obverse with Zeus hurling thunderbolt on the reverse. His successor Euthydemus I (c. 220) maintained this pattern of coinage, substituting for the Zeus reverse a seated Heracles. Heracles also appears as the obverse type on his bronzes with a free horse as the reverse. Under his son and successor Demetrius (c. 195–150) the Bactrian kingdom was extended to the southeast into the Indus valley as far as the Punjab. The silver of Demetrius, both tetradrachms and smaller pieces, shows his portrait bust adorned with an Indian-elephant head-dress; the reverse is a standing figure of a young Heracles facing (Pl. 178).

While Demetrius was extending his conquests into India he was deprived of his Bactrian dominions and even a portion of his conquests in Gandhara by a rival Eucratides (c. 175–155). The kingdom of Demetrius and his successors was henceforth limited to East Gandhara and the Punjab. An unusual feature of the coinage of some of these kings was the use of nickel as a metal for coinage, as for instance by Pantaleon whose nickel pieces have as types a young Dionysus head and a panther. The bronzes struck in Bactria had been of the normal round type but in the Indian territories square bronzes were struck with Greek inscription on the obverse and inscription in Kharoshthi on the reverse, as on coins of Agathocles with types of a lion and a dancing figure (Pl. 179). An unusual type for an inland territory is the figure of Poseidon, found on the reverse of tetradrachms of another king, Antimachus. Under later kings the bilingual feature was extended to silver coinage as well as bronze. On silver coins of Menander the obverse bears his portrait with his name and title in Greek, the reverse a fighting Athena with the same inscription but in Kharoshthi. Both fabric and style deteriorate in the first century until, about 40 B.C., Hippostratus the last of these kings was defeated by the Saka king, Azes I.

Eucratides in his dominions of Bactria and west Gandhara struck an extensive coinage of silver and bronze, both round and square pieces. The types on tetradrachms and some of the smaller silver show the portrait of the king in a helmet adorned with ear and horn of bull and as reverse the Dioscuri charging (Pl. 180). Under Eucratides' successor, Heliocles, the Bactrian possessions were lost to the invading Sakas about 135 and the kingdom of this dynasty was henceforth centred on Kabul. Under a succession of kings, outstanding among whom were Apollodotus and Antialcidas, bilingual silver and bronze with a great variety of types was issued. In the reign of Hermaeus the eastern kingdom was absorbed by the Kushans under their king Kadphises about 40 B.C.

'GREEK IMPERIAL'

The survey of Greek coinage in the widest sense of the term has now been completed. An attempt has been made to outline its various aspects, beginning with the early experiments in coinage in Asia Minor, following its developments in European Greece, its flowering in Italy and Sicily, its extensions in western Europe and North Africa and finally, the more massive issues of the Hellenistic kingdoms from Macedon to Bactria and north-west India. The consolidation of Rome's dominion under Augustus in the late first century B.C. made an end to many of these independent coinages; but Greek coinage of a somewhat different category lived on into the third century A.D. and something of its ramifications is traced in the present section.

The convenient, if not very accurate, term 'Greek Imperial' is normally applied to the diverse and sometimes extensive coinages issued in the eastern dominions of the Roman empire by city mints as distinct from the issues by the mint of Rome or official branches of that mint in the provinces. The principal characteristic of these coinages, as the name implies, is that the inscriptions are in Greek and not Latin, although it is customary to include for convenience in 'Greek Imperial' coinage the issues of colonia or municipia whose inscriptions were usually in Latin. Since in the section on Roman coinage only the Roman issues proper are considered, it is proposed to consider here also the corresponding coin issues in the West which were not Roman issues in the truest sense.

Of the Imperial coinage, gold circulated over the whole empire in both West and East without any real rival. The only other continuous series of gold was that issued by Rome's ally, the kingdom of the Bosporus. This series continued to be struck down into the fourth century A.D., though the metal throughout the centuries became more and more base. The typical gold piece of the Bosporan kings had the portrait of the local king on the obverse and of the Roman emperor on the reverse (Pl. 181). In the West, Roman silver quickly replaced local issues which had no long tradition but in the East a number of series were adapted and continued under the empire. Issues in bronze in the West also soon gave way to Imperial *aes* coinages but again, in the East, the issues of city mints formed the staple currency in bronze.

There were two principal categories of non-Roman coinage, a number of major series in silver and bronze in both East and West which circulated fairly extensively on a provincial basis, and in the East a vast number of more local issues in bronze. These local issues in bronze are themselves of two kinds. Local mints struck an 'imperial' coinage with the portrait and titles of the emperor on obverse and on the reverse a type with local reference but many mints produced at the same time an 'autonomous' coinage with no overt imperial reference.

Of the provincial issues in the East the most extensive issues are those of the great mint of Alexandria in Egypt, issues second only to the massive products of the mint of Rome itself. The issues are also the most long-lived, for they extend from Tiberius down to the monetary reform of Diocletian in A.D. 295. The coinage consisted of tetradrachms, not in pure silver but in billon, an alloy of silver and base metal, tariffed as low as equivalent only to one Roman denarius. The Alexandrian coinage in its earlier stages also included a bronze coinage but in the course of the centuries, as the tetradrachm became more base until its content was almost completely bronze, these parallel issues in bronze ceased. The Alexandrian coinage is remarkably uniform in its basic concept. The obverse carries the portrait of the emperor or one of the members of the Imperial family with name and titles in Greek, the reverse a type more often than not without inscription but with the regnal year indicated by a Greek numeral, preceded by the abbreviation L, for year. A characteristic of this coinage is the range of portraits of Imperial personages not represented on the coinage of Rome, sometimes as obverse type, sometimes as the reverse of a coin of the reigning emperor. Tetradrachms of Nero, for instance, provide portraits of two of his wives, Octavia and Poppaea (Pl. 182). Reverse types, however, more usually carry a representation of a deity or personification as on many Roman issues but seldom does the

reverse make allusion to contemporary events as so often on Roman coins. Types
with specific Egyptian reference receive some prominence such as the deities
Isis and Serapis or the Nile itself. The debased tetradrachms of the later third
century were struck in such vast quantity that these coins, particularly of emperors
from Probus to Diocletian, are amongst the most common coins of antiquity
(Pl. 183).

For Asia the cistophoric tetradrachms began in the Pergamene kingdom and
continued under the republic were struck down to the reign of Hadrian. These
pieces, valued at three denarii, now usually carried the imperial portrait and a
variety of specific reverse types. The most prolific provincial silver issues in this
part of the world, however, were the Syrian tetradrachms, struck principally at
Antioch. The obverse has, of course, the imperial portrait and titles, the reverse
most commonly an eagle facing with out-spread wings (Pl. 184). Antioch struck
this coinage for practically all emperors down to Trebonianus Gallus and Volusian
(A.D. 251–253). Other mints at which these tetradrachms were struck for some
of the earlier emperors are Laodicea ad Mare, Beroea, Seleucia Pieria and Tyre.
A great up-surge of activity in striking this tetradrachm coinage is connected
with the campaigns of Caracalla in the East between 214 and 216 when a complex
of some twenty-eight mints was in action. The products of these mints can be
distinguished by small symbols added on the reverse. A number of these additional
mints remained in operation under his successors.

Other mints in Asia struck imperial provincial silver, though not so continuously or in such quantity. Amisus in Pontus has silver from Hadrian to Severus
and Bithynia for Hadrian only. A number of cities in Cilicia strike in the second
century: Aegaea for Hadrian, Mopsus for Hadrian and Pius, Seleucia for Pius
and up to Caracalla, while Tarsus begins with Domitian and carries on until
Caracalla. Of the major islands Cyprus has a silver series for all three Flavians and
Crete from Caligula to Trajan. The two more important series of silver in Asia
are from Lycia and from Caesarea in Cappadocia. The Lycian series, from
Augustus to Trajan, usually drachms, have the imperial portrait and a lyre reverse;
the Caesarean series from Tiberius to Elagabalus has a variety of reverses but the
most common show Mount Argaeus with, on summit, a naked male figure holding
globe and sceptre. In Mesopotamia a short-lived silver series was issued for Marcus
Aurelius, his co-emperor Lucius Verus and their wives Faustina II and Lucilla.
Provincial bronze coinage was issued consistently at Antioch on the Orontes
from Augustus to Severus Alexander with the imperial portrait on the obverse
and on the reverse a laurel-wreath enclosing the letters S C, which here cannot
be the *senatus consulto* of Roman bronze coins but may stand for *Syriae commune*.
For Augustus another series of bronze has the letters C A within a wreath on the

reverse. On the analogy of the Antiochene bronze these letters may stand for *Commune Asiae*.

Analagous provincial coinages in Europe are in bronze only and have Latin inscriptions. Two of the most extensive were in Greece itself, one at Corinth, the other at Patrae. Bronze of Corinth from Julius Caesar to Galba usually bears the names of the local magistrates, the *duoviri*. A second series extending from Domitian to Gordian III omits the magistrates' names. The traditional Corinthian types of Bellerophon and Pegasus frequently occur. Bronze of Patrae from Augustus to Gordian III has the inscription C.A.A.P. (Colonia Augusta Aroë Patrensis) and a frequent type shows the famous statue of Artemis Laphria. Viminacium in Upper Moesia has a bronze series from Gordian III to Gallienus. The coins show Moesia standing between bull and lion, and bear dates I to XVI of an era extending from A.D. 239 to 257. Further west in Gaul the colony of Nemausus struck bronzes in the reigns of Augustus and Tiberius with the remarkable reverse of a crocodile and palm-tree (Pl. 185). In the same period Lugdunum issued a bronze coinage with imperial head and the famous altar of Lyons dedicated to Rome and Augustus on the reverse. Provincial bronze in Spain has already been mentioned in the section on Spain.

Local issues of bronze coinage in the eastern provinces of the empire make up in their sum total a vast body of coinage. Many of the individual series are quite restricted but the number of cities which struck such coinage runs into hundreds. Almost all the cities, whose earlier coinage has been described, continued striking local bronzes under the empire and in many of the provinces the new peace and security afforded by the empire and the consequent increase in trade brought prosperity and the necessity for local coinage to towns which had not coined before. To survey in any detail this huge coinage would require a volume in itself but, since the coins on the whole show a woeful decline in artistic standard from the earlier Greek series and since, in their diversity, they are of more restricted interest, it is proposed to indicate only the general shape of this coinage, the features of interest which it presents and illustrate some typical and interesting examples.

This local coinage, as has already been mentioned, falls into two general categories. There is an 'imperial' series, struck by many cities, where the obverse always shows the portrait of the emperor or one of the imperial family. Indeed, as on the provincial series at Alexandria, many imperial personages enjoy on local issues rights of coinage not accorded to them on the coins of Rome. The Bithynian youth, Antinous, for instance, the favourite of the emperor Hadrian, appears on the coinage of a number of cities, particularly in Bithynia itself (Pl. 186). The reverse carries the name of the issuing city, usually in the genitive and often the name of

the magistrate, expressed by ἐπι with the genitive. The parallel series of local
bronze at many cities has, usually, the head of a divinity as obverse type or
occasionally the head of some local celebrity, such as Sappho on coins of Mytilene.
Much of this local coinage is unpretentious and presumably represents the issues
for ordinary use but larger and more elaborate issues are clearly connected with
some special occasion. Religious festivals and games provide the inspiration for a
good number of such issues or some outstanding event, such as an imperial visit.

The majority of the local issues are struck in rather low relief and, though on the
imperial series some of the portraits are interesting local interpretations of the
imperial features, the standard of portraiture is generally lower than on the Roman
issues. The great interest of the series and its value to the student of the ancient
world is the wealth of information to be obtained from the great diversity of
reverse types. In the field of religion most of the gods and heroes of Olympus are
represented on one or other city coinage, very often identified with some local
divinity whose name is added to that of the Olympian god. Zeus appears as Zeus
Larasius at some towns in Lydia, as Zeus Lydius at others; Apollo is Apollo
Smintheus at Alexandria Troas and Apollo Tyrimnaeus with his double axe at
Thyatira in Lydia. The great mother-goddess, Cybele, appears frequently on the
coinage of Asian cities, and Artemis, particularly at Ephesus, has a great variety of
representations. Of local versions of deities the conical stone of Elagabal, the sun-
god at Emesa, is of particular interest because of the impact of this worship at
Rome, when its high-priest became emperor in A.D. 218. Coins of Emesa show
this stone in its temple (Pl. 187). In Phrygia the god Mên was widely worshipped
and honoured on the coins of Phrygian cities. A coin of Temenothyrae issued in
the reign of Commodus shows Mên in his Phrygian cap, holding pine-cone and
sceptre in a biga of bulls (Pl. 188).

Another fruitful source of reverse types is ancient myth and legend. The story
of Io is illustrated on coins of Gaza and that of Dirce at Acrasus in Caria. The
heroes of the Trojan war, Hector, Priam and Patroclus, are natural subjects for
the coinage of Ilium, and Phoenician Dido figures on coins of Tyre. The labours
of Heracles had a widespread popularity and were particularly appropriate as
types at the town which bore his name, Heraclea Pontica. An unusual intrusion
into the usual classical repertoire of legends is the Jewish story of the great flood.
A bronze issue from Apamea in Phrygia has on its reverse a chest or ark inscribed
Noe, floating on the water and containing two figures, while the same or similar
two figures stand in front. On top of the ark is a raven and above flies a dove
with a branch in her mouth.

The great range of personifications or 'virtues' which are such a feature of the
Roman coinage is much more restricted on local issues where the only widespread

personification is that of the Tyche or city-goddess. Again, unlike the Roman issues, the great events of history leave little mark on local coinage. The great conquests of Trajan are amongst the few happenings which impressed themselves, as on coins of Ephesus with trophy and despondent figure of Parthia. It is only on occasional issues, too, that the not so infrequent visits of emperors to cities of the East are celebrated. Antioch, which was the headquarters of Severus Alexander for his war against the Persians in A.D. 231, shows the emperor crowning the city Tyche, with the river Orontes at her feet.

Matters of much more local interest supply the bulk of reverses. By good fortune, one of the most popular of reverse types was that which showed some local building of renown; for, in many instances, these coin reverses are the sole pictorial evidence for these buildings. Many of the great shrines of famous cults are pictured on such local coins. The cult of the sun-god Elagabal at Emesa has been mentioned above and a whole range of coins show various views of the temple which housed the sacred stone. The temple has a hexastyle façade with a flight of steps leading to the shrine where the stone stood, shaded by two parasols (Pl. 187). Devotion to the cult of Ephesian Artemis was widespread and receives mention in the Acts of the Apostles. Imperial bronzes of Ephesus not only show the cult figure of Artemis but the great temple itself, depicted on coins of Hadrian with a façade of eight columns. In addition to the cults of the Olympian and local divinities, the emperors also received worship as gods, not as in the West only after their death but in their lifetime. One of the most famous sites of this worship in Asia Minor was at Pergamum where various bronze coins show the temple dedicated to Rome and Augustus. Within the temple stands the figure of Roma crowning the emperor Augustus. In the wide range of archaeological features preserved on coins the famous labyrinth at Cnossus, which had been a favourite reverse on earlier coins, continued to be used on the bronzes of the early Roman empire. Other forms of architecture which find a record on this series of coins include bridges, city-walls and gates and even such a large feature as the harbour at Caesarea Germanica in Bithynia.

The one remaining series of imperial bronzes was that issued by Roman colonies and municipia. These, everywhere in the empire, even in the Greek East, used Latin for the coins' inscriptions. Obverses are devoted to imperial portraits and the range of reverse types is almost as unlimited as that of the other series described above. A common type shows the founder with his team of oxen ploughing the first ceremonial furrow enclosing the new site, as on a coin of *Aelia Capitolina*, the colony founded by Hadrian at Jerusalem after the second revolt of the Jews in A.D. 132–135.

The great political and economic crisis of the empire in the reign of Gallineus

(A.D. 259–268) brought much of this local coinage to an end, replacing it by the uniform issues of branches of the mint of Rome, established in the provinces. In some parts of south Asia Minor a number of local mints, chiefly in Cilicia, continued their activity down to the reign of Tacitus (A.D. 275–276). To fill the gap left by the cessation of local issues the output of the great provincial mint at Alexandria was increased until the monetary reforms of Diocletian in A.D. 295 brought this, too, to an end and substituted regular imperial bronze from an even more extended chain of Roman mints.

ROME

★

Rome

THE REPUBLIC, *c.* 289–31 B.C.

WITH THE exception of rare and infrequent issues of gold coin and an apparently stereotyped series of bronze coins of widely differing weight standards the bulk of the coinage of the Roman Republic consisted of a silver series mainly of denarii. These denarii, superficially so alike, reveal on inspection a bewildering variety of design, complicated by additional elements in the shape of symbols, control marks and monograms. In the centuries following the Renaissance which saw the beginning of the collecting of Roman coins it became the custom to arrange the republican coinage on the basis of the gentile or family name of the moneying official which was the one obvious feature to be remarked on the majority of these silver denarii. The apparent order thus created served its purpose in enabling the body of material to be collected, but by grouping together coins of widely differing dates merely because they were issued by moneyers bearing the same family name and, on the same principle, by divorcing coins bearing different names but of the same period the chronological development of the coinage and the relation to the history of the republic remained for long obscured.

Regrettably this basis of arrangement continues to have its exponents amongst students or rather collectors of republican coinage solely because of its simple nature. Successive studies of this coinage, however, over the last half-century or so have succeeded in reducing the seemingly inchoate issues to an ordered pattern at once relating to and illuminating the course of republican history. Since the coinage in most instances lacks specific allusion to events, the pattern has been established by the application of other criteria.

Some information about the coinage can be gleaned from the ancient authors but, as it is scanty and sometimes contradictory, its interpretation remains controversial. Of more value are the changing weight standards observable in the coinage itself while the development of the types or designs on the coins supply a good guide for the chronology. First comes the standard representation on the denarii of the head of Roma or Bellona as she should perhaps be known and of the Dioscuri, the heavenly twins Pollux and Castor: a further stage is marked by the introduction of other deities and is followed by coinage bearing references to historical events connected with the families to which the moneying magistrates belonged; the final stage is reached with coinage alluding to contemporary events and personalities of whom we have sure knowledge from sources such as Caesar's Commentaries.

COINAGE BEFORE 269 B.C., *AES RUDE* AND *AES SIGNATUM*

The varied beginnings of coinage in Italy provides a useful index to the uneven development of civilization in the peninsula. Along the coast in the south the great cities founded as colonies from Greece had issued splendid series of silver coins as early as the sixth century and in Etruria to the north of Rome coinage began in the fifth century B.C. Rome and the remainder of Italy were still in an earlier stage of civilization and, if any coinage was in use, it was the pieces of *aes rude*, rough lumps of bronze of irregular weight and without any mark of value. At a later stage bronze was cast in a more developed form in the shape of rectangular bars but it is not till the beginning of the third century B.C. that a series of such bars of a roughly regulated weight of about five pounds was issued. These bars are known as *aes signatum* because they bore devices on either side. Their appearance probably coincided with the first establishment at Rome in 289 B.C. of the board of three moneyers known later as the *tresviri aere argento auro flando feriundo*—the three appointed to cast and strike bronze, silver and gold.

The known bars have the following types: (1) Bull on both sides; (2) Shield on both sides; (3) Eagle on thunderbolt—Pegasus; (4) Elephant—pig; (5) Sword —scabbard; (6) Corn-ear—tripod; (7) Tripod—anchor; (8) Trident—caduceus; (9) Trident and dolphins—cocks and stars. The types on some of the bars have a fairly clear meaning. The bull on No. 1 is a reference to the primitive use of cattle as currency which provides the Latin word *pecunia* (money) from *pecus* (cattle). The Indian elephant of No. 4 refers to Pyrrhus of Epirus who used these animals in his invasion of Italy while the sow on the other side recalls the story that the elephants were routed at the battle of Beneventum in 274 B.C. by driving towards them pigs whose smell they could not bear (Pl. 189).

In the next stage, that of the *aes grave*—heavy bronze, the metal was still cast but in circular form and of regular, though roughly adjusted, weight. These heavy bronze coins had a distinctive type on both sides and carried a mark of value. The unit was the as which had the following subdivisions:

As	Mark of value	I	Quadrans	Mark of value	. . .
Semis	,,	S	Sextans	,,	. .
Triens	,,	. . . .	Uncia	,,	.

This series of heavy bronze coins had its beginning at Rome somewhere about 269 B.C., but the heavier weights of some specimens of the other Italian series suggest that the class may have begun earlier and have overlapped the preceding series of bars or *aes signatum*. The *aes grave* from the different districts of Italy have a wide variety of designs, and even in one series from the as down to the uncia the types often change, though usually an element of design or fabric links the whole series. The *aes grave* from Cales in Campania, for instance, has a constant reverse type, a mixing-bowl, but the obverses vary: as, semis and triens—head of Minerva; quadrans—dolphin; sextans—scallop-shell; uncia—club. Typical of picturesque designs on *aes grave* are the lion's head—horse's head from Campania, boar's head—wolf's head from Venusia, or the facing Silenus head—sleeping dog from Hatria (Pl. 190).

THE EARLIEST COINAGE PROPER, 269–211 B.C.

Amongst the scraps of information about the beginnings of Roman coinage given by the ancient writers is the statement in Pliny's *Natural History* that the Romans first issued silver coins in 269 B.C. and that the coins were denarii. Pliny, writing of an event, for him probably not very important which took place some centuries earlier, has confused two happenings; for modern research has shown that the denarius was not introduced till the late third century. There are, however, other silver coins with a Roman connection obviously earlier than the denarius, for these owe much in fabric and style to the coinages of the Greek cities in south Italy and are based on the weight standard introduced by them. The expanding and developing of Rome's power in the first part of the third century, bringing her into contact and conflict with the civilization of the Greek cities, made necessary for her a more developed monetary system than the primitive bronze currency which had hitherto been adequate.

The first coinage proper of the Romans was a series of four silver didrachms of a weight of 7·5 gm. inscribed with the word ROMANO, each with silver litrae and half-litrae as subdividsions, some token bronze and a series of heavy cast-bronze coins or *aes grave*. These four series may have been issued concurrently from different centres and though some of the types on the ROMANO didrachms suggest association with Greek cities in south Italy the mints producing these coins cannot yet be named with certainty. The exception is the series of the didrachm with the head of Hercules and wolf and twin types which contain references to Fabius and Ogulnius who were consuls at Rome in 269 B.C. The mint for this series was most likely Rome itself. The first didrachm series is classified as follows:

A. (Rome). Didrachm: Hercules head—wolf and twins (Pl. 191), litra: Hercules head—Pegasus; as: head of Diana—wheel.

B. Didrachm: Helmeted head of bearded Mars—horse's head; litra: as didrachm; half-litra: helmeted head of Minerva—horse's head; as: young Janus head—head of Mercury.

C. Didrachm: Head of Apollo—galloping horse; litra and half-litra: head of Apollo—Lion; as: Apollo head both sides.

D. Didrachm: Helmeted head of Diana—figure of Victory with small symbol and single or double Greek letter (A—Ω, AA—$\Omega\Omega$); half-litra: similar; as: Head of Diana both sides.

This seems to have been the coinage on which Rome fought the first Punic war. In the second half of the third century, about 235 B.C., the first series of silver didrachms with their accompanying *aes grave* was replaced by another in later style inscribed ROMA and slightly reduced weight standard (6·8 gm.) but still with companion issues of heavy bronzes, based on the libral standard, that is the reduced Latin pound of 272 gm.

A. Rome. Didrachm: young Janus head—quadrigatus (Pl. 192); as: Janus head—prow.

B. Didrachm: Beardless head of Mars—horse's head r.; as: Janus head—Mercury.

C. Didrachm: Apollo head—horse l.; half-litra: similar; as: Apollo head both sides.

D. Didrachm, drachm: Beardless head of Mars, with symbol club—horse; half-litra: similar; as: Head of Diana both sides, symbol—club.

The last three of these series were discontinued about 227 B.C. but the series of the didrachm with the reverse type of the quadrigatus or four-horse chariot continued to be produced, though the accompanying heavy-bronze coins were now put out on a semi-libral or half-pound standard. Of the bronze coins of this standard, the denominations down to the quadrans continued to be cast but denominations from the sextans downwards were struck from dies. Since the period covered by the two series of ROMANO and ROMA didrachms is comparatively short and since there is no strict parallelism of the two series it remains possible that they were not the products of separate mints. As at least one of the early series has a definite association with Rome and one in the second series and that the precise one which continued into the last part of the century, these may well be a series of successive issues all from the mint of Rome. Wherever exactly all the didrachms were struck, the last, the quadrigatus didrachm, was issued at Rome and continued to be issued in great quantity to finance the second struggle against Carthage which began in 219 B.C. In the early years of the war, in 216, came a short emergency issue of gold coin, the first in Rome's history. These were gold staters (6·8 gm.) and half-staters (3·4 gm.) with types showing a young Janus head and two warriors swearing an oath of alliance over a pig held by a third warrior. In the course of the war against Carthage the weight of the cast-bronze coins had been steadily falling until they were issued on a triental standard—the unit, the as, now had the weight of the original triens (a third of a pound) of the original series. In this new series denominations from the triens downwards were struck coins. Early in the war also a smaller silver denomination (3·4 gm.) was introduced, in reality a half of the quadrigatus didrachm but, from its types, a Jupiter head and a figure of Victory crowning a trophy of arms, generally known as a victoriate (Pl. 193). Initially the victoriates had no distinctive marks other than the inscription ROMA but later in the war, as silver supplies grew scant and the *quadrigatus* didrachm sank in weight its place was largely taken by the victoriates marked by letters and monograms which must indicate mints supplementing Rome. The varying signatures are taken to identify the following mints, some of which remain conjectural:

C–M	In Sardinia	⋀R	Metapontum
ꝗ	Corcyra	N	Nola
CROT	Croton	Q	In south Italy
L	Luceria	ꝶ	Rome
⋀	Mateola	ꝟ	Vibo

THE EARLIEST DENARII, *c.* 211–155 B.C.

Rome's first experimental coinage in silver, however, proved inadequate in the stresses of the second war with Carthage. Though there is no explicit documentary evidence relating to the introduction of a new Roman silver coinage, modern research, coupled with new archaeological evidence, supports a date of about 211 B.C. as that of the new coinage. The new system comprised three denominations in silver—the denarius worth ten asses, the quinarius of five asses and the sestertius of two and a half. The companion series of struck-bronze coins had seven denominations from as down to semuncia, based now on a sextantal standard; that is, the major piece, the as, now weighed a sixth of a pound. The denarius issued at a weight of 4·5 gm. equalled ten asses of 54·5 gm. each, giving a ratio of silver to bronze of 1 : 120, and thus in closer conformity to that of the Greek states.

The types of the denarius were, on the obverse, the helmeted head of Roma or Bellona and on the reverse the Dioscuri, Castor and Pollux, the demi-gods whom legend said had helped Rome in the battle of Lake Regillus against the Latins in 497 B.C. The reverse bore the inscription ROMA and on the obverse was the mark of value X—ten asses (Pl. 194). The quinarius and sestertius had identical types but with their own marks of value, Q and II S respectively. The bronze coins continued their traditional types. The reverse was consistently a prow and the word ROMA while varying obverses distinguished the denominations: As—head of Janus (Pl. 195); semis—head of Saturn; triens—head of Minerva; quadrans —head of Hercules; sextans—head of Mercury; uncia—head of Bellona; semuncia —bust of Mercury. The standards were not long maintained and by the middle of the century the denarius had fallen to 4·0 gm. and the bronze to about an ounce. The sestertius was issued for only a few years and soon the quinarius also ceased but its place was taken by a new series of victoriates which at a weight of 2·8 gm. formed a new smaller denomination, probably three-quarters of the denarius.

To defray the costs of the war with Carthage, gold coins also made their appearance in 211 B.C., and in 209 B.C. they were issued extensively. The gold is in three denominations marked ↓, XXXX and XX, equal to 60, 40 and 20 asses, and the types are the head of Mars and an eagle on a thunderbolt (Pl. 198).

The close resemblance of the types of the denarius to the coinage of the Brutii in south Italy has led to a suggestion that the earliest denarii were struck at Rhegium and, on a basis of stylistic variations and the interpretation of some of the letters and monograms on the coins as place names, a variety of mints have been identified for this early denarius coinage. It is possible that in the early second century a system of smaller local mints was required to supplement the production of Rome itself but the centralization which was already the keynote of Roman administration and the existence of only one body of monetary officials in the city itself argues a concentration of minting activity in Rome.

The chronology of the issues in this period can be determined approximately by criteria such as the changes in weight standards outlined above and the presence or absence of the smaller silver denominations. Three main categories emerge: an 'anonymous' series with none but the standard markings described; a series with an additional small symbol on the reverse and a series with a letter or monogram indicating the magistrate responsible for the issue. In general the series follow this order though with some exceptions. Stylistic differences in the helmet and ear-rings worn by Bellona on the obverse of the silver coins also help to establish the sequence. When such criteria are applied to the coinage of this period and allowance made for defective evidence a number of chronological groups can be distinguished and the validity of the sequence is assured by fairly general conformity with the stylistic development of Roma's helmet on the denarii. Some few anomalies probably represent the activity of mints other than Rome.

First Group. Denarius with quinarius, sestertius and bronze. Mostly first type of helmet. Anonymous, L, ꟿ.

Second Group. Denarius with quinarius and bronze. First to third types of helmet. *Symbols:* Adze, anchor, apex and hammer, caduceus, corn-ear, knife, laurel-branch, pentagram, prow, sceptre and feather, spear-head, staff, Victory. *Letters:* ꟼ, B, C, C.ꟼ, (Pl. 196), C. Ꝛ, ꝛ, H, M, ꟽ, ꟿ, Q, V.

Third Group. Denarius with victoriate and bronze. Fourth helmet type. Anonymous. *Symbols:* Club, cornucopiae, crescent, dog, dolphin, helmet, hog, knife, meta (Pl. 197), prow, rudder, sceptre, spear-head, trident.

Fourth Group. Denarius; victoriate and bronze beginning to disappear. Fourth helmet type. Anonymous. *Symbols:* Anchor, corn-ear, pentagram, sceptre (Pl. 198), spear-head.

Fifth Group. Denarius only. *Symbols:* Bull, ear, female head, gryphon, owl, shield and carnyx, wreath. *Letters:* Ʌ, GR, ꟿ, Q.L.C., SX.Q, Ꝛ.

This coinage, which combined a silver system ultimately deriving from the Greek world with bronze issues on the traditional Italian standards, had sufficed for Rome in her expansion in Italy and her struggle against Carthage and was still in being as Rome began to move eastwards into Greece. Use was undoubtedly made there of local coinages already in existence and there are very rare survivors of a special issue of gold coins struck in Greece in honour of the Roman general Flamininus who defeated Philip V of Macedon at Cynoscephalae in 197 B.C. These coins were not an integral part of the Roman coinage system for they were struck on the standard of the Macedonian gold stater but they are of interest as the first coins to carry the portrait of a living Roman.

REDUCED DENARIUS: UNCIAL BRONZE,
c. 155–124 B.C.

A number of changes in weight standards mark out the coinage of approximately the next two decades. The weight of the denarius which had continued to show a tendency to fall was fixed at a new figure of 4·0 gm., which was to remain the standard of the denarius till well into the early empire and at the same time the bronze was reduced to the uncial standard (c. 27·3 gm.), a twelfth of its original weight. The introduction of new reverse types for the denarius further distinguishes the issues of this period. The monopoly of the Dioscuri as a reverse type was broken by the introduction, first of a type showing Diana (or Luna) in biga, then Victory in biga and later a variety of other deities. The use of symbols to indicate issues was practically abandoned in the early part of this series in favour of the monograms of the moneying magistrates with a tendency for more and more of the name to appear on the coins. The lower limit of this present group is marked by a retariffing of the denarius during the tribunate of Gaius Gracchus 123–122 B.C. The style of the coins in this period shows little variation and suggests that if the mint at Rome was supplemented by other mints there was no more than one at this period.

First Group. c. 155–150 B.C. This consists of issues which still include the victoriate, a denomination which disappeared in 150 B.C. *Dioscuri* reverse with (a) symbol— crescent; (b) monogram: ᴀ̄, ᴍᴇ, ꙮ, ᴙ, ᴀᴙ. *Diana* reverse with (a) symbol: fly, feather; (b) monogram: ᴀ/, ᴀ̌, ᴀᴙ.

Second Group. c. 150–146 B.C. The victoriate is no longer issued. A second variety of the reverse, Diana in biga, is issued where Diana holds a goad. *Dioscuri* reverse with (a) symbol—cornucopiae; (b) monogram: ᴀᴙ, CN.Cᴙ, L.COIL, CN.DO, P.ᴀᴇ; *Diana* reverse with (a) symbol—prawn; (b) monogram: TOD. (Pl. 199). To this group also is assigned a series of issues of bronze without the silver denomination because of the form of the moneyer's signatures. These are : ᴙ, ᴀ̄, P.BLAS, A.Cᴁ, CINA, SᴙI, ᴀᴇ, L. MAMILI, Q. ᴀᴀR, Q. ᴍᴇ, ᴀᴀRENA, OPEI, P, Pᴙ , C.Sᴁ, C.Sᴋ, M.TITINI, TᴙD, W , ᴙO.

Third Group. c. 145–124 B.C. The introduction of a new reverse type, Victory in biga, probably refers to the final destruction of Carthage in 146 B.C. Similar obverse style links issues with Dioscuri and other new reverses. No symbols, only moneyers' names. *Dioscuri.* Moneyers: C. ÆSTI, L.CⱽP, Q.ᴁC LIBO, Q.MINV RVF, L.ITI, C.IVNI C.F., M.IVNI, P. PAETVS, C.PLVTI, C.SCR, L.SEᴀ. *Victory in biga,* moneyers: S.AFRA, (Pl. 200), C.CATO, NAT, NATᴀ, C. NVMITORI, SAR, L.SᴀF, P.SⱽA, C.ᴀ C. F. *Diana in biga,* moneyers: FLAVS, ᴿ. *Jupiter in quadriga,* moneyers: CARB, ᴀ RVᶠ, L. MINVCIVS. *Juno in quadriga,* moneyer: C. CⱽR TRIGE. *Juno in biga of goats,* moneyer: C.RENI. *Mars and Nerio in quadriga,* moneyer: CN.GEL. *Hercules in biga of centaurs* moneyer: M.ᴀRELI. *Wolf and twins,* moneyer: SEX. POM. FOSTLVS. *Ionic column,* moneyer: C.AVG.

The great events of this period, the outbreak of the third Punic war followed by the destruction of Carthage, the dissensions in Italy itself and the campaign for reform by Tiberius Gracchus are only dimly reflected in the contemporary coinage. Apart from the new reverse types showing various deities in chariots, some of them such as Hercules not normally portrayed as chariot-borne, this period shows the beginning of the style of reverse type which was to dominate the coinage almost till the end of the republic. The reverses begin to contain allusions to events connected with the history of the moneyer's family. In this vein, the coin of the moneyer Sex. Pom. Fostlus depicts the legend connected with Rome's beginnings in which the shepherd Faustulus finds the twins Romulus and Remus being suckled by the she-wolf (Pl. 201). Similarly the Ionic column on the denarius of C. Augurinus is a reference to one of his ancestors in the fifth century to whom a monument was erected for his services in supplying the Roman people with cheap corn after the death of Spurius Maelius who had tried to bribe the people with free gifts of corn. There may be a contemporary reference here, a hostile comparison of the political activities of the Gracchan brothers to those of the adventurer, Maelius.

THE XVI DENARIUS DOWN TO THE 'SOCIAL' WAR, 123–91 B.C.

The limits of this group are the retariffing of the denarius at 16 asses instead of 10 sometime during the tribunate of Gaius Gracchus (123–122 B.C.) and the coinage associated with the war between Rome and her Latin allies which broke out in 90 B.C. The retariffing is clearly marked on the denarii, for the sign of value, X (10 asses), was changed first to XVI, then after a very short time to ✕. At the same time the bronze as went out of issue and until about 108 B.C. only the denominations from semis down to uncia were issued. One other change in the pattern of denominations in this group was the re-introduction about 104 B.C. of the silver quinarius, not this time with the reverse types of the denarius but with those of the old victoriate, Victory crowning a trophy of arms.

The issues of denarii of some of the moneyers were extensive and on these appear a system of sequence-marks placed on the coins to act in some way as a form of control or check on the output. There was a variety of systems of these sequence-marks—letters of the Greek or Roman alphabet, Roman numerals and symbols. The marks are found placed on the obverse or the reverse and in some issues on both, while different systems are occasionally used in combination. Although the development of the various forms of sequence-marks and their combinations provides some guidance to the order in which the coinage was issued, the evidence which, from this period onwards, is the most valuable for establishing the sequence of issues is that of coin-finds. The presence or absence of moneyers in a long series of finds of denarii of the later second century and onwards has affirmed with reasonable certainty the order in which they held office and issued their coins.

Yet another feature of the denarius coinage which makes its first appearance in this period is the serration or notching of the edge of the coin (Pl. 202). This became a regular practice on some issues after 117 B.C. One explanation advanced is that the serrate issues were meant principally for circulation outside Italy amongst the Celtic and Teutonic tribes to whom such a coinage would appeal as possessing the similar kind of religious significance as the serrated ring-amulets with which they were already familiar. It is more likely that the practice stems from the dissensions of the period in Rome. The democratic party, backed by the knights, stood for good money at a time when there was debasement of the silver and to show that the denarius was of good metal it was issued with this notched edge. That many serrate denarii prove to be in fact plated only demonstrates the ability of the forger even at that time.

As in the previous period, the chief mint is still certainly Rome. Coinage with other characteristics has been assigned to other mints brought into being for special purposes. Amongst these were the issues for the war against Jugurtha in North Africa in 110 B.C. struck probably in south Italy, for the war against the Cimbri from a mint in Cis-Alpine Gaul and for the establishment of new colonies in south Gaul issues from a mint at Narbonne in 118 B.C.

Mint of Rome. Thick and compact flans, at times verging on the dumpy, a typical high relief of the 'Roma' head and the evidence of the finds mark off this group which ends with an issue bearing sequence-marks, introduced towards the end of the century. The earliest issues are clearly those with mark of value XVI which was short-lived; all the remaining issues are marked with the shortened version, ✳ . The obverse type continues to be the head of 'Roma' but the reverse types now show such a rich variety that in this context it is not possible to do more than indicate the more typical coins of the series and comment on some of the more unusual and interesting reverse designs.

The earliest group with the mark XVI contains all three of the regular reverses in use previously, the Dioscuri, Diana in biga and Victory in biga. A peculiar issue is that of L. Atilius where, in place of the usual ROMA on the reverse, is the word NOM which may be the continuation of the moneyer's name Nomentanus (Pl. 203). In the later part of this group, the familiar early reverses give way to types containing allusions to the history of the moneyer's family. The moneyer Sextus Julius Caesar shows Venus in a biga being crowned by Cupid, one of the earliest coin references to the legendary descent of the Julian family from Aeneas, the son of Venus (Pl. 204). Jupiter in a biga of elephants with Victory and wreath above on the denarius of C. Metellus refers back to the victory of L. Caecilius Metellus over the Carthaginians at Panormus when in 251 B.C. he captured their elephants. A whole tableau of citizens voting is presented on the coin of P. Nerva, an allusion to a near contemporary event, the passing in 106 B.C. of a law concerning voting by ballot in certain trials. Towards the close of the group is the issue of N. Fabius Pictor consisting of denarii without, then with a sequence-mark, a changing letter on both obverse and reverse. The final issues, on which the mark of value is almost always missing from the denarius, include the reverse of P. Laeca, showing a soldier appealing from an officer to a citizen. The inscription PROVOCO alludes to the right of appeal (*lex de provocatione*) passed by an earlier P. Porcius Laeca in 199 B.C.

The very end of the century saw a small issue of serrate denarii from Rome but the issues of the decade 100–91 B.C. were of the normal fabric. The earlier coins in this group maintain the head of 'Roma' on obverse but from about 96 B.C. the obverse is also given over to other types, mainly heads of deities as on the coin of C. Fabius with bust of Cybele on the obverse and Victory in biga on the reverse (Pl. 205). The quinarius, reintroduced with the types of the old victoriate, was issued by moneyers C. Fundanius, T. Cloulius (Pl. 206) and P. Sabinus.

Mint in Cisalpine Gaul. Issues with wide flans and heads in low relief, unlike in style to the normal coins of the Rome mint, are shown by finds to have been issued between 109–100 B.C. and constitute a special coinage for the campaigns against the Cimbri and Teutones who had made a number of raids into the province and were finally routed by Marius in 101 B.C. The special nature of the coinage is marked by a number of joint issues signed each by three men who in this special instance took the place of the college of moneyers. One such issue has on the reverse, Victory in biga and the signatures of all three Cn. Fulvius, M. Calidius and Q. Metellus (Pl. 207). Coinage from this mint continued in a second group between 100 and 95 B.C. with special issues. The denarius of M. Porcius Cato with reverse, a seated Victory inscribed VICTRIX, refers to the defeat of the Cimbri and the unusual inscriptions ARG. PVB (argentum publicum) on the coins of L. Sentius and PV (publice) on those of P. Servilius Rufus are those of a special issue.

Mint in South Italy. A group of coins which in their style are reminiscent of some Greek issues may be no more than the work of Greek die-cutters employed at Rome. A mint has been suggested for them in south Italy with its Greek civilization and the base for the campaign being waged against Jugurtha in North Africa *c.* 109–100 B.C. On a coin of this group with bust of Veiovis on obverse and two seated Lares and dog on reverse the monograms Λ and ℞ on the reverse have been explained as Lares Regienses and the mint city, consequently, identified as Rhegium. A striking coin of this group is the denarius of M. Herennius showing a youth carrying an old man on his shoulder, possibly a reference to the story of the brothers Amphinomus and Anapius of Catana who saved the lives of their parents when Mount Etna erupted. The denarius issued by Cn. Blasio is of interest for the head on the obverse has been held to be a portrait of Scipio (Pl. 208).

Mint in South Gaul. A Roman colony was established at Narbonne in 118 B.C. after the victory of Cn. Domitius over the Gauls under Bituitus. Domitius and L. Licinius may have been the commissioners for the founding and a special series of coins of five moneyers signed in addition by both Domitius and Licinius on the reverse may be from a mint in the colony in its early years, *c.* 113–109 B.C. Serration or notching of the edge of the coin aptly makes its first appearance in this series struck in or for Gaul where the tribes, as Tacitus tells, had a fondness for serrate coins showing chariots. The typical coin in this group shows a warrior (perhaps the Gaulish chieftain, Bituitus) in biga on the reverse with the signatures of Domitius and Licinius; the obverse has the usual 'Rome' head and the name of the moneyer, L. Porcius Licinius (Pl. 209).

THE SOCIAL WAR: MARIUS AND SULLA, 91–79 B.C.

The Allies. Despite the attempts of reformers such as the Gracchi Rome continued to refuse to extend the privileges of citizenship to her allies in Picenum, Samnium and Apulia until feelings embittered over long years flared into revolution in 91 B.C., the 'social' war, the war between Rome and her 'socii' her allies. An Italian confederation was formed with headquarters at Corfinium but after initial success the movement collapsed in 88 B.C. The allies issued their own coinage of silver denarii of which two groups can be distinguished, one with Latin inscriptions from a mint in the north-east of their territory, another with Oscan inscription from a mint in Samnium. The types on the coins are a mixture of adaptations of well-known Roman coins and fresh designs. Apt types for an alliance coinage presented on the obverse a head of Italia with inscription ITALIA where the head of 'Roma' had so long appeared and on the reverse warriors varying in number from one to four, standing either side of a standard, swearing an oath of alliance over a pig as on the gold stater of 216 B.C. (see p. 109 above). The mint in Samnium struck issues with such reverses as a bull (Italy) trampling on a she-wolf (Rome) with the inscription ITALIA in Oscan characters (Pl. 210). A further group with similar types is inscribed in Oscan with the names of the allies' generals Q. Pompaedius Silo and C. Papius Mutilus.

Rome. The extensive coinage produced by Rome herself in the years of the war and immediately afterwards is an index of the effort she had to exert to quell the revolt. The coinage of L. Piso Frugi issued at this time is the most massive series produced by one moneyer and is also the coinage with the most elaborate set of sequence-marks. The types show an Apollo head and a naked horseman at the gallop (Pl. 211). The coinage of D. Junius Silanus also struck during the Social war, though not so vast as that of L. Piso Frugi, was a large issue with elaborate sequence-marks. The head of Salus, the preserver, was an appropriate type for the dangers of the time. Internal features of the Roman coinage in this period are the reappearance of the bronze as, reduced now to a semunical standard, a twenty-fourth of the pound and the re-issue of the silver sestertius, both measures introduced by the lex Plautia Papiria in 90 B.C. Bronze coins on this standard ceased about 80 B.C. and rarely reappeared in the republican coinage.

The dissensions between the senatorial and democratic parties at Rome, stilled during the Social war, revived when the danger was removed. Of subsequent events, the march of Sulla on Rome in 88 B.C. and the triumph of the senatorial party, followed by Sulla's departure for his command against Mithridates of Pontus with the consequent return to power of Marius and the 'reign of terror' scarcely show in the coinage. The issues in the Sullan period are those of Q. Titius, Cn. Lentulus, L. Rubrius Dossenus and L. Titurius Sabinus. The types of the latter refer to the earlier clash of Rome with the Sabines and include a rape of the Sabine women, two soldiers bearing off a Sabine woman (Pl. 212). The Marian issues are those of C. Marcius Censorinus, M. Fannius and L. Critonius. An unusual coinage, still in the Marian period, with head of Veiovis and Jupiter in quadriga is signed by all three moneyers of the college, Gargilius, Ogulnius and Vergilius in an order which varies from coin to coin. The return of Sulla to

Italy in 83, and the defeat of the Marians at the battle of the Colline gate in 82 was followed by his dictatorship which lasted till his abdication in 79 and death in 78. In this period there is a similar coinage to that of Gargilius and his college above signed by three moneyers, L. Censorinus, P. Crepusius and C. Limetanus. Separate issues of Crepusius, Censorinus and C. Norbanus are notable for their vast range of sequence-marks. A coinage of serrate denarii in Sulla's dictatorship by Limetanus, A. Postumius Albinus, Q. Antonius Balbus, C. Marius Capito and L. Volteius Strabo was issued for the military actions required against unrest in the provinces, particularly Spain.

Military issues. The East. During Sulla's campaigns against Mithridates of Pontus, and in the following years, coinage was struck for him as imperator—commander— at mints in Asia Minor and Greece. This is almost the earliest instance of Roman coinage to include plentiful issues of gold coins, aurei (10·69 gm.). These coins bear Sulla's name and title of imperator or later of dictator and of either L. Manlius his proquaestor or A. Manlius his quaestor. The aureus with types, head of Roma on obverse and Sulla in quadriga with Victory flying above was struck to mark his triumph over Mithridates (Pl. 213). Athens has been suggested as the mint.

Gaul and Spain. In the west also there were two military issues at the end of the present period. C. Valerius Flaccus propraetor in Gaul issued a denarius coinage with his name and his title of imperator together with the phrase EX S.C. (*ex senatus consulto*—by decree of the Senate). The reverse, a legionary eagle between two military standards, was later revived by Mark Antony. In Spain coinage was struck for the proconsul C. Annius Luscus sent by Sulla in 81 B.C. to put down Sertorius the Marian governor who still held the province. The obverse has the bust of Anna Perenna and Annius' name and rank, while the reverse, Victory in quadriga or biga, is signed by either L. Fabius Hispaniensis or C. Tarquitius, the quaestors of Annius. A little later in 78 B.C. a coinage was struck by C. Caecilius Metellus Pius as imperator in the campaign which he continued against Sertorius in Spain. The obverse, a head of Pietas with stork emblem, refers to his title Pius and the reverse, an elephant, is the badge of the Caecilian family (Pl. 214).

POMPEY THE GREAT, 78–49 B.C.

The coinage in this period was basically one of silver denarii only which were mostly of the same fabric, though there were a few issues of serrate coins. In execution the coinage now reached its highest peak and the imaginative choice of types both for obverse and reverse make it the most richly varied series under the republic. The basic variation in style and fabric is inconsiderable and consistent with the production of the whole regular series from the mint of Rome. Towards the end of the period, issues for Julius Caesar as proconsul in Gaul were struck in the province.

The stirring events of the time find little reference on the coins. After the death of Sulla in 78 and the re-emergence of the democratic party, the senatorial side found a new champion in Pompey who had already acquired fame as a general under Sulla. On Pompey's activities, his defeat of Sertorius in Spain, his crushing of the pirate menace and defeat of Mithridates of Pontus the coins are silent. Only one very rare coinage in gold was struck with Pompey's name in his lifetime. On the obverse is the bust of Africa with elephant-skin head-dress and the inscription MAGNVS—the great—alluding to Pompey. Pompey, holding wreath, stands in a quadriga on the reverse, a reference to the triumph which he celebrated in 61 B.C. (Pl. 215). The fashion was still for the coins to celebrate well-known deeds of the moneyers' ancestors but the tendency grew to allude to men and events of recent history and this paved the way for the coinage portraying and honouring living men which came shortly after this period.

Rome. A number of issues are remarkable not for the content of the coin design but for the continuation and elaboration of the system of sequence-marks. The coins of L. Papius, about 78 B.C., with types, head of Juno Sospita in goat-skin head-dress and gryphon, have different but related symbols on each side, the symbols all being connected with various trades. In 64 B.C. C. Piso Frugi issued a huge series of denarii with the types of Apollo and horseman used by his father L. Piso Frugi in 89 B.C. but with an even more complex set of sequence-marks combining letters, numerals, fractional signs and symbols. As late as 58 B.C. the coinage of L. Porcius Fabatus has a long series of sequence-marks in the form of symbols on both the obverse and reverse depicting again Juno Sospita with goat-skin head-dress and a girl feeding a serpent rearing up before her.

A new feature is a coinage for one moneyer with a whole range of varying types. M. Volteius in 76 B.C. produced a set of types celebrating the five great festival games held every year. The Roman games are denoted by types of Jupiter head and temple of Jupiter Capitolinus in Rome, the *Plebeii* by head of Hercules and Erymanthian boar, the *Cereales* by bust of Bacchus and Ceres in chariot, the *Megalenses* by bust of Attis and Cybele in chariot drawn by lions, and the *Apollinares* by Apollo head and tripod with serpents. Similarly Q. Pomponius Musa, punning on his name, issued a set of nine denarii with Apollo head on the obverse and one of the nine Muses on each reverse. Historical and architectural themes were used by L. Marcius Philippus who represented on his coin an aqueduct on five arches, the *aqua Marcia* said to have been built by Ancus Marcius one of

Rome's early kings whose head appeared on the obverse. Some coins do allude to recent or contemporary events, though not the doings of the leading figures. Faustus Sulla, son the of the dictator, on the occasion of the games given in 60 B.C. in accordance with his father's will, issued coins including one with obverse of Diana and on the reverse Sulla receiving the surrender of Jugurtha by Bocchus (Pl. 216). The coins of M. Scaurus and P. Hypsaeus commemorate the submission of Aretas, the Nabataean king, to Scaurus when he was a legate of Pompey in the East in 62 B.C. Aretas is seen kneeling, holding an olive-branch, while behind stands a camel.

Gaul. A number of special military issues are attributed to Caesar's long series of campaigns in Gaul. One struck in great quantity shows an elephant, the badge of Caesar, trampling on a dragon, representing Gaul. On the reverse of this coin are sacrificial instruments, alluding to Caesar's office of Pontifex Maximus which he had held since 63 B.C. (Pl. 217). A series of gold and silver coins with the head of Venus, the legendary source of the Julian family, and a trophy of Gallic arms is marked ⅃Ⅱ (52), a reference to Caesar's age in the year of issue, 50 B.C. A denarius issue has a similar type but seated below the trophy on the reverse is a captive Gaul, probably Vercingetorix, one of Caesar's greatest opponents in the Gallic campaigns.

POMPEY AND CAESAR, 49–44 B.C.

In this period from the crossing of the Rubicon by Caesar in 49 B.C. and the civil war against Pompey down to the assassination of Caesar on 15th March 44 B.C. the coinage begins to reflect contemporary events with greater immediacy. The great bulk of the coinage still consisted of silver denarii but there were more frequent and extensive issues of gold aurei and the occasional issue of bronze pieces once again. The pattern of the coinage follows closely that of events. In 49 B.C. the Pompeian party still held Rome and issued coinage there but when Pompey withdrew to Greece on Caesar's entry into Italy, the Pompeian coinage was issued from mints in Greece and the East while the Rome mint began its issues for Caesar. There was a brief Pompeian coinage in Spain in 49 B.C. until Caesar's campaign there in the same year and again in 46–45 B.C. during Caesar's campaign against Pompey's sons, culminating in their defeat at Munda. In Africa also a coinage was struck for the Pompeian party up to its defeat at Thapsus in 46 B.C. Most of the military issues in the provinces are marked with the name of the general by virtue of whose imperium, the power of command technically deriving from the Senate, the coins were struck. Even at Rome latterly the coins carry Caesar's name and the various offices which he held. Finally, in the last few months of Caesar's life—in early 44 B.C.—came an issue with not only his name and titles but his portrait as well.

The Pompeian coinage. Rome. Amongst issues of Pompey at Rome in 49 was the denarius of L. Vinicius with head of Concordia and a reverse, Victory with palm-branch adorned with four wreaths, three conferred on Pompey for his victories in three continents and the jewelled wreath given by the Roman people (Pl. 218). A second type, caduceus and palm-branch in saltire was issued by Q. Sicinius, one of the *tresviri*, the moneyers at Rome. *Military mints.* (a) The same Sicinius signs another issue as moneyer but, as the reverse with club of Hercules and lion-skin is also signed by C. Coponius in command of the Rhodian fleet under Pompey, the mint was somewhere in the East. The names of L. Cornelius Lentulus and C. Claudius Marcellus, consuls in 49 B.C. who left Italy with Pompey, appear on three issues, head of Apollo and figure of Jupiter, Trisceles with Medusa head and figure of Jupiter (Pl. 219), Jupiter head and statue of Diana of the Ephesians. Because of the suggestive types, the mints of the last two have been identified as in Sicily and Asia Minor. (b) *Spain.* There were two issues for Pompey's legates in Spain in 49 B.C. before their defeat by Caesar. The first, with types, the head of Numa Popilius and a prow, has the names of Cn. Piso, proquaestor and Pompey as proconsul; the second, bust of Jupiter and sceptre between eagle and dolphin, the names of Varro, proquaestor and Pompey. In the last resistance to Caesar led by Cnaeus and Sextus, the sons of Pompey in 46–45 B.C., coinage was struck with the portrait of Pompey the Great and a figure of Hispania welcoming Cnaeus Pompey, landing from a ship (Pl. 220). (c) *Africa.* The coinage of the Pompeian resistance in Africa was issued by commanders such as Q. Metellus Pius Scipio and M. Porcius Cato. A number of types refer directly to Africa. One coin of Metellus depicts an African elephant (Pl. 221); a second had the head of Africa wearing elephant-skin head-dress.

Coinage of Caesar. Rome. Of the early coinage emphasizing themes of liberty, victory and triumph one of the most striking is the issue by L. Hostilius Saserna in 48 B.C. The obverse is the head of a Gallic warrior, possibly Vercingetorix himself who was exhibited in Caesar's triumph and on the reverse a warrior and his charioteer in a native biga (Pl. 222). Of interest for the history of coinage itself is the representation of its patron Juno Moneta and the instruments used in coinage on an issue by T. Carisius (Pl. 223). Plentiful gold issues in successive years trace the offices held by Caesar. On the aureus of A. Hirtius in 46 Caesar is consul for the third time (COS TER), on that of L. Plancus in 45 he is dictator for the third time and in 44 a third aureus mentions his fourth dictatorship.

Two special features mark out the last issue of Caesar in 44 B.C. The coinage is that of the first college of four moneyers (quattuorviri) who in this year replaced the college of three only and the coins carry the portrait of Caesar. The moneyers are M. Mettius, L. Aemilius Buca, P. Sepullius Macer and C. Cossutius Maridianus and the college functioned in pairs. The coin of Buca with its reverse showing Sulla's dream in which a goddess—Selene or Minerva—offered to put the power of thunder into his hands (Pl. 224) is the only one without the portrait of Caesar. Variations in Caesar's title (Pl. 225) trace the sequence of the remainder to the last group in early March where Caesar has the title *Parens Patriae*, father of his country. Parallel issues by the same moneyers but lasting only into February and emphasizing Caesar's position as general (*imperator*) were possibly connected with his preparations in early 44 for the projected campaign against the Parthians (Pl. 226).

THE TRIUMVIRATE, 44–31 B.C.

The assassination of Caesar removed the one stable element which had maintained order in the last five years and the much diminished authority of the Senate proved incapable of controlling events. Behind the outward maintenance of the old republican forms there developed a struggle for succession to the position and power which Caesar had held. The contenders included Mark Antony, Caesar's lieutenant and his fellow consul in 44 B.C., Lepidus, Caesar's master of horse, and Octavian, Caesar's grand-nephew and adopted heir. In 43 these three formed a triumvirate to control the affairs of the state and the chequered history of this compact and the final emergence of Octavian as the sole and supreme authority can be traced in the coinage of this period. The coins also illustrate a number of side issues—the resistance of Brutus and Cassius, the leaders of the conspiracy against Caesar, until their defeat at Philippi in Greece in 42, and the campaign by Octavian against Sextus Pompey in 38–36 B.C.

In the coinage system itself the trend noted in the previous period for the regular silver series to be supplemented by frequent gold issues becomes more pronounced. Similarly the tendency for the obverse to have a portrait and title becomes almost a rule while the choice of types for the reverse achieves even greater variety. Rare bronze issues of Antony are, to judge from the types, connected with the fleet. Octavian also has a few issues of bronze. Italy and the mint of Rome never passed out of Octavian's control and struck for him and for the members of the triumvirate so long as good relations existed amongst them. Gaul allotted to Antony by the agreement of 43 produced some military issues for him in 43–42 and for some time from 41 onwards for Octavian. The mints which struck for Brutus and Cassius were presumably in Asia Minor which they held for some time, and in Greece during the preparations to resist Octavian and

Antony. Other mints were brought into action to strike for Sextus Pompey in Sicily and for Antony in the East after the new division of provinces in 42 B.C.

Mint of Rome. At least two series issued in 44 B.C., but after Caesar's death, are quite clear. The horseman reverse used for Caesar's last issue by the moneyer P. Sepullius Macer appears with, on obverse, a veiled portrait of Antony who is shown bearded, the convention of mourning. The same reverse is joined with an obverse showing the temple of Caesar's Clemency, decreed late in his life and now dedicated. A coinage later in 44 B.C. includes the issue by the moneyer L. Flaminius Chilo with the unusual inscription IIII VIR PRI (mus) FL (avit). The coins of L. Servius Rufus, M. Arrius Secundus and C. Numenius Vaala in 43 formed the last senatorial issue before the formation of the triumvirate. In 42 an unusually full series of coins was produced by the college of moneyers Clodius, Varus, Mussidius and Regulus. Each moneyer struck two series, one in both gold and silver, with allusive types on both obverse and reverse, the other in gold only, with portraits of the triumviri on the obverse and reverse types appropriate to each triumvir. The portrait of Octavian, for instance, on the aureus issued by Regulus is accompanied by a reverse depicting Aeneas carrying his father Anchises on his shoulder as they escaped from Troy. Octavian's family, the Julians, claimed descent from Aeneas (Pl. 227). Later issues from Rome by Graccus and Vitulus with the portrait of Octavian and the inscription DIVI IVLI F., recorded the deification of Caesar and the recognition of Octavian as his adopted son and heir. The plough on the reverse of Graccus and the calf on that of Vitulus allude to Octavian's settlement of veterans on the land in Italy in 41. The deification theme is repeated on bronze coins with head of Octavian, described as CAESAR DIVI F. on the obverse and on reverse the head of the deified Julius with DIVOS IVLIVS (Pl. 228).

Military issues. Octavian. After the Perusine war in 40 B.C. Octavian visited Gaul to organize the Gallic provinces where a series of coin was issued for him. The various offices held by Octavian and recorded on these coins date the series to the years 40 to 36 B.C. The head of Octavian occupies the obverse and is coupled, in some instances, with the portrait of one of his fellow triumviri Antony and Lepidus on the reverse. Coinage from this mint also honours Octavian's great lieutenant, Agrippa. The fact that in 37 B.C. he was consul elect is recorded on the reverse of issues in both gold and silver where the obverse has the portraits of both Octavian and the deified Julius.

Brutus and Cassius. The coinage of Cassius in his province of Asia makes great play with the theme of liberty, the ostensible basis of the conspiracy against Caesar and the head of Libertas adorns the obverse of the majority of his coins. The names of Aquinus, Lentulus Spinter and Servilius, the legates of Brutus and Cassius, also appear on the coins. The issue, still with the head of Libertas on the obverse but with a crab on the reverse with a rose below refers to the defeat of the Rhodian fleet and the taking of the island by Cassius in 43 B.C. (Pl. 229). The coins of Brutus in Greece are more varied but here too the references to liberty are frequent. The appearance of Caesar's portrait on his coins in his lifetime was evidence to true republicans of his ambition to become king but in a number of issues in the series appears the portrait of Brutus, one of the chief conspirators. On an aureus, the obverse shows his ancestor L. Junius Brutus who expelled the kings from Rome and became the first consul; the reverse has the portrait of Brutus himself (Pl. 230). An even more striking coin is the denarius with a portrait of Brutus on obverse and on the reverse the cap of Liberty flanked by two daggers with the inscription EID MAR (The Ides of March)—a concise statement of the object, the method and date of the assassination (Pl. 230a).

Sextus Pompey. Entrusted by the Senate in 43 B.C. with command of a fleet, Pompey seized and held Sicily against the triumvirate. The coinage of his successful resistance between 42 and 38 carried the portrait of Pompey the Great and reverses of Neptune and Sicilian legend or the portrait of Sextus himself on one side and his father and brother on the other, together with his title of prefect of the fleet (Pl. 231). A truce arranged in 38 B.C. was short-lived and in a second war between 38 and 36 Sextus was ultimately defeated but not before some successes against Octavian. The victory of Sextus at the battle of Messana in 38 B.C. is celebrated by a coinage showing the lighthouse at Messana and a representation of Scylla, the legendary rock in the Messenian straits (Pl. 232).

Mark Antony. Gaul, assigned to Antony in the formation of the triumvirate, issued coins in his name in 43 and 42. The types of the earlier series related to the offices of augur and pontifex maximus held by Antony and Lepidus. The later coins couple the portraits of Antony and Octavian on obverse and reverse. Lucius, the brother of Mark Antony, took up the cause of those dispossessed by Octavian's settlement of the veterans after Philippi. In the Perusine war, in which the dispute culminated, the children of Lucius took refuge in Praeneste and it has been suggested that this is the allusion of the little storks on the reverse of a coin with Mark Antony's portrait, probably struck at Praeneste (Pl. 233). After a fresh division of provinces after Philippi, the East was allotted to Antony and subsequent issues in his name emanate from mints in these provinces. In the first few years despite occasional strained relations there are joint issues with Octavian and in 38–37 B.C. a series of gold coins combine the portrait of Antony with that of Octavia whom he married in 40 B.C. After his conquest of Armenia in 34 B.C. Antony celebrated a triumph in Alexandria and bestowed kingdoms on the sons of Cleopatra, all of which is reflected in the inscriptions and portraits of Antony and Cleopatra on a series of denarii (Pl. 234). After his final breach with Octavian, in the preparations for the inevitable conflict which finally took place at Actium in 31 B.C., Antony struck an extensive series of denarii with less common aurei for use by his forces. The types honour both his army and his fleet; the obverse has a galley and the reverse a legionary eagle between two military standards together with a legion's number (Pl. 235). Coins honouring legions from I to XXX are recorded and as the coins were of baser metal than usual, examples survived in circulation well into the empire.

Octavian's defeat of Antony and Cleopatra at Actium left him the supreme source of power. There is, however, no sharp dividing line between the coinage of the republic and the empire but it is convenient to close the account of the coinage of the republic at this point and consider in the next section how the imperial series was developed from it by Octavian.

THE EMPIRE

The coinage of the Roman empire, like so many Imperial institutions, developed out of the republic. For a proper understanding of the imperial coinage it is necessary, then, to glance back at the coinage system of the republic. Originally, and theoretically until the end of the republic, coinage was produced by the authority of the Senate and was struck by the *tresviri aere argento auro flando feriundo*. Later, in the first century B.C., generals in the field or in their provinces struck coins by virtue of their *imperium*, a power of command which derived ultimately from the Senate. But once begun, this provincial coinage increased in importance until the theoretical senatorial authorization was lost sight of. The issue of coinage in the civil wars between Caesar and Pompey and later in the struggle of the triumvirate was based on powers which were purely autocratic but stemmed from this notional right of an *imperator* to issue coins.

THE JULIO-CLAUDIAN EMPERORS

Augustus, 31 *B.C.–A.D.* 14

Such was the state of affairs in the coinage when Octavian, supreme master of the Roman world after his defeat of Antony at Actium in 31 B.C., turned to the reorganization of the Roman state. As in other fields, Octavian, or Augustus as he was termed after 27 B.C., seems to have felt his way towards the new system of coinage which was finally evolved towards the end of his reign. He could, indeed, have restored the centre of coinage to Rome and, in fact, for a short time this did happen, but a coinage could not be issued at Rome by virtue of the emperor's authority without impinging on the traditional authority of the Senate which Augustus was at pains to respect, and no less could Augustus permit this powerful implement of policy to rest in hands other than his own. In the end, the system evolved was, as will appear, another instance of the Augustan compromise between republican tradition on the one hand and imperial realism and power on the other.

The actual monetary system evolved, as distinct from the system of financial control and mints, grew, too, from the republican system with some modifications. Under the republic, the precious-metal currency was principally in silver, the long series of denarii with a complementary token currency in *aes* (a term used as a convenient, if inexact, description of token money in bronze, brass and copper). From the time of Sulla, about 84 B.C., onwards, the gold aureus was increasingly struck and this gold coinage was continued by Augustus who struck aurei at a standard of forty to a pound and occasional quinarii aurei, or half-pieces. The silver coinage continued with a series of denarii of which 25 made one aureus and as in the case of the gold there were occasional quinarii or half-pieces. In *aes*, the sestertius which continued to be the unit of account was struck in orichalcum or brass at four to the denarius. There were also subsidiary units, the dupondius in brass (2 to a sestertius), the as in copper (4 to a sestertius) and sometimes the quadrans, also in copper (4 to an as).

Augustus seems, as in other fields, to have felt his way to the problem of the control and issue of the coinage and to have developed gradually the system which finally took shape. In the East he continued after Actium his coinage in gold and silver and the unresolved problem of the constitutional position of Augustus in the years 31–27 B.C. between Actium and the formal bestowal of new powers in 27 B.C. accounts for the lack of portrait in this issue which, nevertheless, combines reference to Augustus and his Actian victory. When Augustus resigned his extraordinary powers and was granted the new 'constitutional' powers on which the principate was built, no specific arrangements were made concerning the coinage. The military issues in the East ceased but the provincial silver cistophoric tetradrachms, the equivalent of three denarii, which had been struck in the East since the second century continued to be issued, but now with a portrait of Augustus, and these were supplemented by local bronze coinages. Another group of dated gold and silver was issued in the East about 27 B.C. with definite references to the recovery of Asia and the capture of Egypt (Pl. 236). A further undated series which, with their broad flans and the obverse portrait of Augustus, un-accompanied by an inscription, are in the Greek tradition and must also belong to the East. The other great triumphs of Augustus in the East, the recovery from the Parthians of the standards captured from Crassus, Saxa and Statianus in 53 B.C. and the extension of Roman influence over Armenia are recorded on another Eastern issue about 19 B.C. From this time on, issues of Eastern mintage for Augustus are sparse and spasmodic, for in the West other arrangements for coinage had gradually been taking shape.

In 23 B.C. the constitutional position had been further clarified and the principate of Augustus was now founded on his *imperium* abroad and on the tribunician power at home; and on similar lines the coinage arrangements began to emerge. At home the *aes* coinage was restored in 23 B.C. to the nominal control of the Senate and here begins the long series marked with the distinctive letters S.C.

senatus consulto. As under the republic, the coinage was issued for the Senate by a college of moneyers, but now Augustus, by virute of his tribunician power, is associated in the coinage (Pl. 237). This bronze coinage continued till about 5 B.C.

By virtue of his *imperium* Augustus had, about the same date, inaugurated another coinage in the West, a coinage in bronze and then in gold and silver, issued in the province of Spain (Pl. 238). From about 19 B.C. issues of gold and silver were made at Rome, and in these issues, as in bronze, the senatorial college of moneyers was associated with Augustus, but in the precious metals the emperor's portrait on the obverse shows his pre-eminence. This coinage lasted only till about 12 B.C. when the mint for precious metals at Rome apparently closed down; but, by this time, Augustus' final coinage arrangements were maturing.

On his visit to Gaul in 15–14 B.C. Augustus opened a mint at Lugdunum (Lyons) to strike in gold and silver and here the precious metals appear to have been minted for the rest of the reign. Though it is difficult to accept that no precious metal coinage was struck at Rome, the centre of empire where large administrative payments must have been required, Strabo identifies Lyons as the mint for this coinage and stylistically there appears to be only one series. Amongst the most common issues from this mint are those referring to Augustus' intended heirs, Gaius and Lucius Caesar (Pl. 239) and later, the issues for his ultimate heir, Tiberius, in honour of his triumphs in Pannonia and Germany. To provide bronze coinage for the West, the famous issues with the great altar of Lugdunum were struck there from about 10 B.C. onwards.

Tiberius, A.D. 14–37

In the matter of the coinage Tiberius adhered closely to the policy of Augustus. The precious metals continued to be minted in Gaul while the bronze coinage continued to be produced at Rome. The gold and silver coinage of Tiberius presents little variety for it is represented, mainly, by a single type which shows a veiled, seated figure, commonly identified with Livia, the mother of Tiberius and the widow of Augustus. This is the coin often referred to as the 'tribute penny' as being the most likely coin to have been used by Christ to illustrate his remark, 'render unto Caesar the things that are Caesar's' (Pl. 240). The provincial mint issued a continuation of the series showing the altar of Lugdunum but about A.D. 21 the mint was closed, because, it is said, of the fear that provincial coinage might accentuate the nationalism shown by the revolts of Sacrovir in Gaul and Tacfarinas in Africa, shortly before this.

The mint of Rome issued a bronze coinage in the early years of Tiberius' reign.

The issue had little variety, consisting mainly of asses, some with a portrait of Tiberius and one type with a seated figure, said to be Livia. Probably at this time there was issued the series of asses with the bare-headed bust of the now deified Augustus with the legend DIVVS AVGVSTVS PATER (Pl. 241). The great advance shown in style and ideas in the issues of A.D. 22 may reflect increased imperial control or at least interest in the nominally senatorial mint. A famous sestertius with the legend *Civitatibus Asiae Restitutis* and seated figure of Tiberius recalls the emperor's generosity to the twelve cities of Asia destroyed in an earth-quake in A.D. 17 (Pl. 242). The issues from Rome from now till the end of the reign are noted for the number of persons represented other than the emperor. These include his son Drusus and, on an unusual coin, on top of crossed cornucopiae, the portrait busts of his grandsons, Gemellus and Germanicus. Livia, his mother, is thought to be referred to, if not actually represented, on dupondii with legends *Iustitia* (Pl. 243), *Salus* and *Pietas*. Most unusual types with legends *Clementiae* and *Moderationis* have a small full-face portrait of Tiberius himself in an ornamental shield.

Caligula (Gaius), A.D. 37–41

The final, logical step in the organization of the coinage was taken by Caligula in moving the mint for precious metals from Gaul to Rome shortly after the beginning of his reign so that both the emperor's mint for gold and silver and the nominally senatorial mint for *aes* were now both in Rome. There was a brief issue of *aurei* and *denarii* in A.D. 37 at the mint of Gaul. The reverse of one type shows the head of a deified emperor with radiate crown accompanied by no legend. Sometimes the features are recognizably those of Augustus but some resemble Tiberius whom it is known Caligula at one time wished to have deified (Pl. 244). Another issue also honours his mother, Agrippina I, and his father, Germanicus.

The gold and silver issues of the new mint at Rome continue the series portray-ing other imperial personages. The coins of Caligula almost invariably bear a date on the obverse. In the bronze coinage an innovation is the appearance on the obverse of the sestertius of the emperor's portrait and titles, a practice which remained standard throughout the imperial bronze coinage. Caligula's bronze coinage marks an advance both in portrait and conception and treatment of reverse types in such compositions as Caligula addressing his troops (Pl. 245) or the famous piece depicting the emperor's three sisters, Agrippina, Drusilla and Julia.

The style of the gold and silver coinage of Claudius runs smoothly from that of Caligula's issues to those of Nero, so it would seem that in this reign the only great mint for the precious metals which was active was that of Rome. The majority of the gold and silver coinage is dated according to the tribunician years of Claudius but the conventional and standardized reverses, few in number for Tiberius and Caligula, now give way to a much greater variety of types. The difference in content of the republican and imperial coinages, steadily developing under the earlier emperors, is now quite remarkable. Under the republic the majority of reverse types had been references to the family history of the moneyers who were responsible for striking the coins. Now in the empire, the content is of a different order. The coinage is used by the emperors in more direct fashion to proclaim not only the achievements of the emperor but to make the members of the imperial family familiar to the public; they emphasize the emperor's qualities and policies in the personifications of 'virtues', almost demi-gods such as Providentia (clear-sighted planning), Aequitas (Justice), Annona (the ensuring of the corn supply) and a host of others.

The gold and silver coins of Claudius, many of which can be dated from the titles on the obverse, illustrate this point. Types such as *Constantiae Augustae* (resolution) and *Paci Augustae* (peace) refer to the emperor's character and achievements while notable events of the reign are recorded in such types as the triumphal arch with the inscription *De Britann* in honour of the extension of the empire to Britain (Pl. 246). The issues in bronze in this reign also move more closely in relation to those of the precious metals. Like Tiberius and Caligula, Claudius honoured on his coins other members of his family, some in issues both in gold and silver and also in bronze. Such pieces are those honouring his father, Nero Drusus, and his mother, Antonia (Pl. 247). Towards the end of his reign his marriage to Agrippina II was followed by coins bearing her portrait, in some cases, on the reverse of one of the emperor's own coins. Agrippina prevailed on Claudius to recognize her son Nero as heir-apparent instead of his own son, Britannicus, and a series of coins was issued with the young Nero's portrait, the reverse of one of which gives his title *Princeps Iuventutis*, the almost official title of the heir to the empire.

The most striking feature of the coinage of the first years of Nero's reign is the apparent resurgence of senatorial influence; for even on gold and silver the phrase EX S.C. is found on the reverse. The empress-mother Agrippina, having forced the succession of her own son, Nero, must have found it necessary to push conciliation of the Senate to its limit. When she was forced from power, Nero continued for some time under the tutelage of Seneca and Burrhus and senatorial influence continued strong. In A.D. 63, however, Nero asserted himself as sole ruler and the change is reflected in the coinage by the disappearance from gold and silver of this term indicative of senatorial influence. The following year brought a reform of the coinage. The aureus was reduced to one-forty-fifth of the pound and the denarius to one-ninety-sixth. An experiment was also made of issuing a full series of bronze denominations from sestertius to quadrans in orichalcum but after a very few years a return was made to the Augustan system with a sestertius and a dupondius in orichalcum and an *as* in copper. While it lasted, this was probably the most complete monetary system in imperial times.

The bronze issues at Rome which had been negligible in the latter years of Claudius remained so in Nero's early years, but from A.D. 64 bronze coinage began to be issued again in quantity. About the same time, bronze issues were resumed at the mint in Gaul, issues parallel to those from Rome but distinguished by their flatter fabric and style and by the presence of a small globe at the point of the bust on the obverse.

The early coins show the unique position and influence of Agrippina, the empress-mother, for she appears jointly with Nero on the obverse of gold and silver issues (Pl. 248). The reverse types of the early years are few and conventional, such as Virtus, Roma, Ceres or the wreath enclosing EX S.C. (Pl. 248). The issues from A.D. 64 onwards in their competent design and style mark a great step forward in the art of imperial coinage. Particularly fine is the execution of the portrait and the composition of such unusual types as those showing the newly constructed harbour at Ostia, the congiarium and the temple of Janus, closed to indicate universal peace (Pl. 249). Equally fine pieces in a slightly different style were struck at the mint in Gaul—for example, the triumphal arch (Pl. 250). Even on the smaller bronze denominations types of quality and interest are found on the reverse. On dupondii appear the macellum, the new market constructed by Nero, and a representation of Nero in his favourite guise of Apollo (Pl. 251).

Several months before Nero's death in Rome on 9th June A.D. 68, revolts against his authority had begun in the provinces of the West, in Gaul, Spain and Africa. The revolt in North Africa under Clodius Macer in April was something of an opportunist affair outside the serious movement set on foot in Gaul and Spain and, in October, shortly after Galba became emperor, Macer was quickly put down. In Gaul the revolt against Nero was begun by Vindex in March and was supported by Galba, governor in Spain, and coinage was issued in both provinces to meet the needs of the rebels. From the time of Augustus an emperor had always been found from the Julio-Claudian house and the succession had been determined at Rome but now, with no obvious hereditary successor to Nero, the uncertainty as to the course of the revolt in the months between its beginning and the murder of Nero in June is reflected in a coinage which names no person as claimant to the succession. In addition to these coinages of the early stage of the revolt of Vindex and Galba, the end of the year saw yet another coinage, issued for the troops in Lower Germany in revolt against Galba, the first successful claimant to the succession.

Vindex in Gaul

The coinage of the revolt of Vindex in the spring months of A.D. 68 consists almost entirely of silver denarii with the addition of a few rare issues of aurei. Both these denominations are struck on the standard of Nero's reformed coinage and there is no known bronze coinage associated with the revolt. The mint which produced the coinage is not certain but Vienne has been suggested as a likely centre. In content the coinage bears a superficial resemblance to that of the republic in the absence of a portrait on the obverse and the consequent use of both sides of the coins for allusive types. The actual content reflects something of the dilemma of the revolt, the desire to be rid of Nero, but the uncertainty as to what or who was to replace him. There is a certain amount of borrowing of types from earlier coinages, *Juppiter Custos* from Nero and *Paci Augustae* from Claudius, but the most frequent types for the obverse are the bust of the Genius of the Roman people, *Genius P(opuli) R(omani)* or figures of Minerva, Mars or Victory with the inscription *Salus Generis Humani*. The most common reverses found joined with these are *Mars Ultor*, S.P.Q.R. in oak-wreath, and *Securitas PR* (Pl. 252).

The initiative of Vindex in Gaul was followed by Galba in Spain where a very similar coinage was struck, probably at Tarraco. Here also the series consists only of denarii and less common aurei with no complementary bronze issues. In the absence of an emperor the obverse is normally occupied by a head—again the Genius of the Roman people, Roma herself, Hispania or Bonus Eventus, the god of good fortune, an apt type for the beginning of such an enterprise. A distinctive feature of the series is the frequent use in the inscriptions, on both obverse and reverse, of the dative case in place of the more usual nominative, as in the denarius with obverse *Genio PR* and reverse *Marti Ultori* (Pl. 253). Other reverse types include *Paci PR*—clasped hands holding a winged caduceus, *Roma Renascens*, Roma holding Victory and eagle and S.P.Q.R. in wreath. A particularly spectacular type has on obverse *Concordia Hispaniarum et Galliarum*, busts of Spain and Gaul and on reverse *Victoria PR*, Victory in biga.

A subsidiary group, consisting again of denarii and occasional aurei, is also attributed to the revolt in Spain. The feature here is the use on the obverse of the portrait and titles of the emperor Augustus. The style is quite different from that of contemporary issues of Augustus and, even though some of the reverses repeat Augustan types, similar obverses are used in conjunction with obvious revolt types.

Revolt in Lower Germany

A small series of denarii in crude and simple style with types emphasizing a military connection is attributed to Lower Germany and connected with the beginning of the revolt of the legions in Germany in the autumn of 68 against Galba. Types include deities such as Vesta and Jupiter combined with the essentially military *Fides Exercituum* with type, clasped hands (Pl. 254).

Gallic Revolt

An even smaller series of denarii which makes no mention of Rome or the emperor but in which Gaul and her boar-standard appear is identified as the revolt coinage of Civilis and his Gallic allies in A.D. 68–69. Other types show *Libertas Restituta* and *Mars Adsertor*.

L. Clodius Macer

Macer was legate of Numidia when revolt broke out against Nero in A.D. 68 but on Nero's death he refused support to Galba, invaded Africa, threatening Rome's corn supply and occupied Carthage where a small military series of denarii was struck in his name. Macer made no claim to empire for himself and the coinage used simply his name and portrait on the obverse and a reverse with eagle between standards, copying the famous issue of Mark Antony, honoured one or other of the two legions under his command (Pl. 255).

Galba, spring A.D. 68–January A.D. 69

The coinage of the early stages of the revolt in the West had had a republican flavour with types giving prominence to the *populus Romanus* but Galba was the man to whom the revolt looked to replace Nero. His issues fall into two groups, clearly distinguished on the gold and silver by style, and in all metals by a conventional difference of title on the obverse of the coins. The form on the provincial series always places his name before his title as, for example, *Galba Imperator* or *Ser Galba Imp Aug*, while on the coinage from Rome the title is in the form *Imp Ser Galba Aug*, etc. Titles on the obverses also give the key to the chronologically successive groups of his coinage. From his original acclamation in Spain in the spring of 68 the only title used by Galba on his coins is that of imperator. From the murder of Nero on 9th June and the recognition of Galba as emperor by the Senate, Augustus was added and only after his meeting with the senatorial committee which came to him in Gaul about July did he style himself Caesar. The final form of title includes the office of P(ontifex) M(aximus) assumed sometime towards the end of the year.

Rome. On the recognition of Galba by the Senate in June the mint began the first issue in which he is styled simply *Imp Ser Galba Aug* with sometimes the addition of *Trp*, the *tribunicia potestas*, the administrative power which was one of the bases of the principate. The reverse types take up many of the themes enunciated on the revolt coinage such as *Roma Renascens, Victoria PR, Libertas PR, Salus Gen Humani* and S.P.Q.R. in wreath (Pl. 256). This type was the only one to appear on the aureus; the denarius had the whole range of types while a number of similar types appeared on the bronze. In the second group, after the incorporation of Caesar in the obverse title, an almost identical group of reverses were used for the silver except that a type of *Hispania* replaced *Libertas PR*. The whole series of types also appeared on aurei and to the bronze series of the first group were added types of *Concord Aug* and *Augusta* showing the seated figure of Livia who had been Galba's patroness. The third group with PM added to the obverse title retains these types almost unchanged.

Lyons. The bulk of the remaining coinage forms another regular series distinguished not only by the obverse title beginning with *Galba* or *Ser Galba* and not *Imp* as at Rome but by the portrait which is emaciated and has a large bald forehead and either a small globe at the point of the bust or an extension of the truncation. The precious-metal coinage falls into groups similar to those at Rome but with an extra, early group where Galba before his recognition by the Senate styles himself only imperator. The bronze coinage begins only with the group incorporating Caesar in Galba's title and has its origin in the bronze issues of the parallel group at Rome. The reverse types on gold and silver in all the group repeat many of the themes of the Rome coinage but add a few distinctive provincial types such as *Gallia Hispania* where Gallia, represented as a woman, clasps hands with Hispania in the guise of a warrior. The types of the bronze coins when they begin are those of the Roman issues but in the final group from this mint a series of types not struck at Rome make their appearance. They include elaborate types of *Honos et Virtus* (Pl. 257), *Hispania Clunia* and *Victoria Imperi Romani*.

Otho, January–April, A.D. 69

Galba, though the choice of the provinces and of the Senate, did not have the support of the praetorian cohorts at Rome, who, disgruntled by his parsimony, proclaimed Otho as emperor on 15th January and murdered Galba. Otho's reign was brief, for in the early days of January the German legions proclaimed their own commander Vitellius as emperor and marched on Rome. In April Otho, defeated in battle near Cremona, committed suicide. The issues for Otho from the mint of Rome are in gold and silver only. The portrait of Otho never has the laurel-wreath worn by most emperors and the unusual hair style seems to bear out the statement of Suetonius that he wore a wig. The coinage falls into two groups. The first in both gold and silver gives the emperor's titles on the obverse as *Imp M Otho Caesar Aug Trp* and has reverses *Pax Orbis Terrarum* (Pl. 258), *Securitas PR* and *Victoria Othonis*. The second, omitting the praenomen M(arcus), repeats also on both gold and silver the *Pax* and *Securitas* reverses and adds four new types all with inscription *Pont Max* and types of Aequitas, Ceres, Jupiter and Vesta.

The beginning of revolt against Galba by the legions on the German frontier was manifested by the issue of a small coinage in late 68. Even before Galba had been replaced in Rome by Otho, the German legions, in the first days of January, had saluted as emperor their commander Vitellius who hastened into Italy and defeated Otho in April. The consolidation of Vitellius' short-lived power is made clear by his coinage which falls into two distinct groups, one in Gaul, the other in Rome itself.

Gaul. A small, short-lived issue of both gold and silver coins is distinguished from the main issues in the province by the reverse types. These repeat largely the themes of the revolt coins of late 68 with types of *Fides Exercitum, I O Max Capitolinus* and *Vesta PR Quiritum* and have obverse busts of Vitellius with the Gallic feature of a small globe at the point of the bust. The emperor's title is in the form *A Vitellius Imp German.* It has been suggested that this group was minted at Cologne on the proclamation of Vitellius. The main group of coins also in gold and silver and with the same basic form of obverse inscription has somewhat narrower portrait heads, many facing to the left, but also with the small globe at the point of the bust. A number of the reverse types, some of which are here noticeably elongated, are the same as in the earlier group above but on a group of aurei the emperor's rise to power through the German legions is stressed in types such as *Securitas Imp Germanici, Victoria Imp Germanici* and *Liberis Imp Germanici.* This last shows the busts of the emperor's small daughter and his son who was escorted to meet his father at Lyons and also given the title Germanicus (Pl. 259). This group of coins, continuing stylistic features of Galba's issues from Lyons, was probably struck at the same mint. No bronze sestertii were struck at this mint but there was a small series of *asses* using types similar to those on the precious metals.

Rome. The coins of this mint carry over much of the style of Otho's issues into those of Vitellius. The portrait heads are round, with no great elaboration of the neck truncation, particularly on the aurei and denarii. The portraits are, however, more rugged and realistic. The Rome issues are distinguished by the form of the obverse title, basically *A Vitellius Germ Imp.* There was a small first issue for Vitellius confined to denarii only and comprising only a few reverse types. The obverse has a bare-headed portrait and the titles do not include Augustus. In the second group the emperor's portrait is laureate but he is still not styled Augustus. The reverses of the first group *Concordia PR, XV Vir Sacr fac* and Victory are repeated in both denarii and aurei and to them are added *Jupiter Victor, Libertas Restituta* and *S.P.Q.R. OB C.S.* in oak-wreath, also in both denominations.

Towards the end of the group new reverses were added; *L. Vitellius Cos III Censor* with the portrait of the emperor's distinguished father, and *Liberi Imp Germanici* with busts of the two children. A third group, probably dating from the entry of Vitellius into Rome in July, finally includes the title Augustus in the obverse legend. Both aurei and denarii repeat the reverses of the previous group and add another showing the seated figure of Vitellius senior. Only with this group does the series of magnificent sestertii begin. The portrait heads are in high relief with, often, an indication of a draped bust while the reverse types are strongly drawn and well disposed on the flans. One type similar to that on gold and silver honours the emperor's father but otherwise there is a fresh selection of designs on the bronze coinage with types of *Annona Aug*, emperor and Ceres, *Mars Victor*, *Pax Augusti* and *Victoria Augusti* (Pl. 260).

THE FLAVIAN EMPERORS, A.D. 69–96

The succession to empire had not yet been finally settled, for the victory of Vitellius was quickly followed by the news that the legions in Egypt, Syria and Palestine had declared for Vespasian on 1st July A.D. 69. By the autumn the troops in Moesia and Pannonia who also had gone over to Vespasian had entered Italy and defeated the Vitellians. In December they entered Rome, put Vitellius to death and, though some troops of Vitellius resisted on the Capitoline, on 21st December it was all over and the Senate recognized Vespasian as emperor.

Vespasian, A.D. 69–79

Once again the stages by which the provinces went over to the new emperor are reflected in the issues of coins from provincial mints. A number of mints in the East struck gold and silver for Vespasian from July onwards for a time; precious-metal coins from a mint in Illyricum in 69 have also been identified and when the troops of Vespasian seized north Italy the mint in Gaul began issues for him also. Finally after the capture of Rome the mint there took up coinage for the new emperor.

The East. Antioch in Syria, on the evidence of the historian, Tacitus, immediately began the issue of gold and silver for Vespasian in 69. Of these rare coins some combine portraits of Vespasian and his son Titus on obverse and reverse; others have more usual reverses with types of *Virtus August* or *Aug* in wreath (Pl. 261). An issue of aurei and denarii, dated to A.D. 72–73 by Vespasian's title of *Consul IV*

in an Eastern style has also been assigned to this mint. Coinages of Eastern provenance have been attributed to mints at Tyre and other cities in the East. Yet
other coinages, mostly denarii and only rare aurei, bear marks which indicate
their place of minting. Issues from Ephesus signed EPE in 71 were made for
Vespasian and for both his sons, Titus and Domitian. The monogram >B- indicating the city of Byzantium (now Istanbul) appears on denarii of Vespasian in
70–71. On one issue the emperor's obverse portrait is linked with a reverse *Liberi
Imp Aug Vespas* showing the portraits of his two sons. The earliest denarius
coinage in Asia Minor, beginning in 69 and continuing into 70, is marked with
Ɵ or ᴗ for which no convincing expansion has yet been found.

Illyricum. A small group of denarii distinguished by small obverse portraits
and reverse figures has been attributed to a mint in this area in late 69. Reverse
types such as *Consensus Exercit* two soldiers, *Pacis Event* standing Genius or *Roma
Perpetua* are not shared by other mints.

Gaul. The western provinces fell into Vespasian's hands in the autumn of 69
and the mint of Lyons which had struck successively for Galba and Vitellius
issued a series of aurei and denarii for Vespasian from 69 onwards. Changes in
the emperor's title on the obverse indicate that the mint struck gold and silver
for him until 73, though bronze coinage was continued to the end of the reign.
The portraits tend to be rather heavy and the figures on the reverse types short
and squat; on the bronze coinage the small globe at the point of the bust continues
to be a feature. At this mint the majority of the coinage is in the name of Vespasian
himself and the issues with Titus or Domitian on the obverse during the reign of
their father are less frequent. The first issue for Vespasian carries the simple
obverse title *Imp Caesar Vespasianus Aug* in 69–70; in 70 the formula TRP is added
and subsequently, in 71, PP COS III. In 72 Vespasian's fourth consulship—COS
IIII appears in the title and his additional office of Censor—CEN in 73. The issue
of 70 is also marked by the legend on the reverse indicating Vespasian's second
consulship as on the reverse *Cos Iter trp*, type Fortuna (Pl. 262). Another frequent
type from Lugdunum in aurei and denarii, *Titus et Domitian Caesares Prin Iuven*,
shows the emperor's two sons either riding or seated on curule chairs, and the
successful crushing of the Jewish revolt is celebrated by *Iudaea Devicta*, a Jewess
standing with bound hands by a palm-tree. The bronze coinage largely used
similar reverses to those of Rome in the plentiful series in 71 and 72; then, after
an almost complete cessation of activity, other large issues were made in 77 and
78 when Titus and Domitian share in the coinage.

Rome. The coinage, in all metals, struck at Rome for Vespasian and his sons is
amongst the most aesthetically satisfactory of the Imperial series. The obverse
portraits in good relief have sufficient realism to make them convincing without

making them caricatures, while the reverse types are well proportioned and well disposed in relation to the inscription. Both sons have a substantial share of the coinage struck at Rome, Titus from 71 and Domitian from 73. As the supporters of Vitellius in Rome were defeated only on 21st December 69 it is unlikely that much, if any, coinage for Vespasian appeared till early in the following year. The successive offices held by Vespasian and by his sons and their record in the titles on the obverses mark out the sequence of issues.

A.D. 70. The coinage for this year is for Vespasian only and is practically confined to aurei and denarii. His title on the obverse is simply *Imp Caesar Vespasianus Aug* and the most common reverses are those with legend *Cos Iter Tr Pot* and types of Mars, Neptune or Pax. The reverse *Iudaea* showing a Jewess seated by a trophy refers to the crushing of the Jewish revolt and the capture of Jerusalem in September of this year. A.D. 70–71. The title P(ontifex) M(aximus) dating from Vespasian's election to this office in November 70 is incorporated in his obverse title *Imp Caes Vesp Aug PM* marking the coinage of the second issue and is celebrated on denarii with reverse *Augur Pon Max* showing the sacrificial instruments connected with this office. The large bronze sestertii only now celebrate the success in Palestine with the reverse *Iudaea Capta*, a Jewess seated under a palm-tree with a captive Jew in the background (Pl. 263) and a type, *Fortunae Reduci*, denotes the safe return of Titus from the wars. A.D. 72–73. Vespasian's fourth consulship (Cos IIII) is included in his titles in this issue in which one of the principal themes is the celebration of his triumph for the successful Jewish campaign with types *Victoria Augusti*, figure of Victory and an uninscribed type showing the emperor in his triumphal quadriga. This issue also included coinage for Titus joining in the triumph, either in a quadriga or on horse-back. Later in the issue there is a coinage for Domitian also. The uninscribed reverse with the type of *Spes*, now introduced, was to remain for long the standard type for the heir-apparent, the hope of the dynasty (Pl. 264).

The issues for the remainder of the reign settle down into something of a regular pattern. In general the emperor and his sons have on the obverses titles *Imp Caesar Vespasianus Aug, T. Caesar Imp Vespasian* and *Caesar Aug F. Domitianus* respectively. The main reverses carry legends marking the changing consular offices of the emperor and his sons between A.D. 74 and 79. A good number of the reverses are repeated in successive issues on aurei and denarii with such types as a cow, butting bull, yoke of oxen and eagle on cippus. Domitian frequently has a special reverse *Princeps Iuventutis* with figures of Salus or Vesta. On sestertii the more common types for Vespasian and Titus are those of *Annona, Fortuna* and *Pax*, on dupondii, *Felicitas* and on asses, *Aequitas*. Domitian uses some of these reverses in addition to his special type of *Spes*. Of special interest is the type for Vespasian in gold with reverse *Cos VIIII* showing Victory crowning the emperor and for Titus in silver with reverse *Tr Pot VIII Cos VII*, trophy and captive, both issued in A.D. 79 celebrating the victory of Agricola in Britain.

Titus, A.D. 79–81

On the death of Vespasian on 23rd June 79 Titus became Augustus and Domitian the immediate heir. With the exception of a comparatively small amount of bronze coinage struck by the mint at Lyons for Titus, the coins of this brief reign, both in the precious metals and in bronze, were issued by the Roman mint. In addition to the issues for the emperor and his brothers, there was also coinage for other members of the family, for Julia, the daughter of Titus, for the deified Vespasian and for the deified Domitilla, wife of Vespasian.

Rome. The obverses of both the aurei and denarii of Titus always show the laureate head of the emperor and, apart from a very short issue at the beginning of the reign with obverse title *Imp T Caesar Vespasianus Aug*, carry the title *Imp Titus Caes Vespasian Aug*. The reverses in 79 have inscriptions listing the emperor's titles and largely repeat the types of Ceres, Venus, figure on column, quadriga and capricorn. In A.D. 80 the reverse types represent the sacred couches of the gods, set out in Rome for the services of propitiation following the disaster of the eruption of Vesuvius in this year. A variety of symbols represent the different gods— thunderbolt for Jupiter, corn-ears for Ceres, dolphin and anchor for Neptune (Pl. 265). The bronze coinage for Titus incorporated his offices into the obverse title. The issue for 79 was comparatively small but in 80 there was an extensive range in all the bronze denominations. The sestertii show standard types of Annona, Pax, Vesta and Victoria, a revival of the *Iudaea Capta* of Vespasian's reign and a special type for the completion of the Colosseum (Pl. 266). Dupondii and asses repeat some of these themes with some additions such as Aequitas, Ceres, Salus and Securitas.

The precious-metal issues for Domitian in A.D. 80 show his laureate head with title *Caesar Aug F* (or *Divi F*) *Domitianus*. The chief inscription on the reverse, that of the heir-apparent, *Princeps Iuventutis*, is joined to a variety of types such as Pax, Salus and Minerva. On his bronze coinage Domitian has a range of sestertii without reverse inscription. Amongst the common types are Spes, especially associated with the heir-apparent and Minerva, his favourite deity who also appears frequently on his asses. Titus also struck a small issue for his daughter Julia. Denarii show her diademed and draped bust on the obverse and reverse types of Venus (Pl. 267) and Vesta. There are also rare dupondii with reverse types of Ceres, Concordia and Vesta. Towards the end of the reign a coinage honoured the deified Vespasian. His portrait head on the obverse on aurei and denarii is inscribed *Divus Augustus Vespasianus* and the reverses, inscribed simply SC or EX SC, have types of Victory, a quadriga, or a shield against a column. The complementary bronze coinage, mostly dupondii and asses, has more normal types such as Ceres, Concordia or Aequitas. An extremely rare series of denarii show the portrait bust of the emperor's mother inscribed *Diva Domitilla Augusta* and reverses of Concordia, Pax and Pietas.

An unusual feature of the coinage of this reign is a series of bronze coins described as 'restorations'. They show the portraits of almost all the Imperial personages from Augustus to Galba, while the reverses repeat types of their coinage, accompanied by some form of the basic formula *Imp T Vesp Aug Rest*. There are a number of sestertii but the majority of the pieces are dupondii and asses.

Lyons. A series in bronze only for Titus and Domitian has distinctively heavy portraits and ample reverse figures. The issues, brief for Titus only in 79 and a little more extensive for him and Domitian in 80–81, use the obverse titles and a small selection of the reverse types on the coinage at Rome.

Domitian, A.D. 81–96

On the death of Titus on 13th September A.D. 81 Domitian the third and last of the Flavian emperors became Augustus. The mint at Lyons which had struck only small issues in bronze under Titus issued a brief bronze series for Domitian also but ceased production somewhere about A.D. 82. The mint at Rome remained as the sole issuer of coinage in all metals for Domitian. There were also two small issues for his wife Domitia and a very brief issue for the deified Titus and his daughter Julia.

Rome. Stylistically the coinage of Rome continued at first the small neat portrait heads typical of coinage under Titus but later developed a higher standard of portraiture in good relief with a more naturalistic indication of the bust which is often decorated with a touch of drapery or the *aegis*. This fine style is found equally on the bronze and the precious metal. In the latter the introduction of multiples of eight and four denarii provide a larger flan for the presentation of the portrait. The sequence of the issues is readily determined by the additions and changes in the enumeration of the tribunician power, the consulship and the imperatorial salutations which are recorded more consistently and in greater detail in this than in any other imperial coinage. Basically the obverse title up to 83 is, on gold and silver, in the form *Imp Caes Domitianus Aug PM*; from 84 onwards

Germanicus, in full or abbreviated, is added in honour of successful campaigns in Germany and from 85 the successive tribunician powers (TR P) form part of the obverse title. The majority of the reverse inscriptions complete the record of the emperor's offices. The reverses for 81 continue the types with symbols of the deities issued under Titus in connection with the services of prayer following the disasters of Vesuvius and the Great Fire in Rome in 80. Thereafter for most of the reign the reverses are devoted almost entirely to representations of Domitian's favourite deity, Minerva. She is shown in four poses: (1) brandishing spear and shield; (2) the same but with foot on prow with an owl beside her (Pl. 268); (3) standing holding spear; (4) holding spear and thunderbolt.

The bronze coinage produces some greater variety in reverse types. Minerva appears on issues in 81 and 82 but, after an intermission, a magnificent series of sestertii and smaller denominations celebrate in 85 the victories in Germany. Sestertii with no inscription except the formula S.C. have types such as Victory inscribing a shield on a trophy of arms, the emperor riding down a fallen German (Pl. 269) or accepting surrender from a kneeling warrior. A number of such types are repeated in later issues, probably in connection with later campaigns against the Dacian tribes. The dupondii and asses have many of the standard representations such as Annona, Fortuna or Salus, though the military successes are reflected in reverse types of Mars with Victory and trophy or a vexillum with crossed shields, trumpets and spears. In 88 Domitian's somewhat stereotyped selection of reverses was enlivened by a series of elaborate compositions depicting the ceremonies in connection with the Saecular Games celebrated in this year. These scenes appear on somewhat rare sestertii but are repeated on the comparatively more common dupondii and asses. Representative of such types is the sacrifice scene with the emperor standing by the altar in front of a temple accompanied by the sacrificial victim and musicians (Pl. 270).

The smallest of the bronze denominations, the semisses and quadrantes were struck with varying frequency in most of the reign. Under Domitian they sometimes form part of an issue as in A.D. 85 where, with a simplified form of the emperor's title, the obverse of the semis has a bust of Apollo, with reverse a tripod or raven on branch and the quadrans a bust of Ceres with reverse, corn-ears in modius. Another series of quadrantes with similar obverse and reverse types bears the emperor's name only with no indication of date (Pl. 271). Yet another series of quadrantes has been attributed to the reign of Domitian. These carry no imperial name; the obverse shows the portrait of a deity, the reverse the symbol peculiar to that divinity—Jupiter and his thunderbolt, Minerva and her owl or Neptune and a dolphin.

The coinage for the empress Domitia falls into two groups. The earlier, issued in 82–83, is a series of rare aurei and denarii showing the bust of the empress entitled *Domitia Augusta Imp Domit* with reverse type, a peacock and the inscription *Concordia August*. The second group was struck in 91–92 when, after divorcing Domitia, Domitian was reconciled with her. The reverses are those of the first group but the obverse title reads *Domitia Aug Imp Domitian Aug Germ*. Bronze coinage for Domitia is of the second group only and the reverse types showing Domitia describe her as *Divi Caesaris Mater*, the mother of the Caesar who died in infancy and was deified.

Lyons. There were only two issues of bronze coins from the mint with obverse portraits of the emperors and titles appropriate to the years 81 and 82. Each issue consisted of two sestertii with reverses of Pax and Mars, a dupondius with reverse Roma and an as depicting Ceres on the reverse.

THE ADOPTIVE EMPERORS

For over a hundred years, with the exception of the brief-lived emperors of the Civil wars of A.D. 68–69, two dynasties had provided Rome with her emperors, first the Julio-Claudians, then the Flavians. Domitian, the last of the Flavians, fell in similar circumstances to those of Nero, the last of the Julio-Claudians. Despite popularity with the people and the army, each incurred the hostility of the conservative upper classes and in the end the entourage of each turned against them. The fall of Domitian, however, unlike that of Nero, was not followed by civil wars but by an initial acceptance of Nerva, proclaimed emperor by the Senate. Nerva, an elderly lawyer, found little favour with the army but solved the immediate problem of securing his position by adopting as colleague and heir the army's most able and popular general, Trajan. This practice of adopting as heir a man of ability, irrespective of the claims of dynasty, was continued for several generations and provided Rome with her period of most efficient and prosperous rule.

Nerva, A.D. 96–98

The subsidiary mint at Lyons had been closed down under Domitian in 82 and the whole imperial coinage, as distinct from provincial issues, was produced by the mint of Rome alone for close on the following century. The scheme of the coinage remained much as it had been. Domitian's experiment with multiple denarii was not repeated but there were the usual issues of aurei, of silver denarii and occasional quinarii. Bronze coinage was struck in all denominations including quadrans. The idealized portraiture which had marked much of the coinage of Domitian gives place to a more rugged realism, though the general artistic level remains high.

The pattern of the successive issues can be readily distinguished for, once again, the various offices held by Nerva are recorded in his obverse title. The form in the first issue of gold and silver in 96 is *Imp Nerva Case Aug PM Trp Cos II PP* and this changes only in the enumeration of the offices. Most of the reverse types are chosen from the usual stock—Aequitas, Fortuna, Libertas, though some have a more topical reference such as the introduction of the representation of Justice (Justitia) or clasped hands for the *Concordia Exercituum* (Pl. 272). The same types are repeated in the issues of 96 and 97 but in 98 the reverses have the legend *Imp II Cos IIII PP*. The bronze coinage in this reign runs closely parallel to the gold and silver, both in the form of obverse and the choice of reverse types. A few unusual types found on sestertii only illustrate steps taken by Nerva to alleviate economic conditions in Italy and Rome. The reverse, two mules grazing with the shafts of a wagon in the background, is inscribed *Vehiculatione Italiae Remissa*, an allusion to the cancelling for Italy of the tax levied for the upkeep of imperial communications. Nerva's arrangements for a corn dole to the Roman populace finds record on the reverse, a modius containing wheat-ears, inscribed *Plebei Urbanae Frumento Constituto*. The quadrantes are undated with simple obverse of modius and reverse a winged caduceus. There was also in bronze a small series of 'restored' coins, devoted solely to honouring Augustus.

Trajan, A.D. 98–117

Thanks to Nerva's statesmanlike policy of nominating an acceptable heir his death in January 98 was followed by the succession of Trajan without any of the strife of previous occasions when an emperor had died without a dynastic heir. Trajan was with the army on the Rhine when he succeeded, but the coinage, like other evidence, shows a smooth transition from one reign to the next. The length of this reign has made Trajan's coinage in all metals one of the most common of the imperial series but it appears to have been produced entirely by the mint of Rome. This reign saw the last great conquests and territorial expansion by Rome; but even the needs of the long series of campaigns between 101 and 106 which ended with the creation of the new province of Dacia, or the campaigns between 113 and 117 which created provinces in Armenia and Mesopotamia, did not call into being mints nearer the scene of military action. Trajan's coins have the overall uniformity consistent with the products of one mint only.

Artistically they fall below the level maintained by the Flavians or even Nerva, though some advances in varying presentation of the imperial portrait can be seen. The portrait now appears more often with the bust fully portrayed and clad in the paludamentum or cloak and the cuirass of the soldier.

The range of denominations in the Trajanic coinage continued as before, though the quinarii in both gold and silver become more sporadic and quadrantes less frequent. A great proportion of the reverse types carry stock representations of abstract themes such as Pax, Abundantia or Victory, or they depict familiar deities like Jupiter, Mars and Hercules. The events of the reign, however, do find mention on many issues. The military successes in Dacia and the East, as well as the achievements of Trajan's great building programme in Rome, form the subject of many coin reverses. In addition to the coinage in his own name Trajan honoured on his coins his father Trajan senior, his wife Plotina, his sister Marciana and her daughter Matidia.

The persistence of the fashion of recording a good many of the emperor's offices on either the obverse or reverse of the coins enables the coinage still to be arranged in chronological groups. As the only office consistently mentioned is the consulship, which Trajan held only five times in his reign, some of the groups of coinage cover a good span of years. Various titles such as Dacicus, Optimus and Parthicus accorded to Trajan during his reign help to establish a more detailed sequence of the issues. In the early years the reverses are mostly devoted to types such as Concordia, Fortuna, Felicitas and Pax, with military successes in Germany commemorated by a figure of Germania seated on a shield or referred to by types of Victory and Mars. The title of Dacicus, received by the emperor about 101, does not appear with regularity in his title until the coinage marked by *Cos V*, as of the years 103–111. A portion of this coinage has as reverse inscription *Cos V PP S.P.Q.R. Optimo Principi* with, in some cases, an additional inscription in the exergue containing a specific allusion such as the capture of Dacia, represented as a barbarian seated with hands bound on a pile of arms (Pl. 273). A second part of the coinage in these years emphasizes the honorific title of Optimus accorded to Trajan in 100 with reverses inscribed simply *S.P.Q.R. Optimo Principi*. A later group dated to 112–117 by his sixth consulship, Cos VI on the obverse, in addition to the standard types, show some of Trajan's building in Rome, the Basilica Ulpia, the Forum Trainai and Trajan's column. The extension of the empire to the East finds expression in the later years on coins inscribed additionally *Parthia Capta* and showing two Parthians seated by a trophy.

The pattern of the bronze coinage adheres fairly closely to that of the gold and silver, both in the changes in the obverse and reverse inscriptions and in the choice of types. As in other coinages, however, the reverses of the bronzes tend to be devoted to the more interesting compositions, the wider flans, particularly of the sestertii, lending themselves better to this category. Particularly is this the case with the types commemorating Trajan's public works and buildings. Typical of this class is the picture of the Circus Maximus which, though not in proportion or perspective, contrives to give a general impression of its dimensions and features (Pl. 274).

In the coinage for other members of Trajan's family both the aurei and denarii and, in bronze, the sestertii for his wife Plotina show her portrait entitled *Plotina Aug Imp Traiani*. On the precious metals the more common reverse type in this rare coinage is inscribed with Trajan's titles and shows a figure of Vesta seated. The sestertii have a type of Fides. Most of the coinage for the others is posthumous. Both Marciana and her daughter Matidia are portrayed with extremely elaborate coiffeurs and are described as *Diva Augusta Marciana* or *Diva Augusta Matidia*. The usual reverse for both is inscribed *Consecratio* with the type of an eagle with spread wings. On the coins for Trajan senior the obverse has the portrait and titles of Trajan himself, the reverse the bust of his father inscribed *Divus Pater Traian*.

Trajan also issued a series of 'restored' coins in gold and silver. These include republican coins as well as coins of a selection of the previous emperors—Augustus, Tiberius, Claudius, Galba, Vespasian, Titus and Nerva. The reverse of all of these has the legend *Imp Caes Traian Aug Ger Dac PP Rest*.

Hadrian, A.D. 117–138

Hadrian, for long regarded, though without official nomination, as heir to the empire, was appointed as his successor by Trajan shortly before his death in Cilicia in August 117. Hadrian's policy of consolidation after the military expansion under Trajan led almost immediately to the abandonment of Armenia and Mesopotamia, though Dacia was maintained; and his subsequent detailed inspection and care for the provinces involving his wide travels over the empire receives extensive notice on his coinage. The extensive imperial coinage of the reign, with the probable exception of a small group struck at Antioch, was issued by the mint of Rome alone. In style Hadrian's coins make a smooth transition from those of Trajan. The obverse portraiture undergoes a number of successive changes. The earliest portraits *c.* 117–125, like those of Trajan, are remarkable for their small heads and rather long busts, usually draped and armoured. From 125 to 128 the portrait, a head only with occasional suggestions of draping at the neck, occupies much more of the field of the coin. A subsequent group is distinguished by the absence of the laurel-wreath, though the final issues restore this feature and again show more of the bust. In the earlier groups of the coinage the reverse types show mainly the deities and the usual abstract representations, but towards the end of the reign a number of series are devoted specifically to mention of the provinces and the armies in different areas of the empire.

Hadrian also struck coinage in honour of the deified Trajan and Trajan's wife Plotina. His own wife Sabina is also honoured on coins both in her lifetime and after her death and consecration. There was also a coinage for Lucius Aelius, adopted by Hadrian as his heir in 137 and, following the death of Aelius, for the eventual heir, Antoninus Pius.

The factors which in previous reigns enabled the coinage to be dated with some precision are largely absent on Hadrian's coins. His holding of the tribunician power is not enumerated and the consulship which is recorded was only held twice in his reign by Hadrian. In general, however, the sequence of the coinage moves from the use of a long form of obverse inscription at the beginning to a short form for the later issues.

Some of the specific events in the reign are recorded by coin types. The very first issue includes a reverse with Trajan and Hadrian clasping hands and inscribed *Adoptio*, and in the same issue the type of *Fort(una) Red(ux)* commemorates the return of Hadrian from the East to Rome. A very rare issue in A.D. 121 with the type, a male figure reclining, notes Hadrian's celebration of the Parilia, the games for the birthday of Rome, and is one of the few Roman coinages to carry an express date for it is inscribed *Ann DCCCLXXIIII*, the year 874 of the foundation of the city. The distributions or largesses of the emperor are pictured sometimes on sestertii, sometimes on denarii. The reverse shows the emperor seated on a platform handing the largesse to a citizen, a type that was to become a standard part of coinage in many reigns. But the most famous series of Hadrian's coins, both precious metals and bronze, are those which honour the provinces and the armies and the emperor's visits to the provinces. The provincial series has a reverse, the personification of the province in appropriate dress and accompanied by objects associated with that province. Africa, for example, is shown wearing elephant-skin head-dress and holding a scorpion and cornucopiae with a basket of fruits at her feet (Pl. 275). The emperor's visits are commemorated by a type where Hadrian stands facing a figure of the province who is sacrificing at an altar. The province is distinguished by the inscription, e.g. *Adventui Aug Galliae*. On the army coins the emperor is normally shown standing on a low platform addressing his troops who hold a legionary eagle and standards and the army is named in the inscription, as for example *Exerc(itus) Dacicus* (Pl. 276). Hadrian's care for the provinces is pictured by the series showing him raising a kneeling figure typifying the province and describing him as, e.g. *Restitutor Hispaniae*.

The coinage for Hadrian's wife Sabina has two varieties of obverse portrait; on one her hair is piled high behind a tiara, on the other it falls in a queue down her neck. On the first group the obverse is inscribed simply *Sabina Augusta* but on the second *Sabina Augusta Hadriani Aug PP*. Her reverse types are normally Concordia, Pudicitia and Vesta (Pl. 277) both on the precious metals and the bronze coinage. Sabina, consecrated after her death, was honoured on a coinage where her veiled portrait is entitled *Diva Sabina Augusta* and a new *Consecratio* reverse shows her being carried heavenwards on the wings of an eagle. Lucius Aelius, adopted by Hadrian as his heir in 137, is entitled on the obverse of his coins *L Aelius Caesar*; his portrait, either simply a head or a draped bust, never has the laurel-wreath, a convention which became standard for all later heirs to the emperor (Pl. 278). The reverses of his coins have either the plain statement of his titles *Tr Pot Cos II* or the same with the addition of the name of the personi-fication on the reverse. In addition to Spes, the special type of the heir, Concordia, Pietas and Salus also appear. On the death of Aelius, Hadrian next adopted Antoninus Pius as his Caesar in 138 and coins were issued for him in the few months before Hadrian's death. His obverse portraits follow the conventions of those of Aelius, and Pietas is the most common reverse type for Pius in this coinage.

At the beginning of the reign the deified Trajan is honoured on a coinage mainly in gold combining the portrait of Hadrian on the obverse with that of Trajan, entitled *Divo Traiano Patri* on the reverse. There was also a very rare issue in gold and silver where Plotina, wife of Trajan, appeared on the reverse of coins of Hadrian.

Antoninus Pius, A.D. 138–161

The coins produced in this reign are still in the one uniform style consistent with the output of one mint only, that of Rome. Artistically the coinage never achieves the high level maintained under Hadrian. The portraiture seldom falls below the competent, but is rather monotonous and with the exception of several series connected with special events, the reverse types tend merely to ring the changes on the standard personifications and deities. The conformity in forms of obverse portrait and title on both the precious metals and the bronze coinage which had been becoming the practice in the coinage of at least the last two reigns here becomes more marked. There are some divergences, particularly in the use on the reverses of the bronze coinage of types particularly suited to the broader field of these denominations. The massive issues of this long reign are complicated by large coinages for imperial personages other than Antoninus himself. Earlier reigns had had comparatively small coinages for empresses or Caesar as adjuncts to the main issues but here Marcus Aurelius, adopted early in the reign as Caesar and heir, has a substantial share in the coinage from 140 onwards. There is also a copious coinage for the empress Faustina I early in the reign and a very large issue honouring her after her death in 140-141. The daughter of Antoninus, Faustina II, married to Marcus Aurelius in 145 also has her own coin issues.

With coins being struck for a number of persons simultaneously the difficulties of presenting a comprehensible view of the coinage in short space are great. As in the coinage of Hadrian, the early portion of Antoninus' issues mentions, of the offices of use in dating, only the consulship which Antoninus held only thrice in his reign. Fortunately from 147-148 onwards the reckoning of the emperor's tribunician power is recorded with consistency enabling the sequence of the coinage to be discerned.

In the early issues of the reign a number of less usual personifications are used as reverse types. Minerva returns to the coinage and is joined by Diana with her bow and quiver and Pietas, a favourite type for Antoninus, repeatedly appears (Pl. 279). The first Liberalitas or largesse, distributed on nine occasions by Antoninus, is recorded on the reverse of the sestertius issued in 139 by a picture of the scene. In the same year the emperor's generosity towards the provinces is celebrated on a series of bronzes, mainly sestertii. Of the presents made on the accession of a new emperor, Antoninus remitted half to the provinces and the whole to Italy and the coin reverses show the province personified, accompanied by local symbols and holding out a crown. Part of the issue between 140 and 144 looks forward to the celebration in 148 of the ninth centenary of the foundation of Rome. Aurei and denarii and most denominations of bronze depict the legendary characters and events connected with Rome's early history; Aeneas escaping from Troy holding his son Ascanius by the hand and carrying his father Anchises on his shoulder—a type already used in republican times; Mars descending through the air to the sleeping Rhea Silvia (Pl. 280), and their offspring Romulus and Remus, suckled by the she-wolf. Britain, the scene of almost the only campaign of significance in the reign, is featured on a small issue of sestertii in 143–144. Britannia is shown seated on a rock, holding a standard in one hand with a shield beside her; a similar type is repeated on asses in 154–155.

The coinage for Marcus Aurelius uses practically identical forms of type and and inscription on both the precious metals and the bronze. In the first two issues in which he appears in 139 and early 140 he only shares the coinage with Antoninus who occupies the obverse while Marcus appears on the reverse. His portrait is either only a head or a bust draped and cuirassed but he wears no laurel-wreath. He is described on the coins as *Aurelius Caesar Aug Pii F*—the son of Pius. Later in 140 coinage in the name of Marcus himself begins. The portrait and titles used on the reverse in the earlier joint coinage now appear as the obverse. In 145 his obverse title reverts to the simple *Aurelius Caesar Aug Pii F* which was to remain the norm for the remainder of the reign. The reverses in this issue include a new type of Hilaritas holding palm and cornucopiae, possibly a reference to the marriage of Marcus and Faustina II during the festival of the Hilaria in this year.

Faustina the elder, wife of Antoninus, has one of the most stately portraits of Roman empresses. She is usually shown with draped bust and a most elaborate styling of the hair which lies in wavy loops round her head and is finished off in a tight coil on top of the head. On the coinage struck in her lifetime in the years 138–140 she is entitled on aurei and denarii *Faustina Augusta* or *Faustina Aug Antonini Aug PP*. The latter form with *Pii* added to Antoninus' name is used on bronze. The principal reverses are Concordia and Juno Regina. After her death in 140–141 Faustina was honoured by the greatest posthumous coinages in the Roman series. The portrait of her lifetime coins continues to be used though sometimes it is shown veiled and she is entitled either *Diva Faustina* or *Diva Aug Faustina*. The two main reverse legends are *Aeternitas* and *Augusta*, both of which accompany one of a range of deities or personifications (Pl. 281). A smaller group inscribed *Consecratio* has reverses of a funeral pyre or an eagle bearing the empress heavenwards.

The coinage for Faustina the younger appeared sometime after her marriage to Marcus in 145 but it is noticeable that it is her relationship to her father, the emperor, that is stressed in her title which appears in a variety of the basic form *Faustina Augusta Aug Pii Fil*. Her portrait somewhat resembles that of her mother but her hair is more tightly drawn back from the face and coiled in an elaborate bun at the back of the head. The most common reverse types are Pudicitia, Venus and Concordia, the latter personification being sometimes replaced by the type of a dove, the bird of Venus (Pl. 282).

Another small coinage at the very beginning of the reign honoured the deified Hadrian. The aureus has, as reverse, Hadrian, holding sceptre, being borne skywards by an eagle; on denarii, the reverse shows an eagle on globe. The inscription in both cases is *Consecratio*.

Marcus Aurelius, A.D. 161–180

When Antoninus Pius died in March 161, Marcus Aurelius who had been his appointed heir throughout most of the reign automatically succeeded him. The undisturbed succession in the political field is matched in the coinage by a smooth and undisturbed transition in style. The mint of Rome continues to be the sole producer of the whole imperial series, though this again was a reign with issues of slightly smaller volume not only for Marcus himself but also for his colleague Lucius Verus in the first portion of the reign, for his son and heir Commodus later in the reign, for the empress Faustina the younger and for Lucilla, the wife of Verus. The artistic decline noticed in the coinage of Antoninus Pius continues in this reign where the reverse types particularly are, at best, uninspired. Portraiture on the obverses is the best aspect of the work of the die-cutters. The portraits of Marcus himself with his long, straggly beard are the least successful; the closer beard and tightly curled hair of Verus, the boyish features of the young Commodus and the elaborate hair-styles of Faustina and Lucilla are all more effectively presented.

The pattern of the issues is reasonably straightforward, despite the fact that coinage was issued throughout the reign for at least two personages simultaneously. The regular annual change in the reckoning of the tribunician power of the emperor, faithfully recorded together with the incorporation at a number of points in the reign of honorific titles marking the military successes in the East and in the Danubian campaigns clearly mark out the sequence of the coinage. In the reigns immediately preceding, successive emperors had adopted in their lifetime an heir who participated to an increasing extent in the imperial activities and coinage. The innovation of Marcus was to adopt not a Caesar and heir but, in the person of Lucius Verus, a fellow Augustus and colleague to share the task of empire, and in particular to deal with the war against the Parthians which had broken out as the reign of Antoninus ended. The coinage for the two emperors moves in close parallel and the issues in the precious metals and in bronze maintain an almost identical pattern. The chief difference, apart from the traditional formula, S.C. on the reverse of the bronze coinage, is the tendency for a fuller and less abbreviated form of the imperial titles to be used on the bronze where the greater size of the denominations made this practicable.

The titles for Marcus himself, in any given period, show a number of permutations but there is a distinct pattern for the principal varieties and their combination with the forms of reverse legend. The obverses for Verus conform closely to those of Marcus and the majority of reverse types are common to both. In the coinage of Marcus and Commodus there is a certain degree of conformity and sharing but with a number of divergences. From the beginning of the reign Marcus incorporated the name Antoninus of his adoptive father into his titles and, though the name Marcus, usually only in the abbreviation M, is retained in most of the forms, Aurelius appears only in the longer, fuller forms principally in the earlier issues of the reign.

Ironically, the reign of Marcus Aurelius, the philosopher emperor, was almost completely occupied by warfare; first the campaign against the Parthians in the East, then, in the latter part of the reign, the Marcomannic war. The coin types reflect a considerable part of these events as well as reproducing the standard personifications. The first coinage of Marcus and Verus has a type entitled Concordia showing the emperors clasping hands. The next year, which saw the departure of Verus for the East, produced types of Profectio, Fortuna Redux, Providentia and Salus. By 164 with the Parthians driven out of Armenia both emperors have the title Armeniacus and coinage shows a type of Armenia seated at the foot of a trophy (Pl. 283) and Verus seated on a platform receives Sohaemus to invest him as Rome's vassal king (Pl. 284). After the capture of the Parthian capital, Ctesiphon, and the conclusion of the war a series of Victory types appeared in 166. When Verus returned to Rome the two emperors celebrated a triumph in 167 for the three victories over the Armenians, Parthians and Medians, represented by three trophies on an as of Marcus. Verus died early in 169 as the emperors were returning from the first campaign against the Marcomanni.

From 172 Commodus was associated with his father as Caesar. His coinage in this period includes types appropriate to the heir—Spes and Princeps Iuventutis. He became a full colleague and Augustus in 177 and the coinage, like that of his father, is mainly concerned with the successful conclusion of the Danubian wars.

The coinage of Faustina the younger, struck in the reign of Marcus, continues the obverse portrait used in the reign of Antoninus but now she is entitled simply *Faustina Augusta*. To the reverse types carried over from the previous reign were added a few more, notably Fecunditas, portraying the empress holding two infants, with a child at her side. Faustina who died in 175 when accompanying Marcus on a journey to the East was honoured by a posthumous coinage of considerable size. Her portrait here is sometimes veiled and, as on her mother's consecration coinage, a common reverse is *Aeternitas*. The reverses inscribed *Consecratio* show a funeral pyre, an altar or a peacock with spread tail (Pl. 285). Coinage for Lucilla, daughter of Marcus and wife of Verus, probably ceased on the death of Verus in 169 and her re-marriage. Her portrait bust, similar to that of Faustina the younger but with more wavy hair, is inscribed *Lucilla* or *Lucilla Aug Antonini Aug F*. The reverse types are those which were becoming standard for the imperial ladies, Concordia, Juno Regina, Fecunditas and Venus (Pl. 286).

There were two other small consecration issues, one early in the reign for Antoninus Pius, the second in 169 for Verus. These have the normal reverses of eagle or funeral pyre.

Marcus Aurelius had abandoned the practical politics of adopting a suitable successor in favour of the sentimental claim of hereditary succession and even in his lifetime had raised his young son, Commodus, to the status of an Augustus and colleague. On the death of Marcus in March 180, while still on campaign against the Quadi, the succession of Commodus was not disputed and after patching up an end to the war he returned to Rome. Once again the coinage is clearly that of the Rome mint only and the style and pattern of the coinage is continued without disturbance. The deterioration in design, particularly of the reverses, goes on, noticeably on the denarii, but there is a definite revival in the art of portraiture, perhaps in response to the undoubted good looks of the new emperor. The only other coinage in this period is for the empress Crispina. Issues were probably begun for her before the death of Marcus and continued only until her banishment in 182.

The chronological sequence of the coinage is readily apparent from the changing enumeration of the emperor's offices and titles which form the principal element of the reverse inscriptions. The obverses show a variety of portrait from a simple laureate head to a rather ornately draped and armoured bust and a series of changing titles.

The reputation attached to Commodus by historians of neglect of important affairs in favour of a life of pleasure-seeking finds little reflection in the coinage. The intrigues and conspiracies which succeeded each other and finally led to the assassination of Commodus made little impact on the coin types unless, as in 184 when the treachery of Perennis, the prefect of the guard, was discovered, they were the inspiration for types recording or perhaps appealing for the loyalty of the army—Fides Exercitus and Concordia Militum. Otherwise the coinage on the whole makes use of most of the usual personifications combined with some special types alluding to particular happenings. Of these, military successes in Britain are celebrated in 184 on the reverse of sestertii, one showing the standing figure of Britannia, another inscribed *Vict Brit*, showing Victory inscribing a shield (Pl. 289). This British victory was also the grounds for the inclusion of the honorific Britannicus in the titles of the emperor. In the bronze issues of 183 the reverse of an as with type an elephant and inscription *Munificentia Aug* is thought to record the generosity of Commodus in providing spectacles and games for the populace of Rome. The coinage records that Commodus distributed largesse on nine occasions, two in the reign of his father and seven in his own. The occasions for some, his accession and return to Rome, are self-evident but the reason is not now known for others. The recording of the undertaking and discharge of vows for continued and successful reign is a feature of this coinage. In 185, after five years of reign, the taking of vows for the completion of ten years is shown on denarii. Commodus sacrificing over a lighted tripod is accompanied by the explicit inscription *Vot(a) Susc(epta) Dec(ennalia)* (Pl. 288).

The interest displayed by the emperor in the cults of the various deities finds mention on the coins. A number of such cults from the East which had gained popularity in Rome receive in this reign their first record on coins such as that of the Egyptian deity Serapis, described on a reverse as *Serapidi Conserv Aug*. The favourite deity of Commodus was Hercules who appears on coins with frequency from 183. Towards the end of the reign Commodus came to identify himself with Hercules and his portrait on the obverse sometimes wears the lion-skin head-dress appropriate to Hercules, and in a series towards the end of the reign this portrait is often linked with reverses dedicated to Commodus, the Roman Hercules (Pl. 287).

The brief coinage for the empress Crispina is in the first two years of the reign only. Her portrait is always a draped bust with distinctive coiffeur of hair in stiffly waved ridges with a chignon at the back of the head. The reverse types are mostly those familiar from the earlier ladies of the Antonine house—Concordia, Juno and Venus with the odd new type such as the garlanded and lighted altar, dedicated to the gods of marriage, *Dis Coniugalibus* (Pl. 290).

The coinage for the deified Marcus was struck early in the reign. The reverses are again those usual associated with a consecration, the funeral pyre, the eagle and the eagle bearing the dead emperor aloft.

CIVIL WAR AND THE SEVERAN EMPERORS, A.D. 193–235

Like Nero and Domitian before him, Commodus had alienated the more conservative elements in the state and eventually fell foul of his own immediate following. He was assassinated on the night of the 31st December 192 and with his death ended an era in Roman imperial history. The political and personal excesses of Commodus wrote a sorry ending to the record of the adoptive emperors under whom the empire had had its golden age and his death ushered in an era of increasing autocracy and militarism where emperors were increasingly and more openly dependent on the support of the armies as the basis of rule. In circumstances similar to those in A.D. 68 following the death of Nero, the murder of Commodus was followed by a number of brief reigns until the ultimate victor, this time in the person of Septimius Severus, established a new dynasty which was to provide emperors for approximately the next half-century.

Under Caracalla, the son of Septimius, came the first major alterations in the coinage system since the reform of Nero in A.D. 64. The aureus was reduced in weight and struck at fifty to the pound and a new coin was introduced, the double denarius, often known as the antoninianus, derived from Antoninus, the official name of Caracalla. In other respects coinage continued much as before; gold and silver were struck both in the normal units, aureus and denarius with occasional half-pieces, quinarii of increasing rarity and an occasional multiple aureus was struck. In the *aes* coinage, sestertius, dupondius and as were now the only denominations issued. As before, the civil wars called mints into being in the territory held by various contenders and at least one of them, Antioch in Syria, continued for some time to strike coinage in the fashion of the mint of Rome.

Pertinax, January–March A.D. 193

Commodus died without an heir and Pertinax, the prefect of the city, was proclaimed emperor. The choice, made in Rome, lacked sure support in the provinces and armies and, just as in the case of Galba in A.D. 69, the hostile praetorian guard, having had no say in his proclamation, mutinied and murdered him after only some three months of rule.

The coinage of Pertinax was struck only at Rome. In all metals the portrait is normally a full bust, less commonly a head only and is accompanied by the emperor's name and titles *Imp Caes P Helv Pertin Aug* with the longer form *Pertinax* on bronze. Considerably more originality than usual is displayed in the choice of reverse types. New types are dedicated to *Menti Laudandae*—the goddess Bona Mens, good counsel, to *Opi Divinae*—Ops the goddess of harvest and to *Iano Conservat,* Janus the god of beginnings and the New Year, the day which brought the proclamation of Pertinax (Pl. 291).

Didius Julianus, March–June A.D. 193

The praetorian guard having murdered Pertinax was bribed by Didius to acclaim him emperor and secure his acceptance by the Senate. In April, however, two further contenders with armies to back their claim were proclaimed, Septimius Severus in Pannonia and Pescennius Niger in Syria. When the former advanced into Italy Didius was deposed and executed.

His brief coinage first gives his title as *Imp Caes M Did Iulian Aug* and a second issue adds his other family name Sever(us). Reverse types look hopefully for the support of the army—Concordia Militum and the re-establishment of order— Securitas P.R. and even optimistically describe the emperor as ruler of the world, Rector Orbis. His wife Manlia Scantilla and his daughter Didia Clara also had their own very rare coinages. The former has types of Juno Regina and Pietas, the latter Fortuna Felix and Hilaritas Temporum.

Pescennius Niger, April 193–194/5

Pescennius Niger, governor of Syria, was hailed as emperor by his troops in April 193 after the murder of Pertinax. In the winter of 194–195 Severus, having secured Rome and marched eastwards, defeated Niger in a battle somewhere in Cilicia in which Niger was slain.

Antioch in Syria which for some two centuries had been the mint of an important series of provincial coinage struck a coinage of aurei and denarii of Roman type for Niger. This coinage is, however, quite different both in fabric and style from that issued by the mint at Rome. The flans are somewhat eccentric in shape and the reverse types in particular are poorly struck-up. The portrait of Niger, normally only the head, is crudely drawn, the beard long and straggly and the eye often represented merely as an annulet. His title on coins is basically in the form *Imp Caes C Pesc Niger Iust Aug*, but the various parts tend to be abbreviated or expanded in irregular fashion. The name Iustus may have been part of the emperor's original name and not adopted as an epithet to indicate the emperor's character. The reverse types are an amalgam of stock representations and innovations. The deities who commonly appear are Jupiter, Apollo, Ceres, Mars and Minerva and personifications Fortuna, Felicitas, Salus and Victory. Aptly, in view of the Iustus in the emperor's name, the type of Justitia holding scales and cornucopiae makes its appearance. Spes is qualified with the epithet Bona, which is found also in Bonus Eventus, one of the more frequent types of this rare coinage (Pl. 292). For a civil-war coinage, military types play quite a small rôle, the commonest being a type with trophy and arms, inscribed *Invicto Imperat* or *Invicto Imp Tropaea*.

Clodius Albinus, A.D. 193–197

The potential rivalry of Albinus, governor of Britain in 193, was forestalled by an arrangement under which he was adopted as Caesar by Septimius Severus. The mint of Rome struck coinage for him as part of the issues for Severus between 193 and 195. Late in 195, Albinus, suspicious of the intentions of Severus, was proclaimed Augustus and crossed over to Gaul where the mint of Lyons produced his coinage. In February 197 he was defeated in battle near Lyons.

Rome. On aurei and denarii the portrait of Albinus is of the head only but on bronze coinage more often a full bust, draped and cuirassed. Only very rare gold and silver were struck for him in 193; his title has the form *D Clodius Albin Caes* and the sole reverse, Providentia, shows that he was consul (cos) in that year. The issues of 194–195, adding Septimius to his name, entitle him *D Clod Sept Albin Caes*. Of the reverse types, some of which include *Cos II* in the inscription, the more prominent are Felicitas and Saeculum Frugiferum, a type associated with Hadrumetum, in North Africa, the home of Albinus.

Lyons. The style, particularly of the portrait, is distinct from that of Rome; the head is rounder and the beard tightly curled, not straggly as on the Roman issues. The coins entitle Albinus *Imp Caes D Clo Sep Alb Aug* and many of the reverses in this coinage, confined to aurei and denarii, include reference to his consular office (cos II). The gods given prominence are Jupiter, designated here as Victor, and Mars and to types such as Pax, Providentia and Victory are added less usual personifications of Clementia, the Genius of Lyons, headquarters and mint of Albinus, and a variety of types of Fides, of which Fides Legionum with eagle between two standards is the most common (Pl. 293).

Septimius Severus, A.D. 193–211

The profuse coinage of this comparatively lengthy reign of eighteen years is complicated by the facts that, in the early years, three mints, all in the East, struck coins in addition to Rome and that there shared in the coinage the empress Julia Domna, the two sons Caracalla and Geta and, briefly, Plautilla, the wife of Caracalla. The coinage falls into successive stages. From 193 up to the fall of Albinus in 197, coinage appeared for Septimius and Domna and towards the end of the period for Caracalla as Caesar. From 198 to 209 Caracalla appears as Augustus and Geta as Caesar and Plautilla as consort of Caracalla. From 209 to the death of Septimius at York while on campaign in Britain, Geta's coinage shows him as Augustus also. The greater portion of the coinage was issued at Rome; in the East, mints, identified as Alexandria and Emesa in Syria, were active during the campaign against Niger. The third eastern mint, Laodicea ad Mare, as well as striking for the campaign probably continued for some years more.

Rome. The coinage of the wars of succession has on the precious metals, particularly the denarii, a noticeably thick dumpy flan, almost too small for the dies, and a series of rather stiff portraits. The sequence of the early issues for Septimius is marked out mainly by the enumeration of imperatorial salutations. His titulature has the form *L Sept Sev Pert Aug Imp II* in 194, progressing to an eventual *Imp X* in 199. The reverses feature many of the normal types but the issue of Septimius' first year has a special series honouring the legions. The legion is named in the inscription around the type of a legionary eagle between two standards. Another feature is the emergence of Sol as a frequent type, partly due to the connection of Domna's family with the sun worship at Emesa. After the breach with Albinus, coinage was struck for Caracalla as Caesar with reverses Spes and Princeps Iuventutis, peculiar to the heir. Early coinage for the empress has a peculiarly small portrait bust with title *Iulia Domna Aug* and reverses mainly devoted to Venus.

The next coinage is on somewhat wider flans for the precious metals, normally with large portraits of better style. The successes of Septimius in the Parthian wars are noted by the inclusion of the honorific Parthicus about 200 in his title *Severus Aug Part Max*. This changed soon to *Severus Pius Aug,* the form maintained to the end of the middle period in 209. The sequence of issues is marked by the inclusion in the reverse legend of the changing tribunician power. In a long series of undated coins many of the reverses indicate the joint reign of Septimius and Caracalla by the plural Augg in the inscription. Particular acts of imperial favour towards Italy and to Carthage in the province of the emperor's birth are commemorated by the inscription, in the latter case, *Indulgentia Augg In Carth*, and a type of Dea Caelestis riding on lion (Pl. 294).

Caracalla, created Augustus after the fall of Albinus in 197, is usually entitled *Antoninus Pius Aug*. Septimius by attaching Pius to his own name and Antoninus to that of Caracalla was affiliating himself to the great Antonine dynasty of the second century. The issues of Caracalla can be distinguished by the development of his portrait from that of a boy to that of a young man. Many of his reverses are shared with his father including another type of Sol, described as *Rector Orbis*. The brief coinage for Plautilla was struck between the marriage in 202 and her banishment in 205. Her title is either *Plautillae Augustae* or more commonly *Plautilla Augusta* and as well as types of Venus, Concordia is featured either as a personification or by a scene showing Caracalla and Plautilla clasping hands. Domna, in this period, is designated simply *Iulia Augusta*. Her reverses have types usual to the imperial ladies, such as Fecunditas and Juno as well as Venus, and a particular military type dedicated to her as *Matri Castrorum*. Geta, created Caesar when Caracalla became Augustus, has, most commonly, the title *P Septimius Geta Caes* (Pl. 295).

The coinage of the last few years of the reign is marked for Septimius by the addition of the honorific Britannicus adopted in connection with the campaigns in Britain which finally necessitated the presence of the emperor and his two sons in the province. Both Caracalla and Geta, now an Augustus, also add Britannicus to their titles in this period. The coinage of Domna continues the same obverse style as in the previous period.

Alexandria. A coinage of rare denarii and even rarer aurei of Septimius and Domna has been attributed to this mint in Egypt which declared for Septimius before the end of 193; for the rather elongated obverse portraits, the large reverse types and the lettering have something in common with the provincial coinage of Alexandria. The obverse titles, *Imp Cae L Sep Sev Pert Aug* and *Iulia Domna Aug*, are those of the early years and the inclusion of *Trp II* and *III* in some reverse inscriptions carry the issues up to 195. The reverses of Septimius are mainly military with types of Mars, Fides Legionum and Victory.

Emesa. As Antioch the most likely mint town in Syria was in the hands of Pescennius, series of denarii with Eastern features—almost Greek forms for some letters and an annulet eye—may have been struck at Emesa, the native city of the priestly family of Domna. Septimius has the usual early form of obverse legend in 193 and to this is added *Cos II* in 194 and reverse legends including *Trp III* mark issues in 195. In addition to more usual personifications on the reverses, types similar to those used by Pescennius Niger such as Bona Spes, Bonus Eventus and trophy and arms with legend *Invicto Imp Tropaea* were used. Domna shared some of these unusual reverses but has her own type of Venus Victrix as well.

Laodicea. This city which declared for Septimius is the probable mint of another Eastern series, mainly denarii, in more finished style and with a different obverse title for Septimius, *L Sept Sev Pert Aug Imp.* Typical Eastern reverses such as those at Emesa were used in the earlier issues up to 197. From this point until the last issue in 202 the style and the form of obverse falls more into line with the issues from Rome as does the selection of reverses and the issue of some gold. Coinage for Caracalla, briefly as Caesar then as Augustus and for Geta as Caesar in the style of this mint accompany the issues of their father.

Caracalla and Geta, A.D. 211–212

The brothers, already Augusti in the lifetime of Septimius, returned to Rome from Britain late in 211 and reigned as joint emperors only until February of the next year when Caracalla murdered his brother. This brief coinage was struck only at Rome. The obverse titles are those in use in the last coinage with Septimius

but the numbered tribunician power incorporated in the reverse inscription deter-
mines the attribution of the issues to this period. The success in Britain is still
commemorated by Victory types and Fortuna Redux alludes to the return to
Rome. In this period also falls the consecration coinage for the deified Septimius,
with types of funeral pyre and eagle.

Caracalla alone, A.D. 212–217

Though the reign saw yet another German campaign and a full-scale expedition
against the Parthians, Rome was the sole mint for the coinage. In the issues of 212
Caracalla still retains his British title but in the course of 213 this was dropped and
Felix added. Subsequently in honour of his victories in Germany he took the title
Germanicus, which was to remain in his obverse title till the end. The shorter form
was used on gold and silver, a long form, e.g. *M Aur Antoninus Pius Aug Germ*
on the bronze. Late in 214 a new denomination, the double-denarius, was introduced, larger in flan than the denarius and marked as a double piece by the radiate
crown worn by the emperor, just as the radiate crown on the dupondius marked
it as the double of the as where the head is laureate.

Of the great constitutional change in 212, the extension of citizenship to all
inhabitants of the empire, the coinage makes hardly any mention, though a fairly
common type of Libertas in 213 may refer to this. A type of Victory with wreath
and trophy specifically labelled *Victoria Germanica* honours the successful conclusion of the war in Germany in 213 as does the type with Caracalla in his
triumphal quadriga. In later issues the appearance of Aesculapius and Apollo,
both gods of healing not commonly represented on coins, may reflect the emperor's
ill-health. The sun-god takes an increasingly prominent place on the coins and a
new variety shows him mounting his chariot (Pl. 296). Issues in 217 before the
murder of Caracalla devote a number of reverses to recording victory over the
Parthians, though no real battles had yet been engaged.

The empress-mother, Julia Domna, continued to have a considerable share in
the coinage after the death of Septimius. The issues of this period are marked by
a new obverse title *Iulia Pia Felix Aug*, both on the precious metals and the
bronze. Some of the coinage was probably issued in the joint reign of Caracalla
and Geta but the series which include the new double-denarius are of Caracalla's
sole reign and from 214 onwards. The double-piece for the empress is marked by
the placing of the obverse bust on a crescent. Most of the reverse types are con-
tinuations of previous issues but, possibly parallel to the Sol types for Caracalla,
Domna has a common reverse of the moon-goddess *Luna Lucifera* in a biga.

In April 217 Caracalla was murdered at the instigation, it is said, of the praetorian prefect Macrinus, who feared for his own safety at the emperor's hands. After some hesitation Macrinus was declared emperor by the army in the East and subsequently recognized in Rome by the Senate. Macrinus, the first man of equestrian rank to become emperor, had little opportunity to amend the tyrranical rule of Caracalla, for after a defeat at the hands of the Parthians and a patched-up peace, he in turn was murdered after little more than a year's reign.

The existence of two portrait styles on the coins, a younger, short-bearded portrait and an older portrait with longer beard has prompted the division of the coinage between the mint of Rome and a branch mint at Antioch respectively. A transitional group suggests, however, that Rome was the only mint striking first with a modified portrait of the previous emperor—a familiar phenomenon at the beginning of many reigns—then with a more realistic portrait. Macrinus, adopting himself into the Severan dynasty, added the name *Severus* to his title which appears in the form *Imp C M Opel Sev Macrinus Aug*. The reverse types present little except the conventional representations and the inclusion of types celebrating victory are either anticipatory or merely propaganda for home consumption. The double denarius was also struck by Macrinus, the larger flan allowing miniature compositions such as that of *Iovi Conservatori* with a gigantic Jupiter protecting a tiny figure of the emperor (Pl. 297).

Macrinus appointed his young son Diadumenian as Caesar and to his early titulature *M Opel Diadumenianus Caes* was later added *Ant(oninus)*, indicating the attachment to the dynasty of Caracalla. His reverse types are the conventional Spes and Princeps Iuventutis of the heir. A coinage of great rarity giving Diadumenian the title of Augustus evidences his adoption as a full colleague very shortly before he was murdered together with his father.

Elagabalus, A.D. 218–222

The lack of military success by Macrinus gave opportunity to Julia Maesa, the sister of the former empress Julia Domna, to organize a section of the army to declare as emperor her grandson, known to history as Elagabalus. Macrinus and Diadumenian were defeated, captured and put to death and Elagabalus was recognized at Rome as emperor under the name of Marcus Aurelius Antoninus, the title of Caracalla whose paternity he claimed. Two quite distinctive styles of coinage throughout the whole reign are the products of the mints of Rome and Antioch.

Rome. The style of this coinage is reminiscent of issues of Caracalla, though it gradually develops a more individualistic portrait. An unusual detail is the horn of divine power sometimes placed over the fore-head pointing downwards. In the first issue in 218 the obverse carries a full statement of the emperor's official names *Imp Caes M Aur Antoninus Aug*; this was shortened in successive years by the omission first of the praenomina and then of the title Caesar, but for the final coinage *Pius* was added to the title. The form on the bronze coinage throughout gives the emperor's full name including Pius. The personal excesses and extravagances of the amazing emperor Elagabalus which have been related with such gusto by subsequent historians naturally find no mention on the coins. The only interesting feature in an otherwise conventional coinage is the emphasis given to the cult of sun-god in general and in particular as represented by the sacred black stone from Emesa brought to Rome by Elagabalus who was high-priest of the cult. Reverses showing Elagabalus sacrificing describe him as high-priest and priest of the sun, and the sacred stone is shown being conveyed into the city (Pl. 298).

Coins were also struck for a number of imperial ladies. The emperor's grand-mother Julia Maesa and his mother Julia Soaemias have substantial issues, the former with types of Pietas and Pudicitia (Pl. 299), the latter, Juno, and Venus. There are also rare coinages in successive years for his three wives Julia Paula, Aquilia Severa and Annia Faustina.

Antioch. A number of features distinguish this series. The portrait is weakly executed and has a typical annulet eye and the lettering is less regular; for Elagabalus the most common obverse inscription is *Antoninus Pius Fel Aug*. The cult of Sol is again the interesting feature of the choice of reverse types. On grounds of portrait style some coins of the imperial ladies except Annia Faustina have been attributed to this mint.

Severus Alexander, A.D. 222–235

Julia Maesa, alarmed for the security of the dynasty because of the conduct of Elagabalus, arranged that he should adopt his cousin Severus Alexander as his Caesar in 221 and in early 222 organized his disposal and the proclamation of Alexander as emperor. Apart from a brief issue from Antioch in the first two years, the coinage was produced by the mint of Rome. Caracalla's double-denarius was not struck in this reign.

Rome. The initial issues have portraits resembling those of Elagabalus but as the coinage proceeded it attained a generally higher standard, particularly in portraiture, reminiscent of the better coinages of the second century. The obverse title, beginning with *Imp C M Aur Sev Alexand Aug* is shortened to *Imp Sev Alexand Aug* then to *Imp Alexander Pius Aug*. The reverses are largely conventional with the exception of types alluding to campaigns first against the Parthians and, towards the end of the reign, in Germany. The cult of Sol disappeared in the early issues but later in the reign returns as the most frequent type (Pl. 300). The restoration of public buildings in Rome such as the Colosseum and the Nymphaeum are recorded on the coins and the ceremonial procession in connection with taking up the consulship received mention on each occasion. The issues for his mother, Julia Mamaea, have the conventional types for the empress, Fecunditas, Felicitas, Juno, Venus and Vesta (Pl. 301). His wife Orbiana, banished only two years after the marriage in 226, has a coinage with the one type, Concordia.

Antioch. The coinage from this mint shows the same stylistic features as the Eastern issues of Elagabalus. Many of the reverses are marked with a star and present types such as Fortuna not used at Rome. The mint ceased production in 223.

THE MILITARY EMPERORS, A.D. 235–270

For practically the remainder of the third century there was a swift succession of short-lived emperors or claimants to the office, all of whom issued some form of coinage. A number of major changes occur in the coins and the coinage system. The double-denarius which returned in 238 and almost immediately ousted the denarius itself was increasingly debased till by late mid century it had become a bronze coin with only a silver wash. At about the same time the bronze coinage which had become increasingly smaller ceased entirely. A system of branch mints supplementing the output of Rome gradually spread across the empire. Initially these coinages can still be distinguished only by difference of style but, later on, systems of distinctive symbols and then of abbreviated names or initials mark off the work of each mint. The choice of types became even less meaningful than in earlier centuries, except as demonstrating general trends or alluding to some definite and specific happening, and more or less the same range of types was struck at the various mints.

Maximinus, A.D. 235–238

Alexander and Mamaea were murdered near Mainz at the beginning of the German campaign by a mutinous army which proclaimed as emperor one of the generals, the Thracian Maximinus. The first coinage, which in this reign is from Rome only, presents a portrait which is only a modified and slightly older version of the features of Severus Alexander, but in later issues the portrait is realistic almost to the point of caricature, with beetling brows and jutting chin. The early obverse title *Imp Maximinus Pius Aug* changed in 236 to *Maximinus Pius Aug Germ(anicus)*. The emperor's military successes are the occasion of several reverse types of Victory and specifically a victory in Germany (Pl. 302). The reverse types otherwise are stock representations.

The emperor's son Maximus was appointed Caesar and in addition to the usual type of Princeps Iuventutis has a reverse showing the priestly vessels and implements inscribed *Pietas Aug*, a standard type for the heir in the third century. Consecration coinage for the empress Paulina has a peacock reverse.

Gordian I and II, 22nd March–12th April 238

Discontent with the régime of Maximinus brought a revolt in North Africa in which the proconsul of Africa, Gordian, was acclaimed emperor and associated with himself as Augustus his son, Gordian the younger. They were recognized as emperors in Rome where coins were struck in their name. After only three weeks of rule they were defeated and met their end. They have an identical obverse title, *Imp C(aes) M Ant Gordianus Afr Aug*, but an older, thinner-faced portrait distinguishes the issues of Gordian I (Pl. 303) from those with the rounder features of Gordian II (Pl. 304). The reverse types carry no special message.

Balbinus and Pupienus, 22nd April–29th July 238

The Senate, realizing that the news of their recognition of the Gordians would bring Maximinus down on them from his campaign headquarters in the Balkans, appointed two of their own number, Balbinus and Pupienus, as emperors. Their coinage, issued at Rome, consisted first of denarii and bronze coins and subsequently, in the preparations against Maximinus, the double-denarius was reintroduced. The burly-featured Balbinus has the title *Imp C(aes) D Cael Balbinus Aug* and the full-bearded portrait of Pupienus carries, usually, the names *Imp C(aes) M Clod Pupienus Aug*. The double-denarii stress the co-operation of the two colleagues with types such as Fides Mutua for Balbinus (Pl. 305) and Caritas Mutua for Pupienus (Pl. 306).

Gordian III, 29th July 238–244

The fall of Maximinus was soon followed by the murder of Balbinus and Pupienus by the praetorian guard. Gordian III, who had been Caesar to the latter emperors, became emperor. Coinage was struck for him by an Eastern mint, presumably Antioch, as well as by Rome. From this reign onwards the double-denarius became the principal silver coin, with the denarius reserved for special issues only. Following precedent, the emperor's title begins with a long form but later settles down to a shorter form *Imp Gordianus Pius Fel Aug*. The reverse types ring the changes on the deities and personifications and record the emperor's donatives. With Gordian's departure for the East and the Persian war towards the end of the reign are associated types of Fortuna Redux, Victoria and Mars Propugnator (Pl. 307) on gold and silver and an exhortation of the troops, Adlocutio and Virtus types on the bronze. A special issue of aurei and denarii honoured the marriage of Gordian in 241 to Tranquillina in whose name appeared only a very rare series of double-denarii.

Antioch. Only double-denarii were struck at this mint. The content of their reverse types differs little from that at Rome but the obverse portrait has the characteristics noted on the Eastern portraits of earlier emperors.

Philip I and II, A.D. 244–249

Gordian III was murdered while in the East and succeeded by Philip who associated with himself his son, Philip the younger, first as Caesar and later as full colleague and Augustus. The two mints, active for Gordian, continued to strike for the Philips. The issues at Rome of aurei and double-denarii give Philip's title at *Imp (M Iul) Philippus Aug*, the shorter form being later. The main feature of interest is the special coinage for the celebration in 248 of the millenary of Rome's foundation. The reverses inscribed *Saeculares Augg* picture a variety of animals, probably those which appeared in the games at this time (Pl. 308). In this coinage the numerals I–VI appear on the exergue, marking for the first time the product of the six workshops in the Roman mint. From another issue in the same year with reverses marked with Greek numerals A to S, the division of the facilities of the mint between the two emperors and the empress Octacilia Severa can be observed; four workshops produce for Philip I, one for both Philip II and Otacilia. For the latter, there is a plentiful coinage both in silver and bronze with her own types of Pietas, Pudicitia and Juno Conservatrix. For the first two years the coinage records Philip II as Caesar but from 246 he has the same title as his father from whom his youthful portrait easily distinguishes him (Pl. 309).

Antioch. The coinage of the Eastern mint is again distinguished by the cruder portrait with the peculiar treatment of the eye and a frequent use of portraits facing to the left. Early issues of Philip I can further be distinguished by the use of the unusual, long obverse title *Imp C M Iul Philippus P F Aug P M.* Reverse types such as that celebrating the conclusion of peace with the Persians are peculiar to this mint alone.

A very rare coinage was issued in Syria about 248 for Jotapian one of the many short-lived usurpers in the third century. Pacatian, a usurper in Upper Moesia issued double-denarii from a mint at Viminacium.

Trajan Decius, A.D. 249–251

Decius, one of Philip's successful generals, was acclaimed by his troops and marching into Italy defeated Philip. There are two features of note in this coinage, the appearance of a new mint at Milan and the experiment of a new denomination in the bronze coinage, the double-sestertius.

Rome. The emperor's most common form of title here is *Imp C M Q Traianus Decius Aug* and the emphasis of the reverses is on the emperor's Illyrian origin with types honouring the provinces of Dacia and Pannonia as well as the Genius of the Illyrian army (Pl. 310). Rome also struck for Herennia Etruscilla with the usual empress reverses, for his elder son Etruscus, first as Caesar and later as Augustus and for his younger son, Hostilian, as Caesar.

Milan. The obverse *Imp Cae Tra Dec(ius) Aug* distinguishes the issues of the mint, probably founded in conjunction with the establishment of a military headquarters there to meet the threat of barbarian inroads on the northern frontiers. The principal types are those in praise of the provinces discussed under Rome. To this mint and reign also is attributed a long series of consecration coins honouring emperors from Augustus to Severus Alexander (Pl. 311).

Antioch. Double-denarii with a portrait style associated with this mint were struck for all four members of the family, presumably late in the reign. Amongst types peculiar to this mint are Aequitas, Roma Aeterna and Pudicitia, a type normally associated with the empresses only but here struck for Decius and his sons as well.

When Decius and his elder son were killed in battle against the Goths in 251, Trebonianus Gallus, governor in Moesia, was hailed as emperor by his troops. Hostilian, the surviving son of Decius, was made an Augustus and colleague of Gallus who appointed his own son, Volusian, as Caesar. When Hostilian died of the plague in the same year Volusian was advanced to the rank of Augustus. The three mints of the previous reign continued to strike in this reign. The experimental double-sestertius of Trajan Decius was not repeated, and as the double-denarius by this time had sunk almost to the weight of the denarius, this latter denomination practically ceased to be struck.

Rome. The obverse title for all was in its long form, for Trebonianus *Imp Cae C Vib Treb Gallus Aug* and similarly for Hostilian and later for Volusian. The event which makes its presence felt even on the coin types was the great plague which swept the Roman world; amongst conventional types, special reverses stand out dedicated to Apollo Salutaris, the god of healing, and to Juno Martialis (Pl. 312).

Milan. Coins continuing the style of the previous sign were issued only for Gallus and for Volusian as Augustus, with an obverse title beginning *Imp C C* and with a limited range of reverse types.

Antioch. A relatively substantial coinage here for all three rulers possesses several unusual features. The obverse inscriptions are all in long form and in the case of Hostilian, the unusual spelling recalls the attempts in Greek to transliterate Roman names, as here *C Oval Ostil Mes Covintus Aug*; and a system of marking the product of the various *officinae* or workshops of the mint make its appearance. The marks on both obverse and reverse take the form of dots from one to four or Roman numerals apparently from I to VII. The reverse types repeat the Juno Martialis of Rome but otherwise use the particular selection noted for this mint under Decius.

Aemilian, A.D. 253

The all too common pattern of events in the third century was repeated once again when the general Aemilian after successes in Moesia was proclaimed Augustus by his troops and moving into Italy defeated Gallus. His reign lasted only three months when he in turn fell to Valerian who had been sent by Gallus to bring down reinforcements from Rhaetia. His coinage was struck mainly by the mint of Rome which designates him *Imp Aemilianus Pius Fel Aug*. His reverse types are largely dedicated to the deities, to Apollo, Diana, Hercules, Jupiter, Mars and to Roma Aeterna herself (Pl. 313). A small issue with a different obverse inscription and a slightly different style may have been issued somewhere in Moesia. There is also a very rare coinage for his wife Cornelia Supera with types of Juno and Vesta.

Valerian and Gallienus, A.D. 253–259

Shortly after his defeat of Aemilian and his recognition as Augustus, Valerian appointed his son Gallienus as his colleague. Coinage was resumed again from the mint at Rome, from Milan and from a mint in the East, probably at Antioch. Coinage consisted now of large issues of double-denarii of rather poor silver from all mints, while Rome continued to strike a diminishing volume of bronze coinage and some gold of vastly varying weight. Barbarian attacks on the Rhine frontier and the invasions of the Eastern provinces by the Sassanians under Sapor brought about an administrative division of the empire, Gallienus taking charge of the West, Valerian undertaking the restoration of order in the East. At this time another mint was established at Gallienus' headquarters in the West at Cologne. In this reign disaster overtook the empire; Valerian was captured by the Sassanians in 259 and the Eastern provinces were lost and, as a repercussion, revolt in the West established an independent empire in Gaul.

Coinage was struck for the two emperors, for Salonina, the wife of Gallienus, for Valerian II, his elder son as Caesar, and, after his death in 255, for the younger son Saloninus. At this period the coinage of the various mints carried no specific distinguishing marks except that some Eastern issues are marked by a star or a wreath on the reverse and the attributions to mints depend on differences in style, in the form of obverse inscription and to a lesser extent on the range of reverse types used. In general terms, the long obverse title marks the early issues, successive issues being marked by a progressive shortening of the obverse legend. Personifications familiar from previous coinage still find their place but new concepts make their appearance; Valerian appears as Restitutor Orbis on the Rome coinage or Restitutor Orientis on the Eastern issues (Pl. 314). The similar rôle of Gallienus in the West is marked by a type of Restitutor Galliarum at the mint of Cologne and his successes by a series of Victory types (Pl. 315). The Caesar, Valerian II, has an unusual type for the heir apparent, Iovi Crescenti depicting the legend of the young Jupiter riding on the goat Amalthea (Pl. 316). For Saloninus the reverses are the usual types for the heir such as Spes Publica.

The disasters of 259 not only removed from imperial control provinces both in the East and West and their mints, but the capture of the senior emperor Valerian at Edessa and the death of the heir Saloninus at the taking of Cologne left Gallienus as the sole ruler. The only other personage for whom coinage was struck was the empress Salonina. The mints retained by Gallienus were Rome and Milan but later in the reign a new mint was opened at Siscia in the Balkans; in the East, coinage was still struck for Gallienus, though at a different mint, probably Cyzicus.

Bronze coinage and most of the gold was restricted to Rome but double-denarii, now becoming very debased, were issued by all mints. Most commonly on this coinage Gallienus has as portrait a radiate head only and the shortest obverse title *Gallienus Aug.* The majority of the Roman issues carry on the reverse the mark of the producing workshop. This mark placed either in the exergue or in the field is in the form of a numeral, either Roman (P, S, T, Q, and V to XII) or Greek (A to N). Emphasis is laid on the gods as the emperor's preservers, especially Apollo, Jupiter, Neptune and Diana. The Milan mint began to mark its issues with its initial letter in the exergue with an added letter (P, S, T) to indicate the workshop. The most notable issue here was that honouring the legions, the reverses showing the badge and title of each legion (Pl. 317). Issues of the Eastern mint have, in the exergue, sometimes a tribunician or consular date or the letters S.P.Q.R.

On double-denarii Salonina has a diademed bust set on a crescent and the obverse title (*Corn*) *Salonina Aug.* She has empress types of Fecunditas, Pudicitia and Venus but, at Rome, honours two goddesses, Diana and Juno, as imperial preservers. At Milan one of the most common reverses showing the seated figure of the empress is accompanied by the puzzling inscription *Augusta In Pace* (Pl. 318).

Following the capture of Valerian in 259, the Roman forces in Syria proclaimed emperors Macrian and Quietus. Their coinage, struck by a mint probably at Emesa, was almost solely of double-denarii, with a series of reverse types common to both emperors. These include Rome Aeterna (Pl. 319) and Spes Publica (Pl. 320).

Another usurper, Regalian, struck coins at Carnuntum on the Danube for himself and his wife, Dryantilla.

Claudius who succeeded on the assassination of Gallienus during the siege of Milan in 268 spent his brief reign in action against the Goths till his death from the plague in 270. His coinage is, more or less, a continuation of that of Gallienus but with a different obverse portrait and title. The series of bronze denominations marked with the formula *S C* which had formed a part of the system since its reorganization under Augustus now disappears leaving a coinage mainly of aurei and plentiful issues of billon double-denarii. At Rome most of the issues carry *officina* marks on the reverses which feature conventional personifications and deities (Pl. 321) and make no mention of the Gothic campaigns. The initial letter of the mint at Milan does not appear in this coinage but only the letter indicating the workshop. Siscia continued issuing for Claudius and, in the East, as well as issues carrying on from those of Gallienus at Cyzicus another group can be distinguished with a different obverse portrait and with Greek numerals as *officina* marks in the exergue.

The coinage of Quintillus, who succeeded his brother Claudius for a few months in 270, is mainly an extension of the latter's coinage, with similar features and types. A rare reverse of Pannonia is the only reference to contemporary events. An extensive commemorative coinage for Claudius was also issued with the customary reverses of funeral pyre, eagle and altar (Pl. 322).

THE GALLIC EMPIRE, A.D. 259–274

Postumus, A.D. 259–268

In 259 a revolt headed by Postumus, governor of one of the Germanies, succeeded in establishing an independent empire in the West consisting of Gaul, Spain and probably Britain. The first Gallic emperor, Postumus, issued from the mint which he took over at Cologne a coinage of aurei, billon double-denarii and bronze sestertii. The early issues of Postumus have a rather long, narrow portrait, reminiscent of the coinage of Gallienus and his sons, which had previously been issued by the mint at Cologne; the later portrait is broader and rounder. This Gallic coinage, particularly the gold, is immeasurably superior to the contemporary issues of Rome both in execution and design. The portraits of Postumus on the gold include elaborate helmeted and cuirassed busts, even facing heads and double portraits of Postumus and Hercules. These reverse types, even on the billon coinage, show refreshing innovations with a whole range devoted to local cults of Hercules (Pl. 323). The bronze coinage is not so well executed but has effective portraits and reverse types (Pl. 324). In 268 a brief coinage of double-denarii was struck for Postumus at Milan by Aureolus who revolted against Gallienus.

Laelian, A.D. 268

This usurper was acclaimed emperor by his troops and issued both aurei and billon double-denarii at Mainz where he was besieged by Postumus. The reverses are standard Pax and Victory types (Pl. 325).

Marius, A.D. 268

Postumus, killed at the siege of Mainz, was succeeded by Marius for a brief period, sufficient to produce coinage both in gold and billon with reverses of military flavour such as Concordia Militum and Virtus (Pl. 326).

Victorinus, A.D. 268–270

Though the two styles of coinage for Postumus are successive stages of work of the same mint the issues for Victorinus are of two contemporary styles, produced by two mints, one the mint of Cologne which struck for Postumus and Marius, the other, it is conjectured, at Lyons. The gold issues are remarkable for the variety of treatment of the obverse portrait as on the piece with a half-length bust of the emperor and a similar bust of Victory on the reverse (Pl. 327). A feature of his coinage is another series honouring the legions, this time, more elaborately, on gold coins. To the usual reverse types on billon coins are added a number of types of the sun-god.

Tetricus I and II, A.D. 270–274

The last Gallic emperor and his son of the same name as Caesar, issued coins from both the Gallic mints. The aurei continue the tradition of fine and unusual portraits. The billon, now extremely debased, was struck in quantity, and made use of a great variety of standard reverse types as well as continuing some types of Victorinus. The most frequent appears to be a type of Victory described as Comes Aug. (Pl. 328). The coinage of the younger Tetricus makes use of a number of similar types but most commonly the traditional Caesar types of Princeps Iuventutis and Spes (Pl. 329). In 274 Tetricus, beset with internal difficulties and unremitting barbarian raids, readily submitted to the emperor Aurelian and the independent empire in Gaul was at an end.

The coinage of Tetricus is amongst the most familiar in the Roman series for not only was it issued in quantity but it was widely and profusely imitated throughout the Western provinces. The greater part of the so-called 'barbarous' imitations of Roman radiate coins is based on originals of Tetricus with imitations of the consecration coins of Claudius II forming the next largest single category.

THE RECOVERY OF EMPIRE, A.D. 270–295

Aurelian, A.D. 270–274

In his comparatively brief reign Aurelian effected the almost complete territorial recovery of the empire as it had existed before the disasters of 259. In 271 he gave up Trajan's province of Dacia across the Danube and stabilized the northern frontier and shortly afterwards in a series of campaigns recovered the Eastern provinces which had come under the suzerainty of the Palmyrene rulers, Zenobia and her son Vabalathus; in 274 the Western provinces were regained. As a result of these territorial recoveries, the mint system of the empire was amplified by the addition of the mint in Gaul at Lyons, the mint at Antioch and a new mint in the Balkans at Serdica.

Amongst the measures of reorganization undertaken by Aurelian was a reform of the coinage. The aurei which had been struck at a variety of weights were issued again at a regular weight more or less approaching that of the standard of the earlier period and the billon double-denarius of a better fabric was issued at a weight just under 4 gm. and given a mark of value in the form XX, XX.I or KA (expressed in Greek numerals), perhaps indicating a content of two sestertii or ten *libellae* each.

The coinage before the reform continues to use a wide variety of reverse types but on the reformed billon coinage the types are reduced to a small number and tend to be used by the whole range of mints. At Rome the twelve *officinae* were reduced after the reform to only seven, marked either by Roman or Greek numerals. The consistent appearance of the letter T as the terminal in the exergue mark of one series suggests that the mint at Milan was transferred to Ticinum. Of note amongst reverse types are those describing the emperor as Restitutor Orientis or Restitutor Orbis. The popularity of the cult of Sol is apparent from the frequency of reverses in his honour either as *Sol Invictus* or as *Oriens Aug* (Pl. 330). The coinage of the empress Severina is mainly of the latter part of the reign after the reform, with reverses of Concordia Militum or Concordia Augustorum (Pl. 331).

Tacitus and Florian, A.D. 275–6

When Aurelian fell victim to a military conspiracy, no immediate candidate was proclaimed by the army. The Senate eventually appointed the aged Tacitus as emperor and on his death in Asia Minor in the next year his brother Florian assumed the title but reigned only a few months until defeated by Probus, who held the command in Asia. The same mints as under Aurelian continued to strike in this period, aurei being produced at some mints, but principally at Rome and the new reformed billon coin of Aurelian by all the mints. The cult of the sun-god disappeared from the coinage, whose reverses repeat many of the old conventions. On aurei Roma Aeterna is given prominence (Pl. 332) and on the billon coins a new reverse, Clementia Temporum, was used by both the emperors.

Probus, A.D. 276–282

The proclamation of Probus by his troops was confirmed by the Senate after his defeat of Florian. Gold coinage and the new billon double-denarius was struck by the whole range of mints active in the previous reigns. The tendency for the double-denarii to have a somewhat restricted range of reverse types which were struck by all the mints give place under Probus to a greater variety of reverses which were not necessarily repeated by the several mints. The marks were developed into a complicated system by the addition to the mark, particularly at Rome, of small symbols as thunderbolt, wreath and star. Many of the old familiar representations continued to find their place as reverse types and were reinforced by types which had more recently made their appearance. Sol Invictus figures regularly, usually represented driving his chariot; Clementia Temporum of Tacitus and Florian was continued and types of the emperor as Restitutor Orbis are frequent. The most notable feature of the coinage of Probus is the great variety of obverse types, both of portrait bust and of inscription. On a typical example the obverse legend is *Virtus Probi Aug* and the emperor is shown with crested helmet, elaborately decorated shield on arm and spear over shoulder (Pl. 333).

Carus and family, A.D. 282–285

A mutinous army having again murdered its emperor, its general, Carus, was hailed as emperor in 282 and appointed his sons, first Carinus and later Numerian, as Caesars. In 283 Carus, on his way to war with the Persians, raised both to the rank of Augustus. On the death first of Carus and then of Numerian, Diocletian was proclaimed in their stead and Carinus, who had remained in the West, though successful in battle against Diocletian, was assassinated in 285.

The mint of Serdica which had already ceased operation before the death of Probus is absent from this coinage but all the remaining mints strike for the three members of the family. The elaborate obverses of Probus were not continued nor was the variety of reverse types which are limited to only relatively few at each mint. In the Western mints the types for all three as Augusti are a selection of the more ordinary representations and for Carinus and Numerian as Caesars commonly the type of Princeps Iuventutis. In the East, Clementia Temporum is featured at Cyzicus (Pl. 334) and at Antioch a type of Virtus Augg (g) (a thirdG indicating the three Augusti) shows the emperor receiving a globe from Jupiter (Pl. 335). There was also a small coinage for Magnia Urbica, the wife of Carinus with types of Juno and Venus. Consecration issues were made for Carus and Numerian and for Nigrinian, the grandson of Carus and probably the son of Carinus.

Julian, a usurper proclaimed in Pannonia, issued coins from Siscia in 284–285 with types of Pannonia as well as Felicitas Temporum, Jupiter Conservator and Victory.

Diocletian and his colleagues, A.D. 284–295

The monetary reform of Diocletian in 295–296 is one of the great land-marks in the imperial coinage and the present section gives consideration to the coinage of the reign preceding this reform. In 285 Diocletian chose Maximian as his colleague and made him responsible for the western division of the empire. In 293 he appointed Constantius Chlorus and Galerius as Caesars and seconds-in-command to Maximian and himself respectively. Certain experimental steps towards a reform of the coinage are apparent in the variety of standards at which aurei were struck in this period. Some pieces have the theoretical weight of fifty to the pound (6·55 gm.) of Caracalla's reform; others at Antioch marked with the Greek numeral $\asymp$ were struck at sixty to the pound (5·46 gm.) and a third series, also at Antioch, have the numeral O, at seventy to the pound (4·68 gm.). Otherwise the coinage proceeded as before, the bulk of the issues being still billon antoniniani. Two new mints were opened, at Trier in the West and at Heraclea in Thrace. As in the previous reign, there was greater variety of reverse type in the coinage of the Western mints, though the commonest are types of Jupiter, the patron of Diocletian, and of Hercules, the patron of Maximian. Balkan and Eastern mints repeat some of the more recent innovations such as Clementia Temporum at Siscia, Concordia Militum at Heraclea, Cyzicus and Antioch which has also a type with both Jupiter and Hercules as the imperial preservers. The Caesars have their special type, Princeps Iuventutis at Rome but also share in the reverses of the Augusti.

THE BRITISH EMPIRE, A.D. 286–296

One last coinage in this group is that of the independent empire established in Britain in 286 by Carausius who was assassinated and succeeded by Allectus in 293. The coinage consisted of aurei, a series of good silver at the beginning of the reign of Carausius and billon antoniniani. Carausius controlled the northern coast of Gaul as well as Britain and issued a series of coins without mint-mark from a mint at Boulogne. Two other series were struck at London and Colchester with marks incorporating the initial letters L and C respectively. The early billon coins from the latter two mints were without mark of value but later series included the XXI mark of the ordinary imperial series. Many of the personifications of the Roman coinage find a place on the reverses of Carausius but the greatest emphasis is on the Pax type. Towards the end of the reign coinage was also struck in the names of Diocletian and Maximian and on the reverse types such as *Pax Auggg* for these emperors and Carausius, the triple G stresses the existence of the three rulers (Pl. 336).

The coins of Carausius, particularly in the early series, are in rough but effective style but those of Allectus are more technically finished. Since Boulogne had been retaken by the central empire in 293, the coinage of Allectus was struck by London and Colchester only. Of the reverses of this reign Pax, not so predominant amongst the reverse types, yields the principal place to Laetitia (Pl. 337). An innovation at both mints, a smaller coin with galley type and mint-marks QL and QC, is probably a quinarius.

The monetary reforms carried out by Diocletian in 295–296 established a new coinage system consisting of an aureus struck at sixty to the pound (5·46 gm.) (Pl. 338) and a silver coin marked XCVI indicating that it was struck at ninety-six to the pound (Pl. 339). These were supplemented by a large silvered-bronze coin, commonly called a follis, and possibly a theoretical sestertius of two denarii as it sometimes bears the mark of value XXI. A smaller bronze with radiate head is probably the half of this denomination. More mints were opened to complete a system covering the whole empire. To those existing before the reform were added the mints of London, Aquileia in north Italy, Carthage in North Africa, Thessalonica and Serdica in the Balkans, and in the East, Nicomedia and Alexandria. The coinage at all mints was marked with the initial letter on letters of the mint name except at London, where after the first issue the coins carry no mint-mark.

For the first Tetrarchy of Diocletian and Maximian as Augusti and Constantius and Galerius as Caesars, the aurei show a variety of reverse types from mint to mint but the follis coinage in its beginning has only one reverse *Genio Populi Romani* (Pl. 340). This monolithic system gives way in later issues to more differentiated reverses. Rome has a Moneta type with inscription *Sacra Mon Urb Augg et Caess NN* (Pl. 341), Carthage her own special types such as *Salvis Augg et Caess Aucta Kart* (Pl. 342) and Ticinum another variety of the Moneta type (Pl. 343).

In 305 Diocletian and Maximian abdicated, their Caesars were promoted Augusti and new Caesars Severus and Maximinus Daza were appointed in the West and East respectively. Coinage in gold was of limited quantity and in silver even more so but the follis coinage was struck in quantity. A type *Providentia Deorum Quies Augg* honoured the retired emperors. For both Augusti and Caesars the mints in Britain and Gaul and the Eastern mints continued to issue folles with the Genio reverse but in the central and Balkan mints there were innovations. Rome struck her Moneta type but with an abbreviated legend, and Carthage continued the *Salvis Augg et Caess Fel Kart* type, but at Ticinum and Aquileia the reverse for the Augusti was *Fides Militum* and for the Caesars *Virtus Augg et Caess nn* and at Siscia the patron deities of the Tetrarchies were honoured with types of *Herculi Victori* and *Iovi Conservat*.

The third tetrarchy came into being in 306 on the death of Constantius. Galerius became the senior Augustus and was joined by Severus as Augustus. Constantine who had joined his father Constantius in Britain was proclaimed as Caesar to complete the tetrarchy with Maximinus. The unity of the third tetrarchy was soon disrupted by events and the pattern of its short-lived coinage is essentially that of the second tetrarchy. A feature of note was the reduction in size and weight of the follis towards the end of 306, accompanied on the Genio issue by a shortening of the legend to *Genio Pop Rom* (Pl. 344).

The history of the next seven years and its coinage is complicated by struggles for power tantamount to civil war. In October 306 Maxentius, the son of Maximian, was proclaimed Augustus in Rome and Maximian resumed active rule. The mints in Italy, Rome, Ticinum and Aquileia, and Carthage in North Africa struck coinage for them and for Constantine as Caesar. Severus was defeated and put to death in attempting to recover Italy. In 307 Constantine was appointed Augustus by Maximian and in the following year a new Augustus, Licinius, was created in the East. With the advancement of Maximinus also to the rank of Augustus in 310, no less than six Augusti divided control of the Roman empire.

From 307 when Maxentius quarrelled with his father Maximian, who fled to Constantine, the Italian mints and Carthage struck only for Maxentius and for his son the deified Romulus. In 308 Maxentius closed the mint at Carthage and opened a new mint at Ostia. Considerable issues of aurei were struck at Rome and Ostia with types honouring Hercules, Mars, Victory and the wolf and twins. On some gold issues from Ostia the obverse shows a facing bust (Pl. 345). Silver coinage which was quite meagre repeated a number of these same themes as reverse types. The most frequent type for the reduced follis coinage under Maxentius was the hexastyle temple with figure of Roma inscribed *Conserv Urb Suae* except at Ostia with its own range of types, notably *Aeternitas Aug N*, with types of the Dioscuri and wolf and twins. The follis coinage for the deified Romulus, also a temple type, is inscribed *Aeternae Memoriae*.

The mints of Britain and Gaul controlled by Constantine struck in this period almost solely for himself and for Maximian till his removal in 310. There were practically no silver issues but gold was struck in some quantity, particularly after the defeat of Maxentius in 312, with types honouring Constantine as the restorer of liberty. On the follis coinage in the West the Genio type gave way to types honouring first Mars and then Sol, described as *Soli Invicto Comiti* (Pl. 346). These types were also issued by the mints of Maxentius after they came under Constantine's control. The famous vision of the Cross vouchsafed to Constantine on the eve of the battle of the Milvian bridge in which he defeated Maxentius finds no reflection in the coinage.

The mints from Siscia eastwards struck in the names of Galerius, Maximinus and from 308 for Licinius and accorded to Constantine a better representation on the coins than did Constantine to his rivals in the Western mints. On the aurei there are a number of types honouring the holding of the consulship by various of the emperors, types in commemoration of the discharge of vows and types honouring Jupiter, the patron of Galerius and Maximinus. The follis coinage of reduced module at Eastern mints after the collapse of the third Tetrarchy in 306 has variants of the Genio type, inscribed *Genio Imperatoris* (Pl. 347) and *Genio Caesaris*. Coinage honouring Galeria, the wife of Galerius, has a reverse *Veneri Victrici*. After the death of Galerius in 311, additional types honour Jupiter, Hercules and Sol. Alexandria strikes a special type *Bono Genio Pii Imperatoris*.

THE CONSTANTINIAN DYNASTY, A.D. 313–364

The death of Maximinus in the summer of 313 shortly after his defeat by Licinius left the empire under the control of only two Augusti, Constantine in the West and Licinius in the East. As a result of the civil war in 314, Licinius lost his provinces in Europe with the exception of Thrace and the control of the mints of Siscia and Thessalonica passed to Constantine. In the West, the mint at Ostia was closed in 313 and a new mint opened at Arles in Gaul. A second civil war in 324 left Constantine the sole ruler of the Roman world. Between the two wars, in 317, Crispus and Constantine II, the sons of Constantine, and Licinius II, the son of Licinius were appointed Caesars. Changes in the coinage system included the introduction by Constantine in 312 of a new gold piece, the solidus at seventy-two to the pound (4·5 gm.); the Eastern mints continued to strike the heavier aureus until Constantine's victory over Licinius in 324. The bronze coinage had fallen steadily in weight until about the beginning of this period it had sunk to about 3·5 gm.

Conspicuous amongst the gold coinage of this period are the pieces honouring Constantine's defeat of the Alamanni and Franci (Pl. 348) and the Eastern issues in honour of Jupiter with the remarkable facing portraits of the Licinii (Pl. 349). The bronze coinage of Constantine's mints continues to be devoted mainly to types honouring Sol but shortly after the appointment of the Caesars Sol disappears from the coinage, giving place to Victory types, *Victoriae Laetae Princ Perp* (Pl. 350), types celebrating vows, and the special type at Western mints of *Beata Tranquillitas*. The Licinian bronzes are principally devoted to Jupiter types, but Heraclea strikes a type of a camp gate inscribed *Providentiae Augg* (or *Caess*).

Two other brief coinages in bronze fall within this period, those of Valens and Martinian, appointed as colleagues by Licinius in the civil wars against Constantine, Valens in 314 and Martinian in 324. They share the usual Jupiter types of Licinius.

Constantine reigned as sole Augustus from the defeat of Licinius in 324 till his death in 337 but coinage was also struck for the many members of his family. Crispus and Constantine II were already Caesars at the beginning of this period and the other sons Constantius II and Constans were appointed to the rank in 324 and 333 respectively. Constantine's nephew Delmatius became Caesar in 335 and a second nephew, Hanniballian, held the rank of rex (king) in eastern Asia Minor from the same date. Coinage was struck for Constantine's mother Helena and his step-mother Theodora, as well as for his wife Fausta, until she was put to death together with Crispus in 326. In this period the coinage becomes more uniform and simplified. In the bronze coinage particularly, largely the same type or limited range of types was struck at the same time in all the mints, the issues varying only in the changing mark indicating the place of minting and the particular workshop. Some changes took place in the chain of mints; the mint at London was closed in 326, that at Ticinum in 327 but at the new city of Constantinople in 325 another mint was opened up.

Coinage in silver continued to be rare but gold solidi were struck for all the imperial personages. For the Caesars the normal reverse of Princeps Iuventutis was struck and a series with type of Victory inscribed with the name and title of the Caesar as, for example, *Constantius Caesar* (Pl. 351). Notable amongst the gold issues of Constantine I in this period are those with an unusual obverse portrait in which the emperor is represented with upcast, heavenward-gazing eyes (Pl. 352).

The coinage in bronze, reduced now to a weight of about 2·75 gm., was struck in a much more defined pattern throughout the imperial mints. Between the beginning of the sole reign and the dedication of Constantinople in 330 the main type for both the emperor and the Caesars was a fortified camp-gate inscribed *Providentiae Augg* (or *Caess*). For Helena the chief reverse, used on gold also, was that of *Securitas Republice* (Pl. 353) and for Fausta, the figure of the empress holding two children with inscription *Spes Reipublicae* (Pl. 353a). Between 330 and 335 there were issues in honour of the new capital, Constantinople, with, on obverse, the bust of the city personification inscribed *Constantinopolis* and, on reverse, the figure of Victory on prow (Pl. 354). The ancient capital, Rome, is portrayed on another series inscribed *Urbs Roma* with, on reverse, the wolf and twins (Pl. 355). Constantine, his sons and nephews strike a coinage showing on the reverse, inscribed *Gloria Exercitus*, two standards between two soldiers. In the last two years of the reign the design shows only one standard (Pl. 356).

Following the death of Constantine the Great in 337 his three sons succeeded as joint emperors, Constantine II controlling the western provinces, Constans the central and Constantius II the eastern. Delmatius and Hanniballian were eliminated shortly after Constantine's death.

C.—N

Gold solidi were issued with some frequency, the semis or half-piece only rarely in the reign of the three brothers. Types varied at the different mints; at Trier the army was honoured with a type of Mars inscribed *Virtus Exercitus Gall* (Pl. 357) and at Rome and Constantinople there were reverses of Victory. Silver became more common again, being struck in several denominations, a heavy miliarense of 5·4 gm., a light miliarense of 4·5 gm. and a smaller silver coin, probably a denarius of ninety-six to the pound (3·4 gm.). The bronze coinage continued the *Gloria Exercitus* type as the chief reverse with, at some mints, an additional coinage honouring the dead Constantine. Despite his death-bed baptism into the Christian faith his veiled portrait on the obverse is inscribed in the traditional manner of the deified emperors *Divo Constantino P.*

After the death of Constantine II in 340 the pattern of coinage remained much the same. On the gold coinage Victory types predominated and on the smaller silver denomination a similar type was repeated. On the small bronze pieces the most common reverse in the early years of the reign was on the same theme (Pl. 358). About this time the imperial obverse title substitutes for the *Imp(erator)* used throughout the earlier centuries the new formula *D(ominus) N(oster)*. About 348 a new, heavier bronze denomination was introduced at a weight of 5 gm. These pieces, inscribed on the reverse *Fel Temp Reparatio*, show a variety of themes, and fall into two successive groups. In the first Constans normally has the reverse showing a native being dragged from his hut in the forest (Pl. 359), Constantius the type of emperor holding the labarum, accompanied by two captives. In the later group the reverse for Constans shows the emperor in a galley steered by Victory and that for Constantius a warrior spearing a fallen horseman (Pl. 360). A smaller bronze coinage with the same inscription has as its type a phoenix. The reverse inscription may reflect the fact that this coinage reform coincided with the eleventh centenary of Rome's foundation, celebrated in A.D. 348.

In the West Constans was overthrown in 350 by the usurper Magnentius, who issued coinage from the mints in Gaul, Italy and, for a brief few weeks, from Siscia, both in his own name and in that of his brother Decentius who was appointed Caesar. The principal reverse type on the solidi shows Victory and Libertas supporting a trophy. The silver issues are quite rare, but plentiful bronze issues were struck for both emperors by the Western mints, including a new mint at Amiens. In the last year or so before he was defeated by Constantius in 353 Magnentius introduced a new larger bronze coin with one of the first unequivocal Christian types on Roman coinage, the Chi-Rho, the monogram of Christ, flanked by the letters Alpha and Omega (Pl. 361).

In the confused situation created by the overthrow of Constans in 350, Nepotian, a nephew of Constantine the Great was proclaimed Augustus at Rome but after a single month he was eliminated by Magnentius. While he controlled the mint of Rome, Nepotian issued coinage in gold and bronze with a reverse type *Urbs Roma* (Pl. 362).

In a brief and half-hearted usurpation in the Balkans Vetranio in 350 controlled the mints of Siscia and Thessalonica. Coinage was struck for Constantius as well as Vetranio, who issued rare solidi and a bronze coinage with reverse, Victory crowning the emperor who holds the labarum bearing the Christian monogram, inscribed *Hoc Signo Victor Eris* (Pl. 363), the words associated with Constantine the Great's vision of this symbol on the eve of the battle of the Milvian Bridge in 312.

In this crisis Constantius appointed his cousin Constantius Gallus as Caesar in 351 and having already put down Vetranio pushed Magnentius back into Italy. Control of Italy was regained in 352 and in the following year with the defeat of Magnentius and Decentius in Gaul the whole of the Roman world was once again under the control of Constantius. The mint opened at Amiens by Magnentius was closed down shortly after the victory of Constantius and in the Balkans the mint at Sirmium, reopened to strike for Constantius when Vetranio held control of Siscia, continued issues for Constantius and Gallus in this period. Solidi were issued in considerable quantity with the almost universal reverse type *Gloria Reipublicae* showing Roma and Constantinopolis seated holding a shield recording the vows in connection with the tricennalia, the thirty years of rule by Constantius (Pl. 364). On silver miliarensia issued at the Western mints the army was honoured in a reverse type *Virtus Exercitus* and the smaller silver denominations at central and Eastern as well as Western mints had a simple wreath enclosing a *vota* inscription. The bronze coinage was of slightly lower weight than that instituted in 348 but it continued the inscription *Fel Temp Reparatio*, though limiting the type to the variety showing a warrior spearing a horseman, a type used in common by Constantius and Gallus. Gallus was put to death in 354 and his half-brother, Julian, created Caesar in his place in 355. The coinage of this period was similar to that of the joint reign of Constantius and Gallus but with, latterly, a further reduced bronze coin, still with the warrior and horseman type. A fresh mint was opened at Milan for the issue of gold coinage, probably in 354 when Constantius was in Italy.

Julian was declared Augustus by his troops in 360 and the Western mints struck coinage for him with this title as well as for Constantius though the latter refused recognition to Julian. A clash was obviated by the death of Constantius in 361 and the recognition of Julian as sole emperor. Solidi in some Western issues of Julian continued the *Gloria Reipublicae* reverse of Constantius' coinage but with a *vota* inscription suited to Julian's reign, but the most wide-spread type on solidi was *Virtus Exercitus Romanorum*, showing a soldier with trophy dragging a captive. Silver miliarensia were also struck but the most common denomination was the smaller siliqua of 2·3 gm. which had been introduced towards the end of the reign of Constantius. These siliquae commonly had a reverse of a wreath enclosing a votive inscription. A reform of the bronze coinage about 363 introduced a large denomination similar to that of Magnentius, with reverse type *Securitas Reipub*, a bull (Pl. 365) which, if it represents the bull of Apis is almost the sole indication on the coinage of the pagan revival under Julian.

On the death of Julian while on campaign against the Persians in 363 the army proclaimed Jovian as his successor. Jovian concluded an enforced peace with the Persians but only some months later he died, in early 364. Solidi of Jovian, struck at the more eastern mints, have commonly the single reverse type *Securitas Reipublicae*, Rome and Constantinople holding a shield with a votive inscription. A simple votive inscription in a wreath is also the type featured on the silver siliquae and on the smaller of Jovian's bronze coins. The large bronze pieces of the size introduced by Julian have the reverse *Victoria Romanorum* (Pl. 366).

THE VALENTINIAN AND THEODOSIAN DYNASTIES, A.D. 364–395

Valentinian I proclaimed emperor in 364 in succession to Jovian appointed his brother Valens as colleague, allotting to him responsibility for the Eastern provinces, while he himself dealt with the West and the menace of barbarian inroads there. The principal alterations in the mint system were the re-opening of the mint at Milan, which struck exclusively gold and silver, and the closing down of Sirmium towards the end of 364. The coinage system, particularly in the precious metals, was basically that of the later Constantinian period. In gold the principal unit remained the solidus but there were rare issues of the half-piece, the semis and the piece of 1½ scripulum. Issues in silver included miliarensia, both of the heavy and light standard, but these were rather rare denominations, the chief silver piece being the siliqua of 2 gm. In bronze, the large bronze coin of Julian and Jovian, though issued at the beginning of the reign, soon disappeared leaving the smaller pieces as the bulk issues.

The themes used as reverse types became even more stereotyped and divorced from the rôle of commentary on current events. The gold coinage, however, continued to exhibit more variety of design and to make use of different types at different mints, whereas the silver and even more so the bronze coinage was limited to a few types, repeated almost exactly at all the mints. The theme of reconstruction expressed by an emperor type inscribed *Restitutor Reipublicae* (Pl. 367) was a feature on most denominations and mints at the beginning of the reign but was soon replaced by the common siliqua type *Urbs Roma* in the West and in the smaller bronzes by types *Gloria Romanorum* (Pl. 368) and *Securitas Reipublicae*.

For a brief period in 365–366 the usurper Procopius, a distant kinsman of the emperor Julian, controlled the mints of Constantinople, Heraclea, Cyzicus and Nicomedia. The almost exclusive reverse type on the solidus, the siliqua and the small bronze is an emperor type inscribed *Reparatio Fel Temp*.

The coinage from 367 onwards is marked by the addition of Gratian, the son of Valentinian I, to the college of emperors. In silver and bronze the common types of the previous years continued to be issued and in the case of the senior emperors the post-367 issues are distinguishable only by the extremely elaborate series of mint-marks on the bronze. At the mint of Arelate, Gratian has a special type of his own, *Gloria Novi Saeculi* (Pl. 369). Solidi continued to be struck with some variety of reverse; the most common type in Western types carried over from the previous period showed two seated emperors with Victory behind them with inscription *Victoria Augg* (Pl. 370).

The death of Valentinian I in 375 and the proclamation of his young son, Valentinian II, as Augustus brought little change to the coinage, save the introduction of the portrait and titles of the new emperor but for the new college established in 387 on the death of Valens and the creation of Theodosius as emperor, with charge of the Eastern empire, a number of changes in coin types took place. Although on solidi from Western mints the Victory type of the previous period was retained, at Constantinople a new type, *Concordia Auggg*, showing Constantinopolis seated enthroned was introduced (Pl. 371). A similar type made its appearance on siliquae in the West alongside the existing *Urbs Roma* and another type, still with seated figure of Roma, but inscribed *Virtus Romanorum*. On bronze pieces, somewhat similar to the large coins of Julian's reform, new varieties of reverse included *Reparatio Reipub*, emperor raising kneeling woman (Pl. 372), and *Gloria Romanorum*, emperor in ship steered by Victory, or emperor with standard and captive, the latter reverses being struck by Eastern mints. The next-lower denomination of bronze continued the Concordia type with figures of either Constantinopolis or Roma, while the smallest bronzes commonly showed votive inscriptions.

In 383 Magnus Maximus who commanded in Britain was proclaimed emperor, crossed to Gaul, defeated and put to death the emperor Gratian. Maximus associated his young son Victor with himself as Augustus and they were initially recognized as Augusti in the West by Valentinian II and Theodosius. The latter in this year appointed his own son Arcadius an Augustus. In 387 Maximus invaded Italy but in the following year Theodosius defeated him near Aquileia and shortly afterwards Victor was slain in Gaul. Until the break in 387 the Gallic mints under Maximus struck for the other emperors also but the mints under the control of Theodosius and Valentinian gave scant recognition on the coinage to Maximus and Victor. At the beginning of the uprising Maximus re-opened for a brief period the mint at London which signed its coins *Aug*, the abbreviation for the name Augusta by which London at that time was known. The mint at Sirmium had closed towards the end of the previous period, and that at Siscia ceased operation about 387. Gold was struck much less frequently in this period; in the West most mints issued some solidi but in the East Constantinople alone produced gold coinage. This period saw the introduction of a new gold denomination, the tremissis, the third of the solidus, with a Victory type inscribed *Victoria Augustorum* (Pl. 373). The issue of silver, again with the exception of Constantinople, was also largely confined to the Western mints striking the Concordia and Virtus Romanorum types of the previous period (Pl. 374). On the bronze coinage the types of the larger denomination were retained with an additional emperor and captive variety, inscribed *Virtus Exerciti*. For the empress Flaccilla, wife of Theodosius, bronzes with reverse *Salus Reipublicae* showing either a figure of Victory or the empress (Pl. 375), a type already begun in the previous period, were struck more frequently. On the very smallest bronzes in the West appeared a new type *Spes Romanorum*, a camp-gate for Maximus and Victor (Pl. 376).

On the defeat of Maximus and Victor, Valentinian II, still nominally the senior emperor, was restored as Augustus in the West while Theodosius and Arcadius maintained charge of the Eastern provinces. Relatively small issues of gold were made from Western mints and at Thessalonica there was an issue of solidi with the Concordia reverse while silver, mainly in the form of siliquae with a Roma type, was confined to Western mints. The common bronze issues and the only issues from most Eastern mints were the smallest denominations with two main reverses *Victoria Auggg*, Victory with wreath and palm (Pl. 377), and *Salus Reipublicae*, Victory with trophy and captive (Pl. 378).

Peace was soon broken again in the West with the murder of Valentinian II in 392 and the proclamation of Eugenius the last of the emperors to follow a policy of active support for paganism. He quickly gained control of the West and Italy and in the mints under his control initially issued coinage in the name of Theodosius and Arcadius as well, but he was never recognized by Theodosius who once again invaded Italy and defeated Eugenius in 394. Following the death of Valentinian II, Theodosius advanced his younger son Honorius to the rank of Augustus. Eugenius issued gold from a number of his mints, principally solidi with the now traditional type of two emperors and Victory and large issues of silver siliquae with Roma type. The mint of Sirmium, reopened by Theodosius for his campaign against Eugenius, struck solidi with the Concordia type. In the West bronze issues were confined to the smallest denomination with Victory type but in the East, in addition to the small bronzes inscribed *Salus Reipublicae*, all the mints produced extensive issues of the larger bronzes with the various types inscribed *Gloria Romanorum* (Pl. 379).

DIVISION OF EMPIRE, A.D. 395–491

Although the empire had at times been divided into spheres of responsibility, as in the reign of Valerian and Gallienus in the mid third century and almost consistently from the tetrarchy of Diocletian onwards, there had almost always been one senior emperor to preserve unity. Theodosius was succeeded after his death in 395 by his sons Arcadius and Honorius who assumed responsibility for the East and West respectively, but in the changed political and military circumstances this division became a greater reality. Because of the decline of the West and the encroachment of the barbarian invaders who finally occupied all the Western provinces, the emperors of the East, which succeeded in maintaining itself, generally exercised a superiority. These conditions are reflected both in the coinage itself and in the history of the mints.

In the West solidi were struck chiefly in the Italian mints, including a new mint at Ravenna which now became the seat of the Imperial court. The sole reverse for the emperors, inscribed *Victoria Auggg* showed the emperor with standard and globe, treading down a captive (Pl. 380). The gold tremissis with type of Victory with wreath and palm was also struck by the Italian mints. All the Italian mints struck for both Arcadius and Honorius but Theodosius II, the son of Arcadius, who was appointed Augustus in 402 has gold coinage only at Ravenna. Constantius III, accepted as a colleague by Honorius in 421, issued solidi of the same type at Ravenna. The usurper Constantine III who was proclaimed in Britain in 407 and quickly gained control of Gaul issued his gold coinage from Trier, Lyons and Arles till his death in 411. His successor Jovinus used the same mints to strike solidi of similar type but inscribed *Restitutor Reip.* The amount of coinage in silver declined but siliquae were struck mainly by Italian mints for Arcadius and Honorius and by the Gallic mints for the usurpers in control there. A mint at

Barcelona in Spain struck siliquae with a Victory type during the short-lived usurpation of Maximus in 411. Priscus Attalus who held Rome briefly in 409–410 issued there, as well as solidi on the pattern of those of Honorius, siliquae with a Roma type inscribed *Invicta Roma Aeterna*. Johannes who reigned in 423–425 in succession to Honorius issued his gold and silver only from Ravenna. Bronze coinage was issued in this period mainly in the form of the smallest denomination with a Victory type.

In the East solidi for Arcadius and Honorius and later Theodosius II were struck only at Thessalonica and Constantinople, the reverse type being the seated figure of Constantinopolis inscribed *Concordia Augg(g)*. On solidi of the Eastern mints, the obverse portrait usually shows the young bust of the emperor in helmet and armour and holding spear and shield (Pl. 381) while Western solidi continue the traditional profile bust. Solidi from the Constantinople mint for Eudoxia, wife of Arcadius, show Victory seated writing ✸ on a shield with an inscription *Salus Reipublicae* (Pl. 382). Constantinople was practically the only mint to issue silver in this period, chiefly siliquae with votive inscriptions for Theodosius II. Bronze, however, was struck by all the Eastern mints in various denominations. A widespread issue of the larger bronze for Arcadius and Honorius showed emperor with spear and shield, crowned by Victory (Pl. 383), while there were common issues for Honorius and Theodosius II of the medium denomination with varying emperor types inscribed *Gloria Romanorum* and of the smallest denomination inscribed *Glor Orvis Terrar*.

In contrast to the complexities of the first quarter of the fifth century with coinage in the names of a number of associate or usurping emperors, the outline of the second quarter emerges with some clarity; for the West had only one emperor, Valentinian III from 425 to 455, and in the East the reign of Theodosius II continued to 450 when he was succeeded by Marcian. The system of mints producing coinage for these emperors also became much contracted, reflecting both the loss of a number of mints in the Western provinces to the control of the barbarian invaders and the worsening economic conditions in both West and East.

In the West the mints in Gaul and Lyons and Arelate ceased to function and from Trier there was only a small coinage of silver siliquae and small bronze for Valentinian III. Practically all the coinage of the West was struck at Rome and only some issues of solidi from Ravenna. Solidi retained the traditional inscription *Victoria Auggg* but showed as a type the emperor holding a long cross and treading down a serpent (Pl. 384). The tremissis was issued with a simple type of cross in wreath as well as the traditional Victory type. Solidi were struck for the ladies of Valentinian III's family, for his mother Galla Placidia, his sister Honoria and his wife Eudoxia. Silver siliquae of Valentinian III with a conventional seated-Roma type were a quite small issue but bronze coinage of small denomination was still struck in some quantity. For Valentinian there was a Victory type and a type of camp-gate with inscription *Vot Pub* and for Galla Placidia *Salus Reipublicae* with type, a cross.

In the Eastern empire extensive issues of solidi were produced at Constantinople. Amongst the most common reverses were a long cross supported by Victory with a votive inscription *Vot xx Mult xxx* and a seated figure of Roma accompanied by the legend *Imp xxxxii Cos xvii Pp* (Pl. 385). Such solidi were issued by Theodosius II in his own name and for his sister Pulcheria, his wife Eudocia, his fellow emperor Valentinian III and the latter's mother Galla Placidia. Comparatively rare silver issues, mainly siliquae, also from Constantinople only, had for Theodosius usually a votive reverse and for Eudocia and Pulcheria a simple cross in wreath. Bronze coinage, almost exclusively in the form of the smallest denomination as in the West, was struck by other Eastern mints as well as Constantinople. Common reverses for Theodosius include yet another Victory type but with inscription *Concordia Aug* and a cross in wreath with no legend and for the empresses Eudocia and Pulcheria at Constantinople another *Concordia Aug* reverse with a figure of the enthroned empress.

Coinage for Marcian who succeeded Theodosius II in 450 was struck in gold at Rome and Ravenna with the types of Valentinian III's coinage. In the East, his main reverse on solidi was that of a long cross supported by Victory as on solidi of Theodosius II but now inscribed *Victoria Auggg* (Pl. 386) while tremisses used the reverses, now standard for this denomination, either Victory or a cross in a wreath. Silver issues were small and on the small bronze coins the sole reverse types were variations of the emperor's monogram, a type already introduced under Theodosius II.

The coinage of the concluding decades of the empire gains variety only from the swift succession of emperors, particularly in the West, for the number of mints is restricted and the reverse types remarkably stereotyped. In the West the only mints active were Rome, Ravenna and Milan in Italy and Arles in Gaul briefly between 455 and 465 while in the East gold and silver issues were restricted to Constantinople and the small bronze coinage at other Eastern mints ceased in the reign of Leo I.

The reverse *Victoria Auggg* with emperor treading down a serpent remained the sole type on solidi at Western mints after the death of Valentinian III in 455. It appeared on the gold of Marcian the Eastern emperor whose reign continued till 457, for the Western emperors Petronius Maximus (455), Avitus (455–456), Majorian (457–461), Libius Severus (461–465) and for Leo I who succeeded in the

East in 457. The tremissis when struck was of the variety with cross in wreath on the reverse. The obverse bust was normally a draped and cuirassed bust with pearl diadem on the head in profile except for Majorian, who had an unusual helmeted bust (Pl. 387). Anthemius, emperor in the West from 467 to 472, issued solidi with different reverses inscribed *Salus Reipublicae*; the type at Rome showed three emperors holding a globe and at Ravenna two emperors supporting a long cross. The signature of the mints on the reverse which from the later fourth century had maintained the standard form of the mint initials in the field and COMOB in the exergue, e.g. $\frac{\text{R/M}}{\text{COMOB}}$ at Rome, for Anthemius combined these elements in the exergue, e.g. CORMOB. Olybrius in 472 also introduced a new reverse on the solidi, a cross with inscription *Salus Mundi* (Pl. 388). The emperors Glycerius (473–474) and Julius Nepos (474–475) and the last of the emperors Romulus Augustus (475–476) reverted to the conventional *Victoria Auggg* reverse type (Pl. 389). This reverse was also used for coinage of contemporary Eastern emperors struck in Italian mints down to Zeno (476–491).

The small issues of silver siliquae which were struck in the West had as a type the Christian symbol ✷ in a wreath. Small bronze coinage went on being issued at Rome for some of the emperors, the reverses, as in the case of Libius Severus and Anthemius, adopting the Eastern fashion of a monogram of the emperor's name. After the fall of the last emperor when Rome was controlled by the Ostrogothic king, Theoderic, a series of large bronzes was struck in the name of the Eastern emperor Zeno with, as reverse types, a figure of Roma inscribed *Invicta Roma* (Pl. 390) or types of Victory or wolf and twins without inscription.

In the Eastern empire, the reverse type on gold solidi continued to be *Victoria Auggg*, a long cross supported by Victory. It was struck both for the emperors and for their wives, for Leo I (457–474) and his wife Verina, for Leo II and Zeno (474–475), Basiliscus and his son Marcus (475–476), for Zeno in his second reign (476–491) as well as for Zenonis, wife of Basiliscus, and Ariadne, wife of Zeno. The tremissis was issued by most of the emperors with the Victory-type reverse. Silver issues were extremely rare but bronze coinage was still struck in some quantity. Leo I issued a slightly larger bronze coinage at Constantinople with a type of emperor holding standard and spurning captive, with misspelled legends *Virtus Exrciti* or *Salus Rpublica* and the usual small bronzes both at Constantinople and the other mints in Asia with a punning type of a lion (Pl. 391). For the emperors after Leo only Constantinople struck bronze coins and only the small denomination with the monogram of the emperor as its type.

Here the story of the Roman coinage within the context of an empire extending across the Mediterranean world comes to an end. The Western provinces of

Britain, Gaul, Spain and even Italy had fallen to the control of invaders and their coinage, though deriving from that of the Roman empire, forms the beginning of the coinage of mediaeval Europe. In the East the empire lived on, but its coinage, taking new forms in the reign of Anastasius (491–518), becomes that of the Byzantine empire and also a part of the mediaeval coinage.

EUROPE

★

Europe

THE beginning of European history and European coinage is, by tradition, linked with the deposition in 476 of Romulus Augustus, the last of the Roman emperors in the West but, although this is a convenient milestone in history, the Roman tradition continued to wield influence in the Dark Ages in the matter of coinage as in other fields. In the East, the Eastern empire, known henceforth in history as the Byzantine empire, lived on for almost another millennium, preserving and indeed fossilizing something of the Roman coinage tradition and influencing the development of coinage both in eastern Europe and in western Asia. The barbarian kingdoms in western Europe in Italy, Spain and Gaul used a coinage imitating principally only one denomination of the Roman imperial coinage, the gold tremissis, until about the eighth century.

In most of western Europe gold coinage was replaced, from the eighth century, by coinage of the silver penny, known in different countries by varying forms of the term denier, derived from the Roman denarius. This single denomination lasted until the thirteenth century, when improving trade and economic conditions made possible and necessary the introduction of larger silver pieces of the groat category, of value 4 pennies. The same century saw the return of gold to the majority of European currencies. One of the consequences of the discovery of the New World at the end of the fifteenth century was a vast increase in the supply of bullion for coinage, resulting in the production of even larger pieces of currency such as the Spanish silver dollar or piece of 8 reales. At about the same time the increased exploitation of the silver mines in central Europe gave rise to new large silver coins known as thalers, a term first applied to the large silver coins struck by the Counts of Schlick in Bohemia from the silver from Joachimsthal.

The modern coinage of Europe from the sixteenth century onwards was increasingly produced by machine methods in contrast to the striking of coins by hand by hammer, the method which had persisted since the invention of coinage. The coinage of mediaeval Europe is notable for the great diversity of authorities who struck coins—kings, emperors, feudal and ecclesiastical lords—but in the modern period the replacement of these multifarious coinage authorities by the much smaller number of great national states is reflected by fewer and more stereotyped coinages. The diversity and attractiveness of the most modern coinages has been further lessened by the economic circumstances which have prevailed since the first world war and the withdrawal of gold as a medium of coinage and the increased use of paper money. Since the last world war paper money has increased at the expense of coinage, much of which is now in the form of token or fiduciary pieces, often in base metals which do not lend themselves to the reproduction of good coin design.

BYZANTIUM AND THE EASTERN MEDITERRANEAN

THE BYZANTINE EMPIRE

The Eastern Roman empire which had existed as a more or less separate entity from the end of the fourth century survived the barbarian inroads and the economic collapse of the fifth century which brought disruption to the Western empire. Although the capital of the Eastern empire continued throughout its history to bear the name of Constantinople given to it by its founder, Constantine the Great, by one of the oddities of history the term traditionally applied to the Eastern empire is derived not from Constantinople but from the Greek city of Byzantium where Constantine founded his new city. The part played by the Byzantine empire in the history and development of coinage is a reflection of its more general rôle in the history of Western civilization. The Eastern empire maintained unchanged much of the Roman tradition, in coinage as in other fields, until the reviving civilization of the West was in a state to absorb its lessons.

For centuries the Byzantine empire maintained its frontiers and under Justinian I in the sixth century even regained some of the provinces of the Western empire; it interposed a barrier between Europe and Islam and, to some extent at least, exercised a check on the incursions of Slavs and Magyars into Europe from the East. Though in the course of the centuries the territory and the political influence of the Byzantine empire shrank until in the end the emperors controlled little more than Constantinople and the Peloponnese, almost a thousand years intervened between the sack of Rome by the Vandals and the capture of Constantinople by the Ottoman Turks in 1453. These two events traditionally mark the beginning and the end of the mediaeval history of the West and, throughout the whole period, the influence of Byzantium made itself felt to greater or less degree on the development of civilization. It has been thought appropriate to describe its coinage at the beginning of the European section so that its influence on other coinages can be subsequently traced. The early coinages of the new barbarian kingdoms in Italy, Spain and Gaul were inspired by Byzantine models and, later, in south-eastern Europe the Serbian and Bulgarian coinages were direct derivatives from Byzantium. The Latin kingdoms in the Orient founded by the Crusaders drew much of the inspiration of their coinage from the familiar Byzantine issues and even the early stages of Islamic coinage were little more than adaptations of Byzantine types.

The beginning of the Byzantine series proper dates from the reform of the bronze coinage by Anastasius in 498 but the form of the precious-metal coinage underwent only gradual change. In gold the principal denomination continued to be the solidus of 4·4 gm. of the late Roman empire but by contemporary authorities it was normally described as the nomisma. Since this Byzantine gold piece furnished the main international gold currency in Europe till the thirteenth century, it was often described in the rest of Europe by some form of the term 'bezant'. This nomisma continued to be struck of good metal and to maintain its weight till the reign of Michael VII in 1071 when it tended to become an electrum piece, an alloy of gold and silver. In the early eleventh century a change took place in the fabric and weight of the nomisma. For several reigns a nomisma of the old rather thick fabric but of a weight falling to about 4 gm. was struck alongside a new nomisma of the traditional weight of 4·4 gm., but of thinner, spread fabric of an unusual saucer-like shape, usually referred to as scyphate. Under Alexius I, about 1081, the old nomisma disappeared, as did the consistent high standard of fineness. In this and subsequent reigns until towards the end of the series nomismata were struck in a variety of metals; there were usually some issues in good gold but the majority were either of electrum, billon or even ordinary bronze. In the early centuries of the coinage subdivisions of the nomisma were struck, the half-piece or semissis somewhat infrequently, the tremissis or third more commonly, but these denominations became less regularly issued after Constantine V (741–775) and disappeared completely in the tenth century.

Silver coinage had been rare in the later Roman empire and continued to be equally rare in the Byzantine series. The chief silver coin of about 4·5 gm., the miliarense, was issued only sporadically in the early reigns and was replaced by Heraclius in the early seventh century by a new piece, the hexagram (*c.* 6 gm.). After a lapse of silver coinage Constantine V introduced a new silver coin of about 3 gm., of distinctive flat fabric and with a reverse type always consisting of inscription only. Alexius I abandoned this type in favour of a silver piece of small, thick fabric and about the beginning of the fourteenth century under Andronicus

II came yet another new silver piece, copying both the small, neat fabric and the types of the Venetian grosso. From John V (1341–91) till the end of the series the principal coinage was in rather poor silver with a flat spread fabric.

The reform of Anastasius in 498 produced a new type of bronze coinage forming one of the most distinctive features of the Byzantine series. The innovation lay in the adoption of a bold mark of value, normally in Greek numerals, as the main reverse type. The series consisted of pieces marked with M (40 nummia), K (20), I (10) and E (5). At some of the provincial mints less usual forms are found in some reigns: at Alexandria I B (12), Γ (3) and ΛΓ (33); at Thessalonica I S (16), H (8), Δ (4), Γ (3) and B (2) and at some of the mints the value was indicated by Roman numerals, e.g. XXXX for 40 nummia.

Although the Byzantine coinage was produced for a largely Greek-speaking population, the tradition of Latin inscriptions on the coins continued firm till the beginning of the ninth century when the use of Greek began to infiltrate, but it was not till the reign of Isaac I (1057) that Latin finally disappeared from the coinage.

At the beginning of the Byzantine coinage under Anastasius only three of the Eastern mints which functioned in the late Roman empire were active, namely Constantinople, Nicomedia and Antioch. Under Justin I Thessalonica and Cyzicus were brought back into action, while the reconquests of Justinian I raised the number of mints to some dozen, including centres with such long histories of coin production as Alexandria, Carthage and Rome. From the time of Constans II the active mints dropped sharply in number to five or six and from the early ninth century the official series emanated in practice only from Constantinople. The considerable vicissitudes in the history of the mints will, however, best appear in the more detailed discussion of the development and history of the coinage.

ANASTASIUS TO CONSTANTINE IV, 498–685

This first group of Byzantine coins is defined by a certain unity of treatment of both obverse and reverse types. The tendency, though not an exclusive one, is to depict the emperor or emperors in some form of military dress on the obverse, while the reverse types consist of personifications, usually of Victory or of representations of the cross and are noticeably deficient in those figures of Christ or the saints which are commonly regarded as the essential types of Byzantine coinage.

The coinage in precious metals was struck for Anastasius at the mint of Constantinople only. As the types on the gold denominations remained unchanged throughout the reign it is difficult to distinguish the pieces issued between the beginning of the reign in 491 and the reform of the bronze coinage in 498 from those struck after that date. On the solidus the emperor is portrayed in the conventional late Roman style, a facing bust with head turned slightly to the right, helmeted, with shield at left shoulder and spear over right shoulder. The reverse shows Victory standing to the left, holding a long sceptre terminating in a Christogram and although there was but one emperor the inscription still reads *Victoria auggg*. The mint-mark consisted of a star in the left field and CONOB in the exergue, while the Greek numeral indicating the *officina* was added at the end of the reverse inscription (Pl. 392). In keeping with the earlier fifth-century tradition the obverse of the semis and the tremissis showed the diademed and cuirassed bust of the emperor in profile. The reverse types also continued the earlier conventions for these denominations; on the semis a seated Victory writes a votive inscription on a shield, on the tremissis was a facing Victory, holding wreath and globe. Rare silver coins also had a profile portrait of the emperor and on the reverse a wreath enclosing a votive inscription.

The new bronze coinage on which the reverse consisted primarily of a mark of value was struck at Nicomedia and Antioch, as well as at Constantinople, though not all the four denominations have been recorded from each of the mints. Under Anastasius the denominations M, K and I were struck in two series, a heavy and a lighter, distinguishable also to the eye by their large or small module. The obverse type on all these denominations was the profile bust of the emperor. At Constantinople the major bronze piece of 40 nummia had on the reverse, in addition to the mark of value M, a star to left and right, a cross above, the *officina* letter below and the mint signature CON in the exergue (Pl. 393). In the series of large module the coins of 20 nummia had the mark of value K on the reverse, flanked by a long cross and the *officina* letter, on the 10 nummia coins the Greek numeral I had a pellet on either side, a cross above and an inscription reading *Concord*. The series of small module presenting similar features include a 5 nummia piece on which appeared E with two pellets and an *officina* letter. On all but the 40 nummia piece in this series the mint name was omitted.

At Nicomedia there were only M pieces of the larger module. The distinguishing feature of these pieces and of M pieces of the smaller module, in addition to the mint name, was the disposal of stars to left, right and centre. On the lower denominations, to the left of the mark K a long cross divided the letters N I as did the mark I itself on the 10 nummia pieces. The 40 nummia coins at Antioch had a cross to left, to right and above the M, an *officina* letter below and the mint signature ANTX in the exergue. The only other denomination at Antioch was the 5 nummia where to the right of the mark E, the *officina* letter was disposed between the letters of the signature AN.

Justin I, 518–527

The coinage of Justin followed closely the pattern established by Anastasius. The three denominations in gold and somewhat rare silver were struck only at Constantinople but bronze was issued not only by the three mints active under Anastasius but also by Thessalonica and by Cyzicus, which now resumed minting. The types on the smaller gold pieces remained unchanged but the reverse of the solidus now showed a facing Victory, holding a long cross and a cross on globe, a type which was to be much imitated in the barbarian kingdoms of the West (Pl. 394). Rare silver pieces with the emperor's profile bust on the obverse also showed the standing emperor, nimbate and holding globe or spear and globe on the reverse inscribed *Gloria Romanorum*.

At Constantinople bronzes of the large module were struck only with marks of value M and K. These two larger denominations were rarely struck in the small module, the pieces with I in small amount and only the 5 nummia coins with E in any quantity. On rare pieces with I the standing figure of the emperor occupies the obverse and on the 5 nummia the reverse consisted of ✹ flanked by the *officina* letter and the mark of value E. Thessalonica struck only pieces with M, Nicomedia and Cyzicus only M and K but Antioch issued all four denominations. The 5 nummia coin here was unusual in that the mark of value E was only a minor part of the design which showed the Tyche of Antioch in a distyle shrine with the river-god Orontes at her feet.

JUSTIN I AND JUSTINIAN I, 527

Justin adopted his nephew, Justinian, as his co-emperor in April 527 and for this brief reign, terminated by Justin's death in August, a rare coinage in gold and bronze has survived. In gold the solidus is the only known denomination. On this the reverse type of Justin's sole reign was used again but the obverse set a new style for Byzantine coinage in showing the figures of both emperors. They are represented seated, both nimbate and wearing long robes with both hands clasped on breast or with globe in left hand and right hand on breast. Bronzes with a similar obverse to that of the gold include the 40 nummia at Constantinople and the 20 and 5 nummia at Antioch.

JUSTINIAN I, 527–565

The reign of Justinian witnessed great reconquests of Western provinces which had fallen to the barbarian invaders in the fifth century. In 533 North Africa was invaded and the Vandals under Gelimer were defeated at the battle of Decimum by Justinian's general, Belisarius. In the next year Sicily was retaken and the war carried into Italy itself, held by the Ostrogoths, and Rome was captured in 536. Sardinia and Corsica were restored to the empire and some control regained in south-eastern Spain. It was not, however, until the defeat of the Ostrogothic king, Baduila, by Narses in 553 that Italy was finally secured. This expansion of the empire necessitated an extension of the mint system, mainly by the re-establishment of mints in cities which had earlier possessed imperial mints. In the East the mint at Alexandria resumed the striking of bronze coins, while, in the wake of the conquests, mints were opened at Carthage, in Sicily, at Ravenna and Rome itself.

As in earlier reigns, gold coinage was struck by Justinian principally at Constantinople. The semissis and tremissis maintained their conventional types and the solidus in the earlier part of the reign continued to have the three-quarter-facing bust of the emperor with spear and shield on the obverse and a facing Victory holding long cross and cross on globe on the reverse. A variant reverse showed Victory to left holding a globe surmounted by ✳. In April 538 new types were introduced for the solidus. On the obverse the helmeted bust of Justinian was depicted, completely full-face, holding a cross on globe in his right hand and a decorated shield at his left shoulder. A facing Victory on the reverse held a long cross, the top in the form of P and a cross on globe. A multiple gold piece, equivalent to thirty-six solidi, was struck in 534 in connection with the triumph celebrated by Belisarius for his conquest of North Africa. The obverse was an enlarged version of that on the earlier solidi; the reverse, inscribed *Salus et Gloria Romanorum*, showed the emperor on horse-back, preceded by Victory. This unique piece was, unfortunately, stolen in the theft of pieces from the Paris Cabinet in 1831. The rare silver pieces from Constantinople had the standing, nimbate figure of the emperor as in the preceding reign. The mint at Carthage, re-opened about 534, issued solidi of slightly different style and some silver with either votive reverses or a reverse consisting of a cross, the top terminating in P and the letters alpha and omega to left and right.

The earlier bronze coins of Justinian were of the usual types, a profile bust on obverse and mark of value on reverse. The new full-face bust noted on solidi was adopted for bronze also in 538 and a new feature was introduced on the reverse as well. This consisted of a date in the form of the word *Anno* inscribed vertically to the left of the sign of value and the appropriate numeral to the right (Pl. 395). Thessalonica struck no bronzes of the early variety and the issues after 538 included such unusual denominations as I S (16), H (8), Δ (4), Γ (3) and B (2). After the great earthquake of 528 which damaged the city, Antioch assumed the name Theoupolis which became henceforth the mint-signature also. A series of bronzes here before 539 had a novel obverse type, the emperor seated facing, enthroned. Bronzes issued from Alexandria after decades of inactivity were of unusual denominations—ΑΓ (33), IS (12), S (6) and Γ (3). The bronzes of the new or reopened mints in the West were all of a somewhat outré style. Carthage issued pieces with standard types but some of the smaller denominations departed from the conventional patterns. The reverse of 10 nummia pieces had a facing figure of Victory and a Victory inscription with the mark of value X between two stars in the exergue. On small bronzes attributed to a mint in Sicily the reverse consisted of a cross with a star in each angle.

Justin II, 565–578

The enlarged system of mints brought into action by Justinian continued to coin for his nephew and successor, Justin II. In the gold coinage from Constantinople the smaller denominations are indistinguishable in types and inscriptions from those of Justinian but are of markedly less finished style. Two changes were effected by Justin II in the types of the solidus; the full-face bust on the obverse held a globe, surmounted not by a cross but by a figure of Victory and the reverse, though still inscribed *Victoria Auggg*, substituted for Victory the seated figure of Constantinopolis, holding long sceptre and cross on globe. A second series of gold of different fabric and higher relief has been attributed to Carthage. Rare silver coins from the mint of Constantinople had the obverse type most commonly associated with this reign, the seated, nimbate figures of Justin and his empress, Sophia. The reverse, a half-length figure of Constantinopolis with spear and globe, was inscribed *Salus Mundi*. Silver also was issued by Carthage with types, the emperor's facing bust and inscription, *Felix Res Publ* in a wreath.

At some mints occasional issues of bronze had the bust of Justin only but the predominating obverse type honoured both emperor and empress. They appeared nimbate, seated facing on a double throne, Justin holding a cross on globe and Sophia a cruciform sceptre (Pl. 396). In this reign Carthage again did not always conform to pattern. The obverse presented only the busts and not the full-length figures of Justin and Sophia, with, below, the salutation *Vita* (long life). On some denominations the abbreviation NM (nummia) was incorporated in the reverse design.

TIBERIUS II, 578–582

Justin II had appointed Tiberius Constantine as his Caesar and heir in 574 but coinage in his name was not struck until his accession in 578. A new feature on his gold coinage from Constantinople was the use of the cross as the sole reverse type on all denominations. The cross, shown at the top of a flight of four steps, most probably represented the cross of Calvary on its eminence within the church of the Holy Sepulchre in Jerusalem. Tiberius was represented not only by the conventional facing bust holding cross on globe but also by a portrait showing him in the robes of a consul and holding the consular insignia, the *mappa* and eagle-tipped sceptre (Pl. 397). Silver pieces from Carthage had as reverse types ✳ within a wreath or a cross potent with inscription *Lux Mundi*.

On bronze coins a third type of obverse was used in addition to the two described above. This showed the bust of Tiberius, devoid of additional attributes such as a globe. The reverse type also produced a number of modifications, principally the use of a cursive M on the 40 nummia pieces. A new denomination also made its appearance, the 30 nummia piece, marked not by a Greek numeral but by a Roman XXX. Similarly at some mints XX and X were used in place of the more usual Greek numerals and a new symbol Ч replaced E on the 5 nummia coins.

Maurice Tiberius, 582–602

Shortly before his death in 582 Tiberius Constantine appointed as his successor the general Maurice to whom he married his daughter Constantina. All the mints active in the preceding reigns struck for Maurice with the addition of a mint at Cherson which may have produced some bronze pieces in rather crude style for Justinian but is now definitely identified by its signature on the coins of Maurice. On solidi struck at Constantinople Victory holding cross and globe was restored to the reverse while Maurice was represented by the conventional full-face bust, holding cross and globe and shield, and wearing either a helmet or a crown. Rare solidi commemorating the consulship of Maurice show him seated holding the consular *mappa* and a cross in place of the eagle-tipped sceptre. The semissis and tremissis both had a profile bust and reverse of Victory and cross respectively. The only silver of the reign was issued by the mint at Carthage. The types were the facing, helmeted bust of the emperor and either a small cross with inscription *Salus Mundi* or a cross on steps flanked by alpha and omega, all within a wreath. Carthage also issued silver in the name of the young Theodosius, the son and colleague of Maurice, probably in 596–597 when Maurice made a will bequeathing the empire to Theodosius. These coins had the facing portrait of Theodosius on obverse and on reverse the inscription *Amenitas Dei* or the busts of Maurice and Constantina.

The obverses of the bronze coinage were of the same types as on the gold but the consular portrait was shown holding eagle-tipped sceptre, not cross. On the 40 nummia coins the cursive form of M used by Tiberius II was not continued. An unusual feature on bronzes at Carthage was the inclusion, on the reverse, of the letters NM as an abbreviation for nummia while one series of 20 nummia coins carried a further inscription IND III—indiction year 3, i.e. 584–585. Bronzes of rather rough fabric depicting the standing figures of Maurice and Constantina on the obverse and of Theodosius beside the mark of value on the reverse were issued in two groups. On one the mint-name Cherson is inscribed on the obverse; on the second appears the emperor's name and, though the mint is not mentioned, fabric and style identify it as Cherson also. As well as the usual 40 nummia piece marked M there were denominations marked H or Δ, indicating, in this case, pieces of either 8 or 4 pentanummia, that is 40 or 20 nummia. The bronzes struck for Maurice in Sicily were signed with the name *Sicilia* disposed on the field of the coin or the abbreviation *Cat* for the actual mint, *Catana*.

Phocas, 602–610

An army revolt in 602 placed Phocas on the throne and was followed by the execution of Maurice and all his family. The coinage struck for Phocas by all the mints of the preceding reign except Cherson continued the now well-established pattern of denominations and types with some few departures from convention. The facing bust of Phocas, shown either with cross on globe or with consular insignia, the eagle-tipped sceptre being again replaced by a cross, is bearded in contrast to the portraits of earlier emperors. Earlier bronze coins had, on the obverse, the standing figures of Phocas and his empress, Leontia, the latter always being nimbate, but later issues presented the consular bust of the emperor only.

The reverse of the 40 nummia coins was again marked by a cursive M on the joint issues with Leontia. On the issues with Phocas alone the value was indicated on the reverse by Roman numerals from XXXX downwards.

Heraclius, 610–641

The tyranny of Phocas was brought to an end in the autumn of 610 when Heraclius, son of the Exarch of Africa, crossed with a fleet from Carthage to Constantinople; Phocas was put to death and Heraclius proclaimed emperor. The reign of Heraclius saw the beginning of Byzantine losses in the east. In the early years of the reign Syria and Palestine were overrun by the Persians, in 614 Jerusalem was captured and the Holy Cross removed to Persia and in 617 Alexandria in Egypt was captured. In a series of campaigns between 622 and 628, however, Heraclius regained the lost provinces and recovered the Holy Cross, which he replaced in Jerusalem in 629. But now the empire had to face a new enemy in the east, the rising power of Islam which by 638 had seized the province of Syria and was threatening Egypt. Little of all these happenings was reflected in the coinage except for the intermission of activity at the mints overrun. Two additional mints, however, at Isauria and Cyprus came into use briefly in this reign for the issue of bronze coin.

The coinage of Heraclius falls into three groups, that of Heraclius as sole ruler between 610 and 613, of Heraclius and his son Heraclius Constantine between 613 and 638 and of these two together with the younger son, Heraclonas, from 638. Solidi of Heraclius at Constantinople had as a consistent reverse type the cross on steps linked to a variety of obverses. Early pieces showed Heraclius, alone, first with a very Phocas-like portrait, later with a more individual representation. On the obverses for Heraclius and Constantine the youth and junior status of the son were emphasized by the smallness of his bust (Pl. 398) and on the later pieces, where the obverse was occupied by the standing figure of Heraclius and his two sons, the figures are of noticeably different size. A new silver coin, the hexagram or double miliaresion, first coined in 615, had as obverse either the seated figures of Heraclius and Constantine or later, when Heraclonas also became an Augustus, three standing figures. The reverse, a cross on a globe set on steps, inscribed *Deus adiuta Romanis* (O God, help the Romans), may have reference to the capture of Jerusalem and the removal of the Holy Cross in 614 (Pl. 399). A series of gold coins of similar types to those of Heraclius and Heraclius with Constantine at Constantinople but of rougher style and of thick, dumpy fabric were struck at Carthage (Pl. 400).

Bronze coinage had similar varieties of obverse as had the precious metals: the bust of Heraclius, the standing figures of Heraclius and Constantine, three standing figures—either the two emperors together with the empress Martina or with Heraclonas. An unusual coin of 20 nummia at Carthage showed on obverse the standing figure of Heraclius with cross and globe and the first purely Greek inscription on the Byzantine coinage, ἐν τούτῳ νίκας, a rendering of the Latin *in hoc signo victor eris* (in this sign shalt thou conquer) connected with Constantine's vision before the battle of the Milvian Bridge. Much of the bronze coinage of Heraclius was produced by overstriking earlier pieces and this is particularly evident on the bronzes struck in Sicily.

Constans II, 641–668

The death of Heraclius in 641 was followed within a few months by the death of his eldest son Heraclius Constantine, the expulsion of the empress Martina and her son, Heraclonas, and the proclamation of Constantine III, the son of Heraclius Constantine. Although the emperor's name appears clearly on the coins as Constantine he is known to history by the name of Constans II. The reign saw an abrupt contraction of the mint system from the twelve mints active under Heraclius to only five—Constantinople and the four Western mints at Carthage, in Sicily, at Rome and Ravenna.

The coinage of Constans, like that of Heraclius, falls into three groups as additional members of his family were raised in status. The pattern is exemplified by the coinage of solidi at Constantinople which had a consistent reverse, a cross on steps. From the beginning of the reign until 654 when Constans' son, Constantine IV, was made an Augustus the obverse type showed the bust of Constans only, at first with a short, later with a much larger beard. From 654 the busts of the two emperors occupied the obverse together and, from the elevation of the younger sons, Heraclius and Tiberius, to the rank of Caesar in 659, solidi carried the busts of the seniors on the obverse and the standing figures of the Caesars on either side of the cross on the reverse (Pl. 401), or Constans alone on the obverse and the three sons standing on the reverse. The semissis and tremissis were still struck with a profile portrait of Constans but in a style far removed from that of the Roman period. The hexagram in silver, repeating the *Deus adiuta Romanis* type of Heraclius, disposed the imperial figures as on the three groups of the gold. The bronze, now only of small module, was restricted almost entirely to 40 nummia pieces, marked by both angular and cursive M. Here too the several groups have similar combinations of the imperial family, mostly shown as standing figures.

Much of the bronze coinage, restruck on earlier pieces, was marked *Ananeos*, an abbreviation of the Greek ἀνανέωσις—renovation.

At Carthage gold was also struck in quantity. One series covering the first two groups up to 659 was in a thick, dumpy fabric but a second series in a flat fabric extended through all three groups. Smaller gold denominations of this latter fabric are also attributed to this mint. On the bronze the emperors were mostly represented by busts, not standing figures, and the mark of value was usually denoted by Roman numerals. The long series of bronzes struck in Sicily are notable for the clumsy marks of value and the ogre-like portrait of Constans with a long beard. In Italy solidi of a different, neater style have been attributed to Rome, whose signature as well as that of Ravenna appears on some bronze issues.

Constantine IV, 668–685

Constantine IV who succeeded on the murder of his father in Sicily struck a coinage very similar to that of his father in respect of mints and denominations, though there were a number of changes in type, particularly on the obverse. Constantine IV, known to history as Pogonatus, the bearded, appeared on his early coins quite beardless and even the later bearded portraits did not show him with such a luxuriant beard as Constans II or Heraclius.

His brothers Heraclius and Tiberius were associated with Constantine on his coinage until their deposition in 680, and were represented as standing figures on the reverses. The armoured bust with helmet, spear and shield, last used under Justinian I, by which Constantine is always represented may reflect the military flavour of the reign which witnessed a successful defeat of an Islamic attack on the capital. On the gold of Constantinople the reverse still showed the cross on steps, flanked by the figures of Heraclius and Tiberius, up to 680. The brothers appeared also on the reverse of the silver hexagram with its now traditional types and inscription. Bronze coinage was of large module, restruck on old flans of Justinian I.

Gold attributed to Carthage, of the two distinct fabrics noted in the two preceding reigns, was probably the product of two distinct mints. Bronze from Carthage was struck only rarely but the Sicilian series, close in fabric and style to that of Constans, was a fairly extensive issue. A series of gold in the distinctive Italian style was struck for Constantine as well as bronzes from Rome (Pl. 402) and Ravenna.

The territorial losses of the empire from the time of Heraclius onwards resulted in the loss of a large number of mints and the present period opened with only three imperial mints at Constantinople, Carthage and in Sicily. Coinage of identical types continued to be struck in Italy but is probably not to be regarded as a true imperial issue. From the time of Justinian II there was no bronze coinage signed by Italian mints. By the end of this period Carthage and Sicily were both lost and the sole remaining mint was that of Constantinople. This period also saw the almost complete extinction of bronze coinage. Some attempt had been made in the previous two centuries at realistic portraits, but from the reign of Justinian II the portrait became more and more conventionalized. The outstanding novelty, typologically, was the introduction of representations of Christ.

Iustinian II (First reign), 685–695

The coinage of Justinian II who succeeded his father Constantine IV falls into three clear groups. The first series of gold coins continued the cross on steps reverse but the emperor was portrayed not armoured and helmeted but in mantle and crown. On the second group the obverse was changed to a standing figure of the emperor grasping a cross set on steps and the obverse inscription was altered from the traditional form *D Iustinianus Pe Au* (Perpetuus Augustus) *to D Iustinianus Serv(us) Christi*. On the reverse appeared the facing bust of Christ with long hair and beard, placed against a cross and inscribed *Ihs Christus Rex Regnantium* (Pl. 403). On the smaller gold pieces of which only the tremissis was regularly struck the tradition of a profile bust on the obverse came to an end, being replaced by the appropriate variety of obverse as on the solidi. The conventional reverse and inscription was used on the hexagram of the first coinage but thereafter this denomination also used the standard types used on the gold. Only extremely rare bronze coins of this reign have survived.

Gold struck in North Africa was again of the two distinct fabrics. Solidi of the first two coinages were struck in the thick fabric but solidi and smaller pieces of only the first type in the flat fabric. Practically no bronze was issued at Carthage and Sicilian pieces with their typical widely spread mark of value were not plentiful. Gold coinage of the special style associated with Rome and Italy reproduced the Constantinopolitan types with the exception of the second group.

Leontius II, 695–698

Leontius, an army commander, seized power in 695 and banished Justinian II. For long no coinage was attributed to this emperor, though he is well attested in history, but comparatively recently a series previously attributed to Leo III has been identified as the coinage of Leontius. These pieces are indeed inscribed with the title *D Leon Pe Au*, but they portray a burly and totally different figure to that of the other series with a similar title but properly ascribed to Leo III since they show him in association with his son Constantine V. The gold of Leontius reverted to the cross-on-steps reverse with its conventional inscription *Victoria Augg* and has on obverse the facing bust of the emperor holding either the consular *mappa* and cross on globe or the latter only in his right hand. Pieces with similar types were struck in Rome and very rare bronze has the signature of Ravenna.

Tiberius III, 698–705

The Byzantine forces, ejected from North Africa by the Arabs, mutinied and proclaimed emperor their admiral, Apsimarus, who assumed the official name of Tiberius. On his somewhat rare coinage, practically restricted to gold, the typical obverse portrait showed the bust of Tiberius, crowned and in cuirass and holding a transverse spear and shield. Though Carthage was captured by the Arabs in 698, gold coins in both the fabrics associated with North Africa appeared with the types of Tiberius. An Italian style series of gold was also struck and again some bronze from the mint at Ravenna.

Justinian II (Second reign), 705–711

Justinian when deposed in 695 had had his nose slit, after the barbaric custom of the times, and consequently is usually described in his second reign as Rhinotmetus. In 705 he succeeded in escaping from his exile in Cherson and with the aid of Bulgarian forces recovered his throne and executed both the usurpers, Leontius and Apsimarus. On the obverse of gold coins Justinian, shown again with a facing bust, holds cross on steps and a globe, inscribed *Pax* and surmounted by a cross; the reverse presented a new portrait of Christ with short curly hair and beard. On a rare coinage of this reign the bust of his young son Tiberius was placed beside that of Justinian. Gold of all denominations was struck, rare silver hexagrams with similar types and some bronze with the same obverse but with the usual mark of value reverse. Constantinople was now the only effective mint; North Africa was in Arab hands, Sicily was under threat and Syracuse itself was sacked in 705. Only in Italy, presumably at Rome, was some gold still struck.

Philippicus—Theodosius III, 711–717

Yet another revolt in 711 raised to the throne the Armenian Bardanes, known on his coins as Philippicus. Justinian II was put to death together with his young son Tiberius, the last of the house of Heraclius which had for so long provided emperors for Byzantium. The next few years saw a quick succession of emperors, Philippicus (711–713), Anastasius II (713–716) and Theodosius III (716–717). The coinage of all three was limited to gold and apart from small issues from Rome was struck at Constantinople only. Apart from the obvious difference of title these coinages were distinguished by small variations in the obverse type; all three hold cross on globe in the right hand, Philippicus an eagle-tipped sceptre in his left and the other two the *mappa*.

LEO III—THEOPHILUS, 717–842

This was the period of the iconoclast movement, the rejection of image worship, and, while the exponents of this attitude were in the ascendancy, their influence was extended to the coinage as well, with a consequent disappearance of the image of Christ as a type and its replacement either by a cross or a second portrait of some member of the imperial family. Portraiture became even more conventional than in the preceding period and the portraits of successive rulers are distinguishable, apart from minutiae of dress, by the varying names accompanying them. The coinage, almost entirely of gold with only very rare bronze and silver issues, emanated mainly from Constantinople itself, though issues still came from Rome and elsewhere in Italy.

Leo III, 717–741, the Isaurian

With the re-attribution to Leontius II of the series formerly ascribed to Leo, the coinage of this reign is seen to fall into two groups, of Leo alone and of Leo in association with his son, Constantine V, from 720 onwards. At Constantinople the first group, of solidi only, presented the facing bust of Leo with unusually thin and somewhat spade-shaped features and holding cross on globe and *mappa*, while the reverse continued the conventional cross-on-steps motif. The second group of solidi and rare semisses had a similar portrait of Leo on obverse and a portrait of the young, beardless Constantine V on the reverse (Pl. 404). On bronzes the names of the emperors were for the first time inscribed in Greek and their title was rendered as δεσπότης. Gold coinage attributed to Rome included tremisses as well as solidi in both groups and on some of the issues for Leo and Constantine together the reverse carried a star on the field. Solidi from Rome and elsewhere in Italy were occasionally struck in electrum.

Constantine V, 741–775

Under Constantine the empire successfully resisted the threats to its security by Saracens, Slavs and Bulgars but in 751 Ravenna was finally lost to the Lombards and disappeared from the imperial coinage. The unusual feature of the coinage is the retention of the bust of Leo III as the obverse type and indeed the first group of solidi is identical with the last of the previous reign except that the portrait of Constantine is now bearded and more mature, within the limits of the conventional representation. From 751 when Constantine's son, Leo IV, became Augustus his portrait was added on the reverse of the gold coinage. The 40 nummia coinage in bronze issued in 749–750 revived the practice of placing the regnal year on the reverse, two varieties having either the bust of Constantine on obverse and mark of value and date on reverse or the bust of Leo III on obverse and that of Constantine above the mark of value as reverse. On the joint coinage with Leo IV, after 751, Leo III is relegated to the reverse, Constantine and Leo IV occupying the obverse. New types for the silver coin, commonly called the miliaresion, were introduced consisting simply of cross on steps on obverse and an inscription giving the emperor's name and titles on the reverse (cf. Pl. 405). Despite the inception of a purely Papal coinage in the course of this reign, coinage for Constantine V in the style associated with Rome continued to be issued, though mainly in electrum and even more debased metals.

The iconoclastic policy inaugurated by Leo III and continued by Constantine V did not go unopposed and a revolt of its opponents under Constantine's brother-in-law, Artavasdus, was successful in occupying Constantinople. While Artavasdus, proclaimed emperor, held the city till he was overthrown by Constantine two years later he minted both gold and silver in the name of himself and his son, Nicephorus.

Leo IV, 775–780

The coinage of this reign apparently began a year after Leo's accession when in 776 he associated with himself his infant son, Constantine VI. The coinage was from Constantinople alone and in gold solidi only. Family piety was carried yet a step further on these pieces which portrayed Leo and his son on obverse either with facing busts or as standing figures and on the reverse the busts of Leo III and Constantine V who are described respectively as grandfather and father. The bronze coinage received a similar treatment but the types of the silver miliaresion restricted mention only to the two living rulers (Pl. 405).

Constantine VI and Irene, 780–(797) 802

Constantine VI succeeded as a boy of ten with his mother, the empress Irene, as joint ruler. In 790 Irene was deposed by her son but two years later was reinstated and finally in 797 Constantine was blinded and deposed by Irene who reigned alone till 802. Despite Irene's leanings towards image worship, the forces of iconoclasm were still too strong to permit of an open reversal of policy and the coinage continued to present the same appearance as in preceding reigns. The first issues of gold and bronze at Constantinople resulted in the acme of the family coin, for Constantine and Irene appeared on the obverse and Leo III, Constantine V and Leo IV, the emperor's great-grandfather, grandfather and father on the reverse (Pl. 406). On a second issue only the emperor and Irene were shown on obverse and reverse respectively and only these two received mention in the inscription on the silver miliaresion. In the sole reign of Irene the empress' portrait was placed on both sides of solidi.

Nicephorus I—Theophilus, 802–842

Irene was deposed and succeeded by her treasurer Nicephorus who shared rule with his son, Stauracius, from late 803. The event of the greatest political importance in the reign was the treaty agreed in 803 between Nicephorus and Charlemagne who had been crowned emperor of the Holy Roman empire by the Pope in 800. By this treaty the limits of the two empires in Italy were defined, the exarchate of Ravenna and Rome falling to Charlemagne, the south of Italy remaining in the Byzantine sphere. From this time on, only rather barbarous versions of Byzantine coins were produced in Italy and that only for a few more reigns.

The coinage of Nicephorus alone followed the conventional patterns, a facing bust with cross on steps on the gold and mark of value on the bronze 40 nummia pieces. The gold coins of the joint reign with Stauracius bore the bust of the emperor on obverse and his son on the reverse. The use of the Greek title βασιλεύς (king) which had been used on later issues of Constantine VI became standard under Nicephorus. The title used for Stauracius was that of δεσπότης. The same convention in titles was used in the next reigns, that of Michael I and his son, Theophylactus (811–813), of Leo V and Constantine (813–820) and of Michael II and Theophilus (820–829). Throughout these reigns the pattern both of denominations and types changed but little except that on the reverse of the silver miliaresion from Michael I onwards, the emperors are described as βασιλεῖς ʽΡωμαιῶν— Kings of The Romans.

Certain elements of novelty are, however, apparent in the coinage of Theophilus (829–842). The 'family' type of coin, popular with the Isaurian dynasty, reappeared and solidi with Theophilus himself on the obverse presented either his young son Constantine on the reverse, or Constantine together with a bearded figure who the inscription declares to be Michael, presumably the former emperor, Michael II, father of Theophilus. An extremely rare solidus shows no less than five members of the imperial family. Theophilus with his wife Theodora and daughter Thecla on the obverse and other two daughters, Anna and Anastasia, on the reverse. On solidi with Theophilus alone on the obverse the cross, now in the form of a patriarchal cross, was restored to the reverse and accompanied by a version of the inscription Κύριε βοήθει τῷ σῷ δουλῷ (O Lord, help thy servant) (Pl. 407). Theophilus also replaced the old 40 nummia coin by a new bronze coinage of follis and half-pieces with types, the standing figure of the emperor and on reverse lines of inscription (Pl. 408).

MICHAEL III—JOHN I, 842–976

The coinage of this period reflects the final rejection of iconoclasm, and the triumph of the image worshippers is apparent in the restoration to the coin types of the head of Christ which had appeared earlier in the reign of Justinian II and the introduction of other representations of the Saviour, of the Virgin and of St. Alexander. Although portraiture continued to be conventional, with only occasional attempts at a realistic likeness, more attention was paid to the decorative richness of costume. The consequent magnificence of the coinage in general contrasts with the somewhat stiff and insipid productions of the iconoclastic period. Early in the period, in the reign of Basil I, the rather rude copies of Byzantine coinage which had continued to be struck in the West came to an end. With the exception of Cherson which once again struck some bronze coinage the sole mint for the imperial coinage was Constantinople.

Michael III, 842–867

As Michael was only a child when his father Theophilus died, his mother the empress Theodora exercised the powers of a regency in the early part of the reign. Certainly on the first issue of gold coins Theodora appeared alone on the obverse, the emperor being relegated to the reverse in the company of his sister, Thecla. On the silver miliaresion of this issue the reverse inscription included the names of all three, though here the name of Michael was accorded first place. On the second issue begun about 852 Thecla no longer appeared and Michael and Theodora were represented together on the obverse of the solidus. The reverse of this issue revived the type introduced by Justinian II of the bust of Christ with long hair and beard against a background of the cross. In 856 Michael, already embarking on the course of conduct which was to earn him the sobriquet the 'Drunkard', grew impatient of his mother's control and Theodora was ousted from her position by her brother, Bardas. Though appointed Caesar, Bardas was not associated on the coinage with Michael, who in the third issue appeared alone on the obverse, retaining as reverse the bust of Christ. Miliaresia were struck in the second and third issues with the appropriate changes in the reverse inscriptions but only in the third issue were rare bronzes with mark of value M struck. In 866 Basil I was appointed associate emperor but of the brief joint reign only bronze coinage from Constantinople is on record.

Basil I, 867–886

This coinage is notable for the introduction of a type which was to have a long history both in Byzantine coinage and in coinages imitating Byzantine models. This new reverse type on gold coins of Basil showed the seated figure of Christ with right hand raised in benediction and left hand clasping the book of the Gospels. After a brief initial issue on his own Basil was joined on successive issues by various members of his family. On gold issues the half-length figures of Basil and his son Constantine are shown holding between them a patriarchal cross with the seated Christ on the reverse (Pl. 409), while rarer series with Basil on the obverse have as reverse either Constantine together with the empress Eudocia or the younger sons, Leo and Alexander. Miliaresia of the usual type accompanied the issue of Basil with Constantine. Bronzes with the inscriptional reverse introduced on the follis of Theophilus were issued for Basil alone, for Basil with Constantine and, the most numerous category, for Basil with Constantine and Leo VI. The very rough bronzes struck at Cherson had a cross on steps reverse and the initials of Basil or Basil and Constantine on the obverse.

Leo VI, 886–912

Leo, known to history as the 'Wise because of his reputation for learning and his encouragement of learning, succeeded Basil I, though he was reputed to be the son of Michael III by Eudocia Ingerina before her marriage to Basil. Despite his relatively long reign his coinage remained practically unvaried. The solidus which showed a long bearded portrait of the emperor introduced for the first time on Byzantine coinage a representation of the Virgin who is depicted half-length, lifting up her hands in prayer. This reverse was inscribed with the name of Maria and in the field on either side were abbreviated forms of μήτηρ θεοῦ—Mother of God (Pl. 410). The silver miliaresion preserved its conventional types and bronze follis with inscriptional reverses as on those of Basil had either a seated figure or a bust of Leo as obverse type. Leo's brother, Alexander, though a co-emperor, was represented only on bronze coinage. On the rough bronzes from Cherson also Alexander's initial appeared alongside that of Leo. In 911 Constantine, Leo's son by his fourth wife Zoe, was crowned emperor and appeared with the father on the solidus with type of the two emperors standing. The reverse of this issue reverted to Basil's type of the seated Christ.

Alexander—Romanus II, 912–963

On the rare solidi of Alexander, who reigned for just over a year as the guardian of the young Constantine VII, the emperor was shown being crowned by a saint, his namesake, St. Alexander. The coinage of the remarkably long reign of Constantine VII from 913 to 959, complicated by the intrusion of his father-in-law, Romanus I, as co-emperor and of the sons of Romanus as associates in imperial rule is best dealt with in successive periods. From 913 to 919 Constantine VII reigned with his mother Zoe as regent, the busts of mother and son holding a patriarchal cross between them appearing on gold and bronze with reverse respectively Christ enthroned or an inscription. Between 919 and 921 Romanus I as co-emperor replaced the regent Zoe on solidi while both Constantine and Romanus appeared alone on bronze issues. From 921 Constantine VII was relegated to an inferior position on the coins in relation to Romanus and his sons. On one issue of solidi only Romanus and his son Christopher were represented while on another, where the obverse shows Christ crowning Romanus, Constantine was relegated to the reverse along with Christopher and on silver miliaresia the name of Constantine on the inscription reverse was the last of the three. Later, after 931 on the death of Christopher and the association on the coinage of Romanus' younger sons, Stephen and Constantine, the name of the legitimate emperor again appeared at the end of the list of names on the reverse of the silver miliaresion. The obverse of this issue varied the traditional design by placing a small cross at the centre of the cross on steps (Pl. 411). In 944, however, Romanus was deposed by his two sons who themselves were banished in the next year and Constantine VII was at last left as sole emperor, but after a few months he advanced his son Romanus II to the rank of emperor. On the gold coins of his brief sole reign when his portrait alone occupied the obverse there seems to have been some attempt at a realistic portrayal for the portrait is quite different from the conventional, angular representation of Constantine as he appears together with Romanus II in the joint reign. On the reverse of both issues appeared the bust of Christ against a nimbate cross. Though Romanus II reigned from 959 to 963 the only coins of the reign that survive are bronzes struck at Cherson with the monogram of the emperor on one side and of his infant son Basil on the other.

Nicephorus II—John I Zimisces, 963–976

To the few months of the regency of Theophano, widow of Romanus II, in 963 no coins can be attributed with certainty and in August of that year the soldier Nicephorus became emperor and, though the sons of Romanus II, Basil and Constantine, still remained officially emperors, they were pushed into the background. On an initial issue of gold the solidus or nomisma, as it may now be more convenient to call it, showed the busts of Nicephorus and Basil but a new type was soon introduced on which only Nicephorus appeared, accompanied by the Virgin. A new phrase also made its appearance in the inscription θεότοκε βοήθει—(Mother of God, help Nicephorus). The reverse type continued to be the bust of Christ (Pl. 412). A medallion at the centre of the cross on the miliaresion carried the portrait of Nicephorus only as did the obverse of the bronzes. In 969 a conspiracy brought about the assassination of Nicephorus and the elevation of John I Zimisces. The cult of the Virgin was continued on his coins, the obverse of solidi showing the Virgin crowning John, while a hand of God above blesses him. One type of the miliaresion was devoted entirely to the Virgin: her veiled and nimbate bust occupies the whole of the obverse and she holds before her a medallion with the portrait of the infant Christ while the long inscription on the reverse is also dedicated to her honour. No bronze coins were struck with the name and titles of John or indeed of any of his successors down to Constantine X (1059) but a series of bronzes with the basic types, a nimbate bust of Christ on obverse and an inscription Jesus Christ, King of Kings (in Greek) on the reverse (Pl. 413), are attributed on the grounds of differences of detail and style to the various reigns.

BASIL II AND CONSTANTINE VIII—NICEPHORUS III, 976–1081

The coinage of this period continues much of the tradition of the preceding period but is marked by certain additional features. From late in the reign of Basil II and his brother, nomismata of a new fabric began to be struck. These pieces were thinner and more spread and of the slightly concave or saucer-like shape known as scyphate. These were struck alongside nomismata of the older, thick fabric which persisted throughout the period but finally disppeared under Alexius I in the next period. Silver was struck with increasing rarity and finally ceased, while the only bronze coinages were the varieties of anonymous bronze described above under John I Zimisces.

BASIL II AND CONSTANTINE VIII, 976–(1025) 1028

These two sons of Romanus II who had remained nominally emperors under Nicephorus II and John I came into their own on the death of the latter in 976. Considerable military successes had been won by Nicephorus in the partial re-conquest of Syria including the city of Antioch, by John in his defeat of the Russians and Bulgarians and under Basil the Bulgarians were further defeated and the frontier of the empire once again extended to the Danube. The sole mint for the coinage continued to be Constantinople and the types of the coins were affected in no degree by contemporary events. The only exception as a mint to Constantinople had been Cherson which had continued to strike very rough bronzes but in 989 Cherson was captured by the Russians under Vladimir and this series of bronzes came to an end. Although Basil II was the effective ruler in the joint reign with his brother, the portraits of both appeared on the nomismata, both of the small, thick type and the new scyphate variety, and even on the obverse of the miliaresion small busts of both emperors were placed on either side of the cross on steps. On the gold of the sole reign of Constantine VIII (1025–8) the emperor was represented as a stout Henry VIII-like figure in an elaborately jewelled mantle (Pl. 414).

Romanus III—Michael VI, 1028–57

Romanus III (1028–34) who had married Zoe, the daughter of Constantine VIII, and succeeded as emperor is represented by a somewhat rare coinage. The types of his gold nomismata copied those of John Zimisces, a figure of the Virgin crowning the emperor and an enthroned figure of Christ. No silver coins are on record and bronze attributed to this reign is one of the varieties of the anonymous type. The next emperor, Michael IV (1034–41), whom Zoe married on the death of Romanus was represented on his nomismata by a facing bust with a *manus dei* blessing him, while his nephew and successor, Michael V (1041–2), reverted to the type of Virgin crowning emperor. The empress Zoe, exiled by Michael V, was restored to share rule with her sister Theodora when Michael was deposed in 1042 and only very recently have nomismata of the two sisters come to light. The obverse shows their facing busts adorned with unusual jewelled head-dresses. The coinage of Constantine IX (1042–55) whom Zoe took as her third husband is somewhat more plentiful and varied than that of immediately preceding reigns. Nomismata are of two main classes, first of the older variety with compact fabric with bust of emperor and of Christ, then of the newer, spread and scyphate fabric but with identical types, the reverse changing subsequently to the enthroned Christ. Silver coins represent Constantine on one side and the Virgin—from the inscription the Virgin of Blachernae—in the attitude of prayer on the other (Pl. 415). Bronze, still without emperor's name, had types of Christ and the Virgin. The now aged Theodora reappeared as sole empress for a brief reign of some eighteen months (1055–6). She was represented on nomismata of thick fabric by a facing bust similar to that on her coinage with Zoe and on scyphate nomismata as a standing figure holding a labarum together with the Virgin (Pl. 416). Michael VI (1056–7), nominated by Theodora as her successor, was shown as a tall, facing figure standing on a footstool and holding a jewelled cross, with a bust of the Virgin for reverse type.

Isaac I Comnenus (1057–9) who was proclaimed by the army in the place of Michael VI introduced a welcome note of novelty on his nomismata where he is shown as a standing figure in a short tunic either resting his hand on a sheathed sword or holding a drawn sword over his shoulder (Pl. 417). Isaac abdicated and was replaced by Constantine X Ducas (1059–67). He is usually represented on nomismata by the now familiar type of emperor crowned by the Virgin but the innovation of his reign was the restoration of the imperial portrait and title to some of the bronze coinage. Some issues have the facing bust of the emperor alone, others with a standing figure of Christ on the reverse show Constantine standing with his empress Eudocia holding a labarum between them. On his death Eudocia reigned for some months as regent for her sons, Michael VII and Constantine, all three appearing together on the obverse of nomismata. The early issues of Romanus IV (1067–71) whom Eudocia married are a revival of the 'family' coinage which was a feature of the Heraclian dynasty's issues. No less than six personages are depicted; on the obverse the figure of Christ crowns Romanus and Eudocia while on the reverse stand the three sons of Eudocia—Constantine, Michael VII and Andronicus. Other issues in the thicker, heavier fabric show only Romanus and Eudocia or Romanus alone. On rare silver pieces with Romanus only on the obverse there is an unusually charming reverse of the Virgin and Child (Pl. 418). In this reign the Seljuk Turks were sweeping through Armenia into Syria and at the battle of Manzikert Romanus was captured by the Turkish leader Alp Arslan, and Michael VII (1071–8) the son of Eudocia was proclaimed emperor in his place. The scyphate nomismata bore only Michael's portrait but on the thicker variety, some of them now struck in electrum, the empress Maria appeared with her husband. The coinage of Nicephorus III (1078–81) who succeeded on Michael's abdication is notable for the distinct debasement of the nomismata a large proportion of which were of electrum and not gold. The types were the traditional busts of emperor and of Christ or standing figure of the emperor and an enthroned Christ. An unusual reverse type on bronze coins consisted of a cross with, at its centre, a circle containing a star and in the angles of the cross the initial letters of the inscription Σταυρέ Φύλαττε Νικήφορον Δεσπότην.

The coinage of the Byzantine empire from the reign of Alexius I until the first capture of Constantinople in 1203 by the warriors of the Fourth Crusade and the establishment of the new line of Latin emperors in 1204 presents a distinctive character. Its principal feature, admittedly one which had been developing gradually in the previous period, was the striking of the nomisma in only the scyphate fabric but now, also, almost always in adulterated metal. Bronze coinage was of small module, thick fabric and irregular shape while silver, mostly early in the period only, was of like type. The coinage on the whole was much less carefully produced, and stereotyped and unimaginative designs, restricted largely to imperial figures and those of Christ and the Virgin, are relieved only by the occasional introduction of new figures of saints.

Under Alexius I (1081–1118) the decadence of the empire was temporarily arrested and Alexius contended successfully with the Norman invasions of Illyria and Thessaly, with the continuing struggle against the Seljuk Turks, and finally in 1095 with the Western mercenaries of the First Crusade who were almost as great a menace to the empire as to their infidel enemies. The decadence of the coinage, however, proceeded apace and the continued debasement of the nomisma of the previous two reigns resulted, eventually, in the existence side by side of nomismata of varying intrinsic value, for they were struck in gold, in electrum, billon and even in bronze. The types on this coinage were the bust or standing figure of Alexius and the enthroned figure of Christ or the Virgin. Features of the treatment of the obverse were the extraordinary accentuation on some issues of the jewelled edging of the emperor's robe and the disposition over the field of his name (Pl. 419). Only a very rare issue depicted Alexius with his empress Irene on one side and Christ crowning the emperor's son, John, on the reverse. The small bronzes and silver had types similar to those of the more common nomismata, though some bronzes had, as reverse, a jewelled cross with the initials of the formula beseeching heavenly aid as used on coins of Nicephorus III.

The nomismata of John II (1118–43) of a like variety of metals most commonly have two-figure types on obverse, usually the Virgin crowning the emperor, though on one issue the figure accompanying John and holding with him a patriarchal cross on steps is labelled by the inscription as St. George. Under Manuel I (1143–80) the nomismata followed much the same pattern of fabric and type.

On the issues where the figure of the emperor appeared alone the field is even more than ever occupied by the emperor's mantle and by inscription while the accompanying reverse with a bust of Christ also has an inscription such as Emmanuel in the field. On some of the two-figure types Manuel is accompanied by St. Theodore or St. Demetrius. No coins are known for Alexius II who at the age of thirteen succeeded Manuel in 1180. Andronicus I, a cousin of Manuel, was associated in 1180 with the boy Alexius whom he put to death in 1184, to reign alone only for another year. Andronicus introduced little change in the coin types but on nomismata of Isaac II Angelus (1185–95) a new two-figure type introduced St. Michael, winged and nimbate, as the emperor's companion (Pl. 420). Yet another saint, St. Constantine, appeared beside the emperor on nomismata of Alexius III Angelus (1195–1203) and on the small bronze coinage which had continued to be struck in all these reigns Alexius III placed a bust of St. George with sword on shoulder. The Venetians and the Crusaders who captured Constantinople in 1203 restored Isaac II to the throne together with his son Alexius IV but no coins are known of this reign nor of that of Alexius V who led the rising in Constantinople against the invaders in February 1204, until the final capture and sacking of the city by the Crusaders in April of that year.

LATIN EMPERORS, 1204–61

With the fall of Constantinople in 1204 the empire split up into a number of small states such as the so-called 'empires' of Nicaea, Thessalonica and Trebizond, the coinages of which will be discussed below (pp. 221–2). The new line of 'Latin' emperors who established themselves at Constantinople did not continue the imperial series of coins, currency needs being, apparently, met by other coinages principally that of Venice.

MICHAEL VIII—CONSTANTINE XI, 1261–1453

The coinage of this period carried on the scyphate nomismata of the earlier period but these were even more base and carelessly executed than before. The commercial influence of Constantinople in the eastern Mediterranean had now been replaced by that of Venice and the coinage of the empire suffered a similar eclipse and the later series, influenced by Venetian coinage, became a series of silver pieces of flat fabric with circular inscriptions.

Michael VIII (1261–82), the first of the house of the Palaeologi which provided the emperors of Byzantium down to its fall, ruled a much reduced empire. The types of nomismata, some in gold, some debased, were new to the series. On the obverse the emperor kneels to the front, supported by St. Michael, and is crowned by Christ standing at his side. The reverse, a complete break with the style of previous designs, portrays the walls of Constantinople with, in the centre, the bust of the Virgin, hands raised in prayer (Pl. 421). Bronze scyphate nomismata were of the more traditional type, as were the smaller flat bronzes which showed Michael on one side and, on the other, his son Andronicus II who was associated with him in 1273. On nomismata struck by Andronicus in his sole reign from 1282 to 1295 the emperor was shown abasing himself before Christ, the walls of Constantinople being retained as the reverse. In the joint reign of Andronicus with his son Michael IX (1295–1320) both emperors kneel before Christ on the obverse of the nomismata. On base silver coins which resemble Venetian pieces in fabric and module the types of two standing emperors and the enthroned Christ are accompanied by circular inscriptions in the Western style; similar pieces were issued in the joint reign of Andronicus II with his grandson, Andronicus III (132–58).

During the reign of Andronicus III (1328–41) the Ottoman Turks captured Nicomedia and Nicaea and completed the conquest of Bithynia and the end of the empire was brought appreciably nearer. Only a rare coinage in silver and bronze has survived from this reign and from that of John V (1341–91) under whom the Turkish conquests were extended into the Balkans. No coins were issued for John VI and his son Matthew who set up as rival emperors between 1341 and 1354. A serious attempt to restore the coinage was made by John V (1341–91) to whom is now attributed the majority of the coins formerly given to John VIII (Pl. 422). The main series was in base silver of flat fabric. The nimbate bust of the emperor on the obverse was contained within an ornamented border outside which were two circular inscriptions; on the reverse was a crudely drawn bust of Christ. The empire now consisted only of Constantinople, Thessalonica and the Peloponnese, and Manuel II, seeking aid against the Turks, visited western Europe, including England. In his absence his nephew John VII acted as regent but no coinage was issued in his name.

The last emperor for whom coinage is known was John VIII (1423–8) who continued the silver coinage instituted by his grand-father, John V, as well as small bronze pieces with standing figures of the emperor and Christ. The poor standard of coinage with its caricature of a portrait is amply revealed by comparison with the famous portrait of John VIII by the Italian medallist, Pisanello, when, in 1438, the emperor attended the Council of Ferrara to seek aid from the Pope against the Turks. No effective help was forthcoming and the fortunes of the empire under the last of the Palaeologi, Constantine XI (1448–53), had sunk so low that, apparently, no coinage was issued by him.

Despite the heroic rôle played by Constantine XI in the final assaults of the Turks on Constantinople the city was taken on 29th May 1453 and the Byzantine empire as a political and territorial entity was no more. The thousand years of its existence had spanned the Middle Ages and this eastern continuation of the empire of Rome had lasted up to the threshold of the modern age. In coinage, as in many other fields, it had, throughout this great extent of time, preserved and transmitted to the emerging states of Europe something of Roman tradition, fossilized and conventionalized though it may have been, and in addition its own particular development of coin art and design.

THE EMPIRE OF NICAEA

After the Latin conquest of Constantinople in 1204 a number of separate Byzantine 'empires' were set up. Of these the empire of Theodore Lascaris with its capital at Nicaea was the most important, absorbing in turn the empire of Thessalonica and the despotate of Epirus (see p. 410) and finally in 1261 its ruler Michael Paleologus became emperor of the restored Byzantine empire. The coins of the successive emperors at Nicaea are scyphate nomismata in gold, silver or even bronze of similar fabric to Byzantine issues and with the same fashion of types. The obverse presents two standing figures, the emperor accompanied by one of the saints, usually St. Theodore or St. Constantine, or by Christ or the Virgin, while on the reverse is a figure of Christ or the Virgin (Pl. 423). On smaller bronze pieces of John I Vatatzes (1222–54) the single figure of the emperor appears on the obverse and a bust of St. George on the reverse.

THE EMPIRE OF TREBIZOND

This little empire on the Black Sea was founded also in 1204 by Alexius Comnenus, a member of the imperial Byzantine family, and maintained its existence until it was overwhelmed by the Turks in 1461. The coinage of Trebizond which seems not to have begun till the reign of John I (1235–8) is of pieces known as aspers which have a very typical flat fabric. The types which remain practically consistent throughout Trebizond's history are a standing figure of the emperor on obverse and a figure of St. Eugenius on the reverse (Pl. 424). From about 1300 the same two figures are also represented on horseback and half-pieces of both varieties were struck in most reigns. Particularly in the later reigns a coinage of small bronze pieces, slightly scyphate, accompanies the aspers. The types on the bronzes are most commonly the standing figure of the emperor and a cross, in the angles of which are the letters of the name of St. Eugenius.

THE LATIN ORIENT

The ostensible object of the First Crusade in 1096 was to assist the Byzantine empire against the attacks of the Seljuk Turks and to secure and make accessible to pilgrimage the holy places of Christendom. The partial achievement of these objectives was, however, only incidental to the real purpose of the crusaders, the establishment of a number of feudal principalities and kingdoms. A county centred on Edessa was set up by Baldwin de Bouillon in 1097, Antioch was taken by Bohemond of Taranto in 1098 and made into a principality and Jerusalem itself, captured in 1099 by Geoffrey de Bouillon, later became a kingdom. Another county was created on the capture of Tripoli by Bertrand of Toulouse in 1109 and the whole of the Levant coastal area was brought under crusader dominion. Later crusades wrested the islands of Cyprus and Rhodes as well as other smaller islands from the Byzantine empire and created them into kingdoms or seigneuries. The Levant states were all captured by the Turks before the end of the thirteenth century but the island dominions in some cases survived for at least a century after the capture of Constantinople by the Turks in 1453. The coinages issued by these states show the mingled influence of the Byzantine, western European, Venetian and Arabic coin series.

THE LEVANT

Though the kingdom of Jerusalem was the most important of the crusader states in the Levant its coinage in so far as it has survived is not impressive in quantity or content. Though Geoffrey de Bouillon captured Jerusalem in 1099 and became the head of the new state, the title of king of Jerusalem was first assumed by his brother and successor, Baldwin, in 1100, and it is only under Amaury I (1162–73) that the coinage series proper begins. The coinage consisted solely of deniers and obols in billon after the fashion of the French feudal series and the types for Amaury and for the several monarchs bearing the name of Baldwin are a cross surrounded by the king's name and on the reverse a representation of the church of the Holy Sepulchre with inscription *De Jerusalem*. Deniers of Guy de Lusignan (1186–92), in whose reign Jerusalem was captured by Saladin in 1187, show the facing head of the king and the cupola of the Holy Sepulchre church. Although the kingdom of Jerusalem shrank until it consisted only of a small area of the Levant coast where

Acre was the most important city, coins were still struck with the conventional types by Amaury II (1197–1205) (Pl. 425). The succession to the throne of the kingdom, much disputed in the thirteenth century, passed to the kings of Cyprus in 1286 and in 1291 the last fortress, Acre, was captured by the Saracens.

The kingdom of Jerusalem comprised some twenty seigneuries of which the more important were those of Jaffa and Galilee. All of these possessed the feudal right of coinage but rare pieces of only a few have so far been identified. The coins are billon deniers or obols often with a cross as obverse and an architectural feature such as a church or a city gateway as reverse with the name of the seigneur on the obverse and of the siegneury on the reverse. A further category of coinage associated with the kingdom of Jerusalem is that of the so-called Saracenic besants. One class of these coins are imitations of the Islamic gold dinars; a second series in gold and also in silver have a cross at the centre on one side and the inscriptions in Arabic are proclamations of the Christian faith as well as a record of the mint and date of the coin (Pl. 426).

Edessa was the first important capture by the Crusader army on its march from Constantinople towards the Holy Land. Baldwin de Bouillon became the first Count of Edessa in 1097 and coinage was struck by him and by his successors until the recapture of the area by the Saracens in 1145. The coinage attributed to the Counts of Edessa consists of a series of bronze pieces in a fabric similar to contemporary Byzantine bronzes and borrowing a number of its types from the same source. Attributed to Baldwin I (1097–1100) is a coinage without inscription with the figure of a knight in armour and holding sword and shield on the obverse and sometimes a cross on steps, on the reverse (Pl. 427). Another series bears Baldwin's names inscribed in lines across the obverse field and a third class shows a facing nimbate bust of Christ on obverse and on the reverse a cross with letters of the name of Baldwin in the angles. A further series, again with bust of Christ on the obverse and as reverse type a Latin cross with a small St. Andrew's cross at centre and crescent and globe ornaments, is ascribed, on the basis of local provenance and overstriking on earlier types, to later counts of Edessa (Pl. 428).

Antioch, formerly one of the great cities and mints of the Byzantine empire, was taken in 1098 by Bohemond of Taranto and formed into a principality. The coinage of Bohemond and his successors as princes of Antioch falls into two distinct groups. The issues from Bohemond up to about 1136 are bronze pieces in the Byzantine style with, most usually, the facing bust or standing figure of St. Peter on the obverse. The reverses are either inscriptions across the field in the manner of Byzantine reverses, incorporating the name of the prince, or cross motifs with letters of the prince's name. With Raymond of Poitiers (1136–49) the coinage of

Antioch changed to a series of billon deniers and obols of west European fabric with the name of the prince and the principality in circular inscriptions. The obverse type is frequently a helmeted bust in profile of the prince and the reverse a cross (Pl. 429), but some issues of Bohemond III (1140–1201) have a fleur-de-lis in place of the obverse portrait. The series ended with the recapture of Antioch by the Saracens in 1268.

The coinage of Tripoli dates from the capture of the city by Bertrand of Toulouse in 1109 and the creation of the county of Tripoli as a fief of the kingdom of Jerusalem. Billon deniers and obols of Bertrand have a cross as obverse type and bear his name *Bertrand Co*, while the reverse inscription *Tripolis Civi* is terminated by an arrangement of its last three letters *tas* in the centre. The reverse type for Raymond I (1136–52) is an eight-pointed star. Under Bohemond VI of Antioch who usurped the succession to Tripoli in 1268 silver gros and half-pieces were struck with types of cross and eight-pointed star, while these denominations for Bohemond VII (1274–89) had as reverse type a castle (Pl. 430). Tripoli was captured by the Saracens in 1289.

A Christian kingdom established in Armenia by Rupenus I in 1080 endured until it was overwhelmed by the Turks in 1375 in the reign of Leo VI. The coinage consisted of the gold tahegan, the silver tram and its half-piece, the copper pogh as well as some deniers and obols in billon. The inscriptions on the coins in Armenian give the king's name and title on obverse and the name of the mint, the city of Sis, on the reverse. Of the considerable variety of types the most frequent on gold and silver show the king enthroned, facing, holding cross on globe and sceptre on the obverse and two lions back to back divided by a tall cross (Pl. 431). Other types depict the king on horseback on the obverse and a lion standing with a tall cross behind. Billon coins have as types the king enthroned and cross with smaller cross imposed on the centre.

ISLANDS OF THE MEDITERRANEAN

The island of Cyprus had escaped the attentions of the earlier Crusades but in 1191 Richard of England on his way to the Holy Land captured the island from the Byzantine empire and subsequently sold it for a hundred thousand besants to Guy de Lusignan, erstwhile king of Jerusalem. The Lusignan dynasty reigned in Cyprus for close on three centuries until in 1489 the island passed to Venice and finally in 1570 it was captured by the Turks. In 1268 Hugh III reunited the titles of king of Jerusalem and Cyprus which appear henceforth in the royal titulature on Cypriot coinage. The major unit in the coinage system was the

besant or nomisma of a similar scyphate fabric to that of the contemporary
Byzantine nomisma and, like it, struck in pale gold. The substantial coin, however,
was the silver grosso of which two were equivalent to a besant and in the
divisionary coinage, as well as the half-grosso, the silver carat was also struck at
the rate of six to the half-grosso. The carat itself was tariffed at two billon deniers
and from the reign of Janus (1398–1432) smaller billon coins, known as sizains,
were also issued.

The only coinage of the brief reign of Guy de Lusignan (1192–4) consisted
only of billon deniers inscribed *Rex Guido—De Cipro*. The reverse type was a
cross with annulet in each angle and the obverse either a castle or a star of eight
points. Besants were first struck under Hugh I (1205–18) with the standing figure
of the king holding cross and globe on the obverse and an enthroned, facing
figure of Christ on the reverse, types retained with only minor modifications by
his successors down to Henry II (1285–1324). Copper pieces of uncertain denomination struck for Henry I (1218–53) have a facing crowned head of the king on
obverse and the usual cross reverse; and billon deniers of this reign have cross on
obverse and on the reverse a gateway, similar to that on Genoese coins, but
inscribed with the word *Rex*. The silver grosso was first struck by Henry II
with an obverse type which was to remain standard on this denomination. Henry
was depicted enthroned and facing, crowned and holding sceptre and globe,
while on the reverse was a lion rampant. Amaury, Prince of Tyre, who displaced
his brother Henry between 1291 and 1297 struck grossi with a lion as the obverse
type surrounded by two concentric inscriptions giving his titles as Lord of Tyre
and Governor of Cyprus; on the reverse is a shield with the joint arms of Jerusalem
and Cyprus. Resumed issues of grossi for Henry II had a new reverse type, a cross
with a small cross in each angle, a design which, together with the enthroned
figure of the king on obverse, was to last throughout most of the remaining
coinage of the Lusignan dynasty (Pl. 432). Variations of these standard types are
found on the obverse of grossi of Peter I (1359–69), who holds a sword in place
of a sceptre, and of James II (1460–73), who is shown as a mounted figure holding
a sword.

During the Venetian occupation of Cyprus billon deniers and sizains have as
types the lion of Cyprus with inscription *S. Marcus Venetus* and cross with circular
inscription giving the name of the Doge. During the siege of Famagusta by
the Turks in 1570 the Venetians issued an emergency copper coinage with
type of lion of St. Mark on the obverse which is inscribed *Pro regni Cypri
pressidio* and a four-line inscription on the reverse, *Venetor fides inviolabilis bisante*
(Pl. 433).

In 1204 Leo Gabalas, the Byzantine governor of Rhodes, set himself up as a semi-independent ruler with the title of Caesar. His only coinage consists of rough copper pieces with his name and title inscribed in lines across both obverse and reverse. Coinage of similar successive rulers in Rhodes is of equally crude fabric, often with only a cross design with the letter B in each angle, said to be the device of the Palaeologi, the family from which came the contemporary Byzantine emperors.

A new phase in the history of Rhodes and its coinage began with the seizure of the island by the knights of the Order of St. John of Jerusalem under their grand-master, Fulk de Villaret. Rhodes was held by the Hospitallers until its capture by the Turks in 1522. Gold was struck in the form of ducats closely imitating contemporary Venetian types but the substantive coinage of the Hospitallers consisted of silver grossi and half-pieces and billon deniers. The almost constant type of the obverse of the silver coins was a figure of the grand-master kneeling in prayer before a patriarchal cross on steps, a type undoubtedly inspired by coins of the Byzantine emperors in the thirteenth century; the reverse was occupied by an elaborate cross (Pl. 435). Grand-Master Peter d'Aubusson (1476–1503) introduced silver pieces of large module with types, a shield of arms and standing figure of John the Baptist with an abbreviated form of the inscription *Ecce agnus dei qui tollit peccata mundi*. Similar pieces of Emery d'Amboise (1503–12) bear the Agnus Dei with the banner of the Order of St. John as the reverse type (Pl. 434). A series of billon deniers with types, a church and cross omit the name of the grand-master and are simply inscribed *Magistri Hospitalis—Ierosolemitani Rodi*.

In the early thirteenth century the Byzantine empire was practically powerless to hold and defend the Aegean islands some of which fell to the Turks, some were governed by semi-independent rulers. It was in these circumstances that the Genoese established themselves in Chios and Benedict Zaccharias made himself Lord of Chios in 1304. No coins have survived of Benedict or his son Paleologos and the earliest pieces are of the third generation of the Zaccharias, the brothers Benedict II and Martin, of whom there are rare gold pieces and silver grossi. Chios was regained by a Byzantine fleet in 1329 but was seized again in 1362 by the Genoese company, the Mahone, the members of which, known as the Giustiniani, ruled until the capture of the island by the Turks in 1566. The gold coinage of the Giustiniani consisted of imitations of Venetian gold and silver grossi, and billon deniers had types and legends borrowed from Genoa. The common types are a castle with three towers and a cross; on later pieces the obverse has an eagle above the castle (Pl. 436). The island of Lesbos or Mytilene was ceded in similar circumstances by the Byzantine emperor John V in 1354 to the Genoese Francesco Gattilusio, whose family held the island till its capture by the Turks in 1460. Gold coinage here also imitated the Venetian ducat while small silver pieces bore a cross with letter B in each angle and the Agnus Dei. Copper pieces had a similar obverse and on the reverse an eagle with the tortoise badge of the Gattilusio on its breast. Later copper issues transferred the cross with letter B to the reverse and had as obverse simply the initial of the ruler.

THE BRITISH ISLES

ENGLAND

The coinage of the Celtic tribes in Britain described above (pp. 70–1) ceased with the conquest of the island by the emperor Claudius in A.D. 43 and its incorporation in the Roman empire. The normal Roman coinage issues of gold aurei, silver denarii, bronze alloy sestertii and asses (or their later equivalents) which were universal currency in the Western empire circulated in Britain also. Some of the official issues were widely copied in the less Romanized areas and on the fringes of the province, particularly the bronze coinage of Claudius and the coinage of the later third and the earlier part of the fourth centuries. The brief empire of Carausius and Allectus (pp. 175) brought the issue of Roman coins from mints at London and Colchester and the mint at London continued to strike for the Constantinian emperors up to 325. Though the province was left to fend for itself in the early fifth century, some Roman coinage did find its way into England till about 450.

THE ANGLO-SAXONS

The belief that some categories of barbarous imitations of Roman coinage represent the Dark Age coinage of this country finds no support from archaeological evidence. The civilization and economy of the Saxon invaders and settlers was apparently too primitive to require any indigenous supply of coinage, and currency needs were met by the use of Merovingian gold tremisses imported from the Continent. To judge from evidence such as that of the Sutton Hoo ship burial, which contained Merovingian tremisses issued sometime shortly after 650 but no native coinage, the first Saxon issues are no earlier than the later seventh century. This was a coinage of small gold pieces called thrymsas, struck in imitation of the gold tremisses of the Merovingian kingdom in France, themselves imitations of the gold tremisses of the later Roman empire. The obverse of the thrymsa is generally a diademed bust in profile accompanied sometimes by the name of the moneyer responsible for producing it, while the reverse is usually a cross with, very occasionally, mention of the place where the coin was produced (Pl. 437).

This gold coinage was replaced by or, rather, was debased into a coinage in

228

silver of similar fabric which also derived its types from Roman models. These silver pieces, known as sceattas, were most probably in issue only a little before the end of the seventh century and continued current during much of the eighth century. One of the principal categories of this sceatta coinage is an imitation of a Constantinian bronze coin of the fourth century; the diademed profile bust can still be distinguished on the obverse but the reverse has become a pattern, based on only part of the Roman reverse, namely the standard bearing a votive inscription. On a number of such pieces a Runic inscription on either the obverse or the reverse most probably gives the name of the moneyer (Pl. 438). A second category of sceattas is based on an imitation of the solidus of the Byzantine empire with its reverse of a cross on steps. Such basic designs were elaborated by Saxon art into complicated designs and grotesque forms of birds and animals, providing the types of the other series of sceattas (Pl. 439). In the north an exiguous sceatta coinage was issued both by the kings of Northumbria and by the archbishops of York, both series continuing long after this type of coinage had been abandoned elsewhere in England. The general type of these northern sceattas, which suffered a rapid debasement until they became copper coins, is simply a small cross or pellet in the centre with a circular inscription giving the name of the king or archbishop on obverse and the moneyer on reverse (Pl. 440).

Towards the end of the eighth century this sceatta coinage gave way in its turn to a new money, the silver penny, issued in imitation of and roughly on the same standard as the silver denier, then the current coin throughout most of western Europe in the Carolingian empire. This new coinage, introduced in Kent, was taken up by Offa, king of Mercia, and its appearance coincides roughly with the emergence of the separate Anglo-Saxon kingdoms in England. The new silver coinage of Offa, introduced c. 785, included a group of pieces on which the obverse bears the king's portrait, shown in profile to the right and his name and title, while the reverse is usually a form of floreate cross with the moneyer's name (Pl. 441). Other groups of Offa's coinage are without portrait and show the king's name and that of the moneyer, disposed circularly or in lines across the coin. A rare coinage has the portrait of Offa's queen, Cynethrith. Under one of Offa's successors, Ceolwulf I (822–823/4), the mint of some at least of the Mercian coins is identified by the inclusion of the name of Canterbury on one series of pennies. The Mercian coinage came to an end with the Danish invasions and the rise of Wessex to supremacy in the later ninth century. The kings of Kent, though already subservient to Mercia by the time the silver-penny coinage began, were permitted to issue a coinage in their own names until Kent was seized from Mercia by Wessex in 825. At the mint of Canterbury also coinage was struck for the archbishops of Canterbury from Jaenberht (766–790) to Plegmund (890–914).

The earliest of these coins bear the name of the archbishop on one side and that of their overlord, the King of Mercia, on the other; after Wulfred they have an obverse portrait with the name of the mint or moneyer on the reverse.

Few coins of the kings of East Anglia are known before the reign of Aethelstan (*c.* 825–840). Types for this king include a profile portrait, but the more common types both for him and his successors, Æthelweard (*c.* 840–865) and Edmund (*c.* 865–870), are either cross design or the letters alpha and omega on obverse and reverse respectively. On obverse is usually the king's name and on reverse that of the moneyer. When East Anglia was overrun by the Danes Edmund was slain about 870 but an extensive memorial coinage for the martyred king as St. Edmund was struck by the Danish settlers, during the last decade of the century. The obverse has the letter A as a type with inscription *Sc Eadmund Rex*, the reverse a cross and the moneyer's name (Pl. 442). When by the peace of Wedmore in 878 the Dane, Guthrum, received the kingdom of East Anglia he issued coins under the name of Æthelstan. The kingdom of Northumbria ceased using a sceatta coinage before it was seized by the Viking invaders. The first coinage of the Viking rulers in a Danish kingdom of York was struck at the mint of York which supplies the reverse inscription on some issues of Cnut and Siefred. In addition to the common type of a cross pattée other forms of cross used on this Viking coinage include the patriarchal cross, cross crosslet and cross moline. Coins of Sihtric (*c.* 941–942) and Anlaf (*c.* 927–952) have more unusual types a trefoil-shaped shield on obverse and a Danish standard on reverse, and one series of another Anlaf has as obverse type a raven (Pl. 443).

In the west it was the kingdom of the West Saxons, Wessex, which absorbed in turn the other Saxon kingdoms and created finally a single kingdom in England. The Wessex coinage began under Beorhtric (786–802) and after the seizure of Kent most of the pennies of Ecgberht (802–838) were struck at the mint of Canterbury. When in 829 Ecgberht conquered Mercia he established a mint at London, the name of the city appearing on the reverse of a series of his coins. Pennies of this king which term him *Rex Saxoniorum* and are in a different style were probably struck at Winchester, the capital of Wessex. Coins with somewhat similar types, including some with obverse portrait, were struck for Æthelwulf (838–858) mainly at Canterbury and only briefly at Winchester. A somewhat unusual reverse for Æthelwulf and his successor Æthelbert (858–866) has an open cross with the moneyer's name disposed on the limbs of the cross and in the angles. The coinage of Alfred (871–899) contains a number of rare and unusual designs. These include a piece with a reverse copying the two seated emperors type of a Roman coin and used also by the Viking, Halfdene, and pieces with royal portrait and on the reverse a monogram of the name of London, struck probably after the fortification of London in 886 after its destruction at Viking hands (Pl. 444). A coinage of halfpennies, some with more conventional types, a cross and the king's name and the moneyer's name in two lines on the reverse, is the first instance of this denomination in the English coinage. The successful con-- solidation of the kingdom of Wessex by Alfred in the face of the Danish invaders, whose hold on England was restricted to the Danelaw, the eastern part of England, is reflected in the establishment of new mints at Gloucester and Exeter. The re-conquest of the Danelaw was begun under Alfred's son Edward the Elder (899–924) and though the differentiation of mints upon the coins of Alfred's reign was not continued, a range of new types was introduced on Edward's coinage. These include a hand of Providence, a flower between two leaves, a city gate copied from a Roman bronze-coin type and an ecclesiastical building.

Under Æthelstan (924–939) the kingdom was extended beyond the Humber and the Danish kingdom of York was annexed. Legislation of this reign decreed that a single coinage should be current and that coinage should be struck only within a town. Early issues of the reign still carry only the moneyer's name, usually in two lines across the reverse, but later a circular reverse inscription gives the name of the mint as well as the moneyer. Towards the end of the reign the title *Rex Totius Britanniae*, king of All Britain, was used by Æthelstan on the obverse of his coinage (Pl. 445). The movement towards regular differentiation of the mints on coins suffered a relapse in the reigns of Edmund (939–946) and Edred (946–955), probably because of the continuing trouble in the north where the recently conquered kingdom of York was not finally pacified till 954. The re-established unity of the kingdom and the beneficent rule of Edgar (959–975) produced a prosperity reflected in the coinage, where after some issues of varying design without royal portrait and with only moneyer's name a more settled pattern was established with the king's portrait and title on obverse and in addition to the moneyer's name on the reverse there now regularly appeared that of the mint. Some thirty mints can be identified as participating in his coinage (Pl. 446).

The coins of Edgar's successor, Edward the Martyr, are of one class only, a repetition of the obverse portrait and small cross reverse of Edgar's last type but the long reign of Æthelred II (978–1016), the step-brother whose succession was obtained by the murder of Edward, provides a succession of varying types. In the basic conception of coin types, however, from this point onwards a certain uniformity now obtained in that the obverse was always reserved for the royal portrait and the reverse was generally a design based on the cross motif. The succession of coin types which were changed every few years is evidence of a fiscal plan to secure, at regular and frequent intervals, fresh revenue in the form of payment for the supplying of new coin dies. Since the number of mints had now increased to some seventy-five, each with a number of moneyers—a major mint such as London had as many as fifty—the revenue must have been considerable and the output of coinage vast. This great supply of money was required not only to meet the needs of the prosperous economy of the country but to pay the Dane-geld, the tribute paid to stave off the new Danish invasions which threatened England; and the numerous large hoards of Anglo-Saxon coins found in Scan-dinavia are evidence of the huge payments actually made.

Æthelred's coin types succeeded in introducing a certain variety within the basic concept. The royal portrait was not always a plain diademed portrait but on occasion showed the king in a radiate helmet, cuirassed, and with shield at shoulder—a reminiscence of some Constantinian portraits—while another variety places a sceptre in front of the royal bust. Reverses include a hand of Providence between alpha and omega and cross designs in which the limbs of the cross are formed by double lines to facilitate the division of the coin into halves or quarters for small change (Pl. 447). An extremely rare type, exceptional in not having the royal portrait, bears the Agnus Dei on obverse and a dove on reverse (Pl. 448). These types were once thought to be an allusion to the first millennium which mediaeval superstition anticipated would bring the end of the world.

The Danes under Canute were invading England when Æthelred died in 1016 and the sudden death of the latter's son, Edmund Ironside, left Canute as sole ruler of England. The new dynasty, however, brought little significant change to the coinage. Two varieties of obverse portrait make their appearance showing the king wearing a pointed helmet or a crown, which here makes one of its earliest appearances in the English coinage (Pl. 449). The final issue for Canute has as reverse a cross of four jewels, a type which was carried on by his successor, his natural son, Harold (1035–40) and by his son Harthacanute (1040–2). Both sons have also a coinage where the obverse shows the royal portrait with sceptre. The coinage of Edward the Confessor, the Saxon king restored in 1042, has no less than ten successive issues in the twenty-four years of his reign. A concession to realism in portraiture is the bearded portrait of the last five issues, one of which is a slightly comic facing portrait instead of the usual profile bust, and as a complete innovation one type shows a full-length portrait of the king, enthroned and holding sceptre and globe (Pl. 450). The reverse of this particular issue has in each angle of the cross of the reverse an eagle, often miscalled a martlet. The brief reign of the last of the Saxon kings, Harold II, shows his crowned bust with sceptre and on the reverse the word *Pax* across the field.

The use of coinage to provide a commentary on contemporary events which is such a feature of the Roman series is quite exceptional in mediaeval coinage. Thus the Norman conquest which followed the battle of Hastings in 1066 has left little trace on the coins of William the Conqueror (1066–87). Even the smattering of foreign names amongst the moneyers is little greater than in the reigns of Edward the Confessor and Harold II. The main new feature, besides, of course, William's name as king, is the variety of royal portraits. On the eight principal categories of coinage in William's reign the reverse continued to exhibit a design based on a cross motif and still carried the names of the moneyer and mint but, after the first issue which had a profile bust, the remainder, with one rare exception, presented varieties of the facing portrait which was to remain standard on English coinage for centuries. William is always shown crowned. His portrait appears under a canopy, flanked by two sceptres or two stars or with a sword held in the right hand. The latest issue, which accounts for the greater proportion of William's coinage, shows him crowned and holding the sceptre, while the reverse is a cross with the letters *Paxs* in the angles (Pl. 451). William II (1087–1100) has a coinage with an almost identical form of title on the obverse and coin types varying only in detail from those of his father, and the allocation of five classes of coin to William II is based only on the internal evidence of the coins themselves and on the evidence of coin hoards.

Under Henry I (1100–35) the standard of execution of the coinage shows a marked decline and forgery became more widespread, requiring two major attempts at reform in 1108 and 1125, but, though the issues immediately following the reform show some betterment, the standard quickly fell again. Of the fifteen successive issues of Henry I, only the last few seem to have been of any considerable quantity. Of these the most common shows a facing portrait of the king and a reverse consisting of a quatrefoil cross, ornamented with pellets and with a lis in each quarter (Pl. 452). The civil wars which rent the country during the greater part of the reign of Stephen (1135–54) are probably the cause of the rarity and the poor quality of most of the coinage of this reign. Of the seven issues of Stephen only the first two are at all common. These show a profile bust with sceptre and a cross moline with lis in angles and a facing bust with voided cross with stars in the angles. The number of mints which had continued to decline since the Conquest was now only about fifty and at some of these, when they fell into the hands of rebel barons, barbarous varieties of Stephen's types were struck. Some rare issues of slightly more competent style carry the names of the rebel barons and rare pennies similar to the first issue of Stephen's coinage have the name of the empress Matilda. This daughter of Henry I and widow of the emperor Henry V was subsequently married to Fulk V of Anjou and contested the succession of Stephen to the throne of England.

THE PLANTAGENET KINGS

In 1158, a few years after the succession of Henry II (1154–89), the son of the empress Matilda and the first of the Plantagenet kings, a monetary reform terminated the system of the change of coin types at frequent intervals The coinage of Henry II was, for the greater part of his reign, of a single type, showing on obverse his facing bust and on the reverse a cross with small crosslets in the angles (Pl. 453). This type is commonly called the Tealby type from the large find of coins of this kind made at Tealby in Lincolnshire in 1807. This coinage which lasted until 1180 is susceptible to a division into a succession of chronological groups, based on such criteria as varieties of bust and lettering.

The poor standard of workmanship of the Tealby coins made necessary the introduction in 1180 of a new coinage. Although the new series showed some improvement in the execution of the coinage, there was little advance in the artistic standard of the design, which continued the custom of a facing bust of the king, now holding a sceptre which protrudes into the circular inscription giving the king's name. This coinage derives its name, the Short-Cross coinage, from the reverse type, a cross with short arms and a quatrefoil ornament in each quarter (Pl. 454). The Short-Cross penny remained essentially the same in design until 1247 and, though it was issued by four kings, during the whole issue the king's title on the obverse continued to read *Henricus Rex*. This coinage was current for the latter years of the reign of Henry II (1180–9), the whole reigns of Richard (1189–99) and John (1199–1216) and finally part of the reign of Henry III. As in the case of the Tealby coinage, the arrangement of the Short-Cross coins into chronological groups which can be attributed to the successive reigns depends upon minutiae of design and lettering. The names of the mints and the moneyers still continued to appear on the reverse, revealing a steady diminution of the number of mints in action. Only some thirty mints struck coins of the Tealby type and for the Short-Cross issue the number was reduced to twenty of which the most productive were London, Canterbury, York and Durham.

Towards the close of the Short-Cross issue in 1247 clipping of the coins had become so prevalent that a new issue was decided upon and, in an attempt to prevent clipping, the type of the reverse was altered by extending the cross on the reverse to the edge of the coin, it being ordained that no coin was legal tender, if an arm of the cross was incomplete. The obverse of this Long-Cross coinage still showed a facing bust of the king, only sometimes holding sceptre, but the obverse inscription now most commonly read *Henricus Rex III*; the long arms of the reverse cross cut through the inscription and in each quarter of the reverse were three pellets (Pl. 455). The number of active mints towards the end of the Short-Cross coinage had been few, principally the Royal mints at London and Canterbury; but, after the inception of the new Long-Cross issue, the output required the opening of sixteen mints which functioned only till about 1250. An innovation in this coinage was the striking of a gold penny for Henry III in 1255, probably in imitation of the issue of the gold florin at Florence some five years earlier. The gold penny, struck at London at the value of twenty silver pence, portrayed the enthroned figure of the king on the obverse and, on the reverse, again a long cross but with a rose between the three pellets in each quarter.

In the first seven years of the reign of Edward I (1272–1307) coins of the Long-Cross type continued to be issued without altering the title *Henricus Rex III*, but in 1279 came a new coin type showing a facing bust of the king crowned, with long side-locks of hair and giving Edward's name and titles. Following a change in mint organization the moneyers name disappears from the reverse of the coinage from this time onwards, though the mint name was to remain for several centuries still (Pl. 456). As in the previous single-type coinages, this type, known as the sterling, remained in issue through several reigns—the long reign of Edward I, the reign of Edward II (1307–27) and the early years of Edward III. In this coinage also began the more regular production of halfpennies and farthings of similar design but of respectively smaller module. On a basis of close study of letter forms, minute variations in names, titles and design no less than ten successive groups of coins are attributed to the reign of Edward I and three to the reign of Edward II. The basic distinction is that pennies with the form of name *Edw* are of Edward I, those with the slightly larger form *Edwa* or *Edwar* are of Edward II. In 1279 Edward I introduced a new denomination, the groat or fourpenny piece, with types similar to those of the penny but with two concentric circles of inscription on the reverse, the outer continuing the king's titles, the inner giving the name of the mint of London. This experimental issue was not a success and was of very brief duration.

The growth of trade and the increasing prosperity of the later Middle Ages eventually created in England the economic circumstances which made possible and necessary a permanent coinage in gold, though this stage was not reached until 1344, almost a century after the re-introduction of regular gold coinage on the European continent. The first series of gold coinage consisted of florins of value 6 shillings, which had on the obverse a full-length portrait of the king enthroned and on the reverse a royal cross; the half- and quarter-florins borrowed their names of Leopard and Helm from their obverse types. Difficulties in maintaining this first gold series led to its replacement two years later by the famous gold noble, value 6 shillings and 8 pence, portraying on its obverse the king standing in a ship, supposedly a reference to the battle of Sluys; the reverse is an ornate cross with the letter L, later E, in the centre and a leopard and crown in each quarter.

The Edwardian pennies had a wide circulation on the Continent, particularly in the Low Countries and north Germany and were widely imitated there. The economic difficulties created by the importation of many of these imitations of lower quality were one of the causes of the monetary reform of 1351 which reduced the weight of both the gold and silver coins. Gold nobles, as well as halves, with similar types and quarters with the royal arms as obverse type were struck at this new weight throughout the remainder of the reign. The royal title on the obverse of the coinage contained the claim of the English kings to the French crown but during the eight years following the Treaty of Bretigny in 1361 the French title was omitted, though that of lord of Aquitaine made its appearance. Another new feature on the gold coinage was the use as an inscription on the reverse of a quotation from scripture, namely an abbreviated form of *Jesus autem transiens per medium illorum ibat* (Pl. 457). The monetary reform of 1351 also created larger silver denominations, the groat (fourpence) and half-groat (twopence). The types were an adaption of the abortive groat of 1279, a crowned bust of the king within a tressure of arches and on the reverse the long-cross with pellets in the angles familiar from the penny (Pl. 458). The reverse had two concentric circles of inscription; the inner gave the mint name, the outer another scriptural quotation, *Posui deum adiutorem meum* (Ps. liv. 4). The royal title underwent the same changes on the silver as on the gold. The striking of the coinage was by this time largely concentrated in the mint of London which, as well as striking silver, alone produced the early gold issues of Edward III. Mints at York and Durham struck only silver. At times episcopal mints in these cities struck pence and halfpence, differentiated in design by a feature such as a quatrefoil or a crozier at the centre of the cross on the reverse. In addition to these mints, a mint opened at Calais in 1363, struck both gold and silver coin. The coinage of Richard II (1377–99) is almost identical with that of Edward III except for the eventual replacement of Edward's name by that of Richard.

Under Henry IV (1399–1413) the types and denominations of the coinage continued much the same but the undervaluing of the English currency in relation to foreign coins in the early fifteenth century caused such a drain on coin and bullion that a new coinage of reduced weight both in gold and silver was instituted in 1412 and the mint at Calais was closed down. The types of the coinage, however, suffered no change and, in fact, were repeated with only minor variations of design for Henry V (1413–22) and the first reign of Henry VI (1422–61). The mint at Calais resumed activity under Henry VI between 1424 and 1428, the noble being differentiated, as indeed in earlier reigns, from that struck at London by the appearance of a flag at the stern of the ship on the obverse. The smaller denominations issued by the episcopal mints at York and Durham continued to carry small marks of differentiation such as the cross and letter B beside the neck of the royal portrait on the Durham pennies of Bishop Lawrence Booth (1457–76).

THE HOUSE OF YORK

The lack of immediacy of mediaeval coin types as compared with those of the ancient world is well demonstrated by the minimal effect on the coinage even of the Wars of the Roses. The overthrow of Henry VI of Lancaster by Edward IV of York in 1461 brought no immediate change in the coinage and when changes were made in 1464 they were the result of economic rather than political causes. Two new denominations in gold were introduced at this time. The chief new gold piece, the Rose noble with a value of 10 shillings, had an obverse similar to that of the old noble but had a rose on the side of the ship and a radiate sun at the centre of the reverse cross (Pl. 459). A new gold piece with the same value as the earlier noble was the famous coin called the angel, so called from its obverse portraying St. Michael slaying the dragon; the reverse was a ship bearing a shield with a cross above (Pl. 460). These coins, as well as earlier series, fall into successive groups distinguished by a number of minute differences, principally the initial mark, the small symbol appearing at the beginning of both obverse and reverse inscription. The new coinage of Rose nobles or ryals required the activity of mints outside London and these pieces were struck at York, Bristol, Coventry and Norwich, the issues being distinguished by the initial letter of the mint name appearing in the waves of the obverse design.

The coinage of gold ryals was of short duration; certainly this denomination had ceased to be struck by 1470 when Henry VI was restored for a brief second reign of some six months. The only gold coins of this reign are gold angels and half-angels, mainly from the London mint. The groat was struck at Bristol and York as well as London and smaller silver, except the farthings, from most of these mints. In the second reign of Edward IV (1471–83) a similar range of denominations was struck, differentiated from those of the first reign by a new series of initial marks. The rare coins of the brief reign of the boy king Edward V in 1483 are distinguished from those of his father, Edward IV, only by the initial marks at the head of legends, a boar's head, the personal badge of the king's uncle, Richard, as regent. This coinage was issued only by the London mint but Richard III, who succeeded after the murder of his nephew, issued silver from the provincial mints as well.

THE TUDOR COINAGE

The accession in 1485 of Henry VII, the first of the Tudor monarchs, is conventionally regarded as marking the transition from the mediaeval to the modern in English coinage. The new coinage introduced in 1489 is marked by a notable advance in artistic treatment and by new denominations in both gold and silver. The gold coinage and silver groats were struck only at the mint in London while provincial mints shared in the production of the smaller silver denominations. The episcopal mints at York and Canterbury produced half-groats, pennies and halfpennies, Durham only pennies. The most magnificent of the new coins was the gold sovereign of 20 shillings, whose large flan was eminently suited for displaying the magnificently rich Tudor design with the king enthroned on the obverse and an elaborate Tudor rose and shield of arms on the reverse (Pl. 461). A short issue of gold ryals between 1489 and 1490 had types similar to the ryal of Edward IV but the rose of York was removed from the side of the ship on the obverse and the reverse became a Tudor rose with small shield of arms of France in the centre. The angel and its half introduced by Edward IV were retained, as indeed they were by subsequent Tudor and Stuart monarchs who used them as presentation pieces at the ceremony of touching for the king's evil. A new silver piece struck by Henry VII was the testoon, the forerunner of the later shilling, but it was short-lived and was probably only a trial issue. Towards the end of the reign a new type of groat made its appearance. The use of a realistic profile portrait on this issue shows that the new ideas of the Renaissance were beginning to have effect on the medallic art of England; the reverse was a shield on a long cross (Pl. 462). Yet another innovation was the 'sovereign' penny whose obverse type of the enthroned king was similar to that on the gold sovereign.

The first coinage issues of Henry VIII (1509–47) were almost identical in denominations and types with those of his father, the principal difference being the alteration of the numeral of the title from VII to VIII. One of the very few changes in the early coinage was in the types of the silver farthing. Because of the difficulty in distinguishing between the almost equally small modules of identical design of the halfpenny and farthing, new types, a portcullis obverse and a rose reverse, were placed on the latter denomination from 1523. The vast resources amassed by the careful policy of Henry VII were eventually dissipated by Henry VIII who sought a remedy for his financial difficulties in a debasement of the coinage. In 1523 a new coinage equated in standard to that of foreign countries was issued under the direction of Cardinal Wolsey. The value of the sovereign was increased to 22 shillings and 6 pence and the angel to 7 shillings and 6 pence and a new coin called the crown of the rose was introduced at a value of 4 shillings and 6 pence with types a crowned shield and a rose over a cross. A new, more realistic portrait was used on the new sovereign and half-piece. To maintain a gold denomination of the traditional value of 6 shillings and 8 pence a new piece called the George noble was struck, taking its name from the reverse type which showed St. George slaying the dragon. This denomination and the crown of the rose were of short duration, being replaced by a crown of value 5 shillings, with types a double rose crowned on obverse and a crowned shield of arms on reverse. At first on obverse only but later on both sides of this denomination appear the letters HK, HA or HI, the initials of Henry and his successive queens, Katherine, Anne and Jane. The obverse of the groat received at this time also a new profile portrait of Henry. The issue from the episcopal mint of Wolsey at York has his initials TW on either side of the shield on the reverse with his cardinal's hat below (Pl. 463).

A further debasement was decreed for the coinage issued from 1544 onwards. The principal new feature of this issue was the re-introduction of the testoon. The obverse type presented a facing bust of Henry, an unflattering piece of portraiture showing the large bearded features of the ageing king. A similar change of portrait was also made in the gold sovereign, on the groat (Pl. 464), half-groat and penny.

The practice, remarked already on a number of occasions, of using the types of the previous reign for the first issues of a new reign persisted in some early issues of Edward VI (1547–53) to the extent that even the title of Henry VIII was retained, though on portrait coins such as the half-sovereign the features are those of the boy king, Edward. Consistent attempts were made throughout this reign to restore the standard of the coinage, at least of the gold denominations, though the silver denominations until late in the reign were even more base than in

Henry's reign. The first issues with the name of Edward VI as well as his portrait largely repeat the denominations and types of Henry, the principal innovation being a new shilling piece with a profile portrait obverse and shield on cross reverse. The improved gold coinage between 1549 and 1550 introduced new types for the half, quarter and half-quarter sovereigns. These had on the obverse a profile portrait either bare-headed or crowned and on the reverse a garnished shield and the letters ER. In the further improved coinage in the final years of the reign from 1550 a sovereign of value 30 shillings maintained the traditional types first introduced by Henry VII, but the sovereign of 20 shillings as well as the half-sovereign, the gold crown and half-crown carried a half-length portrait of the king, crowned and holding orb and sceptre. The angel, now valued at 10 shillings, retained its traditional types.

In 1551 the first of the long line of silver crowns was struck with a lively equestrian portrait of the king on obverse, the reverse being the simple shield on long-cross type (Pl. 465). A similar design supplied the reverse for a new issue of fine shillings, sixpences and threepences. These all have a three-quarter facing bust of the king crowned with, in the field, a rose and the appropriate mark of value in Roman numerals (Pl. 466).

In the sole reign of Mary (1553–4) the magnificent sovereign of 30 shillings was issued briefly with the now conventional types and, in addition, a ryal of 15 shillings with the charming, if somewhat incongruous obverse of the queen standing in a ship, while the usual angel and half-piece also found their place in the gold coinage. Silver denominations from groat to penny all have a profile portrait of unusually delicate beauty (Pl. 467). The gold issues of the joint reign of Mary and Philip II of Spain (1554–8) are restricted to the angel and angelet and carry the names of both sovereigns. The shilling and half-shilling have a shield with the joint coat-of-arms on the reverse and an unusual obverse on which the profile busts of Philip and Mary are placed *vis-à-vis* after the manner of coins of Ferdinand and Isabella of Spain (Pl. 468). The early issues of these coins bear, in addition to Mary's titles, Philip's titles of Naples and Spain but these latter were omitted on subsequent issues. On the smaller silver denominations it is only the portrait of Mary which appears, though Philip's name also is included in the inscription.

Following the accession of Elizabeth I in 1558 efforts, not altogether successful, were made to withdraw from circulation the quantities of base money still in circulation. On Elizabethan issues the initial marks which are assignable to specific years provide the key to the sequence of the coinage, and in addition a number of issues carry a clear date in numerals. As well as the sovereign, ryal and angel familiar from previous reigns Elizabeth issued another series in gold consisting of a pound, half-pound, crown and half-crown with crowned portrait and crowned-shield reverse. The crown in silver, introduced by Edward VI but not continued by Mary, was resumed by Elizabeth and the beruffed and crowned portrait with orb and sceptre on this denomination and its half is handsome and regal. An unusual number of smaller denominations in silver were struck in this reign for to the now standard shilling, sixpence (Pl. 469) and threepence as well as the traditional groat, half-groat and penny were added novel pieces of three-halfpence and three-farthings. The types on all these silver denominations were a profile portrait and a shield on cross. Behind the bust on the threepence, three-halfpence and three-farthings was a small rose to distinguish these pieces from the groat, half-groat and penny respectively to which they approximated very closely in size.

All the English coins described up to this point were struck manually by hammer, as had been the practice from the earliest days of coinage, but in the reign of Elizabeth an experiment was made in producing coins by machinery, including a screw-press for stamping them with the dies. Experiment in the mechanical striking of coins had earlier been made in Italy by Leonardo da Vinci and in other continental countries and the innovation in the English coinage was entrusted to the French moneyer Eloye Mestrell. These milled issues included half-pound, crown and half-crown in gold and, in silver, denominations from shilling to half-groat. Restrictive jealousy, however, on the part of the established moneyers ensured that this new method of striking was not adopted at this point in the history of the coinage.

THE STUART AND COMMONWEALTH COINAGE

The coinage of James I is largely undated but the sequence of the issues is apparent from the succession of initial marks. In the first issue (1603–4) James had the title of King of England and Scotland. On the gold coinage of sovereigns and portions the obverse carried the crowned half-length portrait of the king but on the silver crown and half-crown James reverted to the equestrian portrait as on the first issue of this denomination by Edward VI. On smaller silver pieces including the shilling, sixpence, half-groat and penny there was a profile bust with numerals behind the head indicating the value. The halfpenny with portcullis obverse and cross and pellets reverse repeated the types of the Elizabethan halfpenny.

A new issue, at a slightly reduced standard introduced in 1604 in a renewed effort to check the flight abroad of precious metals, has a new royal title, that of King of Great Britain (*Mag. Brit.*). The sovereign of 30 shillings, the ryal, angel and angelet were coined once more in this issue as well as the sovereign of

20 shillings and its parts. An unusual denomination was the thistle crown of 4 shillings with crowned rose and crowned thistle as the two types. These became also the types for silver from half-groat downwards, though the shilling and sixpence continued as in the first issue.

To combat the continued flight of bullion the value of all gold coins was raised by 10 per cent in 1611 but the remedy proved ineffective and a further reduced standard was brought in in 1619. All the gold denominations were coined in this issue except the thistle crown and half-crown. The gold piece of 20 shillings is commonly styled a 'laurel' because the new portrait consisted of a laureate bust in the Roman manner. The 20 shilling piece, its half and quarter had a mark of value behind the bust (Pl. 470).

The first copper pieces in the English coinage were authorized in 1613 when James granted a special licence to Lord Harington to issue copper farthings. These coins bore the royal name and title and had as types two sceptres crowned and a crowned harp (Pl. 471).

The coinage of Charles I continued in general the denominations and types of his father. In gold the now traditional angel of value 10 shillings was struck as well as the gold unite of 20 shillings with its half and quarter. The types on these pieces were a crowned profile bust of the king to left with the mark of value in shillings shown by Roman numerals behind the head and on the reverse the royal arms crowned. The two higher values in silver, the crown and half-crown, had as obverse the king on horseback with sword held upright before him; the reverse was again the royal arms. The lower denominations from shilling to penny had a profile bust similar to that on the gold coins and also carried a mark of value on the obverse. The practice of issuing token copper farthings, begun in the previous reign, was continued. The patent for issuing these had passed to the Duchess of Richmond in 1624 and passed again to Lord Maltravers in 1634. The types of the earlier farthings were crossed sceptres and harp and from 1636 the reverse was a rose (Pl. 472).

The most outstanding hammered coins in this reign were the work of a Frenchman, Nicholas Briot, but even more outstanding in excellence of technique were the coins produced by Briot using the mill and screw-press, methods originally tried out in the reign of Elizabeth I. The silver crown (Pl. 473) exemplifies his work.

Since, with the onset of the Civil War, the Tower mint in London fell into the hands of Parliament in 1642 but continued to strike coinage with the types of Charles until his execution in 1649, mints were established in various provincial centres for the supply of coinage for the Royalists. At a number of these mints silver coinages from the crown downwards was issued with types similar to

those of the Tower-mint coins but some differential other than the slightly
different style is usually included on either obverse or reverse. At York the letters
Ebor distinguished its coins, at Aberystwyth plumes, at Weymouth the letter *W*
and the letters *Ex* on crowns and half-crowns at Exeter. At some other mints,
notably at Shrewsbury, Oxford and Bristol, some unusual denominations and
types were used. The most complete range is that of the Oxford mint. On gold
pieces including a triple unite, a unite and its half-piece the king holds sword and
olive-branch on the obverse while on the reverse appears in abbreviated form the
Declaration, *Religio Protestantium, Leges Angliae, Libertas Parliamenti,* the avowed
policy of the Royalist party (Pl. 474). Silver coins also used this Declaration reverse
with a mark of value above it. The higher denominations from the pound down
to half-crown had an equestrian portrait of the king, the lower denominations
from shilling to penny a profile portrait. At Shrewsbury the only denomination
in gold was the triple unite and silver pieces ranged from the pound to shilling.
The types are similar to those in use at Oxford but are distinguished by different
plumes in the field above the Declaration. Most of the Bristol coinage—in gold
the unite and half-unite, in silver from half-crown to half-groat—was distinguished
by the monogram *Br.* Coinage was struck at other mints, mainly in the West
Country, at Chester, Worcester and possibly on Lundy Island.

During the Civil War, emergency coins were struck at various places while
they were besieged. Since the blanks for these were often produced by cutting up
silver plate the coins were often of unusual lozenge or octagonal shape and since
such irregular and crude pieces lend themselves to easy imitation modern forgeries
of this series are not uncommon. Siege pieces are known for Carlisle, Newark,
Pontefract and Scarborough. Amongst the most common are those of Newark,
lozenge-shaped pieces with the royal initials and crown and mark of value from
half-crown (xxx) to sixpence on the obverse and Newark and the date 1646 on
the reverse (Pl. 474a). The irregular-shaped pieces from Scarborough have a rough
design of the castle and the value stamped on them.

After the execution of Charles I in 1649 a coinage was struck for the Commonwealth with inscriptions wholly in English, the first and last occasion on which
legends in Latin were abandoned. The types, common to all denominations both
in gold and silver, were on obverse the shield of St. George with inscription
The Commonwealth of England and on reverse the shields of St. George and of
Ireland with inscription *God With Us* and a mark of value. These designs are
passable on the gold denominations where the execution was of reasonable
standard (Pl. 475); on the silver the crude workmanship accentuates their banality.
A very fine portrait coinage for Cromwell as Lord Protector was designed by the
medallist Thomas Simon, but it was never put into circulation.

After the Restoration in 1660 the production of hammered coins for Charles II continued for some two years and, as the dies were the work of Thomas Simon, the resultant coins are amongst the most successful of the whole hammered series. On the gold unite of 20 shillings the handsome bust of the king, laureate and with long flowing hair is placed in a well-lettered inscription free from an enclosing line while the crowned and decorated shield of the reverse is similarly disposed. These types are repeated on the half and quarter unite but on the silver denominations, which include only the half-crown, the groat, threepence, half-groat and penny, the royal portrait is crowned and a mark of value was placed behind the head.

With the abandonment of hammered coinage and the introduction in 1662 of coinage generally termed 'milled'—that is produced by machinery, a denominational system was inaugurated which was to remain basically the same for many years. In gold the unit was a new piece called the guinea, the name of which was derived from the source of some of the metal in Guinea in Africa. On some coins the small symbol of an elephant or an elephant and castle are the badge of the Africa Company. There were, as multiples of the guinea, the 5 guinea and 2 guinea piece, and a half-guinea was also struck. The types on all these denominations were the same; on obverse the laureate portrait of the king, on reverse four shields of arms, arranged crosswise, and crossed sceptres (Pl. 476). From this point onward the date of issue was normally included in the reverse inscription. On the edge of the 5 guinea piece (and also the silver crown and half-crown) appeared an incuse inscription e.g. *Decus et tutamen*—an ornament and protection (against clipping) *anno regni quarto decimo*. Since Charles regarded his reign as beginning in 1649, 1662 was his fourteenth regnal year.

The types used for the silver coinage were practically identical. In place of the sceptres in the angles of the cross formed of shields on the reverse of the gold, the angles contained two linked C's on the larger silver denominations from crown down to sixpence. The smaller pieces, the silver fourpence, threepence, twopence and penny had as reverse type the value marked in C's. A new feature of this coinage was the introduction in 1672 of a regal halfpenny and farthing in copper. The king's portrait on the obverse is laureate and cuirassed in the Roman fashion and the inscription reads *Carolus a Carolo*—Charles, the son of Charles. The figure of Britannia which now appeared for the first time on British coinage was probably inspired by the Britannia on coins of Hadrian and Antoninus Pius in the second century but is a very free adaptation of the Roman model (Pl. 477). In the last year of the reign tin farthings with a copper plug were struck with the edge stamped *Nummorum famulus* (a subsidiary coinage).

The coinage of James II (1685–8) showed little change in either denominations or types, apart, of course, from the royal portrait. The portrait of Charles II looked to the right, that of James II to the left, marking the beginning of the tradition of alternate right and left facing regal portraits for successive reigns which has been maintained up till the present. On the larger silver coins the linked C's for Charles II naturally disappeared and the angles were left plain. Similarly the reverses of the lower denominations consisted of the value marked by Roman numerals. The halfpenny and farthing were struck only in tin.

The joint reign of William III and Mary (1688–94) brought some changes in coin types. On all denominations the obverse showed the jugate busts of the king and queen. The reverse of the gold coinage abandoned the shields arranged in cross design and substituted the crowned shield carrying the royal arms with the lion of Nassau imposed on the centre (Pl. 478). The usual reverse on silver coins continued the four shields in cross type but now included the lion of Nassau in the centre of the design. In the angles were the initials *W* and *M* in monogram. On some half-crowns the reverse repeats the single shield type of the gold coinage. In the last year of the reign copper replaced tin as the metal for the halfpenny and farthing.

On gold coinage of the sole reign of William III (1694–1702), as well as the obvious alteration in the obverse portrait, the reverse type was changed to the four shields forming a cross, with the lion of Nassau in the centre as well as crossed sceptres. The types on silver were similar but omitted the crossed sceptres. Owing to the clipping of the hammered money still in circulation it was decided to withdraw this and an extensive recoinage to replace it was ordered in 1695. The new coinage required the work of additional mints at Bristol, Chester, Exeter, Norwich and York until 1698, the product of these mints being marked by the initial letter of the mint placed under the obverse bust (Pl. 479).

The coinage of Anne (1702–14), the last of the Stuart sovereigns, maintained the now settled pattern of denominations and types. On the reverse the arms of Nassau disappeared from the centre of the design and after the Act of Union in 1706 the two shields which previously had contained the arms of Scotland and England respectively now contained each the joint arms. An exceptional feature on part of Anne's coinage is the appearance of the word VIGO under the queen's bust, marking the coins struck in 1702 and 1703 from the gold and silver captured from the Spanish ships at the battle of Vigo Bay in 1702 (Pl. 480). In base metal only the farthing was struck and that only in the last year of the reign. It is perhaps for this reason that the great rarity of Queen Anne farthings has become one of the most persistent numismatic fictions.

The conservatism of British coinage was little affected by the political circumstances, when, on the death of Anne in 1714, the claim to the throne of the son of James II was rejected in favour of George, the Elector of Hanover. The denominational system remained the same except for the introduction of a quarter-guinea and the types underwent little change. The titles of Duke of Brunswick and Luneburg and Elector of the Holy Roman empire held by George before his elevation to the British throne form a new inscription for the coin reverses and one of the four shields on the reverse bore the Hanoverian arms. A number of minor variations appeared on the reverse of silver coins in the course of the reign. Roses and plumes in the angles mark pieces struck from silver obtained from mines in England and Wales while silver coinage of 1723 carries the letters SSC for the disastrous South Sea Company (Pl. 481) and on shillings of 1723–26 the letters WCC stand for the Welsh Copper Company.

The principal innovation on the coinage of George II (1727–60) was the use of a crowned and decorated shield as the reverse type of gold coins. The small letters EIC under the bust indicated the gold coins struck from metal supplied by the East India Company (Pl. 482) and the word LIMA in a similar position devotes coins both in gold and silver struck from the half-million bullion brought back by Anson in 1744 from his round the world voyage. From the year 1729 the smaller silver denominations from fourpence to a penny, whose reverse types from the reign of William and Mary had simply been a crowned numeral giving the value, were no longer struck for normal circulation but only as Maundy coins for distribution by the sovereign on Easter Thursday (Pl. 483). This charitable distribution to persons to the number of the sovereign's age of a like number of silver pennies has been maintained up till the present day. Silver coins of value fourpence, threepence, twopence and a penny with types similar to those in the eighteenth century have continued to be struck in all reigns especially for this ceremony.

The lengthy reign of George III (1760–1820) witnessed a number of changes both in denominations and types. No 5 or 2 guinea pieces were struck for circulation but the guinea and the half were issued extensively. The quarter-guinea was struck only in 1762 but between 1797 and 1813 when there was a dearth of silver coinage a third of a guinea was struck to provide change. The reverse type of this piece was simply the royal crown. On the guinea and the half up to 1786 the reverse type was the crowned and decorated shield continued from the coins of George II but between 1787 and 1799 the shield was changed to a shape which gave rise to the description the 'spade' guinea (Pl. 484). Half-guineas from 1800 to 1813 and guineas in 1813 have the shield of arms enclosed in a ribbon inscribed with the motto of the Order of the Garter.

In the early part of the reign very little silver coinage was struck. The shilling was issued only in 1763 and 1787 and the sixpence only in the latter year. The scant amount of silver available led to the authorization in 1797 of the issue of Spanish dollars with, as a counter-mark, the head of George III. In 1804 the Bank of England was authorized to issue 'Bank Dollars' of value 5 shillings and later in 1811 pieces of 3 shillings and 1 shilling and 6 pence. Copper halfpennies and farthings with the traditional Britannia reverse were issued in some quantity between 1770 and 1775 but a new copper issue was ordered in 1797. This included new denominations, the copper penny and twopence still using the Britannia reverse. Their size and weight plus the broad band round the edge earned them the name of 'cartwheel' coins (Pl. 485). Halfpennies and farthings of similar types were issued in 1799. In a new issue of lighter weight in 1806 and 1807 the twopence was omitted.

A new coinage ordered in 1816 and issued in 1817 introduced the modern sovereign of 20 shillings with its famous design of St. George and the Dragon by the medallist Pistrucci (Pl. 486). On the half-sovereign, however, the reverse continued to be a crowned shield. The types for the silver coinage followed a similar pattern, the Pistrucci design being used for the major piece, the crown, and a shield of arms for the half-crown, shilling and sixpence.

The only denominational change in the coins of George IV (1820–30) was the issue in 1823 of a double sovereign with the St. George and Dragon reverse. This design was also used for the reverse of the ordinary sovereign until 1825 when it was changed to a crowned shield. Shields of varying pattern supplied the reverse of the half-sovereign and of the half-crown, shilling and sixpence while the crown continued to have a St. George reverse. From 1826 the reverse of shillings and six-pences was altered to a lion standing on the crown with the emblems of England, Scotland and Ireland below. These emblems also appeared below Britannia on the copper penny, halfpenny and farthing. For William IV (1830–7) the sovereign and its half had a shield reverse. In silver the crown was not issued and the reverse of the half-crown showed an elaborately draped shield, while the designs of the shillings and sixpences were very pedestrian, being simply the value in words within a wreath. In 1836 the groat or fourpenny piece in silver was revived with a Britannia reverse (Pl. 487).

The coinage of Victoria's long reign (1837–1901) falls into three groups defined by three successive portraits. A young portrait was current from 1837 to 1886, the Jubilee portrait from 1887 to 1892 and the older portrait from 1893 to the end of the reign. On sovereigns and half-sovereigns the familiar reverses first a shield and later St. George and Dragon were used. An unusual reverse appeared on the crown in 1847, the 'Gothic' crown, so called because of the elaborate four-shield reverse within a tressure of arches and the use of Gothic letters in the inscription. The date is given in Roman numerals, also in Gothic script. A new denomination, the florin, was introduced in 1849 as a first step towards a decimal coinage, the reverse stating that it was one-tenth of a pound. This issue, because of the omission from the royal style of the usual formula *Dei gratia*, became known as the 'godless' florin. This was succeeded in 1851 by the 'Gothic' florin where the inscriptions including Roman numerals are in Gothic letters (Pl. 488). Between 1887 and 1890 a brief experiment was made with a denomination of a double florin with conventional shields and sceptre reverse. On other silver denominations the types were either shields or the value of the piece in words. The striking of the silver groat was discontinued in 1856 but its place had been already taken by the silver threepenny which began issue in 1845. The coinage of penny, halfpenny and farthing up to 1860 was in copper with types similar to those of the preceding reigns but from that date bronze was used, the module was reduced to that still current and the date which had previously been on the obverse was transferred to the exergue under Britannia on the reverse.

The only novel design on the coins of Edward VII (1901–10) was the standing facing figure of Britannia on the florin. In the reign of George V (1910–36) the striking for circulation of sovereigns and half-sovereigns came to an end in 1915 and 1917 respectively. A new reverse design for crown pieces between 1928 and 1934 showed a crown within a decorated border and for the crown of 1935 an angular, modernistic version of St. George and the Dragon was used. From 1928 onwards the design for the reverse of shillings and sixpences was changed to a spray of acorns. Coinage for Edward VIII had not been put into circulation when he abdicated in December 1936 but a very few rare examples of twelve-sided threepences in nickel-brass with reverse the plant, thrift, somehow found their way into circulation. The reverse designs for the coins of George VI (1936–52) were mainly variants on the traditional themes. A special Scottish shilling had as its reverse the lion of Scotland, seated facing on a crown and on the silver threepenny was a shield on a rose (Pl. 489). On the bronze coins Britannia yielded place on the halfpenny to Drake's *Golden Hind* and on the farthing to a wren. A special issue of the silver crown with Pistrucci's St. George and Dragon was made in 1951 to mark the fourth centenary of the striking of the first silver crown by Edward VI.

The most notable coin of Queen Elizabeth II to date has been the crown piece issued in the year of her coronation. The obverse design of the queen on horseback recalls the equestrian portrait on the first silver crown and on those of the early Stuart kings (Pl. 490). The obverse used for other denominations marks a welcome return to a more graceful portrait bust in place of the head only of the preceding coinages. In 1961 the farthing was withdrawn from circulation.

ANGLO-GALLIC COINAGE

The convenient if not over-accurate term 'Anglo-Gallic' has been generally adopted to describe the coinage in the name of English rulers for the territories in France which they at different times controlled. These series, though they are unmistakably French in their denominations, types, fabric and style are yet, because of their firm association with English rulers, something distinct; for this reason, as well as for convenience, it has been decided to describe this coinage as an adjunct to the English coinage rather than as an intregal part of the French provincial issues.

The Norman kings issued no certain coinage in their duchy and it was not until the reign of Henry II who by his marriage to Eleanor, Duchess of Aquitaine, secured that duchy and the county of Poitou that the Anglo-Gallic coinage began. Although the marriage took place in 1152, Henry's coinage in Aquitaine began only after his accession to the English throne in 1154, for the coinage issues all accord him the title of king. Silver deniers of Henry are of simple design, his title *Henricus Rex* encircling a cross on the obverse and the name *Aquitanie* in four lines across the field of the reverse (Pl. 491). The smaller obols have only his name around a cross on obverse and his title *Rex* across the reverse. Deniers of Poitou, if issued under Henry, preserved their traditional types and legends with no overt reference to his name and rank.

The French possessions were granted by Henry II to his son, Richard Cœur de Lion in 1168. His deniers and obols are of identical types, his name, with no mention of title, in two lines across the obverse and a cross on the reverse with inscription *Aquitanie*. When Richard became king he relinquished Aquitaine to his mother Eleanor again and to this period is attributed a very common issue of deniers and obols. The types on both are two small crosses with a Gothic M above and an A below on obverse with inscription *Ducisit*; on the reverse is a cross and the name *Aquitanie* (Pl. 492). Though no convincing explanation of the obverse inscription and type letters has yet been advanced, the coins appear to belong to this period. Richard, on his accession, retained his earldom of Poitou and struck deniers and obols with his royal title around a cross as the obverse and *Pictaviensis* in three lines across the reverse. There were a large number of variants of design with occasional annulet in one quarter of the obverse and the series is so extensive that

it is thought to have been continued after Richard's death when his mother
Eleanor assumed the direction of Poitou. On the death of Eleanor, the English
possessions were seized by Philip Augustus of France and no Anglo-Gallic coinage
was issued in the name of John.

In 1225 Henry III by a treaty with Louis IX of France renounced his claims to
Normandy, Anjou and Poitou and received in return lands in the south to form a
duchy of Guienne. This territory never came into his actual possession and no
coins appear to have been struck there for Henry. Henry's son Edward obtained
the province of Gascony as the marriage portion of his wife, Eleanor of Castile.
Deniers and half-deniers of Gascony with types of lion and cross bear his title
Edward(us) Fili(us) H(enrici) Regis Anglie, half on obverse, half on reverse. As a
consequence of repeated quarrels between Edward I after his accession and the
French kings, the English possessions were frequently under French control but
between 1286 and 1292 Aquitaine was securely held and deniers and obols were
struck for Edward at Bordeaux and Guessin. The chief types show the king's
name and royal title with the word *Agl* in the centre of the obverse and a leopard
above and letter E below, while the reverse, a cross with E in one angle, is inscribed *Dux Aquit Burd*, the name of the duchy and the mint town, Bordeaux.
At Guessin the types are a lion or a leopard and a cross with the mint initial G in
the field of reverse or obverse.

No coins appear to have been struck for Edward II in his French possessions
over which he exercised scarcely any hold throughout his reign. For Edward III,
however, there was an extensive coinage, including a variety of denominations
in gold and new, larger denominations in silver. The Anglo-Gallic coinage of
Edward III can, like his English coinage, be divided into periods marked by the
varying use of titles. In 1328, on the death of Charles the Fair of France and the
succession of Philip of Valois, Edward claimed the title of King of France and
inserted it in his titulature on the coins from 1337. In 1360 by the Treaty of
Brétigny Edward waived his claim to the French throne and assumed instead the
title of Lord of Aquitaine. In 1362 Edward raised his son, Edward the Black
Prince, to the rank of Prince of Aquitaine but resumed his lordship of Aquitaine
again in 1372.

A rare issue of gold florins copying the types of the famous coin of Florence
does not bear Edward's name. The obverse has the figure and name of John the
Baptist and the reverse a fleur-de-lis with the title *Dux Aquitanie* and was presumably struck before the change of title under the Treaty of Brétigny. The gold
écu, better known as the chaise from the obverse type which shows the king
seated on a throne is an imitation of a similar series struck by Philip VI of France.
The issue was made sometime from about 1337 and records Edward's title as

King of England and France (Pl. 493). A third type of gold coin known as a leopard after its obverse type was struck from about 1344, again with both the English and French titles; later varieties without the French but with the addition of the Aquitaine title were struck after 1360. The most common of Edward's gold coins, however, was the guiennois struck from 1360 onwards, as the royal titles show. On the obverse the king, crowned and in armour, stands under a Gothic portico. The reverse, as on the chaise and leopard, consisted of an ornate cross but, instead of leopards in every angle, had alternate lis and leopard. On the guiennois the initial of the mint appeared on varying parts of the design—B for Bordeaux at the centre of the reverse cross, P for Poitiers, R for La Rochelle or L for Limoges between the pinnacles of the obverse portico.

The silver and billon coins, like the gold issues, fall into two groups before and after the Treaty of Brétigny. The distinguishing feature here is the form of the Aquitaine title, before 1360 *Dux Aquitanie*, after 1360 *Dominus Aquitanie*. Of the larger silver denomination the gros, the earliest variety, has on obverse a cross within two concentric circles of inscription and on the reverse a lion rampant and the name of the mint. The most common variety was the gros tournois with similar types to those of the coin introduced by Louis IX of France in 1266. The obverse was similar to the lion groat but on the reverse appeared a building with two towers and a spire between and the title Duke of Aquitaine. Other varieties of gros consisted of a cross calvary on obverse and a crown on reverse, or a long cross and a leopard couchant. Demi-gros of these types were also struck. Sterlings and half-sterlings had types very similar to those of the English penny but had a crown in each angle of the reverse and the Aquitaine title in the inscription while the types on the denier and obol were a cross and a leopard passant. After 1360 a coinage with the title *Dominus Aquitanie* had for the gros, demi-gros and sterling the same types, a half-length figure of the king, crowned and holding sword and on the reverse a long cross with three pellets in each angle (Pl. 494). The denier only had different types, a leopard and a cross.

In the campaign in Guienne in 1344 the town of Bergerac was captured by Henry, Earl of Lancaster, to whom Edward III granted the right of striking coin there. Between 1347 and 1352 Henry struck gros and demi-gros of the Tournois type with his titles *Comes Lancastriae* on the obverse and *Dux Bragaivaci* on the reverse. Between 1352 and his death in 1361 Henry's new title of Duke of Lancaster (*Dux Lancaie*) appeared on demi-gros of both the tournois and the leopard variety as well as on sterlings which had his portrait on obverse and, on reverse, a long cross with alternate crown and pellets in the angles.

Edward the Black Prince was created Prince of Aquitaine by Edward III in 1362 and the mint at Bordeaux struck both gold leopards and guiennois of the same types as for Edward III, but in the name of the Black Prince. The title describes him as son of the King of England and Prince of Aquitaine. On his arrival in Aquitaine in 1363 the Black Prince issued a coinage of gold écus of the chaise type from a number of mints of which the most important were La Rochelle, Bordeaux, Limoges and Poitiers. In the following year a new gold coinage of pavilions and half-pieces showed the prince, wearing a chaplet of roses and holding a sword, standing beneath a canopy; the reverse was an ornate cross with lis and leopards in the angles and, at the end of the inscription, the initial letter of the mint. Later in 1368 came a new gold piece, the hardi and its half with a three-quarter-length portrait of the prince, in armour and holding a sword (Pl. 495).

The Black Prince's silver coinage consisted first of a series of gros, demi-gros and sterlings, all with the same types, the half-length figure of the prince in profile with sword in hand on obverse and on reverse a long cross with three pellets in each angle. Accompanying the hardi d'or in 1368 there was issued a hardi d'argent. The obverse was a simplified version of that on the gold piece and the reverse a long cross with alternate lis and leopard in the angles. The most common coinage in billon was one of deniers whose types were a short cross with alternate lis and leopard and a cross pattée.

Because of failing health the Black Prince surrendered his Principality of Aquitaine to Edward III in 1372. The Duke of Lancaster was appointed Lord of Aquitaine in 1373 but by the end of the year the city of Bordeaux was almost the only English hold in the province.

The Anglo-Gallic coinage of Richard II (1377–99) was largely a continuation of the denominations and types of the latest issues of the Black Prince with only the requisite change in the royal title and the substitution, in the portrait, of the king's crown for the prince's circlet. The principal innovation was the double hardi in silver, though the types remained the same as for the ordinary hardi. Henry IV, son of the Duke of Lancaster, who claimed the English throne in 1399 continued the Anglo-Gallic coinage along the lines of his predecessor. Gold was struck only rarely and, apparently, not any half-pieces while in silver the double hardi was issued only in small quantity. A branch of broom on each side of the royal portrait on some of the silver hardis and the substitution of the same symbol for the lis on the reverse formed almost the only changes in the coin designs, but on some billon deniers the branch of broom also took the place of the more usual cross.

Under Henry V the Anglo-Gallic coinage takes on a new aspect. The coinage of earlier English sovereigns in France had been more in the nature of a feudal coinage struck for their possessions, particularly Aquitaine, but Henry V revived with serious intent the claim to the French throne. France, practically in a state of civil war under the mad Charles VI, presented Henry with an occasion for intervention and by 1419 almost the whole of Normandy was in his power and by the Treaty of Troyes in the same year Henry secured the hand of Catherine of France, the regency during the lifetime of Charles VI and the succession to the French throne on Charles' death. Henry's French coinage which is all from mints in Normandy falls into two groups; the first where his title of King of France was still in use, the second, after the Treaty of Troyes, with his new title *Heres*, heir to the French throne.

Gold coins of the first group struck at Rouen, after its capture in 1419, consisted of Moutons d'or of the French type with on obverse the Paschal lamb and banner, its staff dividing the king's name abbreviated and on reverse a floreate cross with lis and leopards in the quarters. A later variety of this coin placed the letter H at the centre of the reverse cross (Pl. 496). In the second group came a new denomination in gold, the salute, named after its type showing the Annunciation. Between Gabriel and the Virgin on the obverse are the quartered arms of France and England, crowned and with the word *Ave* and a sun above; on the reverse a cross calvary divides a lis and a leopard with the initial H below. Silver gros struck at Rouen before the Treaty of Troyes had as types a crown above three lis and a cross with lis terminals and with a crown in the first and a leopard in the fourth quarter. Again the later variety had the initial H at the centre of the reverse cross. The types of the gros after the treaty show a crown above a leopard and three lis and a cross as on earlier gros, with H at centre but no symbols in the angles. Rare half- and quarter-gros were struck in the earlier period. On the double tournois in billon, struck quite commonly at Rouen and St. Lô in the second period the types showed lis over leopard and cross with H at centre. Deniers tournois with crowned leopard and cross types accord Henry the title of king and have, on reverse, the inscription *Turonus Civis*.

Henry VI succeeded to the English throne in 1422 while still an infant of less than one year old, and on the death of Charles VI of France a few weeks later, Henry, by the terms of the Treaty of Troyes, was proclaimed King of France. The coinage struck in his name at the various French mints was a true regal French coinage, more completely so than that of his father, Henry V. Henry VI was accepted as king in the north and east, but the south and west supported the claim of the Dauphin. From 1429 when the French, inspired by Joan of Arc, wrested Orleans from them, the English steadily lost ground, until in 1451 the only French possession left to Henry VI was the town of Calais.

Henry's French coinage included denominations in gold, silver and billon and was struck at some dozen mints of which the most prolific were those at Paris,

Amiens, Chalons, Le Mans and Rouen. The products of the various mints were distinguished by small symbols placed at the beginning of the inscriptions instead of the customary initial cross, a crown for Paris, a lamb at Amiens, a leopard at Rouen and so on. The two gold denominations were the salute and the angelot, valued at two-thirds of the salute. The design on the salute of Henry VI varied on the obverse from that of the original piece struck by Henry V. Gabriel and the Virgin are seen only half-length with two shields with the arms of France and of England below, while the word *Ave* is placed vertically and not horizontally (Pl. 497). The angelot has the same two shields on obverse with, above, a facing angel and on reverse a cross calvary dividing lis and leopard in a plain field.

The major piece in silver was the grand blanc. The design is basically that or the angelot but the angel on the obverse is replaced by the word *Henricus* which appeared also on the reverse below the cross. The petit blanc had only the two shields on the obverse, their outer edges dividing the circular inscription; on the reverse a cross calvary divided the initials HR. In billon a tresin or 3 denier piece was struck somewhat rarely, the more common piece being the denier tournois. The obverse, inscribed simply with the king's name, carried a lis and a leopard, the reverse a cross and inscription *Turonus Francie*. On the denier parisis the king's name abbreviated appeared above lis and leopard on obverse while the reverse was a cross, its arms terminating in lis. In a later issue the king's name was surmounted by a large crown on the obverse and on the reverse a small cross pattée was superimposed on the centre of the larger cross.

With Henry VI the Anglo-Gallic coinage as it has been defined for this section came to an end. Though Calais continued to be held by England until the reign of Mary Tudor the mint there ceased to strike after the reign of Henry VI. Only one other rare series of English coins was struck in France, the silver groats of Henry VIII issued at Tournai in the years from 1513 to 1518 when Henry seized and held that town. One variety showed the profile portrait of the king on obverse and on reverse the English shield on a long cross with the inscription *Civitas Tornacens*, and a unique surviving half-groat presents the same types. A second variety of groat dated 1513 had a crowned-shield obverse and a reverse of elaborate cross with alternate lis and leopard in the angles and initial H at the centre.

SCOTLAND

The autonomous coinage of the kings of Scotland began only in the early twelfth century with the integration of the kingdom within more or less its modern borders by David I (1124–53). Until this time coins found in the more settled southern part of the kingdom are almost without exception those issued by English kings. The base sceattas of the Northumbrian kings whose rule extended well within the modern borders of Scotland are found there and in the Isles as are pennies of later English kings and of the Viking invaders. The coinage of the Norman kings in England also had some currency in Scotland and even after the institution of an independent Scottish coinage. English coinage, particularly Edwardian pennies, as coin hoards from Scotland show, accounted for the greater proportion of coinage in circulation.

The coinage of silver pennies begun by David I are close copies of the contemporary English coins of Stephen both in standard, types and in the extremely poor standard of execution. The obverse shows a crowned portrait of the king in profile with a sceptre in front and has the simple inscription *Davit Rex*. The reverse types are either a cross fleury with pellets in each angle or a cross moline with fleur-de-lis. On the reverse a circular inscription gives the names of the moneyer and the mint town (Pl. 498). There were mints at the capital, Edinburgh, and in the border towns of Berwick and Roxburgh. Henry, the son of David, became Earl of Northumberland in 1139 and issued from mints at Corbridge and Carlisle in his earldom coins of types similar to those of his father but bearing Henry's name and title. The pennies of David's grandson, Malcolm IV (1153–65), have somewhat similar types though one issue copies the contemporary full-face portrait of an issue of Henry II. The long reign of William the Lion (1165–1214) did not produce any great variety of coinage. The obverse continued to show the crowned portrait in profile usually with a sceptre in front but in this reign there was a unique departure from the practice of giving the king's title on the obverse in Latin in the use of a French form *Le Rei Willame*. A reverse type which was to maintain its place for some time in the Scottish coinage was introduced in the latter part of William's reign, namely a voided cross with stars in each angle (Pl. 499). Additional mints brought into action in this reign included Perth and Stirling. The pennies of the next reign, that of Alexander II (1214–49), show no alteration except in the royal name.

The first coinage of Alexander III (1249–86) introduced a number of variations. The reverse was still a voided or double cross with stars in the angles but, following the lead of the English penny reverse, the arms of the cross were lengthened so that they cut across the reverse inscription right to the edge of the coin. On the obverse the king's portrait was also shown bare-headed instead of crowned. The number of mints for this extensive coinage was increased to some fifteen. In 1280 there began a new coinage of greatly improved execution though with only one small change in types, namely the replacement of the stars in the angles of the reverse cross by mullets, stars with a hollow centre (Pl. 500). The inscription on the reverse of this issue gives the conclusion of the royal title *Rex Scotorum* and the moneyer and mint receives no mention. This coinage also saw the introducton of two new denominations, the silver halfpenny and farthing, which had types similar to those of the penny.

The unsettled conditions in Scotland which followed the death of Alexander III in 1286, the imposition of John Baliol (1292–6) as King of Scotland by Edward I of England and the subsequent War of Independence under Robert Bruce (1306–29) are reflected both in the extremely crude coins of John and the rarity of those of Robert Bruce (Pl. 501).

Troubled years for Scotland followed the accession of the five-year-old David II in 1329. Temporarily ousted by Edward III's nominee, Edward Baliol, he took refuge in France and after his return invaded England in 1346 only to be captured and spend eleven years in captivity. The coinage of this period shows a drop in the weight standard from a penny of over 21 grains to 18 grains and is rare in all three denominations. The types repeat those of the preceding reigns. After the return of the king from captivity a new coinage was instituted in 1357 introducing a number of new denominations into the Scottish coinage. The most notable of these was the rare, splendid gold noble whose types imitate those of the English noble first issued in 1351. The types show the king standing facing in a ship on the obverse and on the reverse an elaborate cross within a tressure of arches with lions and crowns in the angles of the cross (Pl. 502). In silver the groat or fourpenny piece and a half-groat were struck for the first time. The obverse type repeated the crowned profile portrait of the king on earlier pennies on the obverse but now enclosed in a tressure of arches and the long cross with mullets in the angles on the reverse; but, in imitation of the English groat, there were two concentric circles of inscription on the reverse. On the noble the reverse inscription had copied exactly that on the English noble but on the groat the outer inscription was original, an abbreviated form of *Dominus Protector Meus et Liberator Meus* (the Lord is my defender and liberator) while the inner gave the name of the mint (Pl. 503). The types on silver pennies in this second issue remained unchanged. A third coinage issue was begun in 1371 on a lower weight standard, the penny being reduced to a little over 15 grains. The noble was not coined in this issue but the groat, its half and the penny were all struck, the only difference in their types being a star either behind the neck of the portrait or on the sceptre handle.

On the death of David II in 1371 the throne passed to his nephew Robert, High Steward of Scotland, who, as Robert II, became the first king of the House of Stuart. The coinage of this reign was simply a continuation of the last issues of David II except that the silver farthing now disappeared from the Scottish coinage. The reign of his successor Robert III (1390–1406) produced some new and interesting coins. In place of the gold noble of David II which, like its English counterpart, had been valued at 6 shillings and 8 pence a new gold crown of value 5 shillings was struck taking its popular name of lion from the obverse type, the lion arms of Scotland on a crowned shield. The reverse showed the patron saint of Scotland, St. Andrew, on the cross between two lis (Pl. 504). The types on the demy or half-piece were the same except that the figure of St. Andrew is absent from the cross on the reverse. The types on the silver coins were also changed bringing them closer to the corresponding English coins. The obverse now had a facing bust and the reverse three pellets in place of a mullet in each angle of the cross. Towards the end of the reign a general reduction was made in the coins of both metals and in silver only the groat, reduced to about 30 grains in weight, was struck.

As James I was a captive in England when Robert III died and was not released until 1424 it seems likely that the coinage in his name did not follow immediately upon his accession. The coinage in gold consisted principally of the demy, whose types were now the lion rampant within a lozenge and on the reverse a St. Andrew's cross with lis on either side, all within an ornate hexagon with quatrefoils in each angle. A much rarer half-demy with similar types was also issued. In silver the groat of value 6 pence presented another facing portrait with sceptre to left and this issue is notable for the variety of ornaments such as lis, saltire or annulet appearing in the field. The reverse introduced a minor variant in its design by placing a lis in alternate angles of the cross. The penny and halfpenny with conventional types was struck at the slightly higher weight of 16 grains but was no longer in good silver but in billon, an alloy of silver and base metal. The first coinage of the reign of James II (1437–60) continued the demies, groats and pennies of the previous reign with only minor variations but a new coinage was ordered in 1451 and as well as new denominations new standards were instituted. The chief gold piece, valued at 6 shillings and 8 pence, was known as a lion, its types being the crowned-lion arms of Scotland in a diamond frame on obverse and a cross with lis in an ornate frame on the reverse. The half-lion had similar types but the obverse shield was uncrowned. The new groat of a value of 8 pence had a crown and three pellets in alternate angles of the reverse cross (Pl. 505). On some billon pennies only alternate angles of the reverse had three pellets. Shortly after the introduction of the new coinage its currency value was raised, the lion to 10 shillings and the groat to 12 pence.

The reign of James III (1460–88) ushers in a period of Scottish coinage presenting a considerable variety of denominations and designs on the gold coinage. Although early Scottish coinage owed much to imitation of English prototypes, and this continued to be true in the case of silver coins, the designs of gold pieces after the first issue of gold nobles are more original. Complete originality cannot be claimed for the gold rider of James III, for similar types can be found on a number of continental series but its adaptation to the Scottish coinage resulted in one of the most graceful coinages. On the obverse the king, in armour, helmeted and crowned rides to the right with drawn sword; the reverse, more pedestrian, is simply a crowned shield on a long cross (Pl. 506). The rider had a value of 23 shillings, and halves and quarters of similar types were also issued. A second original design on the gold piece, of value 18 shillings, showed a unicorn supporting the Scottish arms with on the reverse a large wavy star of twelve points on a cross.

The groats and half-groats of this reign also exhibit some variety and originality. Although some issues maintained the conventional facing bust there were attempts to render a more realistic portrait. The first attempt shows the king's bust three-quarter facing to right and this issue is also notable for the first use of the thistle on Scottish coinage, where it is used in alternate angles of the reverse. A more realistic portrait shows James III with long locks of hair facing three-quarters to left (Pl. 507). The issue of this series in 1485 makes it one of the earliest Renaissance coin portraits in western Europe.

In billon a new coinage of placks and half-placks was introduced. The plack, valued at 4 pence had as obverse a crowned shield in a tressure of arches and as reverse a floreate cross with a saltire at centre and a crown in each angle. The types of the penny remained conventional. Coins known as black farthings were struck in copper with very simple types, first a crown and St. Andrew's cross, later the initials IR crowned and St. Andrew's cross.

The gold unicorn was continued by James IV (1488–1513) with identical types and distinguished only by minute variations and a new gold piece of 14 shillings value was introduced. This piece, though retaining the traditional name of lion, relegated the lion-arms type to the reverse, presenting on the obverse a new version of St. Andrew supporting a cross. The realistic portrait of the groats of James III was continued in the early coinage for James IV but silver coinage in his own name reverted to the conventional facing bust. On some issues of groats and of placks the Arabic numeral 4 or a contracted form of *Quartus* is added to complete the king's name on the obverse.

The first coinage of James V (1513–42) was only of gold unicorns and halves and billon placks with types as in the previous reign. A new coinage in 1526 introduced a gold piece of 20 shillings, termed a crown, with crowned arms of Scotland and a cross fleury with thistles in the angles as types. As these coins were minted at the recently established mint at Holyrood Abbey in Edinburgh they were generally known as abbey crowns. New types were also created for the silver groat, now valued at 1 shilling and 6 pence. The obverse shows the king in profile to right, the reverse the Scottish arms on a long cross, types obviously owing their inspiration to the profile groats of Henry VII of England. A third coinage dating from 1539 contained another of the outstanding pieces of Scottish gold coinage, the ducat of 40 shillings, better known as the bonnet piece after the obverse type where the king is shown wearing a flat bonnet in place of the usual crown (Pl. 508). Very rare two-thirds and one-third bonnet pieces are also known. No silver pieces were struck in this coinage but in billon the now proverbial bawbee worth 6 pence made its first appearance. On the obverse a crowned thistle separates the letter I and numeral 5 while the reverse has a crown on a saltire cross with a lis at either side (Pl. 509).

The vicissitudes of the reign of Mary (1542–67), involving various changes and conjunctions of titles conveniently divide her coinage into successive groups but it cannot be said that the aura of romance with which her career has been invested extended to the designs of her coinage which fall below the more imaginative level of a number of pieces in the preceding reigns. In the earliest group of coinage extending from her accession as an infant of a week old to her marriage with Francis, Dauphin of France, in 1558 her title is simply a form of *Maria Dei Gracia Regina Scottorum*. The first gold pieces of this group are abbey crowns with types similar to those of her father but as their value increased to 22 shillings a new 20 shilling piece was issued in 1543 with a monogram of MR crowned on the obverse and a crowned shield on reverse. Some ten years later a 40 shilling piece, again termed a lion, had on either side of the crowned shield the letters IG, standing for Iacobus Gubernator, James Earl of Arran who was regent of the kingdom in Mary's infancy. The reverse consisted of a very complicated monogram of Maria Regina. The ryal or 3 pound piece which followed two years later in 1555 had the first portrait of Mary on gold coins with the conventional shield reverse (Pl. 510) and in 1553 a testoon of 4 shillings in silver also showed a portrait of Mary, this time crowned. In billon the bawbee and plack were continued with the necessary alteration in the royal initials but the penny, still with a facing portrait, shows clearly the child face of the young queen (Pl. 511).

A new denomination worth a penny-halfpenny took its name of the lion or hard-head from the crowned lion rampant on the reverse.

After her marriage to the Dauphin of France in 1558 Mary's coins carry their joint titles as King and Queen of Scotland and Dauphin and Dauphiness of Vienne, changed on Francis' accession to the French throne in 1559 to King and Queen of France and Scotland. On the obverse of gold ducats their portraits are shown *vis-à-vis* as on some English coins of Philip II and Mary. Billon groats of this period have the unusual reverse of a whole panel of inscription *Iam non sunt duo sed una caro*.

Mary returned to Scotland after the death of Francis in 1560. The coinage of the five years of widowhood consisted entirely of silver testoons with an un-crowned profile portrait and the simple title current on her first group of coins. Mary married her cousin Henry, Lord Darnley, in 1565 and the names of both with their titles of King and Queen of Scotland appeared on their coinage struck only in silver. Very rare ryals of 30 shillings show the busts of Henry and Mary *vis-à-vis* but subsequent ryals and their subdivisions dispensed with portraits and reverted to a crowned shield between thistles as the obverse type. The unusual reverse design showed a tortoise climbing a crowned palm-tree with a scroll inscribed *Dat Gloria Vires* (Glory gives strength) (Pl. 512). In the brief period in 1567 between the death of Darnley and Mary's flight to England and deposition similar ryals were struck with Mary's title as sole ruler.

The Scottish coinage of James VI falls into two separate periods, first from his accession at the age of one year in 1567 till his succession to the English throne in 1603, second as ruler of the United Kingdom. Had the judgement of history depended solely on the evidence of the coinage James VI would have secured a much higher place in esteem than he is usually accorded, for his coinage, par-ticularly in gold, presents an almost bewildering succession of well-conceived and executed designs. The coinage which falls into no less than eight successive groups began with an issue of silver ryals and portions continuing the last series of Mary but altering the reverse type to a sword with a hand in the field rather quaintly pointing to the mark of value, a feature which has lent the name sword dollar to this series. A 20 pound gold piece in the next issue showed the half-length figure of the king above a panel of inscription and the crowned shield of the reverse was accompanied by an inscription giving Virgil's imperial advice, *Parcere subiectis et debellare superbos* (spare the conquered and war down the proud). Silver coins included the thistle dollar, its thistle reverse having the legend *Nemo me impune lacesset* which achieved such popularity that it was later adopted as the motto of the Order of the Thistle. The obverse of the lion noble with its crowned lion seated facing and holding sword and sceptre is the derivation of the type used centuries later on the Scottish shilling of George VI. Perhaps the most remarkable of all the gold coins, however, was the 80 shilling piece of 1591-3. The bust of the king on the obverse wears a strange tall hat and on the reverse a lion holds a sceptre above which is a cloud and Jehovah in Hebrew script (Pl. 513). In the same coinage silver half- and quarter-marks placed the sword and scales of justice on the obverse. In base-metal billon placks and halves as well as the hardhead showed no such imaginative departures from conventional design, but new denominations of twopence and penny in copper have a more than competent obverse portrait.

UNION WITH ENGLAND

When James VI succeeded to the English throne in 1603 the union of the crowns was followed by a union of the coinage as far as the types and denominations were concerned. James' new title was that of King of Great Britain (*Magnae Britanniae*) and as he was the first to bear the name as sovereign of the united kingdom his name is not followed by a numeral. Only minor variants of type differentiate the Scottish from the English coins. The mint-mark thistle always occurs on the Scottish coins and on these pieces the king is shown wearing the Scottish crown. On the two largest silver pieces which had as obverse type the king on horseback the trappings of the horse have a thistle ornament where on the English pieces there is a rose. As the Scottish money was worth one-twelfth of English money, the gold unit, worth 1 pound in England, had a nominal value in Scotland of 12 pounds Scots and the lower denominations values in proportion. Two issues of Scottish coinage are distinguished by differences in the quartering of the shield on the reverse. The first issue between 1604 and 1609 has the Scottish arms in the second quarter, the second issue Scottish arms in the first and fourth quarters. The second coinage had, in addition, twopence and pence in copper with types of thistle and lion rampant.

The first Scottish coinage of Charles I from his accession in 1625 until 1636 retained the denominations and types of his father's coins except for the requisite change in portrait and name. Briot, the French moneyer who in 1631 produced the English coinage using the new coin machinery, was appointed Master of the Scottish mint in 1635 and the following year struck a hammered coinage in Scotland. The issue was in silver only of pieces of half-mark, 40 penny and 20 penny denomination. All had the king's crowned bust on the obverse with mark of value behind the head, a crowned shield on the reverse of the half-mark and a crowned thistle on the other two pieces. Between 1637 and 1642 Briot and his son-in-law, Falconer, struck both in gold and silver with types similar to those of the first coinage but these pieces, produced by the new coining machinery, were of much better workmanship and execution. In copper the twopence or turner, a name probably derived from the French copper coin, the tournois, and the penny repeated the types of James' coins, thistles and lion. From 1632 only the turner was issued with altered types, crown over CR with mark of value II and thistle (Pl. 514).

Although Charles II was crowned at Scone in 1651 his Scottish coinage began only with the Restoration in 1660. No gold coinage was struck but only pieces in silver and copper. The denominations in silver the 4 mark, 2 mark, mark and half-mark all had the same types, the laureate and cuirassed bust of the king on obverse and on reverse a cross formed of four shields; in the angles were linked C's and in the centre the value. In 1675 the types were altered: the king's bust, now laureate and draped, faced to the left and on the reverse the angles were occupied by thistles, the centre by linked C's. Copper coinage included the bawbee of 6 pence with royal bust and crowned thistle and the bodle or turner with types, crown over crossed sword and sceptre and a thistle (Pl. 515). In the short reign of James VII (1658–9) only two silver denominations were issued. The 40 shilling piece had the royal bust with mark of value below and a crowned shield while the 10 shilling piece, though having a similar obverse, had as reverse a St. Andrew's cross with a shield in each angle. A greater range of silver pieces from the 60 shilling to the 5 shilling piece were struck for William and Mary (1689–94). The mark of value remained under the busts of the two sovereigns and the shield on the reverse had the arms of Nassau in the centre. In copper the types of the bawbee repeated those of Charles II but the bodle types were changed to a crowned monogram of WM and a thistle. William's sole reign saw the issue of the last Scottish gold coins, the rare pistoles and half-pistoles with, below the king's portrait on obverse, a small sun rising from the waves (Pl. 516). The silver and copper coins were as those of the joint reign except for the obverse portrait.

The last Scottish coinage proper consisted of the silver 10 and 5 shilling pieces of Anne struck before the Treaty of Union in 1707. The types were as those of the preceding reign except for the removal of the Dutch arms from the centre of the reverse shield (Pl. 517). At the time of the Union, provision was made for the continuation of minting at Edinburgh but now of coinage exactly similar to that struck at the London mint, except for the addition of the mint letter E under the bust on the obverse. Silver coins from crown down to sixpence were struck only for a few years, the last issues of the Scottish mint being made in 1709.

IRELAND

The currency needs of the economy of Ireland in the earlier centuries were satisfied by the use of coinage imported from abroad, chiefly, as hoards show, the Anglo-Saxon coinage of England. These imports were needed not by the Irish who eschewed the use of money but by the Viking settlements in Dublin, Waterford and Limerick after the second Viking invasion of Ireland in 914. The attribution of much of an unusually controversial coinage remains the subject of research but one series clearly belongs to Sihtric, a Viking ruler in Dublin towards the end of the tenth century. Sihtric was a contemporary of Æthelred II and his coins closely imitate that king's types but substitute the name of Sihtric as King of Dublin on the obverse and give Dublin as the mint town on the reverse (Pl. 518). Imitations, both of this imitated coinage and of a number of later English types, extended over a considerable period. A later series of bracteates, that is pieces with a type on one side only, though they carry no inscription appear to be imitations of eleventh-century English coins, notably the *Paxs* type of William the Conqueror (see p. 233).

A consistent series of Irish coinage, however, began only with the conquest of Ireland by Henry II of England. The first issue of this coinage was not in the name of Henry but in that of his son John, whom he created Lord of Ireland in 1177. From mints at Dublin and Waterford silver halfpennies were issued with an obverse type of a round facing head, occupying the full field of the coin and the name of John as *Dom(inus) Yber(niae)*—Lord of Ireland. The reverse was formed of a short cross with an annulet in each angle and an inscription giving the names of the mint and moneyer. The farthings carried no portrait and had only elementary designs of a lozenge and a small cross. The Irish coins of John as king (1199–1216) included pennies, halfpennies and farthings and were issued by a further mint at Limerick as well as those already established. The obverse bore the facing head of the king, similar to that on the English Short-Cross coins but here it was enclosed in a triangular frame while the reverse type, again within a triangle, showed a crescent and a flaming star (Pl. 519). Pence and halfpence for Henry III, not struck till 1248, had an obverse similar to that on John's coins but the reverse was an exact copy of the Long-Cross coins of England. The coinage from the mint of Dublin, Waterford and Cork which carry the name of Edward is attributed to successive groups covering the reigns of the three kings of that name between 1272 and 1377 and distinguished by minutiae of design, particularly of the crown. The obverse portrait on this series still remained framed within a triangle though, again, the reverse followed closely the design of the English Edwardian sterlings.

263

Coinage for Ireland lapsed until the reign of Henry VI (1422–61). In this reign the groat which had been in currency in England for over a century was issued for the first time in Ireland. The types were similar to the English with the necessary changes in the obverse title and in the mint name in the inner of the two reverse inscriptions. The coinage of Edward IV (1461–83) introduced a considerable element of variety in design chiefly on the larger silver denominations. Early groats substituted a crown for the royal portrait and dispensed with the usual double reverse inscription; a single inscription recorded only the mint. The penny design was similarly modified. The Wars of the Roses had almost more effect on Irish than on English coin design for later groats of Edward IV had as types a cross on a rose and a rayed sun. The issues of 1467 and 1468 added to the usual range of denominations a double groat on which the royal portrait returned to the obverse while the reverse showed a rose on sun design (Pl. 520). The reverses of the lower denominations of this issue were also novel; the groat and farthing had a rose at the centre of a cross and on the penny the angles of the cross were filled by two roses and a sun, and two suns and a rose alternately. Although the succeeding issue of silver (c. 1470–8) reverted to the conventional types of facing bust and cross with pellets in the angles, yet another fresh coinage in 1478 introduced further changes in the types. As in the first issue the royal portrait was dispensed with, being replaced by the royal arms and the reverse was altered to three crowns in pale, that is, one above another (Pl. 521). On some pieces the royal name with the English and French titles appears as usual on the obverse, but the coinage struck while the Earl of Kildare, Lord Justice of Ireland, controlled the Irish mints have on both sides only the title *Dominus Hybernie*—Lord of Ireland. No Irish coinage has been attributed with certainty to the three-month reign of Edward V, but for Richard III (1483–5) there were at least two separate issues. Groats and pennies of the first issue had the usual facing bust and coupled with it the rose on cross of one of Edward IV's issues. Later groats copied the royal arms and three crowns in pale types of Edward's last coinage.

TUDOR COINAGE

Henry VII (1485–1509) began his coinage with a repetition of the three-crowns type with the addition of a letter under the lowest crown but the later and more common issues of groat, half-groat and penny have the standard facing bust and cross with pellets types. Successive issues differ mainly in the shape of the king's crown and are remarkable for the crudity of portrait and poor execution of design and lettering. The reign of Henry VIII (1509–47) introduced new types, a new titulature and new denominations to the Irish coinage. A first issue of groats and half-groats, begun about 1526, had, as in several earlier reigns, the royal arms as obverse type but the Irish harp was introduced for the first time as a reverse type. As on English issues the reverse had in addition on either side of the main type the crowned initials of Henry and his successive queens; HK for Henry and Katherine of Aragon, HA for Henry and Anne Boleyn and HI for Henry and Jane Seymour. Groats of similar design but with the initials of Henry only on the reverse give Henry the title of King of Ireland, a style assumed in September 1541. The new denominations were the sixpence, threepence and three-halfpence introduced in 1544 with a bearded three-quarter facing portrait of the king and the royal arms as reverse. Although this issue carried the name of Dublin on the reverse the coinage was in fact struck in London and exported to Dublin.

Irish groats with the name of Edward VI still have a portrait of Henry VIII. In the sole reign of Mary (1553–4) the first Irish shilling was struck with an obverse portrait similar to that on her English coins and on the reverse a crowned harp dividing the crowned initials MR. Groats, half-groats and pennies of this issue had the same basic types. Only the shilling and groat were issued in the joint reign of Mary and Philip, the obverse again being the same as on the English coins, the busts of the two sovereigns *vis-à-vis*. On the now standard harp reverse appeared the crowned initials P and M. Elizabeth's first issue of shillings and groats continued the bust and harp types but in 1561 the reverse type was altered to a crowned shield bearing three harps, while the last issue in 1598 consisting of shilling, sixpence and threepence had as types a shield and harp. These types were also used for copper pennies and halfpennies in 1601.

STUART COINAGE

The Union of the Crowns in 1603 brought little change to the Irish coinage except in the royal titles. The shillings and sixpences, in conformity with the Scottish and English issues, initially the titles of King of England and Scotland in full but from 1605 this form was replaced by the title King of Great Britain.

No regular series of regal silver coins was struck for Ireland in the reign of Charles I but from 1642 a number of emergency issues were made, mostly made from plate called in or seized for the purpose and often of irregular shape similar to some of the siege pieces in England at this time. A coinage known as Inchiquin after Lord Inchiquin, Vice-President of Munster, was of eccentric shape and was stamped on both sides with a circle containing its weight in penny-weights and grains. There were rare gold pieces called pistoles but the series proper consisted of silver coins from crown to groat with additional varieties of the lower denominations carrying annulets to the number of their value in pence. Another series, probably struck at Dublin, consisted of crowns and half-crowns marked with their value in Roman numerals. The most common of these emergency issues, the Ormonde coinage struck by James, Duke of Ormonde, viceroy of Charles in Ireland, ranged from crown down to twopence and had as types a crown over the initials CR and the value in Roman numerals (Pl. 522). A series of crowns and half-crowns issued by the Irish rebels was similar to the Ormonde coinage but substituted a cross for the royal initials on the obverse. Smaller series, mostly in copper, bore the initials or name of the town of issue.

The Commonwealth produced no specific Irish coinage and the issues for Charles II were of a rather sporadic nature. Crowns and half-crowns similar to the Ormonde coins in design but inscribed with Charles II's name and title are thought to have been issued by Ormonde in Ireland shortly after the execution of Charles I. After the Restoration it was not till 1680 that regal coinage was resumed in the shape of copper farthings with the bust of Charles II and a harp reverse. Similar halfpennies were struck for James II until his abdication in 1688 but during his campaigns in Ireland between 1689 and 1691 to recover the throne an emergency coinage was issued, usually known as 'gun money' since the coins, of only nominal value, were in some instances made of brass secured by melting old guns. The crown showed the king, sword in hand, on horseback with as reverse a cross of shield, with a crown at the centre and the date in the form ANŌ DŌM 1690 across the field. The more common denominations from half-crowns to sixpence had the more usual royal bust on the obverse and on the reverse a crown on two sceptres in saltire separating the initials JR ; above was the value in pence, below the month of issue (Pl. 523). Pewter was also pressed into use to strike crown pieces usually with the same types as the 'gun money' crown and also pennies and halfpennies with bust and harp types. During the siege of Limerick in 1691 copper halfpennies were struck there with James II's portrait and a seated figure of Hibernia on the reverse. The only Irish coinage for William III and Mary and for the sole reign of William were copper halfpennies with bust and harp types. For Anne, the last of the Stuart monarchs, there was no Irish coinage.

HANOVERIAN COINAGE

On copper halfpennies and farthings of George I issued between 1722 and 1724 the reverse borrowed the seated figure of Hibernia used on the Limerick coins of James II but the traditional crowned harp returned to the Irish coinage of

George II and the early issues of George III. Because of the great scarcity of silver coin the Bank of Ireland was permitted in 1804 to issue tokens of value 6 shillings with royal portrait and figure of Hibernia and in 1805 tokens of 10 and 5 pence also appeared as well as pieces of 30 pence in 1808. A new copper coinage, consisting of the penny, halfpenny and farthing and produced in 1805, retained the traditional Irish types. Similar copper pence and halfpence struck for George IV in 1822 brought to an end the regal coinage of Ireland.

THE IRISH FREE STATE AND REPUBLIC

The types of the new Irish coinage first issued in 1923 have remained constant up till the present day with only one inscriptional change. The obverse design of all denominations is a harp with an inscription, originally *Saorstát Éireann* but changed in 1939 to *Eire*. The reverse types all depict animals or birds and give the denomination in Irish and the value in figures. The types are: (silver) half-crown—horse, florin—salmon, shilling—bull; (nickel) sixpence—hound, three-pence—hare; (bronze) penny—hen and chicks (Pl. 524), halfpenny—sow and piglets, farthing—woodcock.

BRITISH POSSESSIONS IN EUROPE

Brief mention must be made of several series of coins struck for some of the British islands and for possessions in Europe.

Isle of Man. Copper pennies and halfpennies of the Earl of Derby in 1709 had on obverse the Stanley badge, an eagle on a cap of maintenance and a trisceles. Similar coins were issued by the Duke of Atholl in 1733 and in 1758, the latter issue having a crowned monogram on the obverse. Regal copper coins of George III and Victoria have as types the royal portrait and trisceles.

Lundy. Coles Harman, the owner of Lundy Island, issued in 1929 copper coins with his portrait and a puffin on the reverse, in denominations known as a puffin and a half-puffin (Pl. 525). The issue was discontinued after Coles Harman had been prosecuted under the Coinage Act of 1870.

Guernsey. Copper and bronze coins of eight, four, two and one double-piece were struck from William IV to George VI with types, the arms of Guernsey and value in wreath. The reverse of the eight and four double-coins of the present reign carry Guernsey lilies and a threepenny piece in nickel a Guernsey cow.

Jersey. The copper and bronze coinage has the unusual denominations of one-thirteenth, one-twenty-sixth and one-fifty-second of a shilling on the first issue of Victoria. Later issues are of a twelfth of a shilling and so on. The types are the royal portrait and the island's arms. A twelfth of a shilling, struck in 1949 to commemorate the liberation of the island in 1945 from German occupation, has the inscription *Liberated* 1945. The first issue of Elizabeth II used the same reverse, providing an incompatible combination of obverse and reverse which may puzzle future numismatists (Pl. 526). A nickel fourth of a shilling and a bronze twelfth struck in 1957 revert to the usual arms reverse type.

Gibraltar. The only issue of special coinage was made in 1842. The copper pieces of two, one and a half-quart have the royal head on obverse and a castle with three towers on reverse.

Malta. The issues made for Malta were copper or bronze pieces of the denomination of a third of a farthing with regal portrait and type of Britannia on the reverse. From 1866 the reverse simply states the value in words. The last issue was made in 1913 (Pl. 527).

Ionian Islands. During British administration between 1815 and 1863 coinage with types, a winged lion holding bundle of arrows with Greek inscription on obverse and a seated Britannia on reverse was issued in several denominations of the obol. The obverse of the 30 obol piece in silver was the value in wreath.

Cyprus. Coinage is in denominations of piastres struck in silver, nickel and bronze with the usual royal portrait and reverses bearing a lion shield, two leopards or simply the value. The later issues of George VI included denominations of 2 and 1 shilling. The nickel issues of Elizabeth II are in denominations of 100 mils and divisionary pieces. The reverses on cupro-nickel pieces of 100, 50 and 25 mils are a ship, a fern and a bull's head respectively and on the bronze 3 mils coin a fish.

WESTERN EUROPE

THE NETHERLANDS

The coinage struck in the Netherlands provides here as elsewhere a fair reflection of the historical development of the country. On the collapse of Roman authority in the early fifth century the Netherlands south and west of the Rhine became part of the kingdom of the Franks who in the seventh century extended their domain northwards at the expense of the Saxons and Frisians. The Carolingian dynasty absorbed the whole of the Netherlands which by the division of the Carolingian empire passed to the German empire. Coinage of each of these successive rules was struck at various mints in the Netherlands but from the tenth and eleventh centuries coinage by local seigneuries and bishoprics replaced that of the imperial authority. In the fifteenth century the country came under control of the house of Burgundy and, in the next century, of the house of Hapsburg. The Eighty Years' war, concluded by the Peace of Münster in 1648, brought independence to the seven more northerly provinces until the creation in 1795 under French revolutionary influence of the Batavian republic, followed in 1806 by the kingdom of Holland ruled by Napoleon's brother Louis. In the reshaping of Europe in 1815 a new kingdom of the Netherlands was formed including modern Belgium which seceded in 1830.

The earliest coinage struck by mints in the Netherlands consists of gold tremisses of the Merovingian kings of the Franks. This coinage struck at Duurstede (Dorestad) and Maastricht (Traiectum) is of the type with moneyer's name around a head or bust on obverse and a cross on steps on reverse accompanied by the name of the mint (Pl. 528). In Frisia a coinage of silver sceattas of roughly the same fabric as, and of designs similar to, the Anglo-Saxon sceattas in England was issued in the later seventh and earlier eighth centuries. From about the middle of the eighth century the new silver denier (see p. 286) was struck at Duurstede and Maastricht for Carolingian kings including Pepin, Charlemagne and Louis the Debonair. Duurstede was destroyed by Norse raiders in 871 but silver denars of German kings and emperors continued to be struck at Maastricht and at new mints at Deventer, Tiel (Pl. 529) and Nijmegen.

The eleventh century saw the beginning of two new tendencies in the coinage of the Netherlands. The general increase of the power of the seigneurs as that of the central regal authority in the German empire diminished, made itself apparent in peripheral areas such as the Netherlands earlier than in more central areas and found expression on the coinage in the use of the name and title of the more local authority alongside that of the emperor and, soon, in the disappearance of the imperial name. The bishops of Utrecht and the counts of Friesland were the first to issue a coinage in their own name, followed in the twelfth century by the counts of Holland and Gelderland. The second trend was a reduction in the module and weight of the denar with the consequence that in some series in the thirteenth century the weight had fallen to a half or even a third of its original standard. To judge from the quantities which have survived, the earlier issues were not very substantial but by the thirteenth century the small silver of the counts of Holland was in common issue. The types, as for example of Floris V (1266–96), showed a small portrait head in profile on obverse, accompanied by the inscription *F Co Holandie*, and on the reverse a cross with small flower in each angle and the mint name *Moneta Dordci* (Dordrecht) (Pl. 530). From the small head on the obverse these pieces were termed *kopkens*. The types on the silver of Otto II of Gelderland (1229–71) were a shield and an eagle with the names of the count and the mint of Arnhem on the respective sides. At Utrecht the coins of Bishop Hermann (1150–6) have his bare-headed bust in profile and with crozier on obverse and a cross on reverse. These form the basic types for successive bishops throughout the twelfth and thirteenth centuries.

Towards the end of the thirteenth century the English sterling penny which, unlike the majority of continental issues, had maintained its weight, began to be extensively imitated. In Gelderland sterlings were struck by Renaud I (1271–1326) exactly copying the English types of facing bust and cross reverse but substituting his own name and title and that of the mint, Arnhem. The sterling, where issued, was tariffed at a third of the groot which had also been introduced into the coinage about 1300. Initially, as elsewhere in western Europe, the groot was a close copy of the French gros tournois introduced in 1266 with only such small variations as the placing in the inner inscription of the reverse of his own name in the form *Florentius Co* by Floris V, Count of Holland. Later, in the course of the fourteenth century, more individual types were used such as those of the lion groot issued in Holland, Gelderland and Utrecht. The groot did not escape the inevitable mediaeval tendency towards deterioration and its place as the principal silver coin was taken in the later fourteenth century by a new double groot. The coin was known also as the *plak* or *botdrager* on account of its obverse type which, as on coins of William V, Count of Holland (1346–89), showed a lion with large helmet like a pot; the reverse was a cross with two circles of inscription, the inner reading *Moneta de Holand* (Pl. 531).

At roughly the same time as these new larger silver denominations were introduced into the coinage there began the coinage in gold. As in other lands early gold took the form of close imitations of the Florentine florin but these gold guldens soon gave place to a greater variety of gold denominations and types. In Holland the gulden of William V showed the standing figure of the count and a shield reverse and a gold coinage copying the types of the French *chaise* was also struck. In Gelderland the French *mouton d'or* with its type of the Paschal lamb with pennant was imitated by Edward (1359–71), from 1360 with the title of Duke of Gelderland and under William I of Gelderland (1377–1402) a gold coinage imitating the types of the English noble was also struck. On gold guldens of the bishops of Utrecht in the early fifteenth century a common type was the figure of St. Martin but under Bishop David of Burgundy (1455–94) a special gulden, the Davidsgulden, had as obverse type King David with his harp. On the double-piece the psalmist king is shown enthroned with, below, a shield of arms. The inscription reads *Memento, Domine, David*.

Only a small selection restricted to the more important series has been used to outline the development of mediaeval coinage in the Netherlands but sufficient to demonstrate the considerable variety of denominations and types in concurrent issue. In the fifteenth century, however, there began a certain standardization under the influence of the requirements of commerce and as a consequence of the unification of the more important territorial divisions under the house of Burgundy. Holland came into the possession of Burgundy under Philip the Good, Gelderland was conquered by Charles the Bold in 1474 and the more northerly provinces of Friesland and Overijsel were added by Charles V (1506–55). Uniform types were used for the Burgundian coinage with a local territorial differential added, often in the form of the local title at the end of the obverse inscription, e.g. an abbreviated form of *Comes Hollandiae*—Count of Holland. Philip the Good (1419–67) struck in gold a rider piece and its half with types an armed knight on horse-back and shield on floreate cross (Pl. 532), the lion and its subdivisions with type of heraldic lion seated under a canopy and the Burgundian gulden with a figure of St. Andrew and his cross. In silver the denominations were the double stuiver with types the Burgundian arms on a shield in a trefoil and a floreate cross on reverse and the groot with its double and portions, again with Burgundian arms on obverse but here occupying the whole field. Similar types appeared on the penning struck in billon. The mints in Holland were Dordrecht and the Hague. Under Charles the Bold (1467–77) the mints in Holland were inactive but his new mint at Nijmegen in Gelderland struck his St. Andrew gulden and a new silver piece the vuurijzer with its double and half. The reverse was the usual Burgundian arms on a floreate cross on the double which had on obverse two lions seated *vis-à-vis*; on the smaller pieces the types were a lion's head and cross. The date 1474 on the Gelderland double-vuurijzer is the earliest instance of a date in numerals in the Netherlands coinage. Among new denominations introduced under Philip the Fair (1482–1506) was the silver griffin with griffin rampant on the obverse and two griffins on the double piece. A silver piece of 3 stuivers with shield-on-cross obverse took its name of vlies (fleece) from the reverse type, the jewel of the Order of the Golden Fleece (Pl. 533). The gold Carolus gulden of Charles V (1506–55) showed the half-length figure of the emperor holding sword and globe on obverse and the imperial arms on double-headed eagle on the reverse. The silver gulden has a striking portrait bust of the bearded emperor. A new denomination in copper, the korte also had a portrait head of Charles. In addition to the mints in Holland and Gelderland Charles also operated mints at Leeuwarden in Friesland and Kampen in Overijsel. Amongst the most striking coins of Philip II (1555–98) was the silver daalder with bare-headed portrait and crowned shield of arms on crossed batons(Pl. 534). This far from exhausts the range of coinage, as in addition to the series of which only some of the high-lights have been described, other more local series were also struck.

During the course of the revolt of the Netherlands against Spain the states of Holland in 1575 issued a series of leeuwendaalders with types a half-length armed figure holding a lion shield on obverse and a lion rampant on reverse and making no allusion to the king of Spain in the inscriptions. In accordance with one of the terms of the Pacification of Ghent a new coinage was decreed in 1577. Denominations included the gold gulden and its double, in silver the daalder and its portions as well as the stuiver with its double and half and in copper the liard (Pl. 535) and its half. The types in general continued those previously used on the issues of Philip II and the obverse carried his name and titles and the reverse an inscription *Pace et iustitia*. The majority even of the northern provinces participated in this coinage, but not Holland. Following the union of Holland, Gelderland, Zeeland and Utrecht in 1579 these provinces issued a series of gold nobles on the English pattern and silver daalders with portrait and titles of Philip II on obverse and on the reverse the crowned arms of the particular province with the inscription *Concordia res parvae crescunt* which was to remain a feature of the coinage of the later United Provinces of the Netherlands. Because of lack of confidence in the new coinages a return was made even by Holland, the most intransigent of the provinces, to the issue, once again, of Philip's gold crowns and silver daalders.

The period immediately following the official disowning of Philip's jurisdiction and the creation of the Republic of the United Provinces with William I as stadhouder in 1581 was one of considerable confusion, with each province continuing to issue its own series of coins. In Holland the gold gulden showed the stadhouder holding axe and lion shield on obverse with the arms of Holland on the reverse. The silver daalder and its half also portrayed William but here as a half-length figure with sword on shoulder, while on the reverse a small shield with the provincial arms was surmounted by a many-plumed helmet. The inscriptions on all these denominations were *Vigilate Deo Confidentes* with the date on obverse and *Mo no arg Comit Hol Zel* and the mint differential, here a small rose, the mark of the mint at Dordrecht (Pl. 536). Zeeland struck at this time gold nobles of the usual type and a silver daalder as well as its half-piece. This was known as a kruisdaalder as its main type imitated the Burgundian cross as on coins of Philip II. The silver shilling and its subdivisions showed a half-length armed figure above a shield with the arms of Zeeland. Gold nobles were also issued by Gelderland as well as a gold lion with type of lion rampant holding a banner and shield-on-cross reverse and also a gold rider with its figure of a horseman with raised sword. A similar mounted figure appeared on the silver daalder and half-daalder. Gold nobles were also coined at Utrecht, where the silver daalder had as its obverse a shield and as reverse a small shield on cross. The issues of Friesland and Overijsel had a like range of denominations and types.

The Earl of Leicester as Governor-General of the Netherlands endeavoured to reduce the chaotic monetary system to order. The mints were limited in 1586 to one to each of the seven provinces with an additional mint in west Friesland and a uniform range of denominations and types decreed. In addition to the traditional noble and its parts a new gold ducat was introduced. On the obverse was a full-length armed figure holding sword over shoulder and a bundle of seven arrows, symbolizing the seven provinces, with the inscription *Concordia res parvae crescunt* and the name of the issuing province. The reverse carried a decorated tablet inscribed *Mo ordin provin foeder Belg ad leg imp*. The principal silver coins were the real and its half with types a laureate bust of Leicester and the shields of the six provinces which were in treaty with England, all around the bundle of seven arrows. A cross and the arrows within an oval were the types of the stuiver. The system was, however, of brief duration and towards the end of the century the provinces had reverted to the issue of their individual coinages.

The next attempt to create a regular and uniform system was made by the decree of the States-General in 1602 with much greater success, for the standard, the range of denominations and even of types then established persisted, with but small modifications, till the end of the republic in the late eighteenth century. The gold ducat of Leicester's coinage was revived (Pl. 537) and a double ducat of identical types added. The rider and its half also found a place in the gold coinage, again with its obverse of the horseman with raised sword above a small shield with the arms of the province and, on the other side, a crowned shield with the lion of the Netherlands rampant and holding sword and bunch of arrows. In the eighteenth century the value, 14 gulden and 7 gulden respectively, was placed in the field to left and right of the shield. On the silver rijksdaalder and its half a half-length armed figure, laureate, with sword over shoulder holds ribbons from which depends the shield of the province, while the reverse repeats the reverse type of the rider. A similar reverse but with X - S in the field marked the 10 stuiver piece, which had as obverse an armed figure holding sword and shield of the province. In 1614 were added smaller denominations, the double stuiver and stuiver with obverse, the lion with sword and arrows and, in the case of the double piece, the value 2 - S, and reverse the name of the province in three lines across the field and the date. Later the obverse of the stuiver was changed to a bunch of arrows. The copper duit bore the provincial arms on obverse and the name of the province on reverse (Pl. 538).

New large silver denominations were created in 1659. The silver ducat and half-ducat repeated the now traditional reverse of the crowned shield bearing the Netherlands lion but had as obverse a full-length armed figure with sword and provincial shield. The ducaton and its half has a rider-type obverse with a more than usually elaborate reverse where the crowned lion shield has two lion supporters. The final modification to the system was made in 1680 with the introduction of denominations of 3, 2 and 1 guldens in silver. The obverse, uniform for all the provinces, was the personification of the Netherlands, holding a spear topped with the cap of Liberty and leaning on a bible placed on an altar with the inscription *Hac nitimur, hanc tuemur*. The reverse bore the crowned shield of the issuing province with the value, e.g. I - G in the field (Pl. 539).

Outside the main system of coinage which has been sketched above there existed subsidiary series which space does not permit of detailing. Some provinces such as Friesland and Groningen continued more individual types and Brabant, at this time still a part of the southern Netherlands, used a coinage of which some details are given in the section devoted to Belgium. Imperial cities such as Deventer, Nijmegen and Kampen for a time produced coinage with the name of the Emperor of the Holy Roman empire and in other towns and smaller seigneuries individual coinages persisted for some time.

The spread of revolutionary ideas and the invasion of the Netherlands by the forces of revolutionary France brought to an end the Republic of the United Provinces and the creation in its stead of the new Batavian republic. A new unified coinage was projected but was never issued and each province continued its coinage as before and, even after Napoleon advanced his brother Louis Bonaparte to the status of King of Holland in 1806, two years elapsed before a new series in his name was produced by the sole mint at Utrecht. The types were uniform for all denominations, the bare head of Louis Bonaparte on obverse and a crowned shield. quartered with the lion of the Netherlands and the eagle of France on the reverse with the value in the field. A 20 and 10 gulden piece was struck in gold with head to left, a rijksdaalder, 2½ gulden and 10 stuiver in silver with head to right. The new kingdom was dissolved in 1810 and until 1814 the Netherlands were incorporated in the French empire.

The Congress of Vienna in 1815 created a new kingdom of the Netherlands which included all the provinces of the Low Countries and raised to the throne Prince William of Oranje-Nassau, son of Willem V, the last stadhouder of the United Provinces. Luxemburg which was included in the kingdom became a separate duchy in 1890 on the accession of Queen Wilhelmina, because of the requirements of Salic law. The Belgian provinces revolted and formed a separate kingdom in 1830. The coinage of the new kingdom, issued until 1830 at mints in Utrecht and Brussels, has remained remarkably constant in denominations and types. The gold denominations were the 20 and 10 gulden piece, though the old ducat with its traditional types was struck, principally for use in eastern commerce until just before the last war. Under William I a 3 guilder piece was issued until 1840 from which date the major silver coin has been the rijksdaalder of 2½ guilders, with smaller denominations of 1 and ½ guilder. The types on all these denominations were, and still are where in issue, a portrait head and the crowned shield with the lion of the Netherlands. On denominations of 25, 10, 5 in silver, and 1 and ½ cent in copper the reverse type was the same as on the larger pieces, but the obverse for William I and II was the initial W crowned. Under William III the 25, 10 and 5 cent pieces bore his portrait and the value within a wreath, while the copper cent and its half with types similar to those of his predecessors were replaced by new bronze denominations of 2½, 1 and ½ cent in 1877 with types, the Netherlands lion and value in a wreath.

The long reign of Queen Wilhelmina (1890–1948) who succeeded at the age of ten is marked by five successive obverse portraits, including an early girlish head with long, hanging hair (Pl. 540). In the lower range the bronze denominations were continued with types as under William III but the 5 cent or stuiver in nickel acquired new types, first a crown and value later, an orange-branch and value. The German occupation of Holland produced only a series of zinc coins of the lower denominations 25, 10, 5, 2½ and 1 cent, all with value reverse and stylized obverse types such as the three tulips on the 10 cent piece. A coinage of guilders and subdivisions was struck at the mint of Philadelphia in the United States for the invasion forces and the returning Netherlands government but, since these were of good silver, they quickly disappeared from circulation and their issue was soon suspended. New coins of the lower values were struck for

Queen Wilhelmina in 1948 shortly before her abdication. These all bore the royal portrait; on the nickel 10 cents the reverse was the value with crown, the bronze 5 cents the value against an orange-branch and the 1 cent simply the value (Pl. 541). The coinage for Queen Juliana, begun in 1950, carries her portrait on the obverse and utilizes the same reverses as the final issue for her mother. In 1954 issue of the silver guilder was resumed with its traditional types of portrait and crowned shield bearing the lion of the Netherlands.

BELGIUM

The course of events both historical and numismatic in the areas comprised within modern Belgium follows something the same pattern as those of the Netherlands up to the later sixteenth century. The country formed part of the Merovingian kingdom from the fifth to the mid eighth century and for a time of the Carolingian empire. It was included in the ninth century, in the kingdom of Lotharingia, between the west and east Franks, but on the death of Lothair II it was divided by the Treaty of Meersen in 870 between Charles the Bald of France and Louis the German. Possession alternated between France and Germany until, with its reoccupation by Henry the Fowler in 923, it passed finally to the German empire. The Middle Ages from the tenth century onwards saw the growth of the power of local dukes and lords at the expense of the central authority, culminating in the formation of a powerful state in the fifteenth century first under the house of Burgundy then of Hapsburg. The revolt of the Netherlands provinces against Philip II of Spain in the late sixteenth century which brought independence to the northern Netherlands left the southern provinces still under Spanish dominion. Control passed to the Austrian branch of the Hapsburgs after the War of the Spanish Succession in the eighteenth century. These provinces, absorbed into the France of the Revolution and Napoleon, were made part of the kingdom of the Netherlands in 1815 but seceded, to form an independent kingdom, in 1830.

The Merovingian period of the country's history is represented by the issue of gold tremisses of the category without royal name but with moneyer's name around a profile bust and the name of the mint around the reverse type, usually a cross. The chief mints were at Antwerp, Huy (Pl. 542), Namur and Tournai. The mint of Duurstede to the north seems to have supplied the area's coinage under Pepin, the first of the Carolingians; but the same mints as under the Merovingians with the addition of Liège, Maastricht and Ghent struck for Charlemagne. The most common type of denier has the name *Carolus* in two lines on obverse and that of the mint on the reverse. In the later ninth and early tenth centuries the Belgian mints struck deniers for whichever of the two contending powers was in control (Pl. 543). Denars of the prevailing imperial types were issued for emperors from Otto I (936–973) to Henry III (1039–56) at a range of mints, not all functioning for each emperor, at Dinant, Liège (Pl. 544), Huy, Thuin and Maastricht. Of these only Maastricht remained an imperial mint after Henry III; at the others the rights of coinage had been gifted to or abrogated by ecclesiastical foundations or powerful feudal vassals.

In the course of the eleventh century the coinage of silver deniers and obols of what amount to independent states and ecclesiastical foundations became substantial, but mention can be made here only of the more important and continuing series. In the coinage of the Dukes of Brabant deniers of either Godfrey II (1140–3) or Godfrey III (1143–90) show the half-length figure of the duke holding sword or banner on the obverse and on the reverse either a building or a lion in front of a tree. Henry the Warrior (1190–1235) commemorated his temporary capture of Arnhem from Gelderland by striking deniers there with the mint name *Harnumi* around his facing bust on obverse and the Brabant banner on reverse with inscription *Ban Duc Lou*—banner of the Duke of Louvain, his official territorial title. On the coinage of the thirteenth century consisting mainly of deniers of small module and without inscription the most common types are the lion of Brabant on obverse and a cross with expanding arms on the reverse (Pl. 545). John I added his title in abbreviation *I. Dux* on the reverse of these small deniers and by 1273 had introduced a new coinage of sterlings with on obverse a shield with the Brabant lion and on the reverse a cross with the letters of the name of the moneyer or mint in the angles. The obverse shield after the annexation of Limburg in 1281 bears the joint arms of Brabant and Limburg.

The issues of the bishops of Liège is at once one of the earliest and one of the most persistent of Belgian series, for it continued to be struck right up to the late eighteenth century. On deniers struck at Liège, Visé and Huy the bust and name of the emperor was displaced in the early eleventh century by representations of St. Domitian, St. Lambert or the Virgin. Bishop Theoduin of Bavaria (1048–75) was the first to place his own name on the Liège series. His tonsured bust, facing or in profile, is accompanied by his name while the reverse, usually a cross motif, carries an indication of the mint. On the issues of the bishops of the thirteenth century the obverse carries a facing bust, mitred, holding crozier and raising hand in blessing; the reverse is frequently a church. Under John d'Enghien (1274–81) sterlings with lion shield on obverse were first introduced (Pl. 546). The earliest coins of the counts of Hainaut are the deniers of Rainier V (1013–30) with obverse type a sword and on the reverse a cross accompanied by the mint name *Montes* (Mons). Throughout most of the twelfth and thirteenth centuries the coinage of Hainaut consists of small deniers without inscription and with types, a gateway surmounted by three towers and a cross with crescent and pellet in each angle (Pl. 547). By 1273 sterlings with shield obverse were in issue. The earliest certain coinage of the counts of Namur, deniers of Albert III (1037–1105), carry his profile bust and name on obverse. The reverse of one series has the word *Moneta* in three lines in cross form, qualified by the adjective *Namucensis* (Namur) as a circular inscription. Deniers of Henry the Blind (1139–96) have on obverse a helmeted head in profile with the title *Comes*, and *Namuceso* around a cross reverse. On the issues of the later twelfth and thirteenth centuries the types for successive counts are a castle and a lion with the inscriptions *Marcis*—*Namur*. Sterlings were introduced by Guy de Dampierre (1264–97).

Flanders in the Middle Ages comprised not only the province of Flanders in modern Belgium but the territory included in the two French departments, Nord and Pas-de-Calais, and the marquis, later the Count of Flanders, held his fief from both the empire and France. The earliest coinage of Flanders, coinciding approximately with the end of the Carolingian dynasty, was struck by Arnold II (964–986) at the abbey of St. Bertin in St. Omer. His deniers of rough fabric and execution have the mint name around a head on the obverse and his name around a cross on the reverse. His successor Baldwin IV (989–1036) issued deniers at Ghent and at Bruges; at the latter Baldwin's name is inscribed around a cross on the obverse and on the reverse, with Carolingian temple type, appears the name of St. Donatus and the mint *Sci Donati Bru*. Another series of Baldwin's deniers, with inscription *Bonus Denarius* on the reverse, is ascribed to Arras. Deniers with the inscription *W. A.* and *Insulae* in three lines on obverse and the same name around a cross on reverse are of the mint of Lille and are attributed to Baldwin V (1036–67). The deniers of Robert I (1070–92), of smaller module but much improved workmanship, were struck at St. Omer, Arras and St. Waast, usually with elaborated cross motifs on each side together with the names of the count and the mint. Throughout most of the twelfth and thirteenth centuries the coinage of the counts was restricted to mints at Arras, Ghent, Ghistelles and Ypres but an extensive series of small deniers or mailles was issued by some twenty-seven town and abbey mints with their own individual types, as at Ghent where the obverse showed a helmeted head to left and the reverse a cross and sometimes the mint name *Gant* (Pl. 548).

The introduction of larger denominations in silver and issues in gold in the late twelfth and early thirteenth century marks the beginning of an era in the Belgian coinage, rich both in quantity and in the variety of denominations and artistry of types. In Brabant John I (1268–94) added to his issues of sterlings larger gros denominations, first as close copies of the French gros then with new types, a castle with two towers, around, *Moneta Bruxel* and, in the inner circle, of the reverse *Brabantie Dux*. On the obverse of the half gros the type was the Archangel Michael. The gros of John II (1294–1312) had on obverse either four lions in a quatrefoil or a shield quartered with lions and the small gros, a mounted knight. Gold made its appearance under John III (1312–55) in the form of copies of the lis florin of Florence or the chaise of France. His successor Joan and her husband Wenceslas of Luxemburg issued gold with types of St. Peter, a seated figure of St. Servais or the Paschal Lamb, and Joan, in alliance with Philip le Hardi of Flanders, the gold roosenbeker with its obverse type of the shield of Brabant and Burgundy and above a crown of roses. The coinage of Antony of Burgundy (1406–15) included gold with type a shield supported by lions and in silver the double gros (and parts) known as botdrager after the obverse type a lion with large helmet resembling a pot. The double gros of John IV (1415–27) with type two shields inclined towards each other (Pl. 549) was known as the drielander (three countries) as it was issued in Holland and Hainaut in addition to Brabant. This denomination under Philip of St. Pol (1427–30) was termed a kromstaart, a reference to the twisted tail of the lion rampant on which is placed the obverse shield.

The silver gros was struck in the bishopric of Liège by Hugh III de Chalon (1295–1301), copying closely the gros tournois but with *Leodiensis* around the castle type and *Hugo Episcopus* in the inner circle around the cross but on the small gros the obverse type was an eagle with outstretched wings. A similar eagle type above a small shield was used on gros of Adolf de la Marck (1313–44) and Engelbert de la Marck (1345–64), as well as on the small or two-thirds gros and lower divisions. To Engelbert is also attributed the anonymous gold gulden with the traditional types but inscribed *Sant Petrii* around the lis. Under John d'Arkel (1364–78), however, the gold series proper begins with coins of the mouton d'or type as well as those with St. Peter and shield on obverse. The richest series of this period at Liège is that of John of Bavaria (1390–1418) with coinage in gold of the chaise type, the common St. John gulden and the écu. The larger silver included the griffin with its double and half, named after the obverse type a griffin seated by a shield with long cross over quatrefoil enclosing lions on the reverse. The griffin type was also used on the gold of John of Heinsberg (1419–55) as well as chaise types and guldens with St. Peter and St. Lambert who appear on numerous issues throughout the fifteenth and early sixteenth centuries.

Typical of the new large silver pieces in Hainaut is the gros issued by John I (1232–57) with stylized monogram on obverse, a type repeated by John II (1280–1304) who also issued the small gros with type of mounted knight. An extensive series of gold for William III (1356–89) included pieces of the mouton d'or and rider types and there were some dozen varieties of the silver gros, including still the monogram type and a double gros with the names of the four evangelists *Ioha, Luca, Marc, Mate* on the reverse inscription. The gold angel of William IV (1404–17) showed on obverse an angel holding a shield within a palisade. Typical of the gros coinage issued by the counts of Namur are the coins of John I (1297–1331) with a castle type similar to that on the Brabant gros or with obverse of four lions within a quatrefoil. Under William I (1337–91) silver pieces of the botdrager type were struck as well as the gros with lion obverse and reverse, cross with lion in each angle. William also issued gold guldens showing his half-length figure holding sword under a canopy. This was the only gold issue of Namur until it passed to Philip the Good of Burgundy in 1421.

In Flanders Robert of Béthune (1305–22) struck gros copying the types of the gros tournois, as well as pieces with a mounted figure on the obverse (Pl. 550). The first Flemish gold was issued by Louis de Crécy (1322–46) in the form of angels with type of St. Michael with cross and shield and a dragon under his feet. The richest gold series is that of Louis de Mâle (1346–84) comprising no less than eleven types, including a helmeted lion and a standing figure of the count holding sword under a canopy (Pl. 551). The large silver piece the botdrager—the helmet wearer—with its obverse of lion in large helmet was also issued in Flanders by Louis. Flanders passed to the house of Burgundy on the marriage of Margaret of Flanders to Philip le Hardi in 1384. Amongst his gold coins was the rosenbeeker already described in the coinage of Brabant.

The major provinces, Flanders, Brabant, Hainaut and Namur, passed under the control of the house of Burgundy in the course of the reign of Philip the Good (1419–67) and the existence of a central authority made possible the imposition of a more uniform coinage system. The coinage of the various successive dukes of Burgundy and their Hapsburg successors is described in the Netherlands section (pp. 271–2). During and after the revolt against Philip II of Spain the history of the southern provinces followed a course different from that of the northern provinces, giving rise to a divergent coinage. The coinage agreed by the Pacification of Ghent in 1576 carried the name and titles and, where appropriate, the portrait of Philip on the obverse while the reverse was inscribed with the words *Pace et Iustitia*. This series was struck by the traditional mints of the southern provinces and by new mints at Mons, Tournai and 's Hertogenbosch. Because of the lack of confidence in the various new coinages throughout the Netherlands it was agreed in 1579 to resume issue of Philip's gold écu and silver daalder. When the provinces renounced their allegiance to Philip in July 1581 a coinage was issued at Antwerp and Bruges for Francis of Anjou consisting of a gold écu, a half-écu in silver with portrait of Francis and copper liards and gigots. After the departure of Francis a brief independent coinage of gold lions and silver écus was struck by the states of Brabant and Flanders but, after the reconquest of the southern Netherlands by the Spaniards, coinage of Philip's earlier type was resumed.

A fresh period of coinage opened in 1598 with the cession by Philip II of his Netherlands provinces to the Archduke Albert of Austria and Isabel of Spain. The mints active in this new period were Antwerp, Brussels, Maastricht, 's Hertogenbosch, Bruges, Tournai and later Luxemburg, and the new coinage was issued in the names of both Albert and Isabel. A first issue, begun in 1599, included coins of all three metals. In gold the double ducat bore the two busts *vis-à-vis* in the Spanish style and had as a reverse the archiducal shield within the collar of the Order of the Golden Fleece. This was the reverse also for the later albertin series in gold; here on the double-piece the two rulers were shown enthroned, on the albertin itself were their half-length figures in profile (Pl. 552) and on the half their full-length figures. The large silver ducaton and its half showed the bareheaded busts, jugate, of Albert and Isabel; on the reverse their crowned shield of arms has two lion supporters. The silver patagon established types which were to remain almost constant till the late eighteenth century. The obverse consisted of a cross formed of batons with briquet at centre; above, a crown, below, the jewel of the Order of the Golden Fleece and to left and right a crowned monogram. The same types were also used for the half- and quarter-patagon. The reverse on all was a shield within collar as on the albertin (Pl. 553).

Since Albert and Isabel died without heirs the southern Netherlands reverted to the Spanish crown. The coinage of Philip IV (1621–65) followed the lines laid down by Albert and Isabel except that the obverse on the albertin denominations was changed to the more usual profile bust. A new silver denomination, the escalin, showed on obverse the Flemish lion rampant with raised sword and resting paw on a shield with the arms of Austria and Burgundy. On the reverse were the Spanish arms on a cross of batons. The copper liard (Pl. 554) also carried the Spanish arms on the reverse and had as obverse a crown and the shields of Austria, Burgundy, Flanders (or Brabant) in the form of a cross with briquet at centre. These denominations and types were maintained with the requisite heraldic substitutions through most of the seventeenth and eighteenth centuries, even after the War of the Spanish Succession gave control of the southern Netherlands to the Austrian branch of the Hapsburgs. Some modifications were introduced under Maria Theresa (1740–80) such as the new types on the liard and its double in copper, where the bust of the sovereign appeared on the obverse and the inscription *ad usum Belgii Austriaci* on the reverse. The coinage of the short-lived Belgian revolt in 1790 consisted of a gold lion with obverse type a lion rampant with raised sword and resting paw on shield inscribed *Libertas* and on the reverse a sun surrounded by the shields of the eleven provinces. There was a silver lion of similar types and a florin also with lion obverse but with a reverse showing two arms emerging from the clouds and grasping eleven arrows. The copper liard and its double showed on obverse a lion holding spear topped by the cap of Liberty and an inscription *ad usum Foederati Belgii* on the reverse. This coinage was demonetized in 1791 when the Austrians regained control. Leopold II (1790–2) and Francis II (1792–7) both issued coinage in the Netherlands of the pre-revolutionary types but by 1794 the forward sweep of the French revolutionary forces drove the Austrians out and united the provinces to France, of which they formed a part until the defeat of Napoleon.

The Congress of Vienna united both the southern and northern provinces into one Kingdom of the Netherlands under William I. The coinage of the period is described under the Netherlands above (p. 275), the issues struck in the mint at Brussels being marked by the letter B. The revolution of 1830 established an independent kingdom of Belgium and Leopold of Saxe-Coburg was elected the first king. In 1832 a new coinage was decreed, modelled on the decimal system and the franc unit of the French coinage. On gold and on silver which extended down to a quarter franc the obverse was invariably the royal portrait and the reverse, at first the value in a wreath but, after 1847, the reverse consisted of a crowned shield with the Flemish lion dividing the indication of value. Centime denominations in copper showed a seated lion on obverse and the royal monogram crowned on reverse (Pl. 555). The issues of Leopold II (1865–1909) were similar, except that from 1866 onwards the inscriptions, previously in French only, were presented in Flemish as well. At the end of the nineteenth century centime pieces in cupro-nickel with a central piercing had as obverse two L's crowned and as reverse a branch and value. On the nickel coins of 2 francs and below of Albert (1909–34) from 1923 the obverse presented a figure of Belgium wounded but victorious and the reverse a caduceus and value. The portrait of Leopold III (1934–51) appears only on the higher denominations. The reverse on the 50 franc piece showed the shields of all nine provinces of Belgium but the 5 franc carried only the value. Centime pieces revived the crowned L's of Leopold II's type but added a Roman III at centre, while the reverse consisted of three shields with the value below. These types continued to be used during the German occupation (1940–4) but were struck in zinc instead of copper. Even during the occupation Leopold's portrait continued to appear on the 5 franc piece. On post-war issues the 50 and 20 franc pieces had a head of Mercury with lion reverse and the 5 and 1 franc coins a head of Ceres with an oak-leaf crowned on reverse. The 50 franc piece struck in 1958 in connection with the Brussels exhibition has the portrait of King Baudouin on the obverse and the town-hall of Brussels and the nuclear symbol of the exhibition on the reverse (Pl. 556).

LUXEMBURG

Apart from some very rare deniers of very rough fabric and style attributed to Frederick, Count of Luxemburg (998–1019), the earliest coinage proper is the denier issue of Henry III the Blind (1136–96) with types a horseman with inscription *Hanri* and a castle dividing the legend *Lusenbor*. In the thirteenth century the issues became more substantial, particularly those of Henry IV (1280–8) with the lion shield of the count on obverse and a cross on reverse. In the reign of Henry V (1288–1309) gros denominations were introduced with such types as the castle with two towers, as on the Brussels gros, and the lion within tressure of arches of Robert of Béthune in Flanders. The gold chaise and mouton d'or in the name of John the Blind (1309–46) are perhaps more properly to be ascribed to Bohemia of which he became king by his marriage to Elizabeth of Bohemia in 1309. Of the considerable variety of silver denominations struck by John, the sterling imitating the types of the English sterling penny was struck in such quantity that the term 'Lusshebourne' was used in England to describe all such imitations. Wenceslas I (1353–83) the first to bear the title Duke of Luxemburg issued gold guldens of the Florentine type, as did Wenceslas II (1383–8) who also struck the kromstaart, the gros with obverse type of lion with twisted tail. Luxemburg passed to Philip the Good, Duke of Burgundy, in 1444 and its monetary history from this point is similar to that of the southern provinces of the Netherlands.

In the reshaping of Europe in 1815 the Grand-Duchy of Luxemburg was added to the territory of William I of the Netherlands as compensation for Nassau but by virtue of Salic law forbidding the succession of a female, Luxemburg was detached from the Netherlands on the accession of Queen Wilhelmina in 1890. From 1854 to 1870 copper centimes were issued for William III of the Netherlands as Grand-Duke of Luxemburg with shield and value types and when Luxemburg became an independent grand-duchy in 1890 similar coins were issued for Adolph (1890–1905) and William IV (1905–12). Coins, still only of these denominations, appeared for Marie Adelaide (1912–19) and for Grand-Duchess Charlotte, struck in iron in the 1914–18 war and in the post-war years. The portrait of the grand-duchess appeared on the obverse of 10 and 5 franc pieces in 1929 and her monogram on the 1 franc coin which had as a reverse an iron worker and the state name Letzburg. The same types were used on the coinage resumed in 1946 after the

German occupation and again the shield and value types on the centime denominations.

FRANCE

Since the modern state of France in common with the majority of European countries has behind it some fifteen centuries of historical change and development, it is not always possible to contain the consideration of its successive coinage systems in watertight compartments, but it is sometimes necessary to deal with a political system and its coinage which included part of modern France or of which France formed one portion. A reasonably coherent picture of the coinage of France can, however, be obtained and its growth and development will be considered in a number of fairly clear successive stages (1) the initiative coinage of the barbarian kingdoms which replaced the Roman province of Gaul; (2) the new silver denier coinage of the Carolingian kings and emperors; (3) the denier coinage of the feudal lords and the Capetian kings from Hugh Capet to Louis VIII; (4) the coinage from Louis IX to Charles VIII, marked by the introduction of the larger silver gros and the re-emergence of gold; (5) the coinage of the Bourbons up to the Revolution; and (6) the decimal coinage up to the present day.

VISIGOTHS, BURGUNDIANS AND MEROVINGIANS
(FIFTH CENTURY–751)

The Roman empire in the West lost control of the province of Gaul and its mints in the first decades of the fifth century but a coinage of gold solidi and tremissis or thirds of solidi continued to be struck by the various barbarian kingdoms which were formed in the former Roman province. These gold series reproduced the standard and types of the imperial coinage and many of them are such exact imitations that only an expert eye can distinguish them from the official issues. From a study of minutiae of style a number of such series can be attributed to the various new kingdoms but the placing of additional marks on some issues permit their certain attribution to specific rulers.

When the western Roman empire finally fell in the late fifth century, France was divided amongst three barbarian peoples of whom the Visigoths who controlled Spain held the southern portion. Some tremissis, imitating the types of the Byzantine emperor Anastasius, have in the field letters such as Ꝟ or T, probably indicating mints at Burdigala (Bordeaux) and Tolosa (Toulouse) in Visigothic territory. On some solidi and tremissis struck by the Burgundians in the kingdom

they had established in the Rhône valley appear monograms of their kings
Sigismund (516–524) and Gundobald II (*c.* 524) (Pl.557). Both these tribal kingdoms were, however, of comparatively short duration. The Visigothic kingdom
in France was seized by the Franks under Clovis in 507 and the Burgundian by the
sons of Clovis in 534. Before outlining the coinage of the Merovingian kings of
the Franks who finally united most of France under their rule one further series of
coinage in south France must be noticed. A series of quasi-imperial coins copying
the types of Byzantine emperors from Justin II to Heraclius bear the Roman
figures XXI on solidi and VII on tremissis indicating their content in siliquae
and giving a solidus of about 3·86 gm. compared with the imperial solidus of
4·45 gm. These pieces have an imperial legend and bust, usually in profile on the
obverse, a blundered form of the inscription *Victoria augg* on the reverse with
type, cross on globe. In the reverse field appear the mark of value and letters
indicating the mints, of which the chief were Marseilles (Pl. 558), Arles, Uzès and
Viviers.

The Merovingian kingdom of the Franks comprised four sub-kingdoms;
Neustria in the north and west, Austrasia in the north and east, Aquitaine in the
south-west and Burgundy in the south-east. Space does not permit to trace the
murderous vicissitudes of union and divergence and their reflections in the coinage
but merely to outline the general characteristics of this coinage. No coinage has
been attributed to Clovis and the earliest series is probably that of Theodobert I
(534–548). Gold solidi with a facing portrait of Theodobert with spear and shield
and with the epithet *Victor* added to his name and a Victory type reverse, with
letters in the field indicating the mint, may have been struck on his expedition to
Italy in 539. The more usual regal coinage of the Merovingians consists of tremissis
with a conventional profile portrait and regal name on obverse and on reverse a
Victory type or a cross type with mint letters and the name of the moneyer
(Pl. 559). Since various kings bore the same name and no ordinal number is added
on the coin, the distribution of these pieces over the various kings is dependent
on the study of detail.

Much of the Merovingian coinage shows no direct regal connection but was
issued by ecclesiastical authority. The types remain basically the same but the
inscriptions give the names of monasteries or bishops. The majority of the tremissis coinage from the second half of the sixth century onwards is that of the
moneyers. Around the conventional head on the obverse appears the name of the
moneyer, often accompanied by *monetarius* in variously abbreviated forms; on the
other side is a cross motif with the name of the mint (Pl. 560). The chronological
classification of this Merovingian coinage presents great difficulty and the great
value of the series lies in the wealth of personal and place names recorded. A

considerably smaller class of Merovingian coinage is that of the silver deniers. Originally in the late fifth and early sixth centuries these were imitations of small Roman silver coins, later in the sixth century imitations of Byzantine silver coins of Justinian I and finally in the seventh and early eighth centuries even more degenerate imitations with meaningless inscriptions. In general terms these latter resembled Anglo-Saxon sceattas with which they are found in hoards.

THE CAROLINGIAN KINGS (751–987)

A powerful landed nobility had developed in the various divisions of the Frankish kingdom, the later Merovingian kings had become mere figure-heads and real power lay in the hands of the mayor of the palace. It was, however, not till 751 that the palace mayor, Pepin the Short, took the final step when, with Papal blessing, he was crowned king, the first of the Carolingian dynasty. The Merovingian coinage which had deteriorated in standard and execution was replaced under Pepin by a new coinage of silver deniers. The Merovingian denier like the tremissis had been of small, rather thick module but the new denier had a thinner, spread fabric. The types make it clear that in contrast to most of the Merovingian coinage the issue of coin was once again a royal prerogative, for Pepin's coinage had on obverse only the initials R(ex) P(ipinus) and on reverse the name of the mint (Pl. 561). The denier coinage underwent a change under Charlemagne (781–814) when, owing to the influence of the Arab dirhem circulating in Spain, the fabric became wider and flatter. The denier, struck by Pepin at a weight of about 1·24 gm., was raised by Charlemagne to 2 gm. Twelve such deniers went to one solidus of silver, now only a coin of account, and there were twenty such solidi or two hundred and forty deniers to the pound.

The most common types on deniers of Charlemagne consist of his monogram surrounded by his name and title on obverse, with on reverse a cross and the name of the mint (Pl. 562). Some deniers of Charlemagne show his profile bust in the Roman imperial style and have on the reverse a temple with the inscription *Christiana Religio*, a reference to his coronation as Emperor of the Holy Roman empire on Christmas Day, 800. Deniers of Louis the Pious (814–840) commonly have his name and title around a cross on the obverse with the name of the mint in one or more lines on the reverse. Another class shows his profile portrait on the obverse, while another repeats the temple type of his father. Early coins of Charles the Bald (840–877) are difficult to distinguish from those of Charlemagne but not those struck after about 864, when deniers were struck with on one side the monogram of the royal name surrounded by the phrase *Gratia Di Rex* and on the other the name of the mint city around a cross. The type of the denier became practically immobilized and the issues of subsequent Carolingian kings were largely the same but for the requisite change in name or monogram.

Two further categories of Carolingian coins require mention. Although the intention of the monetary reform at the beginning of this period had been to restore the royal prerogative, it appears that even as early as the reign of Charlemagne himself coinage concessions or grants were being made in favour of abbeys. At first the types were, in the main, royal with the addition of the ecclesiastical mint name but in the tenth century the privilege of issuing a separate coinage began to be conceded. As the power of the Carolingian kings decreased that of the feudal counts increased and, with the stabilization of the denier types, imitation coinage issued by mints other than the true royal mints became more common, some of these 'immobilized' series persisting for several centuries.

HUGH CAPET—LOUIS VIII (987–1226)

In contrast with England where the establishment of a single monarchy was accompanied by a single unified coinage the lack of a strong central monarchy in mediaeval France had, as a corollary, a diffusion of coinage. The Capetian king was originally little more than *primus inter pares* and his coinage, similarly, was only one of many in France and the history of the royal coinage is that of gradual consolidation and increase of authority *vis-à-vis* the feudal issues.

Little more can be done here than sketch the basis and outline of the feudal issues in this period, before turning to trace the main stream of the royal French coinage. In Carolingian times it was not so much the right of coinage that was granted as the profits from coining, but as early as the tenth century independent coinage with the name and style of the feudal lords made its appearance. Amongst the earliest of such issues were those of Richard, Duke of Normandy (943–996), of Hugh Capet as Duke of the Franks (956–987) and Erbert, Count of Mans, about 1000. The right of coinage even when exercised by a duke, a prince or a bishop was basically that of a count. The types are in general derived and developed from those of Carolingian deniers. The cross, either plain or more ornate, was a widespread type as was also the monogram type of Carolingian pieces, the model for the monogram on coins of Erbert, Count of Mans, for instance (Pl. 563). The temple type of Charlemagne though popular on episcopal issues at Lyons, Soissons and Strasbourg was also used on lay issues at Bourges. The profile portrait introduced by Louis the Pious developed into an almost geometric pattern such as on the deniers of Chartres.

Just as at the close of the Merovingian period the king had become a figure-head and real power rested with the palace mayor, so, under the last of the Carolingian monarchs, it was in the hands of the duke of the Franks that power rested. Finally, in 987, with the coronation of Hugh Capet, Duke of the Franks, as king, real and titular power were combined. Although the title of king appears on the coins of Hugh struck after this date, the issues were made by him in his feudal capacity as, for instance, Count of Paris or Count of Sens.

In the coinage of the Capetian kings, in addition to the issues of deniers and obols or half-pieces from mints in the royal domain, the king's name was associated on other issues struck by some of the bishoprics and some feudal lords. The types were usually varieties of the cross or of the developments from Carolingian types which have been discussed above. On the denier parisis of Philippe II Auguste the king's name and title occupies the whole obverse in a circular inscription and an inscription across the field, while on the reverse is a simple cross with the name of the mint, Paris (Pl. 564). Philippe II, under whom the authority of the monarchy was considerably strengthened, extended the centralizing tendency to the coinage, for his deniers, struck in diverse mints such as Arras, Montreuil and Saint Omer, are like in type to the denier parisis. Philippe also in his quality of Count of Tours began striking there the denier tournois. The obverse consisted of his name and title around a cross, the reverse, the castle of Tours and the name of St. Martin (Pl. 565). This was the last reign in which place names commonly appeared on royal issues.

LOUIS IX—CHARLES VIII (1226–1498)

In this period the regal coinage gradually achieved a superior status over the feudal coinage. These latter issues were restricted to their respective feudal domains while regal coinage circulated wherever the royal suzerainty was recognized and an endeavour was made to distinguish the regal from feudal types. In the course of the period, as more territories were united to the crown, the number of feudal issues was reduced, but as the Anglo-Gallic issues (pp. 249–54) illustrate, where coinage rights remained, coinage in other denominations than the early denier developed just as it did in the regal series.

In France in common with the rest of western Europe improved economic circumstances made necessary a large silver denomination. The first of such pieces was the gros tournois, introduced by Louis IX in 1266. This gros of 4·2 gm., valued at 12 deniers tournois, was an enlarged version of the smaller coin: on the obverse was added an additional circle of inscription, an abbreviated form of *Benedictum sit nomen Domini nostri Dei Jesu Christi*, while on the reverse was added a border of twelve fleurs-de-lis (Pl. 566). The extensive series of gold coins of both the Byzantine empire and the Islamic caliphate had rendered this medium familiar and gold coinage was first introduced into the French regal series by St. Louis in the form of the écu d'or, with types a shield with lis and a decorative cross with lis in the angles. In addition to such new denominations, deniers parisis and tournois and mailles or obols of the previous type were also issued. Under Philip IV le Bel (1285–1314) further gold pieces were struck including the angel with its type of the Lamb of God and the chaise d'or which showed the king enthroned, a type which was to be repeated with variations in later reigns and in other coinages (Pl. 567). The gold coinage of Philip VI (1328–50), the first of the house of Valois, is notable for the range of varying types: on the most common, the écu, there appeared for the first time the king holding sword, on the ange a crowned angel treading down a dragon and on the florin St. George on horse-back slaying the dragon. In silver a gros parisis was added, an elaboration of the denier types, the fifteen lis of the reverse border indicating that the piece was tariffed at 15 deniers tournois.

The prosperity evidenced by this coinage suffered a check, however, with the outbreak in 1337 of the Hundred Years' War with England. Much of the still considerable gold coinage of the reign of John the Good (1350–64), particularly the franc d'or with its type of the king in armour on horse-back, was required to pay the ransom of the king who was captured at the battle of Poitiers in 1356. During the captivity of John, his son the Dauphin Charles struck a considerable coinage at the mints of Dauphiné which continued to strike for him after he succeeded in 1364. Typical of this coinage is the gros with the punning reverse type of a dolphin. In the troubled reign of the mad Charles VI (1380–1422) the control of the mints was divided amongst the various contenders for authority, Queen Isabel as regent, the powerful Duke of Burgundy, the Dauphin and Henry V of England who claimed to be the heir of Charles. In the gold coinage the écu à la couronne which was to be become a standard gold piece made its first appearance. The type, as the name implies, was a crowned shield bearing three lis; the reverse was a floreate cross in a tressure of arches with a crown in each spandrel (Pl. 568). On the various gros and blancs the benediction formula of the common inscription was reduced to the form *sit nomen Domini benedictum*. The issues of Henry V and Henry VI of England as kings of France are dealt with in the section on the Anglo-Gallic coinage of the English kings. On his accession in 1422 Charles VII controlled little more than Dauphiné but with the intervention of Joan of Arc, and the relief of Orleans in 1429, began the successful campaigns which by 1453 had driven the English from all their possessions in France except Calais. The principal gold coin of the reign was an écu similar to that of Charles VI but with a crowned lis on either side of the shield and a more ornate reverse. A new piece in silver was the plaque or patard, a double gros struck at Tournai. The types consisted simply of three lis on obverse and a long cross with the letters F R A C disposed in the angles. Louis XI (1461–83) neglected no opportunity of strengthening the now recovered kingdom by re-uniting to it vassal provinces and at the same time the monetary system was considerably simplified. The écu à la couronne was left as the only substantive gold denomination and the varieties of silver and billon coinage were reduced to only a few. The main addition to the coinage under Charles VIII (1483–98) was the Carolus or dizain (10 deniers tournois) with types, a crowned K between lis on obverse and a cross with lis in angles on reverse.

LOUIS XII—REVOLUTION (1498–1792)

From the reign of Louis XII onwards the French coinage begins to discard the features of design associated with mediaevalism and to acquire the characteristics of a modern coinage. The coinage system of Louis XII largely perpetuated that of his predecessor, an interesting novelty on the gold coinage being the écu with a porcupine, the badge of the house of Orleans, on either side of the shield. More significant was the introduction of a new silver piece, the teston, its obverse type a realistic profile portrait of the king revealing the influence of the Renaissance. On some issues of the teston also the traditional Gothic lettering of the inscription was replaced by Latin letters. The reign of Francis I (1515–47) is notable for the administrative reform in the production of coinage by which the differential symbol which had previously marked the product of the several mints was replaced by a letter—A for Paris, B for Rouen, K for Bordeaux—or by a dot placed in varying positions round the inner circle (Pl. 569). At the end of the circular legend was placed the initial or symbol of the mint-master. Modernization of the coinage proceeded further under Henry II (1547–59). The royal portrait was now used on the gold coinage also and on the henri d'or the shield, now displaced from the obverse, was used as a reverse type but the double piece had a new reverse, a cross, the arms formed by the king's initial crowned, with alternate lis and crescent in the angles. The silver testons were issued with a variety of portraits including a simple laureate head or a laureate and armoured bust in the Roman imperial manner and from 1549 onwards the ordinal number of the king was included in his title.

No coinage was issued in the brief reign of Francis II (1559–60) the husband of Mary, Queen of Scots. The gold coinage of his brother, Charles IX (1560–74) in whose reign began the great religious strife which was to trouble France for half a century showed a reversal of practice in omitting the royal portrait, though this appeared regularly on the silver testons and half-pieces. The majority of issues of this and succeeding reigns include the date of issue in figures. In the silver coinage of Henry III (1574–89) a new silver piece made its appearance, the franc and its divisions. These bore the portrait of the king in a ruff on the obverse and his initial at the centre of a decorative cross on the reverse (Pl. 570). In billon the liard had as obverse type the royal initial crowned and set amidst three lis, while on the reverse was a Maltese cross with the dove of the Holy Spirit at the centre. A new coinage of doubles tournois and deniers tournois was struck in bronze. The royal portrait and titles occupied the obverse, three or two lis, according to denomination, the reverse whose inscription simply stated in words the denomination of the coin.

The death of Henry III in 1589, the last of the house of Valois, left the Bourbons in the person of Henry of Navarre next in line of succession. As Henry, however, was a protestant his succession was contested and his uncle Charles, Cardinal of Bourbon, was proclaimed king by the Catholic League. Though the cardinal was already in prison and died in 1590 without recovering his liberty, a certain amount of coinage in all metals was struck for him as Charles X. Henry of Navarre, though he abjured his faith and became a catholic, had to take his kingdom by force of arms in a campaign which lasted until 1598. In his titulature on coins Henry retained, additionally, his title of King of Navarre, a practice followed by all subsequent Bourbon kings. His gold écu was without portrait and had the crowned shield on obverse and an ornate cross on reverse. There were two series in silver. The types of the quarter- and eighth-écu were similar to those of the gold écu but had the mark of value on obverse divided about the shield, while the reverse was a cross, the arms terminating in lis. On the obverse of the second series consisting of half- and quarter-francs was the royal portrait in armour and on reverse the initial H at the centre of four floreate ornaments. Billon dizains and liards of the general types of preceding reigns were struck as well as the double tournois and denier tournois in copper.

The issues of Louis XIII (1610–43) up to 1640 followed closely the pattern of denominations and types in gold and silver of Henry IV's coinage. In the early years of Louis' reign Nicholas Briot, the medallist who later worked for Charles I of England, had made repeated but unsuccessful attempts to have removed the ban imposed in 1585 on striking gold and silver coinage by machine instead of by hammer. By 1640, however, the Paris mint had been won over to the production of machine-struck coins in both gold and silver. In gold the new unit was the louis with royal portrait on obverse and a cross design, formed of pairs of the letter L back to back, crowned and with lis in the angles on the reverse (Pl. 571). Or the multiples of two, four, eight and ten only the double-piece was struck with any frequency, as was the half-piece also. The new silver piece was the écu blanc, more commonly called the louis d'argent with its reverse a crowned shield. Subdivisions of a half, quarter, twelfth and even twenty-fourth were also struck. Throughout the long reign of Louis XIV (1643–1715) the denominations in gold and silver, introduced by his father, remained the staple issues, though with changes and developments of portrait natural for a king who succeeded at the age of five. These portrait changes combined with a number of changes in the detail of the reverse produce no less than ten successive issues of both the louis d'or and the louis d'argent. The final series in silver, begun in 1709, shows the bewigged portrait of the old king and a reverse of three crowns with lis in angles (Pl. 572). A new denomination in copper was the liard, the reverse consisting of the inscription *liard de France* in three lines.

The gold louis continued to be struck under Louis XV (1715–74) with a variety of portraits and reverse types, in one of which the shields of France and Navarre were arranged in the form of a cross, comparable to the reverse design of the English guinea. The silver écu and its subdivisions was also struck with a number of reverse variations and, in copper, a new denomination the sou, with reverse type the crowned shield of France. The coinage of Louis XVI, the last of the Bourbons before the Revolution, falls into two series, a regal series which continued with variations of design the denominations of preceding reigns and from 1791 to 1793 the constitutional series. On this new coinage the king bears the title *Roi des françois*. On both gold and silver the reverse, inscribed *Regne de la loi*, shows a Genius inscribing the constitution and on the more common subdivisions of the silver écu, the quarter and the half, the value, 30 and 15 sols respectively, was added in the field. The date, given in the normal fashion on the obverse, was repeated in the new formula, e.g. *l'an 3 de la liberté* on the reverse. The reverse type of the copper sou of which a double-piece was also struck was composed of the fasces crowned with a cap of Liberty within a laurel-wreath (Pl. 573). Similar types with appropriate change of the mark of value were used for the coinage of 12, 6 and 3 deniers.

FIRST REPUBLIC—FIFTH REPUBLIC (1792–1960)

The initial issues of the First Republic continued the monetary system of the constitutional issues. The silver écu inscribed on the obverse with the new title *République Françoise* and the value, 6 livres, retained the Genius type as the reverse.

The copper sol had an inscribed tablet as obverse and the scales of justice, cap of Liberty and mark of value on reverse. In 1794, however, under the Directory, the decimal system of coinage was adopted with a new unit, the silver franc. In silver only the 5 franc piece was issued with the value in wreath as obverse and a group of Hercules, Liberty and Equality as the reverse, and in copper, which had as types the head of the republic in cap of Liberty and the value in wreath, denominations from 2 decimes to 5 centimes were struck. In the coinage of the Consulate similar reverses were used but the portrait of Napoleon with his title of First Consul appeared on the obverse (Pl. 574) and gold pieces of 40 and 20 francs were added to the range. The coinage of Napoleon as emperor from 1806 onwards varied initially only in his new title, for even the inscription *République Française* was continued until 1808 and the expression of the date in the new era dating until 1807. From 1809 Napoleon appeared with laureate portrait and the reverse bore the inscription *Empire Français*.

With the restoration of the Bourbon monarchy in the person of Louis XVIII in 1814, the decimal coinage system based on the franc was adapted to a regal form. On the issues of the first restoration in 1814–15, Louis was represented by a uniformed bust and on the reverse with its type, the royal shield of France crowned between two laurel-branches was inscribed, e.g. *Pièce de 5 francs*. The portrait of the second restoration was simple a bare head and on the reverse the value was indicated in figures. The denominations in gold were 40 and 20 francs and in silver 5, 2, and 1 franc pieces as well as a half and a quarter. The issues of Charles X (1824–30) followed an identical pattern but the royal arms disappeared from the reverse of the coins of Louis Philippe (1830–48) leaving the value in a wreath of laurel as the sole type. From 1845 the half- and quarter-franc pieces were replaced by 50 and 20 centimes coins.

Almost the sole change effected in the coinage by the expulsion of Louis Philippe and the establishment of the Second Republic was the substitution for the royal portrait of a head of Ceres wearing corn-wreath. With the election of Louis Napoleon as president of the Second Republic in 1851 his bare-headed portrait with simply his name as inscription was adopted for the obverse of the coinage. On the creation of the new French Empire in 1852 Louis Napoleon placed his title *Napoleon III Empereur* on the obverse of the coinage and *Empire Français* on the reverse. The 40 franc piece now disappeared from the gold denominations and pieces of 100 and 50 francs were added at the top of the scale and 10 and 5 in the lower range. In copper, 10, 5, 2 and 1 centime pieces were issued with an imperial eagle as reverse type (Pl. 575). From 1862 the imperial portrait, previously bare-headed, became laureate.

When the Second Empire crashed after the disastrous defeat at Sedan in 1870, the coinage of the Third Republic reverted to the types used by the Second Republic in 1848 with the addition, very soon, of the motto *Liberté, Egalité, Fraternité* to the reverse type. The types remained stable till towards the close of the century when new designs were adopted for all denominations. The head of the republic and the Gallic cock provided the types for the gold 20 and 10 franc pieces while the familiar figure of a sower was placed on the silver coinage, of which the 2 franc piece was now the highest denomination (Pl. 576). The various centime denominations in copper had the head of the republic and an allegorical group. After the first world war, gold coinage ceased for practical purposes and the smaller franc values were replaced by coinage in aluminium bronze. The new coinages of the 1920's and 1930's consisted of various stylized heads of the republic on the obverses and reverses filled with decoration and stating the value.

The Vichy State in France between 1942 and 1944 with its type of a double-headed axe on the franc denominations in aluminium replaced the traditional title with the phrase *État français* and the traditional motto with *Travail, famille, patrie* (Pl. 577). The obverse of the 5 franc piece bore the portrait of Marshal Pétain and his title, Chef de l'État. Only in 1950 was a new post-war coinage introduced. On denominations of 50, 20 and 10 francs in aluminium-bronze the types were identical, a head of the republic on obverse and the Gallic cock and value on the reverse, while a cupro-nickel 100 franc denomination first struck in 1954 had another version of the head of the republic with wheat-ears and value on the reverse. The coinage reform of early 1960 introduced a new franc, tariffed at a hundred of the existing francs and revived for the obverse of the new coin the figure of the Sower, the obverse type of the franc in the first two decades of the century.

ITALY

Because of exceptional circumstances, both historical and geographic, Italy together with the adjacent islands of Sicily and Sardinia has been the scene of more constant flux and change than any other area in Europe. Not only was Italy the cradle of European civilization but Rome, for ever associated in the consciousness of the states which developed in Europe, with ideas of power and empire was also the centre of Christendom. Since in mediaeval times the Mediterranean basin still represented the centre of the world and Italy lay at the cross-roads of the Mediterranean, her history is one long succession of invasion and conquest; and, indeed, it is still less than a century since the final unification took place. The stormy and complicated history of Italy is faithfully reflected in the diversification of Italian coinage issued by successive conquerors, by papal authority, independent city republics and great ruling houses. It is some measure of the complexity of this vast and varied coinage that the ambitious project of compiling a *Corpus* of Italian coinage, instigated and largely personally executed by the late Victor Emmanuel III, has produced some nineteen ponderous volumes but still awaits completion. This present work can hope to do no more than sketch the general development of the successive periods of coinage and high light some of the more important trends and issues.

OSTROGOTHS, BYZANTINES AND LOMBARDS (SIXTH–EIGHTH CENTURIES)

Romulus Augustus, the last of the puppet emperors of Rome, was deposed in 476 by Odovacer, the chief of the Heruli. Coinage in the Roman style issued by Odovacer consists of small silver and bronze coins with his portrait bust and name on obverse and his monogram on the reverse (Pl. 578). The Ostrogoths who had invaded Italy in 489 under their chief Theoderic established themselves as masters of Italy after the assassination of Odovacer in 493. The coinage of this new Ostrogothic kingdom struck in gold, silver and bronze was largely a series imitating the issues of the Roman emperor at Constantinople. Gold solidi issued by Theoderic (493–526) continue to carry the portrait and titles of the Byzantine emperor Anastasius on the obverse and his customary Victory type on reverse and can be distinguished only by their style, though some pieces add Theoderic's monogram at the end of the reverse inscription. A unique triple solidus, however, presents a magnificent facing portrait of Theoderic on the obverse which is inscribed with his name, while the Victory-type reverse also bears his name. The third of the solidus, the gold termissis, was likewise an imitation of the tremissis of Anastasius. Small silver coins, however, bore the monogram of Theoderic on the reverse. Some further divergence takes place on the issues of Athalaric (526–534) who issued bronzes of ten nummi with a bust of Roma, inscribed *Invicta Roma* on the obverse and his full title *Dn Athalaricus Rex* in four lines within a wreath on the reverse. On another variety Athalaric is shown as a standing figure on the reverse. In addition to imitative gold coins and silver pieces with his monogram on the reverse Theodahad (534–536) introduced a large 40 nummi piece in bronze which showed his portrait bust, crowned and with cross on breast on obverse and a figure of Victory on the reverse (Pl. 579). Of the later Ostrogothic kings Baduila (541–552) placed his portrait on both silver and bronze but Theia (552–553), the last king, defeated by Narses the general of Justinian I, maintained the imperial portrait on his silver and placed his own name on the reverse only.

Apart from the series, partly imitative, partly original, just outlined, some larger bronze pieces traditionally called quasi-autonomous since they bear neither imperial nor Ostrogothic names were struck, most probably at Rome in the the reigns of Theoderic and Athalaric. This series has the helmeted bust of Roma on the obverse, inscribed *Invicta Roma*, and, on the larger denomination, an eagle with spread wings and the value XL (40 nummi); on the smaller the wolf and twins of Roman legend with value XX (20 nummi). Coinage struck for the Byzantine emperors at mints in Italy, chiefly Ravenna and Rome, from the time of Justinian I's successful invasion of Italy down to the time of Basil I is described in the chapter on the Byzantine coinage.

Another imitative series akin to that of the Ostrogoths can be noted here, though it has no specific connection with Italy, being the coinage of the Vandals in North Africa which they had overrun after crossing from Spain under their king, Gaiseric, in 429. The coins of Gaiseric (429–477) and Huneric (477–484) are imitations of the silver siliqua of the emperor Honorius and bronzes, marked in Roman numerals with values of 42, 21 and 12 nummi. The obverse of Gaiseric's bronzes show a standing figure of the king with inscription *Kartago* and the reverse a horse's head, similar to that on coins of ancient Carthage, with the value, e.g. XLII. Huneric's bronzes have a standing figure of Carthage and value in wreath. Silver coins of Gunthamund (484–496) and his successors have the portrait and name of the king on obverse and within a wreath on reverse, the value in denarii in denominations of 100, 50 or 25. The last Vandal king to issue such coins (Pl. 580) was Gelimer (530–533) before North Africa was reconquered by the Byzantine empire in 533.

The Byzantine empire was not left long in undisturbed possession of Italy, for in 568 the Lombards who had been used by Byzantium to crush the Ostrogoths returned in force under their king Alboin and assumed effective mastery of Italy at least as far south as the Tiber. Coinage issued by the Lombardic kings initially took the form mainly of imitations of the Byzantine gold tremissis in a distinctive thin fabric, but from the time of Cunincpert (688–700) this coinage of small gold pieces carries the name of the Lombardic king around the rude obverse portrait, usually accompanied on the reverse by a winged figure, holding shield and cross inscribed with the name of St. Michael (Pl. 581). The last of the Lombardic kings, Desiderius (757–774), was compelled to submit to Charlemagne.

Four great Lombard duchies also existed in a state of practical independence in south Italy from the sixth to the eighth centuries. Coinage of the most important of these, the Duchy of Beneventum, consisted again of imitation gold solidi and tremisses. The fabric of this series is also flat and spread and the usual types are a facing bust with a travesty of the imperial name on obverse and a cross on steps on the reverse. Grimoald III (788–806) who was compelled to recognize Charlemagne as his overlord inscribed his own name with the title of *Dux* on the obverse and that of Charlemagne on the reverse (Pl. 582). On his issues from 792 onwards Grimoald adopts the title *Princeps* and omits mention of Charlemagne. Issues of subsequent dukes of Beneventum, usually of silver denari without obverse portrait, continue to use this title till the time of Aio (884–890), the last duke of whom coins have been identified.

Other duchies in south Italy issued a coinage of follari, large bronze coins, modelled on Byzantine issues. Typical examples are the issues of Sergius I, Duke of Naples (840–861) showing his facing bust with cross and globe on obverse and a facing bust of St. Januarius on the reverse (Pl. 583) or of Gisulf I (935–974) struck at Salerno with, as types, the prince's standing figure and a three-line inscription *Opulenta Salerno*.

CAROLINGIAN PERIOD (EIGHTH–TENTH CENTURIES)

In 774 Charlemagne crossed the Alps and forced the submission of Desiderius, King of the Lombards. His earliest coin issues in Italy were imitation tremisses in the style and fabric of the late Lombardic coinage with his name *Dn Carolus Rex*—usually somewhat abbreviated—around a cross on the obverse and the name of the mint inscribed round a star motif on the reverse. These were followed by issues of Charlemagne's silver denier from Italian mints at Florence, Parma, Venice and Milan and later at Rome, Sienna and Lucca. These issues had the name *Carolus* in two lines across the obverse and on the reverse either the letters *RF* accompanied by a small initial of the mint or the name of the mint across the field or disposed in the angles of an ornamental cross. Deniers with the laureate bust of Charlemagne inscribed *Karolus Imp Aug* on obverse and a temple accompanied by the inscription *Xpistiana Religio*, struck after Charlemagne's coronation by the Pope in 800 as Emperor of the Holy Roman empire, were issued by mints at Milan, Pavia and Verona, marked by an initial letter under the obverse bust. The Carolingians who succeeded Charlemagne as emperor also struck deniers at Italian mints including issues of deniers of unusually broad, spread flan, commonly with types cross and temple, probably struck at Milan (Pl. 584). The last of the 'Carolingian' dynasty to issue coins in Italy was Berengarius II as King of Italy in conjunction with his son Adalbert.

The coinage of the popes has its beginnings only at the very end of the eighth century under Adrian I (772–795) who struck a denier coinage, copying Byzantine types with his facing bust and name on obverse and a cross on steps with a version of the *Victoria* inscription on the reverse, together with the letters $\frac{\text{RM}}{\text{COMOB}}$ indicating the mint at Rome. From Leo III (795–816) till the tenth-century papal denari followed a fairly consistent pattern. The obverse carried the name of the current emperor around a monogram frequently representing the word *imperator* or *Roma*, while the reverse bore a monogram of the name of the pope surrounded by the inscription *Scs Petrus*. An exception to this pattern was the coinage of John VIII (872–882) who placed a facing bust of St. Peter on the reverse (Pl. 585), an example followed by Formosus (891–896), John IX (989–900) and Benedict IV (900–903). Under Sergius III (904–911) and Anastasius III (911–913) mention of the emperor is omitted from the coinage and for most of the remainder of the first half of the tenth century there is an absence of papal coinage.

The ninth century also saw the beginning of one of the famous Italian coinages which lasted up to the late eighteenth century; that of Venice. After striking for the Carolingian emperors Louis (814–840) and Lothair I (840–855) Venice in the later part of the century on denari of cross and temple variety omits mention of the emperor's name, using as inscriptions *Pe Salva Venecias* and the general *Ds Cnserua Roman Imp,* while in the tenth century the obverse inscription reads *Christus Imper* and that on the reverse becomes a blundered form of the *Christiana Religio* formula. Mention has been made above (p. 297) of the coinages of the duchies of south Italy in this period.

PERIOD OF THE GERMAN EMPERORS
(TENTH–THIRTEENTH CENTURIES)

With the coronation as emperor of Otto I in 962 after he had deposed Berengarius II, King of Italy, the Holy Roman empire passed to the Saxon kings of Germany, who transmitted it to their successors. Up to the early twelfth century a coinage of denari was struck for these successive emperors at mints in northern Italy at Milan, Pavia, Verona and Lucca. The types continued to be mainly epigraphic, in essence the name of the emperor and the mint around a cross motif on either side (Pl. 586). Even before the twelfth century coinage rights had been granted to a number of important cities in northern and central Italy. After the struggle between the developing city-republics and the imperial authority which culminated with the defeat of Frederick Barbarossa at Legnano in 1176 the treaty of Constance in 1183 according to a long list of cities rights of autonomy, extending in practice to the issue of coinage.

A feature of a number of such coinages is the immobilization, sometimes for centuries, of the coin types current at the time when the grant of coining rights was made. An example of this is the silver coinage of Bologna which received coinage rights from Henry VI in 1191. The obverse inscribed *Enricus* has as its centre the four letters of his title *I P R T*, while the reverse has a circular legend *Bononi* with the final letter *A* of the city name in the centre (Pl. 587). Other city-republics, however, adopted completely autonomous types, as, for instance, Florence which began to coin late in the twelfth century with its characteristic types of John the Baptist on obverse, inscribed *S. Iohannes B* and lily on reverse with inscription *Florentia*. Florence was one of the first cities to add a coinage of gold to the standard silver issues, striking the first of the famous fiorini d'oro or gold florins, still with the same types in 1252 (Pl. 588). Genoa, on the other hand, perpetuated on its coinage throughout the Middle Ages the name of Conrad III who granted coinage rights in 1139. The obverse on the Genoese issues is an example of the punning type; a stylized gateway is inscribed *Ianua*, at the same time a description of the type and the name of the city. Around a cross on the reverse appears the name of Conrad in the form *Cunradi Rex*. Genoa anticipated Florence in the issue of a gold coinage which was authorized as early as 1149, the types reproducing those of the silver coinage (Pl. 589). In 1192 Venice added to her coinage of denari, the grosso, the earliest large silver denomination in the Italian coinage, or matapan. On the obverse St. Mark presents a banner to the doge; a circular inscription on this earliest example includes the name of the doge *H. Dandolo S M Veneti*, while the concluding word *Dux* is inscribed vertically along-side the banner. On the reverse is a seated figure of Christ with the initials IC—XC on either side of the head (Pl. 590). In 1284 the doge Giovanni Dandolo struck the first Venetian gold coin. Here, in contrast to the silver matapan, the doge kneels before St. Mark on the obverse, while the figure of Christ on the reverse is shown standing within an oval frame, accompanied by the inscription *Sit tibi Christe datus, quem tu regis, iste ducatus* (Pl. 591). From the final word of this in-scription the term ducat came to be applied to this and similar gold coins in many lands; the alternative name, zecchino, is derived from the Italian word for mint, *zecca*.

In the south of Italy events had followed quite a different pattern giving rise to coinage of a different kind. In Sicily where the Saracen conquest had begun in 827 a coinage of typical Islamic dirhems was issued at Palermo by the Aghlabids and from the early tenth century till the middle of the eleventh when the Normans in turn conquered Sicily a series of gold rubas was struck for successive Fatimid caliphs, also at Palermo. The Normans first established themselves in south Italy in the first half of the eleventh century at Naples, Amalfi, Capua, Gaeta and Sorrento. Their coins were partly imitations of Arab gold, but mainly copper follari of Byzantine inspiration such as the issue of Roger Borsa, Duke of Apulia

(1085–1111), with facing bust of St. Matthew on obverse and linear inscription *Roger-ius-Dux* on the reverse. Sicily, too, fell to the Normans and eventually in 1130 Roger II of Sicily was crowned in Naples as King of Naples and Sicily, later termed the two Sicilies. As in south Italy the coinage of the Norman kings consisted of the small gold taro with Arabic inscription and the larger copper follaro with Greek inscription. Many of these latter pieces derive their types from Byzantine models but others hark back to even earlier Greek prototypes, as for instance the issue of William II (1166–89) with its obverse of lion's head and reverse with palm-tree and dates (Pl. 592). The Norman dynasty ended with the death of Tancred in 1194 and by 1197 the whole of the Norman kingdom had been conquered by the emperor, Henry VI. The coinage of his son and successor Frederick II (1198–1250), often called 'the first of the moderns', in its quality of design and execution anticipated the work of the Renaissance die-cutters, especially in the case of the gold augustale and its half-piece. The emperor's portrait on the obverse is laureate and cuirassed in the Roman manner while a striking eagle with outstretched wings occupies the reverse. The inscription continued from obverse to reverse reads *Cesar Aug Imp Rom/Fridericus* (Pl. 593).

Papal denari of the later tenth century continued to utilize either the monogram types or bust of St. Peter but on an issue of Benedict VI (972–974) appeared the first papal portrait, a roughly executed facing bust with inscription BE-NE/PA-P in the field while an issue of Benedict VII (974–984) has a temple on the obverse. Coinage lapsed again with the exception of rare pieces of Leo IX (1049–54) and Pascal II (1099–1118). When coinage was resumed at Rome in the late twelfth century it was issued not by the pope but by the senate, and grossi issued by the Senator Brancaleone d'Andalo in 1252 with type a lion to right are inscribed *Senatus PQR* on obverse and *Roma Caput Mundi* around a seated figure of Roma on the reverse.

LATER MIDDLE AGES (THIRTEENTH–FIFTEENTH CENTURIES)

Though Italy was still technically a single kingdom, an appanage of the emperors, in effect it comprised a considerable number of effectively independent constituents—city-states, headed often by powerful families such as the Visconti at Milan, papal possessions and the kingdoms of Naples and Sicily. Imperial coinage as such had, for practical purposes, come to an end and coinage requirements were met by the issues of the several authorities just mentioned.

Genoa continued to strike the coinage described in the preceding section until, with the election of Simon Boccanegra (1339–44) as the first doge, the obverse inscription was altered to read *Dux Ianuensium Primus*. This practice of using simply an ordinal number in place of the doge's name was followed throughout the Genoese coinage. In 1396 Genoa, rent by the quarrels of Guelphs and Ghibellines, gave itself up to the protection of Charles VI of France who continued to coin the typical Genoese denominations and types, only substituting his title *K. Rex Francorum D(ominus) Janue* on the obverse. Genoa resumed her independence in 1409 but in 1422 was conquered by Philip Maria Visconti, Duke of Milan, who added his name on the coinage obverse, together with the wyvern or serpent badge, placed immediately above the gateway type. For most of the fifteenth century Genoa was sometimes independent, sometimes under the domination of France or the dukes of Milan, but the coinage varied only in the obverse designation of the issuing authority.

Another of the important coinage series of north Italy was that of Milan which began an issue of gold florins in the second half of the thirteenth century with the standing figures of St. Protais and St. Gervais separated by the word *Mediolanum*, written vertically on obverse and a standing figure of St. Ambrose on the reverse. Silver coins with cross on obverse took their name of *ambrosini* from the seated figure of St. Ambrose on the reverse. Silver grossi of successive members of the Visconti family as lords of Milan have the seigneur's name between St. Gervais and St. Protais on obverse and seated St. Ambrose on reverse but another variety, such as that of Giovanni-Maria Visconti (1402–12), has the Visconti badge the wyvern between the letters I-M on obverse, a type used also on the smaller soldo.

Venice continued to issue the gold ducat already described but the silver matapan received a new type under the doge Andreas Contarini (1368–82), a star and initial of the minting official on the reverse. The grosso had various modifications of type and in 1423 a new piece, the grossone of 8 soldi, was created with standing or kneeling figure of the doge with banner and half-length figures of St. Mark. The half-grosso with a type of doge on obverse placed the lion of St. Mark on the reverse. The first Venetian copper, the piccolo, was issued by Christopher Moro (1462) with types, bust of the doge and seated lion.

The coinage of the senate at Rome continued and in 1350 the gold florin was added with types imitating those of the Venetian ducat. Here St. Peter hands a banner to a kneeling senator on obverse, while round the figure of Christ in oval frame is inscribed *Roma Caput Mundi SPQR*. The issue of papal coinage at Rome began again in the later thirteenth century. The silver bolognino issued by Urban V (1362–70) had his facing bust on obverse inscribed *Urb PP Qnts* and *In Roma Urbi* inscribed on the reverse. Papal grossoni in the fourteenth century showed the pope seated facing on obverse and two keys crossed on the reverse (Pl. 594). The types on the gold ducat, instituted by Eugenius IV (1431–47) were the arms of the pope, surmounted by crossed keys and tiara and a standing figure of St. Peter. Calistus III (1455–8) on one ducat issue represented St. Peter in a small boat on the reverse.

At Florence the coinage of the gold florin with its types of John the Baptist and lily continued. On the silver grosso, the quarter-grosso and the popolino St. John also occupied the obverse but the reverse is a cross with the lily in the angles. On the large silver cotale of 4 grossi St. John is shown enthroned while the lily provides the reverse. Though the Medici family were lords of Florence from 1434 there is no coinage in their name till the next century.

The kingdom of Naples came into the possession of Charles of Anjou (1266–85) who issued a gold real, inspired by the augustale of Frederick II. The obverse portrait, however, here was crowned, not laureate and the eagle of the augustale reverse was replaced by a shield of lis. Another of the outstanding gold coins of the Middle Ages was the carlin or salute which began issue in 1277. On the obverse, a shield with the joint arms of Anjou and Jerusalem, Charles has the title of King of Jerusalem and Sicily, while the reverse portrays an angel and the Virgin in the Annunciation scene and is accompanied by the inscription *Ave gracia plena dominus tecum* (Pl. 595). This type was also issued in silver. A new silver coin introduced by Charles II (1285–1309) in 1304 showed him seated facing on a lion throne; the coin was known as the gigliato from the lily (*giglia*) in each angle of the floreate cross on reverse. Alfonso I (1435–58) the first of the Aragonese kings of Sicily introduced a new gold ducaton with rider type on obverse but the silver gigliato was continued as the alfonsino with Alfonso's shield of arms replacing the cross with lis in angles on the reverse.

RENAISSANCE TO REVOLUTION
(MID FIFTEENTH–LATE EIGHTEENTH CENTURIES)

The number of individual Italian coinages continued to be great but, with the steady tendency throughout this period towards the growth of larger territorial units, the less important series dwindle and disappear. Features of the coinage are the creation of new, heavy silver denominations, the development of portraiture, the practice of reserving the obverse almost exclusively for the portrait of the ruler and the creation of complete systems of coinage with denominations in gold, silver, base silver alloys and, finally, copper. In this section again only a few of the more outstanding series can be reviewed briefly.

The Duchy of Savoy which provided the dynasty under which the unity of Italy was finally achieved begins to assume importance in the modern period. The teston, a heavy silver piece of 8 grossi, was introduced by Charles I (1482–90) with his profile bust holding sword on obverse and on reverse shield of arms flanked by the word *fe-rt*. Under Charles II (1504–53) the large silver tallero, equivalent to 42 grossi, made its appearance with types, a standing figure of St. Maurice and a shield on cross. Emmanuel Philibert (1553–80) introduced a new monetary system based on the unit of the soldo, the equivalent of the former grosso. As well as the soldo and its subdivisions there were higher denominations up to the lira, equal to 8 soldi with bare-headed bust of the duke on obverse and the inscription *Instar Omnium* within a wreath on the reverse. Gold coinage included a scudo and a filiberto, the latter with shield on obverse and an unusual reverse, an elephant amidst a flock of sheep with the inscription *Infestus infestis*. The silver lira, equivalent to 20 soldi was made the monetary unit by Victor Amadeus I (1630–7) and on coins of this denomination the obverse bust was accompanied by three banners, their shafts set in a crown. The coinage of Charles Emmanuel II (1638–75) and Victor Amadeus II (1675–1730) both began with issues of the dukes with their mothers as regents; and obverses carry their jugate busts. It was in the reign of Victor Amadeus II that, in the settlement of the War of the Spanish Succession, Savoy was granted the kingdom of Sicily which was later exchanged for Sardinia and the title of king, henceforth included in the titulature of his successors. In the coinage instituted by Charles Emmanuel III (1730–73) the basic gold piece was the doppia with multiples up to five, and subdivisions down to a quarter (Pl. 596); in silver the major piece was the scudo of 6 lire, with divisionary pieces down to an eighth. The types were now regularly the conventional bust and arms on all denominations.

Between 1488 and 1527 the control of Genoa was in almost constant contention between the Sforza dukes of Milan and France and the Genoese coinage, though retaining usually its traditional types and denominations, reflects the changing fortunes of this struggle in the inscriptions and the added symbols. The republic re-established with a system of biennial doges continued to produce its traditional coinage until the advent of the Revolution in 1797, though some changes were imported with the system. The obverse now bore the inscription *Dux et guber reipub Genuen* and in the course of the seventeenth century the traditional reverse reference to Conrad disappeared. From about 1638 on the gold doppia, its multiples and subdivisions, the centuries-old gateway type was replaced by that of the Madonna, as also on the silver scudi. From about 1758 multiple lire in gold were struck with Madonna obverse and shield with griffin supporters on the reverse. In common with Venice, Genoa in the eighteenth century produced a number of unusually large multiples in both gold and silver.

Milan under the Sforza dukes in the early modern period played a leading rôle in Italian affairs and has the credit for leading the way in the matter of realistic portraiture in the Reniassance style on coinage. The earliest examples are the portraits of Francesco Sforza (1450–66) but the most famous and the most influential Milanese coinage innovation was the heavy silver teston of Galeazzo Maria Sforza (1468–76) with its striking obverse portrait and its reverse of crested helmet above a shield with the wyvern device of the Sforza family (Pl. 597). Similar types were placed on the gold ducat and the grosso of 8 soldi, though the divisionary silver maintained heraldic devices on both sides. On issues of John Galeazzo Maria under the regency of his uncle Louis Maria, obverse and reverse carry their respective portrait busts. In the struggle between the Empire and France Milan was held first by Louis XII and later by Francis I of France who each coined as Duke of Milan. Francis II Sforza recovered Milan in 1522 but on his death in 1535 it became an imperial fief and, from the time of Philip II a Spanish possession until, in the War of the Spanish Succession it was conquered by Austria by whom it was held till the end of the eighteenth century. Coinage was struck at Milan for the Spanish kings and the Austrian archdukes, usually with portrait-and-arms types.

A number of duchies were created in the beginning of the modern period either by papal or imperial patronage, such as Ferrara, Mantua, Modena and Parma which issued their own coinage, some of them continuing up to the end of the eighteenth century and even later.

Venice continued the issue of its gold zecchino or ducat and its silver grosso but in 1471 the doge Nicholas Tron struck a new heavy silver piece representing in real value the money of account, the lira of 20 soldi. Most unusually this new denomination bore the portrait of the doge himself. Other innovations were the introduction of the gold scudo by Andreas Gritti in 1535 with floreate cross on obverse and shield with lion of St. Mark on the reverse and under Nicholas da Ponto (1578–85) the giustina of 8 lire in silver with lion of St. Mark and kneeling doge on obverse and standing figure of St. Justina on the reverse. A feature of later eighteenth-century coinage was the issue of extremely large multiples of the zecchino, including values up to 100 by Aloysius Mocenigo (1763–78) and Louis Manin (1789–97), the last of the doges of Venice.

Florence maintained its independence and its traditional coinage until, after its siege and conquest by the emperor Charles V, Alexander de Medici was given the title of duke in 1532. For the production of his coinage Alexander had the services of the famous artist Benvenuto Cellini who designed, amongst other denominations, a silver teston with the portrait of Alexander on obverse and standing figures of St. Cosmo and St. Damian (Pl. 598). Cosmo de Medici was created Duke of Tuscany by Pope Pius V in 1569, the duchy including besides Florence such cities as Pisa and Sienna. The tradition of excellence in coinage was maintained under Cosmo, particularly on the silver piastra with its portrait bust and its reverse of St. John the Baptist. The Florentine type of St. John and the lily on the Medici arms furnished the usual coin types, though later, particularly with the extinction of the Medici family in 1737 and the passage of Tuscany to the emperor Francis II, the more conventional bust and arms types are found, particularly on the silver coinage.

Papal coinage was issued at various times at a number of mints in the Papal states such as Bologna, Ferrara, Modena and Parma as well as at Rome itself, though it is only with this latter mint which this section can concern itself. To the denominations in existence in the mid-fifteenth century, the gold ducat or zecchino and the silver grosso and giulio which, originally the grosso largo, received its more common name from Julius II (1503–13). Sixtus IV (1471–84) added a double giulio with profile bust on obverse and Julius II introduced the teston with inscriptional obverse and the figures of SS. Peter and Paul on the reverse (Pl. 599). An even larger silver piece, the piastra, was first struck with frequency by Sixtus V (1585–90) with obverse portrait and on the reverse a scene showing St. Francis receiving the stigmata. The piastra was succeeded as the large silver piece by the silver scudo in the later sixteenth century and continued to be issued till the end of the period under consideration, most frequently with types of bust and arms but also with the papal arms as obverse and with either an inscription, a floreate cross, the Madonna or one of the saints as reverse. On gold the types of St. Peter in a boat and papal arms continued to be favourite types in the later fifteenth and sixteenth centuries and the doppia or double zecchino as exemplified by the issue of Leo X (1513–21) with portrait bust and the Three Wise Men on horse-back was struck with some frequency. From the mid sixteenth century the gold unit was the scudo, often as its name implies with shield reverse, though a considerable variety of other types were also employed. The most common obverse was the portrait of the pope but other types such as the bust of Christ, of St. Peter or St. Paul or a personification of the Church are also found. Copper quattrini which began to be more frequent in the early seventeenth century have the papal arms on obverse and figures of St. Peter or St. Paul on the reverse, but in the half-baiocco later in the century a frequent reverse type is the holy gateway. In the eighteenth century the reverse of the baiocco and its subdivisions is simply the value within a wreath (Pl. 600).

The kingdom of the Two Sicilies was bequeathed by Alfonso I on his death in 1458 in its two parts; Naples passed to his son Ferdinand I (1458–94) and Sicily to his brother John of Aragon. The coinage of Ferdinand is notable for the realistic obverse portrait used both on the gold ducat and on the new heavy silver denomination, the tarin or double-carlin. On the reverse of the carlin itself appeared a new reverse type, St. Michael slaying the dragon with inscription *Iusta tuenda*, probably a reference to victories over the Turks. Small copper coins with crowned bust of Ferdinand are known as cavalli from the reverse of a free horse around which is the inscription *Equitas regni*. Naples, occupied briefly by the French kings Charles VIII in 1495 and Louis XII (1501–3), struck coinage incorporating the French arms. Ferdinand the Catholic who succeeded to Sicily in 1503 expelled the French from Naples and reconstituted the kingdom of the Two Sicilies which remained part of the Spanish dominions until the War of the Spanish Succession in 1700. Notable issues are those of the emperor Charles V. The gold multiples carry his obverse portrait cuirassed and with a crown reminiscent of the radiate crown of the Roman emperors, while the ducat itself shows a laureate bearded head. Charles also began the issue of the silver scudo and its parts with an obverse shield carrying his many quarterings and an ornate cross with crowns at its terminals on the reverse. By the Treaty of Utrecht in 1707 Naples was ceded to Charles of Austria and Sicily was given to Victor Amadeus of Savoy who held it until 1720 when he received Sardinia in exchange from Austria. Amongst unusual issues of Charles of Austria in the Two Sicilies (1720–34) are copper coins of one and two tornesi with eagle obverse and reverses inscribed *Ut facilius* and *Ut commodius*. Victor Amadeus also issued a tornese piece in Sicily with eagle obverse and *Publica commoditas* (Pl. 601) on the reverse. The kingdom was seized again by Spain in 1734 by the Infanta Charles, but on his accession to the Spanish throne in 1759 he ceded the Two Sicilies to his son Ferdinand IV, whose long reign until 1825 carries beyond the period now being considered. In the first portion of his reign until revolutionary France expelled him and set up the Parthenopean republic in 1799 Ferdinand's gold ducats and multiples and silver piastres and portions have bust-and-arms types. Copper coins of various values of tornesi, cavalli or grani have bust or arms obverse and a symbol such as a bunch of grapes and abbreviated value, e.g. C 4 (four cavalli) on the reverse.

MODERN ITALY (1796—1960)

The final period of Italian coinage falls into three phases: first, the series of republics and, later, kingdoms set up during the revolutionary and Napoleonic wars; second, the much reduced number of states after the settlement of Europe in 1815 and, finally, the coinage of united Italy.

The invading French armies created a string of republics, sometimes replacing, sometimes grouping together the existing territorial units. Piedmont became a republic in 1798, Genoa was transformed into the Ligurian republic in 1796, Cispadane and Transpadane republics absorbed the areas south and north of the Po in 1796 and republics also emerged at Rome in 1798 and Naples in 1799. All of these issued coinages of silver scudi or lire and copper soldi with varying representations of Liberty and territorial personifications. Piedmont was annexed to France in 1802, as was the Ligurian republic in 1805, while the Cispadane and Transpadane republics were united in 1797 into the Cisalpine republic which was transformed in turn into the Italian republic with Napoleon as president. In 1805 Napoleon created a kingdom of Italy for which he struck a coinage of silver lire with his portrait on obverse and crowned arms on the reverse and soldi with the iron crown of Lombardy as the reverse type (Pl. 602). On the kingdom of the Two Sicilies, which Ferdinand IV had regained between 1799 and 1805, Napoleon imposed as king, first his brother Joseph (1806–8), then Joachim Murat (1808–15) whose silver lire have portrait and value types. The Grand-Duchy of Tuscany was advanced to the status of the kingdom of Etruria in 1801 and in 1805 Lucca and Piombino were made into principalities for Napoleon's brother-in-law, Felix Bacciochi. The jugate busts of Felix and his wife Elisa Bonaparte appear on issues of silver 5 and 1 franc pieces.

In the settlement of Europe in 1815 the north of Italy comprising Lombardy and Venice was given to Austria. Silver lire carry the portrait of the Austrian emperor and the arms of Lombardy and Venice, while copper centesimi have the iron crown of Lombardy on obverse and the value on the reverse. Lombardy was ceded to Victor Emmanuel II of Sardinia in 1859, Venice in 1866. Coinage for the Grand-Duchy of Tuscany was resumed in 1824 but in 1859 Tuscany also passed to Victor Emmanuel. The papal series, interrupted by the Roman republic of 1798–9, began again in 1800 for Pius VII (1799–1823). The papal portrait and arms form the types on the silver scudi and higher baiocchi values, arms and values the types on the lower copper baiocchi pieces. In the Two Sicilies Ferdinand returned again to the throne with the title now of Ferdinand I and the coinage of piastre and carlini in silver and tornesi in copper was resumed, to continue for his successors until the Garibaldi insurrection joined the Two Sicilies to Italy in 1860.

Victor Emmanuel I of Sardinia recovered his former provinces in Italy in 1814 with the addition of Genoa. On lire in gold and silver the types are royal portrait and arms and on copper centesimi arms and value. On issues of Charles Felix (1821–31) and Charles Albert (1831–49) the arms on the reverse are the plain cross of Savoy. The process of unification under the Sardinian crown culminated with the declaration of Victor Emmanuel II as King of Italy in 1861. The reverse type continued to be the arms of Savoy, accompanied now by the inscription *Regno d'Italia,* though some issues carried simply the value in a wreath. The coinage issues of Victor Emmanuel III (1900–44) after the first world war were restricted to the lower values which have a variety of reverses, some derived from ancient coins of Italy, such as the corn-ear on the 5 centesimi piece which copies the type of the Greek city of Metapontum (Pl. 603). The Fascist era showed a fondness for the type of the Roman eagle or the fasces and after the conquest of Abyssinia in 1936 Victor Emmanuel has the title *Re e imperatore*. The Italian republic formed in 1946 issued various lire denominations with head of the republic and reverses such as bunch of grapes or corn-ear. A new issue in 1951 has symbolic types such as a plough or a bee on the obverse though the head of Italia has returned to the 50 and 100 lire coins issued since 1956.

The papal coinage lapsed from 1871 until the independent state of the Vatican City was set up in 1929 and a coinage of lire and centesimi was issued with either the portrait of the pope or the papal arms on obverse and various religious types on the reverse. Because of inflation only lire values have been struck since the war.

The coinage of Pope John XXIII, issued in 1959, included special pieces of 500 lire in silver and 100 lire in gold with types, the portrait of the pope and arms and value. Lower lire denominations have Pope John's portrait on the obverse and a variety of personifications such as Faith, Hope, Charity and Justice on the reverse.

MALTA

The Knights of St. John, expelled from Rhodes by the Turks in 1523, were granted the possession of Malta by the emperor Charles V in 1530 but, though the emperor later granted the right of coinage, the earliest issues seem to be those of the grand master, Peter del Ponte (1534–5). The earliest coinage was in the form of gold zecchini, adapting the types of the Venetian gold zecchino to show St. John presenting a banner to the kneeling grand master on the obverse and a figure of Christ in an oval frame on the reverse. From the time of John de Homedes (1536–53), in addition to the gold zecchino, there was a coinage in silver in which the basic denomination was the taro of which there were multiples up to 6 tari and also divisionary pieces. The denominations in copper were the grano, its half of 3 piccioli and the picciolo.

The gold zecchino maintained the types described above until the late seventeenth century but the silver carried a variety of designs—the Paschal Lamb, the Maltese cross or the head of John the Baptist on a charger. From the time of Raymond Perellos (1697–1720) multiple zecchini with portrait-and-arms types were issued alongside the traditional zecchino. In the financial difficulties which followed the repulse of the Turkish attack in 1565 tari denominations were struck in copper with a reverse type of clasped hands and inscription *Non aes sed fides*. From the time of Manoel de Vilhena (1727–36) larger silver pieces, a scudo of 12 tari and its double were added to the system, usually with bust-and-arms types (Pl. 604). Copper pieces of various denominations of grani were struck in the eighteenth century with such types as shield of arms and clasped hands or Maltese cross and five crescents on the 5 grani piece. The last issues of the Knights of St. John were those of the grand master, Ferdinand de Hompesch (1797–9). Malta, seized by Britain in the Napoleonic wars, has since then had a British colonial coinage (see p. 268).

SPAIN

The turbulent and complicated course of events in the Iberian peninsula, particularly in the Middle Ages, makes it necessary to present a very brief sketch of the historical background against which the outline of its coinage can be drawn. Roman Spain in common with the rest of the Western empire was occupied in the beginning of the fifth century by various barbarian tribes, principally the Vandals, the Suevi and the Visigoths. The first of these crossed to Africa by the end of the century and need not concern us here but the other two, after an initial period as subject allies of Rome, established independent kingdoms and issued their own coinage. Before the end of the fifth century the Suevi had become subject to the Visigoths and a Visigothic kingdom extended over the whole peninsula. In 711 came the Arab invasion and the occupation of Spain with the exception of the mountainous districts in the north. Christian kingdoms emerged in Leon, Castille, Navarre and Aragon, and Spain was gradually reconquered from the Moors, though the final conquest of Granada took place only in 1492. A single kingdom emerged under Isabella and Ferdinand in 1479 with the exception of Portugal, which had become independent in 1112 and, following the discovery of the New World by Columbus in 1492, a Spanish empire was established, providing a rich supply of precious metals for coinage. The final period begins with the Napoleonic wars in the peninsula in the early nineteenth century.

It is proposed, therefore, to deal with the coinage in the following major divisions: (1) coinage of the Suevi and Visigoths up to 711; (2) coinage of the mediaeval kingdoms up to the union in 1479 (the issues of the caliphates in Spain are included in the section on Islamic coinage); (3) the main Castilian series up to the Peninsular wars; (4) coinage of the nineteenth and twentieth centuries. A final section outlines the more local series continued after the union. The issues for the Spanish

possessions in Europe and the New World are discussed in their appropriate
geographic context.

SUEVI AND VISIGOTHS (FIFTH CENTURY–711)

Coinage attributed to the Suevi consists almost entirely of a series of imitations
of Roman gold, principally the tremissis of the Western emperors with its distinctive types, a cross within a wreath. One unusually articulate imitation of this
type has the inscription *Latina Emeri Munita* on the obverse, showing its place
of minting to be Merida. A rare silver coin with portrait and titles of the emperor
Honorius on obverse is inscribed *Iussu Richiari Regis*, presumably the Suevic king
Richiar, who ruled from 448 to 456. The letters B R on the reverse probably
indicate a mint at Bracara. The authenticity of this coin has been questioned.

The first Visigothic coinage, like that of the Suevi, is an imitation of late Roman
gold, again principally the tremissis, but this time more usually the tremisses of
the Eastern empire with its figure of Victory. The series of imitation tremissis
of the Visigoths in Spain are most distinctive in style. The bust of the profile
portrait is angular, is marked with a cross and cuts through the obverse inscription,
while the figure of Victory on the reverse has a very prominent broad wing. The
inscriptions on this class of imitation in the later fourth and in the fifth century are
blundered forms of the imperial names and legends but beginning with Leovigild
(572–586) Visigothic tremisses carry the king's name. Leovigild's name on the
Victory type is repeated on both obverse and reverse but on other varieties the
reverse carries the name of the mint. Of the whole chain of mints scattered over
the country the most important was the Visigothic capital, Toledo. The most
common type is that with a facing bust on both obverse and reverse (Pl. 605)
while other varieties have on the reverse a cross, a cross on steps or a monogram
of the mint name.

LEON, CASTILLE, ARAGON AND NAVARRE (711–1479)

The small kingdom of the Asturias which succeeded in holding its own from 718
following the Moorish occupation of most of the country had no native coinage.
The old Visigothic coinage continued to circulate, but in the course of the ninth
and tenth centuries, as the reconquest got under way, silver coinage came into
more frequent use. A certain amount may have been in the form of Carolingian
deniers but Arab dirhems supplied the greater quantity. It was, however, not until

the later eleventh century that the resurgent Christian states began the issue of their own billon dineros and obols.

Castille and Leon

The districts of Castille and Leon were erected into kingdoms in 1033 by Sancho III of Navarre for his sons and after a history of alternating separation and union they were finally reunited under Alfonso VI in 1073. Following the increase of the territory of the united kingdom by the capture of Toledo, the old Visigothic capital, in 1085, a coinage of billon dineros and obols was begun by Alfonso VI. The types of the dinero struck at Leon were a cross on obverse with the king's title *Anfus rex* and on the reverse the Christogram and inscription *Toletuo* (Pl. 606). The pieces struck at Toledo had on the reverse two annulets and two stars. Alfonso VI was succeeded by his daughter Urraca (1109–26) some of whose deniers struck at Toledo have her facing portrait, others issued at St. Antonin have a cross type on obverse and two alphas and two omegas in cross pattern on the reverse. Alfonso VII (1126–57) who achieved a temporary ascendancy over Navarre and Aragon took the title of emperor. Dineros struck for him at Leon have a punning type of a lion on the obverse with the mint name below and on the reverse a cross with the new title *Imperator* as a circular inscription. A new mint created at Burgos marked its products with a small letter B placed at the beginning of the inscriptions.

Between 1157 and 1230 Castille and Leon were again separated. One of the most remarkable pieces in this period is a gold morabitin struck by Alfonso VIII (1158–1214), with, on each side, a linear and a circular inscription in Arabic. On the obverse was a cross and a statement of the Christian faith, while the reverse records that it was struck by Alfonso, son of Sancho, at Toledo. It was on dineros of Alfonso VIII also that the castle with three towers which was to become the constant badge of Castille made its first appearance (Pl. 607). Gold was also introduced into the coinage of Leon at about the same time by Ferdinand II (1157–88). This coin showed the crowned portrait of the king in profile with a sceptre in front and a sword behind; on the reverse was the lion with sword above and mint name below and in a circular inscription an abbreviated form of *in nomine patris et filii et spiritus sancti*. These types were also adopted for the dinero. Alfonso IX (1188–1230) issued gold of a similar type but dineros of varying types some with the lion badge but one with the mint name *Leonis* between two lines on a decorated background.

The permanent reunion of Castille and Leon was effected in 1230 by Ferdinand

III whose dineros had a uniform type. On one side was the castle of Castille, on the other the lion of Leon with the royal name *F rex Castille—et Legionis* split between the two (Pl. 608). The main type for his successor, Alfonso X (1252–84), showed the quartered arms of Castille and Leon on one side and a linear inscription *Alfonsus rex Castille et Legionis* on the other. What was probably the first gold dobla with the castle and lion as the two types was also issued in this reign. The billon coronados of Sancho IV (1284–95) with his crowned bust to left and the castle of Castille on the reverse form one of the most plentiful Spanish issues (Pl. 609). The number of mints had now risen to eight including the future capital of Spain, Madrid. The dineros and obols of Ferdinand IV (1295–1312) have as their most usual types the castle and lion set in a tressure of eight arches.

Occasional coinage in gold and in good silver has already been noted but under Alfonso XI (1312–50) issues in these metals became regular form. The gold dobla marked with the numeral XX indicating, most probably, its value as 20 maravedis has the badge of Castille on one side and of Leon on the other with the king's name repeated on each side, the title *Rex Castelle* on the castle side and *Rex Legionis* on the lion side. Identical types were used for the new gros or real in silver. A similar coinage was issued by Peter I the Cruel (1350–68) and in addition a 10 dobla piece with a magnificent, crowned profile portrait and inscription *Dominus michi adiutor et ego dispiciam inimicos meos* and the quartered arms of Castille and Leon together with the royal name and title on the reverse. A new obverse was produced for his silver real, his initial P crowned within a double circle of inscription with the same quotation from scripture as on the multiple dobla (Pl. 610). This was an age of rich magnificence in gold coinage though many of the beautiful multiple doblas must have been intended as presentation pieces and not as ordinary currency. Another example of this gold coinage was the dobla of Henry II (1368–79) which had a new obverse type, the king, armoured and flourishing a sword, on horse-back. Even more striking is the 20 dobla piece of John II (1406–54). On this the knightly figure of the king in armour on horse-back carries a shield adorned with the band and wears a helmet surmounted by the castle of Castille. The royal title, on both sides of the coin, is preceded by the appellation *Dom(i)nus*. A new gold piece, the dobla de la banda, was also introduced in John's reign. The reverse was the usual quartered arms but on the obverse was the shield adorned with a band (Pl. 611). The peak of these gold issues was reached under Henry IV (1454–75) who in addition to the dobla de la banda and the castle-and-lion dobla struck a whole new series known as gold enriques. The reverse was still the quartered arms but on the obverse was the king, crowned and holding sword, seated on his throne with a crowned lion at his feet. The obverse inscription included, for the first time, the king's ordinal number, *Enricus quartus dei gratia rex* and the reverse inscription his very full title *Enricus rex Castille e Legionis et Toleti*. The principal type for the silver real continued to be that introduced by Peter I, in this case the first syllable of the king's name, HEN, crowned. Alfonso of Avila (1465-8), a pretender to the throne, struck gold doblas with the mounted figure obverse and reals with his crowned initial. The coinage of the new kingdom arising from the union in 1474 of Castille under Isabella with Aragon under Ferdinand V begins a new stage in the numismatic history of Spain to be considered in the next section.

Aragon

The kingdom of Aragon was created by Sancho III of Navarre for his son Ramirez in 1035 but only in the reign of Sancho–Ramirez I (1063–94) did its coinage of dineros and obols begin. The types created for this coinage were to remain basic for many reigns and showed the bare head of the king in profile with his name and title, *Sancius rex*, in a circular inscription with on the reverse a tall cross between two floral decorations and the word *Ara-gon* divided on either side of the cross (Pl. 612). A similar coinage was issued by Peter I (1094–1104) and by Alfonso I (1104–34) except that for the latter his portrait was in the form of a bust which divided the hitherto completely circular inscription. The obverse portrait of Peter II (1196–1213) who had been crowned in Rome by Innocent III showed the king wearing crown, while on the reverse the word *Ara-gon* was placed vertically, not horizontally. A crowned portrait was also used by James I the Conqueror (1213–76) who added to his kingdom the territories of Barcelona, Ampurias and Gerona. The obverse inscription carried the kingdom's name while the king's title appeared on the reverse which had a patriarchal cross as type.

Billon coronados with types like those of James I continued to be struck for Peter IV (1335–87) under whom the gold florin was introduced. The types of this denomination reproduced exactly those of the Florentine florin, the figure of St. John the Baptist and the lily of Florence with the addition of the inscription *Arago Rex P*. An identical gold coinage was produced for the successive kings of Aragon, the sole distinguishing feature being the appropriate initial of the king in the inscription. John II (1458–79) created for both his gold and silver, new types, which were to be reproduced on much subsequent Spanish coinage. These were the crowned bust of the king with sceptre and a crowned shield with the arms of Aragon (Pl. 613). A feature of this coinage is the titulature which added to *Aragonum* the initials of the king's other four kingdoms, Navarre, Sicily, Valencia and Majorca.

The issues of Navarre began earlier than those of the other kingdoms which were created for his sons from his possessions by Sancho III (1000-35), who struck the first Navarrese dineros. The types which were copied by the early coins of Aragon showed the king's bare head and on the reverse a tall cross set between two floral ornaments and dividing the word *Navara*. The issues of Garcia III (1035-54) and Sancho IV (1054-76) used identical types with only the requisite change of royal name, though under the latter king the territorial designation was moved from the field of the reverse to form a semi-circular inscription. A new reverse was introduced by Garcia Ramirez IV (1134-50), a simple tall cross with stars in the top two angles, while the reverse for Sancho VI (1150-94) and Sancho VII (1194-1234) showed a crescent surmounted by a small sun. With the marriage of Johanna of Navarre to Philip the Fair of France, Navarre passed for a time to the French crown.

FERDINAND AND ISABELLA—CHARLES IV (1479-1808)

The marriage of Ferdinand II of Aragon and Isabella of Castille in 1479 finally created a single united kingdom of Spain which covered the whole of the Iberian peninsula with the exception of Portugal, which maintained its independence. The coinage issued by the rulers of this united kingdom continues to be known as the Castillian series and forms the national and certainly the most important coinage of Spain. Coinage of the several component kingdoms did, however, continue, with the status rather of a provincial series and will be reviewed in the ultimate division of the present section.

The issues of Ferdinand and Isabella can be said to inaugurate the modern Spanish series, especially after the ordonnance of 1497 which introduced a new monetary system. The obverse type of the gold of which there were a number of multiples of 2, 4, 10 and even 20 ducats showed the crowned busts of Ferdinand and Isabella *vis-à-vis*, a novel design which was to be widely copied in other coinages, notably on that of Mary Tudor and Philip II and of Mary, Queen of Scots, and Francis I. The heraldic motif persisted on the reverse: the shield now bore the quartered arms of Castille and Leon and of Aragon and Sicily, with, below, the arms of Granada, the whole supported on an eagle (Pl. 614). The reverse inscription reads *Sub umbra alarum tuarum protege me*. The types of the silver real were more simple, a crowned F and crowned Y on obverse and reverse respectively. There were also the usual types for the billon blanca and its portions. A new coinage in all metals was instituted in 1497. The new gold unit of which again there were several multiples was known as an excellente and reproduced the types of the earlier ducat but was struck on a slightly different standard. On the half-piece which had identical types except for the absence of the eagle supporter on the reverse the obverse inscription reads *quos deus coniunxit homo non separat* and the names and titles are relegated to the reverse. The designs for the silver real reproduced the shield of arms on the obverse but the new reverse type was composed of Ferdinand's symbol, the yoke, and that of Isabella, a bundle of arrows. Multiples of 2, 4 and 8 reals were also issued, the latter the famous piece of eight which played such a large part in international commerce in this and subsequent centuries. The half- and quarter-real were of simpler design, the yoke on one side, the bundle of arrows on the other. On the billon blanca the types were the royal initials crowned, one on each side. Quite new was a coinage of pieces of 4 and 2 maravedis with obverse the castle of Castille and reverse the lion of Leon. The number of mints was now reduced to seven. Those of Burgos, Cuenca, Granada, Seville and Toledo marked their products with their initial letters; Segovia and Corunna with a symbol of an aqueduct or a shell respectively.

No alteration was made in this coinage after the death of Isabella in 1504 while Ferdinand continued to rule as regent for his daughter Joanna, nor was a new coinage instituted for the short reign of Joanna and her husband Philip, Archduke of Austria, in 1506. This state of affairs continued throughout the minority of Charles I (later the emperor Charles V) and the issues in the name of Ferdinand and Isabella continued even after Charles reached his majority and returned to Spain from the Netherlands in 1517. Only in 1537 was a new coinage issue begun. The types selected for the gold escudo of a slightly reduced fineness set a pattern which was to persist till the middle of the eighteenth century. The obverse inscribed *Ioana et Carolus* was still heraldic, the now extremely complicated arms of Spain composed of the blazons of Leon, Castille, Sicily, Granada, Jerusalem and Navarre. On the reverse was the cross of Jerusalem and the inscription *Hispaniarum reges Siciliae* (Pl. 615). Types which were to become even more familiar on the Spanish issues in the New World were those now settled on the silver real, again the crowned arms of Spain with the names of Joanna and Charles on the obverse and on the reverse the crowned Pillars of Hercules, representing the Straits of Gibraltar, with the motto *plus ultra* in the field, a reference to the discovery of the New World and a circular inscription *Hispaniarum et Indiarum*. As well as the unit, pieces of 2 and 4 reals were also struck. On the half-real the reverse was also the Pillars of Hercules and the obverse simply the initials K I crowned.

Because of the persistent flight of gold from the country the value of the escudo was raised in the reign of Philip II (1556–98) but the design, apart from the change of name, remained the same as on the escudo of Charles I. Pieces of 2 and 4 escudos, commonly known in international exchange as pistoles, were also produced. The real and its multiples up to pieces of eight acquired as reverse type the quartered arms of Leon and Castille (Pl. 616). Even larger multiples of both the gold escudo and the silver real were issued by Philip III (1598–1621). The major gold coin was the onza or 8 escudos and a *cincuentine or* 50 real piece formed the pinnacle of the silver issues. Both gold and silver multiples bore on the obverse the indication of their value in Roman numerals. The appearance of an even larger gold coin the 100 escudo piece (12½ onza) struck for Philip IV (1621–65) is a very inaccurate index of the strength of the Spanish monetary system and of the commercial prosperity of the country. The familiarity evinced by most European literature with Spanish coinage indicates its wide circulation and indeed the great treasure of gold and silver supplied by the New World, once it had been coined in Spain, rapidly found its way out of the country. So long as Spain possessed a practical monopoly of the precious metals her economy bore a specious appearance of prosperity but, once the monopoly was broken, Spain rapidly receded from her position of eminence.

A steady stream of ordonnances aimed at preventing the export of gold and silver coinage as bullion were of little avail and each reign brought further expedients in the revaluing of the denominations. Under Charles II (1665–1700), for instance, a new silver real with multiples of 2, 4 and 8 was issued with its weight reduced by a quarter. The types for these were the crowned arms of Spain with a new reverse, the monogram of the Virgin with a cross above, the type giving rise to the descriptive name, the Maria (Pl. 617). The death of Charles II in 1700 ushered in the War of the Spanish Succession, disputed between Philip of Anjou and the Archduke Charles of Austria. By the Peace of Utrecht in 1713 metropolitan Spain and its overseas colonies were awarded to Philip but the Spanish possessions in the Netherlands, Milan, Sardinia and Naples passed to Austria, and Sicily to Savoy. The initial issues for Philip V (1700–46) maintained the now traditional types for gold and silver except that on the gold the arms of Spain were now impaled with the arms of France. An abortive attempt had been made in 1709 to issue gold with the royal portrait on obverse and finally in 1729 an issue of this nature was produced. The bewigged and armoured bust of Philip V on the obverse is surrounded by a circular inscription, no longer enclosed by lines. The reverse inscription also had no line border and the shield of arms was of different shape with slightly indented sides (Pl. 618). Philip V abdicated in favour of his son Louis I in 1724, but on his death in the same year Philip resumed the crown. The mints for gold and silver were reduced to two only in this reign, namely Madrid and Seville. The rare issues for Louis showed no change in types.

Almost the sole modification in the issues of Ferdinand VI (1746–59) was the use of a head only portrait on the smaller gold pieces. In 1772 a recoinage was carried through: the fineness of both gold and silver was slightly lowered but the most immediately obvious outward change was the use of the royal portrait in all metals and the substitution of modern numerals for the Roman numerals which indicated the denomination of multiple escudos and reals. The coinage of the final reign before the French invasion in 1808, that of Charles IV (1788–1808), continued the now almost traditional types.

JOSEPH BONAPARTE—GENERAL FRANCO (1808–1960)

When Spain was absorbed into the French empire in 1808 Napoleon created his brother, already King of Naples, the new King of Spain. The monetary unit of account on which the coinage system was based was the billon real. Gold pieces of 320 and 80 reals, equivalent to 8 and 2 escudos respectively, were issued with the head of Joseph Bonaparte and the arms of Spain, now with the French imperial eagle at its centre, on the reverse. The same types were used on the silver coinage which ranged from 8 reals (20 billon reals) to 1 real also known as the peseta as well as half- and quarter-reals. Copper coins of 8, 4, 2 and 1 maravedi had the mark of value beside the obverse head and the reverse consisted of a wreath enclosing a floral cross with alternate lion and castle in the angles and eagle at centre. A certain amount of emergency coinage was struck during the Peninsular wars as well as a well-defined series for Ferdinand VII, the king in exile. Gold and silver followed the regular pattern of previous regal issues but the copper maravedis copied the types instituted by Joseph Bonaparte.

The succession of Isabel II (1833–68) daughter of Ferdinand was disputed by his brother who proclaimed himself Charles V and in the civil war, which did not end till 1840, struck a coinage of silver pesetas and copper maravedis at the mint of Segovia. The initial issues of Isabel retained the types and denominations already in use but in 1848 a new decimal coinage created new denominations, though only incidental modifications were effected in the types. The unit was the real and denominations in gold included the doblon or 100 real piece and, later, pieces of 40 and 20 reals; in silver the denominations were the douro and its half of 20 and 10 reals respectively, the peseta and its half of 4 and 2 reals each. All of these had the conventional types, the royal bust and the arms of Spain, the latter after 1850 being placed between crowned pillars with the motto *plus ultra* on the douro and its half. Copper coins for various portions of the real had a portrait obverse and lion-and-castle reverse (Pl. 619). As a third issue of coinage in 1864 had as its unit the silver escudo, the values on the gold denominations were expressed as 10, 4 or 2 escudos and on the silver as 2 and 1 escudo with smaller pieces of 40, 20 and 10 centimos. Copper coinage of various values in centimos now also had the royal portrait as obverse and shield of arms as reverse.

Revolution brought a provisional government between 1868 and 1870. The obverse of its coinage was occupied by a personification of Hispania, a standing figure on the gold, reclining on the silver and seated on the copper. The reverse of the gold and silver was the traditional arms of Spain but on the copper the arms are supported by a lion (Pl. 620). The brief reign of Amadeus I (1870-3), a prince of the Italian royal house, produced gold pieces of 100 and 25 pesetas and silver 5 peseta pieces. Civil war broke out again and the Carlists proclaimed the son of the earlier pretender Charles V as Charles VII for whom silver 5 pesetas and copper centimes were issued. For Alfonso XII, the son of Isabella II, restored to the throne in 1875 coins of traditional type were expressed in pesetas and centimos for the lower values. The main interest of the series for Alfonso XIII (1886-1931), the posthumous son of Alfonso XII, lies in the range of portraits from babyhood onwards (Pl. 621). The traditional designs held their ground till the 1920's when 25 centimo pieces in nickel-bronze were issued with types of a galleon or crown, hammer and olive as obverses and value reverses. The republic (1931-7) used various personifications of Hispania on the now small range of coins of low denominations. The only coins of both sides in the civil war of 1936-9 were small centimo denominations. The current coins of the Franco régime of 10 and 5 centimos retain the historical reverse of the Spanish arms and the mounted figure on the obverse is a modern adaptation of a widespread type of the ancient Celt–Iberian coinage (Pl. 622).

COMPONENT KINGDOMS AFTER 1479

Alongside the main Castilian series which formed the national coinage of Spain subsidiary coinages with a more restricted local issue continued to be struck in the originally independent kingdoms and principalities.

Aragon. Coinage conformed generally to the current monetary regulations and to a certain extent to the ordinary type. On gold coinage the special Aragonese reverse was the crowned arms of Aragon and this type also formed the obverse of silver coins which usually had as their reverse a cross of St. George with, in the angles, the crowned heads of the four Moorish kings said to have been slain by Peter I (1094–1104) at the battle of Alcoraz and used subsequently as the badge of Aragon. The mint for the Aragonese coinage was closed by Philip V in 1730.

Navarre. Ferdinand V on the reconquest of Spanish Navarre in 1512 issued gold ducats with his profile portrait and the arms of Navarre which also supplied the obverse of the silver coinage. Occasional issues were made by the Navarrese mint at Pampeluna for subsequent kings, notably Philip IV in 1652. Coinage finally ceased with the French invasion in 1808.

Valencia. The kingdom, reconquered by James I of Aragon from the Moors in 1238, coined dineros and obols with reverse similar to the Aragonese but with the word *Valencia.* The later and persistent types on both silver and gold were a facing crowned bust and the crowned, diamond-shaped shield with vertical bars. The final coinage was for Charles of Austria (1701–7) one of the claimants in the War of Succession.

Majorca and Minorca. Coinage began only in 1300, though the islands were taken from the Moors in 1239. The types on silver and billon are a facing bust crowned and a tall cross. Peter IV (1343–87) struck a gold real with types, king seated facing and patriarchal cross. The royal title used on coins is that of King of Aragon and Majorca. The latest coinage was for Louis I in 1724.

Catalonia. A denier coinage was struck by a number of independent counts of whom the most important was the Count of Barcelona. The types were a crowned profile bust and a long cross with three pellets and an annulet in alternate angles. This reverse persisted in later issues after the union. The various sieges which Barcelona suffered gave rise to a number of emergency issues.

PORTUGAL

The kingdom of Portugal has its origin in the gift of the district of Lusitania to Henry of Burgundy in 1095 in return for his assistance to Alfonso V of Castille against the Moors. Henry's son Alfonso took the title of King of Portugal after a victory over the Moors in 1139 at Ourique and in 1147 Lisbon, which was to become the capital, was captured. Unlike the other kingdoms in the peninsula, Portugal was not merged in the kingdom of Spain but preserved its independence, except for a relatively short period from 1580 to 1640 when it was held by the Spanish crown.

The Portuguese coinage dates from the establishment of the kingdom by Alfonso I (1112–85) to whom is attributed a gold morabitino or maravedi, whose types refer to the battle of Ourique. On the obverse is the king with raised sword on horse-back with inscription *Regis Portugalensiun* and the reverse is composed of the *quinas,* five small oval shields arranged in the form of a cross. These shields, said to represent the five Moorish kings defeated in the battle, are frequently repeated in the coin types and are the basis of the arms of Portugal. The reverse inscription reads *Moneta Domini Anfsi*. The more usual coinage was that of the billon dinheiro and its half. The usual types are the king's profile portrait and name and a cross with alternate stars and pellets in the angles with inscription *Rex Portugal*. Similar gold maravedis but with slightly different inscription were struck by Sancho I (1185–1211) as well as dinheiros with types, one of the quinas on obverse and on the reverse a long cross cutting the inscription *Po-rt-ug-al* (Pl. 623).

No significant change was effected in the types and denominations issued throughout the thirteenth century and it is only in the reign of Peter I (1357–67) that the issue of larger silver pieces began. These, the tornez and its half, were coins of the gros category. The obverse type was the *quinas* in cross form, the reverse a cross with two concentric circles of inscription on both sides. The rare gold of Ferdinand I (1367–83) is a copy of the French *franc-à-pied;* on obverse the king stands with sword in right hand and rests his left on a shield and on the reverse the *quinas* form a cross. The large silver piece, the barbuda, has a remarkable profile portrait of the king crowned and in helmet with visor closed, while the reverse is a cross with shield at centre and a castle in each angle (Pl. 624). The silver real has the letters F R crowned within a double inscription and the usual *quinas* reverse. Half-pieces of both the barbuda and the real were struck as well as smaller denominations in billon.

The next important alteration in denominations and types took place under Alfonso V (1438–81). The gold cruzado now struck for the first time has as its types the crowned arms of Portugal on obverse and on the reverse a plain cross, types which were to be repeated in several subsequent reigns (Pl. 625). The espadin in gold with its obverse a hand grasping a vertical sword just below the hilt commemorates the institution of the Order of the Sword in 1459, following a successful expedition against the Moors in North Africa. On the silver gros were the arms of Portugal with those of Leon and Castille on the reverse, an indication of the claim of Alfonso to the Spanish throne through his wife Joanna, daughter and heiress of Henry IV of Spain. In addition to the gold cruzado and espadin John II (1481–95) issued an even larger gold piece, the justo, deriving its name from the obverse inscription *Iustus ut palma florebit* surrounding a figure of the king either seated or standing and holding a sword in his right hand. The reverse, the crowned arms, carries John's titles of King of Portugal and Algarve, and Lord of Guinea. The latter refers to the Portuguese holding in Guinea, including a gold mine. The lettering of inscriptions by this time was no longer Gothic but Roman. In addition to silver coinage the copper ceitil was struck with its type of castle, its foot lapped by waves (Pl. 626). Manuel I (1495–1521) issued an even larger piece in gold, the 10 cruzados known as the portuguez. The obverse is the usual crowned arms but the reverse, a cross pattée with the inscription *In hoc signo vinces*, is the first appearance of a type always identified with Portugal. The title with its reference to trade with Ethiopia, Arabia, Persia and India, is an indication of the spread of Portugal's commercial empire. The large silver pieces, the portuguez da prato and its half-piece of value 400 and 200 copper reis were the equivalent of the Spanish piece of eight and the thaler. More common were the silver tostao with types similar to the portuguez in gold (Pl. 627) and the vintem, again with crowned arms obverse but with on reverse the royal initial M crowned. The copper ceitil with its castle type was also in a common issue.

The commercial prosperity of Portugal reached its zenith under Manuel but in the reign of John III (1521–57) the decline began, hastened by the destruction of Lisbon and other cities by the great earthquake. The export of precious-metal coinage led to the suspension of the gold portuguez and the silver tostao which were replaced by a new and less fine gold cruzado which used the cross and *In hoc signo vinces* reverse and a double vintem with the king's name *IO.III* crowned and mark of value XXXX (40 reis). A new copper coinage of large pieces of 10 reis was begun in 1550, the obverse type as usual being the crowned arms and the reverse a large X with the inscription *Rex quintus decimus* (the fifteenth king of Portugal). Another lowering of standard was involved in the issue of the cruzado calvario with its cross-on-steps reverse in 1555 and at the same time new tostaos and smaller denominations with the cross of Aviz as reverse were coined. The final gold type in 1556 showed St. Vincent with palm and ship on the reverse which carried the inscription *Zelator fidei usque ad mortem*, recalling the title of 'zelator fidei' accorded to John by Pope Paul III for his enthusiastic support of the Inquisition (Pl. 628).

The coinage denominations and types remained constant for Sebastian (1557–78) but this reign saw the introduction of coining machinery and the beginning of the practice of placing the date on coins, the earliest recorded being 1562. On the death of Henry I in 1580 a board of governors took charge of the state until the title of the various claimants to the throne had been investigated. Coinage of the usual types was struck by these governors, the obverse inscription reading *Gubernatores Port*, etc. Antonio I, proclaimed king in 1580, was driven out by Philip II of Spain but coinage was struck for him of the ordinary types but of inflated values. In his exile Antonio obtained the striking of his coinage, first at Paris and then at Gorcum in Holland. While Portugal was held by Spain between 1580 and 1640 the special Portuguese coinage was continued with the addition of larger gold pieces of 4 and 2 cruzados, marked on the obverse with the value in

Roman numerals. On the Portuguese issues of the Spanish kings Philip II, III and IV no ordinal number was added to the king's name to distinguish the issues.

In 1640 Portugal successfully revolted against the Spanish kings and John, Duke of Braganza, was proclaimed as John IV of Portugal. Economic difficulties required the raising of the value of current issues under John by counter-marking and a further rise took place under his successor Alfonso VI (1656–83) who was compelled to abdicate and the regency was assumed by Prince Peter. He succeeded as king on Alfonso's death in 1683 but a further extension of the value of the coinage by 20 per cent was required to be made in 1688. The precious metals of Brasil began to flow again into Portugal after the Peace of Utrecht in 1713 and gold cruzados began to be minted at Porto as well as at Lisbon. The products of Porto were marked by the initial P in the angles of the reverse cross. In 1722 John V (1706–50) introduced a new coinage system based on a gold escudo. The types were the royal bust and title and the crowned and decorated arms of Portugal, and denominations included the 10, 5 and ½ escudo as well as the unit (Pl. 629). The types of the silver denominations were now a square shield crowned, together with the mark of value in reis in figures and a cross. Little change in coinage takes place till the joint reign of Mary and Peter III (1777–86) and this only in the use of jugate busts in the gold coins. When Mary, who had reigned alone since 1786, lost her sanity in 1799 John assumed the regency and coined in that capacity.

The French invasion in 1808 drove John into exile in Brasil where he remained even after he became king in 1816, until he was recalled by the insurrection in 1826. The European upheaval had wrought no change in Portuguese coinage which continued the same under Peter IV, the usurper Miguel and Mary II until the issue of her new coinage in 1835. This new system consisted of gold crowns and half-pieces of 5000 and 2500 reis, silver crowns and halves of 1000 and 500 reis, silver tostaos and halves of 200 and 100 reis and coppers of 20, 10 and 5 reis. The types, identical for gold and silver, were the royal bust and the draped and crowned arms of Portugal with mark of value in reis on the reverse. The copper reis types were the arms on obverse and the value in Roman numerals on the reverse (Pl. 630). Under Louis I (1861–89) the royal portrait was also placed on the copper reis and in 1900 the 100 and 50 reis pieces of Charles I (1889–1908) struck in nickel reverted to the arms as obverse type and a value reverse. The last regal issues in Portugal, those of Manuel II (1908–10), found the types still largely immobilized.

The coinage of the republic, declared in 1910, began only in 1914 with a special silver escudo issue showing Liberty holding a torch on obverse and the Portuguese arms on a fasces in wreath on the reverse. The head of Liberty and arms reverse together with mark of value were the types for the ordinary escudo and the smaller centavo coins (Pl. 631). A special issue of 10 escudo pieces in silver in 1928 commemorated, with its mounted knight on the obverse, the battle of Ourique in 1139. Escudos of 10, 5 and 2½ since 1932 have had as types a galleon and a modernistic rendering of the Portuguese arms while the escudo and denominations in centavos in cupro-nickel since 1927 have repeated the Liberty head and value types. The most recent use of the original *quinas* device is on the obverse of 20 and 10 centavo pieces (1942-5) where five square shields, each with five pellets, are arranged in a cross; on the reverse the value is marked with Roman numerals (Pl. 632). A special issue in 1960 commemorates the quincentenary of Henry the Navigator. Silver coins of 5, 10 and 25 escudos carry the portrait of Henry the Navigator on the obverse and the Portuguese arms and value on the reverse.

CENTRAL EUROPE

SWITZERLAND

On the dismemberment of the Roman empire in the West in the fifth century the Roman provinces with which modern Switzerland approximately coincides passed under the control of the Ostrogoths and the Burgundians (p. 284), but after the battle of Tolbiac in 496 Helvetia was incorporated in the Frankish kingdom of the Merovingian kings. Merovingian gold tremisses of the type without regal name but with the name of mint and moneyer were struck at some half-dozen mints in Switzerland; of these the most important were Basel, Geneva (Pl. 633), Sitten and Zürich. Under the Carolingians, however, the number of active mints was reduced to three, Basel, Chur and Zürich, for the issues of the new denier coinage, and in the tenth century mints at Chur, Constance and Zürich struck the silver coinage of successive German emperors. Zürich, for example, coined for Otto I silver denars with cross obverse and imperial name and a reverse bearing the mint name *Turecum* across the field.

In 926 Hermann, Count of Franconia, received the Duchy of Swabia from Henry the Fowler and exercised his privilege of coining at Zürich where denars were struck with the name *Herimannus* around a cross on obverse and the syllables *De-Tu-re-cu* on the arms of the reverse cross. Coinage was continued by his successors, but the tenth century saw the granting of coinage rights to a number of ecclesiastical foundations by various emperors as a means of purchasing support in the long-drawn-out conflicts between emperor and pope. The more important foundations which received these concessions included the bishoprics of Chur, (959) Lausanne and Geneva (tenth century), Basel (1087) and Sitten (1274) and abbeys at Frauenmünster-Zürich (930), St. Ursus-Solothurn (930) and St. Gallen (947). Denar coinage of these ecclesiastical foundations, comparatively rare in the tenth century, was struck with more frequency in the first part of the eleventh century. At Geneva the types were a cross with inscription *Geneva Civitas* and a head of St. Peter inscribed *Scs Petrus;* at Lausanne a temple with *Sedes Lausane* and cross with *Civitas Lausane* and at Basel similar types but with individual inscription. About the middle of the eleventh century the fabric of the denar became thinner so that the reverse type is scarcely decipherable, as at Basel where such coins, semi-bracteates, of Rudolf (1107–22) have a circular inscription *Basilea* around the R on obverse and traces of the same type on the reverse. By the beginning of the thirteenth century a true bracteate coinage was in full flood, often in the form of pieces with a square outline. A wide variety of types include the heads of bishops (Pl. 634) or other ecclesiastical dignitaries, the Paschal Lamb as at St. Gallen (Pl. 635), an ibex at Chur. It was in the thirteenth century that the growing cities began to claim and exercise the right of coinage. Of these Bern in 1228 was the first to receive this privilege but it is only in the thirteenth century that its issues in the form of bracteates with type of bear become substantial. Other city coinages began much later: Basel (1373), Solothurn (1381), St. Gallen and Lucerne (1415) and Zürich (1514).

The bracteate coinage of the Swiss mints gave place in the late fourteenth and in the fifteenth centuries to a new series of small two-sided coins to which were added larger silver denominations of the groschen category and, in some cases, coinage of gold guldens. Basel in 1433 began a coinage of groschen and half-pieces with types, the city arms and inscription *Grossus Basiliensis* and cross with two circles of inscription *Salve regina misericordiae dulcedo vitae* (Pl. 636), and the imperial gulden struck at Basel from 1411 has as types the Madonna and imperial orb accompanied by emperor's name. Bern in the fifteenth century struck a coinage of billon plapparts, equal to 15 hallers with the characteristic city badge, the bear and a cross with inscription *Sanctus Vincencius* as well as a series of batzen, equal to 4 kreuzer, with similar bear type on obverse. Gold guldens which began issue late in the fifteenth century also reproduce the bear on a shield and have a standing figure of St. Vincent on the reverse. Similar billon coinages with their own individual types were struck at Solothurn, Lucerne, St. Gallen and, later, Zürich.

An advance towards unification came in the late fourteenth and fifteenth centuries when the existing association of eight cantons of which the more important were Bern, Lucerne, Zürich and Uri, Schwyz and Unterwalden was joined by five other cantons including Basel, Freiburg and Solothurn and in 1648 Swiss independence was guaranteed by the Treaty of Westphalia. Despite the formation of this association, independent coinages continued to be issued, most of them into the nineteenth century, by the constituent cantons, as well as by a number of cities such as Geneva and St. Gallen and by ecclesiastical foundations such as the bishoprics of Basel and Chur. A good number of these coinages, all with their individual types, include gold issues, particularly at Basel, Bern (Pl. 637), Geneva, Lucerne and Zürich. Silver coinage included the thaler and its half but more frequent was the teston or dicken (Pl. 638). In billon there were a variety of coins such as the groschen and various denominations of the batz (Pl. 639) and kreuzer.

In 1798 Switzerland was invaded by the revolutionary armies of France and a

Helvetic republic was established and a new unified and decimal coinage was instituted with the franc as the unit, divided into 10 batzen, the batz divided in turn into 10 rappen. The system included pieces of 32 and 16 francs in gold; 40, 20, 10 and 5 batzen in silver and in billon the batz, its half and the rap. The types in the denominations down to 5 batzen were a warrior and the value; on the lower denominations the words *Helvet Republ* and the value. In 1803 the cantons, now increased to nineteen in number, were authorized to issue their own coinage again, based still on the franc unit and with a common obverse type and the individual canton arms as reverse. Finally in 1815 the number of cantons rose to twenty-two. The denominational system of the Helvetic republic was maintained in essentials but coinage was mainly in the lower denominations, and only a few cantons struck gold. For the new Swiss Confederation of 1848 a single coinage was instituted and began issue in 1850. The system adopted was identical with the French, the unit being the franc, divided into 100 centimes or rappen. The gold denominations of 10 and 20 francs did not begin issue till 1871 but from 1850 the silver coinage included 5, 2 and 1 and $\frac{1}{2}$ franc pieces, while lower denominations were struck in various alloys. The type used for the obverse on the high denominations is a personificaton of Helvetia, either as a seated figure or a portrait head; on lower denominations appears the arms of the Confederation, a shield bearing a cross. The reverse consists of this shield together with the value on the higher range of pieces or of the value alone on the lower (Pl. 640). This conservative coinage has undergone little subsequent variation except for the issue of a number of special commemorative issues usually of the 5 franc denomination. In the post-war series the bronze 1 and 2 centime coins have a plain cross on obverse and the numeral of value superimposed on a corn-ear.

GERMANY

The presentation of a coherent and informative outline of German coinage throughout the centuries is beset by many difficulties of which not the least are the extent and the diversity of the issues. In the majority of European states a certain initial wide range of diverse coinage, issued by petty kingdoms, or by feudal and ecclesiastical authorities alongside a central authority gives place, usually by the end of the Middle Ages in the late fifteenth century, either to a single national coinage or to a clearly dominant series, supplemented by subsidiary coinages of more restricted local circulation. The German coinage, however, is at the outset complicated by the sheer number of coin issuing authorities. The royal prerogative of striking coin which the Carolingian monarchs had tried to maintain—but with by no means complete success—was rapidly dissipated by their Frankish and Saxon successors as kings of Germany. It was, in any case, a prerogative which their great feudal vassals never completely recognized and in the pursuit of the policy of seeking support from the church to bolster the central regal authority against the powerful dukes part of the price paid by successive kings was first the granting of the profits of coinage and then the acceptance of autonomous coinage on the part of bishoprics, abbeys and monasteries. Later came the extension of this privilege to smaller feudal lords and to communities. On top of all these several rights was that of the Emperor of the Holy Roman empire to strike coins. The problem of presentation becomes greater when coinage of only one denomination, the denar or silver penny, yields place to a variety of coinage systems. The persistence in Germany of numerous political units of which many retained their rights of coinage into the nineteenth century maintains the difficulties of presentation throughout almost the whole of the history of the German series.

Germany is the supreme example in Europe of a state which in modern times is far from being identifiable in a geographic sense with the territories to which Germany in a more general sense can be applied at various periods of history. A certain simplification has, therefore, been effected by detaching from consideration in this section the coinages of, for instance, Bohemia, Austria, parts of Italy and the Low Countries which at various stages of history shared a coinage with areas included in Germany proper.

In default of a detailed consideration of the many component coinages and in an attempt to present a comprehensible outline it is proposed to deal with the German series in a succession of periods: (1) coinages of the Merovingian and the Carolingian kings in so far as they effect Germany; (2) the denar coinage of the Saxon kings of Germany up to 1137; (3) the bracteate coinage of Saxony and parts of Franconia and Swabia to the early decades of the fourteenth century; (4) the denar coinage of the Hohenstaufen period, roughly also to the early fourteenth century in parts of Franconia and Swabia and the West; (5) the groschen and late mediaeval gold; (6) the coinages of the more important modern states from 1500 to the Napoleonic period; (7) State coinage up to 1871; and (8) the coinage of united Germany.

MEROVINGIAN AND CAROLINGIAN COINAGE
(SIXTH–NINTH CENTURIES)

The earliest coinage which can be regarded as German in the sense that it was struck by mints on German soil is that of the Frankish kings who in the sixth century controlled a realm extending, in modern terms, from western Germany to north France. The Frankish coinage like most coinages in western Europe of this period was initially an imitation of Roman imperial gold but a number of pieces while still copying Roman types bear the name and titles of Theodebert I (534–548). In the field of the reverse of a solidus in his name appear the letters COLV, presumably indicating its mintage at *Colonia Ubiorum*, modern Cologne (Pl. 641). The more common series consisted of gold tremisses of which a number in Theodebert's name have monograms marking their issue by mints at Trier, Bonn and Andernach. The most typical series of gold tremisses of the later Merovingian kings of the Franks in the eighth century is that which makes no mention of the king but has, as basic types, a diademed head with inscription recording the moneyer and a cross reverse with the name of the mint. Merovingian mints for this coinage are recorded at Mainz, Strasburg, Trier and Cologne (Pl. 642).

The establishment of the new Carolingian dynasty in succession to the Merovingian by Pepin the Short (752–768) brought also a new coinage of silver pennies (denars). Of the various types issued by Pepin the most common is that with his initials *R(ex) P(ipinus)* on obverse and an indication of the mint on reverse, either as a monogram or as a complete inscription in lines or circularly as on the issue marked *Civ Argent* at Strasburg. Coins of Charlemagne (768–811) with his name in two lines across the obverse bear on the reverse the names of mints at Aachen, Bonn, Mainz (Pl. 643), Cologne and Trier. Charlemagne's title of emperor after his coronation in Rome in 800 appears on coins of Trier, among other of his mints. His profile portrait is inscribed *Karlus Imp Aug* and the city gate of the reverse *Treveris*. Mints at Cologne and Strasburg struck also for Louis the Pious (814–840), an additional cross on the reverse of coins of the latter mint marking, perhaps, episcopal participation in the coinage. The division of the Carolingian empire between the sons of Louis by the Treaty of Verdun in 843 laid the groundwork for the states of France and Germany. The western portion consisting of Neustria and Aquitaine fell to Charles the Bald, the eastern portion— Saxony, Swabia and Bavaria—to Louis the German and a central kingdom made up of Austrasia, Burgundy and Lombardy to Lothar I. The northern portion of this kingdom became the portion of Lothar's son, Lothar II (855–869), and from him stems its name Lotharingia or Lorraine. By the partition of Meersen in 870 the kingdom of Louis the German gained the eastern portion of Lotharingia, roughly modern Lorraine, Belgium and the Netherlands. The German kingdom now created thus secured such mints as Strasburg, Aachen and Cologne which had coined for the two Lothars. In the original eastern portion of the kingdom a new mint had opened for Louis the German at Regensburg, striking the conventional silver penny with obverse type of cross and royal name and reverse, the mint name in lines across the field. Coins of his successor Louis III (876–882) with the mint name of Metz on the reverse have on the obverse the name *Ludovicus* around the cross in the inner circle and the first appearance of the formula *Gratia D - Rex* as an outer inscription. A considerable array of mints at Strasburg, Mainz, Würzburg, Trier and Cologne struck the plenteous issues of Louis the Child (900–911). Of these the Cologne penny with the usual obverse cross and name received a reverse type, the inscription S *Colonia A* in three lines which was to persist as a type for centuries (Pl. 644). The reverse type of the Trier penny, a roughly designed church derived from the temple of Charlemagne's *Christiana religio* deniers, also served as a model for many subsequent issues. The practice of granting the profits of specific mints to episcopal sees had been growing under previous rulers and was considerably extended by Louis the Child, under whom the first step in the creation of autonomous episcopal issues can be seen in the issues of Strasburg where the first syllable of the name of Bishop Odbert (906–913) was added to the mint name on the reverse.

The last issues of the Carolingian or Frankish kings from German mints are those of Charles the Simple, who by extending his eastern frontier to the Rhine in 911 on the death of Louis the Child secured the mints of Cologne, Trier and Metz. Another of the Frankish dynasty, Conrad I, elected successor to Louis the Child, coined, at Regensburg and Mainz, pennies with the church reverse type. On the death of Conrad in 918 the Frankish dynasty ended and the crown was offered to Henry the Fowler, Duke of Saxony.

COINAGE OF THE SAXON KINGS (918–1137)

The most common class of coinage of Henry I (918–936) has the cross with a pellet in each angle and royal name on obverse and the church type and mint name on reverse. From about this time the inscriptions begin to be marked off from the type by an enclosing circle. The final recovery of Lotharingia in 925 resulted in the issue of Henry's coinage from the mints of Strasburg and Metz. The power of the great dukes makes itself apparent in coinage in their own name such as that of Arnulf, Duke of Bavaria, whose issues from Regensburg and Salzburg make no mention of the king. It is probably in the reign of Henry that the issue begins of the so-called Saxon pennies or Wendish pennies. These pieces, a barbarous reproduction of the cross-and-temple types with either no inscriptions or at best a blundered legend, were later coined in great quantity by the Ottonian kings at the mint of Magdeburg (Pl. 645).

Otto I who succeeded in 936 struck at Cologne massive issues with the *Colonia* reverse initiated by Louis the Child. The difficulties in distinguishing the issues of the three successive kings of this name are well exemplified at this mint. In essence, coins with the *Colonia* inscription reverse for Otto I give his name as *Otto Rex*, those of Otto II as *Oddo Imperator*, those of Otto III as *Oddo Rex*. It is this last type which was so widely copied in Rhenish and Westphalian mints. A new mint was created on the eastern borders of Saxony at Magdeburg in 942. The types a cross and a church are inscribed *Otto* and *Atalhet* (Pl. 646) may refer to the marriage of Otto I and Adelheid in 951 but are ascribed by others to Otto III and his grandmother Adelheid under whose tutelage he initially reigned. The extensive issues of this coinage are connected with the exploitation of the silver-mines of the Harz mountains and the mint at Goslar may also have struck this coinage. Otto's policy of strengthening the monarchy by appointing members of his own family to the succession of the dukedoms when the incumbents died created his sons Conrad and Ludolf as dukes of Lotharingia and Swabia and as such they coined at Mainz and Regensburg respectively. On the revolt and defeat of the brothers in 952 Otto appointed his brother Bruno, Archbishop of Cologne, to the duchy of Lotharingia. Bruno's coinage retained the usual royal obverse but placed his own name and title *Bruno Archieps* on the reverse (Pl. 647). Bishop Ulrich of Augsburg who played a leading rôle in the defeat of the Magyars at Lechfeld was the first to strike an episcopal coinage which completely ignored the royal prerogative and used autonomous types. On the obverse around a cross his name *Udulricus Eps* occupied the place usually reserved for the royal name while the reverse was the common church type surrounded by the mint name. The Hungarian defeat ushered in a period of peace in Germany and raised the esteem of the monarchy, both facts represented on a coinage by Otto where the obverse carries the profile bust of the king in royal diadem and the title *Otto Rex Pacificus*.

The extension of the mint system begun by Otto I was continued under Otto II (973–983) and Otto III (983–1002) in whose reigns mints were established at Andernach, Bonn, Dortmund, Hildesheim and Quedlinburg, amongst others. The identification of such mints is often derivable only from the name of the saint which appears on the reverse. The attempt on issues of Otto III who died at the age of twenty-two to convey in his portrait the idea of his youth is an unusual feature in mediaeval coinage where the portrait is usually a mere convention. The beginnings of other episcopal series are seen in the coinages of Bishop Arnulf of Halberstadt and Bishop Bernward of Hildesheim who replace the obverse type of Otto III by their own name and title. An early example of an autonomous coinage by a lesser feudal lord is that of Eckhard, Margrave of

Meissen (985–1002) whose name is inscribed on the obverse of his coins and the mint, Meissen, on the reverse.

A feature of the coinage of Henry II (1002–24) is the more frequent use of a profile bust in diadem or imperial crown as on his issues at the mints of Regensburg in his original duchy of Bavaria. The grants of the profits of coinage, chiefly to episcopal authorities, were considerably restricted in this reign but the process of transmuting this existing privilege into the issue of autonomous coinage increased in tempo, chiefly to the advantage of the bishoprics of Eichstadt, Regensburg and Salzburg. Under Henry the autonomous coinage of lesser feudal lords also showed an increase, chiefly in the west and the Low Countries. An example is the coinage of Graf Heinrich of Stade whose name and title, *Heinricus Com*, is inscribed round a royal bust with radiate helmet and sceptre. The type and the accompanying reverse, an open cross with the letters CRVX in the angles are close copies of an issue of Æthelred II in England and demonstrate the widespread circulation in northern Europe of the Danegeld, the tribute exacted from England. Conrad II (1024–39) pursued a similar policy of sparing issue of the rights to profits of coinage but similarly was unable to prevent the spread of autonomous issues, chiefly ecclesiastical. As well as the ordinary regal issues there were issues such as that at Cologne where the obverse has the crowned and long-bearded portrait of Conrad on obverse and the reverse with mint name inscription has a church type enclosing the letters *Piligri* for Pilgrim, Archbishop of Cologne (Pl. 648). The second stage in the process is illustrated by an issue of Poppo, Archbishop of Trier, where his portrait with crozier in front and his title usurps the regal side of the coin. The reverse is an unusual composition, a hand of God holding the keys of St. Peter with the inscription *S. Petrus*, the letters ETR forming part of the keys.

A new mint with a distinctive type of coinage was set up by Henry III (1039–56) at Goslar in Saxony. On the obverse the king is depicted crowned facing and with a distinctive close-trimmed beard. The reverse presents, unusually, the two facing nimbate busts of SS. Simon and Jude (Pl. 649). Another unusual issue betrays the influence of Byzantine coin types both in the reverse representation of the nimbate bust of the Virgin and the obverse of two facing busts which the inscription with the names of Henry and his father Conrad II demonstrates to be a 'family' type on the Byzantine analogy. The reverse of the Virgin shows the issue to have been struck at Speyer where the cathedral, dedicated to the Virgin, had been begun by Conrad. A greater variety of reverse types begins to be a feature of episcopal as well as regal issues. A particularly picturesque example is that of Coblenz on which the facing portrait of Archbishop Eberhard of Trier (1047–66) is accompanied by a reverse of the church at Coblenz at the junction of the rivers

Moselle and Rhine whose waves are pictured below the church. The reverse inscription, *Confluentia*, identifies the scene. Other archbishops of Cologne whose portraits appear on their coins are Anno who uses an architectural reverse, a view of the church and the city walls and Sigewin who placed on the reverse the gable of the church enclosing a facing portrait of a saint who is named as St. Peter by the inscription above, *Pet-rus*. A Duisburg issue of Henry IV (1056–1105) with crowned profile portrait of the king disposes the letters of the mint name within four circlets on the reverse (Pl. 650).

The long struggle between emperor and pope in the reign of Henry IV and the civil wars to which it gave rise weakened the position of the monarchy and gave opportunity for further assumptions of the rights of coinage, and the deteriorating economic situation led to a reduction in the weight of the silver penny. Though the great quarrel with the pope was finally ended by the Concordat of Worms in 1122 Henry V (1105–24) appears to have coined in remarkably few mints. Of these one was Goslar where the continuing issues of SS. Simon and Jude were given a new obverse, the emperor on horse-back.

The death of Henry V in 1124 gave the German princes the opportunity to insist on their rights of free election. The chief candidates were Frederick of Hohenstaufen, Duke of Swabia, and Lothar of Supplinburg, Duke of Saxony, who was eventually elected, but on his death in 1137 Conrad of Hohenstaufen was elected in his place. The stress and hardships of this civil war following so close on that in the reign of Henry IV are reflected by the coinage. The weight standard, already reduced under Henry IV, sank to almost half its original figure and the fabric underwent considerable change. In lower Saxony and Bavaria especially the flan of the penny became so thin and spread that it could scarce take the imprint of the two dies, and, as in striking, the obverse die was the upper of the two and received the blow from the hammer the obverse often almost obliterated the imprint of the reverse die. For this reason pennies of this type are often referred to as half-bracteates. The issues of Regensburg of this period are remarkable for a selection of types which clearly owe their inspiration to Byzantine and other eastern art forms which the crusaders had brought to the knowledge of western Europe. The type of warrior with bow and arrow shooting a lion is reminiscent of Persian or Sassanian metal work and various facing busts holding sceptres and other objects in their hands are of Byzantine inspiration (Pl. 651).

About the middle of the twelfth century the previous monetary unity based on the silver denar began to be replaced by two different systems. In the West, in the Rhineland, Lotharingia, parts of Franconia and Swabia and in Bavaria a second series of silver pennies of comparable fabric came into issue but in the East, comprising Saxony and the remainder of Franconia and Swabia, the bracteates, a development of the thin spread pennies of the earlier twelfth century became the exclusive type of coinage. The following two sections are devoted to an account of these two systems.

BRACTEATES (*c.* 1150–1350)

The term bracteate derived from *bractea*, a thin metal plate, an explanatory gloss of the later eighteenth century, has become the customary name applied to this class of coinage, though in their period of issue they were regarded as only a form of the denar or silver penny. Indeed coin inscriptions stating that the piece is a *denarius* of a certain person are not infrequent. The bracteate, a development of the thin silver penny of the early twelfth century, is of exceptionally thin fabric and of unusually wide flan. The relative fragility of such a piece led subsequent ages to reject the idea that bracteates were coins and regard them rather as some kind of amulet or token. It is, however, now accepted that those pieces represented real media of exchange and, in fact, there was some continuation of this category of coinage up to almost 1700. The other characteristic feature is that the bracteate has a type in relief on only one side, the other side being an intaglio of the first. The bracteate was produced by hammering a thin plate of silver on a die cut in relief and it is believed that in some series a number of thin plates were imprinted at the one hammering.

In style bracteates have much in common with seals and as a class they are a specific German category of coinage which had little influence on other European coinages except to the immediate south and east. The prolific choice of types is a treasure house of illustration for mediaeval Germany and is a contrast to the almost exclusively heraldic motifs of other coinages of the period. Personages, whether imperial, or secular or episcopal lords, are presented in a variety of attitudes—standing, enthroned or mounted. Saints occur in profusion, either in simple portraits or as participants in a scene descriptive of the legends attached to them. Scenes derived from scripture, as, for example, Adam and Eve in Paradise, also feature as bracteate types. The most widespread motif of all, perhaps, is the architectural, for bracteates abound with representations of buildings of all kinds, chiefly ecclesiastical. The heraldic design also has a share in the bracteate coinage, though a much more restricted share than elsewhere. Initially the inscriptions on bracteates are well lettered and easily legible but later in the thirteenth century the general decline in quality of the bracteate is accompanied by deterioration in the inscriptions which are poorly produced and often blundered. By the fourteenth century the uninscribed bracteate had become more common than the inscribed.

Bracteates were issued, as were the more ordinary silver pennies in the early twelfth century, by a great variety of authorities including the emperor, the great princes and minor feudal lords, as well as bishoprics and other ecclesiastical foundations together with some municipalities. Because of this diversity, which is complicated by the wide variety of types employed, the bracteate coinage is best surveyed on a geographic basis rather than as a strictly chronological development.

Brandenburg

Mention must be made first of the earliest coinage of Brandenburg, a series of half-bracteates of Pribislav who, when converted to Christianity about 1127, used on coins his new name, Henricus. These half-bracteates show his facing bust helmeted and with sword and pennant inscribed *Hein(ricus) Brand(enburgensis)* with on the reverse the bust of his wife entitled in the inscription *Petrissa*. The bracteate series proper begins under Albert the Bear (1134–70) who inherited from Henry. Types include the half-length figure of the Margrave in armour behind a fortified wall between two towers, the Margrave as mounted knight and the standing figures of Albert and his wife Sophia holding a banner between them. His successor, Otto I (1170–84), is presented in various military guises; the most striking is a figure helmeted and holding sword and pennant seated on parapet between two towers with inscription *Otto*. Another type of this reign shows a representation of a walled city clearly inscribed *Brandenburg*. The most common type, however, in subsequent reigns was the standing figure of the Margrave which remained as the obverse when two-sided coins began to supersede bracteates from as early as the thirteenth century.

Pomerania

The issue of bracteates as the only type of coinage began about 1200 and lasted till about the middle of the thirteenth century. Generally the types were the bust of the feudal lord or a building but some more unusual types probably mark the issues of a specific mint as for example the griffin at Stettin.

Prussia

The Teutonic Order, founded on the model of the knights of St. John and the Knights Templar, was rewarded for assistance to one of the Polish dukes against the Borussi or Prussians in 1225 with the sovereignty of that territory. The early coinage of the order consisted of small bracteates with types, a cross or a cross on shield.

Thuringia

One of the earliest and most effective of bracteates is that of Conrad III who is presented as a half-length figure crowned and with sword and lance behind a balustrade and framed between two towers. The piece is inscribed *Cunratus* and *Lampertus*, the name of the king and Lampert, Warden of Gleichen. The equestrian figure, a popular type at various mints in Thuringia, is best examplified in the large bracteate issued at Mulhausen for Hermann of Thuringia (1199–1204) This well-designed and executed piece (Pl. 652) is in contrast to a similar equestrian type issued at Mulhausen for Otto IV (1209–12) on which the angular and disproportionate figures of rider and steed demonstrate the falling off in standard of bracteate design as early as the thirteenth century.

Bracteates of Johann, Bishop of Merseburg, honour the martyrdom of St. Lawrence. The coin face is divided by an arch inscribed *Johannes Episcopus* while, above, the half-length figure of the nimbate saint holds a palm-branch and raises his hand to bless the bishop, who stands beside him holding a crozier. Below the arch is depicted the martyrdom with the saint stretched out on a gridiron above flames stirred by two torturers. Bishop Berthold of Naumburg (1154–61) was depicted on his bracteates with mitre and crozier standing by an altar blessing the chalice, with a sketch of a building with a tower in the background. Another superb example of the ecclesiastical bracteate is that of the abbey of Nordhausen. The double-figure type shows the figure of a saint seated on a low arch and holding a palm-branch and long cross while before him kneels a female figure raising hands in prayer. The inscription *Scs Eustachius Berta Abtissa de Nor* identifies the figures as St. Eustachius and the Abbess Bertha.

The fine series of Otto, Margrave of Meissen (1156–91), derives from the newly discovered silver deposits in the Erzgebirge as does the epithet 'the Rich', usually attached to Otto's name. The armour of the standing figure of Otto is drawn in great detail and the extension of the figure beyond the circle of inscription gives an impression of a third dimension. The inscription *Otto Marchio de Lippzina* is

the first record on coins of the city of Leipzig. The bracteate issues of the archbishops of Erfurt are amongst the most plentiful and continuous as well as the
better executed series. The types are always those of the archbishop and St. Martin
or St. Martin and the beggar. On coins of Henry I (1142–53) the design is divided,
as so often on bracteates, by an arch. Above this is the figure of the saint holding
crozier and cross; below, the archbishop raises his hands in prayer. Sometimes the
archbishop is identified by the inscription *Henri* close to his head, sometimes a circular
inscription gives his full title *Heinricus Eresfordt* (Pl. 653). Towards the end of the
thirteenth century a smaller and rougher series of bracteates came into issue. These
pieces bear the mitred figure of St. Martin, shown seated or standing or half-
length behind a balustrade and are inscribed simply *S. Martinus*.

Lower Saxony

The most important series here is that of Brunswick, particularly the bracteates
issued by Henry the Lion, Duke of Saxony (1142–95). The lion monument
erected in Brunswick in 1166 appears as the principal type on one issue of bracteates, while another commemorates the marriage of Henry to Matilda of England
in 1168. The type is a city gate in the centre of which is the lion, while the busts of
Henry and Matilda appear above the battlements on either side of a tower. A
partly retrograde inscription reads *Heinricus dux leo*. Henry's son Otto who became
the emperor Otto IV (1209–12) coined bracteates at Brunswick, still with the lion
type, and at Hanover, where the type was a large cross with a crown and a lion in
alternate angles and the inscription *Moneta nova domini imperatoris*. In the last decades
of the thirteenth century began the series of uninscribed bracteates with lion type
which constituted the coinage of Brunswick into the fourteenth century, continuing even after 1345 when the city obtained the right to its own coinage.

The lords of Falkenstein and Arnstein made use of the punning type of a falcon
as a type for their bracteate coinage. It appeared as the sole type, occupying the
whole field on an issue for Burchard II (1142–74) but on others it is used as an
emblem in part of the design. One such piece has the falcon flanked by two towers,
superimposed on a scene in which the naked figures of Adam and Eve stand on
either side of the tree of the knowledge of good and evil about which the serpent
is entwined. The regular type on bracteates of the counts of Regenstein and
Blankenburg was their emblem, the antlers of a stag. The earlier issues are inscribed
with name and title as, for example, the *Comes Sifridus de Blankenbruc* of Siegfried
II (1186–1246). The later issues without inscription normally have the figure of
the graf holding the stag's antlers in his hand.

Of episcopal bracteates in lower Saxony those of the bishopric of Halberstadt are amongst the most common. The type is occasionally the bishop himself but most often it is St. Stephen, the patron saint of Halberstadt in a variety of poses. A more than usually ambitious type portraying the stoning of St. Stephen succeeds in crowding no less than five figures into the scene. Another series which made use of multiple figures types was that of the abbey of Quedlinburg, particulary the issues of the Abbess Beatrix III (1286–1308). A fine example shows a building, framing in its openings the seated abbess between two nuns; below, by the abbess' feet, are the busts of a monk and a nun. The important archbishopric of Magdeburg coined a notable series of bracteates which pay particular honour to St. Maurice. Archbishop Wigman (1152–92) uses as types St. Maurice, dressed like a contemporary knight and his own standing figure holding crozier and palm on an issue which has a circular inscription *Wigmannus Archiepisco* and a vertical inscription *Scs Maurc*. Another piece shows Wigman in episcopal dress blessing the Gospel held by up a deacon. As on other series, the standard of coinage declined and the bulk of the bracteates are uninscribed. The archbishops of Magdeburg had a second mint at Halle which also coined bracteates with the type of St. Maurice.

Franconia

The important mints in Wetterau were Frankfort-on-Main and Gelnhausen, both of which struck bracteates for the emperors Frederick I (1152–90) and Henry VI (1190–7). The type is usually the enthroned emperor with his name and title in the surrounding inscription but both Frederick and his wife Beatrix appear as half-length busts on one issue. In the early thirteenth century bracteate coinage here was replaced by the new series of silver pennies. The coinage of the abbey of Fulda from the early twelfth century was in the form of large bracteates which usually represent the abbot alone or, occasionally, with St. Boniface. The earlier pieces such as those of Burchard (1168–76) are finely executed. The vestments of the abbot, seated and holding crozier and Gospel, are drawn in detail and his name *Burcardus Abbas Ful* is given in full. By the next century the module had shrunk and the inscription had disappeared or was reduced to initials (Pl. 654).

Swabia

Most of the issues of the bracteate period in Swabia were from centres such as Basel, Zürich and Constance. The remaining most important series were the imperial and episcopal issues of Augsburg which began in the latter half of the thirteenth century, somewhat later than the bracteates of northern and central Germany. The characteristics of the Augsburg bracteates are a somewhat smaller module, neat execution and a border decorated with crescents, lis and stars. The imperial type is normally the enthroned figure of the emperor holding sceptre and globe but an exceptional two-figure type was used for Philip of Swabia and his Byzantine wife, Irene, who are shown holding between them a cross on globe. On episcopal bracteates the common types are the bust or full-length figure of the bishop, the former occasionally having his hands raised in blessing.

DENAR COINAGE OF THE HOHENSTAUFEN PERIOD (*c.* 1150–1350)

The denar or silver penny which, in its bracteate form became the currency of eastern and central Germany and parts of the south, continued, as a piece with types on both obverse and reverse, to be the medium for western Germany and the greater part of the south. The areas served by this continuation of the silver penny included Frisia, the Rhineland in its wider sense, Lotharingia and Bavaria. It is almost impossible to draw the frontier between the two categories of coinage circulating between the twelfth and fourteenth centuries and to complicate the picture there were a number of areas in which the bracteate and the two-sided penny were in circulation more or less side by side, or in which the issue of bracteates was superseded at a comparatively early stage by coins of the more usual fabric. This second series of silver pennies is of a much reduced module compared with the earlier series of the Frankish and Saxon kings and of a lower standard of both fineness and weight. In artistic merit the new series fails to match up to the earlier and, in comparison with the contemporary bracteate series, particularly in the twelfth century, it must be adjudged a poor second, both as regards conception of design and execution. In general terms the obverse of this silver-penny series presents the portrait of the minting authority, whether secular or ecclesiastical. The portrait, fortunately, is not restricted as it is on much of mediaeval coinage to a bust but can be, in addition, a seated, standing or even a mounted figure with one or other of a number of appropriate attributes such as sword and shield or crozier. The variety of reverse types is, however, considerable, though the majority of them fall under the heading of heraldic.

The description of some of the more important of these silver-penny coinages is based, as was that of the bracteates, on a geographic distribution rather than on a chronological sequence, again because of the complexity of the series arising from its extent and diversity. The somewhat more complicated series which mingle with bracteate issues is considered first and then those of the districts where this silver penny was the exclusive coinage.

(a) Regions with bracteates and denars

Brandenburg

The Margrave of Brandenburg, Otto II (1184–1205), began to issue alongside the bracteates a denar coinage with his portrait bust and a building reverse and under his brother, Albert II (1205–20), the types are a standing figure of the margrave with on the reverse an eagle or a cross and occasionally an indication of the mint, either Brandenburg itself or Stendal. These types set the pattern for the subsequent coinage of Brandenburg in the thirteenth and fourteenth centuries, much of it without inscription (Pl. 655).

Pomerania

Pomerania was converted to Christianity in the reigns of the brothers Bogislav I and Casimir I (1156–80) and its first coinage was of small silver pennies which mention the names of both. Coins with the blundered name of Bogislav alone have as types a building and a cross and some examples mention their mints, situated at Prenzlau and Stettin. On pennies of Bogislav II (1187–1220) and Casimir II (1187–1219) appears the head of St. John inscribed *Scs Johannes* and a building accompanied by the names *Budizlav* and *Kazsmer*. After an intervening issue of bracteates even smaller silver pennies were struck from the latter half of the thirteenth century. These are usually anonymous and the most frequent types are a Gothic A on the obverse and a triangle ornament on the reverse with a head of a griffin in each angle.

Lower Saxony

The later and uninscribed bracteate coinage of the counts of Anhalt in the thirteenth and early fourteenth centuries was accompanied by a series of small silver pennies which used combinations of the great variety of types found on the contemporary bracteates. Some of these are standing figures but the majority are heraldic—a shield surmounted by three peacock feathers with a heart on either side, a helmet with two horns, two keys or towers.

Franconia

At Frankfurt-on-Main, the most important mint in the Wetterau, the issue of silver pennies was a restricted one in comparison with that of bracteates under Frederick I, but in the reign of Frederick II and his son Henry VII silver pennies formed a more substantial issue. The types were the imperial bust and a three-towered building with an arch enclosing a lion. Coins of this type were also struck at Gelnhausen and Oppenheim for these two emperors, as well as a series with eagle within arch on the reverse for Frederick II at Friedberg. Pennies struck for Henry, Landgrave of Hesse (1247–84), during his minority have the portrait and titles of his mother and regent, Sophia, Duchess of Brabant, and either a portrait of the young Henry, a building or the lion of Hesse. Other mints in Franconia which issued the silver penny in this period were Battenberg, Münzenberg and Nassau.

One of the most persistent but monotonous series was that struck by the bishops of Würzburg, for the types are often repetitions of those established on the pennies of Bruno (1034–45), the first bishop to issue an autonomous coinage. From the issues of Emicho (1125–46) till the early fourteenth century the obverse shows the facing bust of the bishop with varying attributes—crozier, Gospel or pennant—and the reverse is one or other of the two types of Bruno, either a building or a monogram of Bruno's name (Pl. 656).

Swabia

The silver pennies of the bishops of Strasburg are small pieces with a raised edge and bear as a rule no episcopal names. Types include the facing bust of the bishop with crozier, simply inscribed *Episcopus* and a building reverse with the mint name *Argentina*. In 1296 Bishop Conrad von Lichtenberg contracted out the coinage to a group of citizens and subsequent issues, though usually with ecclesiastical types, are mostly uninscribed. At the end of the thirteenth century also the imperial mint at Hall began the issue of a series which was to be the model of a number of mints in Swabia, Franconia and Bavaria. The types of the coins which came to be known from their original mint as heller are a hand, the city arms and a cross. A typical square outline surrounds the centre of the flan and the type (Pl. 658).

(b) Regions with only denars

The areas in which the silver penny of more usual fabric and with types on both sides was struck were predominantly in the west and south and many of the mints which issued this coinage lie in territory now included in, for example, the Netherlands and Austria which are dealt with in separate sections. The issues here considered are those mainly of the Rhineland, Westphalia and Bavaria.

Rhineland

The imperial issues of Cologne which had been practically superseded by the episcopal issues since the mid eleventh century were begun again by Frederick I (1152–90). The types are the seated figure of the emperor holding cross on globe and sceptre with a building on the reverse and an inscription *Sa Colonia Paic Mat* (Sancta Colonia Pacis Mater) often in blundered form. A similar imperial coinage was continued throughout the twelfth century. The more prolific coinage, however, continued to be that of the archbishops who, from the time of Philip of Heinsberg (1167–91), are represented with mitre and not bare-headed as before. The complete obverse type is that of the seated figure of the archbishop in mitre, holding crozier and Gospel and an inscription with name and title. The reverse, still the triple-domed building, is now rendered with more care and is inscribed *Sancta Colonia* (Pl. 657). These remained the standard types into the early fourteenth century, though individual issues show a variety of elaborations, particularly of the reverse.

The mint at Aachen also recovered importance under Frederick I who is portrayed seated facing with globe on sword. The reverse, a building, is inscribed *Roma Caput Mundi*. Another issue instituted in 1166 with the facing bust of the emperor on obverse had as its reverse the facing bust of Charlemagne, adorned with large moustache and inscribed *S Carol Imp*, an allusion to his canonization in the preceding year. Versions of these two coins were struck by succeeding emperors. On issues of both William of Holland (1247–56) and of Richard of Cornwall (1257–69) as King of the Romans the obverse figure holds a sceptre instead of a sword or halberd. Under Rudolph of Hapsburg (1273–91) the reverse, a three-towered building and crown, is inscribed *Urbs Aquensis Vince*. The silver pennies of the archbishops of Trier in this period were often pieces of small module, but under Baldwin of Luxemburg (1307–54) a fine series was struck including silver sterlings with types, a facing mitred bust and crossed keys.

The imperial mint at Dortmund struck for Otto IV (1198–1212) a coinage imitating the English short-cross penny of Henry III but with the imperial title and reverse inscription *Tremonia regia*. As at Aachen, the coins of William of Holland and Richard of Cornwall have a seated figure with sceptre and on the reverse the earlier Dortmund type, a building with a central tower. Under Rudolph of Hapsburg the seated emperor was retained as the obverse type but the reverse, a facing head within a triangle, was a copy of contemporary Irish pennies. The head here is that of St. Renaud. On the issues of the bishops of Münster it is under Thierry III (1218–26) that the modern name makes its first appearance, Latinized in the inscription *Monasterium*. The silver pennies of Bishop Ludolf (1227–48) include imitations of the English short-cross penny but with a rose instead of three pellets in the angles. His coinage with types, the seated bishop and head of St. Paul, was the model for issues of his successors. This placing of the relevant saint on the reverse was a feature of other episcopal coinages in Westphalia: St. Peter with key at Osnabruck, St. Liborius at Paderborn, St. Vitus at Corvey.

Lotharingia

The silver pennies of the bishops of Metz of the twelfth century show the decline in module and weight general in the period. The types instituted by Dietrich of Ban (1179–1212), bust of the bishop and blessing hand on crozier, set a pattern for some time but in the course of the thirteenth century gave way to a figure of the bishop raising hand in benediction and a cross with blessing hand superimposed on it. Later issues of the bishopric of Toul were based on the types of Metz but a coinage at Liverdun for Peter of Brixei (1127–68), though it has the usual building type inscribed with his name, *Petrus*, presents a novel reverse, a fish and mint name *Libdun*.

Bavaria

The most important mint of the period was that of Regensburg which was shared both by the bishop and the duke of Bavaria. In 1180 Henry the Lion was compelled by the emperor Frederick I to renounce Bavaria in favour of Otto of Wittelsbach. To him is attributed the uninscribed coins with obverse type, an eagle, the badge of the Wittelsbachs and a figure of the duke on reverse. The joint issues of bishop and duke of the thirteenth century have as their most common types the bust of either bishop or duke on obverse and the busts of both enclosed in separate arches on the reverse. Under Duke Otto III and Bishop Heinrich Roteneck (1277–96) began the coinage with similar types but with the initials H - O added on either side of the obverse bust. Issues of this type continued until late in the fourteenth century.

A feature of coinage in the thirteenth and fourteenth centuries which does not emerge very clearly from the mode of discussion necessarily employed but which requires some emphasis is the growth in the number of cities with coinage rights. These rights were transferred from the original authority—imperial, feudal or ecclesiastical—either by direct sale or by contracting. Amongst the more important in later centuries should be noted the following: Hamburg and Lüneburg 1293, Brunswick 1296, Strasburg 1296, Hanover 1322, Rostock 1325, Frankfurt-on-Main 1346, Göttingen 1351, Hall in 1396 and, in the early fifteenth century, Mainz in 1420.

GROSCHEN AND EARLY GOLD (c. 1300–1500)

In the later thirteenth century the more widespread use of coinage throughout society and the use of larger sums of money which the growth of trade and the general improvement in the economy of western Europe had made necessary rendered inadequate the monetary system of Germany in which the unit was still the silver penny. In the course of trade the larger silver denominations, as well as gold coinage which countries to the west and south had begun to issue in the latter half of the century, had become familiar in Germany as well and set the example for native issues.

The first major silver piece from abroad to exert an influence on German coinage was the French gros tournois of 4·2 gm. instituted by Louis IX in 1266. The obverse, a cross, was surrounded by two concentric circles of inscription, on the inner *Ludovicus Rex,* on the outer *Benedictum sit nomen Domini nostri Dei Jesu Christi*; on the reverse a castle with two towers was inscribed *Turonus Civis* and the enclosing border was decorated with twelve fleur-de-lis. By 1300 these coins commonly known in Germany as groschen had become a familiar currency. The French gros did not only gain wide acceptance but was widely copied. In many cases the original types were retained while the French title on the obverse was replaced by that of the issuing authority or the mint but in other instances the coin was freely adapted and new types such as portraits or arms were substituted for the original French types. The influence of the gros and its copies was most marked in the Rhineland and Westphalia. Another category of groschen in Meissen and Saxony derived its inspiration indirectly through the Bohemian groschen with its types of lion and crown struck by Wenceslas II in 1300. The original Meissen types of a lion and a floral cross were joined in the course of the next two centuries by a wide variety of types some of which gave their names to such coinages as sword groschen or angel groschen. The influence of the Meissen groschen made itself felt also in Hesse and Brunswick.

The imposition of a monetary unity in this period of development was now beyond the waning power of the central authority but, instead, a series of monetary agreements was reached by minting authorities which were striking coin based on an identical standard. In the Rhineland the groschen was the Weisspfennig or Albus with its types of St. Peter and arms of the particular participant in the coinage. Mints in Franconia issued half-groschen of the value of 4 Würzburg pfennige. The Rappenmünzbund united a large number of mints in southern Germany where the groschen which began issue in 1425 had a value of 6 rappen. A similar monetary union in Swabia, including the mints of Würtemburg and Augsburg, struck a coinage of schillings and heller and in the north-east a coinage first of witten of value 4 pfennig and later of schillings was issued in Pomerania, Mecklenburg and east Friesland.

Regular issues of gold coinage made their reappearance in western Europe in 1252 with the introduction by Florence of the florin of 3·5 gm. with its types of St. John the Baptist and the lily, the badge of Florence. This coin, termed a gulden, gained ready acceptance in Germany where it was widely and faithfully copied till the last decades of the fourteenth century. Gradually the types of the Florentine gold piece were altered: the portrait of the feudal lord or bishop replaced St. John on the obverse and the Florentine lily gave place to the issuer's arms. In 1356 the right to issue gold coinage was extended by the emperor to such of the important feudal nobility and electors as had not yet been granted this privilege. Gold coinage as well as silver was the subject of monetary agreements such as that in the Rhineland which established a gold gulden of 3·5 gm. and of the value of 20 Weisspfennigen.

The second great influence on German gold coinage was that of the Venetian ducat with its types of St. Mark and kneeling doge on obverse and figure of Christ in oval frame on the reverse, first introduced in 1284. The popular term applied to this coin is derived from the last word of the reverse inscription *Sit tibi Christe datus, quem tu regis, iste ducatus*. Since the ducat was successful in maintaining its standard as against the fall in weight and fineness which affected the gulden, the term ducat finally triumphed as the acceptable name of the gold piece.

In the course of the fifteenth century the supply of gold bullion became inadequate and this, coupled with the greater exploitation of the silver of the Tyrol, the Erzgebirge and the Schwarzwald provided the conditions for the introduction of still larger silver denominations. Again the impetus of the production of these new silver pieces came from abroad where, in Italy, about 1475 the silver lira was introduced in Venice and the testone in Milan. Pieces similar to the Italian testone were struck in the Rhineland under the name of Dicken, valued at 3 to a gold gulden. In 1484 Sigismund, Duke of Tyrol, struck at the mint of Hall a large piece in silver of the value of the Rhineland gold gulden. All but the final step had now been taken towards the famous large silver pieces, the thalers, whose issue marks the beginning of the modern period of coinage in Germany. Something of the detail of the coinage whose course and development has been briefly sketched is now considered, once again on a geographical basis.

Imperial

By the early fourteenth century the large number of mints from which the emperors had earlier issued coin had shrunk to something just over a dozen and a good number of these struck practically identical types. The coinage of Louis IV of Bavaria (1314–47) who became emperor in 1328 include some of the earliest examples of the adaptation of the French gros tournois. Silver groschen of Louis sometimes substitute only his name *Ludovicus Impr* for that of the French king on the original, but other examples have *Ludovicus Quart* on the obverse and on the reverse round the castle, have either the conclusion of his title *Romanor Imp(er)ator* or the name of the mint. Louis also struck sterlings with facing bust, crowned, at Aachen and silver pennies at Dortmund with the usual types of seated king and bust in triangle. Gold florins were struck by Charles IV (1347–78) at Frankfurt with types of St. John and eagle above shield but under Sigismund (1410–37) gold was struck at some seven German mints. At Frankfurt the usual types of the gold gulden were St. John either with cross and sceptre or holding a lamb on obverse and on the reverse a globe surmounted by a cross (Pl. 659), but another variety had a standing figure of Charlemagne on the obverse. The majority of the mints struck the type of St. John with lamb on the gold gulden but Hamburg had its special obverse type of St. Peter. These continued to be the chief types on the gold of Frederick V (1440–93) and Maximilian I (1493–1519).

The counts of Cleve had received the right of coinage in their own name in 1298 but it was only under John I (1347–68) that a coinage of gold and of larger silver pieces was begun. The gold florin retained the lily type but carried the name of its mint, Büderich, as did the early groschen. Later issues had the count's name, *Johannes Comes*. In the reign of Adolf VI (1394–1448) the county was advanced to the status of a duchy, and the coinage which was mainly of heraldic types carried the new title and from 1436, frequently, a date in Roman numerals. Duke John I (1448–81) introduced on the gold gulden his own standing figure and a quartered shield on a long cross and on the groschen a facing portrait bust between two small shields. John II (1481–1521) continued this coinage until with the introduction of the thaler in 1512 a new mint was opened at Emmerich. The first groschen of the counts of Berg were struck by Adolf VIII (1308–48) at Mulheim with his standing or seated figure on the obverse. Parallel to the imperial groschen struck at Berg was a series in the name of Adolf (Pl. 660). Gerard of Julich (1348–60), who obtained the county of Berg through his marriage to Adolf's heiress, Margaret of Ravensberg, issued groschen with his seated figure holding sceptre and globe and at his feet a shield quartered with lions. As William II (1361–93) was advanced to the rank of duke in 1380 his coinage falls into two categories, first with the title of count, then with that of duke. His gold florin has a half-length figure of the duke on the obverse, as does the groschen struck at Mulheim. This mint issued another type of groschen with as its main type the quartered arms of Julich and Berg with the arms of Ravensberg at the centre. Groschen of the tournois type with inscription *Wilhelmus Comes* were also struck at Remagen. The extensive issues of William are in contrast to those of Adolf (1408–23) whose principal coins were groschen with the arms type. On the death of Reynald IV of Julich in 1423, Adolf succeeded to the duchy of Julich but apart from the inclusion of the new duchy in his title his coinage showed no further change save for the issue of gold florins of St. John and orb type. Gerard VI (1437–75) added groschen with shield and helmet type and issues between 1451 and 1453 are marked with a date in Roman numerals. The gold guldens of William IV (1475–1511) were of several varieties; some carried the standing figure of St. Hubert and an arms reverse, others the types of the Rhineland convention—a standing saint and the arms of the moneying authority surrounded by the arms of the other participants. The coinage of Julich, in this period before its union with Berg, begins with William who has three successive titles: that of count (1329–36), margrave (1336–57) and duke (1357–61). On his groschen as margrave William placed on the obverse the

Three Kings, one kneeling and two standing, and on the reverse the standing Virgin and child between two lion-shields. As duke he issued gold guldens still with lis type and groschen with seated figure and reverse, shield on long cross. William III (1393–1402) struck a variety of groschen including one with his facing bust crowned within a tressure of twelve arches, a type copied from the English groat of Edward III. Gold guldens of Reynald IV (1402–23) were of two principal varieties. The first with obverse of St. John and reverse of the arms of Julich accompanied by the arms of Mainz, Cologne and Trier represented the monetary convention of 1409; the second with obverse of St. Peter had the five shields of the participants in the convention of 1419.

Towards the middle of the fourteenth century the mint of Aachen ceased to be imperial and struck only city coinage. The figure of Charlemagne was the most usual type or the principal component of the type on groschen. The coinage of the archbishops of Cologne, however, was at this time one of the most important of the Rhineland, beginning with the issues of groschen and gold guldens under Walram of Julich (1332–49). The Cologne groschen was already independent, as far as types is concerned, of the original French piece, for it shows the mitred portrait of the bishop with shield on breast on the obverse and carries the name of the mint of Bonn, but the gold gulden still used the original lis device. On groschen William of Genep (1349–62) is represented seated on a chair ornamented with lion-heads with his shield of arms at his feet. The issues of guldens and groschen for Engelbert III (1366–70) are related in type to those of Conon, Archbishop of Trier and Coadjutor of Cologne (1367–8) and later administrator (1368–70). In 1386 a convention was agreed by the archbishops of Cologne, Mainz and Trier and the Count Palatine of the Rhine for the issue of gold guldens which should have the standing figure of St. John on the obverse and on the reverse within a trefoil the arms of the issuer, together with the smaller arms of the remaining members (Pl. 661). In 1417 under Thierry II (1414–63) the figure of St. Peter replaced that of St. John on the gulden and, though in the same year Reynald of Julich joined the convention, the reverse did not include his arms until 1419. A new convention between the three archbishops and the Count Palatine in 1425 did not stipulate the types to be used on the florin, and at Cologne the gulden showed the standing archbishop and the reverse a single shield or else an enthroned Christ and St. Andrew's cross with small shield in each angle. Between 1473 and 1480 when Hermann IV of Hesse was only Vicar of Cologne his guldens used the types of bust of St. Peter and his own arms alone, not those of the convention, but as archbishop (1480–1508) he issued guldens of the types agreed by yet another convention in 1490 which prescribed as types an enthroned Christ and again the conjunction of arms of the participants inscribed

Moneta aurea Rhenen, as well as the date. The types now established lasted through-out the sixteenth century. The grant of coinage to the city of Cologne came only in 1474. The types of the gulden were either a seated Christ with shield of Cologne at feet or the arms of the city on a cross with star in each corner, both having as reverse the imperial globe and the names of the Three Kings, *Jasper, Melchior, Balthesar*. Groschen were, basically, imitations of the French gros with the double inscription of the reverse an abbreviated form of *Grossus Civitatis Colonie/Agrippina olim dicte* (Pl. 662).

At Trier the first issues of the new silver and gold coins were made by Arch-bishop Bohemund (1354–62). The gulden maintained the original types of the Florentine florin, St. John and the lily around which was the archbishop's name and title, *Boemund Arepus*. On the groschen the obverse showed the archbishop seated on a chair ornamented with lion-heads with shield at feet and the reverse the original types and inscriptions of the French gros but with the mint name of Coblenz, *Moneta Confluen*. Conon who had been coadjutor of Bohemund in 1461 and became archbishop in the following year issued guldens with the joined arms of Trier and Minzenberg on reverse and various obverses, including the traditional St. John and St. Peter standing or sitting, holding a long cross and key. As successively coadjutor, administrator and vicar of Cologne between 1367 and 1371 he struck similar guldens with the appropriate variations on his title. In the last period of his rule (1371–88) the types of the gulden were those of the monetary convention described for Cologne above. On Conon's groschen appeared his standing figure, mitred and holding Gospel and crozier, closer imitations of the gros tournois with heraldic types, and a series with half-length portrait of St. Peter and shield of arms (Pl. 663). Guldens of his successors, when they were not using the types prescribed by the Rhenish convention, usually carried representations of St. Peter who also formed the chief type on groschen.

Gerlach of Nassau (1346–71) was responsible for the first regular issues of guldens and groschen at Mainz, though the imitation of the Florentine florin at Mainz had first been struck by Conon of Trier as administrator of Trier (1346–54). Gerlach's guldens continued the florin types on his gold and imitated the French gros on his groschen. St. Martin enthroned was the obverse type for Adolf I of Nassau (1373–90) whose arms appear at St. Martin's feet; the reverse shows a shield with wheel device of Mainz. Adolf's succession was disputed by the emperor and he was not enthroned till 1381. Shortly after this his guldens take on the types of the Rhenish convention and apart from a continuation of a parallel local series with type of St. Martin by Conrad II (1391–6) guldens of Mainz follow the changes of the Rhenish convention already described. Groschen and other silver used types of St. Martin, St. Peter or purely heraldic devices.

In the County Palatine of the Rhine Rupert, Duke of Bavaria (1329–90), transformed the traditional types of the gulden, St. John and the lily, into a figure of St. John but with a reverse formed of his arms in a frame of three arches and three triangles, a combination of types which was to form the basis of the typology of subsequent issues by the monetary convention of the Rhineland (Pl. 664). The types on guldens of successive counts and electors mainly followed the prescriptions of the convention. Under Philip I (1476–1508) the gulden types were the Virgin and Child and three shields with the letter P above; on some of the groschen appeared the bust of Philip.

Swabia

The widespread issue of gold and of silver groschen in the Rhineland which has just been described finds no parallel in Swabia which, in common with the greater part of south Germany, used a currency of smaller silver denominations. The heller was widely struck as well as the pfennig, batzen, kreuzer and schilling. The mint of Hall from which the term heller (or haller) was derived continued the issue of its denars or heller with types of open hand and cross throughout the fourteenth and fifteenth centuries. The larger silver with obverse the double-headed eagle inscribed *Maximilian Romanor Imp* and reverse two shields with cross and hand inscribed *Moneta Nova Swabisch Hal* have a date in Roman numerals above the shields from 1512 onwards. The coinage of the counts of Würtemburg which began in the time of Eberhard II (1344–92) was also exclusively of small silver heller with types of two stag-heads. About the beginning of the fifteenth century Eberhard III issued schillings with arms and cross types at the mint of Stuttgart, but the earliest gold guldens appeared only under Ulric VI (1498–1550) when the types were the standing figure of the duke and a shield of arms (Pl. 665). The bishops of Augsburg throughout the fourteenth and fifteenth centuries struck mainly the pfennig with type the mitred head of the bishop between a cross and a pinecone and the heller with open hand type.

Bavaria

In Bavaria as in Swabia the silver coinage of the later Middle Ages continued to be represented in the main by the original denomination. The silver pennies coined at Munich throughout the period had the punning type of the bust of a monk but the most general type for the dukes of Bavaria was their initial or initials contained within a raised square, the so-called *quadratum supercusum*, already mentioned on the original heller coinage of Hall. The first gold gulden was issued by Albert IV (1465–1508) only in 1506. The types of this coin were the duke kneeling before the Virgin and Child with on the reverse the usual shield of arms with the date above (Pl. 666). Similarly at Regensburg the gold gulden with types, arms and standing figure of St. Peter was first struck for Bishop John III (1507–38) and groschen also began issue only in this reign. The city of Regensburg obtained the right of coinage in the late fourteenth century and the first gulden was struck in 1512 with shield on obverse and standing figure of St. Wolfgang on the reverse.

Franconia

This geographic division had long ceased to have any political connotation but its use is continued from previous sections as a convenient link to coinages already described. The first issues of the burggraves of Nuremberg were made by Albert I in 1361, a pfennig coinage with types of hound's head and lion. In 1396 the Burggrave Frederick VI struck in accordance with a monetary convention with Lambert, Bishop of Bamberg, and Rupert, Count Palatine, a coinage of schillings marked *Moneta maior* and used the arms of the participants as types. The gold gulden introduced by Albert Achilles (1457–86) with its type of St. John holding a lamb and a reverse of four shields was continued by his successors. The mints for this coinage were at Neustadt, Bayreuth and Schwabach, not at Nuremberg itself. In addition to the coinage of the convention with Nuremberg mentioned above, Bishops Lambert (1374–99) and Albert (1399–1421) issued schillings with their own arms and later in the fourteenth century the lion of Bamberg was a frequent type. The first gulden was struck by George III in 1506 with standing figure of St. Henry and reverse, a crown above two shields. The coinage of the bishopric of Würzburg throughout the fourteenth century was a continuation of the pfennig with types, arms and monogram of Bruno described in the previous section. New coinage introduced by Gerard of Schwarzburg (1372–1400) consisted of the gold gulden with types, St. John and shield and the schilling with standing figure of St. Kilian and the bishop's arms of Schwarzburg. Würzburg, as has been already mentioned, shared in the conventional coinage with Bamberg and Nuremberg. Subsequent bishops placed their own arms on the silver coinage (Pl. 667) but the gulden was not issued again till 1506 when Laurence of Bibra (1495–1519) used as the obverse type the figure of St. Kilian.

Thuringia

The pfennig of the principality of Anhalt up to the fifteenth century continued to be the often uninscribed type previously described but on the death of George I in 1474 the principality was divided between Waldemar VI and a number of brothers. A gold gulden of this period shows the standing figure of St. Anne and shield of arms. Groschen with a variety of types including St. Bernard and the Virgin and Child as well as heraldic devices were also issued. The city of Erfurt which obtained the right of coinage in the mid fourteenth century continued to issue a bracteate coinage till well into the fifteenth century when issues of groschen began with type of St. Martin on horse-back. In the margravate of Osterland and Meissen the groschen modelled on the lion groschen of Bohemia probably began issue as early as Frederick I (1274–1320) and the types continued to be used by subsequent margraves. The lion obverse carries the inscription *Grossus Marchionis Misnensis* and the reverse a floral cross is inscribed *Frid Di Gra Turing Langrav* (Pl. 668). Osterland which had been detached as a separate margravate in 1349 was created the Duchy of Saxony and the rank of prince-elector conferred on Frederick in 1423. His groschen normally have as types a helmet on obverse and shield on reverse or lion obverse and floral-cross reverse. Many of the groschen from this point until late in the fifteenth century carry the names of the several contemporary members of the family.

Westphalia

A plentiful issue of groschen from Dortmund in the fifteenth century depicted on the obverse the portrait of the city's patron saint, St. Reynold, with inscription *Sanctus Reinoldus Martir* and on the reverse the imperial eagle. Dortmund also minted gold guldens in the names of the emperors. An issue for Sigismund (1411–38) has a St. John obverse and imperial globe reverse with the emperor's name. Issues for Frederick V between 1470 and 1480 and for Maximilian I in 1500 have the same orb reverse but a standing figure of the emperor as obverse. The new coinage had its first real introduction at Münster under Bishop John III of Simmen (1457–66) who struck gold guldens with bust of St. Paul and on the reverse his arms on a cross, and schillings and their portions in silver with similar types. His successor Henry III (1466–96) issued a similar range of coins but on the silver appeared the types agreed by a monetary convention which included Cologne, Osnabrück, Dortmund and Cleve. These were a shield under a helmet and three shields grouped on the reverse with Gothic letter M at the centre. On the gulden St. Paul remained on the obverse but on the reverse the Gothic letter H, the initial of the bishop's name, was placed at the centre of the three shields. Similar types were used on the gulden (Pl. 669) of Conrad II (1497–1508). The right of coinage granted to the counts of Oldenburg in the first decade of the eleventh century produced at first only a series of uninscribed bracteates with a simple letter O as type. Groschen in the style of the French gros were struck by John XI (1340-45) with the substitution of either the mint name, *Moneta Oldenb*, or the count's name, *Iohanes Comes*. Later in the fourteenth century groschen of Conrad II and Christian VI had as types a bishop raising his hand in blessing and holding the shield of Oldenburg with as reverse the episcopal bust, mitred and holding a sword. A wall with three towers formed the obverse and a cross pattée, with one arm terminating in a point, the reverse of groschen of Nicholas (1425-47). These types were also used on the flindrich or piece of 4 groten struck in the later fifteenth century. The various cantons of east Friesland issued coinage in the names of their respective chiefs who functioned under a variety of titles such as praepositus or domicellus. Coinage of groschen type was struck by a number of these cantons such as Emden where Imelo Abdena (1429–33) has as his types a shield on rampant lion with inscription *Imelo praeposit z capit i Amed* and a long cross on reverse with the letters of the mint name AMED in the angles as well as an inscription, *Moneta Nova in Amed*. Gold was also struck as, for instance, by Udo of Norden (1421–33) with types of St. Ludger and lion shield accompanied by three smaller shields. Later guldens in the fifteenth century usually had types of St. John or St. Peter and the imperial orb.

Lower Saxony

The first groschen of the complicated line of the dukes of Brunswick-Lüneburg was struck by Henry III of Salzerhelden (1427–63) with obverse type a floral cross in a tressure of four arches and inscription *Heinric Dei Gra Dux Br* and reverse a lion supporting a shield and inscription *Grossus Ducis Brunswike*. These remained the chief types in the fifteenth century with occasional variations such as the Madonna or St. Andrew. The cities of Lübeck, Hamburg and Wismar by a monetary convention in 1379 began an issue of witten, pieces of 4 pfennige. The obverse carried the badge of the issuing city, the tower in the case of Hamburg and the mint name, *Moneta Hamburg*, but the reverse, a cross with star at centre and inscription *Benedictus Deus*, was used in common (Pl. 670). In 1381 Rostock and Lüneburg joined the convention. The denomination proved popular and a succession of conventions regulating its issue were made up to the middle of the sixteenth century. In 1432 the same cities agreed to the issue of a series of schillings which had as obverse the appropriate city shield and name and as reverse a cross with quadrant centre. Later in 1468 came an issue of double schillings. At Hamburg this denomination had on obverse the half-length portrait of the Madonna inscribed *Conserva nos Domina* and the three tower arms of the city at the centre of an ornate cross with the mint name around, *Mone nova Hamburge*.

Brandenburg

Throughout most of the fourteenth century the coinage of the margraves of Brandenburg continued to be the small silver pieces with types of margrave holding sword and pennant or other attributes in either hand and an eagle or cross on reverse. When the mark came into the possession of the Hohenzollerns when it was gifted by the emperor Sigismund to Frederick VI of Nuremberg (1415–40) the Brandenburg issues proper consisted still of the so-called *vinkenauge* with types of eagle and helmet, but groschen were also struck at mints including Brandenburg itself. The obverse, the Brandenburg eagle shield, bore the name of Frederick as Elector, *Fredericus Imp Elector*, and the reverse inscribed *Moneta No March Brandbo* carried a quartered shield of arms. Frederick also struck gold guldens where he is entitled *Frideric Margr Bn'gn* and with types, St. John and eagle. On later groschen the obverse a cross with shields in the angles bears the margrave's name; the reverse, an eagle, is inscribed *Grossus novus Brand'bar'*.

Pomerania

Pomerania at this time was divided into the four duchies of Stettin, Wolgast, Barth and Stolp. On the coinage of witten, 4 pfennig pieces, the usual type is a griffin with an inscription, e.g. *Moneta Duc Wolgast*, which does not specify the name of the particular duke. Similarly the schilling bears only the title *Dux Pomeranie* but the shield at the centre of the long cross on either side incorporates the griffin badge and that of the particular duchy. Only towards the end of the fifteenth century are the issues more specific. Bogeslav X, Duke of Stettin (1474–1523), began to issue gold guldens in 1499 with types of Madonna and shield on long cross, the obverse being clearly inscribed *Bogeslaus D G Dux Stettine*. Identical types were repeated on the large silver coins known as bugslawer, but witten of the earlier variety were also continued (Pl. 671).

The coinage of the Teutonic Order in Prussia produced its first major silver piece under Winrich de Kniprode in 1370. This groschen type coinage, termed a halbskoter, had the arms of the grand master of the Order as obverse type with inscription *Moneta Dominorum Prussie* while the reverse, an ornate cross within a tressure of four arches, is inscribed *Honor Magistri iudicium diligat*. This denomination was struck only by Winrich but the other denomination introduced by him, the silver schilling, was continued by his successors. The obverse type was also the shield of the master but bore in addition his name, *Magst Wynrics Primus*; the reverse was the plain shield with cross of the Order with inscription, *Moneta Dnorum Pruci* (Pl. 672).

MODERN COINAGE (*c.* 1500–1806)

The limits of the period whose coinage is now to be considered are marked by the introduction of the large silver coins of the thaler class about the beginning of the sixteenth century and the end of the Holy Roman empire which followed Napoleon's victory at Austerlitz in 1806. The right of coinage remained theoretically still with the emperor and regulations regarding coinage were decreed by the emperor and the seven prince-electors, though, as it will appear, the implementation of these decrees was a matter of some difficulty in view of the considerable political independence enjoyed by the component states of the empire which was divided into ten 'circles'. The outline of the coinage of the period which now follows deals with these circles in succession, with the exception of Burgundy (roughly modern Belgium) and Austria which receive separate treatment. To the German 'circles' must be added Prussia which always held aloof from incorporation in this system.

The first of the large silver coins which have come to be regarded as typical of this period of German coinage was produced in 1484 by Archduke Sigismund in the Tyrol. These large pieces, tariffed at 60 kreuzer, were known as gulden groschen, for their silver value was the equivalent of the gold gulden. Imitation of this coinage, widespread and immediate, included the gulden groschen first struck in 1520 by Graf Stephen Schlick and his brother in Joachimstal with types of St. Joachim with the arms of Schlick at his feet and the lion of Bohemia on the reverse (Pl. 718). The name Joachimsthaler, derived from the place of mintage, was abbreviated into thaler, the generic name applied to all large pieces of this category. The spread of coinage of gulden groschen and thalers of various categories with their subdivisions rendered necessary some attempt to establish a unified coinage system for the empire and the monetary history of the next two centuries is one of a succession of unavailing attempts to create such a system.

The first of these attempts were the regulations promulgated at Esslingen in 1524 by Charles V establishing a silver guldener, tariffed at 8 Cologne marks and equivalent in value to a gold gulden, as well as various subdivisions down to the groschlein which was $\frac{1}{48}$ of the guldener. The types prescribed were the imperial eagle and inscription on the obverse with on the reverse the arms of the issuing authority accompanied by another device and the date. The gold gulden also was to bear the imperial arms on the obverse. This measure was opposed by Austria and by the states in whose territories were ample supplies of silver. A fresh edict in 1551 established a silver gulden of 72 kreuzer and smaller pieces down to 1 kreuzer with an obverse type of the imperial eagle with the value in kreuzer within the imperial globe on its breast, and permission was granted to some states to continue the issue of well-established denominations, such as the albus in the Rhineland or the groschen in Franconia. The silver gulden was retariffed at 60 kreuzers by Ferdinand I in 1559 without change of type. The thaler which had been prescribed was again permitted to be issued in 1566 at a value of 68 kreuzer and this denomination, known as the reichsthaler, soon ousted the silver gulden. Economic chaos aggravated by the Thirty Years' war which broke out in 1618 brought with it a tremendous adulteration of the coinage. This is the period to which the term *kipperzeit* or *wipperzeit* has been applied, the period when clipping and melting down of good coin was the common practice. The monetary system was rescued from anarchy by an ordonnance of Ferdinand II in 1622 which fixed the tariff of the reichsthaler at 90 kreuzer and of the gulden thaler at 80 kreuzer. The three monetary systems adapted their coinages to this standard so that in the south where the money of account was still the Rhenish gulden of 60 kreuzer the thaler of 90 kreuzer was reckoned at 3 groschen or $1\frac{1}{2}$ gold gulden, in the centre where the thaler was the unit, the gulden of account was reckoned at 20 groschen or $\frac{2}{3}$ gulden and finally in the north the mark was reckoned at $\frac{1}{3}$ thaler and divided into 16 schillings. This system also underwent modifications and in 1667 the states with supplies of silver in their territory, namely Saxony, Brandenburg and Brunswick-Lüneburg, established a new convention at Zinna, the outcome of which was the issue of denominations of $\frac{2}{3}$, $\frac{1}{3}$ and $\frac{1}{6}$ thaler pieces. The $\frac{2}{3}$ thaler piece, where the thaler system was in operation, was valued at 24 mariengroschen; where the gulden was the money of account, it equalled 60 kreuzer and in the north 2 marks or 32 schillings. Later agreements altered the evaluation of the basic thaler but not the denominations of $\frac{2}{3}$, $\frac{1}{3}$ and $\frac{1}{6}$ thaler pieces which continued to be issued by the central states, and subsequently the coinage systems of the south were also established on this basis. A convention reached in 1753 between Austria and Bavaria lowered the intrinsic value of the thaler and established a system which included in gold the ducat with its multiples and subdivisions, in silver the new Convention thaler and subdivisions as well as pieces of 20 and 10 kreuzer and groschen of 3 kreuzer value. By 1764 the remaining German states except Prussia and Hanover had adopted this new basis; in the centre and north the silver denominations issued were the new species-thaler with portions from $\frac{2}{3}$ down to $\frac{1}{48}$ thaler pieces. In 1750 Frederick II of Prussia introduced his own system. In gold the 'Frederick' with its half and its double was struck and in silver the reichsthaler, equivalent to 24 groschen and portions from $\frac{1}{2}$ to half-thaler.

The externals of the German coinage in the sixteenth to eighteenth centuries present a certain number of typical features. The increasing use of machinery for the striking of coin had the effect here as elsewhere of the production of a more compact and regular flan and the use of roller dies, particularly in the seventeenth century, imparted a slightly eliptical shape to some of the issues. Gothic script gave way to Roman and most coinages were marked both with a date and their value. Types became to a certain extent more conventional. The obverse was reserved more and more for the portrait bust of the emperor, prince or other issuing authority and heraldic arms formed the common reverse motif, though often in conjunction with a subsidiary type. The large flan of the thaler-type coin and even more of the multiple thaler presented greater scope to the die-cutter than in earlier centuries. These large silver coins often partake largely of the nature of occasion pieces and reverse designs commemorate such events as accessions, coronations, jubilees, victories and even deaths and such pieces are, in effect, medals rather than ordinary pieces of currency. A particularly remarkable series is that of the 'mine thalers' coined by states such as Brunswick-Lüneburg from their rich silver deposits and displaying on these thalers something of the mine-workings. A similar pictorial class of thalers is that which shows a medallic view of the issuing city. The gold ducat in this period presented similar features of treatment on the score of design, particularly some of the lavish multiples of which some are of as high a value as 10 ducats.

Two further external features of the German coinage of this period require mention. The first is the matter of titles. Throughout the centuries a whole chain of titles had become attached to the various princes, dukes and other coin-issuing authorities and on many coin issues all these titles are included in the inscriptions but, as space is limited, the titles and even the name is reduced to a series of initials which are, at first inspection, quite incomprehensible and can be elucidated only by reference to the specialist literature which has been produced on this subject. Some of the more notorious examples require no less than forty initials to enumerate the names and titles of the issuer. An equally bewildering feature, particularly on the smaller denominations, is the use of a complicated monogram as the sole distinguishing type. Such pieces, again, can be identified only by reference to specialist works devoted to their interpretation.

Now that the basic monetary systems and the principal external features of the coinage have been outlined, something of the actual issues of the various state and city coinages will be sketched. At the risk of a little repetition but in the interests of intelligibility the coinages of the various 'circles' of the empire will be considered in succession rather than as one comprehensive chronological development.

Bavaria

The monetary system at the beginning of the sixteenth century consisted of the gold gulden which in the reigns of William IV and Louis X (1516–45) had as types the seated Madonna and shield of arms, of groschen and half-batzen in silver with shield and lion as types and the silver pfennig, a concave uniface piece with shield type. Under Albert V (1550–79) a gold 2 ducat piece was struck with the duke's bust to right with sword over shoulder and a shield reverse. In this reign too the first Bavarian thalers were issued with types of local arms and double-headed eagle in conformity with the imperial ordonnance. On one of the series of 2 ducat pieces of Maximilian I (1598–1651), the duke kneels before the Madonna on the obverse inscribed O *Maria ora pro me* (Pl. 673), and on large 5 ducat pieces stands the full-length figure of the prince-elector, holding sword and globe, while on the reverse is a view of the city of Munich. In this reign the Madonna, patron of Bavaria, appeared also on the thaler coinage. On the kreuzer coinage of Maximilian Emmanuel (1679–1726) the types are the duke's bust on obverse and on reverse a lion supporting a shield with, below in brackets, the value in kreuzer (Pl. 674).

The gold of Charles Albert (1726–44) with bust and Madonna types was the equivalent of the 2 ducat piece and was known as the Carolin of which there were also halves and quarters. Maximilian Joseph (1745–77) issued a kreuzer series with his head inside a circle of laurel and as reverse a shield of arms on a pedestal containing the values 20 or 10. On lower values the shield, contained inside a collar, separated the value, e.g. 3—K. A copper coinage had simple types, the Bavarian arms and the denomination 1 pfennig in words and the date. A similar coinage for Charles Theodore (1777–99) had, in addition, heller pieces in copper with shield type and the word Heller in a diamond-shaped frame. The issues of this and the following reign of Maximilian Joseph IV (1799–1806) conformed to the current European fashion of a portrait head and not a bust.

Regensburg as well as issuing a city coinage with the imperial arms and its own badge of crossed keys on ducats and multiples and portions down to $\frac{1}{32}$ struck issues in gold and silver with the portraits of the emperors. A favourite reverse type in gold and large silver was a view of the city with the bridge over the river (Pl. 675). On the coinage of the archbishops of Salzburg the most common types were basically the figure of St. Rudbert and the bishop's arms. Later in the seventeenth and eighteenth centuries these were much elaborated, particularly on the many multiple gold pieces. The series of silver kreuzer followed the pattern of the Bavarian ducal series; the value in brackets below the reverse type, value on a pedestal and so on. In the eighteenth century the lower denominations began to be struck in copper with shield obverse and the denomination, 1 kreuzer, 2 or 1 pfennig in words on the reverse.

Swabia

Coinage was issued by the bishops of Augsburg up to the early nineteenth century. Ducats and thalers were struck by Alexander Sigismund (1690–1737) and Joseph of Hesse (1740–68) with their portrait busts and arms reverses but for most of the bishops the coinage is only of the smaller kreuzer denominations. The last bishop to coin, Clement Wenceslas (1768–1803), has as types his portrait and on reverse a shield on a pedestal enclosing the value in kreuzer. The kreuzer and smaller denominations were struck in copper with the denomination in words as the reverse type. Augsburg, however, was also one of the imperial mints. Throughout the sixteenth century the common types on gold were the imperial eagle with emperor's name and the pine-cone badge of the city inscribed *Augusta Vindelicorum*. Similar types were also used for the thaler and smaller denominations, the imperial orb, placed on the breast of the eagle enclosing the value of the piece. On a number of eighteenth-century issues in gold when the obverse was consistently occupied by a portrait bust or head the city is represented wearing a mural crown in the fashion of the ancient Greek city Tyche. The pine-cone badge is also occasionally shown supported by two river-gods both on gold and on thalers which, in the seventeenth century, also carried views of the city (Pl. 676). The lower denominations in the eighteenth century were here, as elsewhere, now issued in copper.

The sixteenth century saw at Hall a continuation of the small uniface heller coins with combined types of cross and open hand. A thaler-type coinage struck for Charles V (1519–58) with the usual imperial-eagle obverse had as reverse a shield with cross and open-hand devices side by side. In the seventeenth century ducats, thalers and smaller silver for most of the emperors bore their portrait busts and had on the reverse three scroll shields on which are incorporated the arms of Hall.

The earliest gold gulden of Ulric VI of Würtemburg has been mentioned in the preceding section but a later piece in 1537 has a portrait of the duke in a broad-brimmed hat, reminiscent of the bonnet piece of James V of Scotland (Pl. 677). Gold types otherwise are usually the conventional portrait bust and shield though the gulden of Eberhard Louis (1693–1733) is exceptional in its obverse type of the duke on horse-back. The 2 ducat piece under Charles Alexander (1733–7) was known as a carolin as was that of Charles Albert of Bavaria (see p. 357). In the early eighteenth century the value of the higher denominations of the kreuzer coinage was given by the reverse inscription, e.g. *Landminz* 30 *kreuzer*, round the shield of arms while the lower values were displayed across the field of the reverse. Later kreuzer series follow the pattern of kreuzer reverse types elsewhere with value given in brackets, then on pedestal and so on.

Franconia

One of the more important series in Franconia was that of the bishops of Bamberg. The earliest gold gulden struck by George III in 1506 has already been mentioned but under John Philip (1599–1609) new types were introduced on the double ducat and ducat. On the obverse St. Henry and St. Kunigunde as standing figures hold between them a model of the church but the reverse continued to be a crown above two shields; these types were continued by the immediate successors. On the obverse of the ducat of Francis (1633–42) the seated Madonna was accompanied by the abbreviated inscription *Clypeus omnibus in te sperantibus*. Smaller silver in the seventeenth century also used the St. Henry type as on obverse. He is shown in profile bust, holding an orb inscribed 4 or 2 with a shield of arms reverse. Other silver used the shield as obverse and have as a reverse simply the orb with figure of value, e.g. 84. The thaler coinage in the eighteenth century presented usually the portrait and titles of the bishop with shield-of-arms reverse. In 1800 the thalers of Christoph Franz (1795–1802) take the arms as obverse and show a view of the city on the reverse within a laurel-wreath above the standard, *X Eine feine Mark*. The kreuzer coinage of Adam Frederick (1757–79) with his obverse portrait bust has a standing-Madonna reverse with value (20) below or a shield on pedestal inscribed 20. Copper coinage has a shield obverse and reverse, the field inscribed *I/Leichter/Pfennig* (Pl. 678).

On the coinage of the bishopric of Würzburg the most popular type was that of St. Kilian but after appearing as the obverse type on the earliest guldens in 1506 it was only with the ducat and double ducat of Julius Echter (1573–1617) that he returned to the gold coinage. The reverse of this issue was the Madonna above the imperial eagle holding sceptre and sword. After the mid century St. Kilian gave place on gold to the more usual obverses on gold of a shield of arms or portrait bust. On the smaller silver of the sixteenth and seventeenth centuries St. Kilian remained the principal obverse type combined with shield reverses or orb enclosing the value in figures. The thaler coinage was devoted usually to obverse portraits of the bishops and the reverses to shields of arms with occasional use as under Adam Frederick (1755–79) of a figure of the Madonna inscribed *Patrona Franconiae*. His kreuzer coinage here was similar to that at Bamberg. Copper coinage in the eighteenth century was of the normal pattern, a shield obverse and the value of the denomination in words on the reverse.

The gold coinage of the imperial city of Nuremberg begins as a regular series only in the seventeenth century with obverse types of St. Lawrence or St. Sebaldus and the city arms and, later, with the imperial eagle as obverse type. The gold issues for the emperors normally carry their portrait as obverse type with shields as reverse or late in the eighteenth century a view of the city. The thaler series at Nuremberg is particularly fine and extensive with an unusual range of city views as reverse types. In the earlier part of the series the emperors are usually represented by portraits but in the later eighteenth century by the imperial arms supported on the double-headed eagle. The smaller silver denominations usually have their value indicated on the orb on the breast of the imperial eagle on the obverse.

Upper Rhine

The landgravate and later electorate of Hesse produced one of the most extensive coinages of this circle, first as a unity and later in its two principal branches of Hesse-Cassel and Hesse-Darmstadt. The coinages of William II (1493–1509) and his son Philip (1509–67) account for the first half of the sixteenth century. The gold gulden of both placed the standing figure of St. Elizabeth on the obverse and five or four shields in cross pattern on the reverse. The first issue of thalers in 1502 used the lion arms of Hesse as obverse and again St. Elizabeth holding the model of a church as reverse. On the death of Philip in 1567 Hesse was divided into four portions for his sons but two of the lines died out without heirs by the end of the sixteenth century. On gold ducats of Hesse-Cassel under William V (1627–37) the lion obverse of Hesse is joined by an unusual reverse depicting a storm with lightning, wind and even a waterspout with the inscription *Iehova volente humilis levabor* (Pl. 679), a type also used on some thalers and smaller silver. On the smaller silver denominations of the later seventeenth and the eighteenth centuries the obverse was normally the lion rampant of Hesse or a shield of arms with the field of the reverse inscribed with the value of the piece, e.g. *III/Albus, VIII/Einen/ Rtha* (*Reichsthaler*), etc. On some of these denominations, and on the low denominations in copper only, a monogram appears on the obverse with an inscribed reverse, e.g. *I/Heller/Scheide/Muntz* (Pl. 680). The later thalers have the usual portrait-and-arms types but a novel issue for Frederick II (1760–85) carried on the reverse an eight-pointed star with the lion of Hesse at the centre, a type repeated also on his louis d'or and double piece. In Hesse-Darmstadt the gold coinage produced some novelties of design. The early ducat coins of Ernst Louis (1678–1739) had the standard portrait obverse and shield with lion supporters reverse but later issues adopted from French coinage the device of a cross formed from the initials E L, placed back to back. A similar device was used to form the obverse of the ducats of Louis VIII (1739–68) or else a monogram of two letters L's. Smaller silver, as for Hesse-Cassel, has shield obverse and reverse with field inscribed with the value of the coin, e.g. *X/Kreu/zer*. Some issues for Louis VIII conform to common mid-eighteenth-century pattern and have as types for the higher kreuzer coins an obverse bust and shield reverse with value in brackets below (10) or on the pedestal supporting the shield. The lower denominations for Louis X (1790–1806) had the lion on obverse with the letters H - D and inscribed reverse, the lower kreuzer in silver, the stuber and heller in copper.

Frankfurt-on-Main, an imperial city in this circle, issued a gold coinage both for the city and for a number of the emperors. The imperial connections with the city were strong, as its cathedral was the scene of imperial coronations from 1562 onwards and is pictured on the thaler issue of 1772, and a number of Frankfurt's issues are commemorations of elections and coronations. The early gold pieces have types of St. John with city name and imperial orb with emperor's name. On some seventeenth-century gold the eagle badge of Frankfurt on a decorated shield has the inscription *Nomen domini turris fortissima*, a play on the Latin translation of the city name; on the reverse within a square is inscribed *Ducatus/Novus/ Reipubl./Franc/Furt*. The eagle badge is the common type on smaller silver coupled with the distinctive cross used by Frankfurt as on kreuzer issues of the eighteenth century (Pl. 681). On the smallest silver appeared only the eagle and the word Frankfurt, and across the reverse field the denomination *I/Kreuzer, I/*

Heller, etc. On copper the uninscribed obverse has only the eagle badge with the denomination II or I pfennig on the reverse.

Lower Rhine

Cologne continued to be one of the chief centres of coinage both for the archbishops and electors and for the emperors. The imperial gold had fairly consistent types: the imperial eagle and name on obverse and shield of arms on reverse. An exception was the ducat of Ferdinand III (1637–57) which showed on obverse the standing figure of the emperor with sceptre and globe. Episcopal gold initially maintained its obverse type of the enthroned Christ but an obverse portrait made its appearance on the issues of Salentin of Salm (1567–77) (Pl. 682) and subsequently provided the obverse type, with some exceptions, such as the ducat of Ferdinand of Bavaria (1612–50) where the type was the Madonna. A seated Madonna also appeared as a reverse type on the ducat of Joseph Clement (1686–1723) with inscription *Monstrate esse matrem*. The thaler was struck as early as 1547 at the mint of Deutz for Adolf III with standing figure of St. Peter holding the keys and Gospel on obverse and the archbishop's arms surmounted by helmet on the reverse. These remained basically the thaler types till, again under Salentin, the obverse was given over to a portrait bust. Portraits and shields provided the usual types for both imperial and other thalers except for rare instances of the popular view of the city reverse. On the divisionary silver, types consisted of a shield obverse with the value of the coin forming the reverse. Eighteenth-century copper expressed the lowest denominations with a monogram obverse and inscription $\frac{1}{4}$ /*Stuber* reverse.

The archbishopric of Trier also coined extensively in this period. Throughout the sixteenth century the types of the gold gulden were as described earlier, the enthroned Christ and three shields in a trefoil but new types, a bust of St. Peter and a standing figure of St. Helena, were introduced by Lothar Metternich (1599–1623). The latter type was struck at the new mint in Trier itself (earlier issues had been from Coblenz). From Philip Christopher (1623–62) onwards the types of the gold ducat normally were a portrait bust and arms. The thaler first struck by John VI (1565–7) took as its obverse the half-length figure of St. Peter with key and Gospel above a shield of arms. Thalers of Lothar from his new mint at Trier itself used an obverse type of St. Helena as on his gold. Of the smaller silver coinage the most prolific was the albus or petermännchen with its standing figure of St. Peter and shield reverse (Pl. 683). In the eighteenth century came a kreuzer coinage with obverse bust and a shield reverse with the value in brackets below or on the pedestal supporting the shield. A coinage in copper from 1748 onwards has a monogram as obverse and the value in pfennig (1 to 4) on the reverse.

The third great archbishopric of the Rhineland, Mainz, also continued in the early sixteenth century a gold coinage with the types of the Rhineland convention but from the middle of the century the obverse type became also a shield of arms and from the early seventeenth century a portrait bust was substituted. The earliest thalers issued by Daniel Brendel of Homburg (1555–82) represented the patron saint of Mainz, St. Martin, on horse-back sharing his cloak with a beggar. This type alternated with the imperially decreed types but in the early seventeenth century the use of a portrait as obverse was begun for this denomination also. Smaller silver denominations, particularly in the seventeenth century, occasionally used an obverse portrait and a shield reverse with the kreuzer value marked below, but more often the shield formed the obverse with the reverse devoted to an inscription giving the value, *XII/Kreu/zer, 12/Einen/Reichs/Thaler, II Albus*, etc. As elsewhere in the later eighteenth century the more regular issues consisted of a bust with shield reverse and the value in kreuzer below. Copper pfennig in the eighteenth century had a simple shield or monogram obverse and the value on the reverse, sometimes accompanied by the traditional wheel badge of Mainz.

The coinage of the counts Palatine of the Rhine has a particularly rich variety of gold issues. As early as Frederick II (1544–56) the obverse carried the elector's portrait, often with sword and orb and the ducats and multiple ducats of Frederick V (1610–23) show him on a richly caparisoned horse. The gold carolin and its portions of Charles Philip (1716–42) have on the reverse a cross formed from a double P and interlinked C with arms at the centre. An obverse portrait was used even earlier on the first issue of the thaler by Louis V (1508–44). After a period of issues in conjunction with Trier, Mainz and Cologne, thalers returned to more individual types. The pattern of lower silver denominations conformed to that of other coinages in the 'circle' with the appropriate alterations of bust or shield. As in other coinages the smaller denominations which had currency only in their territory of issue were marked as *Landmunz*, e.g. the reverse of a 20 kreuzer piece inscribed 20 *kr/Chur/Pfalz/Land/Munz* (Pl. 684).

Westphalia

On the coinage of the bishopric of Münster the favourite type is the patron saint St. Paul. He appears either as a standing or a seated figure holding sword and Gospel on the gold guldens of Conrad II at the beginning of the sixteenth century with a reverse of three shields and reappears at frequent intervals in the next two centuries. As a variation Francis of Waldeck (1532–53) used the busts of both St. Peter and St. Paul while in the eighteenth century the obverse was used for the portrait of the bishop. It was under Francis of Waldeck that the thaler also made its first appearance with St. Peter and St. Paul, *vis-à-vis*, either as standing figures or half-length busts but the majority of issues honoured St. Paul only. Later, in the eighteenth century, the obverse-portrait convention gained sway on the thaler issues also. Notable exceptions are the thalers struck during the vacancies of the see when types such as a view of the cathedral or of Charlemagne, its founder were used. Much of the divisionary silver coinage is of the usual types with obverse shield and reverse inscribed with value, though St. Paul with his sword was still occasionally used as a reverse type. The small denominations in copper in the eighteenth century had a half-length portrait of St. Paul with inscription *Mon Cathed Eccles Monaste* with value in pfennig on the reverse.

The bishopric of Paderborn which had ceased to coin in the early fifteenth century began its issues again under Thierry of Furstenberg (1585–1618). On the gold of this episcopal coinage the types are generally an obverse portrait and arms reverse. On thaler issues the episcopal portrait was also used as well as the Madonna and the patron saint of Paderborn, St. Liborius, who replaces the usual obverse portrait even on some eighteenth-century thalers. On the higher thaler divisions the obverse is often a portrait, the reverse the shield of arms with the value below, e.g. ($\frac{1}{6}$), but the smaller denominations more commonly have the arms as obverse and the value as sole reverse type. Such smaller denominations for William Anton of Asseburg (1763–82) use his monogram as the sole obverse type.

A third Westphalian bishopric, Osnabrück, had as its patron St. Peter who on sixteenth- and seventeenth-century gold issues appears as the obverse type, either enthroned or as a seated figure. St. Peter was also honoured on the earliest thalers of Osnabrück issued in 1524 by Eric II and on those of his successors. There was an intermission in the episcopal issues of Osnabrück while the city was in the hands of the Swedes but coinage was resumed under Francis William in 1631. St. Peter still appeared on his gold but the thaler obverse carried an obverse portrait while on smaller silver denominations was a springing horse with value-inscribed reverse. Third-thalers of Ernest Augustus (1662–98) presented on the obverse St. Andrew and his cross, as did also some lower denominations. The issues of Ernest Augustus II (1716–28) are of interest for the appearance of the English royal arms as a type, for Ernest Augustus was also Duke of York.

Since it was to Charlemagne that Aachen owed its original greatness, it is natural to find him as a common type on its gold in the sixteenth and seventeenth centuries, usually with an imperial eagle reverse. Other issues show the standing figure of the emperor and a tablet giving the denomination and mint on the reverse. Charlemagne also figures on thaler issues and the reverses of smaller silver have types of altar and regalia with inscriptions, such as *Locus Coronationis Caesareae* alluding to Aachen as the original scene of imperial coronations. On copper coins of the eighteenth century with reverse giving value and mint, the obverse is simply the imperial eagle. The types on the gold of the imperial city of Dortmund were usually the standing figure of the emperor with imperial orb or eagle reverse while thaler issues had as types the imperial bust and eagle. Smaller silver denominations honour St. Reynold, its patron saint, or have the imperial eagle and value inscribed reverse as do the eighteenth-century copper issues.

St. Hubert continued as the obverse type on the gold of the Duchy of Cleve, Julich and Berg under John III (1511–39) and on small silver as well. Later gold of the sixteenth century had as types five shields of arms and double eagle. The succession of the duchy on the death of John William in 1609 was disputed between John Sigismund of Brandenburg and Philip Louis of Neuburg. The consequent war involved two sieges of Julich which struck issues of emergency siege coins and finally Cleve was apportioned to Brandenburg and Julich-Berg to the count Palatine. Subsequent issues for Julich-Berg have conventional bust and shield types for gold and thaler issues, and arms and inscribed reverses for smaller denominations. As on other eighteenth-century German coinages small denominations of Charles Theodore (1742–99) in billon and copper have a monogram obverse and simple value reverse.

The coinage of the counts of Lippe generally followed the conventional pattern of gold and silver coinage but is notable for copper issues in the seventeenth century under Simon Philip (1636–50) where the types are a rose with inscription *Land Muntz Lippe* and value reverse. The gold coinage of the counts of east Friesland present a variety of types in the sixteenth century, a standing Christ, St. John, St. Ludgerus or portraits of the count or the emperor. The thaler was first issued by Edzard II (1591–9) and on smaller silver the types were usually a shield of arms and the imperial eagle. East Friesland passed to Frederick II of Prussia in 1744 but continued to have its own coinage of small denominations, usually with monogram obverse and simple value reverse.

Upper Saxony

The ramifications of the family of the dukes of Saxony are too vast and complicated to be entered into in detail. In brief, the duchy was divided on the death of Frederick II in 1485 between his two sons Ernest and Albert and their patrimonies were subjected in later generations to further divisions. In the original partition the electorate of Saxony was in the portion of Ernest but was transferred from the Ernestine line to the Albertine by the emperor Charles V in 1547. An additional complicating feature in the coinage of Saxony is the practice of coinage shared among the dividers of a patrimony or shared by the holder of a title with a numerous band of brothers or cousins. In many issues the names of all of these appear and not infrequently their portraits, in some cases as many as eight altogether.

Frederick III (1486–1525) of the Ernestine line coined in his own name as on the groschen with his portrait in flat cap, and reverse an eagle with shield on breast, and also in common with his brother John and his uncle Albert. Later issues he shared with his brother John and his cousin George as, for instance, the groschen with the names of all three on the obverse which had as type an angel over a shield and another shield as reverse, inscribed *Grossus novus ducum Saxonum*. Similarly his brother and successor John (1525–32) shared issues with various members of his family and even with his allies as on the thaler series which has his own portrait with sword over shoulder and titles on obverse and that of his ally Philip of Hesse on the reverse. Further splintering of the Ernestine possessions followed John Frederick's death giving rise to the houses and coinages of Saxe-Gotha, Saxe-Altenburg, Saxe-Eisenach, Saxe-Coburg and Saxe-Weimar. In the coinage of the latter mention may be made of the issues in the name of eight brothers of whom the eldest was John Ernest (Pl. 685). On the gold also of this period (1615–19) the portraits and names of four appear on obverse and four on reverse.

In the coinage of George (1500–39), the representative of the Albertine line at the beginning of the modern period, the types of the gold gulden continued to be those of St. John and the imperial orb, and it was under George that the first thalers of Saxony were issued. The electorate of Saxony was transferred to the Albertine line in the person of Maurice in 1547 and from then on the coinage of Saxony provided one of the most extensive and important series of the German coinage. It has a particularly rich and varied series of gold too numerous to detail. Notable are the ducats and double ducats of John George (1611–56) with their obverse of a crowned portrait of the duke with inscription *Ioh-Georg* in the field and a similar portrait on the reverse but inscribed *Frid-III*, a series in commemoration of the Reformation and of Frederick III, the protector and champion of Luther. A prolific gold coinage was issued by Frederick Augustus I (1694–1733) who was also king of Poland, with a variety of types including a lively equestrian portrait of Frederick. Later gold tended to conform to the conventional bust-and-arms types. Larger silver pieces follow a similar pattern to the gold while the divisionary silver in its upper range generally has bust-and-arms types and, in the lower, shield and value-inscribed reverses, as do the lower denominations in copper in the eighteenth century.

The principality of Anhalt has a similar history of subdivision as has Saxony. In the early sixteenth century its divisions comprised Zerbst, Plötzgau and Dessau under three brothers and Cöthen under a cousin. These princes issued a joint coinage and the busts of all four appear on the first thalers issued for Anhalt. The principality was temporarily united under Joachim Ernest (1570–86) but suffered division again under his sons who established independent principalities in 1603 in Dessau, Plötzgau, Cöthen and Bernburg. The common feature incorporated somewhere in most of the issues of these principalities is the badge of a bear. The coinage of Anhalt-Bernburg is perhaps more extensive than that of the other principalities and typical of the pattern of Anhalt issues. On the gold of Victor Frederick (1721–65) with a shield obverse the reverse shows a bear standing in profile on a wall. These types appear also on thalers, though many use the conventional bust-and-arms types. On smaller silver, particularly the lower denominations, the bear badge forms the obverse with value inscriptions for the reverse and on most of the copper denominations similar types are used, but on some issues both in silver and copper a monogram of the prince's initials replaces the bear.

Amongst the important electorates in the circle of Upper Saxony was that of Brandenburg but as this developed and was incorporated into the kingdom of Prussia, the outline of its coinage is integrated with that of Prussia (see p. 370).

Lower Saxony

The coinage of the house of Brunswick is extensive both because of the various divisions of the line which issued coin but also because of the resources of the Harz mines within its territory. Of the various lines the two major were those of Brunswick-Wolfenbüttel and Brunswick-Lüneburg.

The new types of coinage in silver and gold of the old line of Brunswick-Wolfenbüttel began with Henry II (1514–68) who placed on his gold guldens a shield of arms obverse and a reverse, the 'wildman', an almost naked savage which is a consistent type on coins of Brunswick. The first thalers were also issued by Henry II with portrait-type obverse and wildman with tree-trunk reverse. To coinage of similar type Julius (1568–89) added a large series of multiple thalers known as *juliuslöser* which have two concentric lines of inscription, a line of signs of the zodiac with portrait bust at centre on one side and shield with wildmen supporters on the other. On many of the thalers the wildman holds a lighted candle (Pl. 686). On the divisionary silver of Frederick Ulric (1613–34) the obverse takes the form of his monogram crowned and the reverse a statement of the value. Various pfennig and flitter denominations were struck in copper. The new line of Brunswick-Wolfenbüttel began with Augustus (1635–66). Gold coinage usually has the portrait of the duke as obverse type with occasional departures from the norm in the form of monograms or shields of arms. The reverses take a variety of forms—arms, the wildman device or the springing horse, more common on the coinage of the other branch of Brunswick, or a simple statement of the value of the coin as on pieces of Charles William Ferdinand (1780–1806). The thaler coinage follows a similar course and on the smaller silver with value-inscribed reverses the obverse type is most commonly the wild-man or the springing horse as it is also on the copper pfennig coinages.

The second principal line was that of Brunswick-Lüneburg with Celle. The coinage of this branch gained in importance after the acquisition of the duchy of Grubenhagen in 1617 and a portion of the Harz mines. A gold ducat of Duke Christian, Bishop of Minden (1599–1633), with its obverse type of St. Andrew alludes to the source of the metal in the Andreasberg as does the same type on some of the smaller thaler divisions. Throughout the issues of Brunswick-Lüne-burg the combinations of types on the various denominations are, in general terms, those described under Brunswick-Wolfenbüttel. With the accession of George Louis, Duke of Brunswick-Lüneburg (1698–1727), to the English throne as George I, the four shields of Scotland, England, Ireland and Brunswick-Lüneburg dis-posed in a cross shape as on English gold came into use as a reverse type and the new royal arms of the Hanoverian house figured as an obverse or reverse type on other issues.

The Duchy of Mecklenburg like so many other German duchies underwent a number of subdivisions in the period under consideration. The original duchy was divided into two patrimonies of Mecklenburg-Gustrow and Mecklenburg-Schwerin for the two brothers Henry and Albert in 1520. Prior to the division the two brothers issued a joint coinage bearing both their names but after 1520 each had his individual issues with his own portrait and arms as on the thaler series. Gold issues of Mecklenburg-Gustrow for John Albert II (1611–36) have as types the standing figure of the duke and a shield reverse while for Gustav Adolf (1636–95), named after the great Swedish king, the obverses show the heavily bewigged portrait common to the late seventeenth century. The Gustrow branch ended with the death of Gustav Adolf in 1695. The types on the gold of Mecklen-burg-Schwerin are usually those of portrait bust and arms, though occasionally as under Frederick William (1688–1713) the obverse bore the shield of arms and the reverse the bull's-head badge of Mecklenburg. In the sixteenth and seventeenth centuries the lower silver denominations had the conventional bust-and-shield types or shield-and-value reverse types. On a pfennig coinage in copper as early as Adolf Frederick (1592–1658) the obverse type was the bull's-head badge which was also used in the eighteenth-century pfennig pieces and some of the lower silver denominations. The typical eighteenth-century use of a monogram as obverse type is found for Mecklenburg-Schwerin also. Three further portions of the duchy were split off on the death of Albert Frederick in 1658 but of these only that of Strelitz continued beyond one generation. The coinage issues of Mecklenburg-Strelitz resemble in general terms those described under Mecklenburg-Schwerin.

The Hanseatic city of Lübeck played an important rôle in the economic life of north-west Europe and issued a coinage in conformity with that importance. In agreement with Hamburg, Lüneburg and Wismar, Lübeck abandoned the gold gulden as a monetary basis in preference for a silver coinage based on the gulden-groschen. The Lübeck types for this coinage were the standing figure of the city's patron saint, John the Baptist, within an elliptical frame with a shield of Lübeck at his feet, while on the reverse was the imperial eagle. A little later a new coinage of silver marks and portions was introduced with types, the imperial eagle and the shields of the other three participants in the convention arranged around that of Lübeck. Thaler coinage was issued later still in the sixteenth century together with the usual divisionary denominations. The types most commonly used are John the Baptist and the imperial eagle or orb. Only occasionally on gold does the standing figure or bust of the emperor appear as obverse type. The early sixteenth-century issues of Hamburg have much the same pattern as those of Lübeck with only the requisite change of city type. On the silver mark, for instance, the obverse has a Madonna in place of Lübeck's John the Baptist. Later in the sixteenth century the Madonna still continued to be the type on gold pieces, appearing in some issues on both sides of the coin. The thaler series, however, present the types most usually associated with Hamburg, on the obverse a wall surmounted by three towers, on the reverse the imperial eagle with the value expressed in schillings in a circlet on its breast. This exact combination of types was also used for the sub-divisions of the thaler, and variations of one or other, or both of these, supply the devices for the various denominations throughout Hamburg's coinage. Hamburg has a particularly notable series of multiple ducats, including pieces reproducing on the reverse the type of the Portuguese gold cruzado (see p. 321) but placing the three towers of Hamburg on the obverse, within two concentric circles of inscription containing the city name and the statement that the piece is struck on the basis of the Portuguese coin.

On the issues of Rostock the principal type on coins of all metals is the griffin badge of the city on the gold guldens and later, on the ducats, the griffin obverse is accompanied by a reverse with the imperial eagle and the emperor's name. These are the types of the thaler series also, but on smaller silver of the sixteenth century the reverse has a cross motif often incorporating the initial R in Gothic script while later issues have the customary inscription across the field giving the value of the coin. On copper denominations the obverse is also either the griffin badge or the shield of arms incorporating the griffin device. The issues of the imperial city of Bremen carry the key badge of the city, combined with the imperial eagle. On some of the ducat issues the emperor as a standing figure holding sceptre and globe occupies the obverse while the reverse takes the form of the key on a shield with two lion supporters. The issues of the archbishops of Bremen also feature the key as a badge. The types here on the earlier gold and smaller silver are St. Peter and shield or key, and on later coinages which have a portrait on obverse, the normal reverse is a variously quartered shield incorporating crossed keys.

The archbishops of Magdeburg on gold and thaler coinage generally used the conventional portrait-and-arms types, though some of the silver issues have on their obverse the standing figure of St. Maurice in armour. On smaller silver denominations this figure of the patron saint commonly appears as the obverse. On the issues of the city of Magdeburg the prevailing type is another example of a punning type for it shows the city gateway flanked by two towers between which stands a female figure the *magd* from which the city takes its name. This forms the obverse while the reverse is the imperial eagle or a value inscription.

Prussia

The coinage of the margraves and electors of Brandenburg is included under this heading, as Brandenburg was from 1701 absorbed into the new kingdom of Prussia which earlier had been a duchy belonging to the electors of Brandenburg. The types on the gold coins of Brandenburg are an obverse portrait and shield reverse with occasional variation of obverse in the form of a standing or equestrian figure of the elector as for George William (1619–40). Some ducats of Frederick William (1640–88) have a sceptre-on-shield reverse or a ship—the ship of state—with the inscription *Deo Duce*. On thalers the shield reverse with its great number of quarterings bears witness to the range of smaller principalities which the electors of Brandenburg acquired. On smaller silver denominations the inclusion of this range of titles gives rise to inscriptions which are little more than a long stream of initials.

Prussia was established as a hereditary duchy out of the territory of the Teutonic Order by Albert of Brandenburg, its grand master in 1525, and its coinage series also had its beginnings under Albert. His bust, bare-headed and armoured, forms the obverse of the large groschen, with eagle on shield as the reverse of the 6 groschen piece and inscription giving value for the 3 and 2 groschen denominations. Albert's initial supplies the obverse of the schilling with its inscriptions *Solidus Prussie* and an eagle the reverse. The letter S on the breast of the eagle here and on other of Albert's coins is the initial of Sigismund, King of Poland, of which Prussia was technically a fief and from whom Albert had secured the conversion of Prussia into a hereditary duchy. In 1618 on the death of Albert, Frederick John Sigismund, elector of Brandenburg, became Duke of Prussia and from this point onwards the two territories have an identity of ruler but retain their separate coin types till the beginning of the eighteenth century. In the seventeenth century portrait-and-arms types are used for gold and the higher groschen values in silver and from 1657 when Poland recognized the independence of Prussia the elector's title was altered to *Supremus Prussiae princeps*. Frederick III secured from the emperor Leopold II in 1701 recognition of Prussia as a kingdom and from that date uses on coinage his new title *Fridericus primus rex Borussiae*. The coin types achieve considerable simplification in the eighteenth century for the types used on gold and silver are basically the royal portrait in conjunction with either the Hohenzollern eagle or a shield of arms, particularly under Frederick II the Great (1740–86). The reverse of his gold and of the major silver denominations reflects the military flavour of his reign for the eagle is shown in defiant attitude amidst banners, drums and other military gear (Pl. 687). The lower denominations with values on the reverse have on obverse a shield or crowned monogram which forms the type on copper issues also.

UNIFICATION OF THE COINAGE (1806–71)

In the years immediately following Austerlitz and the end of the Holy Roman empire in 1806 the secularization of the bishoprics of Germany brought to an end many of the historical coinages of Germany and the enforced or voluntary cessation of coinage by the smaller principalities and free cities further reduced the number of series. Almost all the German states with the exception of Prussia were grouped under Napoleon in a Confederation of the Rhine and of these some continued to coin on the same standards as had obtained before 1806. A Confederation of thirty-nine German states emerged from the Congress of Vienna in 1815 but not all of these resumed their rights of coinage and by 1866 when

Prussia defeated Austria at Sadowa these states had been either absorbed by Prussia or allied to her.

In 1871 came the creation of the German empire and of a completely unified monetary system. Between 1815 and 1871, however, a steady process of monetary unification had been taking place. By the convention of Munich in 1837 the southern states of Bavaria, Würtemburg and Hesse adopted a common monetary basis of 24½ guldens to the fine mark, with denominations of a gold gulden, a half-gulden in silver and smaller pieces of 6 and 3 kreuzers as well as lower denominations in baser metals. Other southern states adhered to this convention and a fuller agreement at Dresden in 1839 covering all the states established a two-part system. The essence of the system was that in the northern states, of which the chief were Prussia and Saxony, the thaler which was the basic coin was tariffed at $1\frac{3}{4}$ gulden, and *vice-versa*, in the south in Bavaria, Würtemburg and Hesse the gulden was tariffed at $\frac{4}{7}$ thaler. The equation is better expressed in the arrangement for actual coinage where it was decreed that the major silver piece should be worth 2 thalers or $3\frac{1}{2}$ guldens and should carry a clear statement of this equation. The smaller denominations in silver were fixed as $\frac{2}{3}$, $\frac{1}{3}$ and $\frac{1}{6}$ thalers. A third convention in Vienna in 1857 decreed a system based on the newly agreed pound of 500 grammes adopted by the Zollverein (Customs Union). The old relationship between northern and southern currency was maintained: 2 thalers $= 3\frac{1}{2}$ gulden (south Germany) $=$ 3 gulden (Austria) and 30 Vereinsthalers equalled the zollpfund. Smaller silver consisted of the $\frac{1}{6}$ thaler or the quarter-gulden and lower denominations were struck in billon or copper. Outside the system which was based on a silver unit a gold coinage was also allowed of crown and half-crown denominations at a rate of 50 crowns to the zollpfund.

An exceptional coinage was that of the kingdom of Westphalia which Napoleon created in 1807 from Westphalia with the addition of Hanover, Brunswick and Hesse-Cassel for his youngest brother Jerome. The kingdom collapsed after the battle of Leipzig in 1813 but during its existence it had, alongside the traditional coinage of 10 and 5 thaler pieces in gold, silver thalers and divisionary pieces with obverse portrait of Jerome and value reverses, a coinage on the pattern of the French decimal system. The denominations included gold 40, 20, 10 and 5 pieces; 5, 2 and 1 franc pieces in silver and centime denominations in billon and copper. The types for the francs in gold and silver were similar to those of the French coinage, with the substitution of the portrait and titles of Jerome for those of Napoleon. The centime denominations bore the monogram HN crowned on obverse and the value surrounded by the king's title on reverse (Pl. 688).

During the Napoleonic wars and after the Congress of Vienna in 1815 the number of individual German coinages was reduced to some thirty and by the time of the creation of the German empire in 1871 the number was reduced to about a dozen. The period of unification of the coinage in the nineteenth century was accompanied by a greater standardization of coin types, and the differentiation of the issues of the several coining states consists, in the main, of the varying portraits and titles on the obverse and the distinctive arms on the reverse. In northern Germany the most important coinage was that of Prussia which over-shadowed her neighbours in this as in other aspects. The types on the gold Frederick, which was worth 5 thalers, and on its double and half were the royal bust or head, and eagle perched on military trophies. After the Vienna convention of 1857 gold kronen or crowns were issued with portrait obverse and value in a wreath on the reverse. The types of thalers and their portions were commonly a bust and shield but from 1857 the reverse was changed to the Hohenzollern eagle. The reverse of a number of thalers notes the blessing of the mines with an in-scription *Segen des Mansfeldes Bergbaues*, a type used with appropriate variation on the issues of several other states. Other important coinages in northern Germany were those of Saxony which was made a kingdom in 1806 and Mecklenburg which became a grand-duchy in 1815.

In southern Germany the money of account at the beginning of this period was still the gulden and the gold denomination, the ducat. Bavaria which also became a kingdom in 1806 issued a series of ducats with reverses more picturesque than the conventional shield of arms. In addition to views of the cities of Speyer and Würzburg, representations of river-gods in the classical manner were used for ducats whose metal came, as the inscriptions show, from the Danube, the Rhine or the Iser. Bavarian silver after 1837, in conformity with the Dresden convention, show on their reverse the value in both reckonings, $3\frac{1}{2}$ gulden—2 thaler. From Bavaria also came a long series of thalers with reverses commemorating current happenings or the anniversaries of historical events. The gold coinage of the kingdom of Würtemberg consisted of ducats with the conventional types but also of pieces with the value expressed in guldens as also on the issues of another southern state, the Grand-Duchy of Baden.

UNITED GERMANY (1871–1945)

In 1871 a new coinage was decreed for the German empire based on the gold standard and with a new reichsmark as the monetary unit, the mark being divided into 100 pfennig. The dozen or so subsidiary kingdoms, grand-duchies, princi-palities and free cities which still exercised coining rights struck a coinage of the same standard and of the same types as on the imperial coins but with appropriate change of portrait and titles. The denominations in gold were the 20, 10 and 5 mark pieces; in silver 5, 2 and 1 mark pieces as well as 50 and 20 pfennigs. Lower pfennig denominations were struck in nickel and the 1 and 2 pfennig pieces in copper. The types on the higher denominations were the appropriate portrait and titles on obverse and eagle and value on reverse (Pl. 689). On denominations from 1 mark downwards the types were the eagle and statement of value. More variety was introduced in the issues of the early twentieth century with the appearance of a number of commemorative pieces in the higher values, and in common with the rest of Europe gold ceased to be minted on the outbreak of war in 1914.

The defeat of Germany in 1918 brought the abdication of the emperor and the other ruling princes and the declaration of the German Republic. Little change was effected on the small range of coinage issued in the early years of the republic, for the German eagle and value continued as the types on the 50, 10 and 5 pfennig pieces struck first in silver then in aluminium zinc and even iron. The inflation of the German coinage made itself evident in the issue in 1923 of denominations of 20, 100, 200 and 500 mark pieces. The war years and the inflationary period gave rise to a varied series of local emergency issues not only in metal but in other materials such as the porcelain pieces of Meissen. A new issue of rentenpfennig in late 1923 in denominations from 50 downwards, struck in aluminium, had an obverse of wheat-stalks and a value reverse. In 1924 silver marks from 5 downwards were added with the traditional eagle-and-value types but in addition to these regulation issues almost every year brought new pieces in the 5 and 3 mark denominations commemorating such events as the Graf Zeppelin's world flight, an adaptation of coinage to a practice more usually associated with postage stamps.

The initial issues of the Third Reich created after the rise to power of the Nazi party in 1933 did not bear the party badge. The 5 mark had head of Hindenburg and eagle, the mark and its half an eagle and value but from 1936 the higher mark pieces bore on reverse a stylized eagle perched on a wreath enclosing the swastika badge. The lower denominations with this type as obverse and the value on reverse were first struck in aluminium-bronze but from 1940 till the end of the war only the lowest denominations from 5 pfennig downwards were issued and these in zinc (Pl. 690).

POST-WAR GERMANY

During the allied occupation of Germany between 1945 and 1948 the only German coins to be struck were zinc pieces of 10, 5 and 1 pfennig with similar types to those of the Third Reich but with the omission of the swastika from the obverse. The western zone of Germany between 1948 and 1949 issued the same pfennig denominations in brass with an oak-twig on obverse and inscription *Bank Deutscher Länder* and a value reverse and in 1949–50 a 50 pfennig piece in cupro-nickel with kneeling female figure planting an oak on the obverse. After the creation of the Federal Republic in West Germany these denominations appeared from 1950 with a new obverse inscription *Bundesrepublik Deutschland* (Pl. 691). To these, cupro-nickel denominations coins of 5, 2 and 1 mark were added with a stylized eagle as obverse type and a number of commemorative 5 mark pieces such as that in honour of Schiller in 1955 have been struck.

In Eastern Germany, the German Democratic Republic issued a series of aluminium 10, 5 and 1 pfennig coins with obverse showing the value and inscribed *Deutschland,* the reverse a corn-ear or a cog-wheel. A factory with a plough in the foreground continued the theme of industry and agriculture on the reverse of the 50 pfennig piece (Pl. 692). In 1952 the reverse was changed to a hammer and compasses between corn-ears. In 1956 a cupro-nickel coinage of 1 and 2 mark pieces was added with the hammer-and-compasses design as obverse with inscription *Deutsche Demokratische Republik* and the value on reverse.

AUSTRIA

Charlemagne, expanding his empire eastwards, conquered the Avars occupying the ancient Roman provinces of Noricum and Pannonia Superior and created a new province known as the East Mark or Austria. In 928 Henry the Fowler created as a bar to Hungarian aggression a margravate of Austria which was presented to Leopold of Bamberg and in 1156 Austria was advanced to the status of a duchy for Henry II, Duke of Bavaria. The Austrian coinage began towards the end of the eleventh century in the form of uninscribed denars, frequently semi-bracteate in form and often in a distinctive square shape with rounded corners with a variety of types such as bird, dog's head or cross (Pl. 693). In the course of the thirteenth century facing crowned heads of the dukes begin to appear on these silver coins but only occasionally, as in the case of Ottakar, King of Bohemia as well as Duke of Austria, is the portrait accompanied by an inscription. On this coinage known as Wiener pfennige from their probable place of minting at Vienna the types were changed annually. In 1276 Austria came into the possession of the house of Hapsburg under whom a similar pfennig coinage was continued. Under Rudolf of Hapsburg (1289–91) a coinage of pfennige with his facing portrait accompanied by his name in full, *Rudolf* or the initial *R*, introduced on the reverse the eagle, which in varying forms was to remain a characteristic of Austrian coinage throughout history. From the late fourteenth century the shield of Austria becomes a common type and the regular appearance of at least the initials of the duke facilitates chronological classification.

The title of archduke granted by the emperor in 1453 makes its first appearance on the issues of Albert VI (1457–63). Gold coinage had had its beginning in Austria with the issue by Albert II (1330–58) of florins copying the John the Baptist and lily types of the Florentine gold piece (Pl. 694). A more individual gold gulden was, however, introduced by Albert V who was also emperor between 1437 and 1439. The types here were the half-length figure of the Madonna on obverse and on the reverse an orb surmounted by a cross within a trefoil. Under Frederick III (1458–93) the silver groschen and its half-piece was introduced with an almost constant obverse type of double-headed eagle and a variety of reverse types such as shield, cross or monogram. The provinces of Tyrol, Styria and Carinthia, which had all had independent coinages, had, by the end of the fifteenth century, passed to the archdukes of Austria but coinages for these provinces continued to be issued till the eighteenth century. It was in Tyrol that the first large silver pieces made their appearance, bearing in numerals the date, 1486. This, with the exception of rare trial-pieces dated 1484, is probably the earliest example of this form of dating on European coinage. The obverse shows the standing figure of Archduke Sigismund between seated lion and helmet while on the reverse is the armoured and mounted figure of the archduke within a border of the shields of arms of the Hapsburg possessions (Pl. 695).

The reign of Maximilian (1493–1519) is traditionally regarded as the commencement of the modern coinage of Austria. His gold guldens have, most commonly, types of St. Leopold on obverse and a reverse of five shields of arms, while on the thalers, the first in the long series of this denomination in the Austrian coinage proper, there is a similar reverse to that on the gold but the obverse shows the half-length portrait of Maximilian crowned and holding sceptre and sword, or a bust with a flat cap and the collar of an order about the neck. Under Ferdinand I (1521–64) both Bohemia and Hungary were added to the realms of the archdukes of Austria but the specific coinages struck in and for Bohemia and Hungary receive notice in the separate sections devoted to them. The issues for the Austrian Netherlands and, later, for Austrian possessions in Italy are dealt with similarly. The coinage sketched here is that of Austria proper, struck mainly at the Vienna mint but also in the earlier centuries at provincial mints such as Graz, Klagenfurt and Hall. The general tendency in European national coinages from the sixteenth century onwards was towards standardization of denominations and types and in this respect the Austrian coinage is seen to be one of the most conservative;

for the denominations and types, once established, vary only within narrow limits. The coinage system consisted of a ducat in gold with multiples of 2, 4 and 10 and portions down to an eighth in several reigns; in silver the major piece was the thaler with its half and quarter and smaller denominations expressed in kreuzer, and, for a time, the silver pfennig continued in issue. In the eighteenth century the kreuzer piece and its portions were issued in copper.

The obverse type of the gold ducat throughout most of the sixteenth and seventeenth centuries was the standing figure of the ruler, usually holding sceptre and sword, but the original reverse of a shield gave place to the characteristic double-headed eagle with shield on breast under Rudolf II (1576–1608) (Pl. 696). On double ducats in the seventeenth century the standing figure on the obverse usually has a shield on either side while the 10 ducat obverse bears a portrait bust which, in the eighteenth century, became standard on all gold denominations. The reverse type of the majority of the silver denominations was basically the eagle with shield on breast, the design executed in a variety of fashions throughout the period. An exception is the reverse type for Rudolf II where the eagle is rendered naturalistically rather than heraldically and has on its breast the imperial orb containing a small shield. The large flans of the thaler and its portions present a series of striking and elaborately executed portraits. In the early sixteenth century the portrait bust is shown half-length, crowned and holding sceptre and sword or orb, and subsequent issues reflect the changes of fashion with beruffed and bewigged portraits, often laureate and armoured in the Roman imperial fashion. The considerable degree of realism in this portrait series can be seen in the rendering, almost in caricature, of the famous Hapsburg chin and mouth as on portraits of Leopold I (Pl. 697). The most famous of Austrian thalers is that of Maria Theresa (1740–80), for such was the popularity that this coin gained as a means of exchange in Abyssinia and the Ashanti coast that issues of the thaler with the date 1780 (Pl. 698) continued to be produced for these areas throughout the nineteenth century and in the present century also by mints outside Austria, including Rome at the time of the Italian invasion of Abyssinia and by the Royal Mint in London for the Abyssinian campaign of the recent war.

The smaller divisionary silver other than the half- and quarter-thaler which repeated the types of the thaler itself consisted in the sixteenth century of the sechser and dreier (or groschen), pieces of 6 and 3 kreuzer with bust-and-eagle types, with the value displayed on the eagle's breast. The types of the 2 kreuzer pieces were the imperial orb enclosing the value and shield on eagle. In the seventeenth century denominations of 15, 10 and 6 kreuzer as well as the groschen (3 kreuzer) carry their mark of value in either Roman or Arabic numerals at the base of the portrait obverse or occasionally below the eagle with shield of the reverse

(Pl. 699). Yet another fashion obtains on the eighteenth-century issues. The 30 kreuzer denominations enclose both the types within a diamond-shaped frame while lower denominations have their value enclosed in a small square supporting the eagle-and-shield reverse. On the 20 and 10 kreuzer coins of Leopold II (1790–92) the obverse bust is enclosed within a wreath and the reverse type is flanked by a laurel- and a palm-branch. As on German coinages, the lowest denominations struck in copper in the eighteenth century have as a reverse the simple type of the value in words. After the Austrian defeat by Napoleon at Austerlitz, Francis II renounced the title of emperor of the Holy Roman empire but retained the title of emperor of Austria which he had already assumed in 1804.

The denominations and types of the Austrian coinage after the resettlement of Europe by the Congress of Vienna in 1815 remained practically immobilized except for the requisite changes of obverse portraits and titles for successive monarchs, until the monetary convention of 1857 (see p. 372). Under the terms of this agreement Austria issued a series of *Vereinsmünzen* (Union coinage) consisting of a gold krone and its half-piece with obverse portrait of Franz Joseph (1848–1916) and value within a wreath and a silver thaler and double thaler, still with the conventional types but inscribed as a *Vereinsthaler*. For internal circulation the ducat and 4 ducat pieces continued to be struck but the silver denominations were now the florin and its double, while pieces of 20, 10 and 5 kreuzer were issued in billon and 4, 3 and 2 kreuzer pieces in copper, the latter having the shield and eagle as obverse type and the value in a wreath as the reverse. On this coinage the imperial titulature, hitherto in Latin, was inscribed in German (Pl. 700). In 1870 new denominations in gold were introduced of the value of 8 and 4 florins, the equivalent of the 20 and 10 franc pieces of the Latin Union. The types remained a portrait bust and eagle but the imperial titulature reverted to a Latin form which was also used on the completely new coinage decreed in 1892. This was a coinage on the gold standard with the korona as its monetary unit and consisted of denominations of 20 and 10 koronas in gold, of 5 and 1 korona in silver, in nickel pieces of 20 and 10 hellers, of which 100 equalled a korona and, in bronze, 2 and 1 heller pieces. The types remained basically a portrait head and double-headed eagle on the larger denominations and eagle and value on the lower. The only coinage issues of the short reign of Karl, the last of the reigning emperors and archdukes of Austria (1916–18), were pieces of 20 and 2 hellers in iron with eagle-and-value types.

Although the Hapsburgs were driven to abdicate and an Austrian republic declared in 1918, the new coinage made its appearance only in late 1923. The major coin was the silver schilling with types of the Parliament building and shield and value with divisionary pieces of 1000 kronen in cupro-nickel and 200 and

100 kronen in bronze with value reverses, and obverses a female head in Tyrolean hat, a Teutonic cross and an eagle's head respectively. A second coinage in 1924 created bronze denominations of 5 and 10 groschen with types of cross and Tyrolean head while the types on the silver schilling remained as before, until 1934 when the Austrian eagle reappeared on the obverse. These standard denominations were supplemented by rare multiple schillings in gold (25 and 100) and by a succession of 2 schilling pieces in silver, honouring famous men such as Mozart and Haydn.

Austrian coinage ceased with the loss of independence when, in 1938, Austria was absorbed into the German Third Reich but was resumed in 1946 for the republic restored in 1945. The Austrian eagle returned as the standard obverse on the aluminium schilling and 2 schilling pieces and 50 groschen pieces as well as the zinc 10 groschen. The reverses consist chiefly of the value though the schilling bears a symbolic figure sowing corn (Pl. 701). The larger 5 schilling denomination was added in 1952 and there have been occasional special issues of the 25 schilling denomination in silver, such as that in 1956 in honour of Mozart's bicentenary.

HUNGARY

The parts of the Roman provinces of Pannonia and Dacia which correspond roughly to the Hungary of mediaeval and modern history were engulfed in the fourth century by successive barbarian invasions by the Goths and Huns. No specific coinages have been identified for these peoples nor for the later Avars against whom Charlemagne campaigned and who were, in turn, conquered by the Magyars; only under St. Stephen I (1000–38) of the Arpad dynasty, granted the title of king by Pope Sylvester II, does the Hungarian coinage have its beginning. The three major periods which form the basis of this sketch of the Hungarian issues are: (1) the independent mediaeval kingdom from 1000 to 1527; (2) the union with Austria up to 1918; (3) the modern state of Hungary.

The coins issued by Stephen I are silver denars with the identical type, a cross with a small triangle in the angle of each quadrant on both sides inscribed on the obverse *Stephanus Rex* and on the reverse *Regia Civitas*, the then capital, Gran (Pl. 702). The same types were continued by his successors in the first half of the century but the reverse inscription more frequently reads *Pannonia*. The first regal portraits appeared on the now smaller coins of Salomon (1063–74) either in the form of a facing bust, crowned or a three-quarter-length figure on the obverse (Pl. 703), but the practice did not immediately become regular, for the coins of Geza I (1074–7) revert to the earlier pattern. Ladislas I (1077–95) struck some issues with a facing bust but also introduced a range of new obverse types of which the most striking shows three sceptres each surmounted by a cross and both obverse and reverse carry the king's name and title *Ladislaus Rex*. Up to this point the coinage had consisted of silver denars and obols or half-pieces but under Coloman (1095–1114) the module of the denar was much reduced and the majority of the pieces of this category in the eleventh century are without inscription (Pl. 704).

The place in the Hungarian series of a unique and unusual type of coinage has been the subject of much dispute but it has now been attributed to the period of disputed succession following the death of Bela II in 1141 and is regarded as the issues of Bela's brother, Stephen IV, who usurped the throne between 1162 and 1163 with the assistance of the Byzantine emperor, Manuel I. The coins have indeed the air of Byzantine pieces for they are of a thin, spread bronze fabric, usually slightly scyphate or saucer-shaped. The obverse showing two enthroned figures, crowned, holding sceptre and globe, is inscribed *Rex Bela Sts*—said to be Bela II and Stephen IV—while the reverse depicts the seated Madonna and is inscribed *Sancta Maria* (Pl. 705). These coins and another series of similar fabric but with pseudo-Arabic inscriptions were previously ascribed to the period of the great Mongol invasions in 1241.

In the reign of Bela III (1173–96) the coinage, though continuing to include issues without inscriptions and with rather sketchy types or, rather, ornamental designs, shows the beginnings of a more carefully executed series. In this the name of Bela, disposed across the field or in the angles of a cross, forms the obverse and the simple abbreviation *Rx* the reverse, but under Andrew II (1205–34) and his successors in the thirteenth century a rich variety of types enlivens the Hungarian coinage. There are royal portraits either in the form of a facing or profile bust or an enthroned figure, the Paschal Lamb, equestrian figures and numerous architectural types which recall the types on contemporary German bracteates, and indeed some issues of Bela IV (1235–70) are in the form of small bracteates. The majority of the thirteenth-century issues are without inscriptions and have at best the royal initials as a distinguishing mark. On the death of Andrew III, the last of the Arpad kings in 1301, the Hungarian crown was given first to Wenceslas of Bavaria and then in 1305 to Otto of Bavaria but passed in 1307 to Charles Robert of Anjou whose grandmother was an Arpad princess.

This change of dynasty was coincident with the introduction of a larger silver denomination of the groschen class and the beginning of coinage in gold. The first gold guldens were close imitations of the Florentine florin with the addition of the name of Charles Robert (1307–42) on the obverse but later issues had new types, the king enthroned, holding sceptre and globe and a shield with the combined arms of Anjou and Hungary. The types of this latter issue were also adopted for the new silver groschen (Pl. 706) and for some of the denars and obols, though a number of these perpetuated the range of types current on late thirteenth-century issues. The guldens of Louis I (1342–82) with types, a shield of arms and the standing figures of St. Ladislas holding halberd and globe, set the pattern which was to be followed for centuries on the gold coinage of Hungary (Pl. 707). St. Ladislas also appeared as the reverse type on some groschen in place of the more usual enthroned figure of the king while denars and obols had such types as the crowned bust of the king, shield, lis or cross with double arms, the cross of Anjou. The short reign of Maria (1382–5), the last of the Anjou dynasty, produced only rare guldens and denars.

The crown next devolved upon Sigismund of Brandenburg (1387–1437) who later in 1420 also became King of Bohemia and the shield on his gold guldens is quartered, first with the arms of Hungary and the Brandenburg eagle, later with the lion of Bohemia in addition. Despite the advent of a new line, the form of cross peculiar to the house of Anjou remained as a common type on denars and obols. In the coinage of the next king, Albert of Austria (1437–40), the chief novel feature is the reverse type of denars, four shields of arms within a trefoil, while Wladislas I (1440–4) who was also King of Poland uses the Polish eagle as the obverse on some of his denars. The Hungarian coinage between 1446 and 1453 bears the name of John Hunyad who is entitled in the obverse inscription *Gubernator Ungarie*, governor of Hungary as regent for the infant Ladislas V who succeeded in 1453. The type of the Madonna associated with so many later Hungarian issues was first placed in the coinage by Matthias Corvin (1458–90) as the obverse type instead of the customary shield of arms and also as the reverse on groschen where she is described as *Patrona Ungarie*. This new type was retained by Wladislas II (1490–1516) on guldens, some of which introduced a date into the reverse inscription, and also on groschen and denars. It was Wladislas who also struck the first rare thaler pieces in Hungary. The types here are a shield with no less than ten quarterings and on the reverse the mounted figure of St. Ladislas. A similar coinage, except for the thaler, was struck by Louis II, on whose death in 1526 the Hungarian crown passed to Ferdinand I of Austria. The succession was disputed by John Zapoly of Transylvania who struck a coinage as King of Hungary with the traditional types. Part of Hungary was ceded to John in 1536 but reverted to Ferdinand on John's death in 1540.

From the early sixteenth century onwards Hungary was united with Austria whose archdukes were also kings of Hungary and the coinage system, though similar to that of Austria in its range of denominations, had its own individual types until the late eighteenth century when only some denominations were issued with specific Hungarian types. This Hungarian series was struck at mints at Kremnitz,

Nagybana and Hermannstadt to which Pressburg was added later. The products of these mints are marked in the reverse field by initial letters such as K - B for Kremnitz and N -B for Nagybana. In the sixteenth century the gold ducat maintained its traditional types of the Madonna and St. Ladislas but under Matthias II (1608–18) these were altered to a standing figure of the king, crowned and holding sceptre and orb on reverse or a portrait bust on the obverse, while the Madonna was transferred to the reverse, displacing the type of St. Ladislas (Pl. 708). In the eighteenth century the reverse inscription describes the Madonna as *Patrona Hungariae*. In the seventeenth and eighteenth centuries multiples of the ducat, occasionally as high as ten, were issued and in some reigns a whole range of fractions, notably in that of Maria Theresa for whom ducat fractions down to a sixteenth were coined.

The major coins in silver were the thaler and the half and quarter. For Ferdinand I and Maximilian II the types were a half-length bust with sceptre and sword and a shield of arms surmounted by the Madonna on the reverse, but the thaler reverse of Rudolf II consisted of a similar, somewhat more realistic eagle to that on his Austrian issues. In the seventeenth and eighteenth centuries, however, the types became more stereotyped, a portrait bust and eagle with shield on breast. The reverses for Maria Theresa offer some variety, for they include the Madonna type for this denomination also and a shield with the Hungarian arms on which two angels place a crown. This latter type became the special reverse in the later eighteenth century for the Hungarian thaler, almost the only denomination to be issued with specifically Hungarian types.

Up to about the middle of the seventeenth century the smaller change in silver was in the form of groschen and a continuation of the denar and obol, on all of which the types were the Madonna and shield of arms but in the reign of Leopold I new denominations of 15, 6 and 2 kreuzer were added. The obverse here was the royal portrait beneath which appeared the value in Roman or in Arabic numerals while the reverse was the traditional Madonna (Pl. 709). On a new denomination, the small duarius with a shield obverse, the reverse carried the name of the piece across the field with a small Madonna above. The range of kreuzer denominations was increased in the eighteenth century with pieces of 30, 20, 17 and 10 kreuzers on the reverse of which the value in brackets was placed below the figure of the Madonna or on a pedestal supporting the Madonna type between a laurel- and a palm-branch. Denominations in copper for Maria Theresa included the poltura with Madonna reverse and the gröschel with shield obverse and denomination in words within a decorated frame on the reverse (Pl. 710).

The revolution of the Malcontents between 1704 and 1708 gave rise to a revolt coinage which included gold ducats, silver half-thalers and 20, 10, 4 and 1 poltura pieces in bronze. On silver and gold the royal bust was replaced by the Hungarian arms and the royal name and style by the inscription *Mon Nov Aur (or Arg) Reg Hung* but the Madonna as *Patrona Hungariae* maintained her place on the reverse. The copper pieces took as types a crowned shield with no inscription and the value in Roman figures, sometimes surmounted by a Madonna and the inscription *Pro Libertate*.

In the coinage of the emperors of Austria in the early nineteenth century a return was made to the striking of a number of denominations with traditional Hungarian types. The gold ducat again had its standing figure of the king and the Madonna, the thaler and 20 kreuzer piece, a portrait bust and Madonna. During the Hungarian revolt of 1848 the coinage in gold and silver struck at Kremnitz carried the name and titles of Ferdinand I in Hungarian while the copper kreuzer showed the Hungarian shield and the value, again in Hungarian. The changes in standards and denominations in the later nineteenth century in the long reign of Franz Joseph (1848–1916) are identical with those of the Austrian series (p. 378), but in the systems of 1868 and 1892 the Hungarian series was inscribed in Hungarian and had its own distinctive reverse type. In the 1868 system this took the form of the Hungarian arms where those of Austria were used in the parallel series, while in the gold-standard coinage of 1892 the gold denominations reverted to the traditional Hungarian obverse type of the standing figure of the ruler and a reverse bearing the Hungarian arms with angel supporters. On the reverse of the silver 2 korona denomination two angels hold the crown of Hungary above the denomination name (Pl. 711) and on the nickel or bronze filler pieces, the equivalent of the Austrian hellers, the Hungarian crown forms the obverse.

The Treaty of Versailles established Hungary as a separate state, still nominally a kingdom but without a king and ruled by Admiral Horthy with the title of regent. The immediate post-war coinage consisted only of 20 and 10 filler pieces similar in type to the previous coinage and, like those of the later war years, struck in iron. A new currency, decreed in 1925, consisted of the silver pengo with multiples of 2 and occasionally 5 and sub-denominations of filler in cupro-nickel and bronze. The types of these latter were still the crown and value, those of the pengo the Hungarian shield and value, of the 2 pengo the Madonna and shield crowned by two angels. The 2 pengo piece was also used for special commemorative issues such as that in 1936 in honour of Liszt, or the 5 pengo commemorating, in 1938, the nine-hundredth anniversary of St. Stephen and in 1939 the tenth anniversary of Horthy's rule. Pengos in aluminium and fillers in steel formed the wartime issues of Hungary.

Hungary, declared a republic in 1946, began a new coinage with a new unit, the forint consisting of 100 filler. The reverse type was consistently the value, the obverse of the 1 and 2 forint pieces the Hungarian shield. Special commemorative issues in silver in 1948, in denominations, of 5, 10 and 20 forint, bore the portraits of the heroes of the 1848 revolution. The coinage of the People's republic maintains the system of forint and filler with value reverses and symbolic types on the obverse, such as the dove of peace, ears of corn or a worker (Pl. 712).

CZECHOSLOVAKIA

The modern state of Czechoslovakia which emerged after the first world war has its origins in the ancient provinces of Bohemia and Moravia. The eastward conquests of the Carolingian empire in the eighth and ninth centuries brought these areas into contact with western Europe and in the latter part of the ninth century Christianity secured a footing in Bohemia. The reign of Boleslav I (936–967), Duke of Bohemia, witnessed the absorption of Bohemia into the German empire of Otto I and also brought the first coinage issues of Bohemia. The development of Bohemian coinage followed a course closely parallel to that of the other series within the German empire. A denar or silver-penny coinage was issued in the name of the Duke, or, at certain periods, the King of Bohemia, until in the course of the twelfth century it was replaced by a bracteate coinage. The silver penny with types on both sides began to appear again in the later thirteenth century and about 1300 the larger silver groschen began to be coined by Wenceslas II, while the gold gulden made its appearance under John of Luxemburg (1310–47). The Bohemian coinage entered on a new phase with the devolution of the crown on Ferdinand of Austria in 1526. Though the coinage preserved its identity for some time, it gradually dwindled in importance till it was finally absorbed in that of the Austro-Hungarian empire. An entirely new coinage began with the creation of Czechoslovakia in 1918 and has continued since, except for an intermission during the German occupation between 1939 and 1945.

BOHEMIA AND MORAVIA (*c.* 950–1526)

As Boleslav I, the first Duke of Bohemia to issue coinage, attempted to restore paganism, silver pennies of very rough workmanship and with almost unintelligible inscriptions carry none of the conventional Christian symbols but have types of swords and a bird and may, thus, be earlier than 950 when, after the conquest by Otto I, Christian worship was again permitted. Other and latter issues of Boleslav which incorporate as types the cross or the temple of Carolingian coinage bear his name on obverse and the name of Prague as the mint on the reverse. The most common types for Boleslav II are the hand of God between alpha and omega and a radiate bust copied from the English penny of Æthelred II. The name of the duke on obverse and of the mint on reverse follows the unusual convention of reading outwards from left to right (Pl. 713). A similar coinage was struck by Boleslav III until his capture and blinding by the Duke of Poland who granted Bohemia to his son-in-law Vladivoï, whose silver pennies have a cross type on either side. A distinct Byzantine influence is seen in the coinage of Jaromir (1004–15) who is represented on one issue by a facing bust with a cross in the field while the reverse shows a facing bust of Christ in nimbus with cross. The types of Odalric (1012–37) are a catholic selection including those of Byzantine inspiration, the Carolingian temple and the profile bust derived from English or Scandinavian models.

The earlier issues of Bratislav I (1037–55) of the same module and weight as in preceding reigns reproduce some of the Byzantine facing bust and two-figure types as well as a number of types with cross and bust or figure of St. Wenceslas. Later issues, in common with the general trend in German coinage, were of reduced module and weight and have as their usual type the bust or standing figure of Bratislav on obverse and St. Wenceslas on reverse (Pl. 714). Bratislav divided his territories among his five sons of whom Spytihnew II (1055–61) succeeded him as Duke of Bohemia and then the next son Bratislav II (1061–92). The types under these two dukes remained generally those of the last issue of Bratislav I except that Bratislav II placed on his coins the title of king, which he was granted by the emperor Henry IV in 1086. A new standard both of artistic design and execution was reached under Borzivoi II (1100–7) in a series of small, neat portrait busts, equestrian figures of St. Wenceslas and a kneeling angel holding child (Pl. 715). After a period of disputed succession stability returned under Sobeslas I (1125–40) whose issues are marked by a range of complicated multi-figure types. The title of King of Bohemia appeared again on coins when it was conferred by Frederick I on Duke Wladislas IV in 1158. In the remainder of the twelfth century the workmanship of the coinage deteriorated and in the reign of Przemislas (1192–1230) who became king in 1200 and took the name Ottakar the two-sided silver penny was replaced by the bracteate. Of the variety of types the most common are the facing busts or standing figures of the duke or king between two towers and most issues are without inscription. The bracteate coinage (Pl. 716) lasted throughout the reigns of Wenceslas I (1230–48) and Ottakar II (1248–78) but two-sided silver pennies began to be issued again in the later years of Ottakar II and in the reign of Wenceslas II (1278–1305).

Moravia, sometimes under the Duke of Bohemia, sometimes the portion of one of his sons, was created a margravate in 1182. The silver pennies resemble in type those of Bohemia and have the appropriate name of their ruler and usually of Wenceslas or one of the saints. Moravia also inaugurated a bracteate coinage in the thirteenth century, usually with a lion type.

The first silver groschen of 12 pfennig value were struck in Prague by Florentine artists for Wenceslas II in 1300. This quickly became one of the most popular of late mediaeval coinages which circulated throughout most of Germany and was widely copied, particularly in Poland and in Meissen. The types were a crown with two concentric circles of inscription reading *Wencezlaus Secundus Dei Gratia Rex Bohemie* with the rampant lion of Bohemia with double tail on the reverse inscribed *Grossi Pragenses* (Pl. 717). The first regular series of gold coins were the guldens struck by John of Luxemburg (1310–46) with the standard florin types of St. John and lily. More individual types on the gold of Charles IV (1346–78) showed his facing bust and the Bohemian lion, while one series for Wenceslas IV (1378–1419) is notable for the small, neat Gothic script of its legends around the initial W as obverse type and the lion reverse. With the advent of the Polish Jagellan dynasty under Wladislas II (1471–1516) came the gold ducat with its new types, a standing figure of St. Wenceslas and lion on shield. Groschen types continued much the same and on the small, often uniface, heller coinage appeared the king's initial, sometimes crowned. The ducat of Louis (1516–26) showed little change in types (Pl. 718a) but it was in this reign that the large silver gulden (Pl. 718) struck by the counts of Schlick in Joachimstal in Bohemia gave rise to the term thaler (see p. 354).

BOHEMIA AND MORAVIA UNDER AUSTRIA (1526–1918)

On the death of Louis in battle in 1526 Ferdinand I, Archduke of Austria, was elected king of Bohemia and from this date until the twentieth century the Bohemian throne was hereditary to the Austrian archdukes. Coinage for Bohemia continued to be struck at the mints of Prague, Kuttenberg and, from 1569, at Budweiss, the former principally for gold coinage, the latter two for silver. The Bohemian coinage also preserved to a great extent its individual types. The gold ducat in the sixteenth century still retained the standing figure of St. Wenceslas on the obverse and the lion of Bohemia on the reverse but in the seventeenth and eighteenth centuries Bohemia's saint gave place to a standing figure of the ruler. On early thalers the obverse showed a half-length portrait of the ruler holding sceptre and sword and the reverse an eagle with shield on breast while later issues had sometimes a standing figure on obverse or a more conventional bust. The Prague groschen with their traditional types continued to be issued for some time as well as other smaller divisionary silver pieces usually with types of bust and shield or shield and value. In the eighteenth century the small denominations in gröschel were struck in copper. Under Maria Theresa (1740–80) the types were three shields on obverse and the value on reverse.

A break in the conventional issues of Bohemia came with the revolt of Protestant Bohemia against Matthias II in 1618. The coinage of the revolt, silver pieces of a quarter thaler and less, reverted to the traditional Bohemian types of a crown and lion rampant and had no regnal name but were simply inscribed *Moneta regni Bohemiae*. Frederick V, Count Palatine, was elected king in 1619 and coinage was struck for him in gold and silver before he was driven out by Ferdinand II in 1621. Moravia which had also passed to Austria along with Bohemia in 1526 participated in the revolt against Matthias and struck a coinage of thalers and portions with eagle obverse and inscription *Moneta Nova Marchie Moraviae*. Moravia also followed the example of Bohemia in coining for Frederick, Count Palatine. Another departure from conventional types was supplied by the issue in Bohemia, as in several German states, of 'mining' thalers in several reigns, the reverses recording the source of the metal in the Joachimstal.

REPUBLIC OF CZECHOSLOVAKIA

On the dissolution of the Austro-Hungarian empire in 1918 the Versailles Treaty created a new republic of Czechoslovakia composed of Bohemia, Moravia, Slovakia, part of Silesia and Carpathian Ruthenia. The new coinage system took as its unit the korona struck in cupro-nickel and divisible into 100 haleru of which the 50, 25 and 20 pieces were in cupro-nickel, the 10 and 5 in bronze and the 2 haleru in zinc. In the twenty years between the establishment of Czechoslovakia and its occupation by Germany in 1938 a certain amount of gold was struck in the form of commemorative ducats and multiple ducats. The lower denominations revived the types of the lion of Bohemia and the half-length figure of St. Wenceslas while the higher multiples had on the reverse the mounted figure of the saint. On the ordinary issues the invariable obverse was the Bohemian lion rampant with inscription *Republika Ceskoslovenska* but the reverse types varies on the several denominations. On the korona itself was a kneeling female with sheaf of corn and on the 5 korona a smelting furnace, while higher denominations had reverses of a commemorative nature such as the portrait of Masaryk, the founder of Czechoslovakia, on the 10 korona of 1928. The reverses of the haleru consisted chiefly of the value in numerals with background types such as wheat-ears or a bridge (Pl. 719).

A puppet state of Slovakia set up by the Germans issued its own coinage of korona and haleru between 1939 and 1945. On either obverse or reverse of all its issues appeared the shield of Slovakia with a cross with double arms and inscription *Slovenska Republika*. On the multiple korona in silver the other types were the portrait of President Tiso on the 50 and 20 pieces, Saints Cyril and Methodius on the 20, and the head of Father Hlinka on the 5 piece. The cupro-nickel korona itself had simply the value between two corn-ears. The haleru denominations all bore their value with an additional type—on the 50 a plough, on the 20 Nitra Castle and on the 10 Bratislava Castle—while the 5 had only the numeral of its value. These denominations, first struck in cupro-nickel for the 20 and bronze for the others, were successively issued in bronze, aluminium and finally zinc as the war continued. A separate coinage in zinc was issued between 1940 and 1944 for the remainder of the country which was formed into the protectorate of Bohemia and Moravia. The constant obverse type was the Bohemian lion with the name of the protectorate in German and Czech. On the korona the reverse type bore the value between two branches, on the 50 and 20 haleru the value and wheat-sheaf, and on the 10 haleru the value and a bridge.

The coinage of Czechoslovakia which was restored as an independent state in 1945 resumed the obverse type and style of its pre-occupation issues and also the reverses of the 20 and 50 haleru and the korona. Special reverses of a commemorative nature appeared in successive years on 50 and 100 korona coins including a portrait of Stalin on his seventieth birthday in 1949 after the establishment of the Communist régime. The larger denominations were of silver, the lower of cupro-nickel or bronze, but in 1953 a new issue of various haleru denominations from 25 downwards was struck in aluminium. The types were still the Bohemian lion on obverse but simply the value in numerals on the reverse in a wreath with a star above.

SCANDINAVIA

DENMARK

Coinage came late to all the Scandinavian lands though coin in the form of booty from the more settled lands of Europe found its way to these lands with the returning plunderers and only in the late tenth century do native silver pennies make their appearance, bearing the name of the Danish king Sven (985–1014). The Danish raids on England at this period are reflected in the types of these coins, which copy closely the Anglo-Saxon penny of Æthelred II with its profile bust with sceptre and its cross reverse with the letters *Crux* in the angles (see p. 232). The inscriptions on Sven's coins give, in the Anglo-Saxon fashion, his name and title *Zven Rex ad Dener* on the obverse and on the reverse the mint and moneyer *Godwine M—Andaer*. Under Canute (1014–35), the conqueror of England and Norway, coinage becomes more plentiful but as he usually bears the title *Rex Anglorum* it is difficult to distinguish amongst the issues with the mint name 'Lund' those of London and of Lund in Scandinavia, though the other Danish issues by mints at Roskilde and Viborg are distinctive enough. Under Harthacanute (1036–42), Magnus the Good (1042–7) and Svend Estridsen (1047–75), the continuing English types are joined by designs derived from Byzantine models (Pl. 720) and sometimes a Runic script gives the name of mint and moneyer.

The succession to the Danish throne was in almost constant dispute from the later eleventh century and the troubled times are reflected in the impoverishment of the coinage both in the matter of metallic content and of design and execution. The pennies of Olaf (1086–95) are of a more spread fabric and introduce the facing royal bust which was to continue in use for most of the first half of the next century (Pl. 721). The rider reverse on Olaf's coins is oddly reminiscent of coins of south-east Europe while the Paschal Lamb on issues of Erik Lam (1137–47) is yet another example of the punning type. Waldemar I (1157–82) who restored some degree of unity to the kingdom issued pennies with obverse bust and a building reverse and also began the issue of a bracteate coinage without inscription; some examples have the double portrait of himself and his queen, Sophia. For almost the next century and a half the coinage consisted almost entirely of un-inscribed pennies with a great variety of types—lion, wheel, star, sword, etc.—

but with rarely any lettering to permit of their certain attribution to the successive kings (Pl. 722).

Alongside the regal coinage of Denmark there existed from the reign of Canute (1080–6) an increasing number of episcopal issues. The earliest of these was that of Lund; later came the issues of Roskilde, Ribe and Schleswig. Initially the types are the bust of the king and the bishop but later some of the episcopal issues make no reference to royal authority and have purely episcopal types such as the bishop's crozier.

Not till the reign of Eric of Pomerania (1396–1439) did a proper coinage system replace the undistinguished series of billon or even copper pennies of the fourteenth century. Eric's coinage consisted of pieces in silver of 3 pence and 6 pence, some bracteate and, in copper, the penny. The types were usually simple; a crown with an E in the field or at the centre of the crown. On the sösling or piece of six pennies in 1424 the obverse was a shield with three leopards passant. This also formed the obverse type for the skilling of Christopher of Bavaria (1439–48), with a shield-of-arms reverse. In the interregnum in 1448 the coins bore no royal name but only the inscription *Moneta regni Danie*. The first gold denominations were struck by John I (1481–1513); the noble, showing the king enthroned and a crowned shield of arms, has the unusual obverse inscription *Johannes dei gra rex Danorum iussit me fieri*. The obverse of the gold florin was the standing figure of St. Canute. The skilling, sösling and hvid or blanc continued to be struck in silver (Pl. 723).

The reign of Christian II (1513–23) marks the beginning of the modern period of coinage in Denmark with the introduction of the large silver gulden (sölvgylden) which reproduced the enthroned king and crowned-shield types of the gold noble. The obverse of the silver skilling (Pl. 724) showed a standing figure of the king and that of the hvid his crowned initial. It was in this reign in 1520 that Sweden revolted and secured her independence and in 1523 Christian II was forced to flee from Denmark. The first issues of Frederick I (1524–33) accord him the title *electus rex Danie*, those subsequent to his coronation entitle him *Dei gratia rex Danie*, a distinction which persisted in subsequent reigns until the monarchy was declared hereditary in 1660. Amongst the mint names of his coinage that of Copenhagen makes its appearance. The religious dissensions arising from the Reformation were finally settled by the election of Christian III (1534–59) who issued the large silver mark introducing his profile portrait on the obverse but retaining the crowned shield of Denmark on the reverse. This reign also produced a thaler and half-thaler with types of the half-length figure of the king with sceptre and on the reverse a crowned shield, types similar to those of the Joachimsthaler (see p. 354).

In 1618 the coinage system was altered by the introduction of a new money of account, the corona danica of 8 marks, each of 16 skillings. Silver pieces showed the full-length figure of the king on obverse and a crown on reverse with the inscription *corona danica* (Pl. 725). The gold crown equal to $1\frac{3}{4}$ ducats had as types the crowned shield of Denmark and a crown. An unusual series in this reign consisted of the ducat in gold with multiples and portions and various skilling denominations in silver. These have on obverse the royal portrait or crowned monogram and in three lines on the reverse the words *Iustus Jehovah Iudex*. As the word Jehovah is rendered in Hebrew script this series is usually described as the 'Hebrew' coinage. Among commemorative pieces which are a feature of the coinage a notable issue of Frederick III (1648–70) celebrated the relief of the Swedish siege of Copenhagen in 1659. The obverse consisted of the royal monogram on a rock and the reverse showed a hand emerging from the clouds, grasping a sabre and striking at an arm reaching for the Danish crown.

As in other European countries the coinage in Denmark by the mid seventeenth century had developed into a comparatively regular system. The ducat with various multiples was struck in gold, usually with the royal portrait on the obverse and an heraldic type or crown or monogram on the reverse (Pl. 726). The major silver piece was the speciesdaler, often with a double piece and a half, again usually with royal portrait and heraldic reverse. On the silver krone the royal monogram crowned provided the obverse, as also on the mark and its double. Smaller divisionary silver of various skilling denominations had a variety of obverses, the three-lion shield, lion within wreath or royal monogram and on the reverse appeared the value expressed in figures and words across the field, e.g. *II/Skilling/Danske*. Further simplification came under Christian VII in 1775 with the establishment of the rigsspeciesdaler as the chief silver coin with portions ranging from two-thirds downwards. The types on the higher values were the royal portrait and shield, on the lower the royal monogram and value. From 1812 lower values in skilling with head and value or monogram and value were struck in copper. In 1872 a Scandinavian monetary union established a new system in which the unit was the krone, divided into 100 öre. Multiple kroner of 5, 10 and 20 were struck in gold; in silver, denominations were 2 and 1 krone and smaller pieces down to 10 öre with types royal portrait and shield or value. Smaller öre denominations with monogram and value were struck in bronze (Pl. 727). In common with other series the twentieth-century issues, especially since the 1914–18 war, have seen the disappearance of gold coinage as well as the larger denominations in silver and the replacement of silver and bronze by baser metals. Thus in the contemporary coinage the 2 and 1 krone coins still show the royal portrait and Danish arms but are struck in aluminium-bronze while the öre denominations retain the royal monogram crowned and the value but are struck in cupro-nickel or zinc. A special issue of the silver 2 kroner piece in 1958 with the portraits of King Frederick IX and Princess Margrethe was struck on the occasion of the declaration of the princess as heir to the throne.

ICELAND

Iceland, for long a dependancy of Denmark, began its own separate coinage in 1922. Since Iceland still was included in a union with Denmark this was still a regal coinage. The unit was the krona, divided into 100 aurar and the ordinary coinage until the early 1940's consisted of krona pieces of values 10, 5, 2 and 1 and 25, 10, 5 and 2 aurar, as well as the I eyrir piece struck in cupro-nickel or aluminium-bronze with types, the word *Island* and value on reverse, and either the Icelandic arms, crowned and flanked by the monogram Cx - R of Christian X of Denmark, or the royal monogram crowned on obverse. A number of special pieces of 10, 5 and 2 kronur were struck in silver in 1930. to commemorate the thousandth year of the Althing, the Icelandic Parliament. Iceland proclaimed itself an independent republic in 1941 and a new coinage was issued in 1946. Coins of 2 kronur, 1 krona and 25, 10, 5 aurar and 1 eyrir in aluminium-bronze present the Icelandic arms on the obverse and *Island* and the value on reverse. The arms on the krona values have supporters (Pl. 728); on the eyrir values they are surrounded by two branches of laurel.

NORWAY

As in most of the European lands which had never formed part of the Roman empire coinage in Norway makes its appearance roughly at the same time as Christianity was beginning to make its way into the country. The earliest Norwegian coins are silver pennies attributed to the usurper Hakon Jarl about 990. These, like the earliest Danish coins, are copies of the pennies of Æthelred II of England of the category with profile bust and sceptre and on the reverse, cross with the letters *Crux* in the angles. The inscriptions are usually somewhat blundered but on pennies of similar type struck by Olaf I (996–1000) his name and title *Onlaf rex Nor* appears distinctly. In the early decades of the eleventh century Norway came under Danish domination until its independence was secured by Magnus I (1035–47) who even carried the war into Denmark. Silver pennies of Magnus continued to copy the Anglo-Saxon pennies of Æthelred but also borrowed Byzantine types, especially the figure of Christ. On some of the Æthelred copies a Runic script gives the name of the moneyer, a feature continued on issues for Harald III (1047–66). The copying of the Anglo-Saxon profile type under Harald becomes progressively more incoherent and almost unrecognizable (Pl. 729). In the later eleventh century the fabric of the silver penny became so thin that these coins can almost be classed as semi-bracteates. The types on these pieces are usually a facing crowned bust and some form of the cross motif but, as they are mostly uninscribed, their attribution is a matter of some uncertainty. This coinage was followed by a series of small bracteates with occasional head or cross type (Pl. 731), but more commonly only a letter (Pl. 730) and it was only after some century and a half that coinage with types on both sides reappeared under Magnus VI (1263–80). The types, a neat facing bust, crowned and a cross with rosette in each angle, reflecting the influence of the English sterling penny, were continued under Eric (1280–99) while Hakon V (1299–1319) struck coins with a profile bust and cross fourchée, reminiscent of contemporary Scottish issues. The reverse inscription of some of the latter's coins *Moneta de Asloia* contains the first reference to a mint at Oslo. On other issues of Eric the use, as a reverse type, of the Norwegian lion with axe is one of the early examples of a purely heraldic type on European coinages. A second series of small bracteates, mainly with letter type, supplies the coinage until, on the death of Olaf III in 1387, Norway passed under the control of the Danish kings.

Although with the rare exception of some coins struck by John I (1483–1513) using only his Norwegian title there were no separate issues for Norway during its union with Denmark right up to the early nineteenth century, the Norwegian title always formed part of the royal style on the coinage and the Norwegian lion with axe was a frequent reverse type (Pl. 732). In 1812 Norway was conquered by Sweden and formally ceded by Denmark in 1815. The coinage in the earlier part of the nineteenth century consisted of silver pieces, the speciesdaler and portions and various skilling denominations. The types on the higher denominations were the portrait of the king with the joint Swedish and Norwegian titles and on the reverse the crowned shield with the Norwegian lion. Lower skilling pieces carried the shield on obverse and the value in words on the reverse, the smallest values being struck in copper (Pl. 733). After the Scandinavian monetary convention of 1872 had established as the monetary unit the krone, divided into 100 öre, the pieces of 10 and 20 kroner in gold and 1 and 2 kroner and the higher öre values in silver continued to have the royal portrait and Norwegian arms as types while the lower öre values in silver and the smallest in bronze bore an obverse monogram and a value reverse.

The declaration of Norway as an independent kingdom under Hakon VII in 1905 brought no alteration of the denominational system but was followed naturally by a change of types. On the gold 10 and 20 kroner appeared the crowned, profile bust of the new king with a standing figure of St. Olaf as the reverse type. The silver 1 and 2 kroner carried the bare-headed portrait of the king with as reverse the Norwegian arms surrounded by the collar of the Order of Olaf and, in the case of the 2 kroner, the shields of the provinces. Smaller öre pieces with crowned arms or crowned monogram and value were issued in bronze or, during the first world war, in iron (Pl. 734). Between the two wars the types on the silver krone and higher öre values were a cross formed by four crowned initials and the collar of the Olaf order. A new coinage begun in 1951 has produced cupro-nickel pieces of 1 krone and 50, 25 and 10 öre with crowned initial and Norwegian arms or value and smaller öre values in copper with like types. A coinage of bronze 2 öre pieces in 1959 carry the crowned monogram of Olaf V on obverse and a grouse and the value on the reverse.

SWEDEN

Coinage in Sweden as in the other Scandinavian lands has its beginning towards the end of the tenth century and, like the earliest Danish and Norwegian issues, the silver pennies struck by Olaf Skotkonung (995–1021) are copied from Anglo-Saxon pennies of Æthelred II (Pl. 735). The next series struck for Amund Jacob (1022–50) are copies of the pennies of Canute with as obverse type the royal portrait in profile with pointed helmet and sceptre. These early penny issues were followed by a long series of small bracteate pieces, interspersed with occasional two-type pieces which extended up to the middle of the fourteenth century. The types on these bracteates are simple but of great variety—the royal bust, cross, star, lion, wheel, sword—and only sometimes do these coins bear an inscription permitting their attribution to specific rulers. In the reign of Albert of Mecklenburg (1363–95) a new coinage piece was struck, the örtug, modelled on the north German Witte. The obverse usually took the form of a facing crowned bust of the three-crowns badge of Sweden and the reverse a cross. When, after 1395, Sweden formed part of a united kingdom under the Danish kings the örtug continued to be issued as the principal denomination, the most common types now being the shield with the three crowns of Sweden and the initial of the sovereign (Pl. 736).

The first large silver coins of thaler type which mark the beginning of modern coinage were struck under Sten Sture the younger in 1512. These coins bore the full-length figure in armour of St. Eric on obverse with inscription *S. Ericus Rex Suecie* and on the reverse the crowned arms of Sweden on a long cross with inscription *Mone Stockholme* 1512. The Stockholm revolt of 1520 marked the beginning of Sweden's assertion of her independence from Denmark and in 1521 Gustav Vasa was elected king. The coinage of independent Sweden under Gustav Vasa added to the existing örtug a number of new denominations, notably the silver öre with its types of full-length facing figure of the new king on obverse and on the reverse a crowned shield with the three crowns and two arrows in saltire with a G in the lower angle, the whole on a long cross. Large silver dalers showed the half-length figure of Gustav in profile, holding sword and orb above a shield of arms while the full-length figure of our Lord on the reverse with its inscription beginning *Salvator mundi* earned for this piece the name of Salvatordaler (Pl. 737). This type was continued into the reign of Queen Christina in the mid seventeenth century. Other silver denominations included the mark of 4 öre and half-mark with Gustav's crowned and armoured portrait bust and his shield of arms. The majority of the issues carry the initials of the mints at Stockholm, Abo and Westeraas and in the course of this reign Lombardic lettering gives place to Roman. A series of emergency silver coins on rectangular flans known as klippings struck in 1543, 1556 and 1557 have as types the sheaf badge of Vasa and the value in öre, ranging from 16 to 2. The first Swedish gold coinage was struck by Eric (1560–8) whose gold gulden with its obverse type the laureate and armoured bust of the king and the date 1568 has an allegorical reverse inscribed *Deus dat cui vult*.

In the civil war between Eric and his brothers Johan of Finland and Karl of Südermannland the two brothers issued a series of rectangular klippings with the crowned Vasa badge and their initials on obverse and the three crowns on reverse together with the value expressed in öre. Eric, deposed in 1568, was succeeded by Johan III (1568–92) who issued a rich series of gold and silver which included multiple dalers of values up to 4. Sigismund, son of Johan III, was already King of Poland when he succeeded his father in 1592 but was deposed in 1598 because of his Catholic faith. In the interregnum between 1598 and 1603 part of the Swedish coinage carried no regal name but, instead, the inscription *Moneta Regni Sueciae* while issues between 1604 and 1606 were in the name of Karl, Sigismund's uncle, described as *rex designatus*. The coinage of Gustav II Adolf (1611–32) reflects the dominant rôle which he played in the military history of northern Europe. He struck an extensive series of gold ducats (Pl. 738) with multiples up to five and silver dalers with multiples up to four, as well as divisionary silver ranging from the mark of 8 öre down to the $\frac{1}{12}$ öra or twopenny piece. Copper coinage introduced in 1625 took the form of rectangular pieces marked on obverse with the three crowns and the royal initials and on reverse with the two arrows in saltire crowned, together with the value in öre, a value which represented the intrinsic worth of the piece, not its token value. In addition to the Swedish coinage of Gustav Adolf a rich series was struck in his name at numerous mints in Germany such as Augsburg, Würzburg, Frankfurt-am-Main, Erfurt and Osnabrück.

On some issues of Gustav Adolf's daughter Christina (1633–54) the simple obverse head in laurel-wreath perhaps reflects her known interest in the ancient Roman coinage. Under Christina also began the issue of the copper platmynt, huge plates of copper marked with their intrinsic value. A sign of Sweden's declining political importance and prosperity was the arbitrary raising of the value of the coinage, even in the case of the pieces of copper plate-money under Charles XI (1660–97). Worse followed in the reign of Charles XII (1697–1719) who, after the disastrous defeat at Pultava in 1707 and the loss of most of Sweden's extra-territorial Baltic possessions, was reduced to the issue of paper money in 1715 and, on the advice of Finance Minister Baron Görtz, to the issue of token dalers and half-pieces in copper. This coinage carried some figure of myth or ancient legend on the obverse accompanied by the inscription *Wert och wapen*, while the obverse showed inside a shield the token value of the piece in words. The lack of confidence in the coinage was expressed in the expansion of the issues of copper plate-money of which some examples weigh as much as 20 kilogrammes.

It was not until the reign of Gustav III (1771–92) that a new coinage commanding confidence was introduced. This system was based on the silver rigsdaler species which had as types the royal portrait and the Swedish arms crowned and surrounded by the collar of the Order with the value I - R D in the field. The divisionary pieces were of value of two-thirds of a daler and downwards. All earlier coinages with the exception of the gold ducat and the old speciesdaler were demonetized and the issue of copper plate-money also came to an end. The daler was divided into 48 skillings, each of 4 öre; and pieces of 1 skilling downwards, struck in copper, had as types the royal monogram crowned and crossed arrows and value (Pl. 739). The monetary system and its types remained remarkably consistent even after the advent of Marshal Bernadotte and his succession in 1818 as Charles XIV, though in his reign the fineness of the coinage was lowered in 1830 and divisionary pieces of a quarter and downwards replaced the former subdivisions of the daler. In 1855 under Oscar I (1844–59) a new unit was created, the rigsdaler of 100 öre, equal to a quarter of the species rigsdaler. The types continued to be the royal portrait with the shield of arms and value on reverse for the rigsdaler and its divisions, and the value only as reverse on the lower values in silver (50 to 10 öre) and in copper (5 to $\frac{1}{2}$ öre).

In accordance with the Scandinavian monetary agreement of 1872 described above in the Danish section a new Swedish coinage was begun in 1873. The types on kroner both in gold and silver were the royal portrait and arms, on öre in silver and copper the royal monogram crowned and the value between the three crowns of Sweden. These have continued to be the essential types of Swedish coins with the exception of some special commemorative issues usually in the 2 kroner denomination. The silver öre pieces during the last war modified their types, placing a crown and the country's name on obverse and the value alone on reverse. These denominations of the present sovereign, Gustav VI Adolf (1950–), have transferred the country's name *Sverige* to the reverse but the kroner denominations continue the traditional portrait-and-arms types (Pl. 740).

FINLAND (SUOMI)

In the later nineteenth century a distinctive coinage began to be issued by the czars of Russia as grand-dukes of Finland. The monetary unit was the silver mark, divided into 100 pennia. Denominations of 20 and 10 markaa were struck in gold, of 2 and 1 markaa and 50 and 25 pennia in silver and finally pennia coins of value 10, 5 and 1 in bronze. The types in gold and silver were the imperial eagle of Russia with lion-shield on breast on obverse and the value on reverse; on the bronze the obverse bore the imperial monogram crowned, the reverse, the value. The denominational system was retained when Finland was declared a republic in 1917 but the rampant lion of Finland with uplifted sword replaced the Russian eagle on the obverse. In the post-war coinage which has suffered severe inflation the 1 and 5 markaa coins are struck in iron with a four-loop pattern on obverse, while the 10, 20 and 50 markaa denominations in aluminium-bronze continue to carry the Finnish lion on obverse but have a tree beside the figure of value on the reverse.

EASTERN EUROPE

POLAND

The beginning of a native coinage in Poland as in Scandinavia is roughly coeval with the beginning of the spread of Christianity in the later tenth century. The earliest coinage, in the form of rare silver pieces of the denar or penny type, and of rough execution and style is attributed to Misico I (964–992). The obverse type is a crown accompanied by an inscription in ill-shaped letters giving the name of Misico, while the reverse is the usual mediaeval cross motif. The coinage, however, assumed substantial proportions under Boleslav I (992–1025) who received the title of king from the emperor Otto III in 1000. One issue which has types a cock or perhaps a peacock on obverse and a cross of three lines with a rectangle containing a pellet in the corner of each angle on reverse and on which the inscription of both sides reads only *Princeps Polonie* has been ascribed to Boleslav I. Another with a rough profile portrait and name *Bolizlaus* on obverse and a church on reverse with an attempt to transcribe the name Adelheid is a copy struck in Gnesen of the *Adelheidspfennige* of Otto III (see p. 320). Yet a third coinage with facing bust in the Byzantine style on obverse and an elaborate cross on reverse has the name of Boleslav in Cyrillic script across the obverse field and round the reverse cross and is thought to have been struck in Kiev which was captured by Boleslav.

There is no certain coinage for Misico II (1025–34) nor for his widow Rixa, regent for the young Casimir I, and in 1039 Bratislav I of Bohemia occupied part of Poland including the important towns of Posen and Gnesen. The coinage in circulation in Poland during the reign of Casimir I who was restored in 1041 consists mainly of the so-called *Wendenpfennige*, small silver pieces with turned-up edge and often church-and-cross types. Coins of Boleslav II (1058–81) retain the module and fabric of these *Wendenpfennige* but introduce more individual types such as profile head and rider or facing head and cross. The coinage of Wladislas (1081–1102) with a profile head and building with three towers is somewhat rare but issues of Boleslav III (1102–39) are more plentiful and are struck on a slightly broader flan with a variety of types. Boleslav is shown enthroned and holding sword on shoulder or standing holding sceptre and shield, accompanied by a second figure holding book and raising right hand. The reverse, again, is

398

normally a form of cross. Boleslav III left his kingdom to his four sons of whom Wladislas II (1139–46) was to be recognized as sovereign, but the principal result was to initiate a century of civil war. A small series of silver pieces, usually without inscription, is ascribed to Wladislas II but the issues of the second brother, Boleslav IV (1146–73), who seized the suzerainty are more plentiful and varied, including a series with the facing bust of Boleslav on obverse and the busts of three princes behind a table on reverse (Pl. 741).

The attribution of some bracteates of small module to this Boleslav is not completely assured but certainly in the reign of the third brother, Misico III (1173–7 and 1195–1202), the only coinage is of bracteate fabric. The duke is shown in a great variety of poses—a facing bust, an enthroned or a mounted figure—and in this series the inscriptions are of more than usual interest. Some give the name and title of Misico in Latin, some in Hebrew while others record the Polish form of the name expressed in Hebrew letters (Pl. 742). Under Casimir II (1177–94) this Hebraic form of inscription was not used and such inscriptions as are found on the poor and declining bracteate coinage of the thirteenth and early fourteenth centuries are in Latin. In Silesia which passed to Boleslav the Great, son of Wladislas II, Duke of Poland in 1163, a bracteate coinage was struck during the most of the twelfth century. This series is largely uninscribed and has a rich variety of types: in addition to the usual facing-bust types, a plumed crowned helmet, heraldic beasts and letters are frequently encountered. Towards the end of the century two-sided silver denars re-appear, repeating frequently the types of Silesian bracteates and sometimes inscribed with the name and title of the duke, though more often the coins are without inscription.

Casimir the Great (1333–70) whose reign put an end to the chaos which had reigned in Poland for a century or more was responsible also for re-establishing the Polish coinage. Larger silver denominations were introduced on the model of those in use in western Europe. A groschen coinage of relatively short duration copied closely the groschen of Bohemia (see p. 386). Around the crown on the obverse was inscribed, in two circles, *Kazimirus Primus/Dei Gracia Rex Polonie*, while the reverse, inscribed *Grossi Cracovienses*, replaced the Bohemian lion by the Polish eagle. More substantial were the issues of the half-groschen or kwartnik with types of seated figure of Casimir with orb and sceptre and Polish eagle. This kwartnik remained the standard denomination, though under Wladislav Jagiello (1386–1434) the seated figure was replaced in 1399 by a crown, from which type the denomination is also known as the coronat (Pl. 743). On the quarter-groschen the obverse was reduced to a crowned head while on the denar the types were commonly the initial K and a crown or eagle and crown. The only coinage of Louis I of Hungary as King of Poland (1370–82) is a series of denars with types,

L crowned and eagle but Ladislas Jagiello, Grand-Duke of Lithuania, who succeeded to the Polish crown by marriage to Hedwige, daughter of Louis in 1386,
resumed issue of the kwartnik with types, cross with double transverse bar and
eagle in 1393. This denomination declined in value and was replaced by the
coronat described above. Together with small denars also with crown type,
latterly struck in copper, the coronat continued to be the main Polish denomination
throughout the fifteenth century.

The coinage of gold and of heavy silver pieces by Sigismund I (1506–48) marks
the beginning of Polish coinage in the modern period. A decree of 1526 provided
for small divisionary silver pieces, the denar, the ternar or triple denar, the groschen and its half and in addition large silver pieces of 3 and 6 groschen as well as a
gold ducat. The obverse on the higher denominations from now on is almost
exclusively the crowned portrait bust of the king. The reverse of the ducat showed
the arms of Poland, while on the 6 groschen piece the polish arms had, placed
around it, the arms of various provinces and appendages. Under Sigismund-
Augustus (1548–72) the mint of Cracow was closed and coinage was struck only in
the mints in Lithuania, including the first Polish coin of the thaler category as well
as gold ducats and some large 10 ducat pieces. The death of Sigismund-Augustus
the last of the Jagiellon dynasty was followed by an interregnum of a year, the
short year reign of Henry of Valois and finally by the election of Stephen Batory
of Transylvania in 1576. The coinage system, reformed by Stephen, consisted of
the thaler, its half, 6 and 3 groschen pieces in silver and billon groschen, half-
groschen, schillings and denars. The types on the major denominations were still
the royal bust and arms but the smaller denominations carried a crowned eagle
or the initial S, crowned. The occasional placing of the arms or initials of the
royal treasurers responsible for the issues as subsidiary types on the coins had begun
under Sigismund I but from the time of Stephen Batory this became constant
practice (Pl. 744).

The political importance of Poland and the high standard to which Stephen
Batory had raised the coinage began to decline in the seventeenth century under
Sigismund III (1587–1632), a prince of the royal Swedish house of Vasa. The
value of the silver denominations to which were added new pieces, the ort or
quarter-thaler and the poltoraki or 3 kreuzer piece, depreciated extensively but
gold which still commanded confidence was struck in considerable quantity and in
various multiples, principally of 5 and 10 ducats, though exceptional higher
multiples are recorded (Pl. 745). Under Wladislas IV (1632–48) coinage was
restricted to the ducat, the thaler and its half, all issue of divisionary pieces being
suspended. A projected reform of the coinage by John Casimir (1648–68) on
the basis of a new mark scarcely came to execution. Further depreciation took

the form of issuing schillings in copper, coins known as borotinki (Pl. 746) from their moneyer Borotini; and guldens, of official value 30 groschen but of intrinsic value some 12 groschen, were issued in mass by the moneyers Andrew and Thomas Tympf.

In the seventeenth century Poland had lost Livonia to Sweden and the close tie with Prussia had been broken, while in 1667 Smolensk, Kiev and the Ukraine were ceded to Russia. The continued internal political disturbances and external military pressures are reflected in the mediocre issues of eighteenth-century rulers. Only under Stanislas-Augustus (1764–95), the last of the Polish kings, was the coinage reformed on the basis of the German system with a ducat in gold, a thaler and half in silver as well as pieces of 8, 4 and 2 good groschen (Pl. 747); in addition the groschen and portions were struck in copper. By divisions of Poland between Austria, Prussia and Russia in 1772 and again between Prussia and Russia in 1793 independent Polish coinage came to an end, with the exception of the coins of the Polish revolt in 1831 and of the city of Cracow in 1835. Russia struck a coinage for Poland at the Warsaw mint from 1815 with types the head of the czar and Russian eagle. Higher values of the zloty were struck in gold; values from 10 downwards and groszy values in silver. From 1833 the coinage for Poland was issued on the standard of the Russian rouble. During the first world war a coinage in iron of various values of the fenigow with types, double-headed eagle and value was struck by the Central Powers.

Poland was re-created as an independent republic in 1918 and resumed coinage in 1923. The unit was the zloty of 100 groszy. The types on the zloty and higher groszy values in nickel and the lower groszy values in bronze were the Polish eagle and the value of the coin. Higher values in silver, many of them commemorative issues, have varying historical or allegorical obverses but usually the Polish eagle as reverse. Polish coinage ceased during the German occupation of 1939 to 1945 and new coinage for liberated Poland did not appear till 1949. The denominations and types of the pre-war coinage were revived but the reverses showing the value have an additional ornament of laurel-branches (Pl. 748).

THE BALTIC REPUBLICS

The settlement after the first world war created three independent republics out of the Baltic provinces formerly controlled by czarist Russia. Each of these issued its own coinage until, following the outbreak of the last war, these states were overrun by the Soviet Union.

Estonia. The monetary unit was the kroon, divided first into 100 marks and, after 1927, into 100 senti. Pieces of 2 krooni in silver bore an obverse type showing the castle of Tallinn, the capital, and a shield with three lions passant on the reverse. The kroon piece in aluminium-bronze with similar reverse had a Viking ship on the obverse. The lower denominations in marks or senti had types, the shield of arms and the value.

Latvia. The unit, the lats, was divided into 100 santimi. The normal types both on the silver lats, the 2 and 5 lati pieces as well as the mekel and bronze santimi values were the arms of Latvia with lion and griffin supporters and the value.

Lithuania. The unit was the litas of 100 centu. On silver pieces of 1, 2 and 5 litai and on the bronze coins of values 1, 2 and 5 centai the types were the value on reverse and obverse the Lithuanian horseman.

RUSSIA

Mention has been made of the coinages produced by the Greek colonies on the north coast of the Black Sea (see p. 23) but after these outposts of civilization were overwhelmed by the barbarian flood many centuries elapsed before a native coinage was again struck on Russian soil. Somewhere about the first millennium A.D. the Varangian princes of Kiev began to coin in gold and silver in imitation of the issues of the Byzantine empire. To Vladimir I (988–1015) are attributed gold pieces with his seated figure holding sceptre on obverse accompanied by his name, while a facing bust of Christ with cross in nimbus occupies the reverse. On another variety the reverse displays a trident-shaped object of uncertain significance. The types of this second variety were used on the silver coins also, which, like the gold, were of a flat, spread fabric. Similar silver coins were also issued by Svyatopolka (*c.* 1016) and Jaroslav I (1016–54). No later coinage is known of Kiev which was fragmented by succession disputes into many small principalities and in the early thirteenth century Russia was engulfed by the Mongols of the Golden Horde.

Although the Mongol hold on Russia was not broken until the late fifteenth century a number of native states and duchies of which the more important were those of Moscow, Novgorod, Pskov, Tver and Riasan exercised a sufficient degree of independence to be able to strike their own coinages from sometime in the fourteenth century. The coinage consisted of dengi, small, eccentrically shaped silver pieces. On these the reverse usually carried the word *petschut*—stamp or seal—the names of the duke, of the Mongol overlord and the moneyer. The obverses of this series are of great variety: representations of the duke or prince, an archer, a mounted figure and various animals and birds (Pl. 749). Ivan III, Duke of

Moscow (1462–1505) who broke the Mongol hold in 1477 is credited with the issue of gold ducats copying the types of standing figure of the ruler and shield of arms of the Hungarian ducat but little change was made in the silver denga. Other small silver pieces of irregular shape issued by later dukes have as an obverse type a mounted figure whose lance imparted to these pieces the name of kopeka which was equivalent to 2 dengi. On the reverse an inscription in several lines gives the name of the issuing duke or prince (Pl. 750).

The native coinage was supplemented by extensive use of foreign gold and silver currencies, chiefly the various gold ducats and thalers of western Europe. Under the Czar Alexis Mihailovitch (1645–76) there was an extensive use of over-striking of foreign thaler-type coins to produce silver roubles. The overstriking consisted of an obverse type of the mounted czar and, for the reverse, the double-headed eagle within a square. Countermarking was also extensively used; an oval punch contained the mounted figure of the czar, an oblong punch the date 1655, the first instance of the use of the Christian-era dating, for previously the era used had been that of the creation, determined by the Council of Constantinople in 680 as the year 5508 B.C. Fractions, both overstruck and countermarked, were produced by halving or quartering of thaler-type coins.

The real modernization of the Russian coinage was the work of Peter the Great (1689–1725). The new coinage system was produced for the first time in Russia by mechanical means and a new mint constructed at Moscow in 1711, though subsequently in 1719 the mint organization and machinery was ordered to be moved to Peter's new capital at St. Petersburg. The new system consisted of a gold ducat with laureate bust of the czar and double-headed eagle which was replaced in 1718 by a double gold rouble with a reverse of St. Andrew and his cross (Pl. 751). The major silver piece was the rouble, again with portrait-and-eagle types as on the gold ducat. The reverse was altered in 1724, taking the form of a cross composed of four Π's crowned framing the star of the Order of St. Andrew. The half- and quarter-roubles made use of similar types but the smaller denominations, the grivna (10 kopeks), the 5 kopek piece and the altyn (3 kopeks) had the crowned eagle as obverse and the value in words as the reverse. Kopeks with the old irregular flan were also replaced by circular pieces with the types of St. George and the value (Pl. 752). This denomination was struck in both silver and copper which was the metal also of the denga and the polouchka, both with eagle-and-value types.

These denominations and types have been described in some detail, for subsequent Russian coinage repeats this basic pattern with only some few alterations. Elizabeth I (1741–62) added new gold denominations in the form of 5 and 10 rouble pieces which had as reverse type the imperial eagle at centre with the arms of Moscow, Keizan, Astrakhan and Siberia arranged about it in the form of a cross (Pl. 753). The 10 kopek piece in copper with eagle obverse declares its denomination in words on the reverse above military trophies of flag, drum and cannon while the 2 kopek in copper, still with St. George type, now on the reverse, had the royal monogram crowned between two laurel-branches on the obverse. Further changes in the kopek and other copper denominations took place under Catherine II (1762–96). The kopek and denga in copper were struck with types similar to those described for the 2 kopek of Elizabeth I. Perhaps her most distinctive and certainly most commonly encountered coin is the large 5 kopek piece with crowned monogram on obverse and eagle reverse below which is a scroll carrying, in Russian, the value of the coin (Pl. 754). A copper series struck in 1796 with only royal monogram on obverse has simply the statement of value on the reverse; the denominations include the denga and pieces of 1, 2, 4, 5 and 10 kopeks. Czar Paul I (1796–1801) attempted to reform the Russian coinage on the basis of the Dutch system. The types of the gold ducat were the Russian eagle and on the reverse a tablet, as on the Netherlands ducats, containing an inscription in several lines. In 1797 new types were decreed for the ducat and the rouble, tariffed at the equivalent of 50 Netherlands stuivers. On obverse were four crowned II's in cross form enclosing the letter I, on reverse a tablet as before. The copper denominations continued to carry the royal monogram crowned on obverse and the value and date on the reverse. The innovation was not a success and the new light rouble was replaced by a piece of the previous standard.

An innovation in the reign of Nicholas I (1825–55) was the introduction in 1828 of a coinage in Siberian platinum. The series consisted of pieces of the value of 3, 6 and 12 roubles and had as obverse the Russian eagle with triple crown; on its breast was the shield of St. George and on its wings the arms of the six provinces (Pl. 755). The reverse simply stated the value. Similar types were adopted for the gold and silver roubles also. In 1885 in the reign of Alexander III (1881–91) a new coinage system was created with the silver rouble as the unit, divided into 100 kopeks. Pieces of 5 and 10 roubles were issued in gold, the rouble and divisionary coins down to 5 kopeks in silver and lower kopek denominations in copper. On values down to the quarter-rouble the obverse carried the bare-headed imperial bust, the reverse the Russian eagle and value. On lower values the eagle provided the obverse type, the value in words the reverse. These types remained substantially unchanged for the remainder of the coinage of czarist Russia. A number of commemorative roubles were struck in the early years of the century including an issue in 1913 for the third centenary of Romanov rule. The obverse here bore the three-quarter facing busts of Nicholas II and his ancestor Michael Feodorovitch, while below the double-eagle reverse were the dates 1613–1913.

After the Bolshevik revolution of 1917 a coinage in copper of pieces of 1, 3 and 5 roubles was issued in 1918 with the Russian eagle, now uncrowned on the obverse and the value on reverse but the regular issues of the new Soviet Union began only in 1921. The traditional denominations were retained but the now almost universal types were the hammer and sickle on a globe, all within a wreath of corn-ears on obverse and the value on the reverse (Pl. 756). Denominations of 20, 15 and 10 kopeks were issued in silver, the lower kopek values in copper and subsequently in aluminium-bronze. The higher values, issued in cupro-nickel from 1931, presented a new reverse, a worker holding a shield bearing the value. From 1936 the obverse added a star above its main type and dispensing with the long circular inscription of the earlier issues placed the letters C.C.C.P. beneath the type. All denominations reverted to a simple value reverse. The most recent alteration in 1952 has placed the reverse values of the 10, 15 and 20 kopek pieces within a frame.

THE BALKANS

SERBIA—JUGOSLAVIA

The Serbs who had been conquered by the Bulgars in the early tenth century and together with them had become subject to the Byzantine empire, reasserted their independence as Byzantine power waned in the mid twelfth century. The earliest Serbian coinage is of the silver *grossus* class and betrays Byzantine and Bulgarian influence in its choice of types, a seated Christ and a standing figure of a king accompanied by an inscription in Cyrillic entitling him Stephan. On the grounds that the regal figure does not necessarily refer to the reigning king but to St. Stephen, the coinage has been attributed by some to Vladislav I (1234–40) but by others, with more probability, to Stephan Uros I (1240–72). Of more certain attribution are the coinages in silver on the model of the Venetian matapan with obverse type of seated Christ and on the reverse in place of St. Mark and the doge of the Venetian original, the standing figures of St. Stephen and the king. Issues of this type name the king as either Stephan Uros I (Pl. 757) or Stephan IV Dragutin (1272–75). The latter changed the reverse type to a seated figure of the king with sword on his knees while under Stephan Uros Milutin (1275–1321) and Vladislav II (1316–23) the king is shown holding a fleur-de-lis sceptre and cross on globe The inscriptions under Uros I were usually in Latin but under subsequent rulers the Serbian language and Cyrillic characters were more commonly used.

The next change in type came in the reign of Stephan Dusan (1331–55) who took the title of emperor in 1346. The reverse now was in the form of a helmet surmounted by a cushion bearing a variety of ornaments. Other reverses consisted either of an inscription in several lines in Serbian across the field of the reverse, a reminiscence of the inscribed reverse of the Byzantine silver miliaresion or of the emperor on horse-back, as on Bulgarian coins (Pl. 758). Under Vukachin and his sons in the later fourteenth century and the various members of the dynasty of Brankovitch in the fifteenth the module of the Serbian coinage became much smaller. The established types continued in use were joined by new varieties such as a heraldic lion, the royal monogram or signature, some of which even came to replace the traditional obverse of the seated Christ. The mediaeval history of Serbia ended with its conquest by the Ottoman Turks in 1459.

When Serbia regained its freedom and became an independent kingdom in 1878 the coinage unit adopted was the dinar of 100 paras. Dinar denominations in gold and silver have conventional types of royal portrait head and value within a wreath, but the para denominations in copper, later in cupro-nickel, have on the obverse a double-headed eagle with shield on its breast.

A new kingdom of Jugoslavia was created in 1918 by the addition to Serbia of other provinces formerly part of the Austro-Hungarian empire. The principal alteration in coin types was the use on the reverse of the 10, 20 and 50 dinar pieces in silver of the eagle with shield type (Pl. 759). Under Peter II (1934–45) denominations from the 2 to the half-dinar, struck in aluminium-bronze, substituted a crown for the royal portrait on the obverse. The Republic of Jugoslavia which has existed since 1945 has one set of types on all dinar and para values, namely five small flaming torches within a wreath surmounted by a star on the obverse and the value and date on the reverse within a circle of stars (Pl. 760).

BULGARIA

The first kingdom of Bulgaria which existed from the late seventh century until it was conquered by the Byzantine emperor, Basil II Bulgaroctonos, in 1019 is represented in coinage by a unique gold coin issued by the stratelate Sermo during the struggle against Basil II. The obverse is in the form of the monogram representing the words θεότοκε βοήθει which appear on Byzantine bronzes of the period while the reverse has an inscription in three lines giving Sermo's name and title. With the reassertion of Bulgarian independence a coinage began again under Assen II (1218–44). Almost all the kings of the second kingdom struck both in silver and copper (Michael Assen silver only, Constantine Assen copper only). In the coinage down to 1360 the dominant feature is the representation of Christ on one side of the coins; in the issues from about 1360 to those of the last king, John Chichman (1371–95), a royal monogram is the main feature. Typical of the silver of the first period is the coinage of Assen II showing the standing figures of the king and St. Demetrius on obverse and a standing figure of Christ on the reverse (Pl. 761). The inscriptions are normally in Bulgarian in Cyrillic characters though on the coins of Michael Assen (1242–6) the language used is Latin. On copper coins of Constantine Assen (1257–77) the emperor is shown on obverse as a mounted figure but the reverse remains a bust of Christ. Typical of the second group are the silver coins of Michael Chichman with mounted figure of the emperor on obverse and on the reverse a monogram composed of the Cyrillic letters forming the word czar. Bulgaria was annexed by the Ottoman Turks in 1393.

A third independent kingdom of Bulgaria was formed in 1878 and issued a coinage based on the leva of 100 stotinki. On the leva denominations in gold and silver the types were the royal portrait and the value within a wreath; on the copper or, later, cupro-nickel stotinki values the obverse showed the Bulgarian lion on a shield, crowned (Pl. 762). On the lower leva pieces of Boris III (1918–43) the mediaeval type of king on horse-back was revived on the obverse. On the post-war coinage of Communist Bulgaria the obverse shows the Bulgarian lion within a wreath with star above on the obverse and the value in stotinki together with a corn-ear on the reverse.

ALBANIA

The mediaeval coinage in Albania is represented mainly by the issues of some of the cities of which the most important was Cattaro. Silver coins of the grossus class were struck by some of the Serbian kings, notably Stephan Dusan (1331–55) and Uros IV (1355–67) and later by Louis of Hungary. The types show usually the figure of St. Tryphon within an oval frame on the obverse with inscription *S. Triphon Cataren* and on the other side the seated figure of the king holding fleur-de-lis sceptre and cross on globe (Pl. 763). Between the Serbian and Hungarian issues coinage was issued at Cattaro by Venice with types of St. Mark and his lion. In the fifteenth century Cattaro, as a free city, issued base billon or copper pieces with types of St. Tryphon and a city gateway inscribed *Civitas Catari*. Parts of Albania continued to be held by Venice till 1571 when the whole of the country came under Turkish control.

Although Albania secured its independence from the Turks in 1912 the outbreak of the first world war prevented the setting up of an independent state. The republic of Albania, established in 1925, issued a coinage with the franka as the unit, divided into 5 lek, divided in turn into 40 qindar. Many of the obverse types such as lion's head, eagle's beak (Pl. 764) or helmeted head are modern versions of Ancient Greek coin types. When in 1928 Albania became a kingdom under Zog I the coinage normally showed his portrait on obverse and the value, accompanied by an olive-branch or a double-headed eagle on the reverse. The Communist republic of Albania in the post-war years has coined a series of lek denominations in zinc with double-headed eagle device within a wreath surmounted by star on obverse and value within a circle of stars on the reverse.

BOSNIA

The earliest Bosnian coinage was issued by Ban Stefan Kotromanić (1322–53) in the shape of silver pieces of the kind common to several Balkan countries in this period. The types are again versions of types employed on other Balkan issues, the standing figure of the Ban holding sword and cross inscribed *Stefanus Banus B* and a seated figure of Christ on the reverse. Another variety copies the Serbian type where the king is shown seated with sword on knee. Turtko II (1420–43), who is entitled Rex not Ban on the majority of his issues, struck a series of groschen coins with helmet and small shield on obverse and a standing figure of St. Gregory Nazianensis on the reverse. Thomas Ostojić (1443–61) in addition to groschen of the type just described struck a series of denars with his crowned monogram on the obverse and St. Gregory within an oval frame on the reverse (Pl. 765). Similar coins of Stefan II Tomasević (1461–3) have the helmet with shield type on obverse and a figure of Pope Gregory on the reverse. The last Bosnian issues are those of Nicholas Ujlak (1471–7) who was placed on the Bosnian throne by Matthias Corvin of Hungary. One variety which bears the names of both Nicholas and Matthias carries the typical Madonna figure of Hungarian coins and a shield quartered with the arms of Hungary, Croatia and Bohemia.

MONTENEGRO

Montenegro, now a province of Jugoslavia, when freed from the Turks in 1860 remained an independent kingdom until 1918. The coinage unit was the perper of 100 paras. Perper denominations in gold and silver bore the portrait of Nicholas I (1860–1918) and a mantled shield with double-headed eagle device on the reverse, together with the value. Coins with para values had the eagle and value as types.

ROUMANIA

Wallachia and Moldavia which together account for much of the former Roman province of Dacia and now form part of modern Roumania have no native coinage till the mid fourteenth century. The first coinage in Wallachia was struck by Wladislav I of Bessarabia (1360–73) with the title of Waiwode Trans-alpini. The coins are of the groschen class with types, a shield of arms and an eagle helmet, with inscriptions in Latin (Pl. 766). The coins of later waiwodes down to Wladislav V (1479–92) utilize similar types but with native inscriptions. The issues of the waiwodes of Moldavia begin with coins of Bogdan I (1348–55), copying the Polish kwartnik with on obverse the badge of Moldavia a facing bull's head with a star between the horns (Pl. 767). The inscriptions are usually in Latin except on issues of Alexander II (1449–50) and Bogdan II (1454–6) when Cyrillic characters were used. Moldavia submitted to the Turks in 1513 but after this date some of the waiwodes continued to coin, using the traditional bull's-head type.

The coinage of Roumania as an independent kingdom from 1866 consists of various denominations of the leu which comprised 100 bani. The types most commonly used were the royal portrait and, as reverse, a mantled shield of arms, later a plain shield crowned, together with the value (Pl. 768). On the wartime issues of the second reign of Michael I (1941–8) the obverse has a crown in place of the portrait, the reverse the value within a wreath, though the high values of the inflationary, post-war issues revert to an obverse portrait. The issues of the Communist republic from 1948 onwards utilize the formula common to all the people's republics of eastern Europe.

GREECE

In the partial dismemberment of the Byzantine empire which followed the capture of Constantinople by the armies of the Fourth Crusade in 1204 a number of principalities and duchies established in mainland Greece issued their own coinage until their eventual conquest by the Turks in the fourteenth century. The earliest issues of the principality of *Achaea* are attributed to Guillaume II de Villehardouin (1245–78) but, since on these Achaean coins the inscription giving the name and title is in the form *G. Princeps Achaie*—often further abbreviated but with the prince's name only given as an initial—attribution is often uncertain. The coinage consists of billon and copper pieces with types similar to those of the French denier tournois, a castle with three towers on obverse and a cross on reverse (Pl. 769). This was the almost constant type on all Achaean issues. The issues of the dukes of *Athens* are of greater variety. Billon obols have the gateway type of Genoa on obverse and the initial of the duke on the reverse. The most plentiful series is that of Guy II de la Roche (1287–1308) who struck a coinage copying the types of the denier tournois.

Other portions of the Byzantine empire in Greece were seized by Byzantine overlords. Michael I Angelus Comnenus Ducas established himself as despot at *Epirus* and base nomismata with obverse type Michael and St. Demetrius holding a cross and reverse St. Michael are attributed to this ruler. Epirus passed from the Angeli to the Orsini in 1318 and a series of deniers tournois were issued by John Orsini (1323–35) but the dynasty was extinguished in the struggle with Albania in 1358. Similarly an 'empire' was established at *Thessalonica* by Theodore Angelus Comnenus Ducas. Scyphate nomismata were issued in silver or bronze with Theodore and St. Demetrius on obverse and a seated Christ on reverse. Similar coinages were struck by Manuel and John Angelus until Thessalonica was incorporated into the empire of Nicaea by John I Vatatzes in 1246 (see p. 221).

These and other smaller enclaves, both Latin and Byzantine, were in turn extinguished and with the fall of Constantinople in 1453 all of Greece came under Turkish rule and it was not until after the battle of Navarino in 1827 that an independent Greece was established in 1828. The unit of the new coinage was the silver phoenix of 100 lepta. The types on both the silver and the lepta in copper were the phoenix and value in wreath, together with the name on the reverse of Capo d'Istria to whom the first provisional government was entrusted (Pl. 770). When in 1831 Greece became a monarchy under Otto of Bavaria the drachma was adopted as the new unit. Drachma denominations in gold and silver now bore the royal portrait on obverse with a shield and value on the reverse. Copper lepta had as types the crowned arms and value in wreath. On issues of the republic (1924–35) types taken from Ancient Greek coins such as the helmeted head of Athena on the drachma were adapted to the modern issues (Pl. 771), Demeter and a corn-ear on the 10 drachmae and Poseidon and prow of galley on the 20 drachmae piece. Coinage practically disappeared in the inflation in post-war Greece but, after the monetary reform of 1954 which established a new drachma, pieces of 1, 2 and 5 drachmae were struck in cupro-nickel with the head of King Paul I on obverse and the royal arms, crowned and with supporters, on reverse. Lepta coins in aluminium with a central piercing have the value on the reverse accompanied by a corn-ear, a bunch of grapes or a branch of olive.

THE NEW WORLD

★

The New World

THE first discovery of the New World was made by the Northmen who, in their Iceland voyages in the eleventh century, made land-fall on the coast of North America; but their knowledge received no general publication and quickly passed into oblivion. In 1492, however, Christopher Columbus, with his three ships, accomplished his great expedition and reached the Bahamas and West Indies in his endeavour to sail across the Atlantic and reach India and China. By an award of Pope Alexander VI in 1492, further formulated the following year by the Treaty of Tordesillas, a north to south boundary in America was agreed between Spain and Portugal. The outcome, briefly, was the establishment of Portuguese authority in the area represented approximately by modern Brasil and the extension of the Spanish empire in the course of the sixteenth century over the remainder of South America, Central America, the Caribbean and a considerable area of North America. It was in the north that other European powers, principally Britain and France, were quick to follow the example of Spain and Portugal and establish New World colonies.

As a result of the great colonial wars of the eighteenth century France was compelled to relinquish her American possessions to Britain, although in Canada, above all, the influence of French civilization has persisted till the present day. Later, in the eighteenth century, the disastrous colonial policy of Britain led to the revolt of her American colonists and the creation of the independent United States of America in 1776. A century of steady expansion west and south enlarged the new republic more or less to its present-day boundaries. In Central and South America the percolation of the ideas of the French Revolution and the severance of communications during the Napoleonic wars loosened the ties between Spain and Portugal and their colonies and began the movement which culminated in the establishment in the nineteenth century of the independent republics of today.

The pattern of coinage in the New World mirrors the historical development of the continent which has just been sketched in its barest outline. The great Spanish empire from the sixteenth century was served by a more or less uniform coinage modelled on that of the home-land but struck by a chain of mints, spread throughout the territory, until the creation of the new republics gave rise to a

415

whole series of independent coinages. In the Caribbean, possession of the several islands changed hands on more than one occasion until today's position has been reached of a number of independent states with their individual coinages, while other areas, still administered as colonial possessions, are provided with a colonial coinage. In the north the individual coinages of the several colonies were superseded by a single national coinage on the creation of the United States in 1776 and in Canada the earlier provincial coinages were eventually replaced by a new coinage for the whole country. These coinages will now be examined in some greater detail in geographical succession from north to south.

NORTH AMERICA

CANADA

It is not certain whether the voyages of the Norseman Lief Ericson in the eleventh century brought him to Canada but in 1497, only five years after Columbus discovered the New World, John Cabot made land-fall in Canada. It was left to the French under such adventurers as Cartier and de Champlain to begin the settlement of the Canadian mainland along the St. Lawrence. In 1670 the Hudson's Bay Company was formed and English settlements were made in Hudson Bay, Nova Scotia and Newfoundland. Rivalry between France and England culminated during the Seven Years' war in the capture of Quebec and the French surrender at Montreal in 1760. In 1791 the settled portion of Canada in the east was divided into Lower Canada, predominantly French, and Upper Canada, mainly British, but the two were united in 1840. Expansion westwards in the nineteenth century, accelerated by the great railroad constructions, led to the formation of the other provinces and to the eventual formation of the Dominion of Canada in 1867.

The majority of these happenings find their expression in the coinages current in Canada. The more active French policy of exploration and settlement at the outset of Canada's development is reflected in the provision of a coinage for colonial use, particularly in the Americas. In 1670 in the reign of Louis XIV a series of such coins was struck at Paris in denominations of 15 and 5 sols in silver with types of royal portrait and French arms, similar to those of the ordinary French issues but with a reverse inscription *Gloriam regni tui dicent*. In 1717 copper coins of Louis XV were struck at Perpignan in denominations of 12 and 6 deniers for the American colonies. The obverse carried the usual royal portrait and the reverse a four-line inscription *XII/deniers/Colonies/1717*. Later, in 1721, copper pieces of 9 deniers had as obverse two L's in saltire, crowned, and *Colonies françoises* and the date on reverse (Pl. 772).

For the remainder of the eighteenth century after the submission of the French no specific, official coinage was issued in or for Canada and even the trade-token coinage, of which there is a great variety, where it is dated is, at the earliest, of the first part of the nineteenth century. A series of token coins of a somewhat more official character also made their appearance in the early decades of the nineteenth century, the types varying for each of the several provinces.

In Lower Canada a bilingual series of bank tokens began issue in 1837. The obverse figure in winter clothing has given rise to the name Papineau for this series, after the Papineau who led an uprising in that year and was said to affect this style of dress. The obverse is inscribed in French, *Province du Bas Canada*, with the value (one or two sous), while the reverse is inscribed in English, *Bank Token*, with the value one penny or a halfpenny around arms of St. Andrew's cross with thistle, shamrock, rose and beaver in the angles and the name of the particular issuing bank below (Pl. 773). Another series with a similar reverse but with an obverse giving a view of the bank and inscribed *Bank of Montreal* was issued in 1837–9 and 1842. Quebec Bank tokens of a penny and a halfpenny value in 1852 used the obverse of the first series described but had, on the other side, a personification of Quebec seated below the Heights of Abraham by the edge of the St. Lawrence. The 'bouquet' series of halfpenny or sous tokens takes its name from the bunch of flowers on the obverse which has a variety of inscriptions such as *Trade and Agriculture* or *Agriculture and Commerce*, together with the name of the province of Lower Canada—sometimes in French. The reverse gives the value in either English or French in a wreath. The union of the two portions into the province of Canada in 1840 was followed by an issue of silver cents in 1858 of value 5, 10 and 20 with head of Victoria and value crowned within a wreath (Pl. 774).

In Ontario or Upper Canada a series of halfpenny tokens in copper in 1823 carried the name of the province around the head of George IV, while the seated figure of Britannia on the reverse was accompanied by the value. Between 1850 and 1857 penny and halfpenny tokens of the Bank of Upper Canada had as types St. George and the Dragon and a complex of anchor and sword in saltire above two cornuacopiae, all crowned and with part of the Union flag to the right (Pl. 775). The penny and halfpenny tokens of Nova Scotia bear the name of the province and the portrait of George IV or Victoria and appropriate to the name of the colony, a Scottish thistle as the reverse type (Pl. 776). Later coinage of the cent and its half in 1861 has the portrait and title of Victoria on obverse and crown with date surrounded by wreath border, value and province. The New Brunswick tokens resemble those of Nova Scotia but for the name and the substitution of a sailing ship for the thistle on the reverse, while copper cents in 1861 are identical but for the name. The issues of Newfoundland, which until 1949 remained outside the Dominion, are dealt with below. In British Columbia extremely rare gold pieces of 20 and 10 dollars were struck in 1862 with a crown and the name of the province on obverse and the value in wreath on reverse.

The union of the provinces in 1867 to form the Dominion of Canada brought to an end the series of provincial coinages and the issue of a single coinage for the whole of Canada. Coinage in silver of denominations of 5, 10, 25 and 50 cents was of simple design in the reign of Victoria. Her portrait head in diadem was accompanied by her name and title and the word Canada on obverse, while the reverse carried the value and date within a wreath of maple-leaves, closed by a small crown (Pl. 777). The bronze cent had a similar obverse but with the inscription enclosed within two circles of dots and similar circles on the reverse enclosed a circlet of maple-leaves. The issues of Edward VII were identical except that the obverse bore his portrait bust in imperial robes and crown and the word Canada was transferred to the reverse. The coinage of George V introduced new designs, denominations and metals. Between 1911 and 1919 gold sovereigns struck in Canada with the conventional types were distinguished by a small letter C on the reverse and gold was also coined between 1912 and 1914 in denominations of 5 and 10 dollars with imperial obverse and the arms of Canada flanked by branches of maple on the reverse. The 10, 25 and 50 cent values followed the traditional designs as did the bronze cent initially. The 5 cent, in silver till 1921 and thereafter in nickel, and the bronze cent from 1920 replaced the reverse wreath by two maple-leaves. A silver dollar with reverse showing two voyageurs in canoe in front of a small island with the Northern Lights in the background was first struck for the king's Silver Jubilee in 1935 (Pl. 778).

In common with the coinages of other British dominions and colonies in the reign of George VI the Canadian issues develop a series of reverse types of greater variety and picturesqueness. The dollar retained its type of the voyageurs and on the 50 cents or half-dollar appeared the arms of Canada with lion and unicorn supporters holding, respectively, the Union flag and the fleur-de-lis banner of France. The 25 cents showed a caribou head, the 10 cents a fishing schooner, the 5 cents a beaver and the cent piece maple-leaves. On all these issues the obverse carried a bare-headed portrait of the king. A special silver dollar showing the Parliament buildings at Ottawa was struck to commemorate the royal visit in 1939, and another in 1949 with its reverse the ship of the discoverer, John Cabot, marked the entry of Newfoundland into the Dominion of Canada. The Canadian coinage of Elizabeth II, apart from the change of obverse portrait, has continued the types of the preceding reign. In 1958 the centenary of British Columbia was celebrated by an issue of silver dollars, the reverse of which showed an Indian totem-pole with a background of mountains.

NEWFOUNDLAND

The coinage of Newfoundland was first struck in the reign of Victoria in 1865 and the denominational system consisted ultimately of values of 50, 20, 10 and 5 cents in silver and a cent piece in bronze. The silver pieces carried the royal portrait and title and *Newfoundland* on the obverse and the value within a circlet of leaves on reverse. The cent had as reverse a crown with the value and colony name in a circular inscription. Gold coins of the value of 2 dollars had an obverse similar to the silver coins but on the reverse, carrying the value as a type, had a circular inscription *Two hundred cents—one hundred pence*. The coins of Edward VII and George VI showed the imperial bust common to all commonwealth and colonial issues of their reigns and while retaining the established design of the cent piece had simplified reverses for the other values, the circlet of leaves being replaced by the inscription *Newfoundland*. Only the 5 and 10 cent pieces in silver were struck for George VI, continuing the conventional types but with crowned head and not bust on the obverse. The reverse of the bronze cent was altered to a flower design. The decision of Newfoundland, taken by referendum in 1949, to join the Dominion of Canada was commemorated by the issue of the special silver dollar already described in the Canadian coinage (Pl. 779).

THE UNITED STATES

The story of the settlement of that part of the North American continent which is now represented by the United States of America is one of considerable complexity. England laid claim to North America by virtue of the discovery by John Cabot in 1497 but no extensive settlement took place from England until the early seventeenth century, and that limited to the eastern seaboard. In the meantime other European nations had not been slow to embark on colonization: the Spaniards had pushed north into California and New Mexico, the French had established themselves on the Gulf of Mexico in Louisiana and laid claim to the great hinterland stretching north to the Great Lakes and the Dutch had erected a settlement at New Amsterdam, now New York. Some mention has been made in the Canadian section of the coinages issued by France for her American colonies and those of the Spanish colonial empire are dealt with below (see p. 428). Attention must now be directed to the British settlements in the east and the local coinages which served them.

The first serious attempt at English settlement in America was that of the colonists sent out by Raleigh late in the reign of Elizabeth I but the venture failed, though it still has its memorial in the name of Virginia which was given to the settlement in honour of the virgin queen. A second venture in the reign of James I resulted, eventually, in more permanent settlement, followed by the planting of colonies by the Pilgrim Fathers and others in New England, Massachusetts and Connecticut. The territory granted to Lord Baltimore by Charles I was named Maryland after Charles' queen, Henrietta Maria, while, after the Restoration of 1660, lands to the south of Virginia granted by Charles II were named Carolina in his honour and the Quaker William Penn in 1682 obtained land on the west of the Delaware to which he gave the name Pennsylvania. In 1732, in the reign of George II, a final colony of Georgia was founded in the south. At the end of the great colonial wars France in 1763 gave up her claims to the territory west of the Mississippi.

Unlike France, Britain undertook no coinage for the use of her American colonies and, indeed, in the early stages the primitive circumstances rendered a monetary medium of exchange unnecessary. When the growth of settlement and trade created the need for coinage, these requirements were met here, just as later in the settlements of Australasia and Africa, by the great international trade coinages, particularly the Spanish dollar or piece of eight and its subdivisions which continued to play a part in American coinage till as late as 1857. Although such coinages facilitated exchange where comparatively large sums were involved, there was a growing need for small change for everyday transactions and in default of official provision of such a coinage the defect was remedied by a number of locally produced coins in the various colonies or states as they came to be termed.

Of these one of the earliest, the series known as Hog money after the obverse type, was struck in 1616 not specifically for the continental settlements but for the Sommer Islands in the Bahamas. The coinage in brass was in four denominations, shilling, sixpence, threepence and twopence, and had on the obverse a pig and the value in Roman numerals and a fully-rigged sailing ship on the reverse (Pl. 780). Probably the earliest coinage to be issued in the North American settlements was ordered to be struck near Boston in 1652 for New England. These coins were rough silver disks with nothing but a rectangular stamp with the letters NE on obverse and the value in Roman numerals on the reverse. The denominations were the shilling, sixpence and threepence. Since such a coinage lent itself to forgery and clipping it was replaced in Massachusetts in the same year by a series of the same three denominations but using complete types on either side. There were three varieties of tree which formed the obverse types, namely the willow, the oak and pine. The tree on obverse was accompanied by the inscription *Masathusets in* continued on the reverse *New England An Dom* with the date and value in Roman figures in the centre (Pl. 781). Although only the date 1652 appears on this coinage, it continued to be issued for some thirty years, the three varieties most probably being struck in the order in which they have been named. An extremely rare shilling of the same fabric as the tree coinage used the same types also, except on the obverse which illustrates the story of the Good Samaritan. For Maryland Lord Baltimore produced a coinage of shilling, sixpence and four-pence in silver. The obverse carried his portrait and title *Caecilius Dns Terrae Mariae & ct* and the reverse his arms separating the value in Roman figures with inscription *Crescite et multiplicamini* (Pl. 782). A copper penny, designed but apparently never issued, had a coronet with two pennants on its reverse. Token halfpennies struck in 1694 for Carolina have an elephant on obverse and a five-line inscription *God/preserve/Carolina and/the Lords/Proprietors/* on the reverse.

In addition to these coins and tokens issued for specific states or colonies other series were produced by private enterprise to meet the demand for small change. A series which gained official sanction and wide currency in New Jersey was that of the St. Patrick halfpence and farthings said to have been originally struck in Dublin in 1678. On one side of the halfpenny a kneeling king plays a harp with crown above and is inscribed *Floreat rex;* on the other, St. Patrick inscribed *Ecce grex*, with crozier preaches to a crowd. On the reverse of the farthing inscribed *Quiescat grex* St. Patrick with cross stands before a church. Two other series, in a base alloy principally of brass, were produced by William Wood for more general circulation in America. The obverse of the specifically American series had the bust and titles of George I and a rather attractive reverse design of a full-blown rose inscribed *Rosa americana-utile dulce* (Pl. 783). Denominations of two-pence, penny and halfpenny carried no indication of value but, as in the case of British coppers, were distinguished only by their module. Issues were made in 1722–4. A very similar coinage but with a seated figure with harp, inscribed *Hibernia*, was produced by Wood in the same years. This coinage was originally intended for circulation in Ireland but, proving unpopular there, was shipped to America.

The revolt of Britain's American colonies and the Declaration of Independence in 1776 was followed two years later by the Articles of Confederation which, amongst other measures, left to each state the right to strike coin under the general authority of Congress. In the ten years which elapsed until the legislation of 1792 which provided for a uniform coinage a number of states did, in fact, issue their own coinage in a variety of forms. New Hampshire in fact anticipated events by authorizing in 1776 a coinage of copper cents equivalent to the English halfpence. This coinage with types of a pine-tree and a harp apparently never reached more than pattern stage. The next state to produce coinage was Vermont in 1785 and 1786. Its copper cents had as obverse a plough with mountains and a rising sun in the background with inscription *Vermont respublica* or *Respublica Vermontensium*. The reverse has rays and stars from a central eye while the inscription *Stella quarta decima*—the fourteenth star—alludes to the fact that Vermont was not one of the original thirteen states of the confederation. A new issue begun in 1786 had as types a laureate bust reminiscent of that on British coppers but inscribed *Vermon auctori* and a Britannia-like figure on the reverse with inscription *Inde et Lib.*

Copper cents current in New York were produced, not officially but by private enterprise, in 1786 and 1787. One series copying the laureate bust and Britannia figure of British copper coins was inscribed on obverse *Nova Eboraca* and on reverse *Virt et Lib.* On another an Indian warrior with tomahawk and bow stands on the obverse and an eagle with spread wings on the reverse. In Connecticut copper cents produced between 1785 and 1788 by a private firm under official contract were also based on the types of Georgian copper coins with inscriptions *Auctori Connec* and *Inde et Lib.* Massachusetts, on the other hand, set up its own mint to strike cents in 1787 and 1788 with types of Indian and eagle as at New York but inscribed *Common Wealth* and *Massachusetts*. New Jersey's copper cents struck in 1786–8 by contrast had on obverse a horse's head above a plough with the state name Latinized into *Nova Caesarea* and a shield with inscription *E pluribus unum* on the reverse. In addition to these coinages, which were to a greater or lesser degree official issues, the requirements of small change were met by an extensive series of token pieces of considerable variety. One of the more prolific was the series with a portrait of George Washington coupled with reverses bearing a seated figure, an eagle or a sailing ship. The first coinage of the United States issued by Federal authority was struck in 1787 and is commonly known as the Franklin cent, as it is believed that Benjamin Franklin provided the designs and inscriptions. On one side thirteen linked circles, representing the component states, surround an inner circle inscribed *United States* and containing the words *We are one*; on the other is a sun-dial with sun above, with inscription *Fugio* and the date with, in the exergue, *Mind your business*.

In the discussions which preceded the issue of the first regular coinage for the whole of the United States it was decided that the unit should be the dollar which, in the form of the Spanish dollar or piece of eight, was the most familiar piece of currency in circulation. It was further decided that a decimal system of coinage should be adopted, as advocated by Thomas Jefferson and approved by Washington. In 1792 legislation was passed specifying a coinage system which was to comprise a dollar, its half, quarter, disme or tenth—later popularized into dime— and a half-disme, all in silver. The denominations in gold were the eagle of ten dollars with its half and quarter and token pieces in copper of a cent, the hundreth part of a dollar, as well as a half-cent. A mint for the production of this coinage was established at Philadelphia. Several rare patterns were produced in 1792 but the regular issues date from the following year, though a few years passed before the whole denomination system was produced.

The first gold eagles struck in 1795 carried on the obverse the bust of Liberty wearing her distinctive cap, within a circle of stars representing the states, together with the inscription *Liberty* and the date. The reverse which gave its name to the piece showed an eagle with spread wings on a branch and holding a wreath in its beak with inscription *United States of America*. This reverse was changed in 1797 to a heraldic eagle grasping arrows and an olive-branch in its talons and with shield on breast; above it were the state stars and small clouds as well as the motto *E pluribus unum*. Since this gold coinage was undervalued in relation to prevalent world values, it tended to disappear from circulation and its issue was suspended in 1804. The half-eagle duplicated the types of the eagle itself until 1807 when a left-facing bust of Liberty with round cap inscribed *Liberty* on the cap-band was introduced. At the same time the reverse design was altered: the heraldic eagle was shown three-quarter facing, the motto was raised to a position under the inscription and the value 5 D. was added at the bottom. These types continued substantially unchanged until 1838. On the quarter-eagle the types and their pattern of change were exactly those of the half-piece. Following a reduction of the weight of standard gold in 1834 new mints, established at Dahlonega in Georgia and Charlotte in North Carolina near the sources of gold, joined Philadelphia in the striking of half- and quarter-eagles, their products being marked with their initial letter on the reverse.

The silver dollar was first struck in 1794 with designs similar to those described for the gold coins but with a head of Liberty with long hair on the obverse and an eagle within a wreath on the reverse. A bust of Liberty was introduced in 1795 and in 1798 the heraldic eagle type described on the gold pieces was adopted on the dollar (Pl. 784). Striking of this denomination was suspended in 1803. The half- and quarter-dollar, the dime and its half followed the types of the major piece but, just as in the case of the subdivisions of the gold, continued to be struck after the suspension of the major piece. Issues after about 1807 changed their types to those introduced at that time on the lower gold denominations, including the addition of the value at the bottom of the reverse. The activity of the Philadelphia mint was supplemented from 1838 by the mint at New Orleans which marked its products with O on the reverse. These designs were maintained till the late 1830's.

The copper denominations were the earliest pieces to be struck, both the half-cent and cent being issued in 1793. On the obverse of the half-cent was a long-haired head of Liberty with the Cap of Liberty on a pole behind her head with inscription *United States of America*; the value in words at centre was enclosed in a wreath, while the value, expressed as a fraction $\frac{1}{200}$ (of the dollar), appeared below. The 1793 cent had originally only a head of Liberty on obverse and on reverse a circular chain design enclosing the value in words and as a fraction. Later in the year types identical with those described for the half-cent were substituted. After 1797 the Cap of Liberty disappeared from the obverse and in 1808 a new bust of Liberty with a head-band inscribed with her name was introduced. A circle of stars was also added on the obverse and on the reverse the fractional mark of value was removed. These types remained substantially unchanged till 1857 (Pl. 785).

A new coinage act in 1837 prescribed, amongst other regulations, changes in the precious-metal coin types and was followed shortly afterwards by resumed striking of the gold eagle and the silver dollar. Issues of the eagle began again in 1838 with a coin of reduced weight and module and with modified designs. The obverse in fact carried a type similar to that on contemporary coppers, a head of Liberty with her name inscribed on a head-band instead of round the circumference of the coin which now consisted of a circle of stars. On the reverse was the heraldic eagle with the value, *Ten D*, below. The half- and quarter-eagles had received these modified designs in 1834 but acquired a smaller obverse head on issues in 1839 and 1840 respectively. The quarter retained these types till 1907, the half and the eagle itself until 1866. Additional mints at New Orleans and San Francisco marked their coinage with initials O and S. More obvious changes of type were effected on the silver coins on which the obverse from 1837 onwards showed a seated figure of Liberty holding cap on pole and resting her hand on a shield inscribed with her name. The reverse, as on the gold, was the eagle with value below on the dollar, its half and quarter. The dime and its half had a simple reverse, the value within a wreath. These issues continued until 1866, some issues being marked with the initials of New Orleans or San Francisco.

The coinage of the copper half-cent and large cent was discontinued in 1857, the former for good. The latter was replaced in 1859 by a coin of smaller module in cupro-nickel with an Indian-head obverse and value within wreath on the reverse. A small shield was added at the top of the wreath in 1860 and from 1864 the metal used was bronze. Right up to 1909 these popular types kept the field with only minor variations on lettering (Pl. 786). A new denomination, the 2 cents in copper introduced in 1864, was discontinued in 1872. The obverse with shield type is of interest as being the first instance of the use on coinage of the motto *In God we trust*, on a ribbon above the shield.

Other new smaller-value coins were the 3 cent pieces issued in silver between 1851 and 1873 with types, a shield within a six-pointed star and a roman III within the initial C. The necessity for this unusual denomination appears to have been the fixing of the postal rate at three cents. The denomination was also struck in nickel (1865–95) with Liberty head obverse and III within a wreath on the reverse. Of more moment, however, was the authorization in 1849 of a gold dollar following the great discoveries of gold in California in 1848. The types initially were a Liberty head with riband and value in wreath, changed in 1854 to a head with feathered head-dress (Pl. 787). A multiple piece of 3 dollars with identical types was struck from 1854 to 1889. The gold dollar was also issued until 1889 but the double eagle in gold also introduced in 1849 had a much longer life. The reverse of this piece until 1866 was an ornate heraldic eagle with stars and rays above and value below.

In the Civil War (1860–4) lack of supplies of bullion held up the coinage which was planned by the Confederate States. A small issue of silver half-dollars was in fact prepared in 1861 but never released. This was very much an issue of expediency, consisting of the removal of the reverse type from the national coinage of half-dollars of 1861 and restriking the reverse with a new type. The obverse, therefore, still showed the usual seated figure of Liberty but on the reverse, inscribed *Confederate States of America*, was placed a shield of seven stars and stripes with Cap of Liberty above between two branches. An issue of cents was also planned with value in wreath on reverse and a Liberty head with Confederate inscription on obverse. The cents likewise were never put into circulation and Confederate currency consisted of paper money only.

In 1866 a minor modification was effected in the reverse design of the gold eagle, its double and half as well as the silver dollar with its half and quarter, namely the addition of the motto *In God we trust* first used on the 2 cent piece in 1864. No other change of note was made on the gold pieces till 1907 or on the silver dollar till 1904. An additional mint was opened at Carson City in Nevada in 1870. The half- and quarter-dollar acquired in 1892 a new head of Liberty, treated in more modern style on the obverse and a more frontally presented eagle with stars above on the reverse, types which persisted till 1916. The same obverse head was also used on the dime from 1892 but the half-dime ceased to be struck in 1873, its place having been effectively taken by a new 5 cent piece introduced in 1866 and struck in nickel, the familiar name by which the denomination has come to be known. The types, at first a shield and value in a surround of stars and rays, were changed in 1883 to a Liberty head and a roman V in wreath. Two denominations issued in the later nineteenth century remain to be noted. A 20 cent piece with types of seated Liberty and eagle, struck briefly between 1875 and 1878, was withdrawn because of its similarity to the quarter-dollar. A special series of silver dollars was struck from 1873 for trade in the east. Liberty seated to the left holds a branch on the obverse; on the reverse, with usual eagle type, is inscribed the weight and fineness (480 grains, 900 fine) and the words *Trade Dollar*. Issues ceased in practice in 1878.

The coinage of the United States for something over a century had been extremely conservative and its international impact was due in part to the important part which American commerce had increasingly played throughout the world, and in part to romantic fiction which had rendered the names of its coins familiar to all. The twentieth century, however, brought a striking break in the hitherto conventional and conservative coin designs. Some were extremely successful, others not so inspired but all were at least attempts to break away from the heraldic conventions which still shackle much of modern coinage. Perhaps the most outstanding of these new designs was that for the double gold eagle introduced in 1907. A facing figure of Liberty with torch and branch stands on the obverse while on the reverse is an extremely effective eagle in flight, a design which clearly owes its inspiration to similar types on Ancient Greek coins. Less happy is the standing eagle on the reverse of the half- and quarter-eagle, a reminiscence, surely, of the eagles on Ptolemaic and Seleucid coinage, coupled with an obverse head of Liberty in Indian war-bonnet. Another standing eagle in defiant but clumsy pose was adopted for the half-dollar in 1916 with standing Liberty with flowing drapery on obverse, but the eagle, again in flight, on the quarter is more graceful. Ancient coin types also inspired the designs of the 1916 dime on which the Liberty head wears the winged hat of Mercury and the fasces of the Roman consul occupies the reverse. The nickel of 1913 draws on American types, an Indian head and a buffalo (Pl. 788). The portrait of Lincoln adopted for the obverse of the cent has maintained its popularity until the present day (Pl. 789). The silver dollar, coined again between 1921 and 1935 and presenting a modern rendering of the head of Liberty in radiate crown and a perching eagle, was first issued in 1921 to mark the return of peace.

The economic crisis of the 1930's brought to an end the issue of gold coinage and also of the silver dollar, leaving in circulation the half- and quarter-dollar, the dime, nickel and cent. As legislation of 1890 decreed that changes in coin design should not be made more often than once every twenty-five years the types on some of these remaining denominations, changed after the last war, are likely to go unaltered for a considerable period. The trend in modern times is towards honouring America's famous sons on the various denominations. Lincoln, on the cent, was joined on the quarter-dollar by Washington in 1932, while portraits of Thomas Jefferson appeared on the nickel in 1938, Franklin Roosevelt on the dime in 1946 and Benjamin Franklin on the half-dollar in 1948.

The normal coinage series which has been described has been enlivened from the late nineteenth century by the issue of commemorative pieces, usually of half-dollar value, for such occasions as the tercentenary in 1920 of the landing of the Pilgrim Fathers. These, however, have normally been struck in restricted numbers, presumably for the delectation of coin-collectors. Another and more substantial subsidiary is formed by the gold issues by some of the states and even private companies during the great gold era of the late mid nineteenth century.

CENTRAL AMERICA

It is perhaps not geographically accurate to include Mexico in Central America but since political and numismatic history has separated it firmly from the North American states and linked it equally firmly with Central America and the Spanish New World it has been thought permissible, and certainly desirable, to treat it in this latter context. In addition, since the first mint in the New World for the coinage of the Spanish empire was established at Mexico City and since the issues of that mint were amongst the most prolific and continuous, it will be convenient to give a fairly detailed account of its coinage which will be of general application in the other regions of the Spanish empire in Central and South America.

MEXICO

Shortly after the penetration of Mexico by the Spaniards under Cortès in 1519 the Aztec city of Mexico was captured and destroyed but was soon rebuilt to form, eventually, the capital of the Spanish vice-royalty of New Spain. In 1536 a mint for the Spanish coinage was opened in Mexico City which continued to strike up to and during the war of independence (1810–21). Other provincial mints were established during this unsettled period but Mexico City continued to be the mint for the first Mexican empire of Iturbide (1822–3) and for the republic from 1823 till the present day, as well as for the interlude of the second Mexican empire under Maximilian (1864–7).

The first coinage of the Mexico City mint was in the names of Charles I (the emperor Charles V) and his mother Johanna (1521–56) and consisted of silver coins of 4, 2, 1 and a half-real values. The obverse type, inscribed *Carolus et Iohana Reges*, bore the royal arms of Spain, quartered with the lion of Leon and the castle of Castille, with the small pomegranate of Granada at the point of the shield; to the right appeared the initial M of the mint, surmounted by a small O and to the left the initial of the mint assayer. The reverse, continuing the royal titles *Hispaniarum et Indiarum*, had as type the Pillars of Hercules (representing the Straits of Gibraltar) crowned and standing in the sea, with the motto *Plus Ultra* across the field, and the value, e.g. 4, between the pillars (Pl. 790). Copper coins of 4 and 2 maravedis with the initial K on obverse and I on reverse, each flanked by lion and castle and with the value under the I, were struck but proved so unpopular that they were withdrawn and extremely few examples have survived. Copper was not coined again until the nineteenth century.

The coinage of Philip II (1556–98), in silver only, was furnished with new types. The obverse was still the royal arms crowned but these now bore the quarterings of the many additional states of which Philip was the ruler; beside the shield of arms the value in Roman or Arabic numerals was placed in addition to the initials of the mint and the assayer. The reverse carried a cross with the lion-and-castle device in alternate angles. The half-real, instead of the crowned arms, has a monogram of Philippus. The five values enumerated above continued to be struck, though some pieces of 8 reales have been attributed to this reign. Most of the coinage was of the 'cob' type, that is, not quite circular in shape but somewhat angular, since the flans were produced by slicing from a bar of silver. Under Philip III (1598–1621) and Philip IV (1621–65) the same range of coinage was struck with the same types and since many of the surviving examples of coins of these three Philips are struck on such irregular flans that much of the obverse inscription is often missing, particularly the ordinal number of the king, the exact attribution of these coins is often extremely difficult. An additional difficulty is that the practice of placing the date on the reverse inscription which had begun under Philip II was not always observed.

The first gold coins of the Mexican mint were struck for Charles II (1665–1700) in 1679. The types were almost the same as those of the silver coins except that the lion-and-castle devices in the angles of the reverse cross were replaced by fleur-de-lis and the cross is in the form of a Jerusalem cross. The denominations were the 8 and 4 escudo pieces with a rare 2 escudos also reported. Silver of the established types continued to be struck. For Philip V, the first of the Spanish Bourbons, in his first reign (1700–24) both gold and silver coinage was produced as before, the gold now in four denominations of 8, 4, 2 and 1 escudo pieces (Pl. 792), but not all these denominations have been confirmed for Louis I who succeeded on his father's abdication in 1724. On Louis' death after a reign of only a few months, Philip V resumed the crown and reigned till 1746. New types were introduced on both gold and silver in this second reign and the majority of the coinage was now of circular shape and not of the angular 'cob' variety. The coinage of gold escudos now carried the royal bust and titles on the obverse, while the crowned shield of arms was transferred to the reverse, where the 8 escudo piece had, as an addition, the chain of the Order of the Golden Fleece. The mint mark was also moved from the field to a position in the circular inscription. The silver reales still retained the crowned shield on the obverse but the reverse showed two globes crowned between the Pillars of Hercules on each of which a riband bears a portion of the motto *Plus Ultra* (Pl. 791). On the silver also, the mint initial was incorporated in the inscription. On the silver of Charles III (1760–88) new types appeared in 1773: the obverse had the royal portrait, the reverse crowned arms between pillars with the mark of value now also placed in the inscription. The silver quarter-real or cuartilla was first issued by Charles IV in 1796 with lion on obverse and castle flanked by the mint initial and value on the reverse.

During the revolution which broke out against the Spanish authorities in 1810 royalist provisional mints were established in other cities. Of these only Guadalajara in Nueva Galicia struck gold 8 escudo pieces with mint-mark, initial G accompanied by a small A. Silver was also issued by this mint as well as by mints at Chihuahua, Durango, Guanajunto, Sombrerete and Zacatecas, each of which marked its products with its initial letter. At Chihuahua some of the earliest issues were produced by casting copies from coins of the Mexico City mint. At other cities, such as Nueva Vicaya and Oaxaca, emergency issues with individual types were struck.

The coins issued by the Mexican insurgents include a series in all three metals struck by Morelos, the leader in the south. The types, which have a great number of variations of detail, represent, basically, on the obverse a roughly drawn bow and arrow and the word *Sud* (South) and the value and date on the reverse, accompanied sometimes by the initial M of Morelos. Other coinage was produced by the Supreme National Junta in the years from 1811 to 1814. The first issue of silver 8 real pieces, produced in 1811 by casting, had on obverse an eagle on a bridge of three arches, and was still inscribed with the name of Ferdinand VII; the reverse, a hand holding a bow and arrow with sword and quiver in saltire, was inscribed *Provicional por la suprema junta de America*. On die-struck pieces in 1812 the obverse inscription reads *Vice Ferd VII*, etc. Pieces of 1 real were also produced, as well as some 8 real pieces in copper. Both royalist and insurgent commanders on occasions found it necessary to countermark coinage already in circulation.

When the insurgent forces captured Mexico City in 1821 the Spanish vice-royalty of New Spain ceased to exist and the country assumed the name of Mexico. Augustin Iturbide became head of state, first as a regent and then, in 1822, as emperor of Mexico. On gold coinage of 8 and 4 escudos pieces the new emperor's head was accompanied on the obverse by the inscription *Augustinus Dei Providentia*, while the reverse, showing an eagle perched on a cactus, surrounded by arms or in an oval frame, was inscribed *Mex I Imperator Constitut*. Silver from 8 reales down to a half-real had similar types, the reverse not so elaborate. When Iturbide was compelled to abdicate and flee the country in 1823 Mexico was declared a republic, the form of government which it has maintained with the exception of the years 1864–7 and despite repeated civil wars.

A coinage was struck for the republic of Mexico in gold, silver and copper in the years 1823–64 both at the mint of Mexico and at some eight or nine provincial mints such as Chihuahua and Durango. Gold denominations which included pieces of 8, 4, 2, 1 and ½ escudo had as types a hook-necked eagle with outstretched wings, holding a snake in its beak and standing on a cactus, all between branches of oak and laurel and inscribed on the obverse *Republica Mexicana*. The reverse inscribed *Libertad en la ley*, together with the denomination and the mint initial, showed a hand holding a book surmounted by the Cap of Liberty. In silver the major piece was the 8 reales or peso with smaller values of 4 reales, 2 reales or peseta, 1 real and a half-piece. These had a similar obverse to that of the gold coins but the reverse type was a Cap of Liberty with a background of rays (Pl. 793). The copper cuartino or quarter of a real and the eighth, still with eagle obverse, had value in wreath on reverse. The provincial mints struck these copper denominations in a range of more individual types.

Mexico which had been the scene of one of the earliest European conquests in the New World also witnessed the last European adventure into New World affairs. In the civil dissensions of 1861 Miramon, overthrown by Juarez, appealed to the Catholic powers of Europe and in response Napoleon III of France despatched an expedition which set up a new Mexican empire with the Archduke Maximilian, brother of the Emperor Francis Joseph of Austria, as its emperor. The imperial coinage was based on the decimal system which had already been proposed in 1861. The unit was the peso, divided into 100 centavos. The coinage issued for Maximilian consisted of the peso and pieces of 50, 10 and 5 centavos in silver and a centavo piece in copper. On the peso and its half the portrait head of Maximilian on obverse was inscribed *Maximiliano Emperador*, while the reverse with legend *Imperio Mexicano* and value carried the imperial arms crowned (Pl. 794). The United States, emerging from its own civil war in 1865, refused to recognize Maximilian and ordered Napoleon to evacuate Mexico. The imposed régime, unpopular and deprived of outside support, ended with the execution of Maximilian in 1867 and the restoration of the republic.

The coinage of the restored republic included a range of gold coins of 1, 2½, 5, 10 and 20 peso values with the conventional eagle type on obverse but with the scales of Justice and Cap of Liberty on the reverse. The silver peso and its portions used similar types, though the lower centavo values in silver and the 1 and 2 centavo pieces in copper had simply the value in wreath on the reverse. Nickel coins of 1, 2 and 5 centavo values with bow and quiver obverse were struck only in the years 1882–3. The old piece of 8 reales with eagle and Cap of Liberty type also continued to be struck up to 1897. The official designation of the country, *Estados Unidos Mexicanos*, was placed on the coinage from 1905 but the types suffered little change. The Mexican Civil War of 1913 to 1917 gave rise to a whole range of coinage struck at the mints of the several provinces by the various parties and states which continued to make use of the traditional eagle and Liberty types. The official issues included gold pesos with eagle type and a head of Hidalgo, the leader of the original revolt against Spain. The silver coinage up to 1917 had on the reverse a mounted female figure with wreath and torch and, from 1918 till 1945, the inevitable Cap of Liberty with rays. A special 2 peso piece in silver was first struck in 1921 with a standing figure of Victory on the reverse to commemorate the centenary of independence. A new coinage in 1947 honoured some of Mexico's heroes; the 5 peso bears the head of the Aztec king Cuauhtec and the 1 peso the portrait of Morelos, the revolutionary leader in 1821. Of the very recent Mexican issues silver pieces of 5 and 10 pesos carry the head of Hildago on the reverse, while Cuauhtec in his elaborate head-dress appears on the 50 centavo piece. The great Aztec temple of the Sun provides the reverse on the 20 centavo coin.

GUATEMALA

The captain-generalcy of Guatemala in the Spanish empire comprised the modern states of Guatemala, Costa Rica, Nicaragua, San Salvador and Honduras. A mint was opened at Guatemala in 1733, signing its products with the letter G, and, when a new city of Guatemala was built, the mint, transferred there in 1777, signed NG (Nueva Guatemala). The silver coinage from the reign of Philip V (1700–46) onwards is, apart from the mint-mark, identical with that described under Mexico, much of it until about 1753 being of the rough 'cob' variety. Gold was coined from 1751 onwards, its variations of type being parallel to those of the Mexican issues. The Mexican war for independence was not without its influence in Central America, and Guatemala declared itself independent of Spain in 1821 and became the Confederation of Central America which endured until it splintered in 1832 into the present Central American states. The confederation struck a coinage of pieces of 8 reales and lower values down to the quarter-real in silver. A range of mountain peaks and a rising sun on the obverse is accompanied by the inscription *Republica del Centro de America*, while the reverse with motto *Libre cresca fecundo* has a single tree parting the indication of value (Pl. 795). Nueva Guatemala in Guatemala signed its coins with NG, Tegucigalpa in Honduras with T, Leon in Nicaragua with NR, and San José in Costa Rica with CR.

After the dissolution of the Union in 1832 Guatemala did not issue its own coinage till 1859. The series of peso or 8 reales and divisionary pieces in silver bore the portrait, name and title of its president Rafael Carrera on the obverse and the state arms and value on the reverse. These types were preserved after the death of Carrera in 1865 but his portrait now had the title of *Fundador de la republica de Guatemala*. Later nineteenth-century coinage had as the most persistent types either a head or a seated figure of Liberty and a scroll on crossed arms. The coinage reform of 1924 created a new unit the quetzal in silver with subdivisions and with multiples in gold. The types were on obverse the quetzal, a Central American bird of the parrot family with long tail and resplendent plumage, on a pillar with the value and the same bird perched on a scroll on crossed arms (Pl. 796). Low centavo values in nickel-brass have the bird on scroll on obverse and the value on the reverse.

BRITISH HONDURAS

This British enclave in Spanish Central America grew from original buccaneer settlement, and was finally recognized by Spain in 1798. It acquired colonial status in 1862 but the first coinage was not struck until 1885. This first issue consisted only of copper cents with the head of Victoria and on the reverse the figure 1 with an inscription *British Honduras One Cent* and the date. Higher values of 10, 25 and 50 cents in silver were added in 1894 with equally simple types. Apart from the portraits of the successive monarchs the coinage has remained unchanged till the present day but several metals have been used, including the cupro-nickel of the current coins (Pl. 797).

HONDURAS

Rare silver 2 real pieces were struck at the mint of Tegucigalpa in 1823 with the Spanish arms between two pillars accompanied by the mint name, value and date on obverse, while the reverse carried a cross with lion and castle in the angles. The same mint issued various real values of the republic of Central America in 1830 and 1831 (see p. 432) and the types of mountain peaks and trees were retained on the provisional coinage of Honduras after 1832. Coins of denominations from 8 reales downwards were struck in base metal and inscribed on obverse *Provisional del Est. de Honduras*. In 1869–70 the real and its portions in cupro-nickel carried a harbour scene between two flags on obverse and the value in wreath on reverse (Pl. 798). On the gold peso, with occasional multiples up to 20, issued from 1888 to 1922, there was a Liberty head on obverse and on the reverse arms consisting of a triangle within a circlet inscribed *Republica de Honduras*. The silver peso and lower centavo values from 1882 repeated the arms type on the reverse but showed on obverse a seated figure of Liberty holding flag and scroll. Lower centavo values in bronze with arms-type obverse had a simple value reverse. The coinage decree of 1926 instituted a new unit—the lempira—which, together with the 50 and 20 centavo values, was struck in silver. The types were an Indian head and the Honduras arms, while on the lower centavo pieces in bronze or cupro-nickel the types were the arms and value.

NICARAGUA

Under Spanish dominion the mint of Leon in Nicaragua struck a coinage of silver reales in several values from the later seventeenth century and very rare gold in the later eighteenth century. The types were the standard Spanish colonial designs (see pp. 428–9) and the coins were marked by the signature of the mint NR, usually ligatured. While Nicaragua formed part of the republic of Central America the mint at Leon issued silver 2 real pieces with mountain peaks and tree types (see p. 432) in 1825. In the later nineteenth century the monetary unit was the peso of 100 centavos and silver coinage of 50, 25 and 10 centavos and lower values in cupro-nickel or bronze had as types a triangular frame enclosing mountain peaks, surmounted by a Cap of Liberty on obverse and value in wreath on reverse. In the present century a new unit the cordoba of 100 centavos was created. The new unit took its name from the obverse type the portrait of Cordoba, used on all denominations—the cordoba in silver and centavo values in cupro-nickel or brass. The reverse continued to show the range of mountain peaks with a sun rising behind them (Pl. 799).

SALVADOR

After the break-up of the Republic of Central America a rare provisional coinage was issued for Salvador in 1833–5 of silver 2, 1 and ½ real pieces with volcano on obverse inscribed *Moneda Provisional* and a crowned column on the reverse with inscription *Por la libertad Salv*. Later nineteenth-century coinage was issued with the silver peso of 100 centavos as the unit. Coins of 1 and 3 centavos in copper in 1889 carried the head of President Morazan on the obverse and the value on reverse. The issue begun in 1892 comprised a silver peso and a 50 centavos piece with head of Christopher Columbus on obverse and the arms of Salvador on the reverse and lower centavo values with arms-and-value types. From 1913 the low-value coins revived the obverse portrait of Morazan. The new unit, the colon, taking its name from Colon the Spanish form of Columbus, was instituted in 1925. The colon in silver and the special gold 20 colones piece issued in 1925 celebrate the fourth centenary of Salvador with jugate busts of the early Spanish commander Alvarado and of President Quinonez on the obverse and arms type on the reverse (Pl. 800).

COSTA RICA

As one of the component states in the republic of Central America formed in 1821 Costa Rica participated in the coinage described above under Guatemala (see p. 432). The Costa Rican mint was San José which signed its products with the letters CR. Even after the Central American Federation dissolved, Costa Rica continued to use this same coinage of 2, 1 and ½ real pieces with its types of mountain peaks and tree (Pl. 801) as well as a coinage in gold of 8, 4, 2, 1 and ½ escudo pieces with similar types to those on the silver. In 1849–50 a silver real coinage appeared with new types and inscriptions. The obverse with a facing female bust was inscribed *America Central*, while the reverse, still with the single tree-type, carried the state name *Republica de Costa Rica*. The peso of 100 centavos was adopted as the monetary unit in 1850. The gold escudo, struck also in several multiples as well as in the half-piece or gold peso, now bore the state arms on obverse and an Indian leaning against an inscribed column on the reverse. Silver in the form of the half-peso and similar fractions also had the arms-type obverse but retained the traditional tree-type on the reverse. From 1864 gold coins had the value expressed in pesos as the reverse type though silver coins, expressed in centavo values, continued the arms-and-tree types, changing in 1885 to arms-and-value types.

A new unit, the colon, introduced in 1897 took its name from Cristobal Colon whose portrait appeared on the obverse, accompanied by arms on the reverse on gold pieces of 2, 5, 10 and 20 colones. The divisionary coinage in silver was now expressed in centimos. More modern issues from 1937 onwards with arms-and-value types have been struck in cupro-nickel in denominations of 1 and 2 colones and 50 and 25 centimos. The most recent colones coins are issued in steel.

PANAMA

The isthmus of Panama broke away from Costa Rica in 1903 to conclude with the United States the treaty which enabled the Panama Canal to be constructed. The unit is the balboa, named after the Spanish conquistador whose portrait occupies the obverse of many coin issues. The first coinage in 1904 was of silver centesimos of various values from 50 to 2½ with portrait of Balboa and the arms of Panama on the reverse (Pl. 802). Later minor coins had arms-and-value types but a new coinage in 1930 consisted of a silver balboa and fractions with helmeted bust of the conquistador and standing figure of the republic or arms. Minor values were in base metal with bust of Balboa and value. The fiftieth anniversary of Panama was celebrated in 1953 by a coinage with similar types with an additional inscription *Cincuentenaria* under the bust of Balboa.

SOUTH AMERICA

The early part of the sixteenth century witnessed the gradual conquest of South America by the Spaniards, until by 1541 the whole territory belonged to the Spanish crown, with the exception of Brasil which Portugal had occupied. When, in 1542, Central America was formed into a vice-royalty, a second vice-royalty was set up in South America with its capital at Lima. In 1718 the vice-royalty of New Granada, comprising the northern part of the sub-continent, was created and in 1776 a fourth vice-royalty was established in the south with its capital at Buenos Aires. Coinage for the Spanish empire was struck at a number of South American mints of which the more important were Lima and Potosi. The products of these mints will be described in the separate geographic sections below. During the Napoleonic wars when the Spanish control of the South American colonies was less effective, independence movements began from about 1810 but the establishment of the modern independent states of South America came only a decade or more later.

COLOMBIA

In the Spanish empire Colombia formed part, first of the vice-royalty of Peru and from 1718 of the new vice-royalty of New Granada (Nuevo Reino de Granada). The Spanish mints in this territory were at Popayan and Santa Fé de Bogota. The latter mint began operations in 1622, marking its products with the letters NR, the initials of the province of Nueva Reina. For the first century silver only was coined in real pieces of various values with types, the shield of Castille and Leon on one side and the Pillars of Hercules on the other. The first gold coins were struck in 1756 in the reign of Ferdinand VI with types, portrait bust and arms.

The coinage was, in effect, closely parallel to that described in detail under Mexico (pp. 428–30) and shows the same changes in types. An oddity of the mint was that the coinage for Ferdinand VII up to 1820, though bearing his name and title, continued to have the portrait of his predecessor, Charles IV. The mint at Popayan began coining in 1758, its products being marked with P or PN and, apart from a brief cessation between 1763 and 1767, was active until the end of Spanish dominion under Ferdinand VII. At Popayan as at Bogota coinage was mainly of gold escudos of various values, though silver in the form usually of reales and

437

cuartillos was also issued. The types and their changes followed the pattern of the issues of the Mexico City mint.

The vice-royalty of New Granada made itself independent of Spain in 1811 and struck a coinage of silver pieces of 8 reales and subdivisions. The Indian head on obverse is inscribed *Libertad Americana* and on the reverse the name *Nueva Granada* accompanies a pomegranate, the traditional badge of Granada in Spain (Pl. 803). The Republic of Colombia, formed in 1819 and consisting of Venezuela and Ecuador as well as the modern Colombia, had a coinage of silver reales similar to those just described but with *Republica de Colombia* on obverse. An issue of copper cuartillos with the portrait of Bolivar and the word *Colombia* on the obverse and either a seated or standing figure of Justice with sword and scales carries no date but was produced in 1831 in Birmingham for Colombia (Pl. 804). Gold escudo pieces with multiples up to 8 were also struck with a Liberty head on obverse and the fasces between two cornuacopiae on the reverse, a type which from 1834 supplied the obverse of the silver series which now had a value reverse. The union, however, did not long survive the death of the liberator, Bolivar, in 1830, and split again into its component states in 1836, Colombia adopting now the title of Republica de la Nueva Granada. The Liberty head remained on the obverse of the gold, accompanied by the new state title, while the reverse was formed by the state arms and an inscription giving the value in pesos, together with the mint name of Bogota or Popayan. Silver real denominations showed a condor in flight above a cornucopiae on obverse and value on the reverse. In 1847 as a step towards a decimal coinage the peso was divided into 10 reales of 10 centavos. On the gold denominations a Liberty head and condor above arms supplied the types, the latter type appearing also on the major silver pieces with a value reverse. The republic of New Granada was replaced by the Confederacion Granadina in 1858 but apart from the inscription no change was made in the coin types.

Yet another change, made in 1861 when the title Estados Unidos de Colombia was adopted, brought little alteration to the coins which were struck by a new mint at Medellin, as well as the former mints at Bogota and Popayan. Nickel coins of $2\frac{1}{2}$ and $1\frac{1}{4}$ centavos in 1874 and 1881 had as types a Cap of Liberty and value. In the early twentieth century the title reverted to Republica de Colombia. On multiple gold pesos from 1919 the obverse bore the portrait of Simon Bolivar and the reverse the arms of Colombia, types used also in silver centavo pieces (Pl. 805), while low centavo values in cupro-nickel had Liberty head and value types. A portrait bust of Bolivar in uniform forms the obverse of the post-war 50 and 20 centavo coins in silver and an Indian head that of the 10 centavos in cupro-nickel.

VENEZUELA

The last Spanish captain-general was deposed in 1810 but only some rare emergency coins were issued at that time and, though Venezuela joined in the formation of the republic of New Granada in 1819 (see p. 437), Caracas, held by the Spanish till 1821, struck a few silver reales with lion and castle arms and Pillars of Hercules types. Venezuela became an independent state in 1836 but only in 1843 and again in 1852 did coinage in the name of Venezuela appear in the form of copper centavo and half-centavo pieces with Liberty head and value types. A new currency system, instituted in 1857, was based on the gold venezolano, equivalent to the French 5 franc piece with a silver peso or 10 reales, divided into 100 centavos. Silver only was struck at this time with the head of Liberty and the arms of Venezuela, while the previous copper centavo issue was continued but in reduced module. With the adoption in 1871 of the new title Estados Unidos de Venezuela came also a new coinage. The new monetary unit was the bolivar, taking its name from the liberator, Simon Bolivar, whose portrait appeared on the obverse of gold pieces in multiples from 5 to 100 and in silver from 5 down to ⅕ bolivar (Pl. 806). The reverse was the state arms which also provided the obverse for cupro-nickel coins in lower centavo values which formed the reverse type. This system persisted until 1947 though gold coinage ceased in 1930 and the lower values were expressed as centimos from 1954. The new coinage of 1954 has retained the Bolivar and arms types on its denominations, the bolivar and 50 and 25 centimos in silver.

ECUADOR

For Ecuador as part of the republic of Colombia a coinage of gold escudos and of silver 2, 1 and ½ real pieces was struck at the mint of Quito in 1833 and 1835 with types, fasces between two cornuacopiae inscribed *El Ecuador en Colombia* and the mint name on obverse and a sun above two mountain peaks on the reverse. A similar coinage from 4 to ½ real was struck after the establishment of Ecuador as a separate republic in 1836 with only the necessary alteration of the obverse inscription to *Republica de Ecuador*. A bust of Bolivar and the arms of Ecuador appeared on 4 real pieces in 1844, while a Liberty head obverse was adopted for the range of real pieces from 8 downwards from 1846 onwards. Gold escudos between 1838 and 1843 had Liberty head and mountain-peak types and Bolivar head and arms types from 1845. A new coinage, introduced in 1884, was based on the silver sucre which took its name from the portrait of Sucre, one of Bolivar's lieutenants, which formed its obverse (Pl. 807.) The unit was divided into 10 decimos or 100 centavos. The reverse on the silver coins was the state arms as also on 10 sucre pieces in gold struck in 1899 and 1900. On lower value centavo coins the types were arms and value. These have continued to be the types of Ecuador's coins in the twentieth century, though, following the trend in world coinage, the metals used have become baser, the sucre and its divisionary centavo pieces being struck now in cupro-nickel.

PERU

The original vice-royalty of Peru comprised the whole of Spanish South America until the creation, in the eighteenth century, of the vice-royalties of New Granada in the north and that of the south with its capital at Buenos Aires. The two great Spanish mints were at Lima and Potosi, the latter now in the territory of Bolivia. The latter mint was set up in 1575 for the striking of silver signed with the letter P (Pl. 808). The types on the various real denominations are similar to those struck at Mexico City (p. 428). Gold coinage was first struck in 1779 and continued until 1808 with brief recurrences in the last years before the end of Spanish dominion in 1824. The Lima mint began striking silver at an earlier date, in 1568, with types in general similar to the usual Spanish-American types. The mint was burnt down in 1620 but reopened briefly in 1659 and then from 1684 struck continuously until 1820. Gold coinage began in 1697. With some slight variations the types are as those on the Mexican issues.

Peru declared its independence in 1821 and a coinage of 8 and 4 real pieces was struck at Lima with Virtue and Justice on the obverse and the new state arms consisting of a llama, a tree and a cornucopiae on the reverse. It was not, however, until 1824 that, with the assistance of San Martin, the liberator of Chile, and Bolivar, the liberator of Colombia, that Spanish rule was finally ended. The subsequent coinage of the Republic of Peru included some half-escudo pieces in gold with the state arms on obverse and the value and mint name on reverse and a standing figure of Liberty and the state arms on the escudo and its multiples. These same types were used on the silver real, its multiples and divisionary pieces. The $\frac{1}{4}$ and $\frac{1}{8}$ peso in copper in 1823 had on obverse a llama with mountains and sun in the background and the value on the reverse (Pl. 809). These issues were normally struck by the mint at Lima. Other mints at Arequipa, Cuzco and Pasco issued some silver with these types but also struck silver with a sun as obverse and value on reverse.

In 1857 a new decimal coinage was instituted with the silver sol as the monetary unit. The types now were a seated Liberty and arms on the sol and its portions, including the small dinero and its half. A sun and the value provided the types on the nickel or bronze centavo pieces. These types continued with little change through the nineteenth century and into the twentieth. The gold libra, equivalent to 10 soles, issued from 1898, showed the head of an Inca chief on obverse but still maintained the arms on the reverse, and on coins of 5, 10 and 20 centavos in nickel or brass a head of Liberty or the republic, wearing corn-wreath, appeared on the obverse with a branch and value on the reverse. A special issue of a 50 sol piece in gold in 1930–1 displayed the head of the Inca Manco Capac on obverse and an Inca symbol on the reverse. Since 1950 special issues of gold multiple soles have been struck with seated Liberty and arms types not as pieces of currency but as bullion.

BOLIVIA

General Sucre, one of Bolivar's lieutenants, detached Upper Peru in 1825 and created a new republic with the name of Bolivia. Potosi, one of the great mints in Peru in the Spanish period, was situated in this territory and was used to strike the new Bolivian coinage, supplemented later in 1853 by another mint at La Paz. Gold escudos and multiples honoured Bolivar by placing his bust in uniform on the obverse, clearly labelled with his name below and with an inscription *Libre por la Constitucion*. The reverse showed a mountain with rising sun and a llama in the foreground. The silver sueldo with multiples up to 8 and divisionary pieces also bore the portrait of Bolivar but had a different reverse, two llamas recumbent at the foot of a tree (Pl. 810). A decimal coinage, introduced in 1863, had as its unit the peso or boliviano in silver, divided into 100 centavos with types, an oval shield, flanked by flags and surmounted by a condor on obverse and the value on reverse. Copper centavo values in 1878 had the condor only on the obverse. In 1893 the 5 and 10 centavo pieces in nickel began to be issued with the arms, which are formed from the reverse type of the original Bolivian coins, as obverse and a staff of Aesculapius and value on the reverse and from 1939 a 50 centavo coin with the same types has been struck. The coinage of 1951 consists or 1, 5 and 10 boliviano pieces, all with value reverse and with on obverse the Bolivian types, arms between flags or the bust of Bolivar.

CHILE

Chile was not settled by the Spanish with such expedition as the more northern parts of South America and, though the city of Santiago de Chile was founded in 1541, a mint was not established there till about 1750. The earliest issues, bearing the signature S accompanied by small O, were gold 8 escudo pieces of Ferdinand V and gold of various escudo values continued to be struck with some regularity down to 1817, the types and their changes following fairly closely those described in detail for the Mexican mint. Coinage of the several real values in silver began in 1754.

The struggle for Chilean independence began in 1810 and Spanish control, reimposed in 1814, was finally broken in 1817. The obverse on the coinage of gold escudos, begun in 1824, was a variation of the popular South American type of a mountain range, but here it includes two active volcanoes. On the reverse was a column with two flags in saltire. The silver-real series showed a single volcano on obverse and the column without flags on the reverse (Pl. 811). New types were introduced in 1835 for the gold escudos, a hand resting on the book of the Constitution on obverse and the star shield of Chile with llama and condor supporters. In 1839 the obverse was altered to a figure of Liberty standing by the altar of the Constitution. Silver also received new types in 1838, arms on the obverse and a condor on the reverse. The types of the decimal coinage based on the peso of 10 decimos or 100 centavos were, on silver, arms and a flying condor with a broken chain in its beak, but the gold types remained unchanged. In 1867 the silver peso and its parts took as its obverse a condor beside an oval shield and, as reverse, value in wreath, while low-centavo values with value reverse had a republic head in corn-wreath on obverse. In 1896 a Liberty head and arms were introduced as the types of the gold peso multiples and on silver the obverse was changed to a defiant condor on a mountain peak, a type which persisted till the 1930's. Gold coins were struck in 1926 in denominations of the condor, equivalent to 10 pesos. From 1942 coinage of the peso and centavo values in copper had the portrait bust in uniform of the liberator, Bernardo O'Higgins, on obverse and value reverse. From 1954 the peso and multiples in aluminium have been issued with the same types. The 10 peso coins of 1956 in aluminium have a condor on the obverse and, in a wreath on the reverse, the value 10 *pesos* = 1 *condor*.

ARGENTINA

The movement for independence from Spain began in 1810 and in 1813 a coinage in gold and silver was struck for the Provincias del Rio de la Plata at the mint at Potosi. The Spanish monetary system of gold escudos and silver reales was continued but new types were adopted. The obverse showed a beaming sun and the title *Provincias del Rio de la Plata*, the reverse the new arms, two hands holding a staff surmounted by the Cap of Liberty, accompanied by the inscription *Union y Libertad* (Pl. 812). When Upper Peru was retaken by the Spaniards in 1815 and the mint at Potosi could no longer be used, other mints in the provinces, particularly Rioja, which signed its coins RA, were set up. When de Rosas became dictator in 1836 the name of the state was changed to Republica Argentina Confederada and the types on both gold and silver were altered to the mountain Famatina above crossed flags on obverse and the arms on reverse, flanked, in the case of gold coins, by flags. A brief issue at the outset of the coinage had carried the portrait of de Rosas on the obverse.

The striking of coinage languished from the 1850's and was replaced almost entirely by paper money until a new decimal coinage was decreed in 1881 to be struck by the mint at Buenos Aires. The unit, as elsewhere in South America, was the silver peso of 100 centavos. On gold coins of 5 and $2\frac{1}{2}$ pesos, known as the argentino and its half, as well as on the silver and the low centavo pieces in copper the types were a Liberty head and state arms. In 1896 the 5, 10 and 20 centavo pieces struck in nickel carried the Liberty head and value. These continued to be the principal coins struck up to 1950, though the types were modernized in 1942 and a 50 centavo piece added in 1941. In 1950 the obverse type was changed to a portrait of the liberator San Martin whose centenary, then being celebrated, was mentioned on the reverse also. Subsequent issues have been identical except for the removal of the word *centenario* from the reverse.

URUGUAY

In the course of the independence movements in South America Brasil occupied the left bank of the Rio de la Plata which, after recapture by the new independent state, later Argentina, fell again to Brasil which set up a Cisplatine republic in 1821. In 1828 the independent Republica Oriental del Uruguay was created. Coinage was not issued until 1840 and for long consisted only of 5, 20 and 40 centesimo pieces in copper with a sun obverse and value reverse. In 1869, 1, 2 and 4 centesimos in copper were struck with these same types and in 1877 the silver peso with divisionary pieces in centesimos was added with arms and value types. The gold peso and multiples with identical types was issued in 1870. In 1916 the bust of Artigas, the hero of the liberation, was placed on the obverse of the silver coins and the arms were transferred to the reverse (Pl. 813). The sun and value types of the small centesimo pieces remained unchanged until 1938 but the 10 centavo value received a Liberty head as its obverse in 1930, the centenary of liberation. In 1942 the silver peso was reissued with the Artigas obverse but with a jaguar on the reverse. The new coinage, begun in 1953, of centesimos from value 10 downwards, in cupro-nickel, still honours Artigas on the obverse but has reverted to a simple value in wreath for the reverse.

PARAGUAY

The earliest coinage of Paraguay, the only completely inland state of South America, consisted of an issue of the copper $\frac{1}{12}$ real with types, a lion standing in front of a staff surmounted by the Cap of Liberty on obverse and the value on reverse. Other copper pieces of 1, 2 and 4 centesimos struck in 1870 had a star between two branches on obverse and value reverse, but in 1889 came the first coinage of silver pesos combining the lion and Cap of Liberty and the star types. All the silver issues of the twentieth century till the last war reverted to star-and-value types. On the new coinage in aluminium-bronze, begun in 1944, the various centimo values have had each a different obverse such as the lion and Cap of Liberty on the 50 centimos (Pl.814) or an orchid on the 10 centimos piece The most recent issues begun in 1953 have a scalloped edge and all use the lion type on obverse.

BRASIL

By an award of Pope Alexander and the Treaty of Tordesillas in 1493 the New World was divided by a north to south line, all territory to the east of this line being allocated to Portugal. In exploiting this award the Portuguese discovered Brasil in 1500 and had taken possession of it by 1503. Apart from the seizure of the north of the country by the Dutch between 1624 and 1654 the whole of Brasil remained firmly in Portuguese hands. In the early stages of the development of Brasil such currency requirements as arose were met by the use of coinage from the home country and, towards the end of the seventeenth century, by counter-marking Spanish colonial issues. Eventually in 1694 a coinage for circulation in Brasil was decreed by Peter II. This new coinage, comprising both gold and silver, was modelled in the Portuguese coinage system. The basic denomination in gold was the milreis or piece of 1000 reis with multiples of 2000 and 4000. The pataca of 320 reis was struck in silver, together with its double and half as well as the subsidiary coins known as vintem (20 reis) of which larger 2 and 4 vintem denominations were also issued. The types, also, were analogous to those of the Portuguese coinage. The gold denominations carried on obverse the Portuguese arms crowned, and the reverse, a cross within a quadrilobe. The royal title *Petrus II Dei gratia Portugaliae rex/et Brasiliae dominus* formed a continuous inscription of both obverse and reverse. Silver coins had a similar obverse together with the royal titles in more abbreviated form but the reverse was formed by a globe superimposed on the cross with broad ends, characteristic of Portuguese coinage, and had as inscription an abbreviated form of *Subque signo nata stabit* (Pl. 815). The mint for this first coinage was at Bahia but was transferred in 1699 to Rio de Janeiro.

In 1703 the types of the Portuguese gold coinage were adopted for the Brasilian issues also, differentiated by placing the initial of the mint, R, in the angles of the reverse cross. The initial of Bahia was similarly employed when the mint there was reopened in 1714, while the letter M marked the product of a new mint set up at Villa Rica, the capital of the province of Minas Geraes, in 1724. A specific copper coinage for Brasil was struck from 1715 in Lisbon and from 1729 in Bahia. The obverse bore the royal title and had as type a large crowned X indicating the value. The reverse repeated the globe-on-cross type of the silver but had its individual inscription *Pecunia totum circumit orbem* (Pl. 816). Following the lead of the home coinage Brasilian gold issues changed their types from 1727 to show the royal portrait on obverse and a shield of arms, ornamented and crowned, on the reverse. The Brasilian issues were differentiated by the addition of the mint letters of Rio, Bahia or Minas under the bust.

No essential change of types took place throughout the remainder of the eighteenth century or in the first two decades of the nineteenth, though small modifications were introduced, following the pattern of the home coinage. When John VI, who had been exiled from Portugal by the Napoleonic wars and had remained in Brasil after Napoleon's defeat and his country's liberation, finally returned to Portugal in 1821 he left the government of Brasil to his son, Peter, who was proclaimed emperor of Brasil in the following year. Gold coinage bore his portrait and title as emperor of Brasil on the obverse, while the reverse carried as the arms of Brasil a shield with the globe-on-cross device with the value in reis below. On silver and copper the types consisted of the arms of Brasil and the value in a wreath. Peter I abdicated in favour of his son, Peter II, who reigned from 1831 to 1889, issuing a coinage substantially the same as that of his father (Pl. 817).

In 1889 Brasil was declared a republic with the official title Estados Unidos de Brasil. The types on gold coins issued between 1889 and 1922 were, on the 20 milreis pieces, the head of Liberty in her Phrygian cap on obverse and the five stars of the Southern Cross within a circle of stars on the reverse, and on the 10 milreis piece a similar obverse but with the Southern Cross design of the reverse superimposed on a large five-pointed star. Silver coins of values 500, 1000 and 2000 reis repeated the types of the larger gold denomination and lower values of reis in nickel or bronze took the Southern Cross type as obverse and had simply the value in figures on the reverse. A special issue of the silver denominations in 1900 honoured the fourth centenary of the discovery of Brasil with an obverse showing a galleon of 1500 and round the value on the reverse an inscription 4° *Centenario do descobramento do Brasil*. Another special issue in 1922 commemorated the centenary of Brasil's independence from Portugal with an obverse showing the jugate busts of Peter I, the first emperor of Brasil, and of President Pessoa. The reverse of the silver 2 milreis piece carried the arms of the empire of Brasil and the republic side by side. Yet another commemorative issue was struck in 1932 on the occasion of the fourth centenary of the colonization of Brasil with types showing John III and other personalities connected with the event, a map of South America, marked with the dividing line of Pope Alexander's award in 1493, and a sixteenth-century galleon. Many of the issues of the 1930's carry the portraits of famous Brasilians but the nickel coinage of the new government of President Vargas, set up in 1938, has only his portrait on the obverse and value in a wreath on the reverse.

A currency reform of 1942 introduced a new monetary unit, the cruzeiro of 100 centavos. Cruzeiro denominations in aluminium-bronze have a map of Brasil as obverse and the value between two laurel-branches on the reverse. Centavo values in nickel have Vargas' portrait and value.

THE GUIANAS

The area on the north-east coast of South America known as Guiana was dis-covered about 1500 and this was the one area in South America where European nations other than Spain and Portugal succeeded in establishing colonies in the course of the seventeenth century. The Dutch secured a foothold in 1613, the English in 1650 and the French in 1656.

BRITISH GUIANA

The early currency needs of Guiana were met by the use of the ubiquitous Spanish colonial issues and other major international commercial coinages. Towards the end of the eighteenth century the British settlements at Essequibo and Demerara countermarked Spanish pieces of eight with the letters E & D and the value, expressed in terms of Dutch currency, as 3 guilders. A central piece was punched from these Spanish dollars and itself stamped with the value '3 bits'. The supremacy of Dutch coinage in the area is reflected in the issue in 1809 of a coinage for Essequibo and Demerara consisting of pieces in silver of 3, 2, 1, ½ and ¼ guilder and in copper in 1813 a stiver and half-stiver piece. The types were the bust and titles of George III on obverse with on the reverse the value crowned and the names of Essequibo and Demerara (Pl. 818). A second issue of the silver with slightly modified types was made in 1816 and a similar coinage was struck for William IV. On the issue of 1836 the description on the reverse was changed to British Guiana and the 3 and 2 guilder denominations were abandoned. In the reign of Victoria the only coinage issued specifically for British Guiana was the silver fourpence with types, the royal bust and value in wreath. This denomination has continued to be issued in succeeding reigns up to the present.

FRENCH GUIANA

Uniface billon coins of value 1 sou with a crowned C as type, struck for French Guiana, known as the colony of Cayenne, are undated but were struck in the reign of Louis XV (1715–74). Under Louis XVI billon double sous were issued for Cayenne with his name and title on obverse and, as type, a crown above three lis The reverse, inscribed *Colonie de Cayenne*, bore the value and date (Pl. 819). Copper 10 centimes were issued by Louis XVIII and Louis Philippe with a crowned monogram on obverse and the value on reverse, inscribed *Cayenne française*.

DUTCH GUIANA (SURINAM)

This territory, recognized as a Dutch colony by the Peace of Breda in 1667, normally used either Spanish colonial coinage or that of the home country. In 1679, however, a series of copper doits was issued by the governor Johannes Heinsius. These were in denominations of 4, 2 and 1 stuiver and had on the obverse a small parrot on a branch with the date below (Pl. 820). The reverse was normally smooth but the major piece sometimes was ornamented with a tree design on the reverse. Between 1941 and 1943 coinage of 25, 10, 5 and 1 cent pieces with the types used on the coinage of Holland were struck for use in Surinam and Curaçao by the mint at Philadelphia in the United States which marked its products with a small letter P.

THE CARIBBEAN

The coinages of the islands scattered throughout the Caribbean have usually been issued by the European colonial powers who have at various times possessed them. A number of the larger islands have, however, achieved independence at various times from the nineteenth century onwards and have issued their own individual coinage series.

HAITI

The island of Haiti originally comprised a French colony of St. Domingo in the north-west and a Spanish colony of the same name in the south-east. The whole island was ceded to France in 1795 and until 1804 a colonial coinage in billon was struck for the island. It consisted of billon pieces of 2 escalins or gourdin, an escalin and its half, all with standing figure of Liberty and inscription *République française* on obverse and the value in words on the reverse, inscribed *Colonies de Sainte Domingue*. The north-western portion declared itself an independent empire of Haiti in 1804 under a negro emperor, Jacques Dessalines. He was succeeded in 1806 by a president, Henri Christophe, who issued a base-metal coinage of 15 sols (2 escalins) and 7½ sols (escalin) with types a shield with the monogram of the president and inscription *Libertas Religio Mores* on obverse and standing Liberty, inscribed *Monnoie d'Hayti*, on reverse. The copper cents struck in 1807 show a facing bust of Henri Christophe in uniform and cocked hat on obverse and are inscribed on the reverse, with the value in the field, *Le Gouvernement de Hayti* (Pl. 821). Henri took the title of king in 1812 and ruled as such until 1820, issuing a coinage of silver pieces, mainly the gourde with an occasional double gourde piece. The obverse shows Henri's portrait, the reverse a shield, crowned within a collar, while the inscription *Henri I par la grace de Dieu/Roi d'Hayti* is continued from obverse to reverse and completed by the date, both in its normal form and as an era date from the achievement of independence in 1804.

The south-west portion of the island became a separate republic in 1807 under Alexandre Pétion. The initial coinage of 6, 12 and 25 centimes in silver had as types a palm-tree and trophy of arms and flags, while the reverse, inscribed *République d'Hayti,* had the value enclosed within a ring in the form of a snake. In 1817, or year 14 of independence, Pétion's portrait and name appeared on the obverse, the type with palm-tree and arms being transferred to the reverse, accompanied by the state name and value. Pétion was succeeded as president in 1818 by J. P. Boyer who was recognized in 1820 by the north-western portion, previously ruled by Henri Christophe, and by the eastern portion, which declared itself independent of Spain in 1822. Boyer ruled until 1843 and issued a coinage similar to that of Pétion but with additional denominations of 50 and 100 centimes. Copper coins of 1 and 2 centimes value had as types a fasces dividing the value on obverse and the value within a wreath on reverse.

On the death of Boyer in 1843 the eastern portion broke away and established itself as the Dominican Republic (see below). The north-west portion preserved the name, Republic of Haiti, and its coinage under successive presidents was mainly of copper centime pieces with the fasces type until Faustin, who had been president since 1847, proclaimed himself emperor in 1849. Copper coins of the unusual denomination of 6½ centimes have the crowned bust of Faustin with his title as emperor of Haiti while the reverse is formed by his crowned arms. The empire ended in 1858 when Nicole Geffrard became president. A coinage of 5, 10 and 20 centimes in silver shows his portrait head, while the reverse revives the palm-tree and arms design of Pétion. In 1880 a new monetary system was created with, as its unit, the silver gourde divided into 100 centimes. The types of the gourde and divisionary pieces in silver are a Liberty head with the state name and the year of independence on obverse and the now traditional palm-tree and arms reverse (Pl. 822). The issues of 1904–8 in the form of cupro-nickel pieces of 5, 10, 20 and 50 cents value carried the portrait of the president and had the usual palm-tree reverse. Haiti was occupied by the United States between 1915 and 1934 but when coinage was resumed in 1949 the types of presidential portrait and palm-tree and arms were revived. The nickel 20 centimes of 1956 carry the head of President Magliore on obverse and a palm-tree and arms on the reverse. A similar 10 centimes issue in 1958 had the portrait of President Duvalier on the obverse.

DOMINICAN REPUBLIC

The eastern portion of the island of Haiti declared itself an independent republic with the title of the Dominican Republic in 1844. The earliest coinages in 1844 and 1848 are brass cuartillas or quarter-reales with no types on either side but only the inscription *Republica Dominicana* on the obverse and the value on the reverse. A series of nickel coins in 1877 of low centavo values had as types a cross or arms on obverse and value in wreath on reverse. A new system instituted in 1889 was based on the silver dominicano or franc divided into 100 centesimos. The types on the silver franc, its multiple of 5 francs and its half of 50 centesimos were a Liberty head and arms, and, on the copper 5 and 10 centesimos, arms and value in wreath. In 1897 the peso of 100 centavos was adopted as the monetary unit but the types remained essentially the same. Under the Trujillo régime coinage began again in 1937, utilizing the types of the 1897 issue. On the 1 centavo piece in bronze a palm-tree and the value replaced the Liberty head. The twenty-fifth anniversary of Trujillo's régime was celebrated in 1955 by a special issue of a 30 peso piece in gold and a peso piece in silver with Trujillo's portrait on the obverse.

CUBA

The first coinage to be struck by Cuba after it secured its independence from Spain was a series of silver souvenir pesos in 1897. The obverse carries a female head and is inscribed *Patria y Libertad Souvenir* while the reverse carries the arms and title of the new republic. The next coinage issue, which was not till 1915, consisted of the silver peso in silver with multiples up to 20 on which the types were the head of President Marti on obverse and arms and value on the reverse (Pl. 823). The peso was also issued with a different obverse type, a star on a background of rays, the type used on divisionary pieces in silver down to 10 centavos. Lower value pieces in various metals had as obverse the value as a Roman numeral at the centre of a star. New, modernistic designs were used for the peso between 1934 and 1939. On the obverse the motto *Patria y Libertad* is inscribed in the field beside the bust of Liberty while the state name is similarly disposed beside the arms on the reverse. A special issue of 40, 20 and 10 centavo pieces in 1952 commemorated the fiftieth year of the republic. On the obverse a flag flies before a view of the city. Another special issue in 1953 honouring the centenary of the birth of President Marti has his portrait on the obverse of 50, 25 and 1 centavo pieces.

DANISH WEST INDIES

The Danish possessions in the West Indies consisted of the islands of St. John (1684), St. Thomas (1716) and Ste. Croix (1733) and a special coinage was struck for these colonies until their sale to the United States in 1917. Coinage was first issued in 1740 in the reign of Christian VI in the form of the silver skilling with various multiples. The types on the skilling itself were the crowned monogram of the king with his titles *D. G. Rex Dan. Norv. Van. G.* as inscription on obverse and the value, 1 *skilling danske*, on reverse with inscription *De Dansk. Americ.*

Eyland. Kaab. Mynt. On the higher multiples the reverse type was a three-masted sailing ship (Pl. 824).

These types persisted until the reign of Frederick VII when in 1859 the coinage system was brought into line with that of the United States with the daler of 100 cents as the monetary unit. Silver pieces of 20, 10, 5 and 3 cents now all carried the royal portrait on obverse but the ship reverse was preserved on the 20 and 5 cent coins; a design of sugar-canes appeared on the reverse of the 10 cent piece and the value only on the 3 cent. A copper cent piece had as types the arms and value. The system was slightly modified under Christian IX in 1905 by the introduction of new divisionary denominations of the franc, equal to 20 cents, and the 5 bits, equal to 1 cent. Gold coins of 4 dalers (20 francs) and 10 dalers (50 francs) were struck with royal portrait and seated-female personification. The reverse of the 1 and 2 franc coins in silver showed three native figures standing, while the 50 bit reverse carried only the value and a branch. The lower value coins in nickel and bronze had the crowned monogram on obverse and a design of trident, sickle and Aesculapius' staff on the reverse. These types were retained on subsequent issues, the last of which was a bronze 5 bit piece of Christian X in 1913.

DUTCH WEST INDIES

The Netherlands Antilles group, of which the most important is Curaçao, like most of the Caribbean territories, made use of cut and counter-stamped Spanish silver coinage until the early nineteenth century. The first coinage specially struck for Curaçao was the silver real of 1821 with obverse a stalk of maize and a caduceus in saltire with inscription *Curaçao* (Pl. 825); the reverse carried the value in a wreath. A silver stuiver in 1822 had simply the name of the colony on obverse and the value on reverse.

In the present century small silver pieces of a quarter and a tenth of a guilder were issued in 1900 and 1901 with an obverse portrait of Queen Wilhelmina similar to that of the Dutch coinage and a reverse, crowned arms dividing the value, inscribed *Kolonie Curaçao*. A more extensive coinage was begun in 1944. The major piece was a rijksdaalder similar to that of Holland itself but inscribed on the reverse *Munt van Curaçao*. Lower values of a guilder, a quarter and a tenth of a guilder were also issued in silver. Bronze coins of 1 cent and 2½ cents were also issued with the types of the Dutch denominations but with inscription *Munt van Curaçao*.

From 1952 a coinage in the name of Queen Juliana has been struck for the Netherlands Antilles as a whole. The denominations are the guilder, the quarter and tenth of a guilder in silver and the bronze cent. The types are similar to those of the Dutch coinage but are inscribed on the reverse *Nederlandse Antillen*.

FRENCH WEST INDIES

In addition to the coinage struck by France for general colonial circulation (see p. 416) a special coinage was decreed in 1730 for the Isles du Vent—the Windward Islands—that is Martinique, Guadeloupe, Grenada and St. Lucia. This coinage consisted of two denominations in silver of 12 and 6 sols. The types on both values were the usual royal bust and titles of Louis XV on the obverse and the words *Isles du Vent* disposed across the field of the reverse within three fleur-de-lis and a scroll (Pl. 826). Currency requirements in the French West Indian colonies were supplemented, as they were in the other islands, by the wisdepread use of cut portions of the Spanish silver dollar as well as countermarked Spanish silver coinage. In the later eighteenth and early nineteenth centuries general colonial issues were again used but in the later nineteenth and on several occasions in the present century token coinages of 1 franc and 50 centimes were issued for Guadeloupe and Martinique. The obverse shows the bust of a native woman on the Martinique issue and the reverse carries the value, expressed as, for instance, *Bon poun 1 franc,* in wreath. For Guadeloupe the obverse type is a native head in local head-dress and the reverse has the token value around a palm-frond (Pl. 827).

BRITISH WEST INDIES

Either countermarked Spanish silver dollars, pieces of eight, or portions cut from silver dollars in a variety of shapes were used in a number of British possessions in the West Indies. The islands which have been identified from the monogram or the name in full on such cut and counter-stamped coins include Dominica, Grenada, Guadeloupe and Martinique (temporarily seized from France), Monserrat, Jamaica, Nevis, St. Lucia, St. Vincent, Tobago, Tortola and Trinidad (Pl. 828). For some of the islands special coinage has been issued at various times. At Antigua a copper farthing was struck in 1836 with types, a palm-tree and name on obverse and value on the reverse. The so-called 'Hog money' struck for the Sommer Islands, the name originally given to Bermuda, is described in the section on North America (p. 420) where this coinage also passed current. A copper penny with types, the bust of George III and a sailing ship, was also produced for Bermuda in 1793 and a similar halfpenny for the Bahamas in 1806–7.

For the Barbados a copper penny was issued in 1788 with a quaint crowned head on obverse with inscription *I serve* and a pineapple on the reverse inscribed *Barbadoes Penny* (Pl. 829). In 1792 a penny and halfpenny copied the obverse but with an inscription *Liberty*, while the reverse showed Neptune on a sea-chariot.

Jamaica as the largest and most important island has since 1869 had a special coinage in denominations of penny, halfpenny and farthing, struck in nickel and later in nickel-brass. The types which have remained constant in the successive reigns are the royal portrait and titles on obverse and the arms of the island on reverse with the name of the island and the denomination as inscription (Pl. 830). The last issue was made in 1955 when it was superseded by the coinage of the new British Caribbean Territories (Eastern Group). The obverse on all denominations carries the crowned portrait of Queen Elizabeth II. The reverse of the 50, 25 and 10 cent pieces in nickel shows Britannia in a sea-chariot above the arms of the component territories and is inscribed with the title of the confederation (Pl. 831). A sailing ship provides the reverse of the 5 cent coin in brass, while the 2, 1 and ½ cent pieces have simply the value between two palm-branches on the reverse.

AUSTRALASIA

★

Australasia

ALTHOUGH voyages of exploration in the south Pacific area were begun by several European nations as early as the sixteenth century, systematic emigration and settlement began only in the later eighteenth century. Since the part which coinage had to play in the developing civilizations of Australasia was relatively small, systematic, independent coinages were called into being only in the beginning of the present century.

AUSTRALIA

The coinage requirements of the early settlements from the first at Botany Bay in 1788 onwards were met by the use of the several coins in gold and silver which already had established for themselves a reputation as international currency. Gold pieces included the English guinea, the Portuguese moidore and the Indian mohur, while silver coinage took the form of the ubiquitous Spanish dollar or piece of eight, the Dutch guilder and the English shilling. One of the earliest attempts to set up a regular coinage was made in New South Wales in 1813. From Spanish dollars a circular piece was removed from the centre and stamped with the state name and a crown on one side and the value *Fifteen pence* on the other. Round the hole left in the dollar the state name was stamped on one side and the value *Five shillings* on the other. These dollars are popularly known as ring dollars, the central piece as a bit or dump.

In the nineteenth century, as local settlements developed and spread, a series of token pennies and halfpennies were issued by local traders, both to supply the deficiency of small change and to advertise themselves (Pl. 832). The great gold discoveries in the mid nineteenth century created a crisis in currency supplies and, since the mint machinery required for coinage production was not generally available, roughly shaped gold ingots stamped with their exact weight were recognized as currency in South Australia. The supplies of British coinage in general use were supplemented by the establishment of branches of the Royal Mint at Sydney, Melbourne and Perth for the production of the gold sovereign and half-sovereign. These Australian sovereigns were identical with the British except that they were distinguished by a small initial letter of the mint on the reverse.

When the separate states were federated in 1901 to form the Commonwealth of Australia steps were taken to provide a distinctive Australian coinage but the first issue consisting of the silver florin, shilling, sixpence and threepence did not appear till 1910. On the obverse was the royal portrait in imperial robes and crown, while the reverse bore the Australian arms with kangaroo and emu supporters (Pl. 833). In 1911 the bronze penny and halfpenny were added with value in words as the reverse type. Two special issues of florins were made in the reign of George V to commemorate the opening of the new Parliament House at Canberra in 1927 and the centenary of Victoria and Melbourne in 1935. The former had on the reverse a view of Parliament House, the latter a mounted figure. The coinage of George VI though retaining the heraldic type on the florin adopted a series of more picturesque types on other denominations. Australian wool and wheat are represented by a ram's head and wheat-ears on the shilling and sixpence. On the bronze penny and halfpenny is a jumping kangaroo (Pl. 834). A special silver crown with a crown as reverse type was struck for the Coronation in 1937. The same types continue to be used in the present reign. Special florin issues were made in 1951 on the occasion of the jubilee of the Commonwealth and in 1954 for the visit of Elizabeth II to Australia.

NEW GUINEA

The eastern part of New Guinea was a German colony up to 1914 and had a coinage of gold and silver marks with multiples up to 5 and pieces of 10 and 2 pfennig in copper. The types were a bird of paradise and value and name of the territory within a wreath.

Coinage for New Guinea which has been administered by Australia since the first world war was resumed in 1929. All the denominations are struck with a central piercing and are inscribed with the name of the territory and the value on the reverse. The silver shilling and nickel penny of George V have crossed maces, crowned on obverse, while the sixpence and threepence have the royal monogram crowned. New Guinea was one of the few British coinages to be issued in the name of Edward VIII for whom a copper penny was struck in 1936 with type, crowned monogram (Pl. 835). Issues for George VI repeat the earlier types and so far no coinage of Elizabeth II has been issued.

NEW ZEALAND

The early numismatic history of New Zealand during the period of its settlement, chiefly from Britain, in the nineteenth century is closely akin to that of Australia. The great international currencies detailed in the sketch of early Australian coinage also circulated in New Zealand, supplemented by some of the Australian bronze token coins as well as by British coinage. Independent coinage for New Zealand was first issued in 1933. The obverse on this issue, as on the first Australian, was the royal bust in imperial robes and crown. The half-crown had the arms of New Zealand on the reverse but the other denominations carried more interesting local types such as the kiwi (Pl. 836) on the florin or the Maori warrior on the shilling. A special crown piece was struck in 1935 to commemorate the Waitangi Treaty made a century before with the Maoris. On the reverse a Maori chief shakes hand with a naval officer in dress uniform. On bronze pennies and half-pennies introduced in the coinage of George VI the reverse is a tui bird on a branch. A silver crown with the New Zealand fern badge (Pl. 837) was struck in 1949 for a projected royal visit and in the first coinage of Queen Elizabeth II in 1953 another crown issue with royal monogram, crowned, above a Maori pattern was made in honour of the Coronation.

FIJI

Coinage was first struck for Fiji in 1934 with the usual imperial bust on obverse. The florin carries the island's arms, the sixpence a native vessel and the threepence a sea-turtle (Pl. 838). Nickel pennies and halfpennies have a central hole and only inscriptions on each side. The types have remained unchanged under the next two sovereigns.

HAWAII

Hawaii was annexed by the United States in 1900 and in 1959 became a state of the Union. It was, however, a kingdom from 1791 until 1894 and at times issued its own coinage. Copper cents were struck by King Kamehameha III in 1847 with his facing bust and value in wreath. A more extensive coinage was issued by Kalakauai in 1883, consisting of a silver dollar, its half and quarter and a 10 cent piece. The types were the king's profile portrait and shield of arms (Pl. 839).

AFRICA

★

Africa

THIS section is limited to the consideration of the coinages of the modern, independent states of Africa and of the several European colonies. Coinage in the sense in which it is defined for the purpose of this book was confined before the nineteenth century almost entirely to the northern portion of Africa which had connections with the civilization of the Mediterranean area. The currencies of North Africa in the ancient world are dealt with in the sections on Greek and Roman coins, while the coinages current in North Africa throughout most of the mediaeval and modern periods are discussed in relation to the Near Eastern series of which they are off-shoots. The exception to this classification is the coinage of the kingdom of Abyssinia or Ethiopia which has had a history of independence and an individual coinage since the early Middle Ages.

ABYSSINIA

A series of coins of the Axumite kings of Abyssinia has been identified, ranging from the second half of the third century to the tenth century. The coinage initially is in the form mainly of small gold pieces, deriving their inspiration from the Roman series but carrying regal inscriptions in Greek. The types of this series are a profile bust on either side showing the king usually wearing a distinctive high crown. These Axumite kings were pagan until the conversion of Ezanas in A.D. 330. From this time the inscriptions on the coins incorporate a number of crosses between the syllables e.g. + HZA + NAC + BACI + ΛΕΥC on the obverse and + AΣω + MITωN + BICI + AΛΕ NEΕ i.e. Ezanas, King of the Axumites, of the Alene family (Pl. 840). The series of small gold pieces was supplemented by some bronze issues and very rare silver. A number of changes take place in the sixth and seventh centuries. Greek inscriptions are replaced by Amharic and the coinage degenerates into a bronze series only. The types undergo changes also. In the sixth century the reverse which had previously repeated the obverse-bust type was charged with a cross, and for the latter part of the coinage from the seventh century onwards the obverse showed the figure of the king enthroned in profile and holding a long sceptre, surmounted by a cross (Pl. 841).

In Abyssinia, cut off from Western civilization from the seventh century by the interposition of the Islamic caliphates, the use of coinage lapsed and the striking of Abyssinian coinage was not resumed till the late nineteenth century. Internationally acceptable currencies of other lands undoubtedly circulated in Abyssinia. The most famous of these is the Maria Theresa thaler (Pl. 698) which gained such popularity in East Africa generally and in Abyssinia in particular that this particular denomination has been consistently restruck for use there (see p. 377). Revived contact with the outside world led to the issue of an Abyssinian coinage by Menelik II (1889–1913) in 1894. The system consisted of the talari and subdivisions in silver with the crowned bust of the emperor and the lion of Judah (Pl. 842) with smaller denominations the gersh and its portions in copper. Gold coins of 5, 10 and 20 wark with portrait and lion types, though bearing the portrait of Menelik and dates within his reign, were issued after his death and the gold wark was also struck, though rarely, for his successor the empress Zauditu (1916–30). As well as rare gold the emperor Haile Selassie (1930–36) issued several values of the matona in nickel and bronze before Abyssinia was conquered by Italy in 1936. The emperor's coinage since his restoration in 1941 has consisted of values of 50 cents and downwards. The traditional types of portrait and lion of Judah have been retained but have been modernized (Pl. 843).

EGYPT

Egypt, which in the later stages of Turkish rule had enjoyed the special status of a vice-royalty, became independent under Sultan Husein Kamil in 1915. The monetary unit was the piastre (Pl. 844), divided into 10 millièmes of which, as the name indicates, 1000 constituted an Egyptian pound. As with almost all Islamic coinages portraits were not used as coin types, which consisted of inscriptions in Arabic on both sides, the reverse carrying in addition the denomination name in English and the value in Western figures or as an English word. Multiple piastres up to 20 were struck in silver and a rare 100 piastre piece in 1916 in gold. Millième values from 10 downwards were in cupro-nickel or bronze. Similar piastre coins were issued for Fuad I as Sultan between 1917 and 1922 when Egypt was declared a kingdom. The denominational system remained the same but the obverse carried the profile bust of the king wearing a fez (Pl. 845). The reverse no longer showed the value in Western figures and the millième denominations were issued with an octagonal flan. On the coinage of Farouk I (1936–52) his portrait in uniform and fez was shown facing with the head turned to left. The bronze millième pieces were unusual in having a fluted edge. The coinage of the Egyptian republic established in 1952 is a series of piastres and millièmes in aluminium-bronze with a consistent obverse showing the head of the Sphinx (Pl. 846). The silver 50 piastre issue in 1956 had on obverse a symbolic figure breaking its chains. A special issue of 1 and 5 pound pieces in gold in 1957 have a representation of the Aswan Dam on obverse and the value on reverse. A coinage issued in 1958 consists of denominations in gold of ½, 1 and 5 pounds with the Pharaoh Ramses II in a chariot on obverse and an inscription referring to the creation of the United Arab Republic on the reverse. Silver coins of 25 and 50 piastres have an eagle on obverse and the value divided by a sword on the reverse.

LIBYA

The former Italian colonial territory was created an independent kingdom under its king, Idris I, after the last war. Coins of 1 and 2 piastres and a number of millième denominations have on obverse the portrait of the king in tasselled cap and on the reverse the value in Arabic figures between two palms, with a crown above and the denomination in English below (Pl. 847).

TUNISIA

The coinage of the French protectorate in Tunisia between 1882 and 1891 continued to be piastres in gold and silver of Sultan Ali Bey with Arabic inscriptions on both sides encircled by palms. On the coinage of francs and centimes introduced in 1891 the obverse continued to be inscribed in Arabic but the reverse bore the name of Tunisia and the value in French. The standard of the coinage was altered in 1930 but the types underwent only incidental change. The coinage of independent Tunisia which began issue in 1950 with Arabic inscription and date in both the Christian and Muhammadan reckonings on obverse has a reverse giving the value in francs and the state name both in Western figures and letters (Pl. 848).

MOROCCO

The coinage of silver dirhems of the Sharifi sultans of Morocco under Spanish and French protection in the late nineteenth century was replaced by a series of silver rials and their portions and copper mazunas in 1902. These issues have as types distinctive patterns of a six-pointed star or two interlacing trefoils. In 1921 a coinage based on the French franc began issue. The six-pointed star and other geometric designs supply the usual types and in addition to Arabic inscriptions bear the legends *Empire Cherifien* and *Maroc* and the value expressed in French (Pl. 849).

LIBERIA

The Liberian coinage with its unit of a dollar divided into 100 cents is modelled on that of the United States. The first coinage in 1833 was a series of copper cents with on obverse a naked figure planting a palm-tree by the sea and across the field of the reverse the foundation date 1816. Later nineteenth-century issues of 1 and 2 cent pieces in bronze had types, the head of the republic in cap of Liberty and a palm-tree (Pl. 850). Larger cent values in silver had head of the republic and value in wreath. Current coins in cent values have an elephant on obverse and palm-tree on reverse. On the new coinage of 1960 coins of 25 and 50 cents in silver have the head of a native girl on the obverse and the value on the reverse. The cupro-nickel 5 cents and bronze cent have an elephant obverse and the traditional palm-and-ship reverse.

GHANA

Until it became an independent state in the British Commonwealth in 1957 Ghana comprised the former colonial territory of the Gold Coast in British West Africa. The first coinage of the Gold Coast issued in 1796 consisted of the silver ackey and its parts with the royal monogram on obverse and the arms of the African Company on the reverse. A second issue in 1818 bore the royal portrait. Coinage of British West Africa consisted of a florin (Pl. 851) and shilling with imperial obverse portrait and palm-tree types and the value in wreath on the six-pence and threepence, first in silver, later in brass. The penny, halfpenny and tenth of a penny denominations in nickel and bronze had a central piercing, with royal title and value on one side and the colony's name and two interlocking triangles on the other. This was one of the territories for which coinage in the name of Edward VIII was struck in 1936 (Pl. 852). These types persisted throughout the coinage which still provides the needs of Nigeria and Sierra Leone, though the latter in 1791 had a brief coinage of silver dollars and subdivisions and copper pennies with a crouching lion on obverse and clasped hands on the reverse. Ghana, however, now has a coinage series of its own. The first issue made in 1958 consists of pieces of 10, 2 and 1 shilling values as well as sixpence and threepence, all in cupro-nickel, and the penny and halfpenny in aluminium-bronze. The types are identical on all denominations, the portrait of Ghana's first prime minister, inscribed *Kwame Nkrumah, Civitatis Ghaniensis Conditor* on obverse and a five-pointed star and value on reverse (Pl. 853). The edge of the 10 shilling piece is engraved with *Independence of Ghana* 6 *March* 1956. A special issue, restricted in numbers, of gold coins of the weight of a double sovereign was made to celebrate the declaration of Ghana as a republic on 1st July 1960. The obverse has the portrait of Nkrumah as first president of Ghana and the reverse the arms of Ghana and inscription 1 *July* 1960—*Republic Day.*

SOUTH AFRICA

Prior to the formation of the Union of South Africa in 1910, apart from some copper tokens issued in Cape Town and East London and some rare coins of the Orange Free State which never passed beyond the pattern stage, the only substantial coinage was that of the Transvaal or, to give it its proper title, the South African Republic. Extremely rare gold pound pieces with the portrait of President Burgers and the republic's arms were struck in 1874 but a complete coinage series was issued under the presidency of Kruger between 1892 and 1900. Kruger's portrait appeared on the obverse of all denominations, never accompanied by his name or title but on the pound, the 5 shilling piece and the penny by the inscription *Zuid Afrikaansche Republiek.* The reverse on most denominations carried the arms of the republic, surmounted by an eagle and flanked by banners on the higher values (Pl. 854). The shilling, sixpence and threepence bore the value in wreath on reverse. An oddity of this coinage is that the denomination is always given in English not Afrikaans.

Though formed in 1910, the Union issued its first coinage in 1923, using the British denomination system. The usual imperial bust was used for the obverse of all denominations and while heraldic shields formed the reverse of the half-crown and florin more imaginative and original designs were adopted for other values. The figure of Hope leans on an anchor on the shilling (Pl. 855), six bundles of four rods (the provinces) surround a veldt flower on the sixpence and a sailing ship on the bronze penny and halfpenny (Pl. 856). The reverse carries the name of the country in a bilingual inscription, *South Africa, Zuid Afrika,* the latter form sometimes with the spelling *Suid.* On the issues for George VI the obverse was a bare-headed portrait. Crown pieces struck on the occasion of the royal visit in 1947 have a springbok on the reverse, and crowns in 1952 celebrating the tercentenary of the landing at Capetown of Jan van Riebeck show his ship with

Table Mountain in the background. Similar denominations and types have been issued for Queen Elizabeth II but a decimal coinage based on a unit to be known as the rand was begun in 1961. The bronze cent has as type a Cape cart (Pl. 857).

BRITISH COLONIES

The coinage issued for the colonies of British West Africa has been described above (p. 466). Another series has been struck since the early years of this century to serve the needs of colonies in East Africa. The system, when fully developed, consisted of silver coins of florin, shilling, 50 cents or half-shilling, 25 cents or quarter-shilling values and nickel—later copper—coins of 10, 5 and 1 cent values. The types on the higher values were the imperial bust and a lion, here a real not an heraldic beast, pacing to the right against a background of mountains (Pl. 858), together with the words East Africa and the value. The lower values which have a central hole carry the imperial title and value in words on the obverse and crossed ivory tusks and value in figures on the reverse (Pl. 859). In 1948 the metals of the two categories were changed to nickel and bronze. A separate coinage for Southern Rhodesia and for Northern Rhodesia and Nyasaland, first issued in 1932, uses the British system of denominations. The obverses show the conventional imperial bust or head but the reverses, apart from an heraldic type on the half-crown, have been chosen for their local significance; for the florin an antelope (Pl. 860), the shilling the Zimbabwe bird, the sixpence native axes, the threepence native spears, while the penny and halfpenny with central hole carry a crowned rose on the obverse. This type is a recollection of the rose, in Greek rhodos, used as a punning type on the coinage of ancient Rhodes and used here as yet a further pun on the name of the founder of the colony, Cecil Rhodes (Pl. 861). Rhodes himself is commemorated on a special issue of a silver crown bearing his portrait above the arms of Rhodesia, struck on the centenary of his birth in 1953. The coinage of the new Central African Federation in 1955 has continued the tradition of local types—a fish-eagle, antelope, leopard and flower. The central hole on the halfpenny is flanked by two giraffes and on the penny by two elephants, portrayed rather unfortunately like circus elephants, erect on their hind-legs with upraised trunks (Pl. 862).

Coinage in 1960 for the new dominion of Nigeria retains the types of the half-penny and penny of British West Africa. Higher denominations carry the portrait of Queen Elizabeth II on obverse and a variety of designs on the reverse; on the florin ground-nuts, on the shilling palm-tree fronds, on the sixpence cocoa pods and on the threepence a cotton-flower.

FRENCH COLONIES

The issues for the French colonies in Africa in low denominations of francs and, until the post-war period, of centimes, struck in aluminium or aluminium-bronze, are much more standardized than the British. The obverse, apart from wartime issues, carries the head of the republic and inscription *République française* with, after the war, the addition of *Union française*. The reverse on pre-war issues bore the name of the particular territory—the Cameroons (Pl. 863), French West Africa and Togoland—together with the value and some local attribute. The post-war coinage has followed a similar pattern but usually has a more prominent type on the reverse such as a facing antelope head. Issues have been made for Somaliland and Madagascar in addition to those already enumerated. The coins of the French territories which supported de Gaulle in the war years have the Gallic cock together with the territory's name on the obverse and the cross of Lorraine and value on the reverse. Issues were made for the Cameroons, French Equatorial Africa and Madagascar in 1943.

PORTUGUESE COLONIES

Angola. In various reigns in the nineteenth century from 1814 onwards a coinage of macutas and portions was issued in copper. The obverse carried the *quinas* arms of Portugal on a globe, crowned, together with the royal name and title, while the reverse bore the value and the inscription *Africa Portuguesa*. The issues of the present century are in various centavo denominations with the Portuguese arms on globe and inscription *Angola* on obverse and the value on the reverse. Silver coins of 10 and 20 escudos issued in 1952 have, on the reverse, the broad-ended Portuguese cross with arms on globe at centre.

Mozambique. The nineteenth-century coinage consisted of copper pieces of 20, 40 and 80 reis issued in 1840. The types were the royal arms and title on obverse and on the reverse the value with the inscription *Pecunia totum circumit orbem*. Modern issues in escudo and centavo values have either the arms and name of Mozambique on obverse and the value on reverse or the arms of Portugal on obverse and those of Mozambique and the value on reverse (Pl. 864).

THE CONGO

The Belgian Congo was established initially not as a colony but as a free state by Leopold II in 1885 and the coinage of francs and centimes bore his title as *Roi des Belges et Souverain de l'état independant du Congo*. Silver coins with franc values had Leopold's portrait and the reverse his arms between palm-branches, while the centime pieces with central hole had four double L's back to back, crowned on obverse and a five-pointed star on reverse. By the treaty of 1908 the Congo became a Belgian province and the silver franc of Albert I bears his ordinary title of *Roi des Belges* (Pl. 865). The issues for Leopold III made by the Bank of the Belgian Congo are inscribed with its name and value on the obverse, while the reverse is usually an African elephant. The chaotic situation in the Congo since the granting of independence and the establishment of a republic in July 1960 has so far precluded the issue of new coinage.

SUDAN

The new republic of the Sudan began coinage in 1956. Denominations of 10 piastres in cupro-nickel and 10, 5, 2 and 1 mille in bronze have as types an Arab on camel, as on Sudanese stamps, and the value on the reverse.

THE NEAR EAST

★

The Near East

THE geographical area with which this section is concerned is basically western Asia, bounded by the Mediterranean in the west, the Indus in the east and by the line of the Black Sea and the Caspian Sea to the north and, finally, by the Red Sea and the Indian Ocean to the south. The historical range of the coinage to be considered and some aspects of its territorial spread require more careful definition. Coinages current in western Asia throughout the centuries of Greek and Roman ascendancy, since they have affinities with the coinages of these civilizations, are included in the first two sections of this book. The present section begins with the consideration of the coinage of the Sassanian empire which was established in the early third century A.D. This was the first important coinage in western Asia to utilize a language of types derived from its own culture and civilization. In tracing the coinage of the various dynasties which eventually divided the widespread conquests of Islam it will be necessary to deal with areas outside western Asia which either conquest or conversion brought under Islamic influence, such as North Africa, Spain, parts of eastern Europe and the steppe lands of Asia. The coinages of the Muhammadan invaders of India, however, are described in the context of the other Indian coinages. A further exception, this time territorial, is that the coinages of the Crusader states in the Levant and of Christian Armenia have been incorporated in the section on European coinage.

THE SASSANIAN EMPIRE

About A.D. 200 Papek revolted against the local dynast of Persis (see p. 95) and secured the recognition of his son Sapor. On the death of Papek his second son, Ardashir, rose against Sapor and put him to death and about 212 revolted against his Parthian overlord, Artabanus V. The defeat and death of Artabanus in 224 ended the Arsacid dynasty and Ardashir proclaimed himself 'King of Kings' and initiated in Persia a new Sassanian line of kings which endured until its overthrow by the rising power of Islam in 651.

The coinage of the Sassanian kings throughout something over four centuries remained remarkably consistent in its essentials. Gold, to judge from surviving examples, was struck with no great frequency and is completely absent for many of the kings. Copper, too, was not commonly struck nor were the smaller divisionary pieces in silver. Silver drachms, however, were struck in all reigns, in some of them in massive issues. Sassanian silver had an extremely wide circulation from the Mediterranean coast to the Indus and from the Persian gulf to the Caucasus and together with contemporary Byzantine gold provided the means of exchange for the whole of the Near East.

There is only one basic set of types on the Sassanian coinage. On the obverse appears the portrait bust of the king, joined occasionally by that of his queen and, more rarely, also by that of his heir. Stylistically the portraiture derives from that of the Parthian issues but undergoes considerable change in detail of costume and head-dress in the course of the centuries. This obverse portrait is accompanied, as on the later Parthian issues, by an inscription in Pehlvi giving the king's name and titles. The obverse shows a fire-altar, similar to that on some of the coinage of Persis (see p. 95). The altar is most often shown flanked by two figures, the king and his son, but occasionally stands on its own.

The coinage of Ardashir I (226–240) in addition to issues in gold, silver and bronze includes tetradrachms in potin, the only instance of the use of this base metal in the Sassanian coinage, though this alloy was commonly used in the later Parthian issues, prior to the rise of the Sassanians. The first coinage of Ardashir shows him on the obverse wearing a domed tiara very similar to that of the Parthian kings and his portrait is accompanied by the Pehlvi inscription *the worshipper of Ormuzd, the divine Ardashir, King of Kings of Iran.* On the reverse the fire-altar stands alone and the inscription reads *the fire of Ardashir* (Pl. 866). On other issues Ardashir is depicted wearing either a crown with three crenellated ornaments surmounted by a circular plume of hair or a species of cap, again surmounted by the circular plume, or a kind of plain diadem. Sapor I (240–271), who defeated and captured the Roman emperor Valerian I in the battle near Edessa in 259, is usually shown wearing the crenellated crown and on the reverse the fire-altar is flanked by two figures, possibly the king and a priest.

Bahram I (272–275) wears an unusual head-dress, consisting of a diadem with fire-rays and still surmounted by the circular plume, while on some issues of Bahram II (275–283) the obverse carries the jugate busts of the king and queen (Pl. 867) and a rare series shows the smaller bust of the heir facing that of his parents. Under Hormuzd II (300–309) the head-dress is ornamented with wings, a feature which recurs on some subsequent issues. On the coinage of Firuz (457–483) there began the practice of indicating the regnal year by means of letter numerals placed on the reverse by the fire-altar and from the time of Bahram V

(420–439) other letters placed on the reverse indicate the mint which struck the coin, but, as only the initials are given, the exact interpretation and location of these mints is frequently a matter of uncertainty.

In the earlier coinage the dies from which the coinage was struck coincided almost exactly, as regards size, with the flan but from about the time of Sapor III (383–388) the flans became thinner and more spread so that an unstamped margin was left around the struck portion. On the coinage of Kavad and most of his successors it became customary to place four crescents, equally spaced, on this blank margin, presumably in an attempt to discourage clipping of the coins. The standard both of design and execution gradually deteriorated, particularly in the later sixth and early seventh centuries, resulting in some rather barbaric, if still extremely effective, portraits such as the facing portrait of Chosroes II (590–627), the Sassanian king who captured Jerusalem and carried off the True Cross in A.D. 614 (Pl. 868). In the last century of Sassanian coinage the only denomination struck was the silver drachm of which the issues of Yezdigird III (632–651) is representative (Pl. 869).

THE MUHAMMADAN COINAGE

The coinages which are described in the earlier sections possess two primary features which facilitate their recognition and arrangement: they are, in most cases, equipped with types in the form of representations or designs and are inscribed in languages which are intelligible to a greater or lesser degree to people of Western civilization. When, however, attention is turned to the coinage of the Eastern world, and in particular to that of the Moslem world, little assistance can be gained from the helpful features of Western coinage just mentioned. The Muhammadan coinage, with some few exceptions, avoids, in accordance with religious tenets, the representation of living objects or indeed of any objects at all and both sides of the coins are devoted to inscriptions in scripts and in languages unfamiliar to the generality. The Muhammadan coins possess a certain interest as examples of calligraphic design but their chief value lies in the remarkably full, continuous and dated record they provide of the successive rulers of the various dynasties of the Moslem world; and, as almost all these coins carry a mention of their place of mintage, they supply some indication of the location and the territorial extent of these kingdoms.

In the circumstances, the present section can attempt to do little more than give a description of the typical coinage of the various Muhammadan dynasties within a framework, as far as possible, chronological; but, since many of the dynasties were co-existent, the chronological arrangement must be compounded with a geographical arrangement. The Muhammadan coinage is dealt with in this way in this first section, from its inception in the seventh century up to the nineteenth century, and the emergence of the national states of the present day. A separate, following, section is devoted to the coinages of these states.

IMITATIVE COINAGE:
ARAB-SASSANIAN ARAB-BYZANTINE

The Muhammadan era dates from the year A.D. 622, the year of the Hegira or flight of Muhammad from Mecca to Medina. From this base the new, militant religion of Islam made rapid conquest of the more settled and civilized nations outside Arabia until, within a few decades, Palestine, Syria, Egypt and Persia had all passed to what became, in effect, a new Islamic empire. In the field of coinage the Arab conquerors were at first content to continue to issue coins of the type current in the various areas which they had overrun. In the east, where by 651 Yezdigird III, the last of the Sassanian kings, had met his death by assassination the coinage issued by the Arab governors of the former Sassanian provinces was a copy, almost exclusively in silver, of the Sassanian coinage with its conventional portrait and its reverse of a Zoroastrian fire-altar with two attendants. The most commonly copied coins were those of the last Sassanian king, Yezdigird III, or the famous Chosroes II and can be distinguished from original coinage by the additional inscription in Arabic appearing on the margin of the obverse (Pl. 870). These imitations continued to be produced in the Western provinces of the former Sassanian empire until in the caliphate of Abd al-Malik a new Islamic coinage was introduced in stages from A.D. 696.* In the east, in the province of Tabaristan, coins in the Sassanian style continued to be issued even after the first or Umaiyad caliphate was replaced by the Abbasid dynasty in 749 and in Bokhara these imitations continued as late as the reign of Harun al-Rashid (786–809).

The Western conquests of Islam were at the expense of the Byzantine empire. Damascus was taken in 635 and in a short space of years the rest of Syria, Palestine, Egypt and later the remaining Byzantine provinces in North Africa fell to the Arabs. As happened in the provinces of the Sassanian empire, the administrative and financial systems of the Byzantine empire were taken over and a coinage imitating a selection of Byzantine coinage was issued. Whereas the Sassanian copies were almost wholly in silver, the Byzantine copies were almost exclusively in copper with a small percentage in gold, but none in silver.

The copper 40 nummia piece of Justin II showing the seated figures of the

---

* Dates throughout are given in the Christian not the Muhammudan era.

emperor together with his empress, Sophia, on the obverse and the Greek numeral M = 40 on the reverse (see p. 201) when copied received in place of the imperial legend on the obverse an inscription in Graeco-Latin giving the mint of the coin (Pl. 871). The 40 nummia coins of Heraclius with the standing figure of the emperor holding cross and globe on the obverse (see p. 204) were also extensively copied with the substitution of a Graeco-Latin inscription on the obverse giving the mint name and often an inscription in Arabic on the reverse. Other coins of Heraclius with the emperor together with one or two of his sons were also imitated as well as coins with the half-length portrait of Constans II.

The Byzantine gold which was most commonly copied by the Arabs in North Africa and in Spain was the gold solidus of Heraclius minted at Carthage, with the busts of Heraclius and his son on obverse and a cross on steps on the reverse. In the first stage of imitation the cross was transmuted into the form of a pole with a globe on top on the imitations of the solidus, the semissis or half-piece and on the tremissis or third (Pl. 872). The imitation tremisses struck in Spain are further removed from the originals and frequently have an eight-pointed star on the obverse and a Kufic inscription in the centre as well as round the circumference. One further class of Arab-Byzantine coinage, derivative rather than purely imitative, is that on which the standing figure of the caliph is portrayed on the obverse. This type, usually on copper coins, is a derivation from Byzantine copper coins showing the standing figure of Heraclius holding a long cross in his right hand; the Islamic version shows the figure of the caliph with hand on sword, the attitude in which he delivered the Khutba, or Friday Sermon in the mosque. The reverse sometimes copies the cursive M of the Byzantine original but often takes the form of the pillar with circlet on top, derived from the Byzantine cross-on steps type (Pl. 873).

THE UMAIYAD CALIPHATE

The institution of a new, purely Islamic coinage in place of the imitative issues described above took place in the caliphate of Abd al-Malik. Tradition has it that the stimulus to this coinage reform was supplied by the anti-Moslem policy of the Byzantine emperor, Justin II. In brief the story runs that Byzantium which derived its stock of papyrus from Egypt, now in Arab hands, was displeased to discover that the official headings guaranteeing the papyrus included phrases in Arabic of religious character, such as that there was no god but Allah. To the Byzantine threat to retaliate by placing legends abusive of Muhammad on their gold solidi, which still secured wide circulation in Egypt, the caliph replied by issuing his own gold dinars with Islamic legends.

However much truth there may be in the tradition, it is the case that the first Islamic coins to be issued were gold dinars, in the year A.D. 696–697. Most of these gold dinars carry no mint name but were presumably struck at the caliph's mint at Damascus for they carry a fuller form of inscription than do the half- and third-dinars of which some bear the name of the area of their minting, either Ifrikiya (Africa—mint at Kairawan) or al-Andalus (Spain—mint at Cordoba). The obverse inscription, adapted from the Koran, reads 'There is no god but Allah alone (He has no partner). Muhammad is the Apostle of Allah whom He sent with guidance and the religion of truth (that He may make it victorious over every other religion)'. The fuller form, including the bracketed portion, appears on the dinars struck in the east (Pl. 874); the shortened form on the divisionary pieces with or without mint name issued in the west. The reverse inscriptions on gold struck in east and west differ more widely. On Eastern gold the legend reads 'Allah is One, Allah is the Eternal; He begets not, neither is He begotten', while western issues have the form 'In the name of Allah, the merciful, the compassionate'.

The silver dirhem which was first issued in A.D. 698–699 carries inscriptions of similar type and, almost without exception, has an indication of its mint and the date. In the east a whole range of mints struck the silver dirhem (Pl. 875) the most constantly active being Damascus in Syria and, after its foundation in 703, the new city of Wasit, mid-way between Kufa and Basra in Iraq. In the west no mint towns appear on the dirhems, only the names of the two provinces Ifrikiya and al-Andalus. The signed and dated dirhems carry the formula, e.g. 'In the name of Allah this dirhem was struck in Damascus in the year 79' (A.D. 698–699). Copper was also issued as a coin termed the *fals*, a name clearly deriving from the Roman and Byzantine *follis*. The earliest coppers are inscribed only with religious formulae with no indication of mint or date; these were followed by issues bearing the names of mints in various parts of the Islamic empire as well as by issues without mint name but with a date.

THE ABBASID CALIPHATE

The line of Umaiyad caliphs was replaced by that of the Abbasids in 749 but brought little change to the coinage system or to the details of the coins themselves, except for some alteration in the arrangement of the religious formulae. On the reverse the first part of the formula used under the Umaiyads in the marginal inscription 'Muhammad is the Apostle of Allah', now occupied the centre, replacing the 'Allah is One, Allah is the Eternal' of the Umaiyads. Gold dinars continued to carry no overt indication of their mint town until the ninth century but the silver dirhems, as before, were regularly marked with their place of minting.

Under the caliph al-Mansur (754–775) the name of the heir who was responsible for coinage appeared on the coins and shortly afterwards that of the caliph himself. Later other names came to be added, those of the mint master, of governors and so on. The copper fals also continued, as under the Umaiyads, to carry the names of provincial governors. In the east, in Tabaristan, as already mentioned, Arab-Sassanian imitations were produced by the governors for at least a century after the establishment of the Abbasid caliphate. It was under the Abbasid caliph al-Mansur that the new capital of Baghdad was founded and, of the line of Abbasid caliphs, the name most familiar to the west is that of Harun al-Rashid (Pl. 876).

The Abbasid caliphs, however, were not long able to preserve the unity of their empire and in various provinces governors and generals established themselves as more or less independent rulers, owing only a nominal allegiance to the caliph in Baghdad, then called Medinet-es-Salam. In addition foreign conquerors made themselves master of parts of the Islamic empire and all of these arrogated to themselves the right of coinage, exercising it in the beginning in the name of the caliph. Something of the order of a hundred dynasties exercised rule in the Moslem world at various times but here space permits mention only of the more important in the several geographical divisions.

SPAIN

Although the Abbasid dynasty had replaced that of the Umaiyads in the east, the Arab conquests in Spain never came under their authority, for an independent Umaiyad caliphate continued to exercise rule in Spain until its dissolution in 1031 and its replacement by a number of petty, mutually hostile principalities. The coinage of the Umaiyad caliphs in Spain consisted of gold dinars and silver dirhems of the conventional type struck mainly at the mints of al-Andalus—Cordoba and also at the mint of Medinet-ed-Zahra (Pl. 877). Towards the end of the period the dirhems were struck not in pure silver but in a baser alloy. On the break-up of the caliphate of Cordoba smaller kingdoms were established. The dynasty of the Beni Hamud ruled at Cordoba between 1016 and 1017, that of the Beni Idris at Malaga from 1035 to 1055, the Beni Abbad at Seville from 1023 to 1091 and Beni Hud at Saragossa from 1039 to 1145. These were all in turn overwhelmed by the Christian reconquest of Spain, but while they exercised authority they issued both gold and silver coins from mints in the capital cities of their kingdoms. Successively the Moorish dynasties of the Almoravides and the Almohades in Africa (see below) exercised rule in Spain in the eleventh and twelfth centuries and coined at a number of mints in Spain, including Cordoba,

Murcia and Granada. The dynasty of the Beni Nasra maintained their kingdom of Granada from 1238 until 1492 when Moslem power in Spain was finally overthrown by Ferdinand and Isabella. A change from the hitherto conventional designs is seen on the gold and silver of the kingdom of Granada where the central inscription on both obverse and reverse is enclosed not in a circle but a rectangle (Pl. 878).

NORTH AFRICA

Unlike Spain, North Africa came under the authority of the Abbasid caliphate when it replaced the Umaiyad in 750 but in 800 Ibrahim ben Aghlab who had been appointed governor of the African province by Harun al-Rashid established an independent kingdom which soon comprised Tripoli, Tunis, Algiers and Morocco. The Aghlabite kingdom extended its influence across the Mediterranean, capturing Sicily, Malta and Sardinia in the years between 827 and 866 and in the same period held Bari in Apulia and ravaged Italy. Dinars and dirhems and rarer copper pieces were struck by the several Aghlabite rulers in Africa until the kingdom, already weakened by the establishment of the Idrisid kingdom at Fez in Morocco, was conquered by the Fatimids in 909. Following the Fatimid capture of Egypt in 969 and the removal of their capital from Mahdia on the Gulf of Tunis to Cairo in 972 the former Aghlabite territory was split amongst smaller dynasties, chief of which was that of the Zirids in Tunisia. Sardinia was lost to the Genoese, and Sicily to the Normans in 1061.

A new dynasty, that of the Morabites or Almoravides arose in 1056 and soon controlled the whole of Morocco and, in response to requests for aid from the Moslem kings in Spain, extended their authority over southern Spain. The Morabite coinage is almost entirely of gold dinars struck at mints in Spain such as Cordoba, Seville and Granada and in Africa at Fez and Marrakesh. On the obverse, in addition to the usual profession of faith, is inscribed the name of the ruler with the title Prince of the Moslems, for the Abbasid caliph was still recognized as Prince of the Faithful. The marginal inscription of the reverse gives the mint and date (Pl. 879). The Almoravides were replaced in 1147 by the Muwahids or Almohades who created a kingdom which extended over southern Spain, Morocco, Tunis and Tripoli. The gold dinars of the Almohades are of unusually thin, spread fabric and the central inscription on both sides is contained in a rectangular frame. Marginal inscriptions frequently record not only the name of the reigning monarch but of his ancestors. Silver dirhems which were square in shape are without name of ruler or mint and without date and have no marginal inscriptions (Pl. 880). In Spain the Christian kingdoms, for once united, inflicted a defeat on the

Almohades in 1212 at Las Navas de Tolosa, and in North Africa their kingdom succumbed in 1269 and was divided amongst smaller dynasties, the Marinids in Morocco, the Ziyanids in western Algeria and the Berber Hafsids in eastern Algeria, Tunisia and Tripoli. The coinage of these dynasties was mainly one of gold dinars, usually in the thin spread fabric of previous North African dynasties. On Marinid gold, struck at Fez and Marrakesh, the central area is rectangular and is enclosed by a double frame of two continuous lines. The Ziyanid gold struck at Tlemcen in western Algeria also encloses the central area in a double-lined rectangular frame but on Hafsid dinars struck at Tunis—when a mint can be read— the rectangular central inscription is bounded by a triple frame of which the outer and inner lines are continuous but the central is formed of a row of dots. Rarer silver dirhems of all three dynasties are rectangular in shape and so irregularly cut that it is not always possible to determine the nature of the enclosing frame.

In Morocco the Marinid dynasty was replaced by that of the Wattasids about 1465 and the Hafsids gradually gained the ascendancy over the Ziyanids. In the course of the sixteenth century the whole of North Africa witnessed further changes of rule, this time of greater duration, lasting well down into the nineteenth century. The control of Morocco was disputed between the Wattasids and the Sharifs between 1510 and 1554, the latter finally emerging victorious. To the east, Corsair raiders established smaller kingdoms, nominally vassals of the Ottoman empire of Constantinople, in Algeria in 1556, in Tunis in 1514, in Tripoli in 1551 and in Cyrenaica in 1521. The Sharif coinage of dinars and dirhems begins with types where the central area is enclosed in a rectangular frame but a greater variety of outline makes its way into the coinage—two superimposed squares giving rise to an eight-pointed star design and, much more commonly, two inter-linked triangles, making up a six-pointed star. Multiple dinars and dirhems were also issued and, in the eighteenth century, copper mazunas. On these copper coins with their six-pointed star design the date in the Muhammadan era is given frequently in figures, of the type used in the Western world (Pl. 881). French intervention in Morocco began in 1844 and finally in 1912 the country was divided as protectorates under France and Spain (see p. 465). Coinage was struck by the Ottoman empire (see p. 488) for its North African provinces. Algeria was occupied by France in 1830 and Tunisia in 1883 while Tripolitania and Cyrenaica were seized by Italy in 1912.

EGYPT

The Abbasid caliphs controlled Egypt till about 868 from which date, though nominally recognizing the Abbasid caliph, Egypt was in effect controlled by the Tulunids with their capital at al-Fustat in the Delta. The Tulunids also controlled Syria after 899 and disputed with others the control of the Hejaz. The Tulunid coinage, mainly gold dinars, was issued with the mint names of both Misr–Egypt and Filisteen–Palestine. From about 934 the ruling dynasty was that of the Ikshidids. In 969 came the conquest of Cyrenaica and Egypt by the Fatimids who established their first capital at Mahdia on the Gulf of Tunis until the capture of Cairo in 972. Fatimid dinars struck at Cairo and at Mahdia have a distinctive arrangement of the religious formulae which themselves are unusual, since the Fatimids belonged to the unorthodox Shi'a sect. The circular central area is bounded by a plain circular margin which in turn is encircled by the marginal inscription (Pl. 882). On other issues the centre of the coin is plain and is surrounded by three circular inscriptions. An extensive series of rubas or quarter-dinars was also struck, principally in the island of Sicily (Pl. 883). The Fatimids also controlled parts of Syria from 969 until the First Crusade in 1070. Silver was struck much more rarely by the Fatimid caliphs.

In 1171 a new dynasty, that of the Ayyubids, seized control of Egypt and under its first and most famous ruler, Saladin, recovered control of most of Syria in 1183. Gold dinars of Saladin from mints at Cairo and Alexandria have a small central inscription, surrounded by three circles of inscription (Pl. 884). Silver dirhems and halves of the Damascus mint have a square frame enclosing the central inscription and those struck at Halab have a hexagram or six-pointed-star outline for the central area. Copper coins of Saladin show a feature unusual on Islamic coins in the presence of a type on the obverse, either a recumbent lion or a figure seated cross-legged. These copper coins have an affinity with issues of the Urtukids (see p. 484). The square- or star-shaped central area persists on dirhems of later Fatimid caliphs but gold dinars generally return to the more traditional form of a circular central area enclosed by a marginal inscription. Copper coins with an obverse type were also struck in 1200 for El-Awhad of the Mesopotamian branch of the dynasty. The figure on the obverse is shown either as a half-length bust facing, crowned or wearing a cap with tassels, or as a figure seated cross-legged and holding an orb (Pl. 885).

In 1250 the Mamelukes, the Turkish bodyguard of the Ayyubid caliphs, put forward their own candidate and established a new dynasty which shortly added Syria to its dominions. Shejer-ed-durr, the Turkish concubine of El Salih, the last of the Ayyubids, retained the sovereignty for a few months then made the Mameluke Eybek her husband and sultan. A very rare dinar exists in the name of Shejer-ed-durr alone (Pl. 886). The typical gold dinar of the Mameluke sultans eventually abandoned the use of a marginal inscription and has only lines of inscription across the field on both sides of the coin (Pl. 887). Rarer silver follows much the same pattern but copper pieces have the central inscription enclosed in a triangle or other geometric patterns.

The Mamelukes, first the Bahri dynasty till 1382 and then the Burji, ruled till 1517 when Egypt became part of the empire of the Ottoman Turks. Between 1832 and 1882 Egypt, under Muhammad Ali and his heirs, had a special, semi-independent status in the Turkish empire until, after British and French intervention in the late nineteenth century, it became a British protectorate in 1914 (see p. 464).

ASIA

The effective rule of the Abbasid caliphs in the Asian provinces was of comparatively short duration, though the nominal authority of the Abbasid caliph at Baghdad continued until the Mongol conquest in the thirteenth century. The caliphate was divided into a number of independent kingdoms under various dynasties, each of which struck their own coinage. In the east the Samanids who controlled Transoxiana between 874 and 998 struck a coinage at mints at Samarkand, Egh-Shash and Bokhara. Gold dinars and silver dirhems, produced in quantity, found their way in the course of trade across Russia as far as Scandinavia and have been recorded as finds in England as well. The formulae on these coins are arranged in the conventional pattern, a circular central area surrounded by marginal inscription (Pl. 888). For most of the latter half of the ninth century Khorasan, Afghanistan and much of Persia was controlled by the Saffarids but by the middle of the tenth century the Ghaznavid princes had established their supremacy in the whole of this area and extended it to Transoxiana in the early eleventh century. The Ghaznavid coinage, principally of silver but with a considerable amount of gold, was struck at a range of mints—the capital, Ghaznah, at Balkh in Khorasan and at Mahmudpore and Lahore in northern India. Silver issues from these latter mints have bilingual inscriptions, usually in Arabic on the obverse and Sanskrit on the reverse (Pl. 889). On some of the copper coinage from Indian mints a figure of a bull is incorporated in the rude script on the obverse or a horseman on the reverse. In Mesopotamia effective power was seized between 929 and 945 by the Hamdanids who were succeeded by the Buwahids, a dynasty which maintained itself until about 1094. The Buwahid coinage, mainly silver, was struck at a variety of mints including Shiraz, Medinet-es-Salam, Basra and Oman. The central inscription is contained in a circle bounded by either a dotted or a plain-line border and surrounded by one or two lines of marginal inscription

SELJUKS

In the eleventh century the caliphate was increasingly subjected to invasion by non-Arabic peoples, principally of Turkish origin from the great steppe lands. Penetrating south and west the Turkish Seljuks took possession of Transoxiana, Khorasan, the greater part of Persia, Mesopotamia and Syria by about 1037 and maintained their empire till the Mongol conquests in the mid thirteenth century. Control of part of the eastern areas was maintained by the Ghaznavid princes, succeeded later by the Ghurids, and from the mid twelfth century part of Mesopotamia and most of Persia was held by the Khuwarizim shahs but in Mesopotamia, Syria and Asia Minor various branches of the Seljuks exercised effective control. Up to this point the Muhammadan coinages described have maintained with only minor variations of pattern the conventional types of central and marginal inscriptions only, on both obverse and reverse, but the coinage of the Seljuks and the various Atabegs or generals presents a series of figure types on the majority of issues and a great proportion of the coinage is not in the form of the traditional gold dinars and silver dirhems but of thick heavy copper pieces. The Great Seljuks, who under their sultans Tughril-Beg, then Alp-Arslan and their successors reigned in Persia between 1037 and 1157 and became the protectors of the Abbasid nominal caliph, adhered to the old pattern of coinage in their issues from mints at Nisabur, Medinet-es-Salem and Isfahan.

The Seljuks in Rum (1077–1308), the area in Anatolia which they had conquered from the Byzantine empire, produced, perhaps under the influence of Byzantine coin types, a certain amount of coinage with figure types on the obverse. Some early copper pieces show a mounted warrior with drawn sword and silver coins of Suliman II (1199–1203) struck at the mint of Caesarea carry a mounted figure brandishing a mace and with head in nimbus (Pl. 890). Figure types lapsed after Suliman but under Kay Khusru II (1236–45) a lion surmounted by a sun appeared on the obverse of silver coins (Pl. 891). On the coinage of the Urtukids of Diyarbekr in Mesoptoamia, however, figure types on obverse are the rule and inscriptional types the exception. Though these coins are large, heavy, copper pieces some of them bear the name dirhem and some of them still show traces of silvering. The sources of inspiration of the obverse figure types are as diverse as the great coinage series which had served the area through past ages. A diademed profile portrait is copied from the tetradrachms of the Seleucid kings, a winged Victory shows the influence of Roman coinage (Pl. 892) and a bearded portrait wears the distinctive head-dress of the Sassanian kings. The greatest influence naturally was exerted by the more recent types of Byzantine coins. The two facing busts, one larger and

484

one smaller, stems from the obverses of coins of Heraclius and Constans II while a standing figure of an emperor, crowned by a saint, copies more clearly contemporary Byzantine issues. The facing bust of an enthroned figure (Pl. 893) is a close copy of the bust of the enthroned Christ on many Byzantine issues and the influence of Western coinage, made familiar by contact with the crusaders, is seen in the facing bust wearing trifoliate crown. An unusual figure type which seems to be original as far as coins are concerned is the double-headed eagle (Pl. 894), a type which later found wide popularity in many European coinages. The issues of the Zengids of Mosul include a slightly higher proportion of purely inscriptional coins but thick copper coins with figure obverses were also struck extensively. The choice of obverse figures betrays much the same influences as those noted in the Urtukid coinage but in general the figures are executed in a much cruder style. The coinage of the Begteginids of Arbela is a similar mixture of conventional inscription and figure types.

PERSIA

Roughly contemporary with this unusual figure-type coinage of the Seljuks were the issues of the Khuwarizim shahs who. between 1097 and 1230, controlled part of Mesopotamia and most of Persia. Their coinage in gold and silver followed, in the main, the established inscriptional types but an unusual feature was the introduction of large spread copper coins with either circular or square central area and marginal inscription.

MONGOLS

In the late twelfth century the Mongol nomads in the steppe lands north of the Gobi desert were forced into union under Temujin, the leader of one of the clans. In 1206 Temujin assumed the title, Genghis Khan 'the Very Great King', and under his leadership the Mongols embarked on a career of conquest which soon brought them control of northern China, of Turkestan, of Khorasan and Afghanistan, the outlying provinces of the Khuwarizim shahs, as well as Azerbaijan, Georgia and south Russia. Genghis Khan died in 1227 but under his successors the Mongol conquest was continued until his grandson Kublai Khan held the whole of China and Korea, and Mongol invaders swept over eastern Europe, penetrating as far west as Hungary. In 1256 the Mongols under Hulagu demolished the kingdoms of the Khuwarizim shahs and the Seljuks in Persia and Mesopotamia and their westward advance was checked only by the Mamelukes in Palestine. It was in the course of the conquest that the last titular Abbasid caliph in Baghdad was murdered.

The coinage of the Great Khans, struck for the areas where their southern conquests impinged on the Islamic world, was issued almost exclusively in silver with inscriptions in Arabic. The silver coins of Ghengis Khan himself (1206–27) are pieces of small module (Pl. 895) but coins of the interregnum under Turakina, the widow of Ogotai (1241–6), have a figure type on the obverse, a horseman drawing his bow and accompanied by small figures of a stork and a dog (Pl. 896). The type, reminiscent of a figure-type on the coins of the Seljuks of Rum, is a familiar theme in earlier Sassanian and Persian art. The issues of Mangu (1248–57) are, however, purely inscriptional.

The great Mongol empire eventually divided into a number of independent kingdoms which, for a time, recognized the nominal supremacy of the Great Khan. Most of western Asia from the Mediterranean to the Indus was ruled from 1256 to 1336 by the dynasty of the Il Khans, set up by Hulagu. The Il Khans, converted to Islam, issued a coinage which included some gold and copper but was mainly in the form of silver dirhems (Pl. 897). Something more than fifty mints have been identified on this coinage. Copper coins in the earlier reigns perpetuated some of the figure types of the Urtukid and Zangid coinages and on some later issues the lion and sun of the silver coins of the Seljuks of Rum was used as a type on copper. Gold and silver, however, preserved the traditional inscription types on both obverse and reverse with the central inscription enclosed in a circle, a square or more elaborate geometric forms. On the early coinage of Hulagu (1256–65) the name of Mangu the Great Khan was also inscribed but after the accession of Kublai in 1257 only the title of Great Khan appeared but not his proper name, and from the beginning of the reign of Ghazan (1295–1304) all mention of the Great Khan as overlord was omitted. In addition to the silver dirhem a half-piece was also struck as well as a double piece and occasional higher multiples. The Mongol dirhems were originally issued at the conventional weight of 2·6 gm. but suffered falls in standard to a weight of 2·1 gm. under Ghazan.

The coinage of the khans of the Kipchak Mongols of the Golden Horde, whose various dynasties controlled southern Russia and parts of eastern Europe between 1224 and the final submission to Russia in 1502, is almost exclusively of silver. The types on obverse and reverse consist of a central inscription, usually in a circular frame but without marginal inscription. These silver dirhems are of small module and correspondingly low weight and in somewhat degenerate script (Pl. 898). The hold of Islam on south Russia was completed by the seizure of Astrakhan by Tatar khans in 1438 and by the conquest of Genoese possessions in the Crimea and the Sea of Azov in 1475 by other Tatars. A coinage in silver was struck by these Krim Tatars for some three centuries till their final subjection by Russia in 1783.

After about a century of rule the Mongol empire suffered the same fate which had overtaken the Abbasid caliphate and the Seljuk kingdom, the splintering of its power and the setting up of smaller, semi-independent kingdoms. Persia was controlled by the Jalayrs from 1336 to 1393, Kurdistan by the Muzaffarids (1345–92) and Khorasan by the Sarbadarids (1335–81), while the Kart Mongols ruled Afghanistan until 1389 and the Jagatai Mongols Transoxiana till 1358. The coinage of these dynasties, mostly silver dirhems with only occasional gold dinars, perpetuated the conventional inscriptional types with the central area enclosed in a variety of geometric outlines.

A fresh wave of Mongol conquest began under Timur, better known in Western history as Tamerlane, of Transoxiana, (1369–1404). His conquering armies swept south and east as far as Delhi and westwards through Persia and Mesopotamia, but on Timur's death the more Western conquests were lost. His descendants succeeded in holding central and southern Persia for half a century and Khorasan for the remainder of the fifteenth century, but when Timur's dynasty was replaced by that of the Sheybanids in 1500 Timur's empire had shrunk to the khanate of Bokhara. The principal mint for the Timurid coinage was at Samarkand and the coinage was mainly of silver with some copper issues. In the reign of Timur some silver issues are of the traditional smaller diameter but the majority of Timur's coinage and that of his successors are of larger type (Pl. 899). The silver coins of the Sheybanids in Bokhara in the sixteenth century are of a similar spread fabric as are those of the Astrakhan dynasty which ruled from 1599 till 1785. Most of the coinage of the Mangit dynasty which reigned until Bokhara became tributary to Russia in 1868 is of gold.

THE OTTOMAN EMPIRE

In Phrygia one of the small kingdoms into which the empire of the Seljuks of Rum had disintegrated began to exercise a supremacy over the others under its chief, Othman, in 1299 and within a century the Ottoman Turks were masters of Asia Minor. Although they suffered some reverse at the time of Timur's westward conquests, Ottoman power revived under Murad II (1421–51) and began to extend. Under Muhammad II (1451–81) the Byzantine empire was finally extinguished and Constantinople captured in 1453. The Balkans fell to the Turks in the fifteenth century and the next century saw further Turkish advances westwards into Hungary, and in the same century Syria, Mesopotamia and part of Persia were absorbed into the Ottoman empire. In the early sixteenth century

Egypt was taken and later Tripoli, Tunis and Algiers became Ottoman vassals. The extreme Turkish conquests in Europe were short-lived but the rest of the Ottoman empire survived, with some losses in Africa, until the first world war.

The Ottoman coinage, like almost all other Islamic coinages, is remarkably conservative and almost completely eschews figure types, both obverse and reverse carrying only lines of inscription, usually only horizontally across the field of the coin. At first a simple religious formula was placed on the coins but this was soon dropped and the inscriptions normally record only the name and style of the sultan, the place of minting and frequently the date. The earlier Ottoman coinage omits mint and date but from the time of Murad II (1421–51) these are consistently present. Of the chain of mints throughout the life of the Ottoman empire the most important and prolific were Adrianople and Constantinople in Europe, Aleppo, Damascus, Baghdad and Tiflis in Asia and, in Africa, Cairo, Tripoli, Tunis and Algiers.

Initially the Turkish coinage consisted solely of silver in a denomination known as the akce (Pl. 900), introduced by Urkhan in 1328. The weight of the silver akce was approximately one-third of the silver dirhem of earlier Islamic coinages and the manghir, a copper coin (Pl. 901), was introduced by the next sultan, Murad I (1360–89). The Turkish gold coin, the altun (Pl. 902), was struck for the first time by Muhammad II in 1478 after the capture of Constantinople. Since the altun replaced the Venetian gold zecchino or sequin, which had previously supplied currency needs in gold, the Turkish gold coin has traditionally been referred to in the west as a sequin. The tughra, the monogram of the sultan's names and titles which is a feature of later Turkish coinage (Pl. 903), appeared for the first time under Suleyman I (1520–66) but did not become common until the issues of Muhammad III (1595–1603).

A new, large silver denomination approximating to the thaler class of coinage in Europe was introduced in 1687 by Suleyman II but the weight of 19·5 gm. at which it was issued was only some two-thirds of the normal weight of this category of coin in most European series. The name given to this new denomination, the ghurush or piastre (Pl. 904), recalls the grosso, groschen, etc., of European coinages. Already in 1655 another smaller silver denomination had been introduced, the para. At first the para was equivalent to 4 akces but later as para and akce deteriorated the para was issued at a rate of 40 to the ghurush and the akce at 3 to the para. The para was also issued in a number of multiples of 5 paras of which the more important were the zolota of 30 paras and its double, a double ghurush of 80 paras and the yuzlik of 100 paras. In the reign of Ahmet III (1703–30) the earlier gold altun of 3·4 gm. was replaced by a new gold coin, the funduk altun, which had only the tughra but no formula on the obverse. Subdivisions of this gold coin were also struck. In the same reign a lighter gold coin, the zer mabub, was introduced at a weight of 2·6 gm. (Pl. 905). Subdivisions and multiples of this coin were issued until the coinage reform in the reign of Abdul Mejid (1839–61). Subsequent Turkish coinage is described below in the section on the coinage of the modern states of the Near East.

SHAHS OF PERSIA

The Jalayrids who had ruled Persia until the invasion of the Mongol Timur in 1336 survived as vassals of the Timurid Mongols till 1411. For the remainder of the fifteenth century the control of Persia was disputed between the Timurids and Black Sheep and White Sheep Turcomans, but in 1502 the Safavids under Ismail I gained the ascendancy, establishing the state of Persia which, with vicissitudes of dynasty, has persisted into modern times. The Safavid dynasty ruled until 1736, the final decades being disrupted by the Afghan claimants Mahmud (1722–5) and Ashraf (1725–30), but in 1736 Nadir established a new dynasty of the Afsharis. The Zands at Shiraz who came to power under Kerim Khan in 1750 were finally eclipsed in 1794 by the Kajars at Teheran who had been in revolt since 1779. This last dynasty endured until 1925 when it was replaced by Reza Shah, the first of the present Pahlavi dynasty.

The unit of the Persian gold coinage was the ashrafi (Pl. 906) of a weight of 3·4 gm., roughly that of the contemporary Venetian ducat and similar European gold pieces. In silver the coins were the shahi, the mahmudi equal to 2 shahis and the abbasi (Pl. 907) of 2 mahmudis. The copper kazbegi was tariffed at a tenth of the shahi. Persian gold and silver coinage has initially, like other Islamic issues, exclusively inscription types on both obverse and reverse. The language at first is Arabic. The central area on the obverse is occupied by a religious formula, surrounded, where there is a margin, by the names of the twelve imams, while the reverse gives the royal name and title, together with the mint and the date. Under Abbas I (1587–1629) Persian appears on the reverse. A feature of Persian coinage is the use of a distich or poetic couplet incorporating mention of the shah's name. Nadir (1736–47) introduced a new gold piece, the mohur, on the heavier Indian standard alongside the ashrafi which disappeared from the coinage of Kerim Khan (1750–79) and his successors. A new coinage was instituted by Fath Ali (1797–1834) with the toman as the gold unit and the karan, equal to a tenth of the toman, as the main silver piece. Subdivisions and multiples of the gold toman were also struck.

The next adjustment to the coinage system under Nasr-ed-din in 1877 provides a convenient point to begin the description of the coinage of modern Persia in the section on modern states below. In this reign too the striking of the Persian coinage was restricted to the mint at Teheran, the issues of earlier centuries having been struck at a number of mints of which the most important were Shiraz, Tabriz, Isfahan and Kazvin.

The first departure from the exclusively inscriptional coinage comes only in the early nineteenth century when Fath Ali on double gold tomans of 1823 is depicted on the obverse as a mounted figure and on half-tomans of 1833 as an enthroned figure (Pl. 908). A half-toman of Muhammad in 1846 has on obverse the Persian lion with raised sword, familiar on modern Persian coinage.

Persian copper coinage was issued autonomously until the nineteenth century and differed from the previous metal issues in that the obverse almost always presented a figure type. A common type is the lion surmounted by sun which had originally appeared on coins of the Seljuks of Rum but other issues present a whole menagerie of birds and animals on the obverse (Pl. 909).

GEORGIA

This relatively small mountainous country lying between the Black Sea and the Caspian had a chequered history of successive phases of precarious independence and submission to the empires which rose and fell on its borders, and in the Georgian coinage these vicissitudes of history are reflected. In the classical period the only coinage of the area was that of the Greek colonies on the Black Sea coast (see p. 18) and, later, barbarous imitations of staters of Alexander the Great and Lysimachus and denarii of the early Roman empire.

Georgia became Christian as early as the time of Constantine the Great but it was not the Byzantine empire but the Sassanian which exerted influence on the Georgian coinage which was struck in the seventh century. This took the form of imitations of the Sassanian silver drachm with bust of the Sassanian king on obverse and a version of the fire-altar on the reverse, with, however, the significant addition of a cross above the altar. In 655 Tiflis, the Georgian capital, captured by the Arabs, became a mint for the issue of dirhems of the successive Islamic dynasties until the eleventh century. The growing power of the native Bagratid kings in the south-west from the tenth century is seen in rare silver coins of Bagrat IV (1027–72) and his immediate successors in the early twelfth century. The obverse depicts the facing bust of the Virgin, and the reverse carries an inscription detailing the king's titles (Pl. 910). The decline of Seljuk power gave opportunity for a considerable territorial expansion of the Georgian kingdom. Georgian coinage from

1125 to 1247 consists of copper pieces of thickish fabric. Georgi III (1156–84) appears on the obverse of his coins seated cross-legged and holding a falcon on his right hand but the reverse carries lines of inscription only while from 1184 both sides of the coin have only inscriptions.

The Mongol conquest of 1236 absorbed Georgia, and Mongol dirhems were struck at the mint of Tiflis in the name of the Great Khans and later for the Il Khan dynasty established by Hulagu in 1260. Under the Mongol khan, Abaga (1265–81), and some of his successors, dirhems struck at Tiflis have a Mongol inscription on the obverse but the reverse inscription consists of a Christian formula with a cross at centre (Pl. 911). Georgia came under the control of the Safavid shahs of Persia in the late sixteenth century and Tiflis issued the Persian silver abbasi as well as a series of autonomous copper with figure-type obverse. After a brief Ottoman occupation (1723–35) Georgia was reoccupied by Nadir Shah but in 1744 Georgia was granted independence. The coinage of the last Bagratid kings for the remainder of the eighteenth century are silver abbasis and halves as well as copper pieces in the Persian style. The special coinage after 1800 when Russia took over Georgia was the silver abbasi, its double and half as well as the copper puli. The types are similar on all metals, the mint name of Tiflis with a mural crown above and crossed palm- and olive-branches below on obverse, and a three-line inscription giving value and metal on the reverse (Pl. 912). This coinage was suspended in 1834 in favour of regular Russian issues.

MODERN STATES OF THE NEAR EAST

This section on the coinage of the modern states deal with the issues of states in western Asia since the coinage of other modern Islamic countries in Africa has already been described in the section devoted to Africa. The coinage of the late nineteenth century comes almost entirely from Persia and the Ottoman empire but the division of the latter empire after the first world war created a number of new states, all of which now issue their own coins.

TURKEY

A new Turkish coinage system was instituted in the reign of Abdul Mejid (1839–61) with the piastre as the monetary unit. One hundred piastres made up a lire or pound and the piastre was in turn divided into 40 paras. The types were simple and conservative and practically identical on all metals; the tughra and regnal year above crossed branches on the obverse and on the reverse an inscription stating the mint of the coin—Constantinople for the metropolitan issues—together with the sultan's accession year. Gold was struck in denominations of 5 up to 100 piastres with some exceptional multiples of even higher value. The silver piastre (Pl. 913) was issued in various multiples between 1 and 20 as well as a half-piastre of 20 paras and the copper paras ranged in value from 1 to 40. Succeeding reigns brought little change except in the record of the sultan's accession year while under Muhammad V (1909–18) the para denominations were issued in nickel. The last Turkish sultan, Muhammad VI, struck mostly the gold piastre piece and only the 40 paras denomination in nickel.

The Turkish Republic, set up in 1923, retained the existing monetary system but the details of the types underwent change. On the obverse of gold denominations a large crescent with star between its points enclosed an inscription and the Muhammadan date, while the reverse bore between two branches an inscription and the Christian date. Denominations from 5 to 25 piastres struck in nickel or aluminium-bronze have inscription and date within a spray of wheat-ears on obverse and value flanked by an oak-branch on reverse. The coinage was further modernized in 1933 when a new system of 100 kurus to the lira was adopted. The Latin alphabet was used for inscriptions and Western numerals for the values and the date which was expressed in the Christian reckoning. The obverse of the 25, 50 and 100 kurus carried the portrait of Kemal Ataturk, the founder of the new Turkey. The reverse bore the value, within a crescent and star, for the 100 kurus and divided by a corn-ear for the lower values. Lower value kurus and paras in nickel had crescent-and-star obverse and value reverse. The portrait of the second Turkish president, Ismet Inonu, appeared only on the silver lira of 1940–1. In the post-war coinage, begun in 1947, the only types were crescent and star and value. The lira, the 25 and 50 kurus were issued in silver and the lower values in brass. The 25 kurus issued in 1958 was struck in steel with a peasant woman on the obverse and the value in wreath on the reverse.

SYRIA

The coinage system of Syria which was made a mandated territory of France in 1920 was similar to the Turkish, 100 piastres to the lira. Pieces of 10, 25 and 50 piastres were struck in silver and lower values in nickel and other alloys. Silver coins are inscribed with the value and *Etat de Syrie* on the obverse, while the reverse has an ornate, involved design and the date. Lower values have the state name and date on obverse and value on reverse. Syria, an independent republic from 1944 until its union with Egypt in 1958, adopted as types an eagle with shield on breast on obverse and value at the centre of an ornate design on reverse. Coins of 25 and 50 piastres as well as the lira were struck in silver, lower values in nickel and in 1950 a gold pound and half-pound were issued.

LEBANON

The piastre was adopted as the monetary unit for Lebanon, like Syria a French mandate between 1920 and 1944. Coins of 10, 25 and 50 piastres have as their obverse type a cedar of Lebanon with the state name in French and Arabic, while the reverse bears a double cornucopiae and the value. Similar types are used for values from 2 to 5 piastres struck in bronze but lower values have simply name and value in French on the obverse and in Arabic on the reverse. Lebanon also became an independent republic in 1944 but coins were issued only from 1952. The Lebanese cedar remains the obverse type but, though the higher values, 25 and 50 piastres, have only the value on the reverse, the 10 piastre reverse reproduces the facing lion's head of Ancient Greek issues and the 5 piastre piece an ancient galley (Pl. 914).

ISRAEL (PALESTINE)

The coinage of Palestine which became a mandated territory administered by Britain in 1922 was first issued in 1927. The major unit authorised was a gold pound piece equivalent to a sovereign and comprising 1000 mils. The pound was never coined but subsidiary pieces in multiples of 100 mils and lower were issued, the 100 and 50 mils pieces in silver the lower values in cupro-nickel or nickel-bronze, in most years up to 1946. The types, selected in 1927 and never altered, were on the 100 and 50 mils coins an olive-branch and circular inscription giving the name of the country in English, Hebrew and Arabic on obverse and the value in figures in the centre of the reverse, surrounded by an inscription giving the value in words in the three languages. The 20, 10 and 5 mils pieces were similar but since they had a central perforation they lacked the main central types. The 1 and 2 mils pieces in bronze had the name Palestine in the three languages across the field of the obverse and an olive-branch and circular inscription giving the value on the reverse.

In 1948 mandated Palestine was replaced by the independent state of Israel. In the new coinage first issued in 1949 the pound was divided into 1000 prutah and only the 500 prutah was struck in silver, the lower values using cupro-nickel and other alloys. The reverse on all denominations was consistent, the value and date within a wreath, but the obverses inscribed 'Israel' in Hebrew and Arabic had a varying type for each denomination, some, such as the palm-trees on the 100 prutah or the bunch of grapes on the 25 prutah, reproducing types from coins struck in ancient Palestine (Pl. 915). New issues in 1960 include the 5 pounds in silver with the portrait of Theodor Herzl on obverse, the 1 pound in cupro-nickel with a kibutz on obverse and the 25 prutah with lyre obverse. The reverses in all cases show the value of the coin. In 1960 a new coinage was introduced, based on a system of 100 agurot to the pound.

JORDAN

Coinage was first issued in 1949 on a basis of 1000 fils to the dinar or pound. The types are uniform for all denominations. On the obverse the value in Arabic numerals within a wreath, crowned, is surrounded by an Arabic inscription, while the reverse carries the value in Western numerals and a circular inscription *The Hashemite Kingdom of the Jordan*. The 20, 50 and 100 fils are struck in cupro-nickel, values from 1 to 10 fils in bronze.

IRAQ

Iraq or Mesopotamia, formerly part of the Ottoman empire, was a British mandate after the first world war until it became an independent kingdom in 1932. Its coinage system is similar to that of Jordan, 1000 fils to the dinar. The first Iraqi coinage was struck in 1931, towards the end of the reign of Faisal I (1921–33). The types which are uniform for all denominations and have remained unchanged except for the royal portrait under successive rulers consist of a portrait head accompanied by Arabic inscription on obverse and the value at the centre of the reverse, surrounded by inscriptions and dates arranged in radial segments. The denominations in silver are the 20, 50 and 100 fils, in nickel the 4 and 10 fils and in bronze 1 and 2 fil pieces. Faisal II, who reigned from 1938 until his assassination in 1958, ascended the throne as a minor and his first coinage in 1943 has the portrait of the boy king, but a more adult portrait appears on the second issue in 1953.

IRAN (PERSIA)

In the reign of Nasr-ed-din (1844–96) the almost exclusively inscriptional types of earlier Persian coinage gave place, under the influence of European coinage, to figure types on the obverse, either the portrait of the shah or the Persian lion

with uplifted sword. The major unit in gold was still the toman, divided into 10
karans, each of 20 shahis, which in turn comprised 50 dinars. On some issues of the
gold toman the shah's facing portrait occupied the obverse while the traditional
inscription type remained on the reverse, but other issues of the toman, its multiples
and portions carries the Persian lion type on obverse. The lion obverse with
inscription or value reverse supplied the types for the silver karan denominations
and the dinar denominations in nickel (Pl. 916). This distribution of types over
the denominations remained largely unchanged under succeeding shahs until in
1925 Ahmed, the last of the Kajar shahs, was overthrown by Reza Khan who
instituted the new Pahlavi dynasty. In the reign of Reza Shah (1925–41) a new
coinage was instituted—100 dinars to a rial and 20 rials to the pahlavi. His first
gold pahlavi used the lion-and-inscription types, and later issues a portrait bust
and either inscription or lion types. Rial denominations in silver and dinar pieces in
nickel had lion-and-value designs. The coinage of the present shah, Mohammed
Reza (1942–), has followed much the same pattern and it is only on the gold
pahlavis from 1952 onwards that his portrait has appeared.

SAUDI ARABIA

The kingdom of Saudi Arabia which comprises most of the Arabian peninsula
has had an independent coinage since 1926. The major pieces are the silver rial
and its portions with divisionary coins in cupro-nickel in values of girsh, of which
22 are equivalent to a rial. The types on the silver coins consist of a central and a
marginal inscription, the date and value appearing at the foot of the reverse. On
the girsh denominations there is only a marginal inscription on the obverse but
the reverse with a semi-circular inscription carries also the value and date. An
issue of a gold guinea in 1957 has a palm and two crossed sabres on obverse and
the value on reverse. Similar types appear on cupro-nickel denominations of 4
and 2 piastres.

HEJAZ

This sultanate is now part of Saudi Arabia but it had an independent coinage
issued in 1923 for its last sultan, Hussein ibn Ali (1916–24). As well as the gold
dinar, the silver rial and its portions were issued and in bronze the girsh and
smaller para denominations. The types on all denominations were purely inscriptional, the marginal inscriptions being sometimes continuous, sometimes
divided into segments.

YEMEN

The major unit of this coinage issued since 1923 is the imadi of 40 bogaches, each of 2 halala. The imadi and portions are issued in silver, the bogach and the halala in copper or bronze. Inscriptional types occupy both obverse and reverse and while the reverse has the conventional arrangement of central and marginal inscriptions the inscriptions on the obverse are arranged in an unusual and distinctive pattern. A circular inscription towards the top of obverse is supplemented by two further inscriptions arranged in expanding circles.

MUSCAT AND OMAN

A copper coinage of portions of the anna was struck in the late nineteenth century by Sultan Fessul ibn Turkee but coinage then lapsed until 1940. The present system is based on the rial of 20 baizahs. So far only the half-rial in silver has been struck with types, crossed Arab swords and inscription on obverse, and inscription within a wreath on reverse. Various baizah denominations have been issued with a similar type on obverse and a simplified inscription on reverse. Those lower value coins are struck in nickel and have either a rectangular or a fluted outline.

THE INDIAN
SUB-CONTINENT

★

The Indian Sub-Continent

THE great Indian peninsula, cut off as it is from the rest of the continent of Asia by the semi-circular sweep of the Himalayas and the Hindu Kush, developed a civilization somewhat different from that of either western or eastern Asia. Although India has never been immune from the incursions and influences of other peoples and civilizations and, by the time that the story of Indian coinage begins, had been subjected to several invasions, particularly through the passes of the north-west, sufficient of the individuality of its civilization had survived to impart a different character to its early coinages, especially in the south. In almost all the periods of its history after the introduction of coinage India has comprised an array of separate states, each with its own characteristic coinage; only in the heyday of the Mogul empire in the late sixteenth and in the seventeenth century did India possess anything at all resembling a universal coinage. Even in modern times British India with its unified control and swifter communications preserved until the end vestiges of local coinages in a number of states. This chapter endeavours to sketch the general sweep of development and change of the plethora of coinage covering more than two thousand years of history and to illustrate the detail of the more interesting and important coinages.

ANCIENT INDIA

'PUNCH-MARKED COINS'

One coinage series in the early history of India has already been mentioned, that of the Greek kings of Bactria in north-west India who issued coinage from the third to the first century B.C. (see pp. 95-6); but what in all probability is the earliest series of coins or coin-like objects in India developed independently of external influences. A series of small silver ingots, marked only by three circular dots, as well as heavier bars of silver with marks punched on one side, seem to have been used as an early form of exchange and it has been suggested that they were in use as early as the beginning of the sixth century B.C. They were, in fact, rather later than the beginnings of Western coinage in Asia Minor. These two series of objects are rather rare but the series of small silver pieces known as 'punch-marked coins' had an extensive output, to judge from the quantities which have survived, and from the find records of these coins they enjoyed a circulation over the whole peninsula. These 'punch-marked coins', also called puranas or dharanas, are flat pieces of silver of irregular weight and of either rectangular or circular outline. The earliest examples appear to be those which have small devices punched on one side only and to this category most of the rectangular pieces belong. The next category includes most of the circular pieces which have stamps or punches on both sides (Pl. 917). On this early form of coinage these punches are presumably the badges or signs of merchants and bankers through whose hands they passed. The punches themselves present a whole range of types—birds, animals, other natural objects as well as human figures and religious symbols. There is archaeological evidence for the existence of these 'punch-marked coins' certainly by the mid third century B.C. alongside coins of Bactrian kings, and in south India at least, mixed hoards of these objects and of silver denarii of the early Roman empire witness to their circulation into the beginning of the first century A.D.

EARLY HINDU

In addition to this unusual form of coinage other series conforming more closely to the usual definition of coinage as objects in metal of approximately standard weight with designs on either side appeared in the smaller kingdoms, chiefly in northern India, after the break-up of the Maurya empire at the end of the third century B.C. The majority of these coins are in copper, though some are of lead and the earliest were cast and not struck from dies. On coins of Ajodhya from about 150 B.C. to A.D. 100 the common types are a humped bull together with the name of the rajah in Brahmi script on obverse and religious or solar symbols on the reverse. On coins of Avanti of about the same period the usual obverse type is a standing figure of the king while the reverse is a design of a cross with a circle at each extremity. A conventional tree design within a railing and a humped bull supply the usual types on coins of Kausambi in the second century B.C. (Pl. 918), while copper coins of Taxila have a lion obverse and commonly a blank reverse. The issues of Malwa which extend from the second century B.C. probably as late as the early fourth century A.D. are of smaller module than those just described. The obverse is commonly an inscription in one or two lines across the field but a variety of types—bull, elephant, symbol or rough portrait head—appear on the reverse. Types on the copper coins of the rajahs and satraps of Mathura in the last two centuries B.C. are commonly a standing figure on obverse and an elephant, elephant's head or horse on the reverse.

The first most extensive coinage of Indian origin is that of the Andhra dynasty whose influence controlled a great area from the Godavari river south into Mysore from the late second century B.C. down to the early third century A.D. Coinage is ascribed to rulers as early as the mid second century but issues are plentiful only in the last century B.C. and the first two centuries A.D. A great proportion of the Andhra coinage is in lead, the remainder in potin, an admixture of lead and copper. The commonest types represent a bow and arrow together with inscription giving the ruler's name on the obverse and a *chaitya* or monastery, roughly depicted as tiers of arches on a base and usually flanked by a tree on the reverse (Pl. 919). Other obverses show an elephant, a poorly drawn horse or a lion and in place of the *chaitya* the 'Ujain' symbol, a cross with balls or circles at its terminals, is frequently placed on the reverse.

Off-shoots of the Sakas, the Scythian conquerors of Bactria who were themselves pushed further into north-west India by another Scythian tribe, the Yueh-chi, replaced the Hindu kings of Mathura in the first century A.D. and another of the Scythian chieftains or western satraps as they are called, Chastana, founded a kingdom in Malwa about A.D. 115 and his successors conquered much of the west coast from the Andhras. Coinage struck by Chastana and successive Western satraps is almost exclusively in the form of imitations of the silver drachm of the Indo-Greek kings with a rough portrait on the obverse and a version of the *chaitya* on the reverse. The coins of Chastana have inscriptions in both Nagari and Kharoshthi but on later issues Kharoshthi disappears (Pl. 920). The coinage of the Western satraps came to an end with the conquest of their territories by the Guptas in 395.

INDO-SCYTHIANS AND INDO-PARTHIANS

The Indo-Scythians, driven out of Bactria by the Yueh-chi towards the end of the second century B.C., settled in Sind and about 75 B.C. under their chief, Maues, captured Pushkalavati (Peshawar) in the Punjab. Silver coins of Maues copy some types of the Indo-Greek kings with figures of standing Zeus and Greek inscription on the obverse and a standing Nike or Victory and Kharoshthi inscription on the reverse. Copper coins have the typical Indian rectangular outline and as well as also reproducing types from Indo-Greek coins present some novelties such as elephant on obverse and figure of the king seated cross-legged on stool on the reverse (Pl. 921). Coins of Maues' successors, Azes I, Azilises and Azes II, follow a similar pattern; a frequent obverse type on silver coins depicts the king as a mounted figure (Pl. 922) while the Dioscuri figure frequently on the reverse. Of the Indo-Parthian kings who ruled west of the Indus the most important was Gondophares who struck billon tetradrachms similar to those of the Indo-Scythic kings and with similar types, and copper coins, which presented on obverse a portrait of Gondophares in the Parthian style with a figure of Nike on the reverse. Later kings—Abdagases, Orthagnes and Pakores—issued a very similar coinage.

KUSHANS

In the early first century A.D. the Kushans, a branch of the Yueh-chi tribe, invaded north-west India and under their chief, Kujula Kadphises, put an end to the kingdom of Hermaeus, the last of the Indo-Greek kings, and subsequently, about the middle of the century, occupied part of the kingdom of the Indo-Parthians. Under successive kings—Kujula Kadphises, a nameless king with the title Soter Megas, Vima Kadphises, Kanishka, Huvishka and Vasu-deva—the Kushan kingdom flourished until A.D. 220 and survived with diminished power until the irruption of the White Huns in the late fifth century. The Kushan coinage (except for that of Kujula and Soter Megas in copper only) is of gold and copper, the principal gold unit being struck on the same standard as the contemporary Roman imperial aureus, though double pieces and quarters are also found. The copper coins of Kujula Kadphises were first issued as a joint coinage with Hermaeus, whose portrait and titles in Greek occupied the obverse, while a Kharoshthi legend with the name of Kujula accompanied a standing figure of Heracles. On a later issue the obverse, though still bearing the bust of Hermaeus, is inscribed with Kujula's name. The coinage without king's name, in copper only, presents a diademed bust of a king on obverse and a horseman on the reverse, accompanied by the inscription in Greek, *Basileus Basileon Soter Megas*, 'King of kings, the great Saviour' (Pl. 923). Since the inscription includes no personal name, the precise attribution of this coinage remains in question.

On copper coins of Vima Kadphises the types are a standing figure of the king with hand outstretched over altar on the obverse and a facing figure of the Hindu deity, Siva, and a bull on the reverse. A similar reverse on a double gold stater has as obverse type the figure of the king squatting on a low couch, while on the obverse of the stater itself Vima is shown as a half-length figure. On the gold coins of Kanishka the king is usually represented on the obverse as a standing figure but the reverses present a variety of deities, both Greek and Iranian (Pl. 924). On the coinage of Kujula and Vima the obverse inscription had been in Greek, the reverse in Kharoshthi, but on the issues of Kanishka and his successors only Greek inscriptions appear. The copper coins of Kanishka largely repeat the types of his gold coinage and these types continue with some variations under his successor, Huvishka, whose portrait on gold coins is a half-length figure or a bust and not a standing figure.

THE GUPTA EMPIRE

One of the most magnificent coinages of ancient India is that of the Gupta empire which flourished from the fourth to the sixth century A.D. The splendour of its coinage, which is preponderantly in gold, reflects the prosperity of a kingdom which at its greatest extent stretched from the Himalayas in the north to the river Narbada in the south and from the Jumna in the west to the Brahmaputra in the east; and the artistry of the coins lends weight to the claim that the Gupta period represents one of the peaks of Hindu civilization. The dynasty was founded by Gupta in the territory around Pataliputra (Patna) in the later third century, as the Kushan power began to decline, but the official Gupta era begins only with the accession of Gupta's grandson, Chandragupta I, in 320 and the great territorial expansion took place under his successor, Samudragupta (335–380). It was also in the reign of Samudragupta that the Gupta coinage began to be issued, for the coinage which bears the portrait of Chandragupta I and his wife Kumaradevi was a posthumous issue in the reign of Samudragupta.

The Gupta gold coin is the direct descendant of the Kushan gold stater, itself modelled on the standard of the Roman imperial aureus and gold was the only metal coined by Samudragupta. From the reign of Chandragupta II (380–414) onwards silver coinage was also struck, principally for the western areas of the empire. These silver coins continue in general terms the tradition of the small silver pieces issued both by the Andhras and by the Western satraps (see p. 501). A more restricted copper coinage was issued by Chandragupta II and his successors. The inscriptions on both obverse and reverse of the Gupta coins are in classical Sanskrit.

In types as well as weight-standard the early Gupta gold declares its descent from the gold coins of the Kushan kings whose most constant types of standing figure of the king on obverse and the goddess Lakshmi seated on reverse are repeated on coins of Samudragupta. The types on Samudragupta's coins are not only infinitely better executed than on the later Kushan coins but are considerably modified. On the obverse Samudragupta is shown as a standing figure with nimbus about his head and stretching out hand over altar, while in the background is a standard surmounted by the sacred Garuda bird. The reverse with the goddess Lakshmi, who is also nimbate, is much more ornate and on some specimens is not dissimilar to the much later Byzantine reverse with a seated figure of Christ (Pl. 925). Lakshmi also figures seated on a recumbent lion with her feet on a lotus on the reverse of the coins honouring Samudragupta's parents, Chandragupta I and Kumaradevi, whose figures, both nimbate, stand side by side on the obverse (Pl. 926). On other varieties of Samudragupta's coins the king appears as a standing figure holding either a bow or a battle-axe in his left hand or as a seated figure playing the lyre. On yet another issue the obverse type is a horse standing by a sacrificial post, while on the reverse stands the chief queen holding a sacrificial spear.

Chandragupta II (375–414) under whom the Gupta territory was considerably expanded, principally at the expense of the Western satraps, has an even more plenteous coinage of gold than Samudragupta. The latter's archer type on which the king is shown holding bow is repeated by Chandragupta II but a whole range of new varieties was added to the gold coinage. The king is shown sacrificing at an altar while a small attendant holds a chattra or parasol above him. Another spirited obverse represents the king, armed with a bow, shooting a lion (Pl. 927) and the mounted figure of the king which was a feature of Saka coins was revived by Chandragupta II. The silver coinage of the Western satraps was continued by Chandragupta but whereas the obverse retained the portrait head, which was one of the distinctive features of the small silver coins of both the Andhras and the Western satraps, the equally typical *chaitya* on the reverse of these latter coins was replaced by the Garuda. Copper coins issued by Chandragupta II also picture the Garuda with outstretched wings on the reverse, while on the obverse is a nimbate portrait of the king in profile as either a three-quarter or a half-length figure.

Of new types introduced on the gold by Kumaragupta (414–455) particularly attractive are those which honour the god Karttikeya and his peacock Paravani. On the obverse the standing king feeds the peacock from a bunch of fruit in his hand, while, on the reverse, the god is shown mounted on the peacock (Pl. 928). The silver coinage of Kumaragupta is much more extensive than that of the previous reign and in addition to the Garuda reverse now also pictured the peacock with outstretched wings. The beginning of decline under Skandagupta (455–480), the last of the great Gupta kings, is apparent in the distinct fall in quantity of gold coinage and in the restriction of types largely to two, the archer type and a new obverse on which the king and the goddess Lakshmi stand on either side of the Garuda standard. Skandagupta introduced two new reverses on the silver coins, Siva's bull, Nandi, and an altar. There is further evidence of decline in the base silver in which these coins were struck and in their irregular flans. After Skandagupta's death in 480 only gold coins of the archer type were struck by the Gupta kings down to 560 with a steady decline in technique and in the literacy of the inscriptions.

The devastations of the Huns probably account for the lack of any direct imitations of the Gupta gold coinage by the kingdoms which came after. Only in Gauda in central Bengal was an imitative gold coinage struck by its king, Sasanka (600–625), with types of Siva reclining on his bull Nandi on the obverse and on the reverse the goddess Lakshmi seated on a lotus.

MEDIAEVAL INDIA

The complete collapse of the Roman imperial system in the West in the early fifth century, the invasions of barbarian peoples and the slow re-creation of civilization in the early Middle Ages has its counterpart in India. In the later fifth century in India it was the great Gupta empire which began to disintegrate under the attacks of the Hephthalites or White Huns, a branch of the same Hunnish people which under Attilla had assisted at the downfall of the Roman empire. Somewhat in the same manner as in western Europe, the early Middle Ages in India was a period in which numerous petty kingdoms flourished but, unlike Europe where historical circumstances permitted the coalescing of small states into great national kingdoms, the later Middle Ages in India brought, in the twelfth century, the first of several waves of new conquerors, the Muhammadans who in time established wide sovereignty over most of the sub-continent. The mediaeval coinage of India between the invasions of the Huns and the Muhammadans, particularly in northern India, mirrors the reduced economic circumstances of the period in its dearth of good silver and the absence of any single unifying power in the diversity of issues of which the most typical and important are outlined in this section.

HEPHTHALITES (WHITE HUNS)

The Hephthalites who had established themselves on the Oxus earlier in the fifth century pushed into north-west India where they were temporarily repulsed by Chandragupta II in 455, but by 500 they were established under their leader Toramana in Malwa and under Mihiragula, who succeeded two years later, the conquest of northern India was extended and the capital fixed at Sakala in the Punjab. A revolt of his Indian tributary princes drove out Mihiragula who seized and held Kashmir till his death in 528. The Hephthalite hold on Transoxiana was finally broken by the Sassanian king Chosroes I with the assistance of the Turks in 565. The coinage of the Hephthalites is an imitation in base silver of the silver drachm of the Sassanian kings. The drawing is crude on both the obverse, which carries a portrait bust in elaborate tunic and head-dress, based on the Sassanian model, and on the reverse, which is a version of the Zoroastrian fire-altar with its two attendants. The obverse portrait is accompanied by a symbol resembling a trident usually to the left of the bust. The heads of both the Hephthalite chiefs, Toramana and Mihiragula, who held rule in India appear on coins of this description (Pl. 929) as well as on copper coins reminiscent of those of Chandragupta II with obverse portrait and reverse with a horizontal bar. In place of the type of the Garuda above the bar on Gupta coins appears a solar symbol or a bull on the Hephthalite coppers with the king's name below.

INDO-SASSANIAN

The coinage of the White Huns in India was not the only series which derived its inspiration from Sassanian prototypes. Other imitations of Sassanian issues with inscriptions in Pahlevi and Nagari were produced by minor dynasties which, in the sixth and early seventh centuries, acknowledged Sassanian suzerainty. Typical of this category is the coinage of flat silver pieces with Sassanian-style portrait and a version of the fire-altar which bears the name Napki Malik (Pl. 930). The Sassanian silver drachm was also the original model for a series of thin flat coins with an extremely degenerate and sketchy version of the Sassanian portrait and fire-altar. Smaller but thicker coins in base silver which circulated for a lengthy period in Gujarat and are known as Gadhiya paisa have types which, though they have become elaborate patterns, still show the elements of the original Sassanian types (Pl. 931).

RAJPUT DYNASTIES OF HINDUSTAN AND CENTRAL INDIA

By far the most common coinage in this period is the bull-and-horseman type struck by most of the Rajput dynasties in gradually degenerating style and an increasingly base metal. The types which were first introduced by the Hindu kings of Kabul and Ohind about the middle of the ninth century represent on the obverse a recumbent humped bull with a trident-like symbol on its flank and a Nagari inscription above; on the reverse is a mounted horseman, probably the king, holding a lance pointing downwards and a further inscription in a cursive Bactrian script. The most prolific issue of this coinage, inscribed with the title Samanta-deva, belongs to the early tenth century (Pl. 932). Later bull and horseman coins of this ruler appear in billon while on another Samanta-deva series the types are elephant on obverse and lion with tail curled over back on the reverse.

The second most widespread coinage was in rather base gold with a reverse depicting the seated goddess Lakshmi who had figured so prominently on the Gupta coinage. Here, however, the goddess is portrayed with four not two arms. The obverse consists solely of a three-line inscription in Nagari giving the king's name. The earliest coinage of this category seems to have been struck by Gangeya-deva of the Kalachuri dynasty of Dahala (Jabalpur) in the early eleventh century (1015–40) and then by the Chandella kings of Bunkelkhand in the last half of the century. Coinage of a similar base gold fabric was issued by the kings of Mahaka-sola in the mid-twelfth century, again with line inscriptions giving the king's name on obverse but with a lion-rampant type on the reverse.

The issues of other Rajput dynasties present an admixture of these two cate-gories of coinage. The Tomara dynasty of Ajmir and Delhi in the late tenth and the eleventh centuries struck mainly the bull-and-horseman coins in billon or copper but Kumara-pala-deva (1019–49) has a coinage in base gold with the seated Lakshmi as on the coins of the Kalachuri kings. The Chauhan dynasty which followed the Tomara at Delhi in the later twelfth century confines its issues to bull-and-horseman coinage. The Rathor dynasty of Kanauj in the eleventh and twelfth centuries also had varied issues of copper bull and horseman and base gold seated-goddess coinage but the billon coins of Malaya-varma of Narwar (1220–32) combine types from both classes and show a three-line inscription on obverse and a horseman on reverse. This combination of types was also a feature of the later copper coinages of the maharajahs of Kangra between 1300 and 1625, though the earliest issues are closer copies of the bull-and-horseman coinage.

A rare copper coinage with types, a portrait bust and a vase have been ascribed to a ruler Khingila in Kashmir in the fifth century and copper coins with the Kushan types of king standing by altar on obverse and seated goddess on the reverse have the name Toramana, who may be the Hephthalite chief of the early sixth century. Extremely crude imitations of the standing-king and seated-goddess types were produced in base gold by kings of the Naga dynasty of the eighth century but under subsequent dynasties from the ninth to the twelfth centuries this coinage was struck in copper only (Pl. 933). The coinage of the kings of Nepal of the sixth to eighth centuries was also of copper but presented some variation from the more usual Hindu mediaeval types. The seated goddess still appeared on the reverse of one issue but was combined with a standing-lion type with lotus in front on the reverse. On the other issues the lion on the obverse is winged and there is a sun-type on the reverse.

The coinage of southern India, which was not subjected to the successive waves of invasion and conquest which northern India suffered, developed along quite different lines. The silver punch-marked coinage disappeared in the early decades of the first century A.D. and the currency requirements of south India, to judge from the numerous hoards, appear to have been served by the widespread use of Roman imperial gold coins in the first two centuries A.D. and of silver denarii in the first half of the first century. The frequency with which such Roman aurei were subjected to test by a chisel cut suggests, however, that these gold coins were used as bullion rather than as pieces of currency. Roman and, later, Byzantine solidi were again imported in mass by south India from the later fourth to the fifth century, and in the extreme south as well as in Ceylon the small bronze coins of the fourth-century Roman emperors were used as small change and even imitated locally. This predilection for these two metals is apparent in the native coinages of the early mediaeval period. Gold was struck in two denominations, the heavier hun or pagoda and the smaller fanam, and copper in a denomination known as the kasu, from which the English word cash is ultimately derived. The earliest gold coins are slightly spherical and since, apart from some tiny punch marks, they are completely blank their attribution to specific dynasties and even areas is uncertain, for, in view of the wide circulation of gold coinage, the evidence of hoards for the localization of issues is not of the same value as in the case of copper coins which had a more restricted circulation. Even the next development on the gold coins, the placing of devices on one or both sides, is of little service in the absence of informative inscriptions. Of gold coins of this category the padma-tankas with an obverse design with an eight-petalled lotus at the centre are attributed to the Kadambas in Mysore.

One of the earliest dynasties to whom coinage is attributed, the Chalukyas, reigned in the Deccan from the mid sixth century till their conquest by the Rashtrakutas in 753. Gold pagodas and fanams with the Chalukya badge of a boar were probably struck by the earlier Chalukya rulers but the earliest coinage of certain attribution, with types of lion and trident flanked by two lamps, from the Telugu inscription on the obverse, was issued by Vishnu-Vardana (615–633). The Chalukya power revived and the rulers of the western Chalukya kingdom with its capital at Kalyani issued gold coins in the eleventh and twelfth centuries similar to the lotus-tankas of the Kadambas but with a temple or a lion as the obverse type. The rulers of the eastern Chalukya kingdom from the mid seventh to the eleventh centuries struck gold coins including a series of large, flat gold pieces with a boar device at the centre (Pl. 934) for Saktivarman (1000–12) and Rajaraja (1012–62). The Hoysalas who overthrew the Chalukyas in 753 retained on their gold the lion type which also features on Chalukya coins and the Cholas who conquered the kingdom of the eastern Chalukyas in 1153 also made use of the temple-and-lion types on Chalukya tankas.

Of the Ganga dynasty which ruled in Kalinga from the sixth to the eleventh centuries Antanavarman Chodaganga issued gold fanams with a recumbent bull on the obverse and a Telugu regnal date on the reverse. The pagodas with ornate elephant on obverse and a floral scroll design on the reverse were struck in the ninth century at Orissa by the Chera kings who had settled there after their expulsion from Kongudesa by the Cholas. The coinage of Kadamba chiefs of Goa had as types an inscriptional obverse and a lion reverse. Issues in the late twelfth century for Vishnu Chitta-deva are in gold, for Jayakesin in silver.

TAMIL STATES

Of the Tamil peoples in the extreme south of India the first to attain a position of ascendancy were the Pallavas who issued pagodas and fanams with a maned lion as the chief type. Silver Pallava coins have this lion type also on the obverse and a vase within a circle of rays on the reverse. The history of the Pandyas in Madura is a succession of periods of independence then of subjection to other peoples, first the Pallavas in the eighth century and then the Cholas in the eleventh and twelfth centuries. In the interim period of independence the Pandyas issued both gold and copper coins with either one or two fish on the obverse and an inscription on the reverse (Pl. 935). This fish symbol is also used particularly on copper coins in the thirteenth century when the Pandyas had risen superior to the Cholas whose specific standing-figure type is sometimes incorporated on the coins of the Pandyas. The coinage struck by the Cholas for their Deccan conquests has been mentioned above but on gold and silver coins issued in their own territory on the Coromandel coast in the earlier tenth century the same type, a tiger seated under a canopy and flanked by the two fish of the Pandya coins, appears on both sides (Pl. 936). In a later period of Chola eminence between the eleventh and thirteenth centuries the coinage which is in copper only has a standing figure and a seated figure on the reverse, types copied on the coinage of Ceylon in the twelfth and thirteenth centuries (see p. 531). The coinage of the Chera rulers in Malabar is represented only by extremely rare silver with inscriptions on both sides.

The Muhammadan invasion of northern India in the twelfth century was followed by the establishment of Muhammadan states whose coinage is reviewed in the next section. By the early fourteenth century Muhammadan penetration of southern India had effected the capture of the Pandya capital, Madura, in 1311 and to counter the threat of further conquest the kingdom of Vijayanagar was founded in 1336. Though its greatness was brought to an end by the battle of Talikota in 1565, it survived in attenuated form until the late seventeenth century. Like other south Indian coinages the issues of Vijayanagar are for the most part in gold in which not only the pagoda but its half and quarter were struck. Copper coinage was also issued but on a more restricted scale. On these pagodas whose small dumpy fabric was perpetuated in the pagoda issues of subsequent centuries, both by native states and by European trading companies, the reverse types mostly derive from the Hindu pantheon, while the obverse inscription in Nagari gives the king's name.

One of the earliest of the Vijayanagar pieces is a half-pagoda of Harihara (*c.*1379) with the deities Siva and Parvati seated side by side on the reverse (Pl. 937), a type repeated for Deva Raya II about 1422. On coins of Achuta Raya (1530–42) occurs an unusual type, a double-headed eagle-monster, known as the *Ganda bherunda*, holding up elephants in its beaks and claws. The most popular reverse type is a single seated deity who from his attributes is sometimes Siva, sometimes Vishnu, who also appears standing under a canopy on coins of Rama Raja in the mid sixteenth century. The 'three swami pagoda' which was extensively imitated in later centuries was first issued by Tirumala Raja about 1570 (Pl. 938). The three holy figures of whom the central one stands and the other two are seated have been variously identified as Laksmana with Rama and Sita, or Venkatesvara with his two wives. On copper coins the reverse type is a boar, a device taken over from the Chalukyas.

After the decline of the Vijayanagar kingdom in the sixteenth and seventeenth centuries gold pagodas were issued by the Rajas of Ikkeri. The first of these, Sadasiva Nayaka (1539–75), struck pagodas with the seated figures of Siva and Parvati on the obverse and his name in Nagari script on the reverse, types used by later Nayaka princes until their conquest by Haidar Ali in 1763. On the numerous copper kasu issued by princes in Mysore in this period the most common type was an elephant to left with sun and moon above on the obverse. The reverse consisted of double lines crossing each other at right angles with a circle in the centre (Pl. 939). These 'elephant cash' pieces continued in circulation up until comparatively recent times. The pagodas and fanams struck both by native rulers and by the Dutch and English in south India are described later (see p. 523).

SULTANS OF DELHI

The feature common to Western coinage and to the coinages of ancient India, both of the Hindu states and the successive invaders and conquerors in the north and to the mediaeval coinages of the Rajput dynastes and the states of south India, is the use of a pictorial or heraldic device on at least one side of the coin. The Muhammadan conquest of India which began in the late twelfth century, however, very soon imposed a new pattern on the Indian coinage; for, on the Muhammadan coins of India, just as in the majority of the Islamic coinages of the Near East, the representation of all objects is eschewed and, with some notable exceptions, the types on both sides of the coins consist only of inscriptions composed of religious formulae and details of the ruler, his date and the place of minting. This general pattern of coinage persisted throughout most of the remaining history of Indian coinage under the Muhammadan sultans of Delhi, the Muhammadan states into which that sultanate eventually divided and, later, the Mogul emperors. Only occasional survivals of Hindu coinage break the pattern until the advent of European coinage. The Muhammadan conquest which once again brought India into a relationship with western and central Asia made for easier access to silver supplies and resulted in the eventual return of a widespread use of silver in the Indian coinage.

A Muhammadan kingdom had existed in India in Sind in the north-west since the early eighth century but it was only with the invasions of some three centuries later that a Muhammadan coinage of any importance had currency and was struck in India. In the first quarter of the eleventh century Mahmud of Ghazni invaded and annexed the Punjab (see p. 483) and when, in the middle of the century, the Ghaznavids were ousted from Ghazni by the Ghorids, Lahore became their capital and the mint for small billon coins with the bull, Nandi of the Rajput coinage on the obverse and a Kufic inscription on the reverse. This coinage came to an end with the defeat in 1187 of Khusru Malik, the last of the Ghaznavid rulers of Lahore by the Ghorid prince, Muhammad-ibn-Sam. Muhammad's further advance into India was temporarily halted by his defeat at the battle of Tanesar in 1191 at the hands of Prithviraja of Ajmer and Delhi, but on the same battlefield in the following year Muhammad defeated a confederacy of Indian princes under Prithviraja and the way lay open to the complete conquest of Hindustan.

The replacement of Indian coinage by pure Muhammadan types was, however, not achieved immediately and, indeed, not till after the death of Muhammad. His large silver coins with a small central inscription and three circular inscriptions on both sides are from the Ghazni mint, as are his gold coins with central inscription in square frame and marginal inscriptions in the segments. His Indian coinage consists of imitations of the gold coinage of the Kanauj kings with a degenerate seated Lakshmi type on the obverse and an inscription in Nagari on the reverse. The most prolific of his coinages is the continuation of a version of the Rajput bull and horseman struck in billon or copper, the so-called delhiwalas, with one of the types, more often the horseman, on the obverse and an inscription in Nagari on the reverse (Pl. 940). Muhammad's successor, Kutbu-d-din, who extended and consolidated the Muhammadan conquests in India and established a capital at Delhi, is represented only by a very rare billon coinage of the horseman-and-inscription type. This was also the sole class of coinage for the third sultan, Alam Shah, in 1210.

This derivative bull-and-horseman coinage in base metal was supplemented by Altamsh (1210–35) by issues in silver. The first issue of his silver tankahs showed the sultan on horse-back surrounded by a marginal inscription while the reverse consisted of lines of inscription in Arabic within a dotted circle. Following the receipt of a diploma of investiture from al-Mustansir, the Baghdad caliph in 1228, Altamsh issued a further series of silver tankahs with inscriptions on both sides. The reverse continued to carry the sultan's name and title but the obverse was inscribed 'In the reign of the Imam, al-Mustansir, the commander of the faithful'. These central inscriptions were enclosed in circles with marginal inscriptions giving the mint and the date. The mint calling itself Bilad-al-Hind, 'the cities of Hind', is the first mint to appear in the reign of Altamsh. This form of silver tankah (Pl. 941) was preserved by subsequent sultans down to Balban (1266–86), even though the caliph al-Mustansir died in 1242. The billon or copper coinage which in this reign sometimes carries the name of Delhi as the mint with one of the adaptations of the bull-and-horseman types was also continued with occasional innovations such as on the copper coins of Raziya (1236–9) with bull type on obverse and small central inscription within a circle of rays on the reverse. Of the more usual varieties, that with bull on obverse and horseman on reverse was struck down into the reign of Alau-d-din Mas'aud (1241–6) and that with horseman obverse and inscription reverse till the reign of Nasiru-d-din (1246–65).

A gold coinage with the same types and weight as the silver tankah was first minted by Alau-d-din Mas'aud but his issues and those of his immediate successors were sparse. With the extension of Muhammadan conquest into the rich south, where gold had always formed the chief metal for coinage, Alau-d-din Muham-mad (1296–1316) was enabled to strike a more profuse gold coinage (Pl. 942). The same sultan finally took the step of omitting from the obverse inscription the name of the caliph. In its place came a bombastic inscription acclaiming the sultan as 'the second Alexander, the right hand of the Caliphate'. The arrange-ment of inscriptions was also altered in this reign. Only the obverse now carried a marginal inscription and the reverse field was left free for a linear inscription running from edge to edge of the coin and, since this silver coinage was pro-duced in massive issues, it impresses itself as the typical coinage of the sultans of Delhi (Pl. 943). The coinage of the next effective sultan, Kutbu-d-din Mubarak (1316–20), saw the revival on some issues both of precious metals and billon of the square shape which is a recurrent feature of Indian issues.

The issues of Muhammad-ibn-Tughlaq (1325–51) can claim, on several grounds, to represent the climax of the coinage of the sultans of Delhi. Not only is his by far the most plentiful coinage but it was produced on a higher standard of technical execution and, in addition, it presents a number of features of unusual interest, both in the matter of variety of inscriptions but also in the way of experiments in the coinage system itself. After an initial issue of gold and silver tankahs of the traditional kind, Muhammad-ibn-Tughlaq introduced in 1326 new denominations in gold and silver. In what was evidently an attempt to establish in the coinage the actual relative values of gold and silver in the free market he abandoned the old standard weight of about 11 gm. for both metals and struck a gold dinar at a weight of some 13 gm. and a new silver coin, the adli, weighing approximately 9 gm. The experiment was not a success and in 1332 coinage of the gold and silver tankahs of the old type was resumed. The second experiment between 1329 and 1332 represents one of the earliest attempts to establish a fiduciary coinage. As a substitute for the silver and billon coins, tokens in brass and copper were issued but, despite the cautionary and reassuring in-scriptions such as 'Whoso obeys the Sultan, obeys the Compassionate' (i.e. Allah) and 'Sealed as a tankah of fifty ganis' which appeared on these tokens (Pl. 944), the consequence was widespread forgery and lack of confidence. Some idea of the improbability of the success of such a system in the early fourteenth century can be gained from the realization that it was only in the last century that such fiduciary coinages began to gain acceptance in the Western world and only in the present century have they become of general application. This attempt by Muhammad-ibn-Tughlaq was a genuine monetary experiment and was not dictated by a bankrupt economy, for, on the failure of the scheme, the fiduciary pieces, both genuine and false, were redeemed.

Some of the early issues of Muhammad-ibn-Tughlaq in gold, silver and billon were struck in memory of his father, Ghiyasu-d-din, whose name appears on the inscription with the suffix al-Shahid, 'The Martyr', an ironic addition, since it was by the murder of his father that the sultan secured his accession to the throne. The signature of a variety of mints in addition to Delhi now appeared regularly on the coinage inscriptions and the Kalima, the inscription containing the profession of faith and recording the name of the actual reigning caliph, returns to most of the issues. In addition to a variety of epithets and titles proclaiming his religious adherence Muhammad-ibn-Tughlaq inscribed on some of his issues the names of the first four orthodox caliphs, Abu Bakir, Omar, Usman and Ali.

The extensive billon coinage which present a considerable number of inscriptional varieties appear to have filled the rôle of subsidiary pieces of the silver tankah. In Delhi and the north this denomination was divisible into fifty jaitils and in the south into various values of gani but the weight variations of extant specimens render their assignation to specific denominations a matter of uncertainty.

A steady decline in the political fortunes of the sultans of Delhi took place after the reign of Muhammad-ibn-Tughlaq as, increasingly, the governors of provinces came to regard themselves as independent and to set up their own kingdoms. The shrinkage of precious-metal coinage in the latter half of the fourteenth and in the fifteenth centuries is an index of this decline, for only in the reign of Firoz III (1351–88) was gold coinage issued in any appreciable quantity. These pieces continued to have the somewhat reduced module but thicker fabric which had been introduced under Muhammad-ibn-Tughlaq and which distinguishes such gold issues as were made by the later sultans. Firoz III, like his predecessor, placed on his gold coins the name of the caliph on obverse and on the reverse his own name, accompanied by such titles as 'The deputy of the commander' (i.e. the caliph). In 1359 the name of Fath Khan, his son, is joined with that of Firoz on the gold coins. Silver coinage was struck only in small quantity but billon issues both of Firoz and of Firoz together with Fath Khan were extensive. Silver coinage for the later sultans is practically non-existent and even the billon coinage tended to lose much of its already small silver content, and coinage in copper became more frequent.

In the issues, almost exclusively in billon and copper, of the Lodi dynasty between 1451 and 1526 the only coinage innovation was the introduction of a somewhat larger billon coin by the sultan Bahlol Lodi and hence known as a bahloli (Pl. 945). In 1526 Ibrahim the last of the Lodi dynasty was defeated at Panipat by the Mogul Babar who occupied Hindustan until his death in 1530, when he was succeeded by Humayun.

The coinage of these two Mogul rulers is dealt with in the section on the Mogul coinage below but the story of the coinage of the sultans of Delhi has not yet reached its conclusion, for in 1540, on the expulsion of Humayun, a new dynasty was established by the Afghan Sher Shah (1540–5). The innovations imported into the coinage by this ruler anticipated the system which was later consolidated by the Mogul emperor Akbar. Only rare gold was struck but in silver a new denomination, the rupee, was issued with a broad flan and a weight of 11·5 gm. and some divisionary pieces of the rupee are also found. The obverse retained the Kalima in the central area with the names of the four orthodox caliphs in the marginal segments but the reverse now carried the sultan's name, date and the legend 'May God perpetuate his kingdom', with, below, the sultan's name in Hindi. In the margin was often inscribed the name of one of a whole chain of over twenty mints at which this coinage was struck. The central inscriptions are enclosed on either a circle or a square and frequently incorporate as a mint-mark a small ornament, for instance a four- or five-petalled flower, a swastika or two interlocked triangles (Pl. 946). On occasional issues both of Sher Shah and his successor Islam Shah (1545–52) the coins were struck on a square flan.

A new denomination, the dam, was struck in copper at a weight of 21·5 gm. and of this denomination divisionary pieces down to a sixteenth were also issued. The reverse has a set of inscriptions similar to those on the silver but the obverse inscription abandons the usual Kalima and contents itself with the more general 'In the time of the Commander of the faithful, the protector of the religion of the Requiter' (Pl. 947). Similar silver and copper coinage was struck in the brief reigns of the remaining Suri sultans, Muhammad Adil, Sikandar and Ibrahim in the years between 1552 and the return of Humayun in 1556.

MUHAMMADAN STATES

(THIRTEENTH TO SIXTEENTH CENTURIES)

In some of the constituent provinces of the empire of the sultans of Delhi governors began at quite an early date to issue coinage in their own name and, as the central authority of Delhi declined, a number of these provinces became independent kingdoms which were on occasion retaken by the Delhi sultan but which in most instances endured until the establishment of the Mogul empire in the first half of the sixteenth century. The initial issues of these states are based on the pattern of the Delhi coinage but in time local variants assume the ascendancy. The history of the gradual decay of the precious-metal coinage and the survival of a mainly base-metal coinage of billon or copper which is observed in the Delhi coinage repeats itself in the issues of the Muhammadan states of this period.

From 1202 when it was conquered by the sultans of Delhi Bengal was a single province but in 1310 it was divided into east and west Bengal, until finally in 1339 the whole province became an independent kingdom under Shamsu-d--din Iliyas. A number of governors before the division in 1310 and all of them afterwards issued a coinage almost entirely in silver with only some very rare gold issues. The silver coinage follows closely the pattern of the Delhi coins with the usual Kalima or later the name of al-Mustansir, the last caliph of Baghdad, on the obverse and the local ruler's name and title on the reverse. The issues of the first of the independent sultans of Bengal continue this pattern but in the reign of Sikandar (1358–89) begins the local practice of enclosing the central inscription on one or both sides within geometric outlines of various degrees of elaboration. The coinage of Jalalu-d-din Muhammad (1414–31) is notable for the use of tuhgra characters which, with the strokes elongated right to the edge of the coin, impart a peculiar ridged appearance to the sides on which they are employed (Pl. 948). No less than twenty-four rulers reigned in Bengal, though coinage is not recorded for all, between 1338 and 1538 when it was retaken by Sher Shah, the Suri sultan of Delhi. After the fall of the Delhi branch, an off-shoot of the Suri dynasty continued to rule Bengal from 1552 till 1563. The silver coinage struck in this period has the fine broad flan of the new coinage instituted by Sher Shah (see p. 515). A final dynasty, that of the Afghan Kararanis, held Bengal till the defeat of its last ruler, Daud Shah, in 1576 and the incorporation of Bengal into the empire of Akbar.

JAUNPUR

Jaunpur secured its independence under its governor, the eunuch Khwajah-i-Jahun, in 1394 but the earliest coinage was issued by Ibrahim (1400–40). The main Jaunpur coinage consists of billon and copper pieces similar to the Delhi issues, modified by the practice of the last three rulers of this kingdom Mahmud (1440–56) Muhammad (1456–8) and Husen (1458–76) of issuing 'pedigree' coins, that is, coins on which the name of the ruler's predecessors are added to his own name. After the defeat of Husen and the re-incorporation of Jaunpur into the central empire by Bahlol Lodi in 1476 billon coins in the name of Husen continued to be issued for some thirty years. Rare gold coins of the last three rulers use elongated tughra characters similar to those on the Bengal issues of Jalalu-d-din.

DECCAN

An independent kingdom was established in the Deccan in 1347 by Alau-d-din Hasan, the first of the Bahmani dynasty, with its capital at Kulbarga or Hasanabad. After almost two centuries, in the reign of Mahmud Shah (1482–1518), the kingdom splintered into five smaller sultanates which survived into the seventeenth century. As elsewhere the inspiration of the Deccan coinage is to be found in the Delhi issues, particularly in the case of the silver and the much rarer gold pieces which follow closely the style of the tankahs of Alau-d-din Muhammad, the Delhisultan. Later, from the reign of Ahmad Shah II (1435–57), the coins present on both sides inscriptions detailing the high-sounding epithets assumed in the sultan's title.

MADURA

The most southerly province of the sultans of Delhi was transformed into an independent state by its governor Jalalu-d-din Aghan in 1334 but its existence was short-lived, for it was conquered by the kingdom of Vijayanagar in 1371. Only billon and copper coins similar to those of the Delhi coinage and extremely rare gold pieces were issued in the few decades of independent rule.

MALWA

Dilawar Khan Ghori, the governor of Malwa, set himself up as an independent governor in 1401 but it was only under his son and successor, Hoshang (1405–32), that coinage was begun. Issues in gold, silver and copper by Hoshang and Muhammad I (1432–6) are similar to those of Delhi but under Mahmud (1436–68) billon issues were also introduced and the square shape which characterizes the majority of Malwa coins began to be used. In the sixteenth century all coinage was struck on these square flans. The reverse of Mahmud's coins is divided into two bands by a lengthening of the tail of the final letter in the first line of the inscription (Pl. 949), while, from the time of Ghiyas Shah (1468–1500), both obverse and reverse have this distinctive feature. Ghiyas also introduced the practice of inserting a small ornament in the inscriptions in the same manner as on the Suri coins of Delhi. In 1530 Malwa was conquered by Gujarat and finally in 1560 it was seized by Akbar and incorporated into his empire.

Gujarat, closer to the centre than most of the other provinces, emerged as independent only in the early fifteenth century when a new dynasty was founded by the governor, Zafar Khan, in 1403 but coinage is recorded only from the reign of Ahmad I (1411–43). The coins of Gujarat, unlike those of neighbouring Malwa, are almost always round. Gold figures only infrequently in the coinage, and silver, though struck by most rulers, is restricted, but billon and copper were struck in quantity. Initially coinage follows the Delhi pattern but later the copper coinage in particular was produced in a distinctive thick, dumpy fabric (Pl. 950). Bahadur Shah (1526–36) was able to overrun Malwa in 1530 and add it to his kingdom but it was not until 1572 that Gujarat lost its independence to the Moguls.

KASHMIR

Kashmir, although conquered by the Muhammadans in 1334, did not become part of the empire of the sultans of Delhi but remained an independent kingdom under its own rulers, the first of whom was Shams Shah (1334–7). Kashmir was temporarily subject to the Mogul Humayun between 1541 and 1551 when it regained its independence until Akbar in 1589 added it to his empire. Gold coinage of Kashmir of this period is not common but silver was issued in some quantity with the sultan's name, title and date on the obverse and the mint on the reverse. The silver coins are of an unusual, small square fabric with the reverse divided into a distinctive lozenge pattern (Pl. 951). The plentiful copper coinage also has a characteristic obverse for it is divided by a bar with a kind of double loop in the middle (Pl. 952).

THE MOGUL EMPERORS

The Mogul rulers who established a new empire in India in the mid sixteenth century were descendants of the Mongol Timur or Tamarlane who in the fourteenth century had conquered western Asia and even raided India as far as Delhi. Five generations after Timur, his descendant Babar, driven out of Transoxiana, settled in Afghanistan in 1505 and twenty years later began the invasion of India which terminated with the defeat and death of Ibrahim, Sultan of Delhi, at Panipat in 1526. Before he could consolidate his conquest Babar died in 1530 and his son, Humayun, after years of campaigning, was driven out by Sher Shah, the new Afghan sultan of Delhi in 1542. After thirteen years of exile in Sind, Humayun recovered his conquests and captured Delhi again, but was killed in 1556. The coinage of both Babar and Humayun is mainly of silver dirhems, similar in fabric and types to the Timurid coinage in western Asia (see p. 487). Some small gold pieces were also struck by Humayun and coppers by both Babar and Humayun.

The establishment of the Mogul empire proper dates from the accession in 1556 of Akbar, the son of Humayun. In his long reign he extended his rule successively over the provinces of north and central India and the conquest of the Deccan provinces in the early years of the seventeenth century carried Akbar's empire far to the south before his death in 1605. The political and military achievements of Akbar were matched by a coinage which in extent and quality is ranked amongst the great currencies of history. After a brief issue of coinage of the Timurid type of his predecessors Akbar introduced a coinage which, while new in the completeness of its system covering all metals, yet owed much to the coinage instituted by the Suri sultan, Sher Shah, in 1540. The principal silver coin and perhaps the most famous Mogul coin of all was the silver rupee, adopted from Sher Shah's system, and, like it, supplied with supplementary half-pieces and even lower divisions. Almost equally famous is the new goldpiece, the mohur, of which multiple pieces were also issued, though only very few have survived. The system was completed by issues of the copper dam which also had been first introduced by Sher Shah.

The early issues of Akbar perpetuate the inscriptional types which had been used on most of the earlier Delhi coinage, namely the Kalima and the names of the four early caliphs on the obverse and the name of Akbar with his title and laudatory epithets on the reverse. These inscriptions are contained in a variety of geometric outlines, and usually the date in the form of the Hegira year and always the mint name are included on the reverse legend. These issues were all of the usual round shape (Pl. 953) but this gave place to the square type of coin which is a recurrent feature throughout Indian coinage. The Ilahi or divine era of Akbar was introduced as a dating formula in 1584 and subsequent coins carry this new regnal date together with the name of the Persian solar month in which the coin was struck. Coin types also were changed and after 1579 have the new inscription *Allahu Akbar* on the obverse (Pl. 954), expanded to *Allahu Akbar jalla jalalahu* on some later silver issues. On the coinage from some mints the inscriptions took the form of a distich or poetic couplet, as on some Persian issues, incorporating mention of the names of the emperor and the mint. A few very rare gold issues are notable for the use of a figure type on the obverse, a hawk on a mohur struck at Asir, a duck on a mohur from Agra and, on a half-mohur of the mint at Lahore, the standing figures of Sita and Rama (Pl. 955).

On earlier Muhammadan coinages in India the name of the mint had not invariably found a place in the inscriptions but in the issues of Akbar and on the Mogul coinage generally the mint is more often recorded than not. The steady territorial extension of Akbar's empire was accompanied by an expansion of the mints for his coinage and something over twenty mints are recorded as active in his reign. The presence on the coinage of a combination of mint name and date on the majority of the coins provides useful supplementary evidence for the history of the expansion of Akbar's empire.

Impressive as is Akbar's coinage in its broad sweep and its vastness, it nevertheless yields pride of place to the issues of his successor, Jahangir (1605–28), on the score of interest and artistic merit. The great amount of copper coinage struck by Akbar and earlier sultans of Delhi presumably were sufficient for currency needs, for copper issues by Jahangir are less common but gold and silver were struck in some profusion, in great variety and in both the round and square forms. The early issues of the gold mohur and the silver rupee and their half-pieces had the traditional Kalima on obverse and the emperor's name and titles on the reverse but these types were soon replaced by a couplet legend. A third variety, introduced about 1611 and continuing at most mints till the end of the reign, placed Jahangir's name on the obverse and the date, including the month, as on Akbar's coinage, and the mint on the reverse. For some years the silver rupees of the mint of Agra were struck in alternate months in the round and square form.

An unusual feature of some of Jahangir's issues is the association in the couplet legend of the name of the empress Nur Jahan with that of the emperor. The best of the ordinary issues of Jahangir are outstanding for the distinction and beauty of their calligraphy (Pl. 956) but they are eclipsed by two special series of mohurs. The first in the years between 1611 and 1614 present, most exceptionally on Islamic coins, a series of portraits, mostly of Jahangir himself. One coin, probably unique, shows a three-quarter facing turbanned bust of Akbar with a sun on the reverse (Pl. 957). Jahangir himself with his head in a sort of nimbus is represented by a profile bust with long moustaches, turbanned head and ornate dress, while the reverse has a lion with sun above, very similar to the type on coins of the Seljuks of Rum some centuries before (Pl. 958). On one variety Jahangir holds up a fruit in his left hand and in another a wine-goblet. Yet another issue portrays the emperor seated cross-legged on his throne and holding up wine-goblet on the obverse with either lion and sun or sun only at the centre of inscriptions on the reverse (Pl. 959). In 1618 Jahangir began the issue of his famous Zodiac coins on which the obverse carried the sign of the Zodiac of the particular month in which the coin was issued (Pl. 960). Mohurs of this class were struck up to 1622, principally at the mint of Agra, and rupees only for a portion of 1618 at the mint of Ahmadabad, though sporadic pieces from a few other mints are also recorded.

Mogul coinage, particularly in the form of the silver rupee, continued to be prolific in the reigns of subsequent rulers whose names, because of their impingement on British history, are many of them familiar, such as Aurangzib and Shah Alam in whose reign the Treaty of Allahabad in 1765 ended the reality of the Mogul empire, though the outward form in the person of a puppet Mogul emperor was maintained until the Indian mutiny in 1857. Mohurs and rupees of the later emperors had either the traditional Kalima and title types or more usually a couplet type (Pl. 961).

The policy of farming out the mints which was adopted by Farrukhsiyar (1713–19) marked the end of the monolithic coinage system of the Moguls. The coinage of states acknowledging the nominal suzerainty of the Mogul emperor, and the Mogul-type coinage struck both by the British East India Company and other Europeans in India requires a separate section for adequate discussion.

EUROPEAN COINAGE IN INDIA

The first European expedition to reach India was that of the Portuguese under Vasco da Gama who in 1497 sailed round the Cape of Good Hope and across the Indian Ocean to Calicut, and by the early sixteenth century the first Portuguese settlement was established at Goa. The Portuguese initiative was followed later in the century by the Dutch, French, English and Danes, but it was only in the seventeenth century that trading companies of these powers set up their factories or trading settlements on Indian territory. The political and commercial rivalries of these powers and the consequent wars in Europe had their repercussions on the trading undertakings in India. The wars of the eighteenth century and the Napoleonic wars brought the elimination of the Dutch and French settlements and with the exception of the small Portuguese possessions in Goa the English were left to exercise complete commercial and, finally, political control of the whole of India until the middle of the present century.

The earliest European coinage in India was that of the Portuguese who in the early sixteenth century, in the reign of Emmanuel (1500–21), struck a coinage of half-cruzados in gold with the inscription *Meia* (half) surmounted by a crown on obverse and a globe on the reverse. Gold coinage of John III (1521–57) has a figure of St. Thomas, the legendary early missionary to India, with the inscription *India Tibi Cessit,* while silver coinage of Sebastian I (1557–78) has a figure of St.

Sebastian. No special coinage was issued for Goa while Portugal was under Spanish rule in the later sixteenth and seventeenth centuries but this Spanish connection made familiar in India the ubiquitous coinage of silver reales, particularly the major piece of eight reales. From the eighteenth century onwards the coinage for Goa has consisted of the silver rupia and its portions with types the royal portrait and arms of Portugal (Pl. 962) as well as coinage in copper and other base alloys of the tanga of 60 reis and smaller divisionary pieces. Since 1910 when Portugal became a republic the rupia types have been the arms of Portugal and the broad-ended cross with globe at centre, and on tanga coins the Portuguese arms and the *quinas* shield.

Two series of coinage are associated with the activities of the Dutch trading settlements in India established at Pulicat, Negapatam and Masulipatam in the seventeenth century. The extensive series struck in the Netherlands for the Dutch East India Company, the *Vereenigde Oost-Indische Compagnie* for general circulation in the East consisted in the eighteenth century of ducatoons, guilder and stuiver denominations in silver with the identical types used on the provincial series in the Netherlands (see p. 274) with a monogram of the initials of the company VOC below the reverse type, as well as copper doits with provincial arms on obverse and the company's monogram on the reverse (Pl. 1038). A second series consisted of coinage of local types. Gold pagodas known as Porto Novo pagodas were struck at Negapatam in the seventeenth century with a four-armed deity with the Garuda bird to left and disk with lotus below to the right on the obverse and a convex reverse with granulated surface (Pl. 963). Various copper cash denominations had the company's monogram on obverse and an inscription in Nagari or Tamil on the reverse. At Masulipatam pagodas in the late seventeenth and early eighteenth centuries were of the 'three swami' type with three crowned, standing deities on the obverse and a finely granulated reverse. Pulicat, the last Dutch possession in India, passed into British hands in 1824.

For the Danish possession of Tranquebar on the Coromandel coast, obtained in 1620, coinage was struck from the later seventeenth century in the form of copper cash with obverse type the royal monogram, crowned, and the trading company's initials DOC in monogram on the reverse. Gold pagodas in the eighteenth century had the usual Hindu deity on obverse and at the centre of a granulated reverse the royal monogram, crowned. The silver royalin and its double with monogram-and-value types was added in the later eighteenth century. These silver coins and copper cash were struck in the nineteenth century also, until the cession of Tranquebar to the British East India Company in 1845.

For the French settlement at Pondicherry silver fanams were struck in the eighteenth century with a crown on obverse and five lis on the reverse, as well as copper cash with lis obverse and the name of Pondicherry in Tamil on the reverse. The last issues made in 1836 consisted of silver fanams with cock and crown types and copper cash with types, the Gallic cock on obverse and the date on the reverse. Gold pagodas copying local types were also struck as well as silver rupees of Mogul type with the name of the mint of Arcot. These Arcot rupees copy issues of Mogul emperors from Muhammad (1719–48) with a crescent as a differential mark. The series extends from 1736 to 1839 except for the periods 1761–3 and 1793–1817 when Pondicherry was in English hands.

The British series, extending as it did from 1600 to 1947, is the most extensive European coinage in India. After the success of the early voyages to India, of which the first was in 1591, a Charter was granted to the East India Company by Elizabeth I in 1600 and a special coinage was produced for the company's trade. Because of the supremacy of the Spanish silver coinage in international commerce this new coinage was struck in silver in denominations equivalent to the Spanish 8, 4, 2 and 1 real pieces. The types were the royal arms crowned and a crowned portcullis (Pl. 964). The issue met with little success and over two centuries elapsed before another regal coinage for general circulation in India was produced. In the intervening years coinage of a variety of types and systems was issued on the initiative of the company in the several 'presidencies' under its control.

The three principal trading centres established by the East India Company in the first half of the seventeenth century were in Bengal, at Masulipatam near the mouth of the Godavari on the east coast and at Surat on the west coast. Masulipatam was replaced by Madras after 1640 and Bombay, acquired from Portugal in 1661 as part of the dowry of Charles II's queen, Catherine of Braganza, took the place of Surat. The coinage of gold pagodas at Madras is recorded about 1661 but the exact south Indian types imitated are not yet accurately identified, while the silver fanams with two interlinked C's as type (Pl. 965), traditionally assigned to the reign of Charles II, are now considered to have continued into the eighteenth century. The mint in Bombay became active only in 1671, striking a coinage with a five-line inscription on the reverse and copper pice with similar types were also struck. Silver rupees with types, on obverse a shield containing three ships and the royal arms above and on reverse *Pax Deo* in the field and *Moneta Bombaiensis* around, followed about 1700.

The coinage of Madras in the eighteenth century included further issues of gold pagodas with Hindu deity on obverse and a granulated reverse with a five-pointed star (Pl. 966). Other pagodas, still with granulated reverse, had on obverse the 'three swami' type, that is three crowned deities, standing. At Bombay a coinage of pice, the double and the half with rough designs depicting a crown with GR above and *Bomb* below on obverse and an inscription *Auspicio Regis et Senatus*

Angliae on the reverse was issued in both an undated and a dated series which runs from 1717 to 1771. There followed a series of copper pice from 1772 to 1783 with crown and *Bomb* on obverse and on reverse the company's bale-mark, a heart-shaped design divided diagonally into compartments containing the company's initials V.E.I.C. and surmounted by a mark like the figure **4** (Pl. 967). At the end of the eighteenth century copper coins of 20, 15, 10 and 5 cash, dated 1791 and 1794 with bale-mark on obverse and scales on the reverse, were machine struck as distinct from the rougher, hammer-struck coins of the preceding series. In the early eighteenth century Bombay also took up the minting of silver rupees of Mogul type.

In addition to these several series which have, most of them, clear indications of their issue by the East India Company a number of issues of Mogul type coinage, mostly silver rupees, was produced by the company. The segregation of these coinages and their attribution to mints is not always immediately obvious and presents some difficulties.

As early as 1691 silver rupees and rarer gold pagodas with the types of the Mogul emperor Aurangzib were struck with the mint signature of China-patam, the native name for Madras. Rupees of Chinapatam from 1707, the first year of the emperor Bahadur, carry on the reverse an additional five-pointed star, similar to that on the pagodas attributed to Madras. Another series of rupees with the name of Arcot have the types of Alamgir II (1754–9) but all bear the date of his regnal year 6 and the Hegira date 1172, i.e. 1758–9. This series has on the reverse the lotus-like trisul or trident of Siva and, despite the references contained on the coins, was issued at Madras (Pl. 968). In the presidency of Bombay, Mogul type coinage, again chiefly silver rupees, began to be issued in the reign of Farrukhsiyar (1713–19) whose types are copied. This series continued with copies of coins of succeeding emperors into the reign of Shah Alam, the mint signature in all cases being in the form Mumbai.

In Bengal gold and silver coinage of Mogul type was struck after 1765 at the mint of Calcutta, though the coinage of Shah Alam (1759–1806) which was chosen for copying has the name of the mint of Murshidabad. The coinage of mohurs and rupees struck by the company's mint at Benares presents another variety of the fossilized date such as that noted on the 'Arcot' coins of Madras. The reason for this phenomenon lies in the practice of the moneychangers of deducting a percentage, 'batta', on other than recently issued coins and this 'freezing' was designed to conceal the real date of issue. The Benares coinage copied the coinage of regnal year 26 of Shah Alam but strangely enough, although the regnal year remained fossilized, the Hegira year continued to be changed so that combinations of regnal year and Hegira date range from 6/1203 to 6/1233.

In the early nineteenth century the issue of Mogul-type mohurs and rupees by the company's mints was continued. The 'Arcot' coins from Madras, still with their fossilized date, now had as distinguishing mark the lotus-like trisul or trident of Siva and were struck by machinery in a more Europeanized fabric, complete with milled edge (Pl. 969). An identical issue was made from the mint at Calcutta which had as its differential a rose in place of the trisul. The issues from Bombay replaced the signature Mumbai by that of Surat and used as a differential mark a small crown which was replaced by a four-dot then a five-dot ornament before the introduction of machine-struck coins. The Calcutta coinage with the signature of Murshidabad and marked with the frozen date 19 San of Shah Alam II were also produced in a Europeanized fabric with milled edge from 1793.

In the nineteenth century Madras still issued the pagoda in gold as well as the pagoda and its quarter in silver with an actual pagoda as type and the value in English on obverse and a Hindu deity and inscription in Tamil on the reverse (Pl. 970). A range of silver fanams was also struck. Copper cash of values 20 and lower were issued in 1803 with types the company's arms on obverse and the value in Persian and English on the reverse. Other copper coins in 1807 had the value in Persian script on obverse and in Talugi and Tamil on the reverse. Copper pice at Bombay have the company's arms and scales as types (Pl. 971). The arms of the Company and the value appear on copper pice at Benares and later on divisionary pieces of the anna.

In 1835 the East India Company began a universal coinage for the whole of India with a series of rupees and portions carrying the portrait and titles of William IV on obverse and the value within a wreath accompanied by the Company's name (Pl. 972). A similar issue was struck in the name of Victoria in 1840 The authority of the East India Company was superseded by that of the Crown, following the uprisings of 1857, and thereafter coinage, first issued in 1862, is of purely regal type, the name of the East India Company disappearing from the reverse. In addition to the silver-rupee coinage, copper coins of a quarter-anna and lower were issued with similar portrait-and-value types. The main change in the coinage in Victoria's reign was the use of the title empress after 1877 (Pl. 973). The British imperial coinage in India maintained a conservatism of types under succeeding rulers but the metal of anna pieces was changed to nickel under George VI and some values were issued with a rectangular or a scalloped outline. On the final rupee issues in 1946 and 1947 a new reverse type of a tiger was adopted (Pl. 974).

INDEPENDENT STATES

The authority of the Mogul empire began to decline after the reign of Aurangzib (1659–1707) and the history of India in the eighteenth and nineteenth centuries is one of a multitude of independent states, the majority of which issued their own coinage; and the historical and numismatic picture is further complicated by British intervention which eventually either absorbed these states or permitted their survival as subject allies. The majority of the coinages of these states derive at least their initial inspiration from the Mogul issues, though many subsequently developed more individual types. In this section it will be possible to deal with only some of the more important of these coinages as illustrations of the more general numismatic history of India in this period.

MYSORE

Coinage in Mysore in south India had consisted of gold pagodas with Hindu deity or deities on obverse and inscribed reverse, as well as copper pieces with elephant on obverse and a kind of chequer-board reverse. In 1760 Haidar Ali had usurped Mysore from the Wodeyar dynasty and gold pagodas of local fabric were struck with Haidar Ali's initial on the reverse but this soon became the obverse type with the year and date in Persian on the reverse. The coinage of his son and successor, Tipu Sultan (1782–99), though including gold pagodas of similar type was of an inscriptional character, similar to the Mogul series. Tipu coined the mohur and its half in gold, and in silver the rupee with its double and a whole range of divisionary pieces from a variety of mints of which the most important was Seringapatam. On copper pieces of values from 40 downwards Tipu adopted the elephant device of earlier Mysore coins for the obverse, while the reverse gives the mint and denomination (Pl. 975). With the defeat of Tipu in 1799 Britain was left in supreme control of the Deccan.

OUDH

In 1720 Muhammad Amin, appointed subahdar of Oudh by the Mogul emperor Muhammad Shah, made himself an independent ruler. His descendants, the nawabs of Oudh, controlled the Mogul mint at Benares and its coinage of rupees, still nominally in the name of the emperor. Though Benares was ceded to the East India Company in 1775, coinage with the mint name of Benares continued to be issued by the nawabs. These rupees have as a distinguishing characteristic a small fish and were probably struck in Lucknow the new capital of the nawabs. In 1818 the nawab Ghaziu-d-din Haidar assumed the title of king and began an issue of regal coinage which lasted down to 1856. On mohurs, rupees and copper pieces the obverse is entirely inscriptional but on the reverse at the centre of inscriptions is a figure type in the form of a coat of arms which takes several forms in the various reigns. Under Ghaziu two fish face each other surmounted by a crown, with above two tigers holding pennants, while on coins of the last king, Wajid Ali (1847–56), two mermaids hold clubs and pennants with crown above and crossed swords below (Pl. 976).

BARODA

In western India the Maratha state of Baroda became independent under a ruler with the title of Gaekwar and coinage was struck from the early nineteenth century. The early issues were of silver rupees and copper pice with Persian inscriptions and with a distinctive mark of a scimitar incorporated. Baroda was one of the states permitted to continue coinage after the creation of the British empire in India. Silver rupees had a portrait of the Gaekwar on the obverse and inscription in a wreath on the reverse. Copper pice with inscriptions on both sides still had the distinctive scimitar sign on the obverse.

BIKANIR

The rulers of Bikanir in Rajputana struck coinage of silver rupees and copper from about 1760 of the usual Mogul type with the addition of a series of special distinguishing marks. In 1893 Bikanir was one of the states which issued coinage of silver rupees and copper anna and pice divisionary pieces with portrait of Victoria on the obverse and the name of the local ruler in Nagari and Persian on the reverse.

GWALIOR

Gwalior in central India reached a position of semi-independence in the later eighteenth century and in the reign of Daulat Rao (1794–1824) rupees and pice were issued in the name of the Mogul Muhammad Akbar. On rupees of similar type issued by his successors the reverse inscription is accompanied by a distinguishing symbol like a bow and arrow and copper pice have the trisul or trident of Siva on one side and a spear-head and three-pronged sceptre on the other. In 1893, when coinage in silver by native mints was ended, subsequent issues in

1889–91 of copper half-pice and quarter-annas had as types a coiled cobra with sceptre and trident and the ruler's name and value in Nagari. Quarter-annas from 1913 have had the ruler's portrait on obverse and his arms on reverse with the value in both Nagari and Persian.

INDORE

The Maratha state of Indore came into being under the Holkar dynasty in the mid eighteenth century and a coinage of silver rupees was begun by Ahalya Bai, the queen regent (1765–95). These rupees with the legends of the Mogul emperor Shah Alam were struck at the mint of Maheswar, which has as mark a small leaf, and at Indore or Malharnagar which marked its issues with a sun-face. On copper half-annas of Tukoji Rao II (1844–86) the bull badge of Indore appears on the reverse. Sivaji Rao (1886–1903) issued rupees with his portrait on obverse and on reverse his arms, a rampant horse and bull with sun-face above. The copper half-anna and lower values show the recumbent bull on obverse with the ruler's name and title and the value on the reverse (Pl. 977). Silver coinage was ended in 1902 but small copper denominations continued to be struck in the present century with portrait-and-value types.

HYDERABAD

The nizams of Hyderabad struck silver and gold in the emperor's name with the addition of their own initials but, after 1857, on both the gold ashrafi and the silver rupee the Mogul emperor's name finally was displaced by that of the nizam. Between 1903 and 1911 mohurs and rupees acquired new types, the minareted Char Minar on obverse and a central inscription with elaborate marginal inscription on the reverse (Pl. 978). Copper pice and half-annas had a similar reverse and a tughra obverse. Rupees and coppers of similar types were continued by the nizam, Mir Usman Ali Khan, from 1911 up to 1944.

SIKH LEAGUE

In the north-west a Sikh League was formed to oppose the Persian incursions of Nadir Shah in 1739 and the Afghan Durrani, Shah Ahmad (1748–67), and his successors. Rupees with Persian couplet-type inscription were struck by the League between 1764 and 1777. Silver rupees of the Sikhs in the Punjab issued by mints at Amritsar and Lahore under Ranjit Singh (1799–1839) are of the Persian couplet type but are not inscribed with his name but bear the leaf symbol which distinguishes the Sikh coinage (Pl. 979). Other issues were made from Multan and

Kashmir. Later issues roughly inscribed in Gurmukhi, a Punjabi form of Nagari, were mainly in copper and usually carry the leaf mark. Coinage ended with the annexation of the Punjab in 1849.

NEPAL

Coinage in Nepal in the sixteenth and seventeenth centuries consists of pieces of half-rupee weight with types ultimately derived from the Mogul coinage. The coins have a central square or circle with an elaborately ornamented border. The king's name and title in Nagari appear on the obverse and other formulae and symbols on the reverse. Coinage with similar types was continued after the Gurkha conquest of Nepal in 1768 but included full rupees, and in the nineteenth century gold mohurs and copper coinage with like types were added. In the present century gold and silver coins have been struck with the traditional types (Pl. 980) but on various paisa or pice values in copper a central type, two crossed Gurkha knives, has been adopted. On cupro-nickel rupees of Trivhuvana Vira Vikrama in 1953–4 the ruler's portrait appeared for the first time on the obverse on Nepalese coins and the sun rising behind Mount Everest on the reverse.

AFGHANISTAN

Coinage issued in Afghanistan has been touched upon in the chapter on Muhammadan coinage in the Near Eastern section but a modern-type coinage was introduced under Abd-el-Rahman (1879–1901). On silver rupees with multiples of five as well as divisionary pieces and on copper paisa the usual types are a throne-room on obverse and Tughra on reverse (Pl. 981). A gold denomination known as the amani with similar types was added by Amanullah (1919–29). The principal silver coin in the present system is the afghani, presenting still the throne-room and tughra types. The throne-room appears also on the divisionary coins in base metals for the pul values (100 pul = 1 afghani) but the reverse carries either an inscription or the value in Arabic numerals.

REPUBLICS OF INDIA AND PAKISTAN

When independence was restored by Britain to India in 1947 the sub-continent was divided into two separate states of which the larger, mainly Hindu, retained the name of India, while a smaller state, predominantly Islamic in faith, formed of the north-western provinces together with East Bengal, adopted the name of

Pakistan. The new Dominion of India continued to use coinage identical with the last issues made for British India until the formation of the Republic of India in 1950. The obverse on all denominations of the new coinage has as type the three-lion capital of the Asoka column at Sarnath with inscription *Government of India* in English. The reverse of the rupee, its half and quarter in nickel is the value between two corn-ears while on the 2, 1 and ½ anna coins in nickel the reverse is a humped bull and on the bronze paisa or pice a galloping horse. The new decimal coinage of rupee and paisa makes use of similar types (Pl. 982).

On the coinage of Pakistan the obverse type is a tughra with inscription *Government of Pakistan* in English on all denominations. The reverse of the nickel rupee, its half and quarter is the value in words, surmounted by a crescent and star (Pl. 983). The same reverse was used on the copper-nickel 2 annas and 1 anna coins, the former with a square outline, the latter with fluted edges. The bronze pice, because of its central piercing, had only inscriptions on either side. On new anna, half-anna and pice coins introduced in 1953 the Tughra and crescent and star are combined on the obverse, while the reverse carries the value within a wreath or between two corn-ears. A decimal coinage based on a rupee of 100 paisa was issued in 1961.

CEYLON

Considerations both of geography and history commend placing the sketch of the coinage of Ceylon in this section; for the island lies off the south-east coast of the sub-continent, its history is closely linked with that of south India and its coinage, in almost all periods, follows a pattern not unlike that of India, with the notable exception that the Muhammadan invasions and conquests, which play such a great rôle in India from the thirteenth century onwards, did not extend to Ceylon.

The earliest form of coinage in ancient Ceylon is the purana or flat silver piece stamped with a varying number of small punches representing a whole range of objects. The antiquity of these 'punch-marked' coins remains the subject of dispute but, as in the mainland of India, they may have begun to circulate about the same time as coinage began in the Mediterranean area and certainly were current in the last three centuries B.C. and into the first century A.D. From this class of coinage developed coins on which the various symbols on the punch-marked pieces are united into a single design and small silver pieces, both rectangular and round, are found with such a type struck from a die on one side of the coin only. Some examples of this coinage are in copper also but the more common ancient copper pieces are large, circular coins with a type on both sides. On the obverse the main type is an elephant with symbols above, usually a swastika on a staff surrounded by a railing, a three-branched tree in an enclosure and a *chaitya* or temple. The reverse repeats the swastika and the *chaitya* of the obverse and adds other smaller symbols (Pl. 984). Other less common, smaller copper pieces have a maneless lion on obverse and four dots in a circle on the reverse. A series of roughly rectangular plaques, both cast and struck, with a standing figure of the goddess Lakshmi on one side and the swastika within railing of the coins just described on the other, may also possibly have been used as currency. These several bronze coinages were in use in parallel with the silver 'punch-marked' coins and probably continued to be current till about the sixth or seventh century.

The widespread use of Roman imperial aurei and denarii as either currency or bullion in south India finds a parallel in Ceylon, though on a much reduced scale; and then almost entirely restricted to the earlier period of emperors from Augustus to Nero. Roman and Byzantine gold from the later fourth to the sixth centuries, noted in south India, is found only rarely in Ceylon but small Roman bronze coins from the time of Constantine the Great to the later fifth century are probably more numerous in finds in Ceylon. These types of Roman bronze coins were also widely imitated in the island (Pl. 985) up to the seventh century.

Little is known of the sixth and seventh centuries, the 'Dark Ages' of Ceylon, and the record thereafter for many centuries is of successive invasions by Pandyan and Chola kings of south India, interspersed by occasional successful invasions of south India on the part of Singhalese rulers. In any event, the earliest coinage of mediaeval Ceylon is placed no earlier than the later years of the ninth century and in the tenth century. This is a coinage in gold of which the major piece is the kahavanu with, as fractional pieces, the deka or pala and the even smaller aka. These coins generally carry no regal names or titles. The obverse of the kahavanu shows the figure of Vishnu standing on a lotus plant, holding a flower before his face in the left hand and stretching out the right over a fire-altar or lamp. A similar figure on the reverse squats on a bed-like throne and holds a flower-like object in the left hand (Pl. 986). On the deka or pala a standing figure, possibly Lakshmi, holds in her left hand a vase from which springs a plant but the reverse has only an inscription. The figure on the obverse sometimes holds a lotus in the left hand. Similar types also appear on the smaller aka.

During the Tamil occupation of the northern part of the island in the first part of the eleventh century Singhalese coinage appears to have ceased but gold kahavanus inscribed *Sri Vijaya Bahu* are ascribed to Vijaya Bahu I (1055–1111) as well as similar pieces in base gold or white metal. Under subsequent rulers down to Parakrama Bahu VI (1415–67) the principal coinage takes the form of a development of the kahavanu with steadily degenerating types and in base metal only (Pl. 987). One other series of bronze coins which circulated in Ceylon was that of the kingdom of Jaffna. These coins, dating to the late thirteenth and early fourteenth centuries, have on obverse a recumbent bull surmounted by a crescent and dot and a very crude version of the standing figure on contemporary Singhalese coins.

The first Europeans to secure possessions in Ceylon were the Portuguese who first landed there in 1506, and the whole of the island was under Portuguese control by the end of the century. About the middle of the century the Dutch began to wrest possession of the ports from the Portuguese who were finally driven out in 1658. In the period of Portuguese domination no coinage was struck by the Singhalese. The currencies in use in the sixteenth century were silver larins, the small, thin bars of silver, sometimes turned up at the end like a fish-hook (Pl. 988). The use of this type of coin, originally produced and used in the Persian gulf area and taking its name from the town of Lar, had spread to the eastern sea-board of India and to the Maldive Islands and become one of the chief trading currencies in the Indian Ocean. Gold and silver fanams from south India also had currency as well as European coinages such as the Spanish piece of eight and the Venetian sequin. The silver tangas or double tangas, struck in or for Ceylon by the Portuguese, date from the last few decades of Portuguese domination. The obverse is consistently the crowned arms of Portugal dividing the letters of the mint, e.g. C – L for Colombo, while the common reverse types are the gridiron of St. Lawrence or the standing figure of John the Baptist between the letters S – I (Pl. 989).

The Dutch held Ceylon from 1658 until it was seized in 1795–6 by Britain, whose possession of the island was confirmed by the Treaty of Amiens in 1802. The same admixture of south Indian and European coinages as under the Portuguese continued to pass current, together with the more recent Portuguese tangas, many of which were countermarked with the initials of the Dutch East India Company, the Vereenigde Oost-Indische Compagnie, VOC in monogram (Pl. 989). Towards the end of the seventeenth century a series of thick copper coins of 1 and 2 stuivers in value was struck at Colombo and Jaffna. The type was identical on both sides, a wreath enclosing the abbreviated value, e.g. 1 ST. The next issue of Dutch coinage for Ceylon took place almost a century later. In 1784 an exceptional coinage of silver rupees was struck with inscriptions in Malay Arabic on either side and the date in Western numerals. The earliest of several issues in copper was that in 1783 of the doit or quarter-stuiver with types, the Company's monogram, surmounted by the mint letter C for Colombo on obverse and the value ¼ ST on reverse. A series of copper stuivers and double stuivers between 1783 and 1795 has similar types to those of the doit, except that the denomination on the reverse is written in full, e.g. 1 STUIVER and is accompanied by the date (Pl. 990). These coins carry on obverse the initial letters of mints at Colombo, Galle, Trincomalee and Jaffna. The doit was also struck in lead with monogram obverse and a tree dividing the value or the value only on the reverse.

The Dutch monetary system of a rix-dollar or rijksdaalder of 48 stuivers was continued by the British in the early nineteenth century. The types were identical on all denominations, an elephant with date below on the obverse and on the reverse the value expressed in stuivers with a circular inscription *Government of Ceylon* (Pl. 991). Pieces of 96, 48 and 24 stuivers were struck in silver and of 48, 24 and 12 stuivers in copper. These copper coins are of a thick, dumpy fabric and fluctuate greatly in weight. The silver rix-dollar of George IV in 1821, the first British regal coinage struck for Ceylon, had the royal portrait and titles on the obverse and the elephant and value on the reverse. In the reign of William IV and the first decades of Victoria's reign the small silver three-halfpenny was produced for circulation in Ceylon. The types were similar to the Maundy coins, the royal portrait on obverse and the value crowned within a wreath on the reverse (Pl. 992). The half- and quarter-farthing with the same types as the English farthing were also struck for Ceylon in these reigns (Pl. 993).

In 1892 a new coinage with royal portrait obverse and a palm-tree and value reverse was introduced with denominations of 50, 25 and 10 cents in silver (Pl. 994) and values from 5 cents to a quarter-cent in copper. These types were continued under Edward VII and George V but the palm-tree disappeared from the higher values of George VI. The title emperor was omitted from the royal style on coins struck for Ceylon after its independence was restored in 1947. The last coinage of Ceylon with the portrait of a British monarch was the brass 2 cents issue with scalloped edge in 1955 with the portrait of Elizabeth II.

THE FAR EAST

★

The Far East

THE coinage considered in this section is that of the land-mass of Asia east of India, together with the islands of the Indian Archipelago and Japan. Only one series, the Chinese, is commensurate in its historical duration with the coinages of India, western Asia and Europe, for early currency in most other areas of the Far East takes a primitive form and coinage, in the accepted definition of the term, begins much later and tends to be sporadic. A number of Far Eastern coinages have certain characteristics in common: until relatively modern times they usually were cast from moulds and not struck from dies and were provided with a round or square hole at the centre to permit of their being strung together; certain series, particularly the Chinese, Japanese, Korean and Annamese, are notable for the conservatism of their basic types over long periods of centuries. In the islands of the East Indies and the several states of Farther India and Malaya the establishment of European colonies brought, at various dates from the seventeenth century onwards, coinages of European type and even in the countries of the Farther East which were never subject to European control coinage of European pattern finally displaced the age-old forms of coinage in the late nineteenth century.

CHINA

The well-known claim that the Chinese anticipated by many centuries the invention in the Western world of such things as gunpowder and printing has its parallel in the history of coinage; for ancient Chinese authorities have placed the use of a metallic coinage in China as early as the twentieth century B.C. Whatever the justice of the claims may be in other fields, modern research has not been able to to confirm the existence of true coinage in Chinese civilization earlier than the seventh century B.C. The invention of coinage, then, would seem to be of almost equal antiquity in the West, in India and in the Far East. Coinage in China in the first few centuries is remarkable for the variety of its shapes, but in the course of the third century B.C. Chinese coinage, which, with rare exceptions, is always in copper, acquired its characteristic circular shape with

537

a square hole in the centre which it maintained in essentials for over two thousand years until the late nineteenth century. The development of this, the most homogeneous coinage in the world, is traced mainly in the changing fashion of the inscription on obverse and reverse. Coinage, Westernized both in respect of its system and its fabric, has, since the late nineteenth century, introduced some greater variety into the Chinese issues.

SPADE, WEIGHT OR PU MONEY

China is unique in having preserved in its coinage a stage of monetary development of which only vestiges have survived in other civilizations. The intermediate stage between the barter system of primitive civilization and the general acceptance of metal coins of standard weight stamped with a guaranteeing device produced a coinage—if the term can here be properly used—which consisted of replicas in bronze of the actual agricultural spades which in the earlier period were used for barter. The use of these objects as money has been dated to the early part of the seventh century B.C. and their circulation continued down to the fourth century B.C. These copies of spades have a hollow handle and the shoulders of the spade are square. The most primitive examples have only three lines on either side but more developed specimens are inscribed on the obverse with characters which represent place names or serial signs. Although the place names are of doubtful identification the use of this spade money is associated with northern China.

The pu money, to some examples of which the description weight money is sometimes applied since the characters it bears indicate its weight, is in general terms similar to the spade money, though differing in detail. Pu money is much smaller; it has a flat handle and the shoulders of the spade are sometimes round, sometimes angular and the foot of the spade is indented by either a curve or an angular nick. Like the spade money, pu money usually has characters inscribed on the face only and where these characters represent identifiable place names the area where this form of money was in use is again seen to be north China and more specifically the modern provinces of Shantung, Shansi and Honan. The reverses are frequently plain but sometimes carry the three straight lines as on the spade money or characters representing serial numbers (Pl. 995). Despite the seemingly more developed form which the pu money takes, it too has been ascribed to the period between the seventh and fourth centuries B.C.

Of equal antiquity, that is of the period between the seventh and fourth centuries B.C., is another series of money again small copies of objects used in barter, this time knives. This knife money of cast bronze consists of a slightly curved blade and handle with a ring at the end. The very earliest examples are, like the earliest spade money, uninscribed but most have, on both front and back, characters which indicate the place or province in which they were current and sometimes the value. The areas of currency were again provinces in northern China, principally Shantung and Chihli. The earlier series of knife money was about seven inches long, the later series only about five inches or less. Of the smaller variety a very extensive series bears the name of the city of Ming in the province of Shansi, the modern Chihli (Pl. 996).

Of early coinage of unusual shape mention must be made of the copy in metal of the cowrie which, according to tradition, was issued by the prime minister of the king of Tsu (south Honan) about 600 B.C.

ANCIENT ROUND MONEY

Both the antiquity and the identification of the most ancient forms of round money is debatable. It is questionable whether the most primitive forms, consisting merely of a copper ring with a round hole in the centre, can be classed as coins at all and, since some are completely devoid of inscription or have, at best, only an indication of weight, their attribution to locality and era must be dubious. The series of pieces with round hole which have a place name in addition to the weight in characters on the obverse only (Pl. 997) has more of an air of true coinage and where names have been identified they prove to be in the same area as the spade and knife money already discussed. Traditionally, however, this ancient round money with circular hole is said to have been current from the twelfth to the sixth centuries B.C., thus ante-dating the other ancient types of money.

The next stage in the development of this round money in bronze is represented by the series with a square hole at the centre in place of the circular hole. Some changes in fabric were to take place in the next few centuries but the form this developed in the sixth century B.C. remained the basic form of the bronze round money (Ch'ien or Tsien) until less than a century ago. The earliest examples of this form of round money in the sixth century B.C. have characters indicating value on the obverse only. On one series with the name of the city of Ming on obverse there still appears the word *tao*, 'knife', and presumably it is to be dated to the third century B.C. when the knife money of Ming was being replaced by the new round money.

The definite adoption of round money as the standard coinage dates from the establishment of the new Ch'in dynasty which overthrew the old Chou dynasty about the middle of the third century. The 'First Emperor' Shih Huang Ti (221–209) who built the Great Wall issued bronze coins inscribed with the weight *Pan Liang*, half an ounce or 12 shu (Pl. 998). This coinage of *Pan Liang*, continued under the Han dynasty which succeeded in 206 B.C., but suffered a gradual reduction and debasement. Under the empress Kao in 187 B.C. the weight had fallen to 8 shu, under Wen in 179 B.C. to 4 shu and finally to 3 shu under the emperor Wu in 140.

A coinage reform by the emperor Wu Ti in 118 B.C. demonetized the earlier coinage and substituted a piece of 5 shu, equipped now with a raised rim to prevent filing (Pl. 999). This Wu shu or 5 shu coinage remained the standard currency for some 8 centuries and the chronological arrangement of this series depends on calligraphic criteria. This coinage was issued by some nine regular and twenty-three irregular dynasties which ruled over the whole or parts of China successively or contemporaneously. Exceptions to the usual run of 5 shu coins were the large pieces struck by rulers of the Wu kingdom about A.D. 236 with nominal values of 500 and 1000 shu, and, in A.D. 256, the pieces with nominal value of 100 shu.

The only interruption in this series was the attempt by the usurper Wang Mang (A.D. 7–22) to revive pu and knife money. Both these classes of money are distinguishable from the ancient categories, for they are very much smaller, the pu money measuring only some inch-and-a-half, and the knife money about three inches (Pl. 1000).

NEW ROUND MONEY

Under the emperor Kao Tsu (618–627), the first emperor of the Tang dynasty (618–907), a new type of round money was introduced which gave the coinage of China the form it retained down to the end of the nineteenth century. This new coin, still known as the ch'ien or cash, continued to be cast in bronze. For transactions involving the use of a quantity of these coins, the coins were strung together through their central hole, a string of cash amounting, theoretically, to 100 ch'ien. In practice the number was usually 98 and the slightly lower total of 95 was known as a titsz. Ten strings of cash together made up a tiao, but in no bundle of ten strings might there be included more than two titsz (strings amounting only to 95 cash). The relation of the ch'ien to the tael or silver ounce varied in relation to the market price and the fineness of the silver, with the consequence that the tael might be worth anything from 700 to 2000 cash.

The new round money introduced by Kao Tsu was issued at a standard of ten coins to the liang or ounce of bronze. The inscription on the obverse consisted of four characters which are normally read in the order top, bottom, right and left. The top and bottom characters give the *nien hao* or regnal period, a practice which had been used earlier on the 100 ch'ien in 256 but had not been continued. The characters to right and left read *tung pao* or current money so that the full inscription reads 'the current money of the Kai Yuan period' and this is the formula which, with the requisite alteration of the regnal period, continued in use till the nineteenth century. The reverse of the early tung pao coins was frequently plain but sometimes carried a symbol such as a crescent (Pl. 1001). Tradition has it that on the first wax mould for this coinage the empress Wen Te placed her nail-mark which was later continued as a new moon or crescent. Later issues of Kai Yuan tung pao of the Tang dynasty sometimes have an additional character on the reverse indicating the mint, usually the capital, Layang in Honan.

Complete uniformity, however, was not maintained on the coinage throughout all the centuries, for most dynasties introduced some modification. The issues of the Sung dynasty (960–1280) were produced with three styles of writing, the orthodox, the running hand and the grass character. The coinage of the emperor Hsiao Tsung (1163–89) of the southern Sung dynasty has on the reverse, from the year 1180 to the end of the reign, numerals from seven to sixteen representing the emperor's regnal years. By the early twelfth century the empire of the Sung dynasty was reduced to southern China and the north which, from the early tenth century had been subject to Tatar invasions, was in the hands of the Tatar Chin dynasty with its capital in Peking. In 1213 the Mongols under Ghengis Khan captured Peking and north China and under his successors, notably Kublai Khan, the Mongol empire was extended over south China and Korea. The Mongol dynasty of Yuan issued very little copper money but such issues as there were, were inscribed with Mongol characters. Transactions in this period, as we learn from Marco Polo's account, were conducted with paper money which was extensively used.

Under the Ming dynasty (1368–1644) new heights of literary and artistic achievement were attained, territorial expansion resulted in the conquest of Assam and the sixteenth century saw the first European establishment in China, that of the Portuguese at Macao. The coinage, however, continued its conservative course. A kuan or string of cash now was made up of 400 cash and the coins themselves, with the traditional formula on the obverse, frequently had additional characters on the reverse indicating the place of minting and the value for in addition to the ordinary cash, pieces of value 2, 4, 5 and 10 were issued. The issues of the Ching dynasty (1644–1912) were, until 1900, mainly of the ordinary tung pao coins and, following the practice of the Ming coinage, bore on the reverse the name of the mint. The reverse character is in Manchu script while the obverse characters continue to be orthodox Chinese. In place of the ordinary names of places where coinage was struck the reverse of the coin frequently bears the character Hu, the Board of Revenue, or Kung, the Board of Works. In 1653 additional characters for 1 li or a thousandth part of the tael or ounce, indicating the value of the coin in silver, were added to the obverse and from about this time the reverse frequently gives the name of the mint in both Chinese and Manchu (Pl. 1002). In the financial straits caused by the Tai Ping rebellion between 1812 and 1864 recourse was had from 1851 to the issue of coins with nominal values of 5, 10, 50, 100, 200, 300, 400, 500 and even 1000 cash but the inevitable widespread forgery of these coins led to the abandonment of these large-value pieces under the emperor Kuang Hsu (1875–1900). The Tai Ping rebels who for a time occupied Nanking issued their own copper cash with characters indicating 'the celestial state' on one side and 'sacred currency' on the other and occasionally the character for Ming, the restoration of which dynasty was the professed object of the rebellion.

MODERN TYPE COINS OF THE EMPIRE

The centuries-old cash coinage made of cast bronze with a square hole at the centre was finally replaced in 1900 by a series of cash denominations in struck copper without any central piercing. This modernization of the copper cash coinage was in fact anticipated by a series of machine-struck coins in silver earlier in the nineteenth century. The earliest of the Chinese silver dollars so-called was not an imperial issue but was issued in Formosa during the revolution begun by Chang Wen in 1837. The types were the bust of the long-bearded god of longevity on obverse with characters indicating the reign of the emperor Tao Kwang and the value 7 mace and 2 candareens, while the reverse showed a sacrificial vase on three legs and Manchu characters giving the place of minting. A series of imperial silver coins struck at provincial mints for a range of provinces began issue in the last decade of the nineteenth century. In addition to the major piece the dollar of 7 mace and 3 candareens there were divisionary pieces of 50, 20, 10 and 5 cash. The types were uniform for all denominations apart from the statement of value. On the obverse in the centre four Chinese characters denote 'Valuable coin of the Kuang Hsu régime' and at the very centre are four smaller Manchu characters with the same meaning, while the circular inscription gives the province name and the value of the denomination. The reverse carries the imperial emblem, a flying dragon and a circular inscription in English giving the name of the province and the value (Pl. 1003). The first provincial series was struck for Kwantung (Canton) in 1889 and was followed by issues in other provinces in the next ten years.

This imperial provincial series in silver was accompanied by copper cash in denominations of 20, 10, 5 and 1 with similar types to those of the copper, usually incorporating at the centre of the obverse the provincial symbol. In the early years of the present century an issue of imperial coins by the central authority was produced in modern style. On the silver tael and denominations of 5, 2 and 1½ mace between 1903 and 1906 the obverse carried Chinese and Manchu characters as on the provincial silver, while the circular characters are the equivalent of the empire of China and the value. The reverse with flying-dragon type has inscription in Chinese and in English *Tai-Ching-Ti-Kuo Silver Coin*, i.e. imperial Chinese silver coin. A rare tael in gold was also struck in this issue. A silver dollar with like types but inscribed in English *One dollar* on the obverse was issued in 1907 and divisionary pieces of 50, 20 and 10 cents between 1907 and 1911. The issue was completed by coins of 20, 10, 5 and 1 cash in copper (Pl. 1004). A second series of copper cash with inscription *Hu Poo* and the cash denomination in English was issued by the authority of the Board of Revenue.

REPUBLIC OF CHINA

Revolution broke out in China in 1911; China was declared a republic in January 1912 and in February Hsuen Tung, the last Manchu emperor, abdicated. Despite the part played in the republican movement by Sun Yat Sen, the assembly at Peking elected Yuan Shih Kai the first president. The attempt of Yuan Shih Kai to have himself elevated to the position of emperor in 1915 miscarried but caused the revolt of Yunan and other southern provinces. Sun Yat Sen became president in 1921 and after his death in 1925 Chiang Kai Shek, as leader of the Kuomintang party, headed affairs until the Communist régime came to power in 1948. The coinage system remained much as it had been with the dollar and subsidiary pieces issued in silver and cash denominations in copper. The portrait of Sun Yat Sen was placed on the obverse of silver dollars and lower values in 1912 with a reverse inscribed in English *The Republic of China One Dollar*. The types on the copper cash in 1912 had the appropriate inscription in English on the reverse and crossed flags on the obverse; these types persisted on the 20 cash piece till 1922.

The first issue of the silver dollar for Yuan Shih Kai in 1912 showing his uniformed bust facing on obverse, and characters indicating the value 1 yuan at centre and a circular inscription giving the value, 1 dollar, in English. The issues for Yuan Shih Kai from 1914 on the dollar and lower values showed his profile bust on obverse and an open wreath enclosing characters on the reverse (Pl. 1005). The various changes of régime and separatist movements in the provinces have also found representation on coinage issues in modern China. The use of pictorial types on the reverse is seen on issues shortly before the last war. Silver dollars with portrait of Sun Yat Sen have a Chinese junk with spread sails on the reverse and other dollars and half-pieces have a representation of the ancient pu money as reverse type. Lower-value coins of cent denominations also use this reverse between 1935 and 1941 (Pl. 1006).

The Communist régimes in Hupeh, Anhwei and Honan in 1932 and in Szechuan and Shensi provinces in 1934 issued some silver dollars with hammer and sickle on globe as obverse type and propaganda inscription on the reverse. Copper coins in denominations of 500 and 200 cash had a hammer and sickle in a five-pointed star on obverse and value on reverse. The currency of Communist China consisted of paper money until the issue in 1955 of aluminium coins of 1, 2 and 5 fen with types five stars above a mausoleum on obverse and the value on the reverse.

The coinage of Nationalist China in Formosa, issued since 1949 in various values of the chiao in aluminium and bronze, has as types the portrait of Sun Yat Sen on obverse and a map of the island of Formosa on the reverse.

TIBET

China and, later on, Nepal have always provided for the wants of Tibet in regard to coinage and even from the eighteenth century when coins were struck in Tibet itself the influence of Nepalese and Chinese coinage is obvious. It had been the practice for bullion to be sent from Tibet to Nepal in exchange for coinage but after the advent of the Ghurka dynasty in Nepal (see p. 529) its currency proved not so acceptable and in the later eighteenth century silver coins were struck in Tibet itself. The types on these were derived from the Nepalese and had an eight-petalled flower at the centre surrounded by eight fleurets containing Buddhist emblems on the obverse and on the reverse a leaf-scroll design also surrounded by eight fleurets containing emblems. Between 1788 and 1793 degenerate copies of this coinage were issued. Resumed Chinese intervention in Tibet in 1793 was followed by a coinage of cast-silver pieces, copying the basic elements of the Tibeto-Nepalese coinage but with square at centre of the obverse surrounded by four fleurets and four Chinese characters. The reverse was of similar design but with Tibetan characters.

In the early years of the present century silver rupees and portions struck in the province of Szechuan for Tibet had the portrait of a mandarin on obverse and characters within a scroll wreath on the reverse. In 1909 new types appeared on the silver srang and on copper pieces of 2½ and 7½ skar. At the centre of the obverse was a Chinese lion surrounded by eight fleurets containing symbols, while the reverse, with a symbol at the centre, had a surround of inscription and outside this, on the silver only, fleurets with symbols. These remained basically the types in later issues which included a 20 srang piece in gold, the 5 sho in silver as well as the sho and skar values in copper (Pl. 1007). Since 1935 on various srang values in silver and sho pieces in copper the central type on obverse has been the lion with a background of mountains.

JAPAN

The history of Japanese coinage is much briefer than that of the Chinese series, for no regular issues of coins were made before the early eighth century A.D. This first coinage was a cast-bronze series similar to the contemporary Chinese, but after only some two-and-a-half centuries official coinage came to an end. The coinage, resumed again in the sixteenth century, consisted not only of cast-bronze pieces but of gold and silver, differing in fabric and shape from the almost universal round coins. In the later nineteenth century when Japan adopted a general Westernizing policy the traditional coinage forms were replaced from 1869 by a new system of Western type and fabric.

EARLY ISSUES (c. 708–958)

The first coins to be cast in a uniform pattern consisted of both silver and bronze but the silver was produced only for one year, while the copper issues continued for half a century. The bronze coin, produced in the reign of the empress Genmyo in the first year of Wado, is termed the wado kaiko after the four-character inscription on the obverse. This Japanese coinage bears a close resemblance to tung pao coins introduced in China by the emperor Kao Tsu (618–627) of the Tang dynasty. The characters on the Japanese coin, however, are read clockwise and are interpreted as 'Japanese copper initial treasure'. The denomination of this early coin is the sen, a term which has survived in the Japanese coinage till the present day. This wado kaiko coinage falls into two groups: an early class of rougher execution and a second category of better workmanship and quality dating from the use of Chinese craftsmen in 720 (Pl. 1008).

In 760 coins were issued in gold, silver and bronze but no certainly genuine examples of the silver taihei genpo have survived and only a unique specimen of the gold kaiki shoho in the imperial collection. The bronze issue with characters mannen tsuho were tariffed at the rate of 1 to 10 of the earlier copper pieces. All in all, no less than twelve varieties of bronze coinage were produced between 708 and 958, successive issues showing a progressive deterioration both in execution and in metallic content down to the small kengen daiho of 958 (Pl. 1009). Between the mid tenth century and the mid sixteenth century no official coinage was produced in Japan. Currency needs in this period were met by the continued circulation of some of the bronze sen of the twelve dynastic types mentioned above and by counterfeits of this coinage as well as by the acceptance and use of bronze coinage from China and Korea.

SHOGUNATE (SIXTEENTH TO NINETEENTH CENTURIES)

In this period when imperial authority was eclipsed and real power was in the hands of a succession of powerful semi-feudal military overlords, Japanese coinage resumed and developed along most individual lines. The beginnings of the coinage system which developed and persisted in the Tokugawa shogunate from 1599 to 1867 can be discerned in the issues under the military dictatorship of Toyotomi Hideyoshi (1582–98). Cast copper or bronze coins of the traditional type and known as eiraku sen had been issued from about 1570 and were continued under Toyotomi and in fact were minted in China for export to Japan till as late as about 1640 (Pl. 1010). The innovation of the reign, however, was the issue of gold coinage. Gold had for long been used in currency in the form of thin gold plates, but only as bullion. Under Toyotomi these gold plates were developed into a coinage by marking oval-shaped, flat gold pieces with the kiri-flower crest on the edge at top and bottom and inscribing them in Indian ink with their value and the signature of the mint superintendent. The first recorded date of issue of these gold obans is 1586. Extremely rare rudimentary silver coins also appeared in the form of small slabs of silver known as chogin.

Under the Tokugawa shogunate (1599–1867) several denominations of gold in the form of flat oval plates were used. Nominally the major piece contained ten of the standard units of value, the gold ryo, and were stamped as of this value but the gold content was always considerably lower. Of the obans of the various periods the Keicho (1600–95), the Genroku (1095–1710) and the Tempo (1838–60) passed current only at 8 ryo and 2 bu (the bu was a fourth part of the ryo), while the rare Kyoho oban (1725–1838) was current at 7 ryo and 2 bu; but in the economic circumstances which pertained just before the nineteenth-century currency reform the mannen oban (1860–2) reached an exchange value of 25 ryo. These obans followed much the same pattern as the original issue of Toyotomi with inscription in Indian ink but usually had four stamps, one at the centre of each edge, and three stamps on the reverse. The goryoban or half-oban was issued only in 1837 in the Tempo period. The koban or tenth of the oban, of which there were nine issues between 1601 and 1860, carries no guaranteeing inscription in ink and the arrangement of the stamps or seals is different. The kiri stamp was placed at the edge at top and bottom only inside a fan-shaped frame and not a circular one as on the oban; two rectangular stamps were placed one below the top, the other above the bottom kiri stamp. The reverse also carried a central stamp and a second smaller stamp indicating the era of issue (Pl. 1011). On smaller rectangular gold pieces of 2 bu and 1 bu the stamps cover most of the surface area.

The silver used as currency in this period partook even more of the nature of bullion than did the gold and scarcely qualifies to be considered as coinage. One category, the chogin, was in the form of oval-shaped blocks of silver some two to three inches long with guaranteeing stamps on the obverse or face and stamps indicating the era of issue at each end of the obverse. A second category consisted of bean-shaped silver pieces, called mameita gin, stamped with a representation of Diakokusama, the God of Plenty, on obverse and, frequently, a stamp designating the era on the reverse. Of the rectangular silver pieces issued in the later eighteenth and in the nineteenth century the most common is the ichibu gin or 1 bu in silver (Pl. 1012) issued in 1837, 1859 and finally in 1868.

The bronze eiraku tsuho which was already in issue in the time of Toyotomi continued in circulation till about 1640 but the basic bronze coin throughout most of the period was the kanei tsuho (Pl. 1013) which was produced from 1626 until 1863 with four characters on the obverse and wave-like lines on the reverse. Some of the later issues of this coin were in brass or iron. The copper bunkyu eiho, again with characters on obverse and wave-like reverse, of value 4 mon, was cast from 1863 up to the coinage reform of 1869.

MODERN COINAGE (1868–1960)

The fall of the Tokugawa shogunate and the restoration of imperial authority in the person of the emperor Mutsuhito in 1868 opened the new Meiji (enlightened government) era and brought the introduction of a new decimal coinage of European pattern. The new monetary unit was the yen, divisible into 100 sen, each of 10 rin. The first issue of the new coinage was made in 1870 and consisted of the yen and pieces of 50, 20, 10 and 5 sen in silver with a dragon-type obverse with circular character inscription rendering the country, era and value, and a chrysanthemum in an open wreath on the reverse (Pl. 1014). In 1872 the gold yen with multiples up to 20 was produced, with similar dragon obverse but with the sun-in-wreath reverse type flanked by pennants. In 1873–4 the silver denominations were reduced in size and the rayed sun on reverse was replaced by three characters indicating the value. Copper pieces of 2, 1 and ½ sen with similar types were now also added to the system at this time as well as the 1 rin piece with chrysanthemum obverse and character reverse indicating the value. The types on the gold were changed in 1891 to a sun on obverse and on reverse value in wreath closed by chrysanthemum. On sen values in silver from 1907 the obverse type became a sun in a circle of cherry-blossom.

In the reign of emperor Yoshihito (1912–26) gold denominations, restricted to 5 and 20 yen, continued the existing types but ceased issue, the 20 yen in 1920 and the 5 yen in 1924. Divisionary sen values in silver returned to the dragon-type obverse between 1912 and 1917, as did the yen in silver in its last year of issue in 1912. The only silver coin later in the reign was the 50 sen piece with sun obverse and value between two mythical birds of longevity on the reverse (Pl. 1015). The bronze sen and 5 rin pieces of this reign had as obverse type the kiri-flower crest which had appeared on the gold obans and kobans of the shogunate. The coins of emperor Hirohito (1926–) included a short issue of gold 5 and 20 yen with traditional types in 1929–31. The silver 50 sen also remained unchanged as did the bronze sen whose types were now repeated on 5 and 10 sen denominations. Coinage in silver and bronze ended in 1937, and from 1938 until the end of the war coinage consisted mainly of 5 and 1 sen denominations in aluminium and even in tin in 1944–5. On the 1 sen piece of 1941–3 the types were Mount Fujiyama and value. The post-war coinage has introduced two new features, the indication of value in Western numerals and the use of pictorial types (Pl. 1016).

KOREA

The great peninsula of Korea under the name of Chao-hsien was a fief of the Chinese empire until the early fourth century A.D. when the Kao clan took possession of it. No Korean coinage was produced until the eleventh century when cast copper or bronze pieces with fabric and types similar to those of the contemporary Sung dynasty in China were issued. Early issues have plain reverse and four characters on the obverse reading *San han tung pao*, 'Currency of the Three Han', that is the three provinces of Korai, Petsi and Shinra which were united into one kingdom of Korea by Ouang in the eleventh century. Li Chengkuei who usurped the throne and acknowledged the sovereignty of Hung Wu, the first emperor of the Ming dynasty of China (1368–98), restored the old territorial designation Chao-hsien which reappears in the four-character inscription *Chao-hsien tung pao* on cast-bronze coins which had an extended circulation (Pl. 1017). For most of the seventeenth and eighteenth centuries the Korean kings were tributary to Japan. From the end of the eighteenth century a regular bronze coinage was issued with four-character inscription *Chang ping tung pao*, 'Currency of the Chang ping', the new dynastic style now adopted. This coinage was produced by a number of mints which placed on the reverse of the coins numerals indicating the sequence of issues and a series of elaborate mint-marks (Pl. 1018).

In the late nineteenth century in the reign of the emperor Tai (1863–97) a modern, Europeanized coinage was introduced. The first issue in 1891 consisted of the rare silver whan and copper pieces of 5 and 10 mun, all with types similar to contemporary Japanese issues, namely a dragon on obverse and value in an open wreath on the reverse. The inscription on the obverse included a statement of the value in English. The 1894 issue was of 1 and 5 yang pieces in silver and 1 and 5 fun coins in copper with types the same as before but for the new denomination names. A new unit, the won, divisible into 100 chon was introduced in the coinage of 1905–6. Gold denominations of 10 and 20 won as well as the half-won and coins of 5, 10 and 20 chon continued to have the same types but the bronze chon and its half had a phoenix as obverse type (Pl. 1019). A final issue of reduced weight was produced before the annexation of Korea by Japan in 1910. On coins of South Korea in 1959 the 100 hwan in cupro-nickel carried the portrait of Singman Rhee on obverse and two peacocks and value on the reverse. The cupro-nickel 50 hwan had as types a war galley and value and the bronze 10 hwan a rose and the value. The 10 and 5 yang coins in aluminium of North Korea in 1959 had types, arms in wreath and value.

BURMA

Coinage in Burma was not issued with any frequency or regularity until comparatively modern times but some relatively common series of coins are attributed to earlier periods of Burmese history. Perhaps the earliest is a series of flat silver pieces produced by late mediaeval dynasties in Arakan in west Burma. On the obverse is a recumbent humped bull with an inscription above in Nagari and on the reverse the trisul or trident of Siva. Both types are enclosed in a circle of dots (Pl. 1020). Silver coins with the Kalima on obverse and ruler's name and title on the reverse in Kufic script are attributed to rulers of Arakan who in the sixteenth century were tributary to the Muhammadan kings of Bengal. A third series of silver coins of rulers of Arakan was issued from the early seventeenth to the late eighteenth century. These large, flat silver pieces only have inscriptions on both sides giving the date and title in Burmese on obverse and the ruler's name on the reverse in Persian and Nagari. From about 1638 the coins have the same inscription, indicating date and title in Burmese on both sides.

To Pegu and Tenasserim in southern Burma is attributed a series of coin-like pieces some two inches in diameter, made of a mixture of lead and tin. On the obverse is the fabulous animal, a mixture of horse and deer, known in Burmese as *To*. The reverse has a wheel at the centre, surmounted by an inscription in Pali, using Burmese letters. On another series of like pieces the obverse carries the hansa or sacred bird. Metal weights in use in Arakan up to the nineteenth century were in the shape of this bird. A series of smaller coins in silver with the sankh or shell of Vishnu on the obverse and the trisul of Siva on the reverse have been attributed to Pegu as early as the eighth century.

The coinage of the kings of Burma proper begins only in the later nineteenth century and has a Western fabric. The first issue in 1852 for Mindon Ming (1852–78) consisted of the silver rupee with divisionary pieces down to the sixteenth. The common appellation of peacock rupees for these coins is inspired by the obverse type of a peacock with tail in splendour, while the reverse is simply the value in wreath (Pl. 1021). A copper quarter-anna in 1865 had similar types but on the obverse of the half-anna in 1869 appeared the Burmese lion which also formed the obverse for the 2½ mu in gold in 1866. The issue of the gold rupee and multiples of 2 and 5 rupees in 1880 for Thebaw (1878–85) used the peacock type on obverse. Burma, incorporated in Britain's Indian empire in the late nineteenth century, had no individual coinage until the restoration of Burmese independence in 1948. The Republic of Burma adopted for its first coinage of nickel pieces from 8 annas down to half-anna in 1949, the traditional Burmese lion on obverse and value in wreath on the reverse. The types were retained on the new coinage of 1952 based on the kyat (rupee), divisible into 100 pyas. In this, as in the 1949 coinage, some of the lower values are struck on a square flan or have a scalloped outline (Pl. 1022).

SIAM

The earliest currency of Siam is not a true coinage within the terms of our definition for it was in the form of silver bracelets which are assigned to the period of the seventh to the ninth century. An even more unusual currency is the silver *ka'kim*, conical in shape but with a piercing. Silver bars or *lats* with stamps on the upper surface also were used as currency. Yet another category of silver currency in Siam is the bat or tical, a bullet-shaped piece with turned-in ends (Pl. 1023). The bat, however, qualifies to be rated as a coin as pieces of this kind carry a number of guaranteeing stamps, have consistent weight standards and some issues are furnished with divisionary pieces. It is thought that the introduction of this class of coinage may have taken place as early as the beginning of the fourteenth century and a classification of this coinage has been made, attributing various of the marks stamped on the coins to specific kings. This 'bullet' coinage continued to be produced up to the late nineteenth century and overlapped the introduction of a European-type coinage by the Siamese king, Mongkut (1851–68).

The unit of the new coinage retained the name of tical or bat and was divided into 8 fuang, each of 8 att. The types on the first issue were identical for all denominations, on the obverse the tall Siamese crown flanked by ornate umbrellas and leaf-scrolls and on the reverse an elephant at the centre of a *chakram* or wheel design (Pl. 1024). Coins of 8, 4 and 2 bat were struck in gold, the bat and portions down to a sixteenth in silver and 2 and 4 att in copper. Similar coinage was issued for Chulalongkorn (1868–1910) at the outset of the reign, except that the leaf-scrolls disappeared from the obverse; but a new coinage in 1888 placed the king's portrait with his name and titles on the obverse and Siamese royal arms on the reverse on the silver denominations. A subsidiary nickel coinage in values of 20 down to 2½ satang, a hundred of which now formed a bat, had a facing elephant on obverse and value in wreath on the reverse. The facing elephant was also adopted on this ruler's final issue of the silver bat and on the silver of his successor Rama VI (1910–25). Satang pieces, now with a central piercing, had inscription on obverse and *chakra* design on the reverse. Only slight modifications were effected on the issues of Prajadhipok (1925–33) but the coinage of Ananda Mahidol (1933–46), in satang values only, showed, on the issues of 1946, the portrait of the young king on obverse and a facing winged deity on the reverse. The satang coins in aluminium-bronze of the present sovereign, Phumiphol, show his portrait on obverse and the royal arms on the reverse (Pl. 1025).

MALAYA

Indigenous coinage of the Malay peninsula is somewhat scanty or perhaps it would be more true to say that knowledge of this coinage is still very imperfect. A coinage has been identified of the sultans of Kedah, consisting of base silver pieces with Malay and Arabic inscriptions with dates ranging from the seventeenth to the eighteenth century. A further series from Kedah is in the form of tin coins with a central hole with Malay and Arabic inscriptions on the obverse and dates in the early nineteenth century on the reverse. Coins of the sultans of Johore of much the same period are of an unusual octagonal shape (Pl. 1026). Another coinage in tin was issued by the rajahs of Patani in the first half of the nineteenth century. These coins are pieces of about an inch in diameter with a large hole at the centre with a Malay inscription giving the place name on the obverse and an Arabic inscription with date on the reverse. Tin coins of similar fabric were also issued at Sanggora with inscription in Chinese characters on the obverse and in Malay and Arabic on the reverse. The most unusual coinage in Malaya is the 'tin-hat' money of Pahang, also in the earlier nineteenth century. These pieces, in shape like a square-sided hat with sloping sides and a broad brim, were produced in three denominations with inscriptions stamped on the brim. The ampat or 4 cent piece measures some three inches across, the dua or 2 cent piece an inch-and-a-half and the satu or 1 cent piece one inch.

The next phase of coinage in Malaya is that of the East India Company and of the British domination of the peninsula. For the island of Pulu Penang just off the western coast, secured as a trading settlement in the later eighteenth century, the East India Company issued a coinage in 1788. This consisted of the half, quarter and tenth of a dollar in silver and the cent, quarter and tenth of a cent in copper. The types were similar on all denominations; on the obverse was the company's bale-mark, a heart-shaped frame, divided diagonally into compartments containing the initials of the company, the whole surmounted by a symbol like the figure 4, while the reverse carried an inscription in Persian (Pl. 1027). The company's arms and inscription in wreath formed the types of the copper cent in 1810 and the 2, 1 and ½ pice in 1825 and 1828. Only one issue of copper coins of 1 and 2 kapangs was made for Malacca in 1831 with types a cock on obverse and inscription on reverse.

For Malaya generally an issue of the copper cent and its portions in 1845 carried the portrait of Victoria on obverse and the name of the East India Company and the value on the reverse. On a similar issue in 1862 the name of the East India Company had disappeared and was replaced by that of the India Straits in a circular inscription around the value figure. Later in Victoria's reign the name was again altered to the Straits Settlements but the types otherwise remained unchanged in an issue in silver of coins of 50, 20, 10 and 5 cents (Pl. 1028). This pattern of types continued under Edward VII on copper and silver except for the dollar which had a leaf-and-scroll reverse. Another silver dollar may be mentioned here, although it was issued not specifically for the Straits Settlements but for all Far

Eastern trade. This 'British dollar' has a standing Britannia on obverse with the words *One Dollar* as the sole inscription, while the reverse has leaf-and-scroll design similar to that of the Straits Settlements dollar. This dollar, first issued in 1895, was struck at intervals up to 1935 (Pl. 1029). There was little change except in obverse portraits in the coinage of the succeeding reigns except that the copper cent was struck on a square flan from 1919 and the half-cent from 1932. From 1939 the reverse inscription was altered to *Commissioners of Currency Malaya* and the 1954 coinage with the obverse portrait of Queen Elizabeth II was inscribed on the reverse *Malaya and British Borneo* (Pl. 1030).

INDO-CHINA

This territorial designation includes, in terms of modern states, the kingdoms of Cambodia and Laos and the Republic of Vietnam which, since 1954, has been partitioned into South Vietnam and Communist North Vietnam. The numismatic history of Indo-China falls into three phases, indigenous coinage, principally of the Annamese kingdom, the coinage of Indo-China as a French colony and finally the issues of the new independent states.

Since Annam from its earliest history was a tributary of the Chinese empire its coinage for many centuries was similar to the Chinese, namely a series of copper or bronze cast coins of cash denomination with character inscriptions on the obverse and sometimes on the reverse and with a square central hole (Pl. 1031). The earliest series of these copper cash are ascribed to the later tenth century and, with changes of the characters inscribed on the obverse, similar coins were issued up to the time of French colonization in the nineteenth century. A further category of coinage, mainly of nineteenth-century date, is that of the silver taels and portions of Europeanized fabric with types, a rayed sun at the centre of the obverse with four characters around and a dragon on the reverse. This class of silver money was used as presentation money by the Annamese kings. Another unusual coinage in later Annam consists of silver bars inscribed with characters on both back and front (Pl. 1032). The kingdom of Cambodia issued a modern-type coinage in 1860 with the portrait of King Norodom I and his title in French on the obverse, and the royal arms and a native-script legend with the value in French also on the reverse. The franc with multiples up to 5 francs (piastre) and divisionary pieces were struck in silver and 5 and 10 centimes in bronze, all with the same types (Pl. 1033).

A French colonial coinage was issued from 1879 to 1885 for Cochin China with a piastre and fractions expressed in centimes in silver as well as a bronze centime piece. The types were the seated figure of the republic and the value, the inscriptions all being in French. A bronze sapeque or cash was also issued with obverse inscription in French and reverse inscription in Chinese. A zinc sapeque of like types was produced for Tonkin in 1905 and the sapeque, cast in copper or brass, continued to be issued with traditional Annamese types at intervals up to 1926 in the reign of the French puppet ruler, Bao Dai. From 1885 a French colonial coinage was produced for the whole area with types similar to those described for Cochin China but now with the name of Indo-China on the reverse (Pl. 1034). The issues for Indo-China by the Vichy government were confined to centime values struck in zinc. The post-war coinage with obverse bust of the republic and rice-shoots on the reverse was in cupro-nickel for the piastre and aluminium for the centime values.

The first coinage of the modern kingdom of Cambodia in 1953 revived types which had appeared on the rare coins of ancient Cambodia, such as the mythical bird on the 10 centime obverse. The reverse on all values carried the state name in French and value in native script and in French. The Laotian issue in 1952 continued, as did the Cambodian, the piastre and centime system and used such types as a monument showing the foreparts of three elephants on the obverse of the 20 centime coin. In Vietnam the piastre was rechristened the dong, divided into 10 hao, each of 10 xu or su. On the coinage of 1953 the obverse of various xu values carries three female portraits, representing the constituent states of Cochin-China, Annam and Tonkin.

EAST INDIES

Coinage native to the islands of the Indian Archipelago, now mostly grouped in the state of Indonesia, is comparatively rare, and substantive issues of coinage associated with the islands first make their appearance with the spread of the activities of the Dutch East India Company. After the issues produced by the company, there followed the coinage of the colony of the Dutch East Indies and finally the issues of the independent state of Indonesia from 1950.

The most ancient coinage of the islands is a series of small gold pieces, similar in fabric to the fanams of south India but stamped with characters in an incuse. These pieces have been identified as coins of the Hindu period in Java as early as the tenth century. Another series of similar fabric but slightly larger in module and struck in silver is placed after the gold coins and certainly had ceased by about the thirteenth century when the currency commonly in use was the bronze Chinese cash. A series of coin-like pieces in brass with a square hole at the centre have as the general type two 'deities' with a tree above on the one side and a collection of symbols on the other. These pieces were used as temple money not as regular coinage and, though some are of a certain antiquity, they continued to be produced until comparatively modern times. Coins known as pitis were issued in tin with a round hole at centre by some of the small constituent states of Java (Pl. 1035). Coins of this category in Bantam in the eighteenth century have an inscription on obverse and a blank reverse. Similar coins from Cheribon, also in the eighteenth century, have either an inscription formed by four Chinese characters or the name *Cheribon* in Western script.

In the island of Sumatra small gold and silver pagoda-like pieces similar to those described above in Java are attributed to Fantsour. A somewhat more substantial series of coins is that of the sultans of Atjih who struck a coinage in gold from the sixteenth to the eighteenth centuries with inscriptions in local script on the obverse and in Arabic on the reverse (Pl. 1036). Other coinage in Sumatra is mainly in the form of tin pitis. Those issued by Siyak in the seventeenth and eighteenth centuries have a large circular hole at the centre and resemble washers, as do those of Djambi, though some of the latter have an octagonal outline. The tin pitis of Palembang, some round, some octagonal, have a much smaller central hole. On all the piti coinage only the obverse carries an inscription.

The islands further to the east have even fewer coinage series. Copper or bronze cash of Chinese type were issued in Borneo in the seventeenth century and in the late eighteenth and early nineteenth centuries there was a coinage imitating the copper doits of the East India Company. The obverse usually retained a fair copy of the company's monogram but the shield on the reverse, in place of displaying the arms of one of the provinces of the Netherlands, as on the originals, bears an Arabic inscription. The only coinage of any consequence in the Celebes is that of the sultans of Macassar who in the sixteenth and seventeenth centuries struck a gold coinage with inscriptions on both sides.

The beginnings of Dutch coinage for trade in the East are remarkably similar to the English 'portcullis' silver (see p. 523). The issue, made like the English in 1601, also consisted of silver coins equivalent to the Spanish 8, 4, 2 and 1 real coins, with fractional pieces of a ½ and a ¼. The coins issued by the United Amsterdam Company had the arms of the province of Holland and inscription *Insignia Hollandiae* and the value on obverse, and the arms of Amsterdam and inscription *Et Civitatis Amstelredamensis* on the reverse. Like the similar English coinage this issue was not long continued. The next coinage, produced in 1645, consisted of silver pieces of 48, 24 and 12 stuivers with wreath and sword on obverse and the initials of the East India Company, the Vereenigde Oost-Indische Compagnie, VOC, in monogram on the reverse. In the eighteenth century coinage of silver ducatoons, 3 and 1 guilder pieces was struck with the identical types of the provincial issues in the Netherlands but with the VOC monogram placed below the provincial arms on the reverse (Pl. 1037). A parallel series of copper doits had the company's monogram on obverse and the provincial arms on the reverse (Pl. 1038).

In addition to such coinages produced in the Netherlands for use in the East Indies rupees in silver and gold coins struck from silver-rupee dies were issued in Java with Arabic and Javanese inscriptions in the later eighteenth century. In the last years of the eighteenth century an emergency coinage of copper 'bonks' was struck. These were rough lumps cut from rods of copper and stamped with the value 1 S (1 stuiver) or 2 S (2 stuivers) on the obverse and the date, ranging from 1796 to 1799, on the reverse (Pl. 1039). In the same period doits were issued in tin with VOC on obverse and the value 1 doit on the reverse.

The decline of the company coincided approximately with the establishment of the Batavian Republic in the Netherlands and the next coinage for the East Indies struck in 1802 bears the inscriptions of the republican period. Denominations in silver ranged from the guilder down to the sixteenth of the guilder and had as types a sailing ship on obverse with the inscription *Indiae Batavorum* and on the reverse the arms of Holland with legend *Mo Arg Ord Foed Belg Hol* (Pl. 1040). Copper doits and half-doits of this issue replaced the traditional VOC monogram on the reverse by *Indiae Batav* and the date, while the provincial arms of the obverse were flanked by the figures $5-\frac{1}{16}$ G or $5-\frac{1}{32}$ G, indicating that 5 doits or 10 half-doits equalled one sixteenth of a guilder. This was an error, for the guilder of this issue was current at 24 stuivers (96 doits) not 20 (80 doits) as indicated on the coins; the value should have read $6-\frac{1}{16}$ G. In the early years of the 1800's rupees and halves with inscriptional types were also issued and copper 'bonks' of 1 and 2 stuiver values. In the reign of Napoleon's brother Louis as King of Holland copper doits were issued with his initials LN in monogram on the obverse and Java and the date 1810 on the reverse. The stuiver and half had similar types with the value, e.g. 1–St., flanking the monogram on the obverse and 'bonks' of 1 and 2 stuivers were also issued in the same year.

During the British occupation of the Dutch East Indies from 1811 to 1816 gold rupees and halves were struck with the inscription 'Money of the English Coy' in Javanese on the obverse and Arabic on the reverse. On the copper stuiver, its half and quarter the obverse carried the East India Company's bale-mark containing the letters VEIC and surmounted by B on the obverse and *Java* and date on the reverse (Pl. 1042). Lead doits in 1813–14 were marked with the company's initials on the obverse and the value and *Java* on the reverse.

From the recovery of the East Indies possessions in 1816 a regal coinage was issued for use in the islands. Under William I (1815–40) the types on the guilder and its divisions were similar to those of the Netherlands itself but with *Nederlandsch Indie* added under the arms on the reverse. The copper cent altered its types to arms and value on obverse and *Nederl. Indie* on the reverse. For William III (1849–90) further standardization of types and values took place. In silver the $\frac{1}{4}$, $\frac{1}{10}$ and $\frac{1}{20}$ guilder were issued and the $2\frac{1}{2}$, 1 and $\frac{1}{2}$ cent in copper; on all, the types were arms, *Nederlandsch Indie* and value on obverse, and inscriptions in Javanese, Malay and Arabic on the reverse with no mention of the ruler's name. A similar coinage was issued in the reign of Queen Wilhelmina (Pl. 1041) from 1890 until the capture of the Dutch East Indies by the Japanese in 1941 and then briefly after the liberation of the islands in 1945.

The islands became the independent republic of Indonesia in 1950. The unit of the new coinage is the rupiah of 100 sen. On aluminium coins of 10 and 25 sen issued in 1952 the types are an heraldic eagle with shield of arms obverse and the state name, value and date on the reverse. Lower sen values with central hole have inscriptions on obverse and value on the reverse.

Coinage has also been issued for various British possessions in the East Indies. In Sumatra where the British East India Company had been established since 1686, copper coins of 3, 2 and 1 kapang in 1786 had as types the bale-mark on obverse and value and date in Arabic on the reverse. On a later issue in 1810 the obverse was changed to the company's arms. Copper kapangs for the island of Labuan off the north coast of Borneo had similar types except that the company's arms on obverse were accompanied by *Island of Sultana* and not the company's name. A cock and a many-pointed star were the types on the copper kapang of Celebes in 1834. The British North Borneo Company issued copper cents in 1891 with the company's arms on obverse and the value in wreath on the reverse. Later, when North Borneo became a British colony, the arms were retained as obverse type but the company's name was replaced by *State of North Borneo* accompanying the value on the reverse. Various cent values were issued between 1903 and 1941. Sarawak, ruled by the Brooke family as rajahs, had a coinage with the rajah's portrait and name on the obverse and value in wreath on the reverse. The cent and its portions in copper and higher values in silver were issued for three successive Brooke rajahs between 1863 and 1937 (Pl. 1043).

HONG KONG

Coinage has been issued for the British colony since 1863. The types on various cent values 5 to 50 in silver and on the cent in copper were the royal portrait and the colony's name and value in English and Chinese (Pl. 1044). A silver dollar and its half were struck between 1865 and 1868 with regal-portrait obverse and a scroll design enclosing Chinese characters on the reverse, together with the inscription, e.g. *One Dollar Hong Kong*. In subsequent reigns the silver dollar was not issued and the simple types of the lower-value coins have been retained. From the reign of George V only denominations of 10 cents and below have been struck.

THE PHILIPPINES

For the Spanish colony of the Philippine Islands, the earliest coinage was issued under Charles III in 1766 in the form of copper quartos with a castle and inscription *Cuidad de Man(ila)* on obverse and the arms of the Philippines on the reverse. In the first half of the nineteenth century coinage continued to be of copper quartos, the usual types being a crowned lion on obverse and arms of Spain on the reverse. For Isabel II (1833–70) this copper-quarto coinage was reinforced by issues in gold of the peso and multiples up to 4 and of silver coins of 50, 20 and 10 centimos values. The types on all were the royal portrait on obverse and on reverse the Spanish arms with an additional inscription, *Filippinas*, below the shield. Similar silver coins and the gold 4 pesos were struck for Alfonso XII (1875–85) and in 1897 the last Spanish coinage for the Philippines was the silver peso of Alfonso XIII.

Following the Spanish-American war, the Philippines were bought by the United States in 1898. On the peso and centavo values from 50 down to 10 in silver the obverse showed a standing female figure with a volcano in the background, while the reverse carried the arms and title of the United States of America. A seated male figure and the volcano appeared on the nickel 5 centavos and the bronze centavo and its half, all of which had the same reverse as the silver coins (Pl. 1045). The issues after the creation of the Commonwealth of the Philippines in 1935 continued the denominations, less the peso, and the types of the earlier coinage, but the arms of the United States on the reverse were replaced by those of the Commonwealth. A special issue of the silver peso in 1935 had on its obverse the jugate busts of President Roosevelt and President Quezon of the Philippines. In 1936 the silver peso and its half bore the busts of Governor-General Murphy and President Quezon. After the liberation of the islands from the Japanese the Philippines became an independent republic in 1946. The first coinage of silver peso and 50 centavos in silver in 1947 with arms-and-value reverse carried on the obverse the portrait of General MacArthur inscribed *Defender and Liberator of the Philippines*.

A new cupro-nickel coinage was issued in 1958. The 25 and 50 centavos pieces repeated the types of female figure and volcano on reverse and the 1, 5 and 10 centavos coins the seated male figure and volcano which had appeared on earlier coins. The obverse, the usual shield of arms, now has an inscription *Central Bank of the Philippines*.

TOKENS, COUNTERS, COIN-WEIGHTS, ETC.

Tokens, Counters, Coin-Weights, Etc.

A GENERAL account of the world's coinage would not be complete without some mention of certain categories of objects which resemble coins in fabric and shape and, like coins, have types or designs and inscriptions stamped on one or both faces. These various series are generally of late mediaeval or of modern date and, since most of them were produced in quantity, they furnish some of the most common objects that come under the notice of the general collector. These coin-like objects, which lie on the periphery of coinage proper, range from the series of unofficial or token coinages, through pieces used as aids to reckoning both for purposes of commerce and gaming, to the mass of metallic objects which, before the age of the newspaper and the photograph, were circulated for purposes of commercial advertisement or political propaganda and satire.

Although the most common categories of this kind of material are associated with the modern period and with the Western world, a number of such marginal series are found attached to the coinages of the ancient world and the East. In the late Roman empire a series of coin-like objects in bronze, roughly of the size of the sestertius of the imperial period and known as contorniates because of the turned-up rim on many examples, was produced in the late fourth century A.D. Many of these contorniates carry portraits of emperors, most frequently Augustus and Nero, but portraits of famous Romans such as the poet Horace are also found, as well as other famous men of antiquity such as Alexander the Great. The considerable variety of reverse types includes such interesting representations as an ancient organ but the most common scenes are those associated with the circus and the Roman games (Pl. 1046). It is possible that the contorniates represent some form of tickets for the games, but it is also suggested that they played a more subtle part as propaganda for the old ways of Rome and against the rising power of Christianity. Other Roman pieces in base metal presenting a number of erotic scenes are, for lack of a better explanation, classed as brothel-tickets. The most plentiful series is that of the lead *tesserae* or tickets, small pieces of about the size of a sixpence, with types, usually a simple object, on either side (Pl. 1047). In the late Roman empire, when official bronze coinage was in short supply, these *tesserae* were used as small change in private transactions and as counters in games of chance.

Associated with the coinages of the Far East, particularly those of China and Annam, are the cast-bronze pieces of similar fabric to the coins but, in most cases, of larger module and carrying, in addition to the characters similar to those on the coins, figure types which were absent from the coinage till the present century. A number of these types are human and animal figures but the most common are representations of the various figures of the zodiacal circle. Though resembling coins, and possibly on occasion being used as coins, these pieces were produced primarily as charms or amulets. The Near East has produced a series of coin-like objects made of glass. These pieces are particularly associated with Egypt and are connected with coinage in as much as they are approximately of the module of coins, reproduce the weights of coin denominations and carry inscriptions similar to those on the coins (Pl. 1048). The coinage series to which these pieces run parallel range from the Umaiyad caliphate through the Abbasid and Fatimid caliphates and continue, though not with such frequency, under the Ayyubid and Mameluke dynasties in Egypt. Those Arab glass pieces, however, are not coins but weights, and glass was chosen as the medium in which to make them because of its imperviousness to wear.

Easily the most common and the most widespread in the Western world is the series of pieces which are coins in every sense, except that their issue and their guarantee lacked the authority of state and government. One special category of such unofficial issues comprises coins struck in the emergency of a siege in earlier centuries. When, in a beleaguered town, the supply of coinage failed, recourse was had either to countermarking any available pieces of coinage or to placing a guaranteeing stamp on pieces of precious metal, most usually silver plate. Such siege-pieces have been mentioned in the descriptions of several of the coinages in the preceding sections as, for instance, the siege-pieces produced during the Civil War in England (Pl. 474a).

Three periods in the history of British coinage, when the supply of officially produced small change failed, are marked by extensive series of unofficial pieces. The first of these periods was between the end of the Civil War in 1649 and the introduction of new copper coinage by Charles II in 1672. In the reigns of James I and Charles I attempts had been made to remedy the deficiency of small change by the issue of official token farthings (see p. 242) but these had not proved popular. After 1649 the dearth of coins for small, everyday transactions led to the production of 'tradesmen's tokens' in denominations of a halfpenny and a farthing. Some series were issued for local circulation by cities and towns, but, as the common name for these pieces indicates, they were most frequently produced by tradesfolk—shopkeepers and innkeepers. The varieties of this series are innumerable but in general the obverse had, in a circular inscription, the name of the issuer and usually the date, and, as a type, some object connected with his trade, while the reverse inscription stated the village or town with, at the centre, the value of the token. A typical example is the token of John Warner of the 'Dolphin and Bell' in Aldersgate Street in London. The obverse has at centre a dolphin and a bell and is inscribed *John Warner* 1668; the reverse continues the inscription *Aldersgate Street* and has across the field *His/halfe/Penny* (Pl. 1049). These tokens, produced in most towns and in many villages of almost every county in England, are valuable documents for local history, particularly for that of London where tokens detailed the very street in which a particular tradesman carried on business.

A famine in small change in the late eighteenth century was the occasion of the second great issue of tokens, mostly halfpennies with a good proportion of pennies but few farthings. These tokens lack the local interest of the seventeenth-century issues, for, though they were produced for currency in various localities, they were made at a few centres. The earliest and most common issue is that of the Anglesey tokens. These were made from copper from the Parys mine in Anglesey and the obverse of this series bears the bust of a Druid as the eighteenth century visualized him; for the antiquarians no doubt recalled that the island of Mona or Anglesey was the scene of the final suppression of the Druids in Britain by the Romans. The edge of these coins is usually stamped with the names of the places where such tokens were acceptable as payment. The local flavour is, however, not completely absent and types often refer to the history of the places where they were current as, for instance, the portrait of John of Gaunt, Duke of Lancaster, on Lancaster's tokens or Lady Godiva on tokens of Coventry (Pl. 1050).

The final series in the early nineteenth century is, in some ways, a continuation of the late eighteenth-century issues. The deficiencies of copper coinage had to some extent been remedied by official issues, but the silver famine which occasioned such expedients as the countermarking of Spanish silver dollars for currency in England and the issue of bank tokens in silver (see p. 247) made necessary the issue of tokens for higher denominations. A good number of token pennies continued to be produced but silver tokens, usually of the value of a shilling or sixpence, were also issued by firms and municipalities (Pl. 1051).

Such unofficial or token coinages were not confined to Britian. The early currency needs of developing countries such as New Zealand, Australia, Canada and the

United States were all met by the use of token coins until the provisions of an adequate supply of official coinage. Tokens for local circulation were issued until quite recent times by many Chambers of Commerce in municipalities in European countries and tokens for the operation of slot machines and meters have and, in some cases, still are provided by electricity, gas and telephone companies. In the United States the imposition of a sales tax in some of the states led to the production of local sales-tax tokens where the sales-tax percentage resulted in a price which could not be paid exactly by using current denominations (Pl. 1052).

A special series of American pieces known as 'Hard-Times' tokens were pressed into service as money of necessity in the period roughly from 1834 to 1841 when copper small change was scarce. The pieces themselves were put out, not as token coins, but as political medallets containing satirical comment on the controversy about the United States Bank and the politics of Presidents Jackson and Van Buren. One of the more common examples shows on one side a tortoise carrying a chest labelled 'Sub-Treasury' with a caption below reading *Fiscal Agent* and dated 1837, while a circular inscription reads *Executive Experiment*. The other side has a jackass as type—a reference to President Jackson and his alleged mulishness —and is inscribed *I follow in the steps of my illustrious predecessor* (Pl. 1053). The obverse satirizes Jackson's hostility to the Bank and the wording of the reverse was taken from the inaugural declaration of Van Buren.

Other types of token have also been used not so much as unofficial coinage but to represent temporary payments. Many of the hop-gardens and orchards of Kent in the nineteenth century had each their own individual tokens which were given out to the hop- or fruit-pickers as tallies for given quantities picked during the harvest, and, at the end of the season, redeemed for cash. These tokens are ordinarily in base metals, frequently in lead or tin, and carry little more than the initials of the farmer and the quantity for which they were a tally. A few are more elaborate with full-length inscriptions with the names of the farmer and his farm on one side and of the producing firm on the other. Another whole range of coin-like pieces were used in the later seventeenth and the eighteenth centuries as metal tickets or passes for admission to theatres and pleasure gardens. A special type of admission-piece is represented by the communion tokens used by Presbyterian churches, particularly in Scotland, in the last century. These tokens of authorization to partake of communion were normally small oval pieces of lead or pewter with the name of the particular church and sometimes its minister on the face, and on the reverse either a brief quotation from or the reference to the passage in Corinthians (I Cor. xi, 24) which describes the institution of the sacrament by Jesus at the Last Supper (Pl. 1054).

Until the fifteenth century, when the use of numerals as we know them became widespread, calculations were made by means of the cumbersome Roman numerals. Various aids in reckoning were used such as the abacus, a frame with rows of beads on wires, long used for teaching elementary arithmetic in schools, and still used in the commerce of the Far East. A second method, that of the reckoning- or casting-board, reproduced the same principles as the abacus but replaced the wires and beads by a division of the board into squares like a chequer-board and the use of metal counters placed in the appropriate squares. In the later Middle Ages these metal counters or disks in copper or brass imitated coins in appearance and types. Reckoning- or casting-counters are known also by their French name of jettons, for the system originated in France in the thirteenth century. Early jettons copy the types of contemporary coins and frequently reproduce one of the familiar religious phrases such as *Ave Maria Gracia Plena* found on coins. The inscriptions on many jettons are illiterate and reproduce only in a general way the letters of the original phrases. The types of the Anglo-Gallic coins of the late mediaeval period were also much copied on reckoning-counters (Pl. 1055) but the only English coins copied were those of the 'sterling' type coinage of Edward III and his successors, a facing crowned bust and a cross with three pellets in each angle on the reverse (Pl. 1056). Such jettons are some-times referred to in England as 'wardrobe counters', the Wardrobe being a royal department which dealt with money and accounts. Since reckoning-counters are frequently found on the site of old ecclesiastical buildings they are sometimes called 'Abbey Tokens'.

In France special series of jettons, some struck with considerable finish and using well-designed types, were produced for various government departments but the majority of counters tend to be utilitarian. In the thirteenth and fourteenth centuries jettons were produced in most countries of west Europe but from the later fourteenth century Nuremberg in Germany became the principal source of supply. These German *rechenpfennige* in the sixteenth century were largely produced by a few families such as Laufer, Schultes and Krauwinckel whose names appear on one side of the piece. The most common Nuremberg counters are those of Hans Krauwinckel (1586–1635). A design of crowns and fleur-de-lis is accom-panied on the obverse by his name *Hans Krauwinckel In Nur.*, while the reverse, the Reichsapfel—a cross on globe, in a trilobe—is inscribed *Gott allein die Eere sei* (Pl. 1057).

In the days before the universal use of fiduciary coinage, coins in precious metal, especially gold, were coins without frontiers and frequently circulated well beyond the limits of the state which issued them. Since the production of coinage by machinery and the provision of a milled edge became standard practice only in the seventeenth century, coins were frequently clipped or rubbed to remove part of their metal so that in transactions it was necessary to check the weight of the pieces involved. The weights used were generally of brass and initially reproduced on one side the characteristic type of the coin to be checked, as, for instance, St. Michael slaying the dragon on the English gold angel. The general practice later simply inscribed the name of the coin to be checked on the face of the weight. One of the most common coin-weights encountered in England is that used to check the eighteenth-century Portuguese moidore. The obverse here still reproduces the portrait and titles of John V of Portugal and the reverse states plainly the amount it was worth in England, namely, *Three pounds twelve* (Pl. 1058).

A great variety of pieces of coin-like appearance were made to be used as counters in card games. By far the most common are the imitations in brass of the guineas and half-guineas of George III issued between 1787 and 1800 and, from the shape of the shield on the reverse, known as 'Spade-guineas'. These brass imitations, in order to avoid a charge of forgery, do not reproduce the exact inscriptions, detailing the king's name and titles, but are frequently only a jumble of letters or, commonly, the phrase *In Memory of the Good Old Days* and commonly have an incongruous date (Pl. 1059). Other small brass playing-card counters combine impossible coin-types such as the portrait of Victoria and the imperial German eagle. Pieces with types such as the three-plumed crest of the Prince of Wales and inscription *The Prince of Wales model half-sovereign* are probably relics of Victorian children's games rather than card-counters.

The account of such coin-like pieces could be extended to great length but must be concluded now with the mention of three very common items which are a source of great puzzlement to the general collector. Small copper pieces with a small silver disk at the centre have every appearance of being a coin and indeed have the portrait and titles of Victoria on obverse and the words *Model penny* on the reverse. These pieces were unofficial issues made about 1840 when discussion was raging about the possibility of issuing a less cumbersome and heavy penny. It was advocated that, by the addition of the small silver disk to these small coppers, the intrinsic metal value of the coin would be maintained at one penny but the scheme was never adopted. A second common piece of the nineteenth century is the imitation in brass of the sovereign of Victoria. The obverse has the ordinary portrait of Victoria but the inscription *Victoria Regina* replaces the official form and title, while the reverse replaces the St. George and dragon type by a crowned horseman and a three-headed dragon, accompanied by the inscription *To Hanover* and the date 1837. This was originally a satirical medallet issued on the occasion of the departure of the Duke of Cumberland to become King of Hanover. Because of the similarity of the piece to the true sovereign it was taken up and produced in quantity and passed as a sovereign on race-courses and so on where money changes hands quickly (Pl. 1060). The final piece, a little more unusual in appearance, is a brass Hindu amulet or piece of temple-money. On one side are the standing figures of Rama and Lakshama; on the other Rama and his wife Sita sit enthroned with courtiers around and the monkey-god, Hanuman, below. These pieces, known as 'Ramatankas', are sometimes silvered but, despite their unusual designs, they are modern pieces, produced in quantity and, consequently, of little value (Pl. 1061).

Select Bibliography

GENERAL

COMENCINI, M. *Coins of the modern world*, 1870–1936. London, 1937.

FORRER, L. S. *The art of collecting coins*. London, 1955.

FREY, A. R. *Dictionary of numismatic names*. New York, 1947.

FRIEDBERG, R. *Gold coins of the world*, *A.D.* 600–1958. New York, 1958.

FRIEDENSBURG, F. *Die Münzen in der Kulturgeschichte*. Berlin, 1926.

GRIERSON, P. *Coins and medals. A select bibliography*. London, 1954.

LAGERQUIST, L. O. and NATHOORST-BÖOS, E. *Mynt och medaljer och annam numismatik*. Stockholm, 1960.

LANE-POOLE, S. *Coins and medals: their place in history*. London, 1894.

LINECAR, H. W. A. *Coins*. London, 1955.

MACDONALD, G. *The evolution of coinage*. London, 1935.

MARTINORI, R. *La Moneta*. Rome, 1915.

MILNE, J. G., SUTHERLAND, C. H. V. and THOMPSON, J. D. A. *Coin collecting*. Oxford, 1951.

RAWLINGS, G. B. *Coins and how to know them*. London, 1935.

RAYMOND, W. *Coins of the world—Nineteenth-century issues*. New York, 1953.

RAYMOND, W. *Coins of the world—Twentieth-century issues*. New York, 1952.

RENTZMANN, W. *Numismatisches Legenden-Lexicon des Mittelalters und der Neuzeit*. Berlin, 1865–6.

SALLET, A. VON. *Münzen und Medaillen*. Berlin, 1898.

SCHLICKEYSEN, F. W. A. *Erklärung der Abkürzungen auf Münzen der neueren Zeit, des Mittelalters und des Alterthums*. Berlin, 1896.

SCHRÖTTER, F. VON. *Wörterbuch der Münzkunde*. Berlin-Leipzig, 1930.

SUTHERLAND, C. H. V. *Art in Coinage*. London, 1955.

YEOMAN, R. S. *A catalogue of modern world coins*. 3rd edition. Racine, 1959.

PARTICULAR

GREEK

General

BABELON, E. *Traité des monnaies grecques et romaines.* Iere Partie, Vol. I. *Introduction.* Paris, 1901; 2e Partie, Vols. I–IV. *Description historique.* Paris, 1907–32.

GARDNER, P. *A history of ancient coinage, 700–300 B.C.* Oxford, 1918.

HANDS, A. W. *Common Greek coins.* London, 1908.

HEAD, B. V. *Historia Numorum. A manual of Greek coins.* 3rd edition. Oxford, 1911.

HILL, G. F. *Historical Greek coins.* London, 1906.

MILNE, J. G. *Greek coinage.* Oxford, 1931.

SELTMAN, C. T. *Greek coins. A history of metallic currency and coinage down to the fall of the Hellenistic kingdoms.* 2nd edition. London, 1954.

Catalogues

Catalogue of Greek coins in the British Museum. London: R. S. Poole, *Italy,* 1873; R. S. Poole, B. V. Head and P. Gardner, *Sicily,* 1876; B. V. Head and P. Gardner, *Thrace,* 1877; P. Gardner, *Seleucid Kings of Syria,* 1878; B. V. Head, *Macedonia,* 1879; P. Gardner, *Thessaly to Aetolia,* 1883; R. S. Poole, *Ptolemaic Kings of Egypt,* 1883; B. V. Head, *Central Greece,* 1884; W. Wroth, *Crete and the Aegean Islands,* 1886; P. Gardner, *Peloponnesus,* 1887; B. V. Head, *Attica, Megaris, Aegina,* 1888; B. V. Head, *Corinth,* 1889; W. Wroth, *Pontus and Paphlagonia,* 1889; W. Wroth, *Mysia,* 1892; R. S. Poole, *Alexandria and the Nomes,* 1892; B. V. Head, *Ionia,* 1892; W. Wroth, *Troas, Aeolis and Lesbos,* 1894; B. V. Head, *Caria and the Islands,* 1897; G. F. Hill, *Lycia, Pomphylia and Pisidia,* 1897; W. Wroth, *Galatia, Cappadocia and Syria,* 1899; G. F. Hill, *Lycaonia, Isauria and Cilicia,* 1900; B. V. Head, *Lydia,* 1902; W. Wroth, *Parthia,* 1903; G. F. Hill, *Cyprus,* 1904; B. V. Head, *Phrygia,* 1906; G. F. Hill, *Phoenicia,* 1910; G. F. Hill, *Palestine,* 1914; G. F. Hill, *Arabia, Mesopotamia and Persia,* 1922; E. S. G. Robinson, *Cyrenaica,* 1927.

Catalogue of Indian coins in the British Museum. P. Gardner, *The coins of the Greek and Scythic kings of Bactria and India,* 1886.

British Museum. *A guide to the principal coins of the Greeks from c. 700 B.C. to A.D. 270,* 2nd edition, London, 1959.

Special works covering the fields not yet included in British Museum catalogues.

AFRICA

MAZARD, J. *Corpus Nummorum Numidiae Mauretaniaeque.* Paris, 1955.
MULLER, L. *Numismatique de l'ancienne Afrique.* Copenhagen, 1860–2.

SPAIN

HEISS, A. *Description générale des monnaies antiques d'Espagne.* Paris, 1870.

GAUL

BLANCHET, A. *Traité des monnaies gauloises.* Paris, 1905.
MURET, E. and CHABOUILLET, M. A. *Catalogue des monnaies gauloises de la Bibliothèque Nationale.* Paris, 1889.
TOUR, H. DE LA. *Atlas des monnaies gauloises.* Paris, 1892.

BRITAIN

EVANS, J. *The coinage of the Ancient Britons.* London, 1864. Supplement, 1890.
MACK, R. P. *The coinage of Ancient Britain.* London, 1953.

EASTERN CELTS

FORRER, R. *Keltische Numismatik der Rhein- und Donaulande.* Strassburg, 1908.
PINK, K. *Einführung in die keltische Münzkunde mit besonderer Berücksichtigung Österreichs.* Vienna, 1950.

ROMAN

General

HILL, G. F. *Historical Roman coins.* London, 1909.
MATTINGLY, H. *Roman coins from the earliest times to the fall of the Western Empire.* 2nd edition. London, 1960.

Republic

BABELON, E. *Description historique et chronologique des monnaies de la république romaine.* 2 vols. Paris, 1885–6.

BAHRFELDT, M. VON. *Die römische Goldmünzenprägung während der Republik und unter Augustus.* Halle, 1923.

HAEBERLIN, E. J. *Aes Grave. Das Schwergeld Roms und Mittelitaliens.* 2 vols. Frankfurt, 1910.

SYDENHAM, E. A. *The coinage of the Roman Republic.* London, 1952.

THOMSEN, R. *Early Roman coinage. A study of the chronology*: I. *The Evidence.* Copenhagen, 1957; II. *Synthesis I;* III. *Synthesis II.* Copenhagen, 1961.

Empire

ALFÖLDI, A. *Die Kontorniaten.* Budapest, 1943.

BERNHART, M. *Handbuch zur Münzkunde der römischen Kaiserzeit.* 2 vols. Halle, 1926.

BOLIN, S. *State and currency in the Roman Empire to* A.D. 300. Stockholm, 1959.

CARSON, R. A. G., HILL, P. V. and KENT, J. P. C. *Late Roman bronze coinage.* London, 1960.

COHEN, H. *Description historique des monnaies frappées sous l'empire romain.* 8 vols. Paris, 1880–92.

ELMER, G. *Die Münzprägung der gallischen Kaiser in Köln, Trier und Mailand.* Bonn, 1941.

GRANT, M. *From Imperium to Auctoritas.* Cambridge, 1946.

MAURICE, J. *Numismatique constantinienne.* 3 vols. Paris, 1908–12.

STRACK, P. L. *Untersuchung zur römischen Reichsprägung des zweiten Jahrhunderts.* 3 vols. Stuttgart, 1931–7.

SUTHERLAND, C. H. V. *Coinage in Roman imperial policy.* London, 1951.

SUTHERLAND, C. H. V. *Coinage and currency in Roman Britain.* London, 1937.

Catalogues, etc.

CARSON, R. A. G. *Coins of the Roman Empire in the British Museum.* Vol. VI. *Serverus Alexander–Balbinus and Pupienus.* London, 1962,

GRUEBER, H. A. *Coins of the Roman Republic in the British Museum.* 3 vols. London, 1910.

MATTINGLY, H. *Coins of the Roman Empire in the British Museum.* 5 vols. London: I. *Augustus–Vitellius,* 1923; II. *Vespasian–Domitian,* 1930; III. *Nerva–Hadrian,* 1936; IV. *Antoninus Pius–Commodus,* 1940; V. *Pertinax–Elagabalus,* 1950.

MATTINGLY, H., SYDENHAM, E. A. and others. *The Roman imperial coinage.* London: I. *Augustus–Vitellius,* 1923; II. *Vespasian–Hadrian,* 1926; III. *Antoninus Pius–Commodus,* 1930; IV. *Pertinax–Aemilian,* 3 parts, 1936–49; V. *Valerian I–Diocletian,* 2 parts, 1927–33; IX. *Valentinian I–Theodosius I,* 1951.

EUROPE

General

DAVENPORT, J. S. *European crowns since* 1800. Buffalo, 1947.

ENGEL, A. and SUERRRE, R. *Traité du numismatique du moyen âge.* 3 vols. Paris, 1891–1905.

ENGEL, A. and SERRURE, R. *Traité du numismatique moderne et contemporaine.* 2 vols. Paris, 1897–9.

HAZLITT, W. *The coinage of the European continent.* London, 1893.

LUSCHIN VON EBENGREUTH, A. *Allgemeine Münzkunde und Geldgeschichte.* Munich, 1924.

Particular

BYZANTINE, ETC.

GOODACRE, H. *A handbook of the coinage of the Byzantine Empire.* 2nd edition. London, 1957.

LANGLOIS, V. *Numismatique de l'Arménie du moyen âge.* Paris, 1855.

LONGUET, H. *Introduction à la numismatique Byzantine.* London, 1961

SCHLUMBERGER, G. *Numismatique de l'Orient latin.* With supplement. Paris, 1878–82.

WROTH, W. *Catalogue of Imperial Byzantine coins in the British Museum.* 2 vols. London, 1908.

WROTH, W. *Catalogue of the coins of the Vandals, Ostrogoths and Lombards, and of the empires of Thessalonica, Nicaea and Trebizand, in the British Museum.* London, 1911.

GREAT BRITAIN AND IRELAND

England

BROOKE, G. C. *English Coins.* 3rd edition. London, 1950.

DOLLEY, R. H. M. ed. *Anglo-Saxon coins: studies presented to Sir Frank Stenton.* London, 1961.

GRUEBER, H. A. *Handbook of the coins of Great Britain and Ireland in the British Museum.* London, 1899

HILDEBRAND, B. E. *Anglosachsiska mynt i Svenska Kongliga Myntkabinettet, funna i Sveriges jord.* 2nd edition. Stockholm, 1881.

OMAN, C. *The Coinage of England,* Oxford, 1931.

SUTHERLAND, C. H. V. *Anglo-Saxon gold coinage in the light of the Crondall hoard.* London, 1948.

Catalogues

ALLEN, D. F. *Catalogue of English coins in the British Museum. The cross and crosslets* ('*Tealby*') *type of Henry II.* London, 1951.

BROOKE, G. C. *Catalogue of English coins in the British Museum. The Norman kings.* 2 vols. London, 1916.

KEARY, C. F. and GRUEBER, H. A. *Catalogue of English coins in the British Museum. Anglo-Saxon series.* 2 vols. London, 1887–93.

PECK, C. W. *English copper, tin and bronze coins in the British Museum, 1558–1958.* London, 1960.

Sylloge of coins of the British Isles. P. Grierson, *Fitzwilliam Museum, Cambridge, Pt. I. Ancient British and Anglo-Saxon coins.* London, 1958; A. S. Robertson, *Hunterian and Coats collections, University of Glasgow, Pt. I. Anglo-Saxon coins.* London, 1961.

Scotland

BURNS, E. *The coinage of Scotland.* 2 vols. Edinburgh, 1887.

STEWART, I. H. *The Scottish coinage.* London, 1955.

Ireland

NELSON, P. *Coinage of Ireland in copper, tin and pewter,* 1460–1826. London, 1905.

NOLAN, P. *A monetary history of Ireland.* 2 vols. London, 1926–8.

WESTERN EUROPE

Netherlands

CHIJS, P. O. VAN DER. *De munten der Nederlanden van de vroegste tijden tot aan de Pacificatie van Gend.* 9 vols. Haarlem, 1851–66.

GELDER, H. E. VAN and HOC, M. *Les monnaies des Pays-Bas bourgonignons et espagnols* 1434–1713. Amsterdam, 1960.

SCHULMAN, J. *Handboek van de Nederlandse munten van* 1795–1945. Amsterdam, 1946.

VERKADE, P. *Muntboek bevattende de namen en afbeeldingen van munten, geslagen in de zeven voormalig vereenigde nederlandsche provincien, sedert den Vrede van Gent tot op onzen tijd.* Schiedam, 1848.

Belgium

CHALON, R. *Recherches sur les monnaies des comtes de Hainaut.* Brussels, 1848

CHALON, R. *Recherches sur les monnaies des comtes de Namur.* Brussels, 1860.

CHESTRET DE HANEFFE, J. DE. *Numismatique de la principauté de Liège.* Brussels, 1890.

DUPRIEZ, C. *Monnaies et essais monétaires du royaume de Belgique et du Congo Belge.* 2 vols. Brussels, 1949.

WITTE, A. DE. *Histoire monétaire des comtes de Louvain, ducs de Brabant.* 3 vols. Antwerp, 1894–9.

Luxemburg

BERNAYS, E. and VANNERUS, J. *Histoire monétaire du comté puis duché de Luxembourg et ses fiefs.* Brussels, 1910.

France

BLANCHET, A. and DIEUDONNÉ, A. *Manuel de numismatique française.* 4 vols. Paris, 1912–36.

CARON, E. *Monniaes féodales françaises.* Paris, 1882.

DIEUDONNÉ, A. *Les monnaies françaises.* Paris, 1923.

HOFFMAN, H. *Les monnaies royales de France.* Paris, 1878.

LAFAURIE, J. *Les monnaies des rois de France. Hugues Capet—Louis XII.* Paris, 1951.

LAFAURIE, J. and PRIEUR, P. *Les monnaies des rois de France. François I—Henri IV.* Paris, 1956.

POEY D'AVANT, F. *Les monnaies féodales de la France.* 3 vols. Paris, 1858–62.

PROU, M. *Les monnaies mérovingiennes. Catalogue des monnaies françaises de la Bibliothèque Nationale.* Paris, 1892.

PROU, M. *Les monnaies carolingiennes. Catalogue des monnaies françaises de la Bibliothèque Nationale.* Paris, 1896.

Italy

CAGIATI, M. *Le monete del reame delle Due Sicilie da Carlo I d'Angio a Vittorio Emanuele I.* Naples, 1911–37.

Corpus Nummorum Italicorum. vols. I–XIX. Rome, 1910–40.

PAPADOPOLI, N. *Le monete di Venezia.* 3 vols. Venice, 1893–1919.

SAMBON, G. *Repertorio generale delle monete coniate in Italia.* Part I. Paris, 1912.

SAMBON, A. *Recueil des monnaies médievales du sud d'Italie avant la domination des Normands.* Paris, 1919.

SCHEMBRI, H. C. *Coins and medals of the Knights of Malta.* London, 1908.

SPAZIANI TESTA, G. *Ducatoni, piastre, scudi, talleri e loro multipli battuti in zecche italiane e da italiani all' estero.* vol. I. *Casa Savoia.* Rome, 1951; vol. II. *Romani Pontefici.* Rome, 1952.

Spain

DASI, T. *Estudio de los reales a ocho.* 5 vols. Valencia, 1950–1.

FARRES, O. G. *Historia de la moneda Hispanola.* Madrid, 1960.

HEISS, A. *Descripcion general de las monedas hispano-cristianas desde la invasion de los Arabes.* 3 vols. Madrid, 1865–9.

MATEU Y LLOPIS, F. *La moneda espanola.* Barcelona, 1946.

MILES, G. C. *The coinage of the Visigoths in Spain.* New York, 1952.

Portugal

FERRARO VAZ, J. *Catalogo das moedas portuguesas. Portugal continental* 1648–1948. Lisbon, 1948.

REIS, P. B. *Preçário das moedas portuguesas de* 1140–1640. Lisbon, 1956; ditto *de* 1640–1940. Lisbon, 1957.

TEIXEIRA DE ARAGAO, A. C. *Descripçao geral e historica das moedas cunhadas em nome dos reis, regentes e governadores de Portugal.* 3 vols. Lisbon, 1874–80.

CENTRAL EUROPE

Switzerland

CORAGGIONI, L. *Münzgeschichte der Schweiz.* Geneva, 1896.

DEMOLE, E. *Histoire monétaire de Genève de* 1535 *à* 1848. 2 vols. Geneva, 1887–92.

POOLE, R. S. *A descriptive catalogue of the Swiss coins in the South Kensington Museum.* London, 1878.

SCHWARZ, D. W. H. *Münz- und Geldgeschichte Zürichs im Mittelalter.* Aarau, 1940.

TOBLER-MEYER, W. *Die Münz- und Medaillen-Sammlung des Herrn Hans Wunderly von Muralt.* 5 vols. Zürich, 1896–8.

WEISSENRIEDER, F. X. 100 *Jahre Schweizerisches Münzwesen* 1850–1950. Bern, 1950.

Germany

General

CRAIG, W. D. *Germanic coinages. Charlemagne through William II.* California, 1952.

DANNENBERG, H. *Die deutschen Münzen der sächsischen und fränkischen Kaiserzeit.* 4 vols. Berlin, 1876–1905.

DAVENPORT, J. S. *German Talers*, 1700–1800. Galesburg, 1958.

DAVENPORT, J. S. *German Talers since* 1800. Galesburg, 1949.

DAVENPORT, J. S. *Oversize Multiple Talers of the Brunswick Duchies and Saxe Lauenberg.* Galesburg, 1956.

GEBHART, H. *Die deutschen Münzen des Mittelalters und der Neuzeit.* Berlin, 1929.

JAEGER, K. *Die deutschen Reichsmünzen seit* 1871. Basel, 1959.

SCHLUMBERGER, G. L. *Les bractéates d'Allemagne.* Paris, 1874.

SUHLE, A. *Die deutschen Münzen des Mittelalters.* Berlin, 1936.

Regional

BAHRFELDT, E. *Brandenburgisch-preussische Münzstudien.* 2 vols. Berlin, 1913–30.

BERGHAUS, P. *Währungsgrenzen des Westfälischen Oberwesergebietes im Spätmittelalter.* Hamburg, 1951.

CAHN, J. *Der Rappenmünzbund.* Heidelberg, 1901.

FIALA, E. *Münzen und Medaillen der Welfischen Lande.* 7 vols. Prague, 1906–19.

JESSE, W. *Der Wendische Münzverein.* Lübeck, 1928.

NOSS, A. and HÄVERNICK, W. *Die Münzen und Medaillen von Köln.* 4 vols. Cologne, 1913–35.

Austria

HANS, J. *Zwei Jahrhunderte Maria-Theresen Thaler* 1751–1951. Klagenfurt, 1950.

JAECKEL, P. *Die Münzprägungen des Hauses Hapsburg* 1780–1918 *und der Bundesrepublik Österreich* 1918–56. Basel, 1956.

LOEHR, A. *Österreichische Geldgeschichte.* Vienna, 1946.

MILLER ZU AICHHOLZ, C. VON, LOEHR, A. and HOLZMAIR, E. *Österreichische Münzprägungen* 1519–1938. 2nd edition. Vienna, 1948.

Hungary

RETHY, L. *Corpus Nummorum Hungariae.* German edition. Graz, 1958.

Czechoslovakia

FIALA, E. *Beschreibung der Sammlung bömischer Münzen und Medaillen des Max Donebauer.* 2 vols. Prague, 1895–8.

NOHEJLOVA–PRATOVA, E. *Krása České Minče.* Prague, 1955.

TURNWALD, K. *České a moravské denáry a brakteáty.* Prague, 1949.

SCANDINAVIA
Denmark

GALSTER, G. *Die Münzen Dänemarks, bis etwa* 1625. Halle, 1939.

HAUBERG, P. *Myntforhold og udmyntninger i Danmark indtil* 1146. Copenhagen, 1900.

HOLM, J. C. *Danmarks Mønter* 1848–1947. Copenhagen, 1947.

MANSFELD-BULLNER, H. V. *Afbildninger af samtlige hidtil kjendte Danske mønter fra tidsrummet* 1241–1377. Copenhagen, 1954.

SCHOU, H. H. *Beskrivelske af danske og norske mønter,* 1488–1814, *og danske mønter* 1815–1923. Copenhagen, 1926.

WILCKE, J. *Daler, mark og kroner* 1481–1914. Copenhagen, 1931.

Norway

BJØRNSTAD, O. C. and HOLST, H. *Norges mynter efter* 1814. Oslo, 1927.

SCHIVE, C. J. *Norges mynter i middelalderen.* Christiania, 1865.

Sweden

APPELGREN, T. G. *Gustav Vasas mynt.* Stockholm, 1933.

GLUCK, H. and HESSELBLAD, G. G. *Artalsforteckning over Svenska mynt med värdering-spriser: Gustaf Vasa—Gustaf VI,* 1521–1959. Stockholm, 1959.

LINDGREN, T. *Sveriges mynt* 1719–1776. Stockholm, 1953.

WALLROTH, K. A. *Sveriges mynt* 1449–1917. Stockholm, 1918.

EASTERN EUROPE
Poland

GUMOWSKI, M. *Handbuch des polnischen Numismatik.* German edition. Graz, 1960.

HUTTEN-CZAPSKI, E. *Catalogue de la collection des médailles et monnaies polonaises.* 3 vols. Reprint. Graz, 1957.

KIRMIS, M. *Handbuch der polnischen Münzkunde.* Posen, 1892.

Baltic Republics

PLATZBARDIS, A. *Die Münzen und das Papiergeld Estlands, Lettlands, Litauens.* Stockholm, 1953.

Russia

CHAUDOIR, S. DE. *Aperçu sur les monnaies russes et sur les monnaies étrangères qui ont eu cours en Russie.* 3 vols. St. Petersburg, 1836–7.

DENIS, C. *Catalogue des monnaies émises sur le territoire de la Russie,* 1914–25. Paris, 1926.

PETROV, V. I. *Catalogue des monnaies russes.* 2nd. edition. Moscow, 1899.

SEVERIN, H. M. *Gold and platinum coinage of imperial Russia from 1701–1911.* New York, 1958.

BALKANS

LJUBIĆ, S. *Opis jugoslavenskih novaca.* Zagreb, 1875.

MARIĆ, R. *Études de numismatique serbe* (In Russian with French summary). Belgrade, 1956.

MOUCHMOV, N. A. *Numismatique et sigillographie bulgare.* Sofia, 1924.

RENGJEO, I. *Corpus der mittelalterlichen Münzen von Kroatien, Slavonien, Dalmatien und Bosnien.* Reprint. Graz, 1959.

EUROPEAN COLONIAL

British

ATKINS, J. *The coins and tokens of the possessions and colonies of the British Empire.* London, 1899.

LINECAR, H. W. A. *British Commonwealth Coinage.* London, 1959.

PRIDMORE, F. *The coins of the British Commonwealth of Nations.* Part I. European territories. London, 1960.

WRIGHT, L. V. W. *Colonial and Commonwealth coinage.* London, 1959.

French

MAZARD, J. *Histoire monétaire et numismatique des colonies de l'Union française.* Paris, 1953.

Spanish

MEDINA, J. T. *Las monedas coloniales hispano-americanas.* Santiago, 1919.

Dutch

SCHOLTEN, C. *The coins of the Dutch Overseas Territories, 1610–1948.* Amsterdam, 1953.

NEW WORLD
General

ADAMS, E. H. *Catalogue of the collection of Julius Guttag, comprising the coinage of Mexico, Central America, South America and the West Indies.* New York, 1929.

RAYMOND, W. *Spanish-American gold coins.* New York, 1936.

RAYMOND, W. *The gold coins of North and South America.* New York, 1937.

RAYMOND, W. *The silver dollars of North and South America.* New York, 1939.

WEYL, A. *Katalog der Jules Fonrobert'schen Sammlung überseeischer Münzen und Medaillen.* vols. 1–3. Berlin, 1878–9.

Particular

NORTH AMERICA
Canada

CHARLTON, J. E. 1960 *Standard catalogue of Canadian coins, tokens and paper money.* Toronto, 1960.

TAYLOR, H. C. and JAMES, S. *A guide book of Canadian coins, currency and tokens.* 2nd edition. Winnipeg, 1960.

United States

CROSBY, S. S. *The early coins of America.* Boston, 1878.

NOE, S. P. *The New England and Willow Tree coinage of Massachusetts.* New York, 1943.

NOE, S. P. *The Oak Tree coinage of Massachusetts.* New York, 1947.

NOE, S. P. *The Pine Tree coinage of Massachusetts.* New York, 1952.

YEOMAN, R. S. *A guide book of United States coins.* 14th edition. Racine, 1960.

Mexico

MEEK, W. T. *The exchange media of colonial Mexico.* New York, 1948.

PRADEAU, F. *Historia numismatica de Mexico desde la epoca precortesiana hasta 1823.* Mexico City, 1950.

CENTRAL AMERICA

GURDIAN, R. *Contribucion al estudio de las monedas de Costa Rica.* San José, 1958.

PROBER, K. *Historia numismatica de Guatemala.* Sao Paulo, 1954.

LEITAO, S. *Catalogo de moedas brasileiros de* 1643–1957. Rio de Janeiro, 1957.

MEDINA, J. T. *Las monedas chilenas.* Santiago, 1902.

MEILI, J. *Das brazilianische Geldwesen.* 3 vols. Zürich, 1897–1905.

ROSA, A. *Medallas y monedas de la republica Argentina.* Buenos Aires, 1898.

SALLES OLIVIERA, A. DE. *Moedas do Brasil.* vol. I. *Moedas y barras de ouro.* Sao Paulo, 1944.

TAULLARD, A. *Monedas de la republica Argentina.* Buenos Aires, 1924.

WEST INDIES

LISMORE, T. *The coinage of Cuba.* Havana, 1955.

WOOD, H. *The coinage of the West Indies with special reference to the cut and counter-stamped pieces.* New York, 1914.

AUSTRALASIA

General

ANDREW, A. *Australasian tokens and coins.* Sydney, 1921.

SUTHERLAND, A. *Numismatic history of New Zealand.* New Plymouth, 1939–41.

WEYL, A. *Katalog der Jules Fonrobert'schen Sammlung überseeischer Münzen und Medaillen.* Vol. 4. Berlin, 1879.

AFRICA

General

WEYL, A. *Katalog der Jules Fonrobert'schen Sammlung überseeischer Münzen und Medaillen.* Vol. 4. Berlin, 1879.

Special

ANZANI, A. *Numismatica Auxumita.* Reprinted from *Rivista Italiana di Numismatica.* Milan, 1926.

KAPLAN, A. *Catalogue of the coins of South Africa.* Germiston, 1950.

PARSONS, H. A. *The colonial coinages of British Africa with the adjacent islands.* London, 1950.

NEAR EAST

GÖBL, R. *Aufbau der Münzprägung.* (Sassanian coinage) in *Ein Asiatischer Staat* by F. Altheim and R. Stiehl. Wiesbaden, 1954.

HAZARD, H. W. *The numismatic history of late mediaeval North Africa.* New York, 1952.

LANE POOLE, S. *Catalogue of Oriental coins in the British Museum.* 10 vols. London: I. The Eastern Khaleefehs, 1875; II. Amawee Khaleefehs of Spain and lesser Spanish dynasties; Ghaznawees, Buweyhees, etc., 1876; III. The Turkuman houses of the Seljook, Urtuk, Zengee, etc., 1877; IV. The Fatimee Khaleefehs, the Ayyoobees and the Memlook Sultans, 1879; V. The Moors of Africa and Spain; Kings and Imams of the Yemen, 1880; VI. The Mongols, 1881; VII. Bukhara (Transoxiana), 1882; VIII. Othmanlee Sultans, 1883; IX. Additions to vols. I-IV, 1889; X. Additions to vols. V-VIII, 1890.

LANE POOLE, S. *Catalogue of the coins of the Shahs of Persia in the British Museum.* London, 1877.

LANG, D. M. *Studies in the numismatic history of Georgia in Transcaucasia.* New York, 1955.

LAVOIX, H. *Catalogue des monnaies musulmanes de la Bibliothèque Nationale.* 3 vols. Paris, 1887–96. I. *The Eastern Caliphs;* II. *Spain and Africa;* III. *Egypt and Syria.*

MAYER, L. A. *Bibliography of Moslem numismatics, India excluded.* London, 1939.

NÜTZEL, H. *Katalog der orientalischen Münzen (Königliche Museen zu Berlin).* 2 vols. Berlin, 1898–1902. I. *The Eastern Caliphs;* II. *Spain and Western North Africa.*

PARUCK, F. D. J. *Sassanian coins.* Bombay, 1924.

RABINO DI BORGOMALE, H. L. *Coins, medals and seals of the Shahs of Iran,* 1500–1941. Hertford, 1941.

RIVERO, C. M. DEL. *La moneda arabigo-española.* Madrid, 1933.

VALENTINE, W. E. *Modern copper coins of the Muhammadan states.* London, 1911.

WALKER, J. *Catalogue of the Muhammadan coins in the British Museum.* 2 vols. London: I. *A catalogue of the Arab-Sassanian coins.* 1941; II. *A catalogue of the Arab-Byzantine and post-reform Umaiyad coins.* 1956.

INDIA

BROWN, C. J. *The Coins of India.* Calcutta, 1922.

CODRINGTON, H. W. *Ceylon coins and currency.* Colombo, 1924.

ELLIOTT, W. *Coins of southern India.* London, 1886.

SINGHAL, C. R. *Bibliography of Indian coins.* Part I. *Non-Muhammadan series;* Part II. *Muhammadan and later series.* Bombay, 1950–2.

VALENTINE, W. H. *The copper coins of India.* 2 vols. London, 1914–20.

Catalogues

Catalogue of Indian coins in the British Museum. 7 vols. London: P. Gardner, *The coins of the Greek and Scythic kings of Bactria and India,* 1886; J. Allan, *The coins of ancient India,* 1936; E. J. Rapson, *The coins of the Andhra dynasty, the Western Ksatrapas,* etc., 1908; J. Allan, *The coins of the Gupta dynasties and of Sasanka, king of Gauda,* 1914; S. Lane Poole, *The coins of the sultans of Delhi,* 1894; do., *The coins of the Mohammadan states of India,* 1885; do., *The coins of the Moghul emperors,* 1892.

Catalogue of the coins in the Indian Museum, Calcutta, 4 vols. Oxford: V. A. Smith, *The early foreign dynasties and the Guptas,* etc. 1906; H. N. Wright, *The sultans of Delhi and contemporary dynasties in India,* 1907; do., *The Mughal emperors of India,* 1908; J. Allan, ed., *Coins of the Native States of India,* (i) *Coins of Awadh* (C. J. Brown), (ii) *Coins of Mysore and South India,* (J. R. Henderson), (iii) *Bombay, Rajputana and Central India* (W. H. Valentine), 1928.

Catalogue of the coins in the Punjab Museum, Lahore. 3 vols. Oxford; 1914–34: R. B. Whitehead, I. *Indo-Greek coins;* II. *Coins of the Moghul emperors;* III. *Coins of Nadir Shah and the Durrani dynasty.*

Catalogue of coins in the Central Museum, Madras. 4 vols. Madras, 1888–90. E. Thurston, I. *Mysore;* II. *Roman, Indo-Portuguese and Ceylon;* III. *Sultans of Delhi;* IV. *East India Company.*

Catalogue of coins in the Provincial Museum, Lucknow. I. C. J. Brown, *Coins of the Guptas,* etc., Allahabad, 1920; II. P. Dyal, *Coins of the Sultans of Delhi,* Allahabad 1925; III. C. J. Brown, *Coins of the Mughal emperors,* Oxford, 1920.

FAR EAST

COUPERIE, A. T. DE LA. *Catalogue of Chinese coins from the seventh century* B.C. *to* A.D. 621 *included in the collection in the British Museum.* London, 1892.

JACOBS, N. and VERMEULE, C. C. *Japanese coinage.* New York, 1953.

KANN, E. *Illustrated catalog of Chinese coins.* Los Angeles, 1954.

LE MAY, R. *The Coinage of Siam.* Bangkok, 1932.

LOCKHART, J. H. S. *The currency of the Far East from the earliest times up to the present day.* 3 vols. Hong Kong, 1895–8.

LOCKHART, J. H. S. *The Stewart Lockhart collection of Chinese coins.* Shanghai, 1915.

MILLIES, H. C. *Recherches sur les monnaies des indigènes de l'archipel Indien et de la peninsule malaie.* The Hague, 1871.

MUNRO, N. G. *Coins of Japan.* Yokohama, 1904.

PHAYRE, A. P. *Coins of Arakan, of Pegu, and of Burma.* (*Numismata Orientalia.* vol. 3. Part I.). London, 1882.

SCHJOTH, F. *The currency of the Far East.* London, 1929.

SCHROEDER, A. *Annam, Etudes numismatiques.* Paris, 1905.

TOKENS, ETC.

BARNARD, F. P. *The casting-counter and the counting-board.* Oxford, 1916.

BOYNE, W. *Trade tokens issued in the seventeenth century in England, Wales and Ireland.* Revised edition by C. G. Williamson. 2 vols. London, 1889–92.

DALTON, R. and HAMER, H. S. *The provincial token coinage of the eighteenth century.* 14 Parts. London, 1910–18.

DAVIS, W. J. *The nineteenth century token coinage of Great Britain, Ireland, the Channel. Islands and the Isle of Man.* London, 1904.

DIEUDONNÉ, A. *Manuel des poids monétaires.* Paris, 1925.

MILES, G. C. *Early Arab glass weights and stamps.* New York, 1948.

SHEPPARD, T. and MUSHAM, J. F. *Money scales and weights.* London, 1923.

Illustrations

(The coins are illustrated by courtesy of the Trustees of the British Museum.)
The metal of each coin is indicated by the following abbreviations:

N=gold
R=silver
$Æ$=bronze
Al.=aluminium

Al.br.=aluminium-
 bronze
Bill.=billon
CK=Cupro-nickel

El.=electrum
K=nickel
P=lead
Pot.=potin

GREEK COINS, PLATES 1–13

ROMAN COINS, PLATES 14–25

(a) REPUBLIC

(The denarius is of silver, the aureus and solidus of gold.)

(b) EMPIRE

COINS OF THE NEW WORLD, PLATES 48–51

COINS OF AFRICA, PLATES 52–53

NEAR EASTERN COINS, PLATES 54–56

COINS OF INDIA, PLATES 57–60

COINS OF THE FAR EAST, PLATES 61—63

TOKENS, JETTONS, ETC., PLATE 64

Index

PLATE 1

GREEK COINS

PLATE 2

18   19

20   21

22   23   24

25   26   27

28   29   30

31   32

33   34

GREEK COINS

PLATE 3

GREEK COINS

PLATE 4

PLATE 5

GREEK COINS

PLATE 6

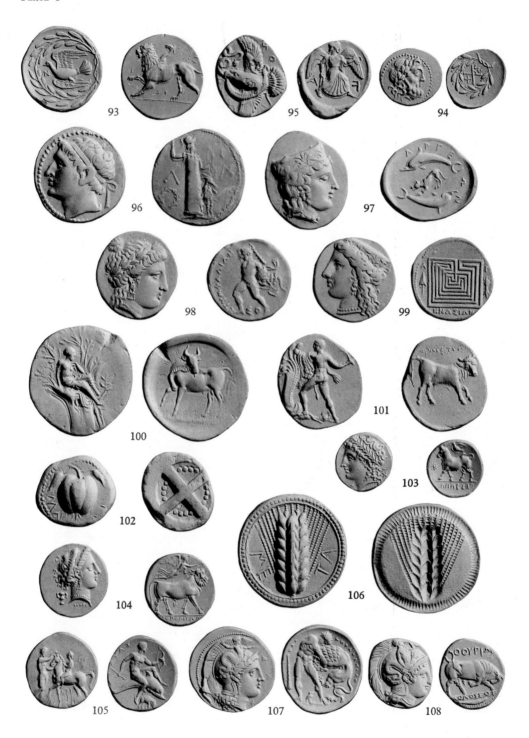

93   95   94

96   97

98   99

100   101

103

102   104   106

105   107   108

GREEK COINS

PLATE 7

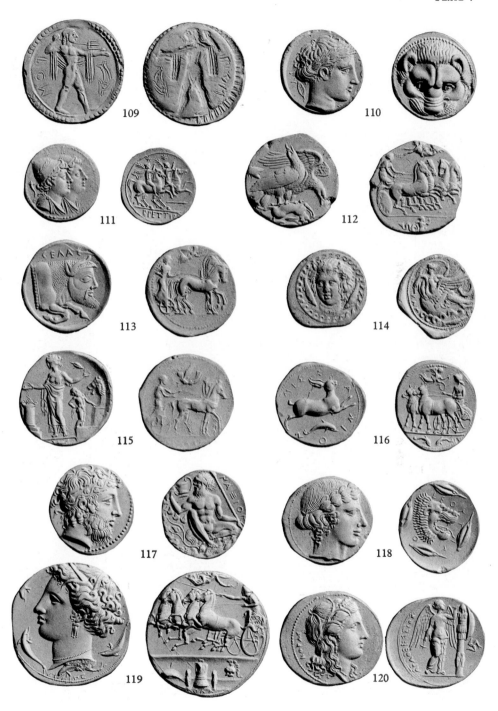

109

110

111

112

113

114

115

116

117

118

119

120

GREEK COINS

PLATE 8

GREEK COINS

PLATE 9

PLATE 10

154 155 156 157 158 159 160 161 162 163 164 165

GREEK COINS

PLATE 11

166   167

168   169

170   172

173

171   174

175   176

GREEK COINS

PLATE 12

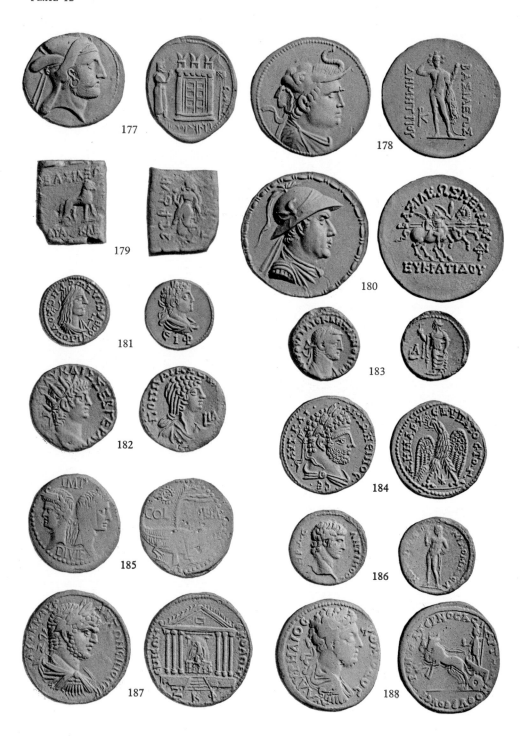

177

178

179

180

181

182

183

184

185

186

187

188

GREEK COINS

PLATE 13

189

190

ROMAN REPUBLICAN COINS

PLATE 14

191

192

193

194

195

196

198 197 199

200 201 202

203 204 205

206 207 208

209 210 211

ROMAN REPUBLICAN COINS

PLATE 15

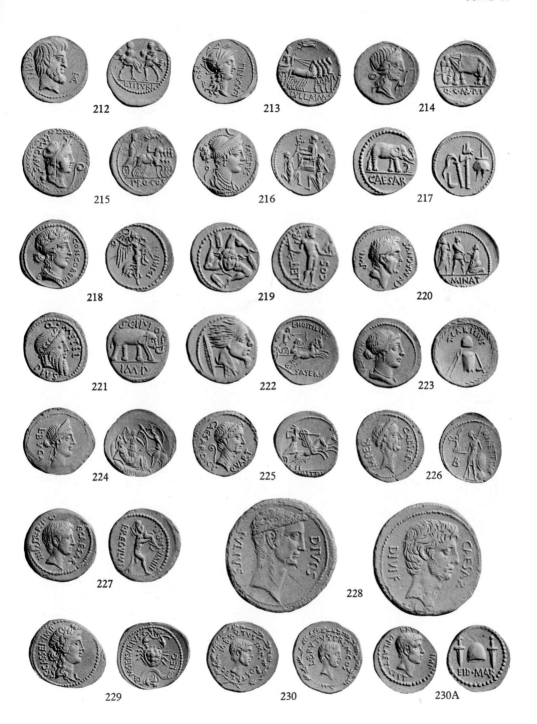

212

213

214

215

216

217

218

219

220

221

222

223

224

225

226

227

228

229

230

230A

ROMAN REPUBLICAN COINS

PLATE 16

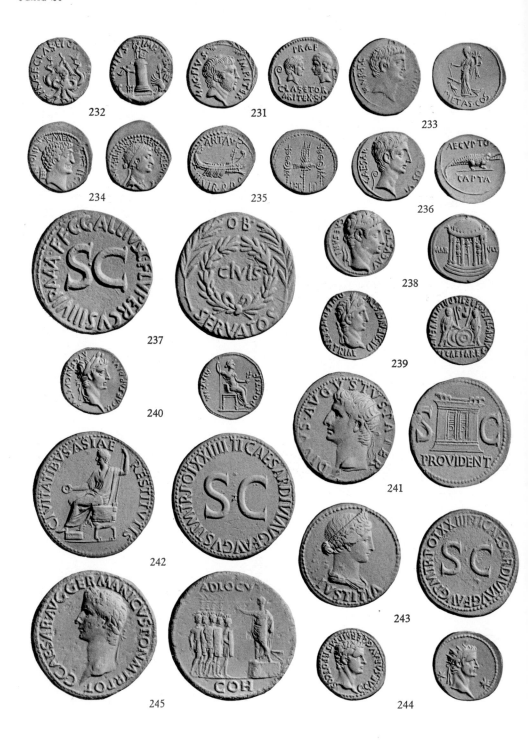

232
231
233
234
235
236
237
238
239
240
241
242
243
245
244

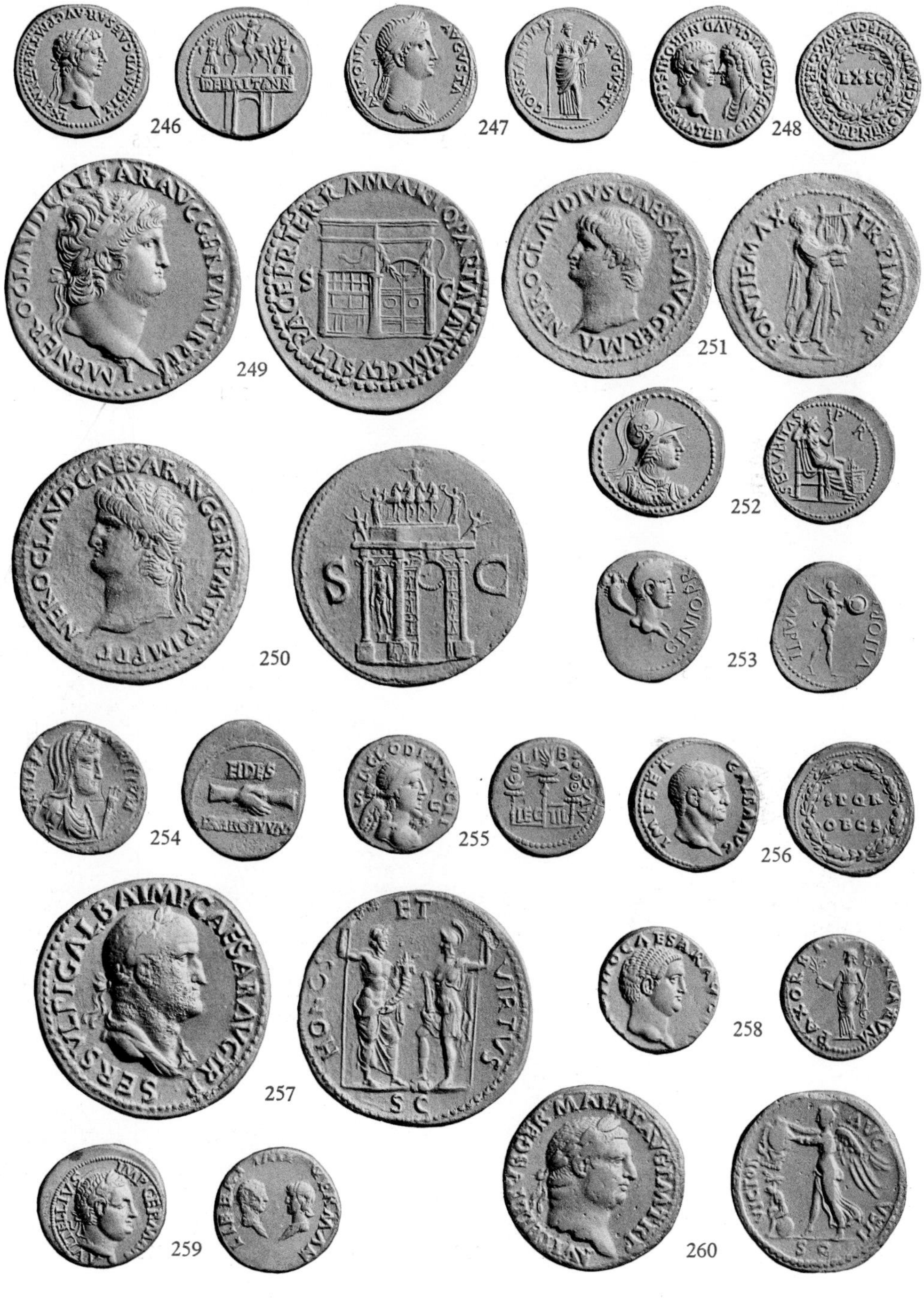

246 247 248 249 250 251 252 253 254 255 256 257 258 259 260

ROMAN IMPERIAL COINS

PLATE 18

PLATE 19

274

275

276

277

278

279

281

280

282

283

284

285

286

288

287

289

ROMAN IMPERIAL COINS

PLATE 20

PLATE 21

308   309

311

310   313

312   315

314   317

316   318

319   320

321   322

ROMAN IMPERIAL COINS

PLATE 22

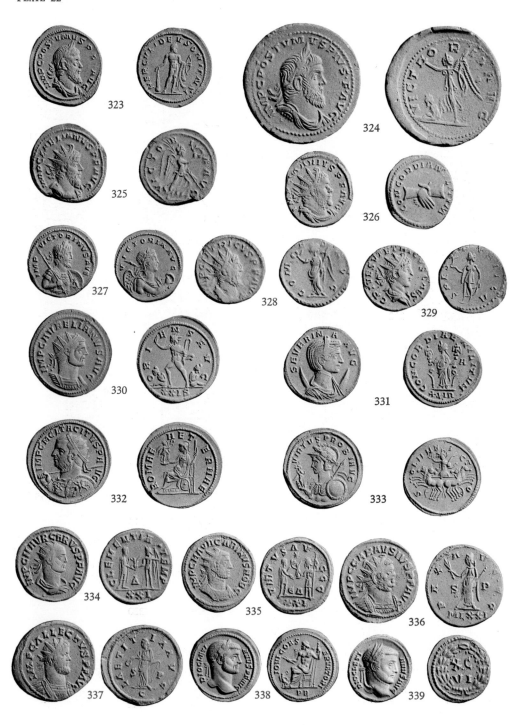

323

324

325

326

327

328

329

330

331

332

333

334

335

336

337

338

339

PLATE 23

340   341

342   343

344   345

346   347   348

350   349   351

352   353   353A

ROMAN IMPERIAL COINS

PLATE 24

354 355 356
357 358 359
360 361
362 363
364 365
366 367
368 369 370

ROMAN IMPERIAL COINS

PLATE 25

ROMAN IMPERIAL COINS

PLATE 26

392

394

397

393

395

396

398

399

400

401

402

403

404

405

406

407

408

PLATE 27

409 410 412 411 413 416 414 415 417 418 419 420 421 423 422 424

EUROPEAN COINS : BYZANTIUM, NICAEA, TREBIZOND

PLATE 28

425   426   427

428   429   430

431   432

433   434

435   436   437

438

439

440

441   442   443

444   445   446

EUROPEAN COINS : LATIN ORIENT, ENGLAND

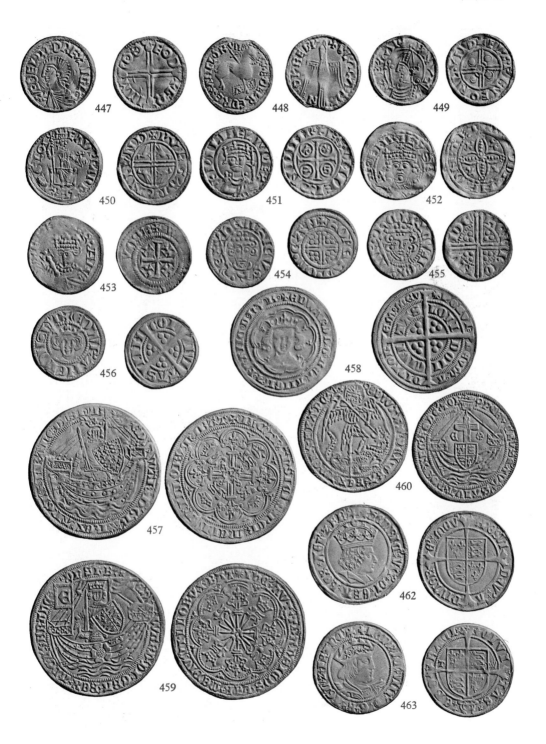

PLATE 29

447   448   449
450   451   452
453   454   455
456   458
457   460
459   462
463

PLATE 30

461

464

466

465

467

468

469

470

471   472

473

474

475

EUROPEAN COINS : ENGLAND, GREAT BRITAIN

PLATE 31

474A

476

477

478

479

480

481

482

483

484

485

486

487

488

489

490

EUROPEAN COINS : GREAT BRITAIN

PLATE 32

PLATE 33

EUROPEAN COINS : SCOTLAND AND IRELAND

PLATE 34

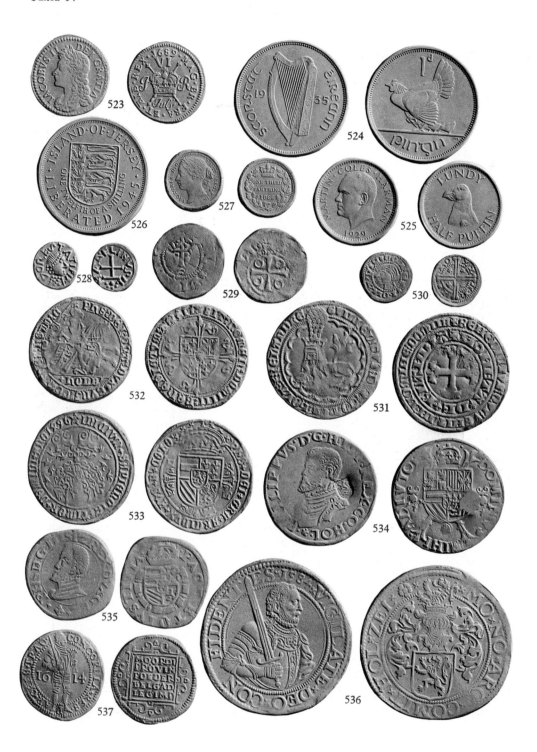

EUROPEAN COINS : IRELAND, NETHERLANDS

PLATE 35

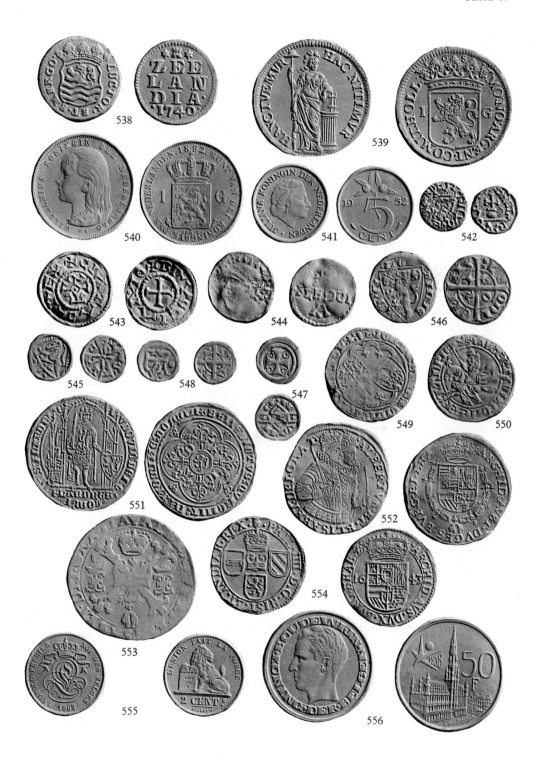

EUROPEAN COINS : NETHERLANDS, BELGIUM

PLATE 36

557

558

559

560

561

562

563

564

565

566

567

568

569

570

571

573

572

PLATE 37

574   575
576   577   578
580   579   581
582   583   586
584   585
587   588   589
590   591   592

EUROPEAN COINS : FRANCE, ITALY

PLATE 38

593

594

595

597

598

596

599

600

601

602

603

604

607

605

606

608

609

610

612

EUROPEAN COINS : ITALY, SPAIN

PLATE 39

611

613

614

616

615

617

618

619

620

621

622

623

624

625

EUROPEAN COINS : SPAIN, PORTUGAL

PLATE 40

626
627
628
630
629
631
632
633
634
635
636
638
637
639
640
642
641
643
644

EUROPEAN COINS : PORTUGAL, SWITZERLAND, GERMANY

PLATE 41

645

646

647

648

649

650

651

652

653

654

655

656

657

658

659

660

661

662

663

664

EUROPEAN COINS : GERMANY

PLATE 42

665

666

667

668

669

670

671

672

673

674

675

676

677

678

679

680

681

EUROPEAN COINS : GERMANY

PLATE 43

682 683 684
685 687 688 689 690 691 692 686 693 696 694 695 697

EUROPEAN COINS : GERMANY, AUSTRIA

PLATE 44

698 699 700 701 702 703 704 705 706 707 708 709 710 711 712 713 714 715

EUROPEAN COINS : AUSTRIA, HUNGARY, CZECHOSLOVAKIA

PLATE 45

716   717   718A

718   719

720

721   722   723

724   725

727   728

729   726

730   731   732

EUROPEAN COINS : CZECHOSLOVAKIA, DENMARK, ICELAND, NORWAY

PLATE 46

733   734   735   736   737   738   739   740   741   742   743   744   745   746   747   748   749   750   751   752   753

EUROPEAN COINS : NORWAY, SWEDEN, POLAND, RUSSIA

PLATE 47

EUROPEAN COINS : RUSSIA, BALKANS

PLATE 48

772

COLONIES FRANÇOISES 1721 H

773 PROVINCE DU BAS CANADA · UN · SOU

BANK · TOKEN · CONCORDIA SALUS · 1837 · HALF PENNY

775 BANK OF UPPER CANADA 1859 · BANK · TOKEN · ONE · HALF · PENNY

774 VICTORIA DEI GRATIA REGINA CANADA · 20 CENTS 1858

776 PROVINCE OF NOVA SCOTIA · HALFPENNY TOKEN 1832

777 VICTORIA DEI GRATIA REGINA CANADA · 25 CENTS 1874

778 CANADA 1935 DOLLAR

779 CANADA FLOREAT TERRA NOVA 1949 DOLLAR

780

881 MASATHUSIN

1652 XII

782 CECILIUS · DNS · TERRÆ MARIÆ &c

783 ROSA · AMERICANA · 1723 UTILE · DULCI

784 LIBERTY 1799 · UNITED STATES OF AMERICA

GEORGIUS · D · G · MAG · BRI · FR · ET · HIB · REX

GULIELMUS · DEI · GRATIA X II

NEW WORLD COINS : NORTH AMERICA

PLATE 49

785 786 787
788 789 790
791 792
793 794
795 796 798
797 799 800

NEW WORLD COINS : NORTH AND CENTRAL AMERICA

PLATE 50

801

802

803

804

805

806

807

809

808

811

810

812

813

814

815

NEW WORLD COINS : CENTRAL AND SOUTH AMERICA

PLATE 51

816

817

818

819

820   821   822

823   824   825

826   827   828

829   830   831

NEW WORLD COINS : SOUTH AMERICA, CARIBBEAN

PLATE 52

AUSTRALASIAN COINS ; AFRICAN COINS

PLATE 53

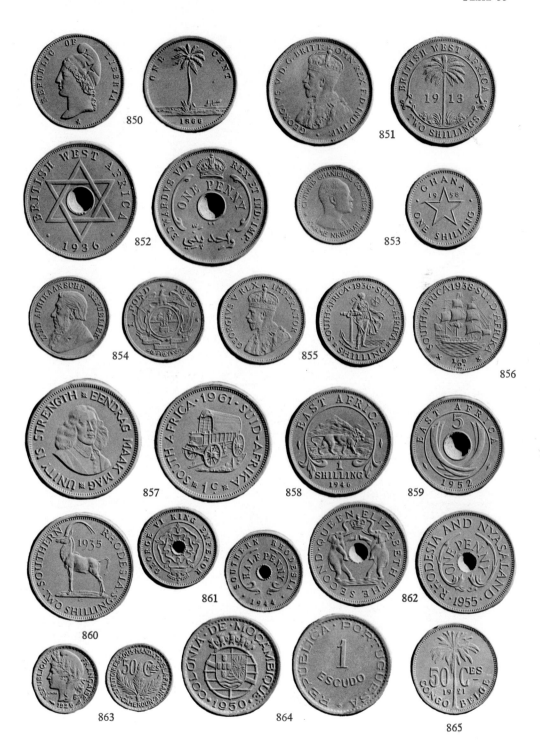

PLATE 54

PLATE 55

881

882

883

884

885

886

887

888

889

890

891

892

893

894

895

896

897

898

899

900

901

NEAR EASTERN COINS

PLATE 56

PLATE 57

917

918

919

920

921

922

923

924

925

926

927

928

929

930

931

932

933

934

935

936

INDIAN COINS

PLATE 58

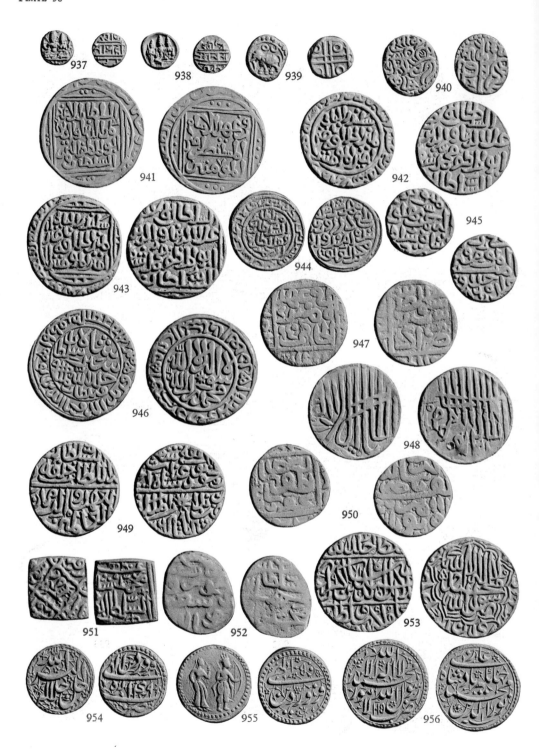

937   938   939   940
941   942
943   944   945
946   947   948
949   950
951   952   953
954   955   956

PLATE 59

INDIAN COINS

PLATE 60

INDIAN AND SINGHALESE COINS

PLATE 61

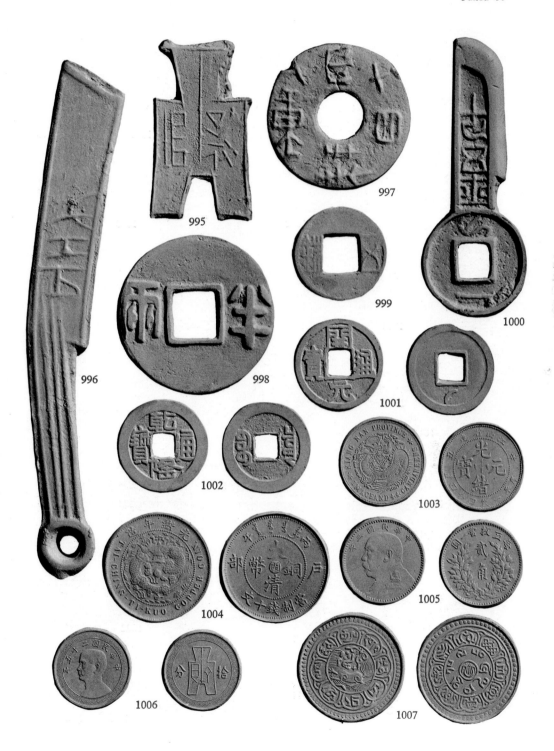

FAR EASTERN COINS

PLATE 62

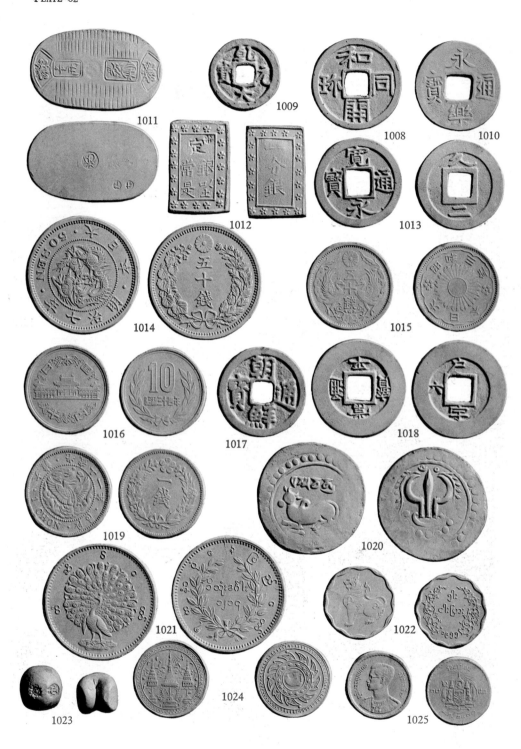

PLATE 63

FAR EASTERN COINS

PLATE 64